The Hudson Valley & Catskill Mountains

Including Albany & Saratoga Springs

— ONLY THE BEST PLACES —

2018-2019

JOANNE MICHAELS

A Guide For Discerning Travelers, Families and Local Residents.

The Newburgh Waterfront.

View from Cold Spring.

The Hudson Valley & Catskill Mountains

Including Albany & Saratoga Springs

— ONLY THE BEST PLACES —

2018-2019

JOANNE MICHAELS

JMB Publications
Woodstock, New York

I would like to hear from readers of this guidebook. Please contact me at
JMB PUBLICATIONS, PO Box 425, Woodstock, NY 12498, or by email @
contact@joannemichaels.com.

Tenth Edition

Hudson Valley & Catskill Mountains: Only the Best Places
ISBN: 978-0-9619429-5-3

Cover photo by Nick Zungoli, Exposures Gallery, Sugar Loaf, NY
Interior photographs by the author unless otherwise specified
Maps by Moore Creative Design
Cover and interior design by Thom Hermance
Composition by Color Page, Kingston, NY

Published by JMB Publications, PO Box 425, Woodstock, NY 12498
Distributed by JMB Publications
Printed in the United States of America

In memory of John Heard, a great friend, fellow traveler and inspiration…

And to my fellow explorers and armchair travelers, with special thanks to Arthur Davis III, Erik Michaels-Ober and Helen Levine, who have shared adventures with me in the Catskills, as well as up and down the Hudson River Valley—and beyond!

Cooper Lake in Woodstock.

The Beekman Arms in Rhinbeck.

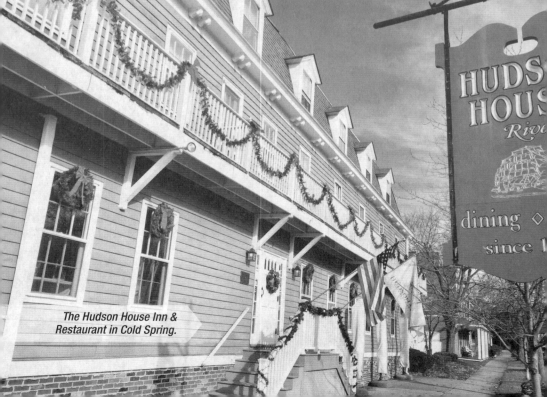

The Hudson House Inn &
Restaurant in Cold Spring.

AN IMPORTANT
NOTE TO READERS

No entries for any establishments in this book have been solicited or paid for. I selected lodging and dining places based on their merits alone. There is no charge to innkeepers or restaurant owners for inclusion. The decision to feature a business or site has to do with quality alone: This book is truly the best of the region.

Over the past 38 years, both as editor-in-chief of Hudson Valley magazine and currently as president of a regional book distribution company, I have lived in the Catskills and annually travel thousands of miles throughout the region. The wide-ranging contacts I have made during these decades are invaluable. My experience will ensure the trips of those who use this guide are richer and more varied than those who simply grab certain give away publications: some pander to advertisers or promote minor attractions.

I urge you to keep the book in your car…and enjoy!

PRICES

Please don't hold me, or the owners of various businesses mentioned in the book, responsible for general price categories listed as of press time in 2018. Changes are inevitable. Additionally, state and local taxes should be added to all prices.

The price rating system is simple and provides general guidelines to travelers. By their nature, restaurants included in the Eating Out sections are generally inexpensive. For entrees in the restaurant sections, in general:

$—The majority of entrees cost $15 and under

$$—Most entrees cost $15-25

$$$—Most entrees cost over $25

For inns and bed & breakfasts (per room before tax):

$—Means most rooms run $150 and under

$$—Means $150-$250

$$$—Means above $250

LET ME KNOW!

Over the 30 years this book has been in print, I have received many letters from readers throughout the U.S. If you would like to share any of your experiences, please contact me at PO Box 425, Woodstock, NY 12498, or email contact@joannemichaels.com

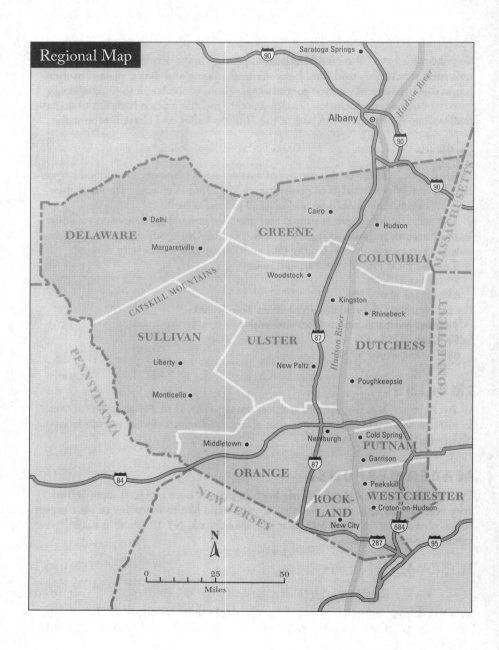

Regional Map

Saratoga Springs

Hudson River

90

Albany

90

90

MASSACHUSETTS

Cairo

DELAWARE

Delhi

GREENE

Hudson

Margaretville

COLUMBIA

CATSKILL MOUNTAINS

Woodstock

Kingston

Rhinebeck

CONNECTICUT

Hudson River

PENNSYLVANIA

SULLIVAN

ULSTER

87

DUTCHESS

Liberty

New Paltz

Poughkeepsie

Monticello

Middletown

Newburgh

Cold Spring

PUTNAM

87

Garrison

ORANGE

Peekskill

WESTCHESTER

NEW JERSEY

ROCK-LAND

Croton-on-Hudson

84

New City

684

287

95

N

0   25   50
Miles

MAPS

A Guide For Discerning Travelers, Families and Local Residents

CONTENTS

ACKNOWLEDGMENTS

It is never possible to thank everyone who helps a book of this kind come to life: for every person I mention, several more were behind the scenes, answering questions, mailing information, offering suggestions, and opening their homes to me.

I am particularly thankful to a few members of Hudson Valley county government departments: Nancy Lutz of Dutchess County Tourism, and Chris White, Deputy Director of Ulster County Planning Department as well as Aaron Bennett, Ulster County Environmental Planning Department, were especially helpful. Bruce Conklin and Frank Smith at Putnam County Tourism offered assistance; (Frank spent one of his last afternoons on the job sharing information with me; for that I am grateful.) Annamaria Bellantoni of the Saratoga County Chamber of Commerce and Darryl Leggieri, Marketing Director of the Saratoga Hilton, were wonderfully welcoming.

The following people, who regularly travel throughout the Hudson Valley and Catskills, gave me excellent recommendations, information and support: Alan Chartock, president of Northeast Public Radio, Bruce Moor, M.D., Betsy & Al Bergman, Mark Cuddy, Nancy Michaels, Helen Levine and Ellen Messer.

Nick Zungoli did a wonderful job on the cover photograph and after 45 years in the publishing business I have learned a cover truly sells a book.

Frank Campagna at Color Page in Kingston, New York, was willing to consider several new ideas. His advice and guidance were invaluable. Bruce Sconzo and Deborah Downes, who work with Frank, assisted me through the printing process. Both were always patient and responsive to my questions and concerns. Thom Hermance created a beautiful design and put in several hours making this book easy to use.

Many people gave their opinions and the names of their favorite places, based on years of growing up and living in their respective towns. They probably didn't realize at the time how helpful they were. These locals got me off the beaten track where I discovered charming neighborhood restaurants, tranquil back roads, and a swimming spot or hiking area I probably never would have found on my own. So this book, aside from being the most comprehensive guide to the phenomenal region I've always called home, is also a gift to all the people of the Hudson Valley, Catskills, Albany, and Saratoga Springs.

Charles DeSimone and Eric Burger of Barnes & Noble have been amazing in recognizing this "local book".

As you will discover, I didn't hold back telling the truth about a less than stellar aspect of a restaurant or lodging option. So many of our legislators—and even journalists—these days are bought and paid for. I have never been one of them and have been known throughout the region for "telling it like it is." You will glean the benefit of my discrimination—and honesty—throughout these pages. This guidebook has been in print for 30 years: the book you have is its 10th edition. No entry here was purchased and the work has always been a labor of love!

Bed and breakfasts have proliferated throughout The Hudson Valley. This book does not recommend *airbnb* establishments due to the fact there is no standard of quality aside from online comments. The recommendations of the B&Bs and hotels listed in this guidebook are for places that have been in business for years and have a long-standing reputation for quality. The selections chosen are particularly charming or special in some way. Reduced mid-week and off-season rates are offered by most. I welcome feedback from all travelers!

INTRODUCTION

Although I am certainly not the first traveler to recognize the scenic wonders of the Hudson Valley and Catskills, I am proud to say I have remained at the forefront of reminding people some of the most beautiful sights in the world are, literally, at their back doors.

A close friend once commented that by writing about these regional treasures, I am causing them to be overrun with tourists. He suggested I keep these special places to myself, or they will risk being ruined. I cannot deny there are times when I have the impulse not to include a deserted swimming place I frequent in summer, or an "undiscovered" eatery on a back road I stopped at one day, but I know sharing this information is what makes my book the best one available.

For 30 years, various editions of my guide have enriched the travels of thousands of people visiting the region. Once in a while readers take the time to write a letter, sharing their experience of a particular inn or historic site. I have never heard anything but praise for the beauty of the Hudson Valley and Catskills—even if, on occasion, a particular restaurant didn't live up to their expectations.

When people think of this area, many imagine mysterious mountains where Rip Van Winkle slept away the years, lush valleys where bobcats roamed, or even huge hotels where the entertainment and food never stopped. True, these are part of the region's story, but after traveling hundreds of thousands of miles on back roads and main highways, in snow, fog, sun and rain, I have come to the conclusion that practically nowhere else in America can one enjoy such startling beauty, rich history and variety of cultural activities to be found in the Hudson Valley and Catskill Mountains.

And because there is so much to see and do, I chose to include only what I consider the best—be it food, inns, hiking trails, or history. At places of interest, I looked for unusual exhibits or special events. When evaluating restaurants, inns, hotels and B&Bs, I looked for value, distinctiveness, quality, cleanliness, and courtesy. Farm stands, whether large or small, had to show pride in their produce. I have intentionally avoided corporate entities when recommending lodging and dining options. More often than not, they are run by unimaginative drones who care little about the region and the bounty offered to visitors.

I have traveled the area in all seasons, talked to hundreds of people and visited every historic and cultural site in this guide. In a few cases, if I couldn't experience a place myself, I talked to experts whose judgment I relied on to ensure you are getting the best recommendations.

There are many different types of travelers, so this book offers a large number of places for visiting and dining. I have tried to select a variety to please people of all ages and all budgets. Some sites are free while others have rather expensive admission charges, but all are the best of their type.

Keep in mind lunches may cost considerably less than dinners; single lodging rates may be higher or lower depending on the establishment; and in some places special rates are available to groups, those over the age of 65, or mid-week. If an attraction or restaurant is omitted, that doesn't reflect a negative review. It is possible the place may have recently opened. Therefore, please contact me so future editions of the guidebook will be as complete and accurate as possible.

All sites included in this guide are within a day's drive of New York City and New Jersey. Many are a few hours by car from Boston and Philadelphia. The book is arranged by county beginning with those on the west side of the Hudson River, heading north to Albany and Saratoga Springs, and continuing south of Albany on the east side of the Hudson. You can be with the crowds or be utterly alone on a mountaintop. You can consume crunchy apples and creamy goat cheese, hike, kayak, or just take a walk along the Hudson River. The climate is fairly temperate and the views are extraordinary.

Many places of interest are seasonal, as are several outdoor activities, but many sites are open year-round. Summer events, in particular, are often held rain or shine; however, I strongly suggest you plan ahead and check schedules before making a long trip.

At the beginning of each chapter I have listed phone numbers and websites for tourism departments in every county. You may want to contact one or two for specific information when you return home.

The Hudson Valley and Catskill Mountains offer such a range of sights and activities virtually all visitors enjoy their stay. Take your time exploring my favorite region—-my childhood home (Shrub Oak in northern Westchester County), and where I have returned to live (Woodstock) since 1980. And remember: share your suggestions and discoveries with me at PO Box 425, Woodstock, NY 12498 or email contact@joannemichaels.com.

Don't forget to keep the book in your car so it is always available to guide you while traveling through this special place on the planet!

Joanne Michaels, Woodstock, NY
February 2018

IF YOU HAVE...

2-3 DAYS IN THE HUDSON VALLEY, YOU MUST SEE:

1. Olana/City of Hudson
2. FDR Home/Vanderbilt Mansion/ERVK
3. Walkway Over the Hudson
4. West Point (USMA)
5. Village of Woodstock/KTD Monastery
6. Mohonk Mountain House

4-5 DAYS IN THE HUDSON VALLEY, YOU MUST SEE:

1. Olana/City of Hudson
2. FDR Home/Vanderbilt Mansion/ERVK
3. Walkway Over the Hudson
4. Village of Rhinebeck
5. Village of Woodstock/KTD Monastery
6. Mohonk Mountain House
7. Bannerman Island/Cruise on Hudson
8. West Point (USMA)
9. Opus 40/Village of Saugerties
10. Huguenot Stone Houses/New Paltz

6-8 DAYS IN THE HUDSON VALLEY, YOU MUST SEE:

1. Olana/City of Hudson
2. FDR Home/Vanderbilt Mansion/ERVK
3. Walkway Over the Hudson/Rhinebeck
4. Village of Woodstock/ KTD Monastery
5. Mohonk Mountain House/High Falls
6. Bannerman Island-Cruise Hudson
7. West Point (USMA)
8. Opus 40/Village of Saugerties
9. Huguenot Stone Houses/New Paltz
10. Villages of Nyack & Piermont
11. Village of Millerton
12. City of Saratoga Springs

The Stony Point Lighthouse.

ROCKLAND COUNTY

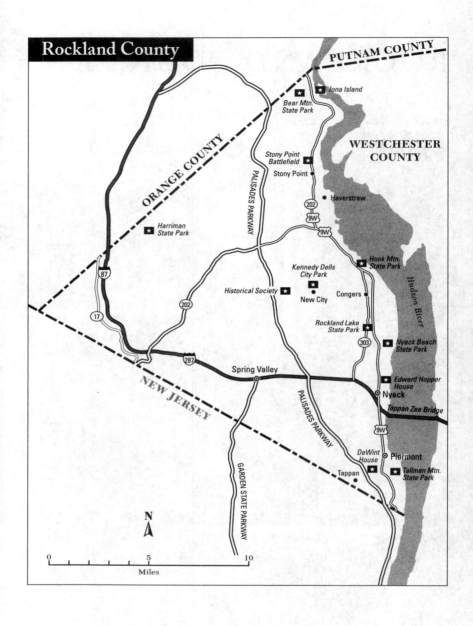

1

Rockland County

PUTNAM COUNTY

Iona Island

Bear Mtn.
State Park

WESTCHESTER
COUNTY

Stony Point
Battlefield

Stony Point

202
9W

Haverstraw

9W

ORANGE COUNTY

PALISADES PARKWAY

Harriman
State Park

87

Hook Mtn.
State Park

Kennedy Dells
City Park

Historical Society

New City

Congers

17

202

Rockland Lake
State Park

303

Nyack Beach
State Park

Hudson River

287

Spring Valley

Edward Hopper
House

Nyack

NEW JERSEY

Tappan Zee Bridge

9W

PALISADES PARKWAY

DeWint
House

Piermont

Tappan

Tallman Mtn.
State Park

GARDEN STATE PARKWAY

N

0   5   10
Miles

ROCKLAND COUNTY

Only 176 square miles in size, Rockland County packs a lot into its area. It seems everywhere you look in Rockland there is a park, from the tiny vest-pocket squares of green in towns and villages to the great spaces of Bear Mountain. Only 30 miles north of New York City, Rockland has preserved many of its forests, wetlands, mountains, and historic sites and still offers residents and visitors 32,000 acres of parkland. Wealthy patrons, civic leaders, and citizen activists joined forces to prevent Bear Mountain and High Tor from becoming a prison site and a quarry, respectively. Today, the fruits of those early environmental battles are seen and enjoyed by all. Hundreds of miles of hiking and biking trails wind through estuarine marshes, along the Hudson River, and up over dramatic peaks. Lakes and streams teem with wildlife and plant lovers will delight in the explosion of color and scent that marks the spring wildflower season. Stony Point Battlefield, the mountaintop meadow where American troops defeated the British redcoats, is very much as it was more than 200 years ago.

In small towns and villages throughout the county, houses have been preserved with care and a sense of history. Visitors feel as if they have stepped back in time. While touring Rockland, you will hear again and again the names of those who made history and are still remembered in ceremonies and festivals throughout the county: George Washington, Benedict Arnold, John André, and even Captain Kidd!

VISITOR INFORMATION

Rockland County Tourism (845-709-7300; 18 New Hempstead Road, New City 10956; www.explorerocklandny.com.

Visitor Center: Palisades Parkway Tourist Information Center (845-786-5003), between exits 16 and 17 on the Palisades Interstate Parkway. The center offers trail and road maps, hiking and travel information, including NYS fishing licenses. Open April through October; daily 8-6; November through March, daily 8-5.

Nyack Chamber of Commerce (845-353-2221), PO Box 677, Nyack 10960; www.nyackchamber.org.

Arts Council of Rockland County (845-598-9421); 55 West Railroad Avenue, Garnerville 10923; www.artscouncilofrockland.org.

Historical Society of Rockland County (845-634-9629), 20 Zukor Road, New City 10956; www.rocklandhistory.org.

HOW TO GET THERE

By car: From the upper deck of the George Washington Bridge, follow signs to the Palisades Parkway. Take exit 9E, the New York State Thruway, which leads to Interstate I-87 South. Get off at exit 11, Nyack, the last exit before the Tappan Zee Bridge. Make a left off the exit onto Route 59 (becomes Main Street).

By bus: **Rockland Coaches** (845-356-0877) operates buses that travel daily from the Port Authority in Manhattan at 20 minutes past the hour, to Route 9W in Nyack. **Transport of Rockland** (845-364-3333) operates a bus line servicing ten routes within Rockland County and offers service to the Westchester towns of Tarrytown and White Plains. Some of these buses stop at the Metro North train station, where travelers can make connections to Manhattan.

MEDICAL EMERGENCY

Nyack Hospital (845-348-2000), 160 North Midland Avenue, Nyack 10960.

Good Samaritan Hospital (845-368-5000), 255 Lafayette Avenue, Suffern. Poison Control Center (800-222-1222); Rabies Information (845-364-2594).

VILLAGES

Nyack. Located off the NYS Thruway at exit 11, the last exit before the Tappan Zee Bridge. First settled by the Nyack Indians, who moved there from Brooklyn, Nyack soon became home to the Dutch, who began to farm the region. When steamboats arrived, making river travel easier, Nyack became a center for shipping and boatbuilding. The town is now known as an antiques and arts center, home to dozens of shops that offer the finest furniture, jewelry, crafts, and artwork.

To see Nyack's charming architectural heritage, begin at South Broadway, near the Nyack Public Library, one of the libraries built with funds from the Carnegie Foundation at the turn of the 20th century. Next to the library is a Queen Anne-style house with a tower and fine shingle work. Heading north, at 46 South Broadway, Couch Court is an unusual late-19th century building that sports a towerlike cupola. The Presbyterian church was built in 1838 in

The Flywheel at the Flywheel Park in Piermont is the actual piece of machinery that helped provide power for the first factory in town, the Piermont Paper Company, over a century ago.

the Greek Revival style, in which columns and symmetry were used in an effort to capture what was considered the ancient purity of Greece. Down the street a little farther, look for the Tappan Zee Theatre, built when movies were silent and vaudeville shows were the rage. Across the street, the Reformed church has a clock tower that dates from 1850. On Burd Street a plaque on the bank tells a little of the history of Nyack. On North Broadway you'll see the Congregation of the Sons of Israel, a synagogue founded in 1870. A side trip down and around Van Houten Road (it turns into Castle Heights) runs past riverfront homes and offers a magnificent view of the Hudson. Continue your drive up North Broadway, passing splendid mansions and lovely 18th-century homes, to Hook Mountain State Park.

The village of Nyack sponsors special events throughout the year, including a farmers' market every Thursday 8am-2pm, May through November, in the municipal parking lots at Main and Cedar streets, rain or shine; there are arts and antiques street fairs during the spring and fall, a Halloween parade and other happenings. A series of spring walking tours includes a guided walk through Oak Hill Cemetery, which contains the burial sites of Helen Hayes, Edward Hopper, Ben Hecht, Carson McCullers, and many other fascinating people who made Nyack their home. For information regarding dates and times, check the website, friendsofthenyacks.org.

Piermont. This is one of my favorite villages in Rockland and many travelers neglect to take a detour there. Located about four miles south of Nyack, you can follow Piermont Avenue from Nyack and drive along the Hudson River right into town. The village became somewhat renowned after Woody Allen filmed *The Purple Rose of Cairo* (1985) here. The Piermont Flywheel Gallery (845-365-6411), open Thursday through Sunday, 1-6pm, on the pier, is just one of many intriguing places to see fine art and photography here. The best way to experience Piermont is to park the car and wander along Piermont Avenue and the waterfront area. The village is chock-full of interesting shops and galleries.

Haverstraw. The brickworks that lined the Hudson in the 19th century made this town, located north of Nyack, known as the brick-making capital of the world. Barges once carried bricks to New York City. When cement became a more popular building material, the town deteriorated, like many places with economies based around changing industries. Today Haverstraw is in the midst of an exciting renaissance. Upscale businesses and restaurants are moving into newly renovated storefronts. A downtown walking tour offers a sample of some fine Central American cuisine. At 91 Broadway a restored brick firehouse is now the **Arts Alliance of Haverstraw** (845-786-0253), open Monday through Friday 10-5; Saturday and Sunday by appointment. Don't miss the **Garnerville Arts and Industrial Center** (845-947-1155), 55 West Railroad Avenue, a renovated factory complex filled with an array of art galleries, crafts shops, and cabinetmakers. **The Haverstraw Brick Museum** (845-947-3505), at 12 Main Street, gives a detailed overview of the town's past, when it was home to more than 40 brickyards. **Emeline Park**, at the foot of Main Street, is the perfect place to rest after strolling; you will be treated to wonderful river views. Traveling by ferry is also an option for commuters in Haverstraw. A direct ferry service is available between Haverstraw and Ossining. For a schedule, check www.nywaterway.com.

Tappan. The local government here was the first in New York State to establish by ordinance a historic district. A walk down Main Street in Tappan will reveal the result, with many 18th- and 19th-century structures still standing tall. The **Tappan Library**, a frame house dating from the mid-18th century, boasts a restored colonial garden. John André was imprisoned in the **Yoast Mabie Tavern**, built in 1755, although Washington's instructions were that André be treated civilly. Just beyond the tavern look for the **Killoran House**, a town house built in 1835 with the bricks taken from a dismantled church. In the middle of Main Street, where it meets Old Tappan Road, the village green was the site of the public stocks and the liberty pole, depending on the mood of the townspeople at the time. The nearby **Reformed Church of Tappan** stands on the site where

André was tried and convicted of spying. Although André requested he be shot as a soldier, the tribunal ordered him hanged as a spy, since to do otherwise would have been to cast doubt upon his guilt. In the nearby burying grounds you will find many old tombstones. Farther up the road is the **Demming-Latrelle House**, best known as the home of the man who manufactured the first canned baby food.

WHAT TO SEE

Edward Hopper House Art Center (845-358-0774; www.edwardhopperhouse. org), 82 North Broadway, Nyack. Open Wednesday through Sunday noon-5. Admission charged; under age 16 free. The American realist painter Edward Hopper was born in Nyack in 1882 and as a youth spent much of his time in the village. Several of his paintings feature local landmarks, and he taught painting classes at the house, which was built by his grandfather. When he died in 1967, Hopper was buried in the Oak Hill Cemetery. His boyhood home was rescued from demolition not long after his death, and today it is a community arts and cultural center. Exhibits include works by Hopper and other American painters, and concerts are given in the gardens of the Hopper House each summer. Art classes and workshops are given for both adults and children.

The Haverstraw Brick Museum on Main Street is open on weekend afternoons year-round and tells the story of the town's major industry in decades past.

DeWint House National Shrine and George Washington Masonic Historic Site (845-359-1359; www.dewinthouse.com), 20 Livingston Avenue (near Oak Tree Road), Tappan. Open year-round, daily, except Monday, 10-4. Free. Constructed in 1700 of Holland brick and sandstone, the DeWint House boasts the pitched roof and tile fireplace common in well-to-do Dutch homes of the period. Although the house is important architecturally, it is best known as George Washington's headquarters and as a shrine to Washington's participation in the fraternal organization known as the Masons. It was also here that Washington, after refusing to commute the sentence, stayed the day that British spy Major John André was hanged. It is recorded that Washington asked that the shutters to his room be closed—the same shutters covering the window today. When the house was purchased by the Masons, the owner said family tradition held that several of the items in the house were there at the time of Washington's war, along with the story of his membership in the Masons. A small carriage-house museum also contains period artifacts and exhibits, and trees around the site have been marked with identification tags. Information on a self-guided walking tour of Tappan is also available at the carriage house.

Camp Shanks World War II Museum (845-638-5419; www.rockvets.com), 20 Greenbush Road, Orangeburg. Open Memorial Day weekend through Labor Day, Saturday and Sunday noon-4. Free. This site was the processing center for more than a million soldiers who shipped overseas from the Piermont Pier to Normandy. Now a small museum, it tells the story of military life at the camp through exhibits and a visit to a barracks.

Historical Society of Rockland County (845-634-9629; www.rocklandhistory. org), 20 Zukor Road, New City. Open Wednesday through Friday and Sunday noon-4. Jacob Blauvelt House is open by appointment only. Admission. This site features a history museum and the 1832 Jacob Blauvelt House. Rotating exhibits and programs throughout the year display the history of Rockland County. The museum shop offers a good selection of local history publications.

Holocaust Museum Center for Tolerance & Education (845-574-4099; www.holocauststudies.org), 145 College Road, Suffern. Library Media Center open Monday through Thursday, 10-3; closed on national and Jewish holidays. Free. Visitors to this museum will be humbled and moved by powerful images of the Holocaust and the strength shown by its survivors. A permanent exhibit examines the history and effects of the Holocaust, while videos and artwork bring home the personal horrors of this period. A research library is available for public use.

Stony Point Battlefield (845-786-2521; www.palisadesparkconservancy.org), 44 Battlefield Road, Stony Point (located on Park Road, off Route 9W). Open mid-April through October, Wednesday through Saturday 10-4:30; Sunday noon-4:30. Grounds open until 5. Free, although there is a parking fee on weekends and a charge for special events. When George Washington felt he had to demonstrate that American troops were determine to stand up to the superior British forces in the Hudson Highlands, he sent in General Wayne to prove the point. In July 1779, Wayne led the elite troops of the Corps of Light Infantry in an attack on the British at Stony Point. During a midnight raid, the Americans routed the British from their beds and challenged their reputation as an invincible fighting force. A self-guided walking tour of the battlefield takes visitors through a wildly beautiful park where remnants of British fortifications still survive. Trails are marked with plaques explaining the battle, and you will pass the 1826 Stony Point Lighthouse, used for more than a century to aid ships on the Hudson. It was restored in 1995. The museum offers exhibits and original memorabilia illustrating the tactics and strategies that brought victory to the Americans. Dogwoods bloom along the paths, and special events, like military encampments and holiday celebrations, are held in the spring, summer and fall.

ACTIVITIES

BASEBALL

Provident Bank Park/Home of the Rockland Boulders (845-364-0009; www.rocklandboulders.com), 1 Provident Bank Drive, Pomona. This impressive stadium opened in 2011 and overlooks the scenic Ramapo Mountains. Home to the Rockland Boulders, an independent professional minor league baseball team, the ballpark features extra-wide seats, a large food court, a special kids' zone and an exciting atmosphere. If you are a baseball fan, make sure to take in a game when you are in the area. The season runs from mid-May through early September and the prices are reasonable. A full schedule is posted on the website.

BICYCLING

Rockland Lake and Tallman State Park both have paved bicycle paths. Although Bear Mountain State Park and Harriman State Park offer a number of challenging bike routes, both can get extremely congested on weekends. Another option is Nyack Beach State Park, located off Route 9W with access from Broadway in Upper Nyack. This park runs along the Hudson River and the paths are flat, with fine views. Hook Mountain State Park also offers biking paths with scenic river views. To get there, go east on North Broadway in Nyack; the park is located at the end of the road. Bike Route 9 starts in Manhattan then crosses the George Washington Bridge and goes north along the Hudson River, crossing back over the river at the Bear Mountain Bridge. Bike Route 9 is part of the Hudson Valley Greenway.

FARM STANDS AND PICK-YOUR-OWN FARMS

Although Rockland County is small there are still a half dozen outlets for local fruits and vegetables.

Auntie El's Farm Market (845-753-2122), 171 Route 17, Sloatsburg. Open year-round, daily 8am-7pm. This market offers an enormous array of fruits and vegetables from Rockland County farms.

Dr. Davies Farm (845-268-7020) Two Locations—Route 9W, Congers; 306 Route 304, Congers. Both places are open daily 8:30-6. You can pick your own apples in the fall and then select from a wide variety of berries, pumpkins, plums, and other goodies at the farm stand. The Davies, a community-minded family who are involved in the arts in the county, own the oldest farm in Rockland dating back to 1836. The produce is excellent and the farm is well worth a stop. "Dr. Davies" was owner Niles Davies' *grandmother*, by the way, not a common occupation for a woman in the early 20th century! Note: Only cash or checks accepted… no credit cards.

The Hand and Hoe, at the Fellowship Community (845-356-8494), 241 Hungry Hollow Road, Chestnut Ridge. Organic fruits and vegetables sold Friday only, noon-5.

Nyack Farmers Market, the municipal parking lot at Main and Cedar streets, Nyack. Held May through November, every Thursday 8-2, rain or shine. This is a great place to stock up for the weekend. The market attracts farmers from throughout the region and offers an enormous variety of produce as well as specialty foods.

The Orchards at Concklin (845-354-0369), 2 South Mountain Road, Pomona. Open March through December. This farm has been in business since 1712. You can harvest your own apples and pumpkins in September and October. Open daily 9-5.

Van Houten Farms and Garden Center (845-735-4689), 68 Sickletown Road, Pearl River. Open March through December, daily, 9-6:30, with fruits, vegetables and holiday greenery in season.

FISHING

The state parks allow fishing, but you will have to check with them for their individual regulations and restrictions. Fishing is also allowed in the Ramapo River, which has a long trout season. Route 17 has parking areas, and the waters north of Ramapo are considered good fishing spots. On Route 202 near Suffern, watch for the Mahwah River and the parking areas along its bank. Minisceongo Creek has good fishing from the Rosman Brige. New York State fishing licenses are required for all state parks except for crabbing and angling in the Hudson River.

GOLF

Blue Hill Golf Course (845-735-2094), 285 Blue Hill Road, Pearl River. Open weekdays 7am-dusk; weekends 6:30am-dusk. Operated by the town of

Orangetown, they boast 27 holes and have a restaurant on the premises. This course is a good choice for beginners.

Philip J. Rotella Memorial Golf Course (845-354-1616), 100 Thiells Mount Ivy Road, Thiells. Open weekdays 7am-7pm; weekends 6am-7pm. Named for a former Haverstraw town supervisor, this challenging 18-hole championship golf course underwent a $3 million renovation in recent years. Duffers will enjoy a view of the Hudson River from one of the tees. Owned and operated by the town of Haverstraw.

Rockland Lake State Park Champion Golf Course (845-268-7275), 100 Route 9W, Congers. Open April through October weekdays 7am-dusk; weekends and holidays 6am-dusk. There are actually two golf courses at this state park, including an 18-hole par-3 course and an 18-hole full-size course. It is advised to call 10 days in advance to reserve weekend tee times. There is a clubhouse, driving range, pro shop and snack bar here.

Spook Rock Golf Course (845-357-6466), 233 Spook Rock Road, Suffern. Open weekdays 7am-dusk; weekends 6am-dusk. This 18-hole championship course was built in 1969; it is owned and operated by the town of Ramapo. There is a driving range open 7am-7pm and two practice greens.

Tappan Golf Center (845-359-0642), 116 Route 303, Tappan. Open year-round, daily 6:30am-10pm, this 18-hole miniature golf course is a great place to go with the kids.

HIKING/WALKING

Almost every park has hiking trails that wind through the woods or over mountains. Some unusual trails, set up to commemorate the American Revolution, also provide ways to get to know local history. The 1777 Trail, the 1777E Trail and the 1777W Trail — known collectively as the **Bicentennial Trails** — are all less than three miles in length. Located in Bear Mountain and Harriman state parks, the trails are accessed from Route 9W, one mile north of Tompkins Cove. Look for the diamond-shaped white blazes with red numbers. This is also the starting area for the **Timp-Torne Trail,** a 10-mile hike that offers spectacular views down the Hudson River all the way to New York City. The trail ends at the Bear Mountain Inn. The shorter **Anthony Wayne Trail,** a three-mile loop marked with white blazes, can be found in Harriman State Park (exit 17 off the Palisades Interstate Parkway). Another popular trail is the **Pine Meadow Trail,** which begins at the Reeves Meadow Visitors Center on Seven Lakes Drive in Harriman State Park near Sloatsburg. If you want to climb Bear Mountain, take the **Major Welch Trail** from the Bear Mountain Inn.

Buttermilk Falls Park, in Nyack, has trails from the parking lot to the falls themselves, a lovely place in early spring.

Kennedy Dells Park, Main Street, one mile north of New City (watch for signs), was once part of film producer Adolph Zukor's estate. Along with hiking trails, there is also a trail for people with disabilities.

Dutch Garden, at the County Office Building, New Hempstead Road, New City, is a three-acre historic site with gardens and walking paths.

Shorter walks may be taken in **Betsy Ross Park,** Tappan; **Tackamack North** and **Tackamack South** parks, Clausland Mountain Road, Blauvelt; and along the **Erie Trail,** which runs from Sparkill to Grandview along abandoned railroad tracks. **Mount Ivy,** off Route 202, Pomona, is a rails-to-trails park, with hiking along the old tracks and a wetlands and nature study center.

PARKS

Bear Mountain State Park (845-786-2701). Take exit 19 off the Palisades Interstate Parkway or Route 9W. Open daily, year-round. Parking fee. Part of the vast Palisades Interstate Park System, Bear Mountain shares almost 54,000 acres with its neighbor, **Harriman State Park.** Noted on maps since the mid-18th century, Bear Mountain has been known as Bear Hill, Bread Tray, and Bare Mountain (presumably because of a bald peak). Once the site of Revolutionary War forts Clinton and Montgomery, the area the park now covers was slated to become the home of Sing Sing Prison until public outcry and political pressure persuaded the state to change its plans early in the 20th century. Since then a parkway system has made the park accessible to the hundreds of thousands who visit each year, and several lakes add to the park's outdoor appeal. Visitors to the park will find a four-season outdoor wonderland featuring a wide program of activities and special events, including swimming, fishing, hiking, boating (rowboats and paddle boats), sledding, and cross-country skiing. At the **Trailside Museum and Zoo,** located across the street from the Bear Mountain Inn (watch for signs; see Lodging), exhibits and programs describe the Native American, military, and natural history of the area. (There are even mastodon remains!) Open year-round, daily 10-4:30. Donation requested. Across the field from the Bear Mountain Inn, a beautiful **carousel** has been built and it's housed in a stone-and-timber Adirondack-style building. Children may climb aboard carved animals native to the Hudson Valley—raccoons, bears, deer, eagles, fox, river otters, and bobcats—for an old-fashioned ride on this full-size merry-go-round. (Note: There is a small charge for carousel rides.)

The self-guided trail is the oldest continuously run trail in the country. The short trail also features a unique zoo with wildlife in natural settings, including a beaver lodge (which has been cut away for easy viewing), a reptile house, and trees, shrubs, and plants with identification tags. On into the park, visitors may want to bike or drive along the scenic inter-park roads.

Harriman State Park, with rock formations dating back one billion years, has also become a center for geology buffs. For many years geological researchers neglected the New York region, but that has changed, thanks in large part to the efforts of Dr. Alexander Gates, who discovered garnets in the park dating back more than two million years. Gates and his research team have done geological mapping at Harriman, which is pretty much as it was 12,000 years ago when the last glacier retreated.

Hook Mountain and Nyack Beach State Park (845-268-3020). To reach Hook Mountain State Park, take North Broadway, in Nyack, east to the end; follow signs. To reach Nyack Beach State Park, take Route 9W from Broadway. Both parks are open daily dawn to dusk; free. Hook Mountain has been referred to by the Dutch colonists as Verdrietige (tedious) Hook because the winds could change rapidly and leave a boat adrift in the river. The area was also a favorite campground of Native Americans because of its wealth of oysters. For modern visitors the park provides a place to picnic, hike, bike, and enjoy scenic views of the Hudson. A hawk watch is held every spring and fall, and local lore suggests the park is haunted by the ghost of the Guardian of the Mountain, a Native American medicine man who appears during the full moon each September and chants at the ancient harvest festival. Nyack Beach State Park is open for hiking, kayaking, picnicking, and fishing; the views of the river are outstanding.

Piermont Marsh and Tallman Mountain State Park (845-359-0544), Rockland Road, off Route 9W, in Sparkkill, near Piermont, north of Palisades Interstate Parkway, exit 4. Piermont Marsh can be reached through Tallman Mountain State Park by following the bike path or from the Erie Pier in the village of Piermont. Admission fee. This nature preserve covers more than 1000 acres of tidal marsh, mountain, and river and is considered one of the most important fish-breeding areas along the Hudson. Wildflowers, such as the spectacular rose mallow, abound in portions of the marsh, and this is a prime bird-watching locale in all seasons. The area along the marsh is a marvelous place to view the river and a hike up the mountain offers a stunning panorama for photographers. Tallman Mountain State Park is a wonderful place to spend a summer day—along with its natural wonders, the park has complete recreational facilities, including bike paths, an 18-hole miniature-golf course, tennis courts, and hiking trails. Even some human-made ponds have become home for many varieties of reptiles and amphibians; ironically, the ponds were to have been part of a tank storage area for a large oil company earlier in the 20th century. Today, especially in spring, the ponds hum with the sounds of frogs, and the woods come alive with birdcalls.

Rockland Lake State Park (845-268-3020), Route 9W, Rockland Lake exit, Congers. Open year-round, daily 8am-dusk. Use fee. Another jewel in the crown of the Palisades Interstate Park System, this popular recreation area is located at the base of Hook Mountain. The lake was once the site of an ice farm, which provided a harvest of pure, clear ice for nearly a century before the advent of modern refrigeration. The park is a wonderful place to explore: in addition to hiking, you can enjoy swimming, jogging, fishing, biking, boating and golf. Rowboats are available to rent by the hour. During the winter, go ice skating on the lake or cross-country skiing and sledding on some of the challenging hills. At the nature center you will discover live animals and exhibits, special events and programs throughout the summer, and guided tours along the wetlands walkway (3.25 miles around the lake). Just outside the center, marked nature trails run along a boardwalk and contain Braille interpretation stops for the blind and visually impaired. Wildflowers and birds are particularly vibrant during the spring, but there are wonders to discover here any time of year.

LODGING

Bear Mountain Inn (845-786-2731), 3020 Seven Lakes Drive, Bear Mountain 10911. ($$$) There are fifteen deluxe guestrooms and suites in this majestic landmark hotel originally built in 1915 overlooking the shores of Hessian Lake. A beautiful stone and timber structure, the ambiance combines rustic mountainside elegance with all the creature comforts of home. An array of recreational activities on the premises will delight visitors year-round, including swimming in the outdoor pool, hiking, cross-country skiing and ice-skating on the outdoor rink. There are lovely walking paths around the hotel, and guests may enjoy a short stroll in addition to longer day hikes. All rooms are equipped with 32-inch cable TV, high-speed Wi-Fi Internet access, and kitchenette with microwave and refrigerator. Pets are strictly prohibited.

Bricktown Inn (845-429-8447), 112 Hudson Avenue, Haverstraw 10927. ($$) This renovated brick Colonial home built in the mid-1800s features a mansard roof, striking mahogany staircase, plaster moldings, and high ceilings. Four guest rooms include private baths and air-conditioning, and are decorated with antiques and family heirlooms. A separate parlor has a TV and Wi-Fi. The parlor is designed for conversation and comfort and includes a baby grand piano. The Garden Room is a great place to read, relax, or watch a move from the extensive DVD collection. Guests get excellent value for the money here.

Casa Hudson (845-219-1698), 34 First Street, Haverstraw 10927. ($$)
This newly restored 1850s Italianate villa on the Hudson River is a modern
interpretation of bed & breakfast hospitality. Owners Andrea Caccuro, a
former fashion executive, and her husband, Nelson Diaz, an artist, have done
a fantastic job creating an atmosphere where guests feel welcome. Each of the
three rooms with eclectic decor has a combination lock, private bath and free
Wi-Fi. One room has views of a private beach on the Hudson River. There
are no televisions. A brickyard owner built the home almost 200 years ago
and a stay here combines all the modern amenities with a feeling of stepping
back in time. There's fresh fruit and a variety of pastries for breakfast; on
occasion, locally made tamales will be offered as well! (Pasta making classes
and chef demonstrations with communal dinners are given at certain times
of the year, so inquire, if you're interested.)

Time Hotel (845-675-8700), 400 High Avenue, Nyack 10960. ($$$) First
opened in 2016, this 133-room, four-story boutique hotel with loft-style
accommodations, a rooftop bar & lounge, is located just off the NY State
Thruway (exit 11) and situated in a renovated plastics factory building. Rooms
are spacious and there is a decent restaurant (Bobby Van's) specializing in
steak and seafood on the premises, but the walls are thin and when the hotel
is crowded this can be an issue. This hotel will appeal more to millennial
travelers and those who aren't looking for first-rate service.

*Michelle Natale, owner of Bricktown Inn Bed & Breakfast in Haverstraw, goes all out at the
holidays with her fantastic Christmas decorations and Victorian High Tea.*

Rockland County has a number of fine chain hotels and the following eight are the ones I recommend:

Crowne Plaza Suffern (845) 357-4800, 3 Executive Boulevard, Suffern 10901. ($$$); crowneplaza.com.

Doubletree by Hilton Hotel Nanuet (845) 623-6000, 425 Route 59, Nanuet 10954. ($$$); doubletree3.hilton.com.

Hampton Inn (845) 623-2800, 260 West Route 59, Nanuet 10954. ($$$); Nanuet.hamptoninn.com

Hilton Garden Inn (845) 623-6000, 623-6000, 270 West Route 59, Nanuet 10954. ($$$) Nanuet.stayhgi.com

Hilton Pearl River (845-735-9000), 500 Veterans Memorial Highway, Pearl River 10965. ($$$) 3.hilton.com

HNA Palisades Premier Conference Center (845-732-6000), 334 Route 9W, Palisades 10964. ($$$) hnapalisades.com

Holiday Inn Orangeburg (845-359-7000), 329 Route 303, Orangeburg 10962. ($$) holidayinn.com

Marriot Fairfield Inn (845-426-2000), 100 Spring Valley Marketplace, Spring Valley 10977. ($$) qualityinn.com/springvalley

WHERE TO EAT

DINING OUT

Alain's Bistro (845-535-3315), 9 Ingalls Street, Nyack. ($$$) Open daily noon-10; Saturday 5-10. When you enter this authentic cozy bistro, you feel far from its strip mall locale. The cuisine is authentic French Alsatian with such offerings as onion soup, country paté, steak frites, duck leg confit, braised short ribs and pan-seared diver scallops. Desserts are not to be missed and include apple tart, crème brulee and sorbet. Do not take the kids, please!

Babe's (845-429-8647), 73 East Railroad Avenue, West Haverstraw. ($$) Open daily 11am-midnight. This establishment welcomes diners with a pink and green neon sign that dates back to 1928, when it was Tony's Luncheonette. The current owners took over in 2000 and returned the restaurant to its speakeasy period looks. The menu offers traditional favorites, including salads, burgers, and ribs, with an array of hearty fish dishes as well as meat, pasta, and chicken entrees. Everything is prepared to order, and diners won't walk away hungry. Good value for the money. People with children will feel comfortable here.

Banchetto Feast (845-624-3070), 75 West Route 59, Nanuet. ($$) Open daily 11am-11pm. An informal Italian restaurant located in the Nanuet Mall, Banchetto's menu includes pasta, chicken, veal and seafood dishes, all expertly prepared. There are several lunch and dinner specials weekday evenings. The spaghetti with white clam sauce was my favorite here and I wish I had tried their "salad pizza," which sounded interesting. Some diners will be pleasantly surprised to discover whole-wheat pasta may be substituted for the usual variety. Children welcome.

Bombay Grill (845-323-4049), 261 South Little Tor Road, New City. ($) Open daily for lunch 11:30-2:30; dinner 5-9:30. The lunch and dinner buffet here have an enthusiastic local following, and the price is extremely reasonable. The tandoori chicken and chicken tikka masala are both flavorful and are prepared with the right amount of spiciness. There are several curry dishes offered as well as both butter and garlic *nan*. Vegetarians will be pleased to discover a number of options.

Alain's French Bistro on Ingalls Street (Route 59) in Nyack is popular with both local residents and travelers.

Confetti (845-365-1911), 200 Ash Street, Piermont. ($$) Open daily noon-10; Friday and Saturday until 11; Sunday until 8. Just steps away from the Piermont waterfront, this restaurant specializes in authentic Italian dishes created the way they are prepared in Italy. Branzino (sea bass), saltimbocca, and filet mignon are specialties of the house. Chef-owner, Arturo Lepore, recommends the chicken country style (a mélange of homemade sausage, potatoes and an array of vegetables). On the lighter side, a variety of salads, pizzas, and *paninis* are offered. The breads, pastas, and desserts are all homemade on the premises. Children welcome.

Freelance Café and Wine Bar (845-365-3250), 506 Piermont Avenue, Piermont. ($$) Open daily, except Monday, for lunch, noon-3; dinner 5:30-10:30. Next door to Xavier's, this informal eatery offers American specialties like coconut shrimp in a sharp mustard sauce, grilled chicken salad and tiramisu. The service is excellent and it is a popular place with locals.

Giulio's (845-359-3657), 154 Washington Street, Tappan. ($$) Open daily for dinner 5-10. Fine Northern Italian cuisine is served in this century-old Victorian house. There is a candlelit setting at dinner making this one of the more romantic places in Rockland. Sample the Valdostana vitello (veal stuffed with prosciutto and cheese in a champagne sauce) or the scampi Giulio (jumbo shrimp sautéed with fresh mushrooms). Children are welcome. Reservations are suggested.

Hudson House (845-353-1355), 134 Main Street, Nyack. ($$$) Open for dinner Tuesday through Thursday 5:30-10; Friday and Saturday until 11; Sunday 4:30-9:30. Brunch is served Saturday & Sunday 11:30-3:30. Located across the street from the Helen Hayes Performing Arts Center, this building was originally a jail in the 19th century and late became the Nyack Village Hall. The chef, A Culinary Institute graduate, features contemporary American cuisine served with an imaginative flair. Not recommended for children.

Il Fresco (845-398-0200), 15 Kings Highway, Orangeburg. ($$) Open for lunch Monday through Friday 11:30-2:30; dinner daily 5-9:30. Sunday 3-9. Located in a restored 1728 farmhouse with several fireplaces and quaint rooms, this restaurant is a neighborhood favorite and offers a romantic ambience. They feature imaginative Italian cuisine, with the emphasis on fresh local ingredients. There is an excellent wine cellar here and the martini list is impressive. Not recommended for children.

Il Portico (845-365-2100), 89 Main Street, Tappan. ($$) Open Wednesday through Sunday noon-9. There are different fish specials every day at this cozy spot featuring Northern Italian cuisine. The most popular dishes are the veal D'Vinci (with prosciutto and mozzarella) and the linguine a la Genovese (with pesto). The tiramisu and ricotta cheesecake are made fresh on the premises. Portico means porch, by the way! Children are welcome.

La Cascada (845-429-0347), 35 Main Street, Haverstraw. ($) Open daily, 10am-midnight. If you have a hankering for authentic Ecuadorian cuisine, or just want to try it, this is the place to go. Every dish is well-prepared, whether you order steak or chicken with rice, beans and salad, or any of the pork dishes. There are about 40 seats and children are always welcome.

Marcello's Ristorante (845-357-9108), 21 Lafayette Avenue, Suffern. ($$) Open for lunch Monday through Friday noon-2:30; dinner daily 5-9:30. The chef-owner, Marcello, travels to Italy twice each year and brings back new ideas for the continually changing menu. Every dish at this elegant spot is cooked to order, and all pastas are homemade. The seafood ravioli and veal chop with sage are just a couple of the superb house specialties.

Piermont is located on the Hudson River; the Tappan Zee Bridge is visible from the village, even on a foggy afternoon.

Maura's Kitchen (845-535-3533), 81-83 South Broadway, Nyack. ($$) Open Tuesday through Sunday noon-9:30; Monday 5-9pm. This Peruvian restaurant and bar is in a new location as of spring 2017, but the fare remains excellent. Peruvian specialties, tapas and unusual entrees will delight both adventurous diners and those who are reluctant to try anything new!

Old '76 House (845-359-5476), 110 Main Street, Tappan. ($$) Open daily 11am-10pm. Located in a restored 1753 sandstone and brick house, this restaurant boasts beamed ceilings, fireplaces surrounded by Dutch tiles, and a colonial atmosphere. Legend says British major John Andrew was imprisoned here during the Revolution. The traditional American and Continental food is well prepared and entrees include a variety of steak and seafood selections.

Restaurant X & Bully Boy Bar (845-268-6555), 117 South Route 303, Congers. ($$$) Open for lunch Tuesday through Friday noon-2:30; dinner Tuesday through Thursday 5:30-10; Friday and Saturday until 11; Sunday 5-8. This charming country restaurant with lush landscaping and pond has four dining rooms, each with its own distinctive atmosphere. The modern American cuisine with an international flair includes dinner entrees like Pacific ahi tuna, classic beef Wellington, and prosciutto-wrapped Alaskan halibut. This is a lovely place to celebrate a special occasion. Not recommended for children.

Sho Chiku Sushi (845-362-6031), 14 Thiells Mount Ivy Road, Pomona. ($$) Open daily noon-10; lunch buffet Sunday through Friday noon-3; dinner buffet Monday 5-10. This Japanese restaurant has been in business for over 20 years and their sushi and sashimi is renowned by local residents.

Sidewalk Bistro (845-680-6460), 482 Piermont Avenue, Piermont. ($$). Open daily for lunch and dinner noon-10, this consistently solid French bistro offers lovely outdoor dining on the sidewalk in town and in their backyard garden. There are also elegant dining rooms where diners may enjoy favorites like brochette Provencale (shrimp, scallops, polenta grilled asparagus, and fennel). There's bouillabaisse Marseillaise, and mussels in white wine, as well as thin crust individual pizza. The burgers are Kobe beef, for those who prefer American fare. Desserts are superb. Wine list is pricey.

Thai House (845-358-9100), 12 Park Street, Nyack. ($$) Open for lunch Friday through Sunday 11:30-2:30; dinner served daily 5:30-10; until 11 Friday and Saturday. Enjoy beautifully presented Thai dishes whether you are eating in the restaurant or getting take-out. The vegetables here are always cooked perfectly— al dente. Those who enjoy Thai food should not pass up this gem with reasonable prices and good service.

The Turning Point (845-359-1089), 468 Piermont Avenue, Piermont. ($$) Open daily 11-5:30 and also for light fare (burgers, salads, pasta) during musical performances. Check website, turningpointcafe.com, for schedule. The venue has been a hangout for creative people for decades.

Two Henrys (845-735-9000), 500 Veterans Memorial Drive, Pearl River. ($$) Open daily for breakfast 7-11:30; lunch 11:30-3; dinner 5-10. Located in the Pearl River Hilton, this elegant restaurant has a strong local following. The dining room overlooks a golf course, and the relaxing view further enhances the gracious imaginative American cuisine. All entrees served with homemade bread. Don't skip the luscious desserts that include chocolate peanut butter pie! Reservations are suggested for dinner.

Two Spear Street (845-353-7733), 2 Spear Street, Nyack. ($$) Open for dinner Wednesday through Saturday 5-10; Sunday brunch 11-4; dinner 4-9. This family-owned and operated restaurant is delightful. The cuisine is New American with a touch of grandmother's comfort food, and it's served in an intimate atmosphere. Entrees range from baked macaroni and cheese and rib eye steak to veal cordon bleu and whole roasted red snapper. Not recommended for children.

Union Restaurant & Bar Latino (845-429-4354), 22-24 New Main Street, Haverstraw. ($$) Open Tuesday through Saturday for lunch noon-3; dinner 5:30-10; Friday and Saturday until 11; Sunday noon-9. Enjoy American cuisine with a Latin flair prepared by chef-owners who previously worked at **Xavier's** and **Freelance Café,** two of the county's finest restaurants. The atmosphere is inviting with elaborate tin ceilings, rear skylight, dark wood and romantic lighting. The menu features Cuban-inspired dishes such as Tilapia al Sarten (panko-encrusted fillet served over a spinach and white bean ragout) and tuna ceviche with fresh mango cilantro, and coconut milk. I enjoyed an excellent meal here; however, the service can be slow on crowded weekend nights in the summer so be forewarned!

Velo Bistro & Wine Bar (845-353-7667), 12 North Broadway, Nyack. ($$) Open daily except Sunday for lunch noon-3; dinner 5-10:30. Enjoy New American cuisine with a French and Italian accent. Some house favorites include tuna tartare, chianti risotto with black truffle, chicken on a bed of broccoli rabe, and salmon fillet over beet-infused couscous. There is an excellent selection of wines by the glass. The pizza is a great choice if you want a lighter meal.

Wasabi (845-358-7977), 110 Main Street, Nyack. ($$) Open Monday through Friday for lunch noon-2:30; dinner 5-10 Saturday 5-11; Sunday 1-9:30. You can enjoy fine sushi, sashimi, tempura, negimaki, teriyaki and vegetarian dishes at this charming restaurant with elegantly simple Japanese décor. Everything is fresh and made to order before your eyes.

Xavier's at Piermont (845-359-7007), 506 Piermont Avenue, Piermont. ($$$) Open for lunch Tuesday through Friday & Sunday noon-2; dinner 5:30-10; Sunday until 9. Closed Monday. An intimate, beautiful spot that's a perfect place for people who enjoy fine dining. The imaginative menu features Continental cuisine with choices like roast pigeon with truffle sauce and fettuccine with fennel sausage and white grapes. For dessert, there is maple walnut soufflé, a house specialty. Don't bring the kids!

EATING OUT

Agnello's (845-639-5373), 170 North Main Street, New City. ($) Open daily 11:30-9; Sunday 2-9. This is an excellent eatery specializing in coal-fired brick-oven pizza "you can't refuse!"

There are no slices here but everything is made to order from the freshest ingredients. Dozens of choices will delight pizza lovers and there are whole-wheat and gluten-free options to choose from. The atmosphere is classy so don't expect a hole-in-the-wall joint! Check out the $9.95 lunch specials that include a small pizza, salad and a drink during weekdays. Children are welcome.

Anna's Bakery (845-268-7540), 12 Old Haverstraw Road, Congers. ($) Open Tuesday through Saturday, 6am-6pm; Sunday 6-2; Closed Monday. This is the place to go for excellent Italian pastries and cookies and brownies. I love the red velvet whoopee pie. Anna has an edge, but locals claim it comes with the fine baked goods!

Art Café (845-353-4230), 65 South Broadway, Nyack. ($). Open daily 7am-10pm. This vegetarian café specializes in Mediterranean cuisine with largely organic ingredients and serves breakfast and lunch all day. There is always an omelet selection and the soup of the day is a popular choice. Borekas (phyllo dough stuffed with Bulgarian cheese) is a house specialty. The hummus is quite good and there's always a cheese plate to accompany bagels, muffins or croissants. The excellent coffee draws local residents who stop by daily.

Blu Fig New City (845-708-5686), 191 South Main Street; **Blu Fig Stony Point** (845-786-7800), 32 South Liberty Drive. ($) Open daily at both locations 11-10. These eateries/coffeehouses feature brick-oven pizzas, pasta dishes, salads, sandwiches and Mediterranean entrees. Everything is prepared to order and parents will feel comfortable here with the kids.

Bunbury's Coffee Shop (845-398-9715), 460 Piermont Avenue, Piermont. ($) Open Monday through Friday 6:30-6; Saturday and Sunday 7-6. The early morning crowd in town grabs coffee along with muffins and croissants here. The coffee, array of teas and baked goods, are all quite good. A cozy atmosphere prevails if you choose to sit and read the newspaper.

Deli Central (845-786-3601), 65 South Liberty Drive (Route 9W), Stony Point. ($) Open daily 4:30am-6pm. This is the place to stop if you are planning a picnic at Bear Mountain or Harriman State Park. There are over-stuffed sandwiches of all kinds, fresh deli salads and "boo boos," tortillas bursting with several kinds of meats, whatever you like, made to order. The deli is renowned for their generous servings and decent quality. A mainstay for locals, children are welcome.

Didier Dumas Patisserie (845-353-2031), 163 Main Street, Nyack. ($) Open daily 6:30am-9pm; Friday & Saturday until 11pm. The baked goods (croissants, brioches, fresh fruit tarts, layered mousse cakes), as well as superb café au lait, will make you feel transported to France. There are tasty savory treats that include an array of sandwiches too.

El Bandido (845-425-6622), 196 Route 59, Spring Valley. ($) Open daily 111am-midnight. Strolling guitar players add to the fun ambiance at this colorful Mexican eatery, where the portions are generous and the margaritas are first-rate.

Hogan's Family Diner (845-429-9603), 56 South Liberty Drive (Route 9W), Stony Point. ($) Open daily 6am-10pm. Friday & Saturday until 11. The food here is a cut above the usual diner fare. They always offer several specials and portions are large. It's a favorite among local residents and some popular entrees are the prime rib, eggplant *parmigiana*, pot roast and lamb chops. Breakfasts are hearty and the diner is bustling in the early morning hours.

Khan's Mongolian Barbecue (845-359-8004), 588 Route 303, Blauvelt. ($) Open daily, except Monday, for lunch noon-2; dinner 5-9:30; Sunday 4-9 only. Just off the NYS Thruway exit 12, this is one of the better Mongolian barbecue restaurants I have tried. Choose your own ingredients and sauces, and watch while the chef creates a delectable meal before your eyes. The buffet is a bargain and includes appetizers, soup, barbecue, and dessert. The all-inclusive price is exceedingly reasonable. Don't pass on this place if you are traveling with children.

Latin Star Restaurant (845-429-1113), 39 Broadway, Haverstraw. ($) Open daily 5am-9:30pm. The menu is quite extensive in this diner-like establishment specializing in Spanish specialties for breakfast, lunch and dinner.

The Mountain House (845-359-9191), 333 Route 340, Sparkill. ($) Open daily for lunch and dinner, noon-10. While the fare is basic Italian American—burgers, salads and pastas—the specialty of the house is the thin-crust pizza. A perfect place to go with young children.

Nyack Main Essentials (845-512-8692), 145 Main Street, Nyack. ($) Open daily 9am-9pm; closed Sunday. If you enjoy a healthy meal that doesn't compromise on taste, this reasonably priced eatery specializing in Caribbean vegan cuisine is the place to go. There are several salads, kebabs, wraps, freshly squeezed juices, and smoothies; everything is prepared to order. Kids are welcome.

Tacos Marianita (845-942-1295), 10 West Street, Haverstraw. ($) Open daily 11:30-10. If you crave authentic Mexican favorites—tacos, fajitas, enchiladas, or burritos—don't miss this informal eatery known by local residents for consistently turning out terrific food. Kids welcome.

Temptations Café (845-353-3355), 80½ Main Street, Nyack. ($) Open Monday through Thursday 11:30am-10pm; Friday and Saturday until 11. Sunday 8am-9pm. Those with a sweet

Union Restaurant on New Main Street in Haverstraw specializes in Latin cuisine and is renowned for great food.

tooth won't want to pass on this café. There are scores of dessert selections in addition to a wide variety of ice creams, frozen yogurts, cappuccinos, and exotic coffees. The light menu features soups, quiches, salads and sandwiches.

True Food (845-480-5710), 166 Main Street, Nyack. ($) Open daily 8:30am-8:30pm; Sunday until 7:30pm. Organic homemade fare including yucca lasagna, fish tacos, veggie burgers, fresh baked goods, smoothies, juices, coffee, chai and ginger tea. Fair trade, vegan locally sourced ingredients: everything is freshly prepared and tasty. Children welcome.

Rockland Bakery (845-623-5800), 94 Demarest Mill Road, Nanuet. ($) Open daily 6am-10:30pm. This award-winning bakery is one of the largest in the Northeast with an enormous assortment of breads, pies, cakes, cookies and bagels. Everything is super-fresh and high quality.

TFS (The Filling Station) Burger Works (845-786-9000), 45 South Route 9W, West Haverstraw. ($) Open daily 11:30-9. 2nd location—243 Route 9W, Palisades (845-359-9000), Open daily 11:30-9; until 10 Friday & Saturday.

The organic beef burgers include a blend of brisket, hanger steak and short rib from free-range black-angus beef (no antibiotics or hormones). The meat is ground fresh daily and cooked medium, unless otherwise requested. Other fare includes sesame chicken salad, wings and boneless chicken bites. For an inexpensive, decent family meal, this is a wonderful choice.

FOR BEER AFICIONADOS

Defiant Brewery (845-920-8602), 6 Dexter Plaza, Pearl River. ($) Open Monday through Friday, 2-midnight; Thursday & Friday until 2am; Saturday & Sunday noon-midnight; Saturday until 2am. There are a dozen beers on tap and the offerings are constantly changing. The owners continually come up with new brews. From the smokehouse, there's pulled pork, brisket, baby back ribs, wings and hot dogs—and a mac and cheese bowl for vegetarians!

Growler & Gill (845-507-0899), 148 Route 59, Nanuet. ($) Open Monday through Thursday 4-11; Friday & Saturday noon-11; Sunday noon-8. This is truly an innovative establishment—part bar with 24 rotating beers on tap and over 500 (in bottles) from around the world, part retail store. There is an excellent selection of high-end microbrews as well as small batch wines by the glass or bottle. You can pair the terrific fare (chili, pork sliders, German brats and kraut, fish & chips, quesadillas, burgers or pizza) with one of their fine beers. Beer lovers won't want to miss this spot!

ENTERTAINMENT

Levity Live Comedy Club (845-353-5400; levintylive.com), 4210 Palisades Center Drive, Space A-401, West Nyack. This club opened in 2012 and features some of the heaviest hitters in stand-up, including performers from *Saturday Night Live*. Check the website for a full schedule.

Nyack Village Theatre (845-826-2639; nyackvillagetheatre.com), 94 Main Street, Nyack. This community hub offers a potpourri of entertainment including films, music, poetry, and drama. There are intriguing performances year-round, so check the website to find out what's happening.

Penguin Rep (845-786-2873; penguinrep.org), 7 Crickettown Road, Stony Point. In 1977 an empty 100-year-old barn in Stony Point became home of Rockland's first year-round non-profit professional theater. There are 108 seats in 12 rows, all with a great view of the stage. The *New York Times* called Penguin Rep "the gutsiest little theater." The high-quality material and first-class productions are shown on the website.

Rivertown Film Society (845-353-2568; rivertownfilm.org), 58 Depew Avenue, Nyack. This is the place to go for first-rate independent films, including documentaries rarely offered in commercial theaters. Nyack is lucky to have this venue and the website lists the schedule.

Rockland Center for the Arts (845-358-0877; rocklandartcenter.org), 27 South Greenbush Road, West Nyack. Open Monday through Friday 9-5; Saturday 10-4; closed Sunday. Known as ROCA by locals, this non-profit cultural organization has sponsored exhibits, theater, summer camp for kids and extensive classes and workshops in a school for the arts (painting, sculpture, crafts, and fashion) since 1947. Travelers will enjoy strolling through the galleries as well as the Catherine Konner Sculpture Park which is open daily year-round from dawn to dusk.

The Nyack Village Theatre on Main Street offers comedy as well as musical and dramatic performances year-round.

SELECTIVE SHOPPING

Nyack has many shops that are worth a visit, and an entire day can be spent strolling the shopping district and enjoying the antiques and artwork on display. Most stores are open daily except Monday, but call ahead if you are planning to visit. The following establishments are my favorites, but there are many more to wander through.

Hickory, Dickory Dock (845-358-7474), 43 South Broadway, has clocks that tick, clocks that tock—hundreds of selections!

ML Gifts & Accessories (845-358-1293), 75 South Broadway. An eclectic collection of contemporary clothing, jewelry, footwear, and gift items in a range of prices may be found here. Make sure to stop in while walking around the village.

The Original Christopher's Antiques (845-358-9574), 71 South Broadway, is a fine gift shop with all kinds of unique items, including antiques, dried flowers and more.

The Palisades Center (845-348-1000), 1000 Palisades Center Drive, West Nyack. This three million square foot, four-level shopping mall offers over 250 shops under one roof. There are 25 eateries and an NHL-size ice-skating rink, a Ferris wheel, movie complex and an IMAX theater. Located off exit 12 of the NYS Thruway, the mall is open Monday through Saturday 10-9:30; Sunday 11-7.

Squash Blossom (845-353-0550), 49 Burd Street, offers Native American jewelry and crafts.

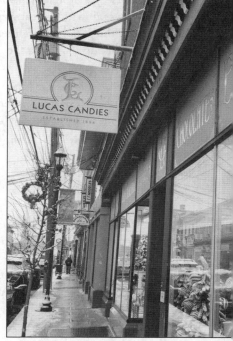

Piermont is smaller than Nyack, yet both are ideal for shopping excursions. The town is best experienced by walking down Piermont Avenue and around the waterfront area. There are several interesting boutiques, specialty stores, art galleries and restaurants. The village **farmers' market** (914-923-4837) is held from late April through mid-

For over 100 years, Lucas Candies in Haverstraw has been creating fine confections.

November every Sunday 9:30-3, rain or shine on Ash Street. Visitors will find plenty of parking available here.

SPECIAL EVENTS

Throughout the course of the year, various local organizations sponsor concerts, parades, art shows, street fairs, and walking tours. It is impossible to list them all. Some of my favorite annual events in Nyack include the **Springfest** street fair in April, the **Septemberfest** street fair, the **Hawk Watch** at Hook Mountain in September, and the **Halloween Parade** in October. The **farmers' market** in Nyack is held May through November, on Thursdays, rain or shine. If you are planning a trip to Rockland County, check the website (rockland.org) for a complete list of special events.

Hudson River view from the village of Piermont.

View from the Newburgh Waterfront looking north.

ORANGE COUNTY

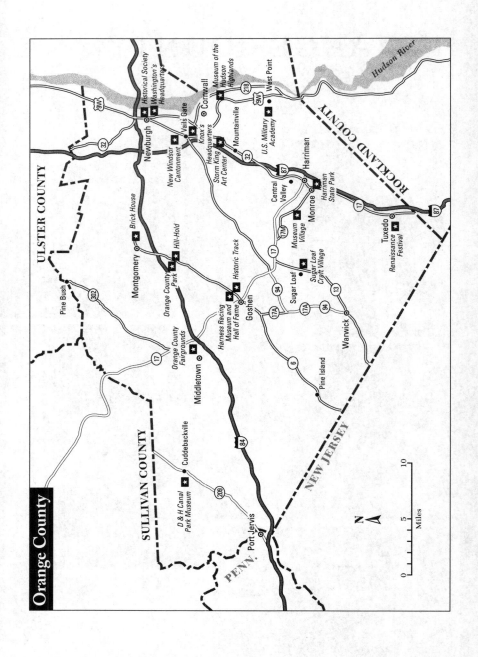

2

Orange County

ORANGE COUNTY

Visitors are reminded in every village and every park in Orange County that this is a place that cherishes its history. Museums, restorations, and historic exhibits are everywhere, from the Native American displays in the Goshen Courthouse to the collection of military equipment at West Point. You can imagine the life of a Revolutionary War soldier as he waited out the bitter winters in a wooden hut or watch as a costumed group of interpreters reenacts a battle that helped turn the tide of the American Revolution.

Orange County is also a place where the agricultural heritage of New York is still strong, a place where vegetable farming is a way of life for families and has been for generations. Stop at a farm and take home some just-picked peaches, or join the fun at the Onion Festival in the Black Dirt area, a unique farming district where some of the best of New York State's produce is grown. A drive through this region in early summer gives new meaning to the word bountiful.

Several wineries and breweries have sprung up in recent years in Orange County. They welcome visitors year-round but the wineries are particularly fun to visit at harvest time in autumn.

VISITOR INFORMATION

Orange County Tourism (845-615-3860; orangetourism.org), 99 Main Street, Goshen 10924.

Park Visitor Center & Bookstore (845-786-5003;palisadesparkconservancy. org), between exits 16 and 17 on Palisades Interstate Parkway. Pick up trail and road maps, hiking guides, local history and nature books. Open daily: April through October 8-6; November through March 8-5.

HOW TO GET THERE

By car: Orange County is accessible from exits 16 (Harriman) and 17 (Newburgh) off I-87; the New York State (NYS) Thruway, coming from the north or south; as well as from I-84 coming from points east and west. Route 17, which joins the Thruway at Suffern, is another route that goes into the county.

By bus and train: Adirondack Trailways (1-800-858-8555; trailwaysny.com) runs buses from Port Authority in New York City to Kingston and Newburgh.

Check the website for complete schedule. **New Jersey Transit** (973-275-5555 or 800-626-RIDE; njtransit.com) runs buses from Manhattan and Newark Airport to Greenwood Lake and Warwick and trains (Port Jervis line) from Pennsylvania Station in Manhattan to Tuxedo, Harriman, Salisbury Mills, Campbell Hall, Middletown, Otisville and Port Jervis. **Short Line/Coach USA** (800-631-8405; coachusa.com/shortline), offers commuter service from Port Authority in New York City to over 20 towns in Orange County. Overnight packages and day trip destinations to West Point, the wineries, Woodbury Common outlets and other places of interest are available. Check the website. **Metro North** (Hudson Line, 212-532-4900; mta.info), stops in Beacon going to and from Grand Central Station in Manhattan. An inexpensive bus shuttle service across the Hudson from Newburgh connects with the trains but doesn't operate on holidays. There is a **ferry service** (845-569-4024; nywaterway.com/NewburghtoBeaconRoute.) connecting the Newburgh waterfront with Beacon, but ferries run only during commuter hours.

By air: Stewart International Airport (845-838-8200), 1180 First Street, New Windsor; services major cities throughout the eastern United States as well as northern European countries.

MEDICAL EMERGENCY

Orange Regional Medical Center (845-333-1000), 707 East Main Street, Middletown.

St. Anthony's Community Hospital (845-986-2276), 15 Maple Avenue, Warwick.

St. Luke's Cornwall Hospital (845-561-4400), 70 Dubois Street, Newburgh; (845-534-7711), 19 Laurel Avenue, Cornwall.

TO SEE

Harness Racing Museum and Hall of Fame (845-294-6330; harnessmuseum. com), 240 Main Street, Goshen. Open year-round, daily 10-5; closed Easter, Thanksgiving, Christmas and New Year's Day. Free. Messenger and Hambletonian, pacers, trotters, and standard-bred horses—all call to mind the speed and grace to be found on a trotting track, and the history and color of the sport can be discovered at this unique museum established in 1951. Trotters and pacers (trotters move their right front and left rear legs at the same time; pacers move both legs on one side at the same time) have long been a part of American history. Such notable figures as George Washington, Abraham Lincoln, and Ulysses S. Grant spent time breeding and racing these swift horses. At the Harness Racing Museum and Hall of Fame, the history of the sport can be traced through dioramas, prints, exhibits, and statues displayed throughout the former Good Time Stables building. Galleries include displays of Currier and Ives prints, 19th and 20th century fine art, famous racing silks, the Greyhound Gallery (featuring harness racing's "Horse of the Century") and the sport's national Hall of Fame where dozens of small lifelike statues recall the greatest participants (human and four-legged) in the sport. Restored stalls have full-size replicas of horses and their equipment, while you can see the sulkies and sleighs the horses once pulled (it wasn't unheard of to drive a horse many miles, then race it, then drive it home to the farm). There is even a room that reproduces the interior of the clubhouse from the nearby Historic Track. The room is so well maintained you expect to hear the rustle of programs and the voices of members discussing the best bet of the day. There are films and shows throughout the museum, changing gallery exhibits, and the world's only 3-D harness racing simulator that makes you feel you are the driver in a race. You can even feel the wind blowing through your hair!

Historic Track (845-294-5333; goshenhistorictrack.com), 44 Park Place, Goshen. Open year-round, daily 10-5. Located directly behind the Harness Racing Museum and Hall of Fame, this is the only sports facility in the country that is a National Historic Landmark. The Historic Track has been hosting meets since the 1830s. Although the Grand Circuit races visit here only once a year, the track is used as a training facility, so you may be able to see pacers, trotters, and a local blacksmith at work, no matter when you visit! The track is such a local institution that some of the private boxes have been passed down in families for generations.

A view of the Hudson River from one of the restaurants that line the Newburgh waterfront.

Hudson Highlands Nature Museum (845-534-5506; hhnaturemuseum.org), PO Box 451, Cornwall with 2 locations: The **Wildlife Education Center** (25 Boulevard, Cornwall-on-Hudson) is open year-round from Friday through Sunday, noon-4; and the **Quest Visitors Center** (174 Angola Road, Cornwall) at the **Outdoor Discovery Center** open May through October, Saturday and Sunday 10-4. There are programs for children at both sites. The **Wildlife Education Center** has a "Meet the Animals" program every Saturday and Sunday at 2:30. Admission fee. To get to the **Wildlife Education Center**, take Route 9W to the Angola Road exit. At the rotary in Cornwall, take the first right onto Hasbrouck Avenue and go to the end. Follow the signs. The **Outdoor Discovery Center** is on Route 9W, just after the Angola Road exit. The **Wildlife Education Center** is an excellent site to visit with children who love animals and want to learn more about their lives and habitats. The changing exhibits in the center are geared to children's interests. The Hall of Animals has an indoor mini zoo that houses small animals native to the Hudson Valley. Several amphibians, reptiles, small mammals and birds, crawl, creep and, in the case of Edgar Allan Crow, talk. Outside the site, there are well-marked easy trails to follow. At the **Outdoor Discovery Center,** families will enjoy hiking trails. Through riddles, hands-on activities and field notes, visitors will learn about nature in an interactive way. The four Quest trails cover woodlands, meadows, and wetlands with ponds and streams. The museum is also known for summer camp and weekend programs for families. Teachers will enjoy the environmental education classes offered to school groups. Strollers can navigate the **Wildlife Education Center** and some trails at the **Outdoor Discovery Center.**

Motorcyclepedia (845-569-9065; motorcyclepediamuseum.org), 250 Lake Street, Newburgh. Open year-round, Friday through Sunday 10-5. Admission fee. Gerald Doering and his son, Edward, opened this motorcycle museum in 2011, featuring 400 bikes along with vintage photographs, posters, and lots of memorabilia. Several exhibit rooms include early American motorcycles dating back to 1865, as well as chopper bikes and Indian motorcycles built between 1902 and 1953. There is a military section as well as several Harley-Davidson models. A re-creation of the Captain America chopper from the film *Easy Rider* is also in one of the galleries. The "Wall of Death," an exciting live demonstration given approximately every six months, always on a Saturday, requires reservations for any of the four shows given on that day. Those who desire a guided tour of the museum can make arrangements by calling in advance. Even those who aren't motorcycle aficionados will find this an interesting place to visit.

Museum Village (845-782-8247; museumvillage.org), 1010 Route 17M, Monroe. Open July and August, daily except Monday, 11-4; mid-April-mid-June and September to mid-November, Saturday & Sunday 11-4. Special events are held throughout the year; and have included a circus, a mineral show, and America's birthday. Check website for a schedule. Admission. The daily life of preindustrial America has been preserved and re-created at this fascinating museum comprised of buildings and equipment moved to the site from other parts of the Hudson Valley. Set up like a small crossroads village, the museum is considered to have one of the largest sites devoted to the folk arts of everyday America. More than 20 buildings house crafts, equipment, and agricultural displays. At the blacksmith's shop, artisans hammer and pound hot metal into a door latch or horseshoe. In the newspaper office, the master printer and the printer's devil (apprentice) are composing the weekly newspaper, and in the potter's workshop butter churns and mugs take shape on the wheel. Costumed guides answer questions; photos, prints and tools trace the history of Orange County. The museum is a favorite place for children. For a fun time set even further back in history, visit the mastodon, the most complete skeleton of this 11,000 year-old animal in New York State. Every Labor Day weekend there is a Civil War encampment, the largest in the Northeast, and it includes battles, camping demonstrations, and drills.

Storm King Art Center (845-534-3115; stormkingartcenter.org), Mountainville (street address for GPS is 1 Museum Road, New Windsor). Take the NYS Thruway to exit 16; the center is off Route 32 north, on Old Pleasant Hill Road. Watch for signs. Open April through mid-November; indoor galleries open mid-May 11:30-5:30. Admission. Special events include classical concerts, garden talks and family activities; check the website for up-to-date schedule. This 500-acre park and museum has one of the world's largest displays of outdoor sculpture. The permanent collection contains dozens of works by several contemporary artists, including Isamu Noguchi, Louise Nevelson, Alexander Calder, David Smith, and Mark di Suvero. The surrounding landscape is lovely, with a backdrop of Schunnemunk Mountain. This is truly one of the most impressive stops in the region and should not be missed. Trams and elevators make the grounds handicapped accessible.

HISTORIC HOMES

Brick House (845-457-4921; hillholdandbrickhouse.org), 850 Route 17K, Montgomery. Open June through Sunday of Labor Day weekend, Saturday & Sunday 10-4. Admission. A treasure trove of early American furniture and decorative arts owned by the same family since 1768. Nor run by Orange

County, the house, a red Georgian mansion constructed with bricks imported from England, is considered one of the finest private homes built between New York City and Albany in the 18th century. It was a meeting site for colonial officers during the Revolution, and many of the original furnishings are still intact. Pieces include a very rare 17th-century chest, fine crystal, Lafayette china (produced to honor the French hero) and an Eli Terry shelf clock. Brick House is the site of a large autumn antiques show: see website for details.

Constitution Island and the Warner House (845-446-8676; constitutionisland. org). Take Route 9W to West Point, enter the U.S. Military Academy gate, and take the first right past the Hotel Thayer. The dock and a large parking lot are at the end of the street. Tours are offered mid-June through late September, Wednesday and Thursday afternoons at 1 and 2pm only. Call for reservations—only 40 people per tour are permitted. There are occasionally weekend tours and special events that begin in Cold Spring (Putnam County). Buses for Constitution Island leave from the south end of the Cold Spring Metro North train station every ten minutes from 10am to 3pm. Check the website to confirm schedule. Admission. To visit this site, take the boat from West Point to Constitution Island. There you will find a 17-room Victorian mansion, home to the Warner family from 1836 to 1915. The daughters, Anna and Susan, grew up on the island and were best known for their writing. Anna penned many hymns, including "Jesus Loves Me," and Susan's Wide Wide World was a bestseller. After their father lost his fortune, the sisters stayed on in their home, living frugally and teaching Sunday school courses to West Point cadets, who never forgot the two spinsters. Their home is now a museum filled with their original possessions. Also on the island are the remains of Fort Constitution, a Revolutionary War-era fort, and the Anna B. Warner Memorial Garden, which is particularly lovely in late June. The surrounding Hudson River is glorious any time. If you visit the West Point cemetery, look for the sisters' graves; they were buried near their beloved home.

Gomez Mill House (845-236-3126; gomez.org), 11 Mill House Road, Marlboro. Open mid-April through mid-November, Wednesday through Sunday 10-4 with tours at 10:15, 11:30 and 1:45. Admission. The oldest surviving Jewish residence in America, and the oldest house in Orange County, this was the home of Lewis Moses Gomez, who arrived in America in 1703 and became a prosperous businessman. He built a stone trading post north of Newburgh, the site of the house, in 1714. In addition to the home, visitors will see the icehouse, root cellar, and restored mill and dam. Continuously inhabited for nearly 300 years, the Gomez house has been a fur trading post and a home to merchants, farmers, and craftspeople.

Hill-Hold (845-29102404; hillholdandbrickhouse.org), 211 Route 416, Campbell Hall. Open mid-May through early October, Friday through Sunday 10-4. Admission. Once a section of a 30,000-acre estate, the land Hill-Hold stands on was presented to William Bull, an English stonemason, as a wedding present in the early 18th century. His son, Thomas Bull, built the home. Fortunately for lovers of 18th-century architecture, later family members donated the house and most of its furnishings to the county. The large Georgian mansion is graced by elegant wood and stonework, with barrel-backed cupboards, paneling, and deep-silled windows. Rooms are furnished with many original Chippendale, Queen Anne, and Empire pieces. Two kitchens are still extant in the house: one in the basement and a newer one, added in 1800, in a separate stone wing. Like most manor houses of the era, Hill-Hold was the center of a thriving farm. Surrounding the farmhouse are the original outbuildings, including the granary, barn, summer kitchen, wagon house, smokehouse, and, of course, the privy. On the working farm, sheep, cows, chickens, and geese are tended. Children will enjoy the farm animals, and flower lovers should spend some time in the summer gardens. Also on the site is the Goosetown School, a one-room schoolhouse still used for educational programs on daily life in the 19th century.

HISTORIC SITES

Clove Furnace (845-351-4696), 21 Clove Furnace Drive, Arden. Open year-round, Monday through Friday 9-11 and 1-4; weekends by appointment only. Free. Although not a very active historic site, this is an unusual one: a small museum devoted to the history of iron making in rural New York is on the premises. The restored hot-blast furnace dates from 1854 and was used to produce artillery pieces during the Civil War. Exhibits outline the story of mining and iron, and there are displays related to Orange County history (some include rare Parrott artillery pieces). An enlightening stop for those interested in the commercial development of what was once a major American industry.

Knox's Headquarters (845-561-5498; nysparks.com/historicsites), 289 Forge Hill Road (Route 94), Vails Gate. Open Memorial Day through Labor Day, Wednesday through Saturday 10-5; Sunday 1-5; grounds open daily. Admission. For several periods during the Revolution, the Ellison family's stone house served as headquarters for the colonial officers in the area. Generals Henry Knox, Horatio Gates, and Nathanael Greene were only a few of the men who met in the house and planned campaigns in the gracious rooms. Today it is furnished with military camp beds and folding desks such as those that displaced the Ellisons' fine 18th-century furniture. There are also two short hiking trails here that are perfect for families traveling with young children.

New Windsor Cantonment (845-561-1765; nysparks.com/historicsites), 374 Temple Hill Road (off Routes 32 and 300), Vails Gate. Open April through October Monday through Saturday 10-5; Sunday 1-5. Admission. Washington's troops waited out the last months of the Revolutionary War here in anticipation of an announced cessation of hostilities. More than 10,000 soldiers, officers, cooks, and blacksmiths, along with their wives and other camp followers, constructed the snug log cabins, outbuildings, and a meeting hall, and here Washington quelled a mutiny of his troops, who resented Congress's slowness with wages and pensions. After the war, the buildings were auctioned off for the lumber, and the land remained unused until the state acquired 70 acres and began restoration of the site.

A visit to the cantonment today provides a look into the everyday life of Revolutionary soldiers. Displays depict the difficulties faced by both the troops and their leaders. The purple Heart, which Washington presented to several soldiers, has its own Hall of Honor. A walkway leads from the orientation center to the rebuilt parade grounds and buildings. Costumed guides go about their business blacksmithing, drilling, cooking and even entertaining (a fife player may be on hand). There are also demonstrations of 18th century medical procedures. Although many of the buildings have been reconstructed from sketches that remain from the era, one is original. It had been carted away to become an addition to a local house, and there it remained for a century and a half, until its importance was realized, and it was returned to the site. Just across the road, on the west side of Route 300, are a small museum and re-created campgrounds that illustrate the lives of the enlisted men during the war.

United States Military Academy (visitors center 845-938-2638; usma.edu), 600 Thayer Road (off Route 9W, just north of Bear Mountain State Park, follow signs), West Point. Visitors Center is open daily 9-4:45, except Thanksgiving, Christmas, and New Year's Day. The post is open year-round, except major holidays; the museum is open year-round, daily 10:30-4:15. Free. (There is a charge for a bus tour of the post. To make arrangements for an organized tour, call 845-556-4724, West Point Tours, a private company.) Situated on the bluffs overlooking the Hudson River, this is where the nation's army officers have been trained since 1802; where Benedict Arnold attempted to bring the British to power; where such distinguished cadets as Robert E. Lee, Ulysses S. Grant, and Douglas MacArthur once marched. It is where James Whistler and Edgar Allan Poe discovered they had other talents. Tradition is important here and that is what you will find; from the Long Gray Line of cadets, to the quiet cemetery and imposing stone barracks.

It is difficult to see all of West Point in one visit. There are statues, museums, chapels, and points of interest everywhere you turn. But even if you can't stay overnight, use your time well, and make your first stop the visitors center on Main Street, near the Thayer Gate entrance. Maps, schedules of events and a display and movie about the cadets' lives at the Point are available at the center. You can also pick up the USMA bus tour which leaves every 20 minutes and lasts nearly an hour in the summer season. (The frequency of the tours changes seasonally.)

A must-see is the **West Point Museum** (845-938-3590), which is in Olmstead Hall. This is the oldest military museum in the country and its holdings are among the largest in the world. Dioramas, permanent and changing exhibits, and thousands of artifacts are found throughout vast galleries, each with its own theme: the history of war, American warfare, weapons, the history of West Point. Visitors may see anything from a Stone Age hunting ax to the equipment used in Vietnam. Because the museum has so many collections, displays are changed frequently. Outside on the post itself, Trophy Point recalls the dead of the Civil War, there is also a 150-ton chain that was used to close off the Hudson River to British ships during the American Revolution. Although the attempt was unsuccessful, the chain represents the ingenuity that made America the victor. To the rear of the memorial is the Plain, the drilling area once used by Baron von Steuben to train and parade troops. It is still used on Saturday for full-dress parades by the cadets.

The **Cadet Chapel** contains stained glass windows, the largest church organ in the world, and an overpowering sense of the men and women who have worshipped there. Another restored section of the Point is **Fort Putnam**, which was used as a fortification in the Revolutionary War and offers exhibits on the lives of soldiers of the time, as well as a show

West Point Museum at Olmsted Hall at the US Military Academy, West Point.

about the battles fought in the area. There is also a panoramic view of the surrounding mountains from this point.

West Point is famous for its football games, played at Michie Stadium. Tickets have to be purchased in advance online. In addition to football, there are basketball, hockey and lacrosse games. Call the box office or check the website for a complete schedule (845-446-4996; goarmysports.com).

Concerts are given throughout the summer at various sites on the post. Most are free and include the West Point Military Band. The concerts are well worth the trip. However, **Eisenhower Hall Theatre**, on the grounds of the USMA, has shows that range from musical revivals and classic country to dramatic theater and rock stars. Call 845-938-4159 or check ikehall.com).

Just south of the academy is a Revolutionary War site, **Fort Montgomery Historic Site** (845-446-2134), which offers magnificent views of the Hudson River, interpretive signs describing the "turning point" battle that occurred here centuries ago, and a pedestrian suspension bridge permitting access to Fort Clinton in the Trailside Museum and Zoo at Bear Mountain State Park. This is a wonderful destination for history buffs. The site is maintained by the Palisades Interstate Parks Commission.

One of the cannons at the Fort Montgomery State Historic Site.

Washington's Headquarters (845-562-1195; nysparks.state.ny.us/sites), 84 Liberty Street, Newburgh. Take Route 17 from NYS Thruway exit 17, to downtown Newburgh; watch for signs. Open Monday and Wednesday through Saturday 10-5; Sunday 1-5. Check the website for a schedule of special celebrations. Admission. If Jonathan Hasbrouck's stone mansion set on a bluff overlooking the Hudson River could speak, it would say Martha and George Washington slept here. In fact, the end of the American Revolution was announced on the grounds. Construction began in 1750 but was not finished until 1782, when Washington's troops added a gunpowder laboratory, a barracks, a privy, and a larger kitchen. Washington remained here for nearly a year and a half, waiting for the British to leave New York under the terms of surrender. The house and grounds were acquired by the government in 1848, and on opening day, July 4, 1850, Washington's Headquarters became America's first National Historic Site. (In the adjacent museum, opened in 1910, is an exhibit called "First in the Nation," which highlights the site's history of more than 150 years. The galleries were renovated and reopened in 2012 with new exhibits of artifacts from the museum's permanent collection)

The story of the Revolutionary War truly comes alive inside Hasbrouck House, where Washington is seen as a man who endured problems, boredom, and loss of the privacy that was so dear to him. The house was owned by Tryntje Hasbrouck, a widow who received notice of her eviction with a "sullen silence," according to historical records. Visitors are guided through the eight rooms where Washington and his staff lived and worked. The dining rooms where George and Martha ate their meals still contains the original jambless Dutch Fireplace, open on three sides. The plain bedrooms and offices are sparsely furnished, and a field bed with its tent-like covering speaks clearly of the winter cold, while bedrooms show that not everyone was fortunate enough to have a room. The grounds are well kept and offer wide views up and down the Hudson. Special events are held throughout the year and include kite-flying days, Martha Washington's birthday, and, of course, George Washington's birthday festivities in February.

SCENIC DRIVES

The term scenic drive in Orange County is redundant. There are so many well-maintained roads where the pace is unhurried and the views are phenomenal. Just about any drive around the county on back roads is certain to please. Even the Thruway softens up a bit as it moves through the Harriman area—drivers will see deer at twilight and apple blossoms on the orchards' trees in spring. Route 9W is an attractive road, but the section known as **Old Storm King Highway**, between West Point and Cornwall, is truly spectacular.

For a lovely country drive past lakes and trees, start at Harriman and take Route 6 east across Bear Mountain State Park to the Bear Mountain Bridge. From there, 9W north offers vibrant river views on its way through West Point, Cornwall, and into Newburgh. Once in Newburgh, look for Route 32 around Cronomer Hill Park, a breathtaking sight in summer and fall.

Another scenic highway is **Hawk's Nest Drive**, Route 92, near Sparrow Bush. The road runs along the Delaware River for a short distance, but you can then follow Route 209 north to the Delaware & Hudson Canal Park. (see Parks).

A different type of view is found along Route 17A, which cuts through the rich **Black Dirt Farm Region** around Pine Island. Kane Road near 17A in Warwick goes up Mount Peter between Warwick and Greenwood Lake, offering great views of the valley. This area is a major skyway for migrating hawks. If you follow Route 6 from Goshen to Pine Island, you will travel through one of the largest onion producing areas in America. More than 14,000 acres of vegetable farms with several farm stands along the way, the Black Dirt region was formed from a glacial lake more than 12,000 years ago. The area was once called "the drowned lands" before it was drained to create the farmland it is today.

WINERIES, BREWERIES, DISTILLERIES AND CIDERIES

The following places in Orange County are my favorites. Most are open year-round, but do call ahead to check operating hours when you intend to visit. Schedules change depending on the season. In recent years, many establishments have sprung up. I feel these are the best in the county in their category and their products are described in detail on their websites.

WINERIES

Baldwin Vineyards (845-744-2226;baldwinvineyards.com), 176 Hardenburgh Road, Pine Bush.

Brotherhood Winery (845-496-3661; brotherhood-winery.com), 100 Brotherhood Plaza Drive, Washingtonville.

Demarest Hill Winery (845-986-4723; demaresthillwinery.com), 81 Pine Island Turnpike, Warwick.

Palaia Winery (845-9228-5384; palaiawinery.com), 10 Sweet Clover Road, Highland Mills.

Several special events are listed on shawangunkwinetrail.com, so go to the website, particularly if you are visiting during the autumn harvest season.

BREWERIES

In recent years a number of breweries have sprung up in Orange County. These are the ones I've visited and found to have interesting selections for beer lovers.

Equilibrium Brewery (845-775-4216; eqbrew.com), 22 Henry Street, Middletown. The M.I.T. graduates/owners here follow scientific principles to balance taste and flavor. Their beers are easy to drink, but pack lots of body. There are seven beers available in the newly opened gastropub and tasting room at the brewery. This is a particularly inspired addition to the microbrewery scene in the Hudson Valley.

Newburgh Brewing Company (845-569-BEER; newburghbrewing.com), 88 Colden Street, Newburgh.

Pine Island Brewery & Taproom (845-288-2646;kraftifybrewing.com), 682 County Route 1, Pine Island.

Rushing Duck Brewery (845-610-5440; rushingduck.com), 1 Battiato Lane, Chester.

Westtown Brew Works (845-381-3496; westtownbrewworks.com), 236 Schefflers Road, Westtown.

DISTILLERIES

Apple Dave's Distillery (845-772-1242; appledavesdistrillery.com), 82 Four Corners Road, Warwick.

Orange County Distillery (845-651-2929; orangecountydistrillery.com), 19B Maloney Lane, Goshen.

CIDERIES

Angry Orchard (888-845-3311; angryorchard.com), 2241 Albany Post Road, Walden.

Orchard Hill Cider Mill (845-374-2468; orchardhillnyc.com), 29 Soons Circle, New Hampton.

ACTIVITIES

BALLOONING AND HELICOPTER TOURS

The balloon companies listed here all run flights out of Randall Airport (100 Airport Road, New Hampton); advance reservations are necessary. The price is approximately $300 per person and one can experience an unusual, dramatic way to view the Hudson Valley's rolling hills, forests, and farmlands. All are fully insured and operate with FAA certified pilots.

The helicopter tour company offers 30-minute and one-hour sightseeing flights in two- and four-seat planes. Prices depend on the length of the flight and number of passengers.

Above the Clouds (845-692-2556;abovethecloudsinc.com), PO Box 4816, Middletown 10941.

Hudson Valley Enchanted Balloon Tours (845-649-9654; enchantedballoons.com), 14 Franklin Lane, Otisville 10963.

Independent Helicopters (845-549-3755; independenthelicopters.com), Stewart International Airport, 1035 Firth Street, New Windsor.

Wandering Winds Hot Air Balloon Adventures (845-754-8540; wanderingwindshotairballoons.com), PO Box 239, Cuddebackville 12729. A woman-owned and operated company!

BOAT CRUISES

One of the best ways to see the Hudson is from the river itself. As far back as the early days of European settlement in the region, the Hudson River catered to tourists in addition to being a major trade route. Today, a few companies offer travelers a relaxing way to take in the scenery while cruising. Check websites for special theme cruises as well as the variety of tours available.

Bannerman's Castle/Pollepel Island Cruise & Tour (800-979-3370; bannermancastle.org), Newburgh Landing, Newburgh. From May through October, Saturday and Sunday at 11am, this 2 ½ hour excursion includes a walking tour of the island where Bannerman Castle was built in 1901. Visitors have a chance to walk along trails and see the castle up close along with the unique vegetation on the island. A guide takes visitors, wearing hardhats, on a tour that has been closed to the public for decades. This is a spectacular excursion and any visitor should make plans to go, if traveling during the six month period when the tour operates.

Hudson River Adventures/Pride of the Hudson (845-363-4550/845-220-2120; prideofthehudson.com), 90 Front Street, Newburgh. From May through October, Wednesday through Sunday, the *Pride of the Hudson* departs from Newburgh Landing. Bannerman's Castle rises from the north side of Pollepel Island like a medieval fantasy and is one of the most intriguing sights on the Hudson River. Travelers can discover the mystery and history of the castle during the 40-minute narration as the boat approaches the island.

The River Rose (845-562-1967; riverrosecruises.com), Newburgh Landing, Newburgh. This two-deck Mississippi-style paddleboat plies the Hudson from May through October, Friday through Sunday. It's a particularly nice excursion during fall foliage season with magnificent views of Breakneck Ridge and Storm King Mountain.

The Newburgh Waterfront is a wonderful place to visit, even if you aren't interested in embarking on a cruise. The paved walkway to the river offers spectacular views of Bannerman Island, Storm King Mountain and Mount Beacon. There are several shops and restaurants where one can dine alfresco in the warm weather. **The Downing Film Center** (845-561-3686; downingfilmcenter.com), 19 Front Street, occupies 1200 square-feet of the lower level of a large building that once housed an art gallery. The 55-seat theater features independent, foreign and classic films. About half the seats are recliners that rock, so arrive early to enjoy one! Patrons are permitted to take food and drinks inside the theater and sit at small tables while watching films. Reservations are suggested, particularly on weekends.

During weekday morning and evening rush hours a ferry goes across the river to the Beacon train station; it's a nice round-trip excursion if you don't have time for a sightseeing trip! (From the NYS Thruway exit 17 take I-84 east to exit 10 just before the Newburgh-Beacon Bridge. Make a right off the exit and a left at the next light. Continue a short way to the waterfront.)

CANOEING AND KAYAKING

The Delaware River may not have the same cachet as the Colorado, but it can offer a beautiful day of canoeing or kayaking. Most rentals are in the western part of the county and offer trips from mid-April through October. Trips may range from drifting idylls to challenging whitewater in the spring.

Kittatinny Canoes (1-800-FLOATKC; kittatinny.com), 3854 Route 97, Barryville. They rent canoes, kayaks and will help you organize a safe successful outing, even if you are a first-timer. Ask about river conditions before you go.

Landers Delaware River Trips (800-252-3925; landersrivertrips.com), 5961 Route 97, Narrrowsburg. Canoeing, kayaking and rafting rentals. I canoed the Delaware River from Narrowsburg to Matamoras with friends back in 1983. Landers suggested we break up the 35-mile trip by camping mid-way at their riverfront campground. This was definitely a memorable experience. Make sure to bring a hat and plenty of sunscreen!

Silver Canoe (845-856-7055; silvercanoe.com), 37 South Maple Avenue, Port Jervis. Raft, canoe and kayak rentals on the Delaware. Transport and pickup are included in their rates and all age groups are welcome.

Skip's Dockside Marina (845-477-8410; skipsdocksidemarina.com), 65 Ten Eyck Avnue, Greenwood Lake. Canoe, kayak and paddleboat rentals. There is also a picnic area and snack stand.

I recommend two tour/guide outfitters, especially if you are interested in going out on the Hudson River which can be quite tricky with its tides.

Mountain Valley Guides (845-661-1923), 2 Idlewild Avenue, Cornwall-on-Hudson, organizes kayaking trips out of Cornwall-on-Hudson, Hastings and Rye, for paddlers of all abilities. They supply the necessary equipment for these excursions that include two-hour children-only trips (ages 9-14), family outings and sunset paddles.

Storm King Adventure Tours (845-534-7800), 178 Hudson Street, Cornwall-on-Hudson, is the place to go for a three-or four-hour trip through Moodna Marsh or an excursion to Bannerman Island. They will tailor an outing on the river to your liking and supply all necessary equipment. If you would like to combine kayaking and hiking, they specialize in both and will organize an excellent adventure incorporating a full day of the two activities.

FARM STANDS AND PICK-YOUR-OWN FARMS

Few people know that Velveeta cheese was created at a factory on Mill Pond Parkway in Monroe in 1917. Because so much of Orange County is agricultural (the Black Dirt area produces half of the onions grown in New York State), you will find dozens of farm stands here. Some specialize in one particular fruit or vegetable while others offer a wide variety, but everything is as fresh as it gets. Try to plan a trip to Orange County Onion Festival if you are visiting in September. Pine Island is transformed.

The Pine Island area offers several top-drawer farm stands and pick-your-own farms.

One of my favorite stops in the area is **Scheuermann Farms** (845-258-4221), 73 Little York Road, Warwick, off County Road 1, a fifth-generation family farm offering top-quality fruits and vegetables, as well as flowers….all grown on the farm.

Apple Dave's Orchards (845-986-1684), 82 Four Corners Road, Warwick, has lots going on. There are pick-your-own apples and pumpkins in season, a farms store, free wagon rides and puppet show for the kids. There's a picnic area, farm animals and rose gardens. If you are visiting Sugar Loaf, this farm is only a few miles from the village.

Blooming Hill Organic Farm (845-782-7310), 1251 Route 208, Blooming Grove is a family owned and operated organic farm with a farm stand, bakery and grill. On the banks of the Wallkill River, there are dozens of organically grown fruits and vegetables for sale. By all means plan on having a bite at the small café; they serve breakfast and lunch and the owner is a terrific character and will make you feel at home. He will usually be found at the grill!

Overlook Farm Market (845-562-5780), 5417 Route 9W, Newburgh, sells local apples, peaches, nectarines, pumpkins, and a variety of home-baked pies, cakes and cookies. You can pick your own apples and enjoy a picnic lunch on the grounds in the fall. Children will enjoy the petting zoo.

The Fox Ridge Christmas-Tree Farm (845-986-3771), 17 Kays Way, Warwick, has seven varieties of Christmas trees and they supply everything you need to cut your own during early December.

The Maples Farm (845-344-0330), 749 Route 17M, Middletown (their shop includes homemade fudge, baked goods and crafts). A year-round country store with pumpkin picking and a haunted barn in October; trees, wreaths and poinsettias in December.

Pine View Farm (845-656-1942), 575 Jackson Avenue, New Windsor. Here you can cut your own balsam, Canaan and Fraser fir, and blue, white and Norway spruce. There are candy canes, coloring books, and live animals for the children every weekend in December.

Bellvale Farms (845-988-5414;bellvalefarms.com), 75 Bellvale Lakes Road, Warwick, has guided tours of this 200-year-old family dairy farm. There is also milking and calf feeding which will delight children. The tours are given June through October, Sunday only, at 12:30pm and reservations are required.

Shalimar Alpacas (845-258-0851; shalimaralpacas.com), 164 East Ridge Road, Warwick. This family owned farm is open on Saturday and Sunday 11-4 for the public to meet these delightful creatures. There is also a country store that sells yarn and all types of hand-wove items.

Farmers' markets bloom in Orange County. These are some of the larger ones; others can be found in several towns throughout the county.

Cornwall Farmers' Market (845-534-2070), Town Hall (183 Main Street), June through October, Wednesday, noon-6.

The Goshen Farmers' Market (845-294-5557) is held in Village Square, 33 Park Place, June through October, Friday, 10-5.

Warwick Valley Farmers' Market (845-988-7912), South Street parking lot, mid-May through mid-November, Sunday, 9-2.

GOLF

The following six courses are open to the public and welcome visitors to Orange County.

Hickory Hill Golf Course (845-988-9501;orangecountynyparks.com), 156 Route 17A, Warwick. This 18-hole course, par 72, has a pro shop and driving range on the premises.

Mansion Ridge Golf Club (845-782-7888;mansionridgegc.com), 1292 Orange Turnpike, Monroe. This is New York's only Jack Nicklaus Signature Design course open to the public. At one time, a 220-acre estate, this 6,889-yard championship course features stunning rock formations and great scenery. The stone-barn clubhouse has a pro shop and restaurant. Open April through November, daily, dawn to dusk.

Scenic Farms Golf Course (845-258-4455;scenicfarmsgolf.com), 525 Glenwood Road, Pine Island. This professional designed nine-hole executive golf course is excellent for beginners and challenging for advanced golfers. There is a driving range and practice putting and chipping greens. Open April through November, weekdays 7am-8pm; weekends 6:30am-10pm.

Stony Ford Golf Course (845-457-4949;orangecountynyparks.com), 550 Route 416, Hamptonburgh. Located in Thomas Bull Memorial Park, just south of Montgomery, this 18-hole course is open March through November, daily dawn to dusk.

Wallkill Golf Club (845-361-1022; townofwallkillgolfclub.com),40 Sands Road, Middletown; exit 119 off Route 17 West. Open April through November, this 18-hole championship course is fairly challenging. There's a driving range and restaurant on the premises.

West Point Golf Course (845-938-2435;westpointmwr.com), Route 9W & 218, West Point (on the outskirts of the USMA). Founded in 1948, this hilly course has a practice green with pitching and chipping areas. The course is open April through November. It is best to call a few days in advance for a tee time.

HIKING

In Orange County the trails range from easy to advanced and offer river views, woodlands and meadows. There are several county parks, preserves and community recreation areas with hiking trails. The first section of the Appalachian Trail was founded at Bear Mountain in 1923, and a portion of it offers spectacular views of Greenwood Lake as it weaves through the southwest section of the county. The Palisades Interstate Park (parks.ny.gov) can supply you with maps and general information.

For those hiking the **Appalachian Trail**, there are four bunks available at a hostel in Unionville from late April through early November. To make reservations, call 845-786-2701, ext. 242.

Black Rock Forest, Route 9W, north of West Point in Cornwall has marked and unmarked trails that vary in length; decent hiking skill is required here, however.

The **Heritage Trail** is a converted railbed of the Erie Railroad. One can walk or bike this scenic route, which passes through Chester, Goshen and Monroe. All three towns have entrances to the trails, and most of the 19 miles is paved. It is also handicapped accessible.

The **Highlands Trail** is a rugged 35-mile trail that starts in Cornwall-on-Hudson, traverses the scenic highlands, continues over Schunnemunk Mountain, through Black Rock Forest, to the top of Storm King Mountain.

Two parks have trails of varying difficulty: **Schunnemunk,** Route 32 in Highland Mills, has six marked trails, the longest of which is eight miles. **Winding Hills Park**, 1847 Route 17K, Montgomery, has trails, a picnic area and a nature study area.

Sterling Forest State Park, 116 Old Forge Road, Tuxedo, has the 8-mile **Sterling Ridge Trail,** the 3-mile **Allis Trail**, the 4-mile **Indian Hill Loop**, 7 miles of the **Appalachian Trail**, and 10 miles of the **Highlands Trail**. The U.S. Senator Frank R. Lautenberg Visitor Center is located at the south end of Sterling Lake and has dioramas, displays, and a gift shop.

Stewart State Forest, in the town of New Windsor, has semi-paved areas for walking, running, mountain biking and horseback riding. There are three areas along Route 207, between Drury Lane and Route 208, to pull of the highway and access the trailheads.

HORSEBACK RIDING

Clove Acres Stables (845-496-8655), 299 Mountain Lodge Road, Monroe, specializes in English riding. The family atmosphere makes this place ideal for the youngest riders.

Ivy Rock Farms (845-534-0365), 99 Purdys Lane, New Windsor, is an 85-acre facility open daily year-round for lessons with an indoor arena as well as hundreds of miles of trails. They offer something called "trail lessons" and will take you out on some of their trails if you are competent to handle the ride. This is a good choice for those who haven't been riding in a while and would like to learn something in addition to going out for a ride.

Juckas Stables (845-361-1429), 1204 Route 302, Bullville. This establishment has been in business for over 50 years. Their lovely trails are open year-round, and both English and Western lessons are offered. There is a friendly, informal atmosphere with qualified staff.

Old Field Farm (845-294-6339), 349 Sarah Wells Trail, Goshen, offers lessons and horse shows with English riding, hunters, jumpers and equitation.

SWIMMING

Bear Mountain State Park Pool (845-786-2701); 55 Hessian Drive, Bear Mountain and **Lake Tiorati Beach** (Harriman State Park; 845-351-2568). Admission. Open from mid-June through Labor Day, these swimming areas are particularly appealing to those traveling with young children. Lake Tiorati has a nice beach area with showers, food, grills, and designated picnic areas.

Hil-Mar Lodge (845-496-4869), 1 Hil-Mar Lane, Salisbury Mills, offers a large pool with snack bar, game room, picnic tables, tennis and a playground. There is an admission fee and covered event spaces for rent. Open Memorial Day through June, Saturday & Sunday, noon-6; July through Labor Day, open daily noon-6.

Thomas P. Morahan Beach (986-1124), Windemere Avenue, Greenwood Lake. Admission. Enjoy lake swimming (with lifeguards) on Greenwood Lake. Picnic areas and volleyball courts are a couple of other amenities. Open Memorial Day weekend through late June, weekends only 11-7; late June through Labor Day, daily 11-7.

WINTER SPORTS

ICE SKATING

Bear Mountain State Park (845-786-2701, ext. 266;bearmountainicerink. com), 3006 Seven Lakes Drive (off Route 9W), Bear Mountain. Admission; under age five, free. This outdoor rink offers public sessions of an hour and a half from late October to early March. Skate rentals available.

Several lakes in Orange County have skating (at no charge) weather permitting. It is imperative to make sure conditions are safe; do call before going. **Chadwick Lake** (845-564-7815), 1702 Route 300, Newburgh; **Fancher-Davidge Park** (845-346-4180), 130 Lake Avenue, Middletown; lights for night skating; **Mill Pond** (845-782-8341), Route 17M, Monroe; safe skating here is indicated by a green flag; when the red flag is up, no skating is permitted. **Thomas Bull Memorial Park** (845-457-4949), 211 Route 416, Montgomery; skating on a man-made outdoor rink for hockey and pond for free skating at this county park.

Ice Time (845-567-0005), 21 Lakeside Road, Newburgh. Open year-round. Public skating sessions are Wednesday 11:30-1:30; Saturday and Sunday 2-4.

SKIING

Mount Peter (845-986-4940), 51 Old Mount Peter Road, Warwick. There is a vertical drop of 400 feet here, three chairlifts, a carpet lift and a rope tow. With eight downhill slopes and fourteen trails for skiing and snowboarding, it is an excellent choice for beginners. There's a café, pub and two lodges. Open daily in season 9am-9pm; until 5pm Sunday.

Tuxedo Ridge (845-351-1122), 581 Route 17A West, Tuxedo. Open mid-December through mid-March with night skiing every day. The vertical drop is 450 feet; there are four double chair lifts and six slopes to delight both skiers and snowboarders. Snowmaking, rentals and restaurant/lodge. Monday through Thursday, noon-9; Friday & Saturday 10-10; Saturday 9am-10pm; Sunday 9-9.

PARKS

Delaware & Hudson Canal Park (845-614-3830), 58 Hoag Road, Cuddebackville (off Route 209, ten miles south of Wurtsboro). Open year-round dawn to dusk. The *Neversink Valley Area Museum* in the park is open April through October, Friday through Sunday noon-4, and by appointment. Admission. This 300-acre park, a registered National Historic Landmark, recalls an era when coal, lumber, and other goods were moved from Pennsylvania to New York City by a combination of water, mules, and backbreaking labor. Huge barges were often run as family businesses, with the crew consisting of parents and children. And there wasn't much room for profit, since the barges moved at a leisurely three miles per hour.

There are hiking trails, fishing areas, and a one-mile walking path next to the canal. The park sponsors seasonal events that evoke life in old-time New York State. Demonstrations have included ice cutting, story evenings and nature walks. The museum has exhibits about the canal and its people and is located in a restored blacksmith's house near the aqueduct; other buildings include a lockkeeper's house, a canal store, and a full-size replica of a canal barge.

Indian Hill (845-473-4440), Orange Turnpike, Tuxedo. (From exit 16, NYS Thruway, take Route 17 south. Make a right on County Route 19, also known as Orange Turnpike. After one mile, the entrance is on the right.) The fascinating ruins of a 19th century iron furnace can be seen at this 500-acre park. The trails include a 4-mile loop traversing hardwood forest and rock outcroppings. There are panoramic views of the Ramapo River Valley and Harriman State Park.

Kowawese Unique Area at Plum Point (845-615-3830), 90 Plum Point Lane, New Windsor. (Take Route 9W to Plum Point Lane, which is north of the intersection of Routes 9W and 94.) This 102-acre park on the Hudson River provides magnificent vistas of the Hudson Valley gorge, Bannerman's Castle, Mount Beacon and Storm King Mountain. There is also 2000 feet of sandy beach. Those who travel by canoe or kayak on the Hudson from here can see the historic homestead of one of George Washington's lieutenants, the Squire Nicoll house, which dates from 1735 (not open to visitors). Visitors are welcome daily April through November 8-dusk.

Orange County Arboretum (845-615-3828), 211 Route 416, Montgomery. Open daily year-round, dawn to dusk. There are 35 acres of planned gardens, cascading waters, amazing trees and flowers as well as a September 11th Memorial to the 44 Orange County residents who perished that day. This is a beautiful place to stop and stroll during your Hudson Valley travels!

LODGING

Ashford Cottage (845-986-6162/258-7167), 25 Oakland Avenue, Warwick 10990. ($$) Three charming rooms, all with private baths are available in this stone cottage in the center of Warwick. There are several restaurants and boutiques within walking distance. The owners prepare a full breakfast and you may choose the most convenient time to be served. In summer, guests enjoy an outdoor pool and media rooms with a large-screen TV. An excellent choice for a cozy romantic getaway; not a good place for those traveling with children. Open year-round.

Bear Mountain Bridge Motel (845-446-2472). 1041 Route 9W, Fort Montgomery 10922. ($). There are only five rooms in this small motel with dining options nearby. The location is great: two miles south of West Point, near Bear Mountain State Park. Open year-round.

Bear Mountain Inn (845-786-2731), 3020 Seven Lakes Drive, Bear Mountain 10911. ($$) Located at the edge of Bear Mountain State Park, there are 44 recently renovated rooms in this historic 1915 inn renowned for its rustic luxury. Guests are within walking distance of the park's rowboat docks, swimming pool, nature trains, ice-skating rink, Trailside Museums and Zoo. Full service restaurant and bar, lounges, gift shop on the premises. Open year-round.

Breezy Point Inn (845-477-8100), 620 Jersey Avenue (Route 210), Greenwood Lake 10925. ($) Open year-round, there are four basic rooms overlooking Greenwood Lake in this informal, reasonably priced inn. The restaurant on the premises serves German-American fare; lakefront dining on the deck in the warm weather months.

Caldwell House Bed & Breakfast (845-496-2954), 25 Orrs Mills Road, Salisbury Mills 12577. ($$$) For a deluxe B&B experience, this renovated 1803 home furnished with fine antiques on seven landscaped acres (with fireplaces in some rooms and a spa) makes a great escape. There are 14 air-conditioned rooms, all with private baths, TV; one has a Jacuzzi. The four-poster beds have handmade linens. Open year-round.

Cider Mill Inn (845-258-3044), 207 Glenwood Road, Pine Island 10969. ($$) There are three rooms, all with private bath, in a meticulously restored 1865 Victorian farmhouse, formerly a working dairy farm and apple orchard, hence the name. The lodgings offer down comforters, spa robes and hot tub in addition to a full gourmet breakfast. Children over the age of 12 are welcome. Open year-round.

Cromwell Manor (845-534-7136), 174 Angola Road, Cornwall 12518 ($$$) This renovated inn, a historic country estate, dates from 1820. It is situated on seven acres of woodland and gardens close to West Point and Stewart Airport. The twelve rooms and suites (all with private bath) are beautifully decorated with period antiques. Many rooms have a working fireplace and Jacuzzi, and all are air-conditioned. A full breakfast is served in the dining room or on the veranda. Step back in time without sacrificing modern amenities. The inn is only a short drive from West Point and the Storm King Art Center, as well as the charming village of Cornwall. Jones Farm Country Store is next door. Open year-round.

Goldsmith Denniston House (845-562-8076), 227 Montgomery Street, Newburgh 12550. ($$) This Federal-style house was built circa 1820 for a local attorney. In the 1880s a bay window and marble fireplaces were added. It was opened as a bed & breakfast in 2004. The four bedrooms are decorated in various styles; from Federal to Victorian, each air-conditioned room has a queen-size bed and private bath. Three have fireplaces. Behind the house is a spacious patio where breakfast is served in warm weather. Open year-round.

Hambletonian House (845-469-6425), 19 High Street, Chester 10918. $$) This elegant Victorian home, built in 1850, is situated on a hill surrounded by trees and gardens. The period furnishings transport guests back in time to an era when the pace was slower. A full breakfast is served on the porch in season or in the spacious dining room. There are two air-conditioned rooms, each with a private bath. Open year-round.

Peach Grove Inn (845-986-7411), 1572 Route 17A, Warwick 10990 ($$) This restored 1850 Greek Revival home overlooks a 200-acre farm. There are six large rooms, all with private baths. The full breakfast features delicious home-baked breads and cakes. A great place to slow down and escape from everything! Open year-round.

Pine Bush House (845-744-3641), 215 Maple Avenue, Pine Bush 12566. ($$) Housed in a Victorian home built in 1904, this elegant B&B takes visitors back to another era. There are four bedrooms and one suite, some with steam showers or Jacuzzi, and all with private baths, fireplaces, flat-screen TVs, and high-speed wireless Internet access. A four-course gourmet breakfast is served. A short walk takes guests to the center of Pine Bush. Not recommended for children. Open February through December.

Sleepy Valley Inn (845-986-7829), 117 Sleepy Valley Road, Warwick 10990. ($$) There are four rooms in a large carriage house here on eight park-like acres surrounded by forest. All rooms are furnished with antiques and have private baths and Jacuzzis; three have fireplaces. A full breakfast is served; open year-round. This is a good choice for those who treasure privacy.

Stagecoach Inn (845-294-5526), 268 Main Street, Goshen 10924. ($$) A former stagecoach stop dating back to 1747, this inn is located in the middle of a country town, a few minutes' walk from shopping, dining, and the racetrack. It is also one of America's oldest continuously operating inns. Six rooms, all with private bath, and a stone veranda, overlook three acres of manicured lawns. A full breakfast is served and the inn is open year-round.

Sunday brunch is popular at the Hotel Thayer's MacArthur's Riverview Restaurant.

Storm King Lodge (845-534-9421), 100 Pleasant Hill Road, Mountainville 10953 ($$) This spacious comfortable country lodge, the converted carriage house of a former estate, has views of Storm King Mountain and is only a few minutes away from the Storm King Art Center and West Point. The setting is stunning with colorful gardens, a grand outdoor pool open to guests, and gorgeous mountain views. The six guest rooms have private baths; a few have a fireplace. There is a two-bedroom cottage on the property, the perfect choice for families. The cozy ambience reflects the warmth of the family that operates the lodge. Gay and Hal Janks have been in the area for years and won't steer you wrong with their suggestions. Open year-round.

Thayer Hotel (845-446-4731), 674 Thayer Road, West Point 10996. ($$) The Thayer reflects a time of grandeur, with many guest rooms overlooking one of the most scenic parts of the Hudson River. There are 151 rooms with 23 recently renovated executive suites. Breakfast is not included in the room rate, but *MacArthur's Riverview Restaurant* serves breakfast on the terrace in the warm weather and one can enjoy a panoramic view of the Hudson Valley. The *Zulu Time Rooftop Bar & Lounge* is another place to relax and enjoy the Hudson River views. Open year-round.

Warwick Valley (845-987-7255), 24 Maple Avenue, Warwick 10990. ($$) The six rooms in this 1900 Colonial Revival home have private baths and are decorated with antiques and country furniture. A full breakfast is served to guests on the covered porch. Open year-round.

Waterstone Inn (845-477-3535), 62 Sterling Road, Greenwood Lake 10925. ($$) Located on lovely Greenwood Lake, where guests can even arrive dockside, there are five renovated guest rooms, all named after steamships and renowned local citizens. All rooms have private baths, air-conditioning and TV, and most have Jacuzzis. Beautiful lake and mountain views are delightful in all rooms. Open year-round.

WHERE TO EAT

DINING OUT
Cornwall and Newburgh Area
(Eastern Orange County)

Canterbury Brook Inn (845-534-9658), 331 Main Street, Cornwall. ($$) Open for dinner Tuesday through Saturday 5-9 with specially priced dinners Tuesday through Thursday. Hans and Kim Baumann offer up a touch of Switzerland in Cornwall. The fine Continental cuisine may be enjoyed while overlooking

Canterbury Brook, or dining fireside in the cooler months. Specialties of the house include roast duckling, classic Wiener schnitzel, fondue and an array of fresh-fish entrees. Desserts are truly spectacular.

Captain Jake's River House (845-565-3939), 40 Front Street, Newburgh. ($$) Open daily noon-9; Friday & Saturday until 10, for lunch and dinner. This is the place to go for seafood. The raw clams and oysters are excellent. My favorite is the lobster fettuccine. In the warm weather months it's delightful to dine al-fresco as the Hudson River views are spectacular. Service can be slow on busy summer weekends.

Cena 2000 (845-561-7676)50 Front Street, Newburgh. ($$) Open daily 11:30-10. Northern Italian Tuscan cuisine is featured here; fresh fish, pasta, seafood, filet mignon and veal chops are some of the entrees. Desserts include homemade gelatos, tiramisu and Italian pastries. Hudson River waterfront dining May through October. Reservations are recommended. Not very child friendly, but kids are accommodated.

Citrus (845-787-4947), 1004 Route 94, New Windsor. ($$) Open daily for lunch 11:30-2:30; dinner 5-10. An interesting combination—Indian and Thai food in lovely surroundings. There are samosas, curry dishes and several Thai classics. The best bargain is the daily lunch buffet, as diners will get to sample a taste of many intriguing items on the menu. Children are welcome.

Canterbury Brook Inn on Main Street in Cornwall serves dinner Tuesday through Saturday with prix fixe specials Tuesday through Thursday nights.

Il Cenacolo (845-564-4494), 228 South Plank Road, Newburgh. ($$$) Open for lunch weekdays, except Tuesday, noon-2:30; dinner 5:30-9, until 11 Friday & Saturday; Sunday 4-9. Fine Northern Italian cuisine is the fare at this excellent restaurant based on an Italian supper room. There are a variety of pasta dishes as well as traditional favorites. Save room for the homemade desserts. Don't bring children; reservations required.

Lake View House (845-566-7100) 205 Lakeside Road, Newburgh. ($$) Open daily for dinner, except Tuesday, from 5; lunch served weekdays, except Tuesday noon-2:30. Watch the sun set over Orange Lake while dining at a restaurant in operation since 1899. The chef-owner specializes in traditional American fare. Hearty soups, salads, and sandwiches are served for lunch. Children are welcome here.

Liberty Street Bistro (845-562-3900), 97 Liberty Street, Newburgh. ($$$) Open Wednesday through Sunday for lunch noon-3. Dinner served daily, except Tuesday 5-9; Sunday 3-7. This is a culinary treasure operated by Culinary Institute-trained Michael Kelly, an experienced award-winning chef. The restaurant offers French-American, bistro-style cuisine with a touch of German influence. This is a terrific addition to the growing restaurant scene in Newburgh. Leave the kids home!

Machu Picchu Peruvian Restaurant (845-562-6478), 301 Broadway, Newburgh. ($) Open daily, except Tuesday, 11-10. After traveling to Machu Picchu in 1984 and finding it one of the most amazing places on the planet, I was intrigued by the name of this restaurant. I wasn't disappointed. There are breakfast specialties here—the tacu tacu dish (eggs cooked with fresh garlic, diced tomatoes, onions, rice and beans) is quite tasty, as well as hearty soups and fish stews that are a meal in themselves for lunch. The entrees, served with rice and beans, including chicken, lamb, steak and seafood. Children are welcome.

Mama Theresa's (845-561-6262) 374 Windsor Highway, New Windsor. ($) Open Monday through Saturday 11-10; Sunday noon-9. This is the place to go for first-rate Italian home cooking. Everything is made fresh on the premises— pasta, calzones, Stromboli, and more. Whether you want pizza, pasta, veal, chicken or seafood, it is excellent. *Mangia*!

River Grill (845-561-9444), 40 Front Street, Newburgh. ($$) Open daily for lunch noon-3; dinner 5-9; till 10 Friday and Saturday; Sunday noon-9. Mark Mallia, the chef-owner, offers an array of seafood, steaks, chops, rack of lamb, and a good selection of pasta dishes. The River Grill Calamari is lightly coated in their own special blend of seasoned flour and served with two sauces; a spicy *fra diavolo* and a chive horseradish. Enjoy the wonderful river view from the bar and most parts of the restaurant.

Schlesinger's Steak House (845-561-1762), 475 Temple Hill Road, New Windsor. ($$) Open for lunch and dinner daily 4-9; 10 Friday & Saturday. Savor corn-fed Iowa beef, hand-cut and aged on the premises. The restaurant is located in the historic Brewster House (circa 1762) which dates from the Revolutionary War, when it was used as officers' quarters. In addition to steaks, the menu offers seafood, barbecued ribs, chicken, and pasta dishes. Children's menu.

Yobo (845-564-3848), 1297 Route 300, Newburgh. ($$) Open daily for lunch and dinner 11-10. Serving Asian cuisine since 1980, this restaurant has a waterfall inside its walls, and the sound of the running water is relaxing and reminiscent of the Far East. One of my favorite dishes is the Thai firecracker seafood with a blend of hot-and-sweet-flavored sauce mixing scallions, cilantro, and peppers with seafood, served over a bed of vermicelli noodles. There are wonderful soups as well as sushi and Korean and Indonesian favorites. Children welcome.

Montgomery and Goshen
(Central Orange County)

Camillo's at the Crossroads (845-457-5482), 2215 Route 108, Montgomery. ($$) Open for dinner Tuesday through Sunday, 5-9; until 10 Friday and Saturday. American regional cuisine is offered at this spacious restaurant housed in a convenient location "at the crossroads" of State Route 208 and I-84. The pan-roasted organic chicken and Portobello mushroom in port wine sauce are popular entrees. The pastas are excellent; my favorite is the rigatoni Bolognese. Desserts are classic and include selections like apple crisp and chocolate mousse. Children's menu available.

Catherine's (845-294-8707), 153 West Main Street, Goshen. ($$) Open for lunch Wednesday through Friday 11:30-2:30; dinner Wednesday through Saturday 5:30-9. Contemporary American cuisine here includes a variety of pasta and seafood specialties served in a comfortable country setting. Portions are generous. The restaurant is housed in a historic building that dates from 1869.

88 Charles Street (845-457-9850), 88 Charles Street, Montgomery. ($$) Open daily 11:30-10. The outstanding Northern Italian cuisine here features, veal, chicken, pasta, seafood and steaks. Large portions, reasonable prices, romantic atmosphere.

Magoya Japanese Restaurant (845-469-7874), 41 Brookside Avenue, Chester. ($$$) Open daily 11:30-10. This is the place to go for excellent fresh sushi in casual surroundings. They offer a wide selection of rolls as well as sashimi and various combinations of both. There are teriyaki dishes for diners who prefer cooked entrees.

Stagecoach Inn (845-294-5526), 268 Main Street, Goshen. ($$$) Open Wednesday through Saturday for lunch 11-3; dinner 5pm on. Sunday brunch 10-2; dinner from 4:30. Casual elegance in one of the most historic structures in Goshen. Diners will enjoy salmon, scallops, filet mignon, pork tenderloin and other classic entrees, all beautifully prepared. There is an inn as well as a restaurant on the premises and both are well-managed and worth visiting!

Wildfire Grill (845-457-3770), 74 Clinton Street, Montgomery. ($$) Open Wednesday through Monday for lunch 11:30-3; dinner 5-10. This cozy spot has an open kitchen, and Black Angus meats are one of the specialties of the house. The lamb is first-rate and on occasional you will find ostrich and buffalo on the menu. For lunch there are wraps, pizzas, burgers, and homemade fries. The chef was formerly a pastry chef, so make sure to try one of the signature desserts. I enjoy the filo-wrapped crème brûlée topped with fresh berries and the flourless chocolate espresso torte. Children's menu.

Zona Rosa (845-778-6696), 39 Main Street (Route 52), Walden. ($) Open for dinner Sunday through Thursday 4-10; lunch and dinner Friday and Saturday noon-11. The Mexican food here is quite good—as are the prices. There is a nice selection of entrees, including chicken and beef burritos, chimichangas, and enchiladas. The salsa and cheese quesadillas are tasty and the sangria is made with decent wine from Spain. Children welcome.

Central Valley and Warwick
(South-Central Orange County)

Chateau Hathorn (845-986-6099), 33 Hathorn Road, Warwick. ($$$) Open for dinner Wednesday through Saturday 5-9:30; Sunday 3-8. Enjoy Continental cuisine with a French touch in a restored mansion dating from the 1700s. The menu changes seasonally, but the rack of lamb and chateaubriand are specialties of the house. Desserts are not to be missed. Local and organic ingredients are used when possible. Not recommended for children.

Coquito (845-544-2700), 31 Forester Avenue, Warwick. ($$) Open Tuesday through Sunday 11-9. This eatery specializes in upscale Puerto Rican cooking. The empanadas, seafood stew (lobster, scallops, and shrimp), and flan were excellent when I dined there. Friday nights there is live jazz and Saturday features Latin bands. If you are in the Warwick area on a weekend, this is a fun place to dine.

Crystal Inn (845-258-4232), 12 Amity Road, Warwick ($$) Open for dinner Wednesday through Sunday 4-9. The contemporary American fare here, served in a casual atmosphere, is first-rate. The emphasis is on fresh, organic ingredients. Although there is a large menu, fish lovers will enjoy the wide-ranging choices including snapper, salmon, sea bass, and scallops. All desserts are homemade on the premises. Tasting menu available. Children welcome.

Iron Forge Inn (845-986-3411), Iron Forge Road, Bellvale. ($$) Open for dinner Thursday through Saturday 5-9; Sunday 3-8. Brunch served Sunday 11-1. At the foot of Mount Peter, this historic inn is located on the site of a

Yesterday's on Main Street in Warwick is a popular place for drinks and hearty comfort food.

forge in a Revolutionary-era home dating from 1760. For the past half century it has been known for fine country dining. There are five intimate dining rooms with a warm colonial ambience; the adjoining Tap Room has a lovely bar and fireplace. Contemporary American cuisine that varies seasonally is the fare here. One winter menu included braised short rib of beef, duck breast, five onion and escarole lasagna, and organic salmon: all are prepared creatively. If you prefer light fare, the Tap Room has a pub menu with quesadillas, burgers, wings and grilled chicken sandwiches. Children welcome.

Landmark Inn (845-986-5444), 526 Route 94 North, Warwick. ($$) Open daily, except Monday, for dinner 5-9:30. Enjoy contemporary American cuisine in a historic house that dates from 1779. Choose from a wide variety of dishes, including steaks, seafood, chicken, and veal. Make sure to save room for the phenomenal desserts.

Yesterdays (845-986-9933), 29 Main Street, Warwick ($) Open daily 11:30-10. This family-owned Irish pub with a full menu of comfort food (burgers, salads, wraps and more) is a popular place to grab a bite with town residents. I enjoyed their delicious shepherd's pie made with lamb, a nice surprise, as well as one of the many beers on tap. Children are welcome.

Middletown
(Western Orange County)

Blue Finn Grill & Sushi (845-342-5542), 157 Dolson Avenue, Middletown. ($$) Open Monday through Friday 11:30-9; Saturday & Sunday 3-9. American cuisine with an Asian accent; steaks, seafood, and sushi are the mainstays. Ginger-crusted salmon and soy-marinated sizzling steaks are a couple of the house specialties.

The sushi bar will delight those seeking Japanese fare. A children's menu is available.

John's Harvest Inn (845-343-6630), 629 North Street, Middletown. ($$) Open Wednesday through Saturday 5-9; Sunday 3-8. The Continental cuisine here is decent and the portions are hearty. The fresh seafood and veal dishes are specialties of the house. There are more than 100 clocks decorating the walks in this cozy spot, which is popular with local residents.

Nina (845-344-6800), 27 West Main Street, Middletown. ($$) Open daily 11:30-9:30; Sunday 10:30-8. Eclectic American cuisine with a large menu including steak, seafood, lamb, chicken, and veal entrees. The shrimp asparagus risotto is renowned. For lunch I enjoyed the Tuscan summer sandwich (grilled chicken with sun-dried tomato, basil pesto and mozzarella cheese on focaccia).

Saffron Fine Indian Cuisine (845-344-0005), 130 Dolson Avenue, Middletown. ($$) Open daily for lunch buffet 11:30-2:30; dinner 5-10. This is the only Indian/Pakistani restaurant in Orange County, and it's serving up excellent cuisine at moderate prices with classy décor (despite the fact it's in a strip mall). The lunch buffet is a bargain and offers a huge selection of Indian dishes. This is definitely a great addition to the dining scene in Middletown. Children are always welcome.

Something Sweet Café (845-343-2233), 17 North Street, Middletown. ($) Open Monday 11-4; Tuesday through Thursday 11-8; Friday and Saturday 11-10. Closed Sunday. Imaginative creations include Israeli couscous on a bed of baby arugula with grilled shrimp, and baked four cheese farfalle pasta. The desserts are sumptuous and include a chocolate-raspberry parfait and hazelnut-praline mousse. This café is a reason to go to downtown Middletown!

EATING OUT

Newburgh

New Windsor and Cornwall

Café Fiesta (845-928-2151), 547 Route 32, Highland Mills. ($$) Open daily 11-10. This informal Mexican family restaurant with colorful décor offers a wide-ranging menu, including American fare. In addition to tacos, burritos, chimichangas, and quesadillas, there are vegetarian selections, low-fat dishes, and daily specials. Everything here is made from scratch. Portions are generous, and prices are reasonable. If you're hungry at lunchtime, try the grand burrito, a giant flour tortilla stuffed with "the works!"

Café Pitti (845-565-1444), 40 Front Street, Newburgh ($$) Open daily for lunch and dinner 11:30-10. This is a wonderful place to go in the warm weather as you can sit outside on the terrace by the waterfront and watch the boats pass on the Hudson. The interior is casual, a place to enjoy salads, personal thin-crust pizza, and paninis. For dessert, there's gelato, cappuccino cake, and sorbet. Children are welcome.

Commodore's (845-561-3960), 482 Broadway, Newburgh. ($) Open daily 10-6. Closed Sunday. Located in an old-fashioned ice-cream parlor, Commodore's has been in business and run by the same family since 1935. They are famous for their handmade chocolates and candies. There are the usual delicious classics like marzipan and truffles, as well as Swedish fudge and almond bark. In late November call to find out when they start handmade candy cane demonstrations held on weekends noon-4.

Fiddlestix Café (845-534-3866), 319 Main Street, Cornwall. Open daily 7-3; Saturday and Sunday, 8-3. The pancakes, eggs, soups and sandwiches are quite good, but the service needs improvement. A good place to call in advance for take-out!

Hudson Street Café (845-534-2450), 237 Hudson Street, Cornwall-on-Hudson. ($) Open daily 8-3. This is the kind of place I love. They offer locally grown and fresh organic food at affordable prices. Breakfast and lunch selections include soups, salads, omelets, wraps, and sandwiches. All include imaginative variations on standard fare. The offerings are consistently good and this eatery is popular with local residents, families and travelers.

Nature's Pantry (845-465-4945), 436 Blooming Grove Turnpike, New Windsor. ($) Open daily 8am-9pm; Saturday until 7; Sunday until 6. This is one of my favorite health food emporiums (it's enormous) and the prices are discounted. Owner Damian Masterson, is always at the store keeping things on track. He does a fantastic job bringing first-rate produce as well as personal care products and take-out to local residents and travelers. So if you are in New Windsor or the West Point area, make sure to stop in and stock up! I always do…

Painter's Tavern (845-534-2109), 266 Hudson Street, Cornwall-on-Hudson. ($$) Open for lunch and dinner Monday through Saturday 11-10; Sunday 10-9. Perfect for any meal, there are nightly dinner specials, along with creative variations on burgers, sandwiches, and salads. There are dozens of imported and domestic beers, bottled and on tap. This establishment has been popular in town with locals for decades. Children are welcome.

Prima Pizza (845-534-7003), 252 Main Street, Cornwall. Open daily 11-10. A family restaurant for many years, owner Anthony Scalise, regularly airmails brick-oven-cooked pizzas to places as far as California. Everything is made fresh on the premises. There are calzones, subs, salads, and an array of pasta dishes. It would be a good idea if Anthony used china plates with real silverware. It's often difficult cutting the pizza with plastic!

Wherehouse (845-561-7240), 119 Liberty Street, Newburgh ($) Open daily noon to midnight, Sunday hours may differ. This is the place for comfort food—ribs, pulled pork, and juicy burgers, as well as several vegetarian selections, including an array of salads, and homemade desserts. The Wherehouse Nachos are popular in Newburgh. The eatery is located a couple of blocks from the waterfront. Children are welcome.

Woody's Farm to Table (845-534-1111), 30 Quaker Avenue, Cornwall. ($) Open daily 11:30-8:30. Those who fantasize about fast food burgers that are actually healthy will appreciate Woody's natural beef. They serve locally raised, grass fed/grain finished beef burgers, hormone-free chicken, local Pine Island onions, and Pennsylvania mushrooms. Milk shakes and malts are made with Jane's ice cream and milk from Hudson Valley dairies. Fries are cooked in trans fat-free canola oil. Located in a restored 1910 building, Woody's atmosphere is casual, with an open kitchen. This is a great place to stop when traveling with young children, and the prices are exceedingly reasonable.

Central Orange County

Goshen

Craft 47 (845-360-5253), 47 West Main Street, Goshen. ($$) Open Tuesday through Sunday noon-10; Sunday until 8. Enjoy American-style small plates and flatbreads paired with one of the dozen craft beers on tap or a glass of wine.

Elsie's Luncheonette (845-294-5765), 130 West Main Street, Goshen. ($) Open daily 6am-2pm. This old-fashioned gathering place for locals specializes in comfort food. For breakfast, the waffles, pancakes and omelets are good choices. Lunch offerings are similar to diner fare and include fresh meat loaf or turkey and mashed potatoes, and a choice of homemade soups. The kids will love it. Service can be slow when it's crowded, so you're forewarned!

Allan's Falafel (845-469-1714), 115 Main Street, Chester. ($) Open daily, except Monday, 11:30-8. This relaxed Israeli restaurant serves kebabs, shawarma, falafel and other classics in an informal atmosphere. Everything is prepared fresh and they have beer and wine available as well.

Hacienda (845-294-9795), 1753 Route 17M, Goshen. ($) Open daily 11-10. This establishment is owned and operated by the chef, who turns out authentic Mexican fare—tacos, burritos, enchiladas—served in a casual atmosphere. The margaritas are excellent and the food is quite good. The restaurant is housed in a restored Victorian mansion with a lovely fireplace. Children are welcome.

Vinum Café (845-496-9001), 84 Brotherhood Plaza Drive, Washingtonville. ($) Open Wednesday through Sunday noon-9. Enjoy a cheese platter and glass of wine, or dessert and a cappuccino, outdoors on the patio at the Brotherhood

Winery. The café offers a full menu for dinner, but it's a great spot to stop and relax after wine tasting.

Sugar Loaf & Warwick

Bellvale Farms Creamery (845-988-1818), 385 Route 17A, Warwick. ($) This family farm produces and sells its own ice cream. Open for ice cream April through October, daily noon-9; the main dairy barn is open June through October, Sunday at 12:30pm, for tours, when visitors may see baby calves being fed and cows getting milked. There are also Holstein cows, a fresh-vegetable stand during the summer, pick-your-own pumpkins and hayrides in the fall. This is a great stop for those traveling with children. Closed in the winter months.

Conscious Fork (845-988-KALE), 20 McEwen Street, Warwick. ($) Open year-round, daily 10-6. This farm-to-table vegan juice bar and market serves up smoothies and an array of juice specials. Their Whole Bowl involves patrons choosing grains, proteins, and vegetables topped with sauces to create their own tasty salads. The chef, Jamie Manza, worked at Blue Hill at Stone Barns, and the offerings are first-rate—and healthy.

Jean Claude's Bakery & Dessert Café (845-986-8900), 25 Elm Street, Warwick. ($) Open Wednesday through Saturday 8-6; Sunday 8-3. Those who love fine French pastries, brioche, fruit tarts, petits fours, baba au rhum, cream puffs, and handmade truffles should stop at this fantastic bakery and sample the excellent offerings.

ENTERTAINMENT

Eisenhower Hall Theatre (845-938-4159; eisenhowerhall.com), 655 Pitcher Road, West Point. This is the second largest theater in the country (Radio City Music Hall is the biggest), and it offers a variety of entertainment, including Broadway touring companies, comedy, pop, rock and classical music. It is also a venue for ballet and opera.

Joker's Comedy Club (845-345-1039; jokerscomedyclubny.com), 78 Brookside Avenue, Chester. This club showcases fine comedic talent from all over the metropolitan region—and beyond. The shows are on Friday and Saturday nights, and food is offered along with drinks. Their spinach artichoke dip is quite good! Check the website for a schedule.

The Paramount Theatre (845-346-4195; middletownparamount.com), 17 South Street, Middletown. This venue offers films, music, dance, theater and children's performances year-round. The website gives a current schedule.

Railroad Playhouse (845-565-3791; rrplayhouse.org), 27 South Water Street, Newburgh. This unusual noteworthy theater is open year-round and showcases award-winning emerging new playwrights. The offerings range from comedy to drama and a schedule of performances is available on their website.

Ritz Theater (845-784-1199; safe-harbors.org), 107 Broadway, Newburgh. There is an eclectic mix of entertainment being presented in this beautifully renovated theater—folk music, performance artists of all kinds, and children's programs.

SELECTIVE SHOPPING

ANTIQUES

The love of history found across Orange County extends to a love of antiques and collectibles, and many shops cater to the connoisseur. Some of my favorites are the following places:

Arnell's Jewelry & Gift Shop (845-477-8747), 88 Windermere Avenue, Greenwood Lake. Open Monday through Saturday 10-5. There are two floors of antique furniture here along with a large quantity of glass and silver.

Newhard's on Main Street in Warwick has been in business for decades and has been owned by the same family.

Country Heritage Antiques Center (845-744-3792), 112 Maple Avenue, Pine Bush. Open Friday through Sunday 11-5:30 or by appointment. Furniture of all types is the specialty here. There is a good-size collection of armoires, cupboards, desks, bookcases, china closets, dressers, beds, tables and chairs.

Montgomery—A number of antiques and novelty stores have clustered in this historic village in recent years making it a great stop for those who want to take a break from traveling. It's a nice place to stroll and browse, whether you are traveling north or south. Make sure to stop in at the **Clinton Shops** (845-457-5392), 84 Clinton Street, is a multi-dealer center open daily year-round 11-5, except Wednesday. The **Montgomery Antique Center** (845-457-7100), 40 Railroad Avenue, has 2800 square feet of antiques and just about anyone will find something of interest here.

Tuxedo—There are several antiques dealers in this interesting town. My favorite is **Vera Johnson Antiques** (845-351-4466), 538 Route 17, one mile north of the village. Open Thursday through Monday 11:30-5, there are collectibles and all kinds of jewelry. **BackHome Antiques** (845-915-3505), Tuxedo Park, is a multi-dealer shop in a 3500 square foot space offering artwork, mid-century modern antiques, jewelry and pottery. Open Saturday through Monday 11-6.

ART GALLERIES There are several galleries in Sugar Loaf, Cornwall and Warwick and the best way to see them is to walk around the villages: they are designed for exploration on foot! Those listed here are somewhat off-the-beaten-track.

Ann Street Gallery (845-784-1146) 104 Ann Street, Newburgh. Open Wednesday & Thursday 9-5; Friday & Saturday 11-5. This non-profit gallery specializes in contemporary art and shows both emerging and established artists. The focus is on cross-cultural and intergenerational subjects.

Exposures Gallery (845-469-9382), 1357 Kings Highway, Sugar Loaf. Open Wednesday through Sunday 11-5. Hudson Valley landscape photographer Nick Zungoli

Main Street in Warwick, a popular village with several fine shops and restaurants.

displays his photos of the region as well as those of his travels throughout the world. The gallery is located in one of the original Sugar Loaf houses. This is a must stop for visitors to Sugar Loaf.

The Gallery at ORMC (845-333-2385), 707 East Main Street, Middletown. Open daily 8am-8pm. Hudson Valley artists are showcased in this new hospital with a collection of regional artists on display throughout the facility.

Wallkill River School of Art (845-457-2787), 232 Ward Street, Montgomery. Open Monday through Saturday 12-6. This artist's cooperative specializes in outdoor paintings of Orange County, in the style of the Hudson River School. There are changing exhibits monthly and art classes are available.

AUCTIONS

Auctions are usually held on a regular basis, whether once a month or once a week. Estate sales offer everything from Persian rugs to eccentric collectibles. Flea markets are another business springing up on warm weather weekends.

Mark Vail Auction Services (845-744-2120; markvailauction.com), 188 Kelly Avenue, Pine Bush, has antiques and estate auctions twice a month. They have been in business for over 30 years and the website lists a calendar of auction dates.

Flannery's Auction & Estate Services (845-744-2233; flanneryestateservices. com), 26 Recreation Park Road, Pine Bush. This company has been in business since 2002. Their estate business and auction services dovetail. Website contains a complete schedule; auctions are usually conducted twice each month during the summer and less frequently at other times of the year.

Old Red Barn Auctions (845-754-7122; oldredbarnauction.com), 35 Route 211, Cuddebackville, has weekend auctions in a historic red barn dating back to the early 1800s on the first Saturday of the month. The website lists a full schedule.

CRAFTS

Clearwaters Distinctive Gifts & Jones Farm Country Store (845-534-4445), 190 Angola Road, Cornwall. Open daily year-round weekdays 8-6; weekends until 5. Since 1914 this fifth-generation family farm has served the Hudson Valley with homegrown produce, fresh eggs, maple syrup, honey, preserves, coffees, and many gourmet items. Grandma Phoebe's kitchen features homemade baked goods, cream and butter fudge and wonderful apple cider doughnuts. There is now a café where you can enjoy the fantastic cookies and have a coffee after a busy day traveling around West Point! Children are always welcome to visit the animals and enjoy the observation beehive. The second floor of the store is an enormous gift shop with books, china, novelty items, and wonderful handcrafted goods. This store is an interesting stop in Cornwall, a lovely village with a number of fine shops and eateries.

Sugar Loaf Crafts Village (sugarloafny.com). Take exit 16 off the NYS Thruway to Route 17, and go west for 8 miles to exit 127; follow the signs. Open year-round, Tuesday through Sunday 11-5. Named for the local mountain that is shaped the way sugar was during colonial times, Sugar Loaf, with its bare crest, has been the subject of unusual speculation. Originally the mountain was a Native American burial ground, and over the years various relics and bones have been uncovered in the area. Once a bustling stagecoach and river stop, the area lost its prominence when the railroads bypassed it in the mid-19th century. But in recent years, Sugar Loaf has regained its spirit. Home to dozens of craftspeople and artists who live and work in several fo the buildings along Kings Highway and Woods Road, the village is a terrific place to find a special gift or add to a collection. Visitors will find handcrafted stained glass, pottery, paintings, photography, and jewelry. As befits an art colony, there are crafts fairs and art shows throughout the year, as well as a fall festival and holiday caroling at Christmas. The village is charming; an excellent place to spend an afternoon talking to a number of artists at work in their studios. Visitors will do lots of walking, so keep that in mind. Parking is at either end of the village in well-marked lots.

FACTORY OUTLETS

If you tire of taking in the beauty of Orange County, there is always shopping to enjoy—and plenty of it. Factory outlets have come a long way from the dingy shops of the past, so perhaps stop at the renowned **Woodbury Common** (845-928-4000), 498 Red Apple Court (off Route 32), Central Valley. Open daily year-round, except major holidays, 9am-9pm. There are over 200 stores in this colonial-style mall, selling everything from shoes, clothing, sweaters and watches, to toys, wallets, crystal, and stockings. The mall sponsors special events throughout the year, and there is a large food court.

Gillinder Glass (845-856-5375), 39 Erie Street, Port Jervis. Open Monday through Saturday 9:30-5:30; Sunday noon-4. Call ahead for group visit information. Here visitors are offered a rare chance to watch glass being heated, molded, shaped, and cooled into fine collectibles. The factory, which has an on-site shop, has a viewing area, and the furnaces glow as the craftspeople use the same techniques employed a century ago. After a tour, stop by the Tri-States Monument (at the junction of the Neversink and Delaware rivers, Laurel Grove Cemetery), Just under the I-84 bridge is a rock on which you can stand in three states (New York, New Jersey and Pennsylvania) at once; it also marks the boundary between New York and New Jersey.

TWG Fabric and Home Decorating Center (845-343-3423), 115 Wisner Avenue, Middletown. This outlet specializes in decorative fabrics and is an exclusive importer of 60-inch lace. They are open Monday through Thursday 9:30-6; Friday until 1; Sunday 11-4. Closed Saturday.

SPECIAL EVENTS

April: **Brigade of the American Revolution Spring Encampment** (845-4561-1765; parks.ny.gov), New Windsor Cantonment, 374 Temple Hill Road, Vails Gate. The last encampment of the Continental Army is reenacted. This event is usually scheduled for a weekend in mid-April on both Saturday and Sunday between 10am and 4pm. Check the website for exact date. Admission.

July: **Orange County Fair** (845-343-4826; orangecountyfair.com), 239 Wisner Avenue (fairgrounds), Middletown. One of the oldest county fairs in New York State, this one started as an agricultural display between 1818 and 1825. Local interest didn't begin to build until 1841, when the New York State Agricultural Society entered the picture. From then on the fair was a hit. The 1841 extravaganza featured horses, cows, pigs, farm exhibits, and races. A visit to the fair today will turn up top-name entertainment, scores of food booths, thrilling rides and some unique events such as pig racing, where swift-footed swine dash for the purse—a cookie! Native American shows, stock-car racing and petting zoos are also on-site, along with the finest local produce and livestock.

July-September: **New York Renaissance Faire** (845-351-5171, after June 1st; renfair.com), 600 Route 17A, Sterling Forest, Tuxedo Park. Watch for signs. Open late July through mid-September, weekends only. Call for exact dates and hours. Admission. Knights and ladies, sorcerers and their apprentices, fools and varlets, bumpkins and wantons all gather on the glorious grounds of Sterling Forest to re-create the lusty days of a merry olde English fair. The festival runs for eight consecutive weekends and presents a colorful, noisy look at a misty period of time somewhere between King Arthur and Shakespeare. Falconers show off the skills of their birds, and opera and Shakespeare are presented at the Globe Theatre. Maid Marian flirts with

Robin Hood, ladies dance beneath a maypole, and the rose gardens are open for strolling. Craftspeople display and sell their wares and the aroma of steak on a stake, mead and cheese pie flavor the air. There are jugglers, knife throwers, mud fights, and a living chess game in which the pieces wander the gardens to their squares. The actors play their roles throughout the entire festival, so authenticity combines with the personal touch. Kids adore the noise and action, and there is enough to see and do for everyone in the family.

September: **Orange County Onion Festival**; (845-651-4266) is held annually, rain or shine, on the Sunday of Labor Day weekend at the Pavilion in Pine Island. Admission. There is always live music, which often includes Jimmy Sturr and his orchestra whose specialty is polka music.

New York Renaissance Faire , Sterling Forest, Tuxedo Park, NY

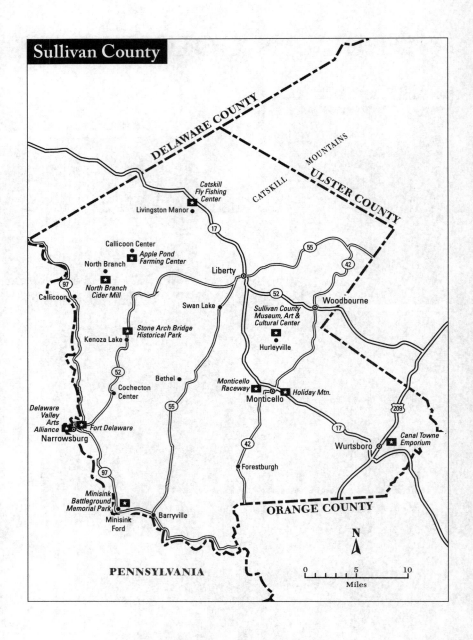

Sullivan County

DELAWARE COUNTY

CATSKILL MOUNTAINS

ULSTER COUNTY

Catskill Fly Fishing Center

Livingston Manor

17

Callicoon Center

55

42

North Branch

Apple Pond Farming Center

97

North Branch Cider Mill

Liberty

52

Callicoon

Woodbourne

Swan Lake

Sullivan County Museum, Art & Cultural Center

Stone Arch Bridge Historical Park

Kenoza Lake

Hurleyville

52

Bethel

Monticello Raceway

Holiday Mtn.

Cochecton Center

Monticello

55

209

Delaware Valley Arts Alliance

Fort Delaware

42

17

Narrowsburg

Forestburgh

Canal Towne Emporium

Wurtsboro

97

Minisink Battleground Memorial Park

Minisink Ford

Barryville

ORANGE COUNTY

PENNSYLVANIA

N

0   5   10
Miles

SULLIVAN COUNTY

Only 90 miles northwest of New York City lies Sullivan County; 1000 square miles of outdoors treasures. The Delaware River snakes along the county border and down into Pennsylvania, where the rugged, untamed countryside is home to bald eagles. To the north, visitors will discover the charm of tranquil, silvery lakes, lush forests, and narrow valleys where tiny villages nestle alongside bubbling streams. Sullivan also offers some of the world's best trout fishing, and on opening day of the season—rain or snow—rods and flies are taken from basements and garages across the county in pursuit of the annual dream of catching "the big one." Only a small percentage of the county is considered agricultural, but there are dairy and pick-your-own farms as well as abundant orchards. A drive through Sullivan County is a reminder that not too long ago this area was the frontier, a place where bears, bobcats, and the mysterious panther haunted the uneasy sleep of woodsmen and pioneers.

VISITOR INFORMATION

Sullivan County Visitors Association (845-747-4449; 800-882-CATS; scva. net), County Government Center, 100 Sullivan Avenue, Ferndale 12734.

Sullivan County Chamber of Commerce (845-791-4200; catskills.com), 196 Bridgeville Road, Monticello 12701.

Liberty Chamber of Commerce (845-292-9797; libertychamber.org), P.O. Box 147, Liberty 12754.

Roscoe Chamber of Commerce (roscoeny.com), P.O. Box 443, Roscoe 12776.

GETTING THERE

By car: Sullivan County is accessible from Route 17 (the future Route 86) and Route 209. You can pick up Route 17 at NYS Thruway exit 16 (Harriman).

By bus: **Rolling V Transportation Services** (845-434-0511; 800-999-6593), 5008 Main Street, South Fallsburg, provides bus and limo services for the local area as well as long distance **Short Line/Coach USA** (800-631-8405; shortlinebus.com) 45 Sturgis Road, Monticello, offers frequent express service from the Port Authority Bus Terminal in Manhattan as well as other parts of the metropolitan area.

By air: **Stewart International Airport** (845-564-2100), 1035 First Street, New Windsor, has service to major East Coast cities daily. Charter service and private aircraft can be accommodated at **Sullivan County International Airport** (845-583-6600), 57 Route 183A, White Lake, and **Wurtsboro Airport** (845-888-2791), 50 Barone Road, Wurtsboro.

MEDICAL EMERGENCY

Catskill Regional Medical Center (845-794-3300), 68 Harris Bushville Road, Harris, or **Grover Hermann Division** (845-887-5530), 8881 Route 97, Callicoon.

MAJOR SITES TO SEE

Bethel Woods Center for the Arts (800-745-3000; 845-583-2000; bethelwoodscenter.org), 200 Hurd Road, Bethel. Open Memorial Day weekend through Labor Day daily 10-7, with extended hours on concert days; the rest of the year, Thursday through Sunday 10-5. A full performance schedule is listed on the website.

The actual **Woodstock Festival Site**, now part of Bethel Woods Center for the Arts, is on Hurd Road, in Bethel, NOT in Woodstock (Ulster County), more than 50 miles away. This is where it happened: three days of peace, mud,

The Woodstock Festival Site Museum in Bethel.

Time and the Valleys Museum exhibit, Grahamsville.

and rock'n'roll, where 400,000 gathered in August 1969. This state-of-the-art performance venue (including an interpretive center/museum) opened in 2006 and features jazz, classical and country music, as well as rock. There are 4800 seats under a pavilion and lawn space for up to 12,000; the 6348-square foot stage is twice the size of the one in Radio City Music Hall. Bethel and the surrounding countryside is beautiful, a good place for a leisurely drive, a walk, or a picnic. The self-guided tour of the museum is a must-see for anyone who lived through the 1960s, as well as those who are interested in the decade. The museum is beautifully designed for wandering and is filled with displays, videos, and audiovisual experiences, as well as a 21-minute film, *Woodstock: The Music.* The high-definition images and surround sound in this captivating film capture the highlights of the 1969 festival. Additionally, the performing artists of the concert reflect on these inspiring and emotional experiences nearly a half-century ago.

Catskill Fly-Fishing Center and Museum (845-439-4810; catskillflyfishing. org), 1031 Old Route 17, Livingston Manor. Open year-round: April through October, daily 10-4:30; November through March, Wednesday through Saturday, 10-4. Admission. Dry fly-fishing enthusiasts will certainly find a lot to do in Sullivan County, where they will discover some of the best trout streams in the nation. Visitors should not miss this museum, located on 53 acres along Willowemoc Creek. There is a changing exhibit of fly-fishing equipment such as rods, reels and flies; memorabilia, a library, and a hall of fame. It also presents the story of Lee Wulff, a streamside legend, who brought elegance and science to the fly-fishing art. Special appearances by well-known anglers and craftspeople take place during the summer season, and there are special events, including workshops, seminars, and just-plain-fun get-togethers.

Sullivan County Museum and Historical Society (845-434-8044; paththroughhistory.iloveny.com), 265 Main Street, Hurleyville. Open year-round, except January, Tuesday through Saturday 10-4; Sunday 1-4. An array of changing exhibits complements the permanent ones that related the history of the region. One focuses on Frederick Albert Cook, an early 20th-century explorer who, in addition to being a physician and anthropologist, was the first American to travel to both the North and South Poles. The website lists a variety of special events at the museum year-round. This is one of the few places in the area that offers several fun activities during the winter months.

Time and the Valleys Museum (845-985-7700; timeandthevalleysmuseum.org), 332 Main Street, Grahamsville. Open Memorial Day through Labor Day, Thursday through Sunday, noon-4 and weekends in September. Admission. This wonderful museum is chock full of interactive engaging exhibits, a local history research room and museum shop. If you ever wondered how New York City gets its waters from Catskill reservoirs, this is the place to go. Learn about the high price local residents paid (and still pay) to provide that water to urban dwellers in New York. If you wondered how those tunnels were built, this is the place to find out. While children will enjoy this stop, everyone will find it interesting, particularly those of us who live in the Catskills!

HISTORIC SITES

Apple Pond Farm and Renewable Energy Education Center (845-482-4764; applepondfarm.com), 80 Hahn Road, Callicoon Center. Open year-round, Thursday through Sunday, by appointment. Admission. Today more farms are run with advanced technology as older agricultural methods and theories are slowly being lost in an avalanche of computer information. But there are still some farmers who cherish the old ways and believe that if the land is worked well, it will yield a bountiful harvest. At Apple Pond, an educational center and working farm, visitors can judge for themselves the merits of organic farming practices, wind turbines, renewable energy sources, and sustainable agricultural practices. Visitors can enjoy one of several different tours, including Farming with Kids, Solar Sundays, and Alotta Ricotta, a cheese-making tour. The farm is stocked with sheep, milking goats, and free-range chickens. Special activities like renewable-energy and gardening workshops, spinning, and cheese-making demonstrations and classes are held throughout the year, and all activities require reservations. The website has a list of special events. There is a pet-friendly four-bedroom, two bath guesthouse at the farm available for rental year-round, and visitors can participate in farm activities. Don't expect a quaint little restoration here; do expect to get some mud on your shoes!

Fort Delaware Museum of Colonial History (845-252-6660), 6615 Route 97, Narrowsburg. Open Memorial Day weekend; weekends in June; late June until Labor Day, Friday through Monday 9-5; Sunday noon-5. Admission. Much attention is paid to the people who settled the main cities of New York, but those who decided to take on the wilderness are often forgotten. At the Fort Delaware Museum, the daily life of the backwoods settler is explored through exhibits, crafts demonstrations, and tours. The fort is a reconstruction of the original frontier settlement of Cushetunk on the Delaware River with its stockades and stout log homes, which offered the only protection from Native Americans and, later, English troops. The fort consists of a small settlement entirely surrounded by high log walls, or stockades. During the tour, visitors see the blockhouses (where arms and ammunition were stored), settlers' cabins, a meetinghouse, a blacksmith shop, a candle shed, a loom shed, and more. Outside the fort walls you'll find a small garden planted with crops typical of the era. Costumed guides and staff members demonstrate skills and crafts from the period, including candle making, blacksmithing and even weaponry. Special events are scheduled throughout the season. Your visit may include a show by Revolutionary War soldiers, weavers, or cooks. There is an excellent gift shop here, so make sure to check it out.

Minisink Battleground Memorial Park (845-807-0287), County Route 168, Minisink Ford. Open mid-May through mid-October, daily 8-dusk. Free. One of the unusual and forgotten Revolutionary War Battlegrounds in the region, this site offers visitors a chance to walk along trails that tell stories of both nature and combat. In July 1779, the area's most important historic battle took place. A group of American rebels were defeated by Mohawks in a massacre that took almost 50 lives. In an eerie postscript, the bones of the dead were not gathered and buried until more than 40 years after the battle because the area was wilderness, and not many people visited.

Today the 56-acre park has three walking trails from which to explore its history and the surrounding natural setting. The blazed trails have descriptive markers that tell the story of the area, and written trail guides can be picked up at the interpretive center. The **Battleground Trail** depicts the tactics and strategy of a woodland skirmish and includes stops at Sentinel Rock, where the lone American defender was killed; Hospital Rock, where a rebel doctor lost his life while tending to his wounded charges; and Indian Rock, which legend says was set up to commemorate the dead. The **Woodland Trail** meanders through wetlands, dense foliage, and a variety of ferns. The park map points out the trail's flora and describes some of the animal life you may encounter, such as foxes, wood frogs, raccoons, and maybe even a bald eagle. On the **Old Quarry/Rockshelter Trail**, discover the logging, quarrying, and Native American histories of this section through trail markers. You may also want to visit the battleground in time for the small memorial service held each July 22nd, the anniversary of the night, to honor those who fell here.

Roebling's Suspension Bridge. Look for the historical marker opposite the entrance to the Minisink Battleground. Built by the designer of the Brooklyn Bridge, this crossing on the Delaware River is the oldest of its kind still standing. The aqueduct was constructed because canal boats and logging rafts kept crashing into one another on the river; the aqueduct would actually carry the canal boats over the river itself. The aqueduct was turned into a bridge crossing in the late 19th century, and today it still carries traffic across to Pennsylvania.

SCENIC DRIVES

Sullivan County has more than 1000 square miles of countryside, so just about any drive through the county will take you past exquisite views that change dramatically with the seasons. The earliest blush of spring may be enjoyed by driving along any back road, or even on Route 17; summer is lush and lazy anywhere you turn; fall splashes the meadows and forests with color; and winter here is strikingly beautiful. Sullivan County Tourism offers details theme driving tours in their literature. Check the website, scva.net. The following trips are my favorites.

If you want to travel the southernmost section of the county and see some spectacular river and mountain scenery, start your tour in Monticello. From there head south on Route 42 to Sackett Lake Road (you pass through a town called Squirrel Corners), and keep heading south to Forestburgh Road, where you will make a right. This is the reservoir area of **Mongaup Falls**, a good spot to sight bald eagles. At Route 97 head west along the snaking river drive known as **Hawk's Nest**, with its views of New York and Pennsylvania; you will pass **Minisink Battleground Park** and **Roebling's Suspension Bridge**. Head north on Route 52 to Liberty, where you can pick up Route 17 back to Monticello.

Another drive, which will take you past some of the few remaining **covered bridges** in the county, begins at Livingston Manor (exit 96 off Route 17). Turn onto Old Route 17 from the Vantran covered bridge, built in 1860, and one of the few existing bridges constructed in the lattice-truss and queen post styles. Go back to Livingston Manor and follow the signs east from town along DeBruce Road to Willowemoc, which has a covered bridge built in 1860 in Livingston Manor, then cut in half and moved to its present site in 1913. From Willowemoc take Pole Road to West Branch Road, which leads into Claryville. The Halls Mills covered bridge, built in 1912, is on Claryville Road over the Neversink River. Head south from Claryville to Route 55, then west back to Liberty.

Another sight worth making time to see is **Tomasco Falls**, often called the Niagara of Sullivan County. These spectacular waterworks are a refreshing sight on a hot spring or summer's day but are particularly dramatic after heavy rains. To get there, take Route 209 to Kerhonkson. Turn onto County Route 55, and follow to Mountaindale. The falls are visible from this road.

Other roads that offer outstanding views include State Routes 209, 55 and 55A. Route 17 is the major north-south road through the county and provides access to most of the region's scenic areas and byways.

WINERIES, BREWERIES AND DISTILLERIES

Bashakill Vineyards (845-888-5858; bashakillvineyards.com), 1131 South Road, Wurtsboro. Open April through December Saturday and Sunday noon-6. This is Sullivan County's first commercial winery and they offer both white and red wines. There is also live music most days when the winery is in operation. They are also now a farm brewery serving two styles of beers: a full-bodied stout aged in red wine barrels and the other is a cream-ale. Leashed dogs are welcome!

Catskill Distilling Company (845-583-3141; catskilldistilling.com), 2037 Route 178, Bethel. Open year-round Saturday and Sunday noon-5: weekdays by appointment. The owner, Monte Sachs, a veterinarian as well as a distiller, is occasionally on hand to take visitors on a tour of the facility where he created Peace Vodka in the same town where the 1969 Woodstock Festival took place. Artisan distilled spirits from New York

A wood sculpture that stands inside the Dancing Cat Saloon, a restaurant adjoining the Catskill Distilling Company in Bethel.

State-grown products include bourbon, grappa, and gin. Opened in 2010, there are now eight spirits from locally grown grains, fruits and botanicals. The products here have no additives!

Prohibition Distillery (917-685-8989; prohibitiondistillery.com), 10 Union Street, Roscoe. Open daily year-round; 11-5; Friday & Saturday until 8; Sunday open at noon. This award-winning craft-distillery and makers of Bootlegger 21 vodka, gin and bourbon, offers tastings and tours. The owner is enthusiastic about the products and will happily answer any questions you may have. Those who love spirits should definitely stop here.

Roscoe NY Beer Company (607-290-5002; roscoebeercompany.com), 145 Rockland Road, Roscoe. Open year-round, but call for hours: they vary with the season. This brewery, created by people who love the outdoors and their community in Roscoe, has a spacious storefront and self-serve tap wall, full-service tasting bar, and lounge area. It's a good place to relax and enjoy a drink after walking around town.

ACTIVITIES

Those who are new to outdoor activities like biking, hiking and kayaking may want to contact two excellent outfitters in Sullivan County for maps, guidance and equipment rentals. **Ridgeback Sports** (845-887-3048), 34 A Dorrer Drive, Callicoon and **Morgan Outdoors** (845-439-5507), 46 Main Street, Livingston Manor, are both open year-round daily.

BICYCLING

Liberty O&W Rail Trail (845-292-5111), at the intersection of Chestnut and West streets, Liberty. Open year-round. Free. This rustic trail is excellent for biking or walking and was formerly part of the O&W Rail Line. It's a great choice for families with young children. There are benches along the way where bikers can stop and rest. Map boards at the end points guide you. The trail has four trailheads across three different sections.

Rails-To-Trails (845-434-8810) Greenfield Road, Woodridge. Open year-round. Free. This four mile rail trail leads west and east of the village of Woodridge. No motorized vehicles are permitted and it is open for walking, biking and cross-country skiing.

Walnut Mountain Park (845-292-7690), 73 Walnut Mountain Road, Liberty. Open daily 8-dusk. This 265-acre public park has miles of hiking and biking trails that are perfect for snowshoeing and cross-country skiing in the winter. There are great views, picnic areas, a softball field and playground.

CANOEING, KAYAKING, AND RAFTING

Canoeists, kayakers, and rafters enjoy the Delaware River's rapids from spring to fall. Both the Upper Delaware (from Hancock to Port Jervis) and the main section of the river (from Port Jervis to the Chesapeake) are used for recreation, although there are sections that are particularly good for novices and the less adventurous. As with any other water sport, a few guidelines and suggestions will make your trip comfortable and safe. Most rental agencies require you know how to swim and insist flotation gear be worn by anyone in a canoe or raft—it may look harmless, but the Delaware can reach depths of fifteen feet. For your own comfort, take along sunscreen, lightweight sneakers, extra clothing, snacks, and a hat. If you go early in the season, the water may be higher and colder than if you go in late July or August. The following companies rent equipment, and some offer a return trip to your starting point. Although you don't always need to make a reservation on busy summer and holiday weekends, it pays to call before you go. Rates are often lower midweek.

Kittatinny River Trips (845-557-8611), 3854 Route 97, Barryville, is one of the oldest (over 75 years) operating canoe-rental companies and they are family-owned and operated. They also rent rafts, tubes, and kayaks. They have seven locations and two riverfront campgrounds. Open daily April through October 8-6. The **Kittatinny Zip Lines**, open May through October, two 3000-foot dual racing zip lines, extend from the mountaintop overlooking the Delaware River Valley down to the valley floor. After a raft or canoe trip, this is an exciting way to end the day!

Lander's River Trips (845-252-3925; 800-252-3925), 5961 State Route 97, Narrowsburg, has three campgrounds for guests in addition to full river equipment (canoes, tubes, kayaks and rafts) for rent. Open daily April through October 8-6.

The following companies also rent equipment: **Jerry's Three River Canoe & Campground** (845-557-6078), 2333 Route 97, Pond Eddy; **Indian Head Canoes** (845-557-8777), 3883 Route 97, Barryville; **Reber's River Trips** (845-557-3332), 3351 Route 97, Barryville.

FARM STANDS AND PICK-YOUR-OWN

Nothing tastes like fruits and vegetables that still have the blush of the sun and the mist of the morning on them. Harvesting begins in Sullivan County in late spring with asparagus and berries, and ends in late fall with pumpkins and apples (although some stands stock local eggs, maple syrup, and honey year-round). Hours vary with the season and type of harvest, and not all stands are open daily, so it is suggested you call before making a special trip. There are several small, family-run farm stands that carry only one or two items and they are open for only a few weeks a year. Keep an eye out for these too when you're driving around. They often have unusual selections or heirloom varieties. Whether you pick the produce yourself or buy from a roadside stand, the selection and quality in Sullivan County are excellent.

Many area farmers attend **the Sullivan County Area Farmers Market** (845-292-6180), with locations in several towns: in Barryville, behind the River Market, mid-May to late October, Saturday 10-1; In Callicoon the outdoor market is held May through October at 23 Dorrer Drive; November through April at 8 Creamery Road, Sunday 11-2. In Monticello, at North & Jefferson Streets parking lot July through October, Monday 11-2; in Roscoe at Niforatos Field May through October, Sunday 10-2.

Buck Brook Alpacas (845-807-3104), 99 Bestenhelder Road, Roscoe. A family owned farm between North Branch and Roscoe with over 50 alpacas in a variety of colors. The farm started in 2013. You must call in advance to schedule a visit. There is a farm store and they are open year-round.

Butterfly Botanicals (845-733-7713), 363 Petticoat Lane, Bloomingburg. Open mid-May through mid-October, daily 8-6. There are live butterfly exhibits here and a hands-on educational environment that will particularly delight the kids. There are also perennials and annuals for sale in the greenhouse.

Diehl's Farm Market (845-887-4935; 807-3131), 625 Gabel Road, Callicoon, is a well-stocked market with a full range of local crops, from apples to eggs and dairy products. Open daily year-round; call for hours.

Silver Heights Farm (845-482-3608), 216 Eggler Road, Jeffersonville. This organic nursery specializes in transplants of unusual and heirloom vegetables and flowers. They have over 250 kinds of tomatoes and a great selection of peppers. Open April through mid-September; Tuesday through Saturday. Call for hours.

Sonoma Falls Cider Mill & Country Market (845-439-4949), 140 Old Liberty Road, Morsston. There's a seven-tier waterfall here with hiking trails, fishing (for fee per pound), and apple cider pressing, with snow tubing and ice skating in the winter months. During maple syrup season, this is a great place to see tapping of the trees. The store offers local produce, gifts, and ice cream. There is also a café on the premises that serves breakfast and lunch.

Vita's Farm & Garden Market (845-482-5776, 4789 Route 52, Jeffersonville, is open May through October, daily 9-6; weekends only through December. A large selection of annuals, perennials and unique plants may be found here along with gifts, crafts, local produce and home-baked goods.

Some farms offer visitors the chance to select and cut their own Christmas trees. You can bring your own saw or rent one for the day. Dress warmly, bring rope to tie the tree to the car, and have a nice holiday! Do call ahead for directions, hours, and prices. The **Pine Farm** (607-591-5507), 121 Eagin Road, Youngsville, has quality trees and wreaths and has been in the same family since the mid-1800s. They are open on weekends between Thanksgiving and Christmas from 10am to dusk. **Trees of the Woods** (845-482-4528), 135 Leins Road, Callicoon Center, is run by the ex-personal assistant to Steven Speilberg's mother. A native of Grahamsville, he returned to Sullivan County after an interesting career in LA and New York. Open weekends between Thanksgiving and Christmas, 10-dusk.

FISHING

Sullivan County is an angler's paradise. The famed Willowemoc and Beaverkill streams produce prize-winning trout each year in addition to being recognized

as the cradle of American fly-fishing. The Delaware River offers its rich bounty to the patient angler, as do Mongaup Creek and Russell Brook. Then there are the ice lakes of the county, with such entrancing names as Kiamesha, Kenoza, Swan, and Waneta. There are hundreds of fine fishing areas in Sullivan County and too little space to do them all justice. The following general information, however, will assist you in finding the perfect spot to enjoy a rocky stream, a sunny sky, and, just maybe, a record catch!

The county's streams and rivers are famed for their brook, brown, and rainbow trout, but bass, pickerel, walleye, and shad are also plentiful. All streams on state land are open to the public; other streams often have public fishing rights through state easements, which are indicated by signs. New York State requires

Catskill Fly-Fishing Center and Museum.

fishing licenses for anyone over 16, as well as special reservoir permits (call 866-933-2257 or go to dec.ny.gov/permits for information). Lake fishing is also popular in Sullivan, but there are separate use fees charged, and some lakes are privately owned by hotels or resorts, so check on the site before you fish.

The Beaverkill is one of the best known trout streams in the world and may be reached from Roscoe, Livingston Manor, Lew Beach, Beaverkill, and Rockland. Fly-fishing tackle may be purchased in Roscoe at the **Beaverkill Angler** (607-498-5194), 64 Stewart Avenue. Make sure to stop in at **Roscoe Little Store** (607-498-5553), 59 Stewart Avenue, the oldest sporting goods and variety store in the county. In addition to licenses, tackle, live bait, and clothing, they carry all kinds of specialty items, toys, and gifts. The store is fun to explore and is open year-round, daily 9-5:30. Or call **White Clouds Beaverkill Fly-Fishing School** (607-498-4611) in Roscoe. This private school offers students a chance to learn casting, fly tying, and moving water fishing techniques. You can schedule lessons to meet your needs. **Baxter House River Outfitters and Guide Service** (607-290-4022), 2012 Old Route 17, Roscoe is a fly-fishing guide service and is open daily April through November. **The Wulff School of Fly-Fishing** (845-439-5020), Livingston Manor, is located in the beautiful upper Beaverkill Valley, set on 100 acres. The school has a building designed to meet teaching requirements. In addition to fly-fishing, you can learn wading, streamcraft, and obstacle casting. If you have time, enjoy fishing in the Delaware River's main stem and its east and west branches, as well as the no-kill stretches of the Beaverkill and Willowemoc rivers.

RIVERS AND STREAMS (SOME LOCATIONS)

Willowemoc Creek is found between Roscoe and Livingston Manor, along Old Route 17. Mongaup Creek runs from Livingston Manor to Mongaup Pond. The Neversink River is at Claryville on County Routes 19 and 15, and you can pick up the Delaware River at East Branch on Route 17. Among the lakes are Kenoza Lake (Route 52, Kenoza Lake Village), Swington Bridge Lake (Route 17B, Mongaup Valley), Swan Lake (Route 55, between Liberty and Kauneonga Lake), White Lake (junction of Routes 17B and 55), Waneta Lake (County Route 15 in Deckertown), Cable Lake (Route 17 northwest of Roscoe, end of Russel Brook), and Kiamesha Lake (Route 42, Kiamesha).

The Beaverkill Trout Hatchery (845-439-4947), 22 Alder Creek Road, Livingston Manor, is a fish hatchery that has been in the same family for five generations. Call in advance to make arrangements to take a tour. They are open April through September, Saturday and Sunday 8-5 for fish and pay pond. They also sell fresh and smoked trout which is excellent.

The New York State Fish Hatchery (845-439-4328), 402 Mongaup Road, Livingston Manor, is a great place to take school classes as tours are only available for groups. Brown trout are raised here for distribution throughout the state. Open year-round 9-4; holidays and weekends in the summer months 8-noon.

GOLF

The beauty of Sullivan County's farm country carries over to its golf courses. Many resorts have outstanding courses that are open to the public. Well-known championship courses at Grossinger's, Villa Roma, and Lochmor coexist here with family-friendly nine-hole courses like Twin Village. It is always best to call ahead to confirm hours and see if reservations are required for a tee time.

Grossinger Country Club (845-292-9000), 26 Route 52 East, Liberty, has 27 holes of golf, a driving range and putting greens, and full facilities. Rated 4 ½ stars by *Golf Digest*.

Swan Lake Golf and Country Club (845-292-0323), 38 Eagle Drive, Swan Lake, is an 18-hole PGA-rated course nestled high in the Catskills. Open April through November, daily 7-6.

Tennanah Lake Golf & Tennis Club (607-498-5000), 100 Fairway View Drive, Roscoe, an 18-hole par-72 course, practice facility and driving range. They offer club rentals and lessons for novices. Open April through October, daily 7am-9:30pm.

Villa Roma Resort & Conference Center (845-887-4880), 356 Villa Roma Road, Callicoon, has a par-71 6514-yard, 18-hole course, a putting green and full facilities. The course is open April through mid-November but call for hours.

Public courses include **Sullivan County Golf & Country Club** (845-292-9584), 2514 Route 52, Liberty; **Tarry Brae** (845-434-2620), 387 Pleasant Valley Road, South Fallsburg; and the **Lochmor Golf Course** (845-434-1257), 586 Loch Sheldrake-Hurleyville Road, Loch Sheldrake, with its par-71, 18-hole course.

HARNESS RACING

Monticello Casino and Raceway (845-794-4100; monticellocasinoandraceway. com), 204 Route 17B, Monticello. Open year-round, Monday through Thursday 10am-2am; until 4am Friday through Sunday. There are over 1000 slot machines here, as well as electronic table games including roulette. There is also live entertainment, live harness racing, and simulcasting of thoroughbred and harness races. There are two restaurants on the premises. The entertainment schedule is posted on the website.

HORSEBACK RIDING

Bridle Hill Farm (845-482-3993), 190 Hemmer Road, Jeffersonville. Open year-round daily 7am-9pm. There is an indoor arena here, as well as lessons for all ages from beginner through advanced. There are miles of trails here, and great care is taken to match every rider with the right horse for his/her ability. Lessons and trail rides are combined, and the owners make a special effort to give young riders a great experience.

Rolling Stone Ranch (845-583-1100), 282 West Shore Road, Bethel. Open Saturday and Sunday year-round; daily late June through Labor Day. There are indoor and outdoor riding arenas here and trail riding for students who take lessons.

SOARING

Wurtsboro Airport (845-888-2791), 50 Barone Road, Wurtsboro. Open daily, weather permitting. Established in 1928, this airport is home to the oldest soaring site in the country. Soaring is done in sailplanes, motor-less craft towed into the air and released. The pilot then sails the plane on the air currents—sometimes for hours—before gliding in for a landing. A 20-minute demonstration flight with a certified pilot can be arranged. If you enjoy the sport and want to learn, flight instruction is available.

WINTER SPORTS

CROSS COUNTRY SKIING

There are so many places to cross-country ski in Sullivan County that you would have to spend several winters here to try all of the trails. Many local parks allow skiing for free, but often the trails are not groomed and there are no nearby rentals. At the large resorts some trails are open for a fee to day visitors, but if you are uncertain of the hotel's policy, it is suggested you call ahead. Policies also change from year to year. Also refer to the Bicycling Section since the rail trails are great places to cross-country ski.

The DeBruce (845-439-3900), 982 DeBruce Road, DeBruce, has miles of cross-country trails, unmapped and unmarked within the Catskill Park. It is located near Mongaup State Park.

The 160-acre **Town of Thompson Park** (845-796-3606), Old Liberty Road, 1.5 miles past the Monticello Post Office; the 110-acre **Hanofee Park** (845-292-7690), on Sunset Lake Road, off Route 52 east, in Liberty, where you will find about three miles of ungroomed trails; and 265-acre **Walnut Mountain Park** (845-292-7690), Liberty, with ungroomed trails. You need to bring your own equipment here; there are no services.

DOWNHILL SKIING

While downhill skiing in Sullivan County does not revolve around large resorts like Hunter or Windham, it does have a few centers that offer fun for travelers of all ages.

Holiday Mountain Ski Area (845-796-3161), 99 Holiday Mountain Road, Monticello (exit 107 off Route 17 at Bridgeville), has both day and night skiing, 15 slopes, 100 percent snowmaking, and a vertical drop of 400 feet. The longest run is 3500 feet and both beginners and advanced skiers will enjoy the slopes here; cross country skiing is allowed and so is snowboarding. A ski shop, snack bar, and parking are available. Open mid-December through mid-March, Tuesday through Thursday 3-9; Friday noon-9; Saturday and Sunday 9-9. Closed Monday.

Villa Roma Resort & Conference Center (845-887-4880), 356 Villa Roma Road, Callicoon. There are four slopes, a double chairlift and T-bar, snowboarding, rentals, lessons, night skiing, and a snow tube run for those who prefer not to schuss down the slopes. The resort has snowmaking capability and is open to the public, not just guests of the hotel.

ICE FISHING

Every winter various organizations sponsor ice fishing contests. The King of the Ice contest is held every February and is sponsored by the Sullivan County Conservation Club. Call 845-747-4449 for up-to-date information before you go.

PARKS

Bashakill Wildlife Management Area (845-256-3098), South and Haven Roads, Wurtsboro. Located just south of town. Open year-round, daily dawn to dusk. Free. This 3107-acre tranquil wildlife habitat and recreation area where visitors can fish, boat, bird-watch, and hike, is one of the largest wetlands in the state of New York. The Bashakill is a famous stream in the history of Sullivan County, renowned for decades as teeming with fish. The area is managed by the DEC, and it is often passed by.

Lake Superior State Park (845-583-7908/807-0287), Dr. Duggan Road, Bethel (off Route 17B, 10 miles west of Route 17 exit 104). Open year-round; beach area is open Memorial Day weekend through Labor Day daily 9am-dusk (fee for beach area). This state park offers boating, boat rentals, fishing and picnic facilities, in addition to swimming. The beach is a perfect stop for families traveling with children.

The Stone Arch Bridge, made of hand-cut stone, in Kenoza Lake outside Jeffersonville, was built in 1873 and spans the East Branch of the Callicoon Creek.

Stone Arch Bridge Historical Park (845-807-0287), intersection of Routes 52 and 52A, Kenoza Lake. Open year-round Free. This three-arched stone bridge spanning Callicoon Creek, is the only remaining one like it in the U.S. Built in 1872 by two German stonemasons, the bridge was constructed from hand-cut local stone and supported without an outer framework. Replacing an earlier wooden span that finally collapsed from the constant weight of wagonloads of lumber, the Stone Arch Bridge gained fame not only for its graceful design and unusual construction, but also for a bizarre murder that took place on it in 1892. A local farmer, believing his brother-in-law had put a hex on him, convinced his son only the brother-in-law's death could life the curse. So the young man carried out the murder and dumped the body into the river. The case drew enormous publicity because of the witchcraft angle, and there have been reports of a ghost appearing on the bridge! Today, visitors fish from the banks, picnic on shore, or just walk through the 10-acre landscaped park and along the nature trails. Children will enjoy the small play area.

LODGING

Sullivan County is probably best known throughout the world for the Catskills resorts that flourished there for nearly a century. While some hotels, like Kutsher's, still welcome guests, others, like the Concord, have shut their doors. The region still offers a wide variety of resorts, bed and breakfasts, inns and bungalows, from inexpensive to luxury accommodations.

Resorts World Catskills Hotel & Casino (833-586-9358), 888 Resorts World Drive, Monticello 12701. ($$$) On the site of the old Concord Hotel, the resort features Adelaar, a one billion dollar integrated entertainment and lifestyle complex, cutting edge slot machines, classic table games, an 80,000-square-foot casino, 400 luxury hotel rooms and full service spa.

These are my favorite places to stay in Sullivan County. I have visited most and stayed overnight at several. They are all top-notch.

Bradstan Country Hotel (845-583-4114), 1561 Route 17B, White Lake 12786. ($$) There are five rooms in this informal country hotel overlooking beautiful White Lake. It is the perfect place to stay if you are going to Bethel Woods Center for a concert and don't want to drive home late at night. All rooms are filled with antiques and have private baths. A gourmet breakfast is served in the morning and special diets can be accommodated with advance notice. Open daily, May through October.

Catskill Mountains Resort (845-456-0195), 211 Mail Road, Barryville 12719. ($$$) This new addition to the Sullivan County hotel scene is truly fantastic. Enjoy luxury whether in a suite in the Main House or a beautifully appointed cabin. There is a full-service spa and restsaurant on the premises and Chef Pascal has worked in Manhattan at Veal d'Or as well as several Michelin starred restaurants in France, Switzerland and London. Guests may also enjoy the Olympic-size pool as well as the hiking and biking trails surrounding the resort. Open year-round.

The DeBruce (845-439-3900), 982 DeBruce Road, DeBruce 12758. ($$) Off Route 17 (exit 96). This inn, which dates back to the turn of the 19th century, is located on the banks of the Willowemoc Creek within the Catskill Forest Preserve. The 14 guest rooms have been completely renovated recently and both a gourmet breakfast and dinner are served daily by a fabulous young chef. Foodies take notice! This is a getaway to explore. Open year-round for single night stays or multiple evenings.

Ecce Bed & Breakfast (845-557-8562), 19 Silverfish Road, Barryville 12719. ($$$) "Ecce" is Latin for behold and rightly so as a description of this award-winning mountain house perched on a bluff 300 feet above the Delaware River with panoramic views of both the New York and Pennsylvania mountains at every turn. Five guest rooms all have private baths, (some with whirlpool tubs), TV, refrigerator, and Internet access. A wood-burning fireplace in the living room creates a warm, inviting atmosphere. There's a wonderful gourmet breakfast and guests will enjoy exploring the beautiful hiking trails on this 60-acre property as well as

The Inn at Lake Joseph in Forestburgh, former retreat of Cardinal Spellman.

kayaking and canoeing on the Delaware River nearby. The owners are always on site and pay attention to all the details. Open year-round.

Horse & Hounds (908-309-2799), 385 Hurd Road, Bethel, 12720. ($$) The attraction here is the lakefront property with boating, fishing, kayaking and swimming. There is an antiques-filled great room with a large fireplace and scenic views as well as a wrap-around front porch. The four rooms are beautifully appointed and the there is a full breakfast in the morning. Open year-round.

Inn at Lake Joseph (845-791-9506), 162 St. Joseph's Road, Forestburgh 12777. ($$$) Located off County Road 108, off Route 42, this 19th-century Victorian mountain retreat nestled in the Catskills and surrounded by acres of forest, this inn was built by a prosperous businessman who then sold the house to the Roman Catholic Church, which used it as a retreat for Cardinals Hayes and Spellman. A private 250-acre spring-fed lake offers swimming, kayaking, boating and fishing. There are two tennis courts, an outdoor pool and lovely hiking trails on the property. I spent a night here (in the Cardinal's bedroom) in 2017 and it is truly a magnificent property with wonderful owners who go out of their way to make every guest in their 16-room mansion feel at home. Highly recommended.

Kenoza Lake View Manor (845-482-2089), 56 Swiss Hill Road, Kenoza Lake 12750. ($$) This is an unusual place to stay: a large 15-room manor house with simple furnishings, a comfortable, homey ambiance, located on a quiet pastoral 16-acre property. There are hardwood floors, area rugs and lots of windows. A wonderful breakfast of omelets and fresh muffins is served in the morning. A family owned and operated establishment (it's not an inn, hotel or motel), America and her husband live on the property with their children. There is definitely the feeling of being a guest at a friend's rambling home! Open year-round. Children are welcome.

Nine River Road (845-887-0042), 9 River Road, Callicoon 12723. ($$) This beautifully decorated riverside house opened in 2016. An 1884-vintage house on the Delaware River, once home to a furniture store, has eight spacious rooms spread out on three floors, some with claw-foot tubs and river views. There is canoeing, swimming and tubing on the river. It's only a short walk to the numerous restaurants, galleries and shops in the center of Callicoon.

North Branch Inn (845-482-2339), 869 North Branch Road, North Branch 12766. ($$) Designer/owner Victoria Lesser has beautifully restored this 1860s inn, complete with juice bar/café on the main floor (the baked goods are excellent). All five rooms have private baths and children over the age of 12 are welcome. Open year-round.

Roscoe Motel (845-607-498-5220), 2054 Old Route 17, Roscoe 12776. ($) Located near some of the most famous fishing waters in the country, this is a funky motel that's inexpensive and provides the necessary amenities. A great place to stay if you're traveling with young children or just want basic accommodations. Open year-round.

Samba Inn (845-482-5900) 4893 Main Street, Jeffersonville 12748. ($) There are two efficiencies with kitchenette and cable wifi on the Callicoon Creek behind the Samba Café. The owners of the restaurant renovated this lovely guesthouse, a perfect place for families to stay while traveling through the county. The village of Jeffersonville is just steps away. Your hosts, Andrea and Tim Corcoran, are friendly and aim to please. They own and operate a café and Samba Marketplace which is chock full of local products, books and interesting gifts. Open year-round; children and pets welcome.

Stone Wall Acres (845-482-4930), 142 Eagin Road, Youngsville 12791. ($$) There's one carriage house here and it's furnished in original antiques, the perfect place for those seeking a secluded getaway. You'll feel transported to England, being surrounded by a country garden on six private acres. The carriage house has a living room/dining room, loft bedroom, and fireplace. Breakfast may be served there, in the main-house dining room, or poolside on the patio, depending on your preference. Open year-round.

WHERE TO EAT

Sullivan, although not a large county, has few major roads and is time-consuming to navigate. Therefore, the Dining Section for this county is organized by location.

DINING OUT

Southeastern Sullivan
(Monticello, Rock Hill)

Albella Restaurant (845-794-8866), 50 Jefferson Street, Monticello. ($$) Open year-round; Tuesday through Friday 10:30am-10pm; Saturday & Sunday 3-10. Closed Monday. Enjoy homemade pasta, fresh seafood, veal chops and steaks in lovely surroundings. There's also pizza and a bar menu for those who want lighter fare. Enjoy good Italian food at reasonable prices here.

Bernie's Holiday Restaurant (845-796-3333). 277 Rock Hill Drive, Rock Hill. ($$) Open Wednesday through Sunday for dinner 4-10. One of the largest restaurants in Sullivan County and also one of the best. The specialties here are steaks and seafood and the portions are generous. Children welcome.

Ciao Bella (845-796-4110), 46 Forestburgh Road, Monticello. ($$) Open daily for dinner 4-10. The Italian fare here is absolutely first-rate. I enjoyed the homemade Funghi Ravioli (stuffed with porcini mushrooms in a delicious sauce). They offer gluten free and whole wheat pastas and the choices are unusual and prepared to order. There is a wide selection of entrees and appetizers; excellent calamari as well as beef, chicken and veal dishes. Desserts are not to be overlooked here!

Southwestern Sullivan
(Barryville, Kauneonga Lake, Narrowsburg, White Lake)

Dancing Cat Saloon (at the Catskill Distilling Company) (845-583-3141), 2037 Route 17B, Bethel. ($$) Open Wednesday and Thursday 5-10; Friday and Saturday noon-10; Sunday 11-8. This is a fun place to dine and they have an enormous menu that includes burgers, wings, chili salads, and pizza. Their handcrafted spirits, like Peace Vodka, are a terrific accompaniment to the meal. There is a wide selection of cocktails and distilled spirits. The atmosphere is casual and the prices are quite reasonable.

Heron Restaurant (845-252-3333), 40 Main Street, Narrowsburg. ($$) Open Thursday through Sunday for lunch 11-3 and dinner 5:30-10. ($$) Since opening in 2012, this lovely restaurant along the banks of the Delaware River specializes in American cuisine created with ingredients from local farms.

There are lots of comfort food choices and their desserts are all made from scratch. This is the place to go after kayaking or canoeing!

Local Table and Tap (845-583-3020), 3 Horseshoe Lake Road, Kauneonga Lake. ($$) Open daily, except Tuesday, noon-9. This is one of my favorite restaurants in Sullivan County. There is something here to please every taste—steaks, organic chicken, imaginative salads and more. This is a perfect stop to make before heading out to a concert at Bethel Woods.

Northwestern Sullivan
(Callicoon, Jeffersonville, Livingston Manor, North Branch, Roscoe)

Arnold House Tavern (845-439-5070), 839 Shandelee Road, Livingston Manor. ($$) Open daily at 5pm; from noon on weekends. Local ingredients predominate, including trout from local streams. The comfort food served includes hearty soups, sandwiches and salads. There's outdoor dining on the deck in the warm weather and children are welcome.

Beaverkill Valley Inn (845-439-4844), 7 Barnhart Road, Livingston Manor. ($$) Open for breakfast, lunch and dinner. Breakfast and lunch is served buffet style; dinner is served by reservation only. Trout is the specialty of the house in this historic inn on the banks of the Beaverkill River, along with farm-raised chicken, beef, lamb and seasonal vegetables.

Matthews on Main (845-887-5636), 19 Lower Main Street, Cochecton. ($$) Open daily 11-9. This bright-red building with green and tan trim, houses this chef-owned family restaurant featuring fine fare at reasonable prices. The beautifully renovated building dates from 1865, and outdoor dining on the deck is where one can order lunch all night. There are international selections—fresh fish, duck, prime rib and sesame-crusted salmon. Desserts are all made from scratch on the premises and includes cakes, pies and sorbets. A casual, comfortable spot with a full bar and beautiful tin ceilings, management welcomes children.

Michelangelo's Restaurant (845-482-3900), 4900 Route 52 (Main Street), Jeffersonville. ($$) Open Monday through Saturday 11-9. The Southern Italian cooking features Neapolitan specialties like eggplant parmigiana and eggplant rollotini. All sauces are fresh and homemade. I sampled the linguine Michelangelo: pasta topped with arugula, jumbo shrimp, cherry peppers and a light tomato sauce. Desserts include cannoli, tiramisu, and dessert…if you have room!

North Branch Inn Bar Room & Restaurant (845-483-2339), 869 North Branch Road, North Branch. ($$) Open year-round, daily 5:30-9; until 10 Friday and Saturday; Sunday Brunch 11-3.

The menu here focuses on American favorites: everything is locally sourced so the menu changes seasonally depending on what is available. The bar serves only American made drinks. There are long, custom-made tables for communal dining. An interesting stop for travelers to Sullivan County!

Raimondo's (607-498-4702), 3 Stewart Avenue, Roscoe. ($$) Open daily 11-10 for lunch and dinner. This old-fashioned Italian restaurant offers everything from the basics (pizza and pasta) to more elaborate dishes. A couple of house specialties are linguine with crabmeat and veal with wild mushrooms and asparagus, topped with provolone cheese. This is a popular dining spot among local residents.

Riverside Café (607-498-5305), 16624 Route 17, Roscoe. ($$) Open for dinner daily May through October, 5-10; Sunday from noon-9. Enjoy a meal overlooking the Beaverkill stream while dining in this cozy eatery. The basic American cuisine includes hearty selections like grilled pork tenderloin, rack of lamb, baked stuffed brook trout, steak and lobster. All breads and desserts are baked fresh daily.

Rockland House (607-498-4240), 159 Rockland Road (Route 206, Roscoe. ($$) Open April through January, daily 5-9; until 10 Friday and Saturday. You may see the sign on Route 206 before approaching this long-established restaurant: Eat Here or We'll Both Starve. The specialties of the house are prime rib and a 10-ounce lobster tail. The salad bar has more than 30 items to choose from, and the homemade soups and breads are delicious. The spacious dining room with cathedral ceilings has long been a gathering place for local residents who have been patronizing this landmark steakhouse for decades. Children's menu.

Tavern on Main (845-482-2380), 4919 Route 52, Jeffersonville. Open Wednesday through Sunday 11-9. The building first opened as a hotel back in 1907. After extensive renovations in 2017, it reopened as a restaurant serving classic American favorites along with creative fare. Owners Lauren and Michael are passionate about their new business and offer several local craft beers. Children are welcome.

Northeastern Sullivan
(Hurleyville, Liberty)

Nardi's (845-434-8051), 205 Main Street, Hurleyville. ($) Open year-round, daily 11:30-10. This reasonably priced Italian American restaurant, known locally for its large portions specializes in steak, seafood, pasta, and pizza. It's a great spot for lunch or dinner if you're traveling with children.

Pickled Owl Gastropub (845-693-5322), 218 Main Street, Hurleyville. ($) Open daily, except Tuesday, 11:30-9:30. Enjoy the hipster ambiance in this comfortable spot with excellent service. The fare is all farm-to-table and there are dozens of craft beers to choose from, along with live music. Less traditional than many Sullivan County eateries, but a welcome change!

Picolo Paese (845-292-7210), 271 Route 52, Liberty. ($$) Open for lunch Tuesday through Friday noon-3; dinner served daily 4:30-10. This elegant, yet moderately priced, Northern Italian restaurant features fresh homemade pasta, seafood, chicken, veal, and imaginative appetizers. The chef-owner creates terrific daily specials I highly recommend.

EATING OUT

Benji & Jakes (845-583-4031), 5 Horseshoe Lake Road, Kauneonga Lake ($) Open Wednesday 4-9; Thursday through Monday noon-9. The brick oven pizza is the specialty of the house, located on a beautiful tranquil lake. In the warm weather, dine alfresco. The beer-battered jalapeño onion rings are one of my favorite dishes. There's pizza with fire-roasted eggplant sauce which I thoroughly enjoyed. You can also create your own pizza from an array of wonderful farm-fresh items.

Blue Horizon Diner (845-796-2210), 4445 Route 42 North, Monticello. ($) Open daily 7am-10pm. While you can order the usual diner fare here (burgers, sandwiches, salads), they are known for sautéed dishes (shrimp and scallop scampi), as well as steaks and lobsters. There are always daily and early bird specials.

Brew (845-796-2222), 280 Rock Hill Drive, Rock Hill. ($) Open daily year-round Tuesday through Saturday 11:30-9:30; on Sunday 11:30-8. Enjoy several craft beers on tap and fine New York spirits in a relaxed atmosphere at this eatery. The fare includes Angus beef burgers, Murray's chicken and salads with fresh local ingredients. A great stop if you're hungry and don't want to spend a lot but desire a high quality meal. Children welcome.

Brother Bruno Pizza & Restaurant (845-791-4600), 4050 Thompson Square, Monticello. ($) Open daily 11-9. This Italian American restaurant specializes in pizza and calzones as well as the standard favorites: lasagna, manicotti, and an array of other pasta dishes. Children welcome.

Chocolate Mousse Café & Bakery (845-557-3611), 3461 Route 97, Barryville. ($) Open daily 9-9; Sunday 11-5. Located in the historic Spring House Commons, this is a great place to enjoy homemade fare (soups, salads, and sandwiches for lunch, or pancakes, waffles and omelets for breakfast), that is both healthy and delicious. They are, of course, renowned for their chocolate mousse cake. In the warm weather, there's outdoor dining along the Delaware River. Children welcome.

Coffee Creation (845-252-6688), 25 Main Street, Narrowsburg. ($) Open daily 7-5; Saturday until 6. Enjoy hearty breakfast sandwiches, bagels, pastries, and hot oatmeal (breakfast is served all day). For lunch there are soups, salads, and wraps, mostly from locally grown ingredients. There's a casual atmosphere, WiFi, couches to lounge on, and tables available on the outdoor patio in the warm weather months. This eatery is truly a town hub.

The Corner Ice Cream Shop & Grill (845-557-3321), 577 Route 55, Eldred. ($) Open daily 11-8; later in the summer months. This combination ice cream-souvenir shop offers 16 flavors of Perry's and Edy's ice cream, as well as milk shakes, sundaes, and root beer floats. There are several types of paninis, if you are interested in non-sugar sustenance. Children will enjoy a stop here.

DeFilippi's Bakery & Café (845-791-4103), 506 Broadway, Monticello. ($) Open daily year round 6am-4pm. This delightful bakery/café offers a terrific variety of lunch specials including wraps, sandwiches, salads and great desserts. I have stopped here a few times on my way through Sullivan County and the fare and service are always excellent.

Floyd & Bobo's Bakery and Snack Palace (845-292-6200), 98 North Main Street, Liberty. ($) Open Tuesday through Saturday 7-5; Sunday 7-1. The comfort food here is tasty and fresh, and the owners aim to please. Whether you want a muffin or egg sandwich for breakfast, or chicken salad for lunch, it will be freshly prepared. The atmosphere is relaxed and casual. Children are welcome.

Java Love Coffee Roasting Company (845-583-4082), 10 Horseshoe Lake Road Kauneonga Lake ($) Open year-round, daily 7-5. This is the place to go for excellent coffee in the Bethel area.

Liberty Diner & Restaurant (845-292-8973), 30 Sullivan Avenue, Liberty. ($) Open daily 6am-midnight; until 2am Friday and Saturday. You will find the standard diner fare here in this combination diner/restaurant with two large dining rooms. A local oasis.

Rolling River Café (845-747-4123), 25 Cooley Road, Parksville. ($) Open year-round, Wednesday through Friday 5-9; Saturday and Sunday noon-9. This delightful café features hearty international favorites made from local organic ingredients. There is an art gallery on the premises and outdoor dining in the warm weather. Live music on weekends.

Roscoe Diner (607-498-4405), 1908 Old Route 17, Roscoe. ($) Open daily 6am-10pm. This Greek diner is a local mainstay, and their spanakopita, pastitsio, and moussaka are first-rate. In addition to the usual diner fare, there is a variety of broiled fish, wraps, burgers, and homemade soups. All baking is done on the premises and desserts are decent. The chocolate Bavarian cheesecake is huge—and a favorite choice among local residents.

Sonoma Falls Cider Mill (845-439-4949), 140 Old Liberty Road, Morsston. ($) Open daily 9-5 (later in the summer months). This is a busy place and a great spot for a picnic. There is a seven-tier waterfall, hiking trails, a country store, and freshly pressed apple cider (you can watch the process on weekend afternoons). The store offers jams, jellies, and maple syrup along with fresh produce and local meats. Breakfast and lunch items are available. The kids will love it here and can run around a bit after being confined in the car on your travels!

Soy Asian Cuisine (845-707-4233), 512 Broadway, Monticello. ($) Open year-round Tuesday through Saturday 11-10; Sunday noon-9. Fresh high-quality ingredients distinguish this Asian restaurant. Perfect for take-out or eating in with lunch specials daily from 11-3:30.

Yulan Country Store (845-557-0425), 218 Airport Road, Yulan. ($) Open year-round, Monday through Saturday 5:30-3; Sunday until 1. This is a deli with all the usual offerings. What makes it special is the owner, Hank, who is renowned for his sausage, egg, and cheese breakfast sandwich. The doughnuts here are first-rate, if you want something sweet.

ENTERTAINMENT

ARTS

Sullivan County has a long tradition of supporting the arts, and the cultural programs and shows offered throughout the region are quite good.

The Delaware Arts Center (845-252-7576; DelawareValleyArtsAlliance.org), is headquartered in the historic Arlington Hotel in Narrowsburg, 37 Main Street, which is on the National Register of Historic Places. Its gallery is open year-round for exhibits and special events, so call for a schedule. This is also the home of the Delaware Valley Arts Alliance, the arts council for Sullivan County.

The Catskill Art Society (845-436-4227; catskillartsociety.org), 48 Main Street, Livingston Manor, sponsors art, studio and architectural tours, workshops and other activities. The website lists a full schedule.

The Sullivan County Museum and Historical Society (845-434-8044; SCNYHistory.org), 265 Main Street, Hurleyville, is open year-round Tuesday through Saturday 10-4:30; Sunday 1-4:30. There are several items of local historical interest on display and the work of artists who are from Sullivan County.

A Sixties scene from the Woodstock Festival Site Museum in Bethel.

PERFORMING ARTS

Bethel Woods Center for the Arts (845-583-2000; BethelWoods Center. org), 200 Hurd Road, Bethel, is a major tourist attraction in Sullivan County from May through Labor Day when top entertainment is offered in a beautiful outdoor venue.

NACL Theatre (845-557-0694; NACL.org), 110 Highland Lake Road, Highland Lake. The North American Cultural Laboratory is a group that has been offering community theatrical productions year-round in the county since 1997. Check the website for a full schedule.

Forestburgh Playhouse (845-794-1194; fbplayhouse.org), 39 Forestburgh Road, Forestburgh, offers drama, comedies and musicals with post-show cabaret and cocktails in an adjoining tavern. The entertainment runs from late June through Labor Day. Closed Monday. Check website for the summer schedule.

Seelig Theatre at Sullivan County Community College (845-434-5750; SunySullivan.edu), 112 College Road, Loch Sheldrake, has dance, theater and musicals as part of a series along with holiday offerings and family shows.

The Delaware Valley Opera (845-252-3136; delawarevalleyopera.org) is headquartered at 170 Main Street, Narrowsburg. Two operas, one in July and one in August, are presented each summer at the Tusten Theatre, 210 Bridge Street in Narrowsburg. This 150-seat theater also offers jazz, classical, folk, and theater performances. The theater is also home to the **Delaware Valley Chamber Orchestra** (845-252-7272), which presents works of local composers every October.

SELECTIVE SHOPPING

There are some specialty shops and flea markets to be discovered while browsing the streets of Sullivan County's quaint villages, such as Narrowsburg, Roscoe, and Wurtsboro. There are ten fine artisans on the **Sullivan County Pottery Trail.** Those interested in meeting these craftspeople and visiting their studios to see how pots, plates, bowls, vases, and more are created should follow this special itinerary. To obtain a trail map, contact the Sullivan County Visitors Association.

If you are in Wurtsboro, make sure to stop in to the **Canal Towne Emporium** (845-888-2100), 107 Sullivan Street. They are open year-round, daily 10-5. They sell fine furniture, handcrafted items and decorative accessories.

Catskill Mountain Sugar House (845-985-7815), 227 Glade Hill Road, Grahamsville, is open year-round but call first. This is where you can buy all types of maple products (candy, syrup and sugar) and honey at reasonable prices. During the month of March, take a tour of the sugarhouse and see how syrup is produced.

Cutting Garden (845-482-3333), 4055 Route 52, Youngsville. Open Memorial Day weekend through Columbus Day, Friday through Monday, 11-5; rest of the year, weekends only, 11-5. Closed in January. This is a place to pick your own flowers and vegetables in season. They also sell vintage furniture, kitchenware, collectibles, and work by local artisans. Fair trade products and gifts are also available.

Justus Asthalter Maple Syrup (845-292-8569), 865 Aden Road, Parksville. Open daily during March and April, 10-5; other times, by appointment. Tour the sugarhouse and discover how maple syrup is made in the Catskills. There's a store with maple syrup, candy and several other treats. Children will be delighted.

River Gallery (845-252-3238), 8 Main Street, Narrowsburg. Open year-round, daily 11-5; Friday until 7; Saturday until 8; Sunday until 6. This terrific gallery features an eclectic mix of Asian and American antiques, home décor, and local Delaware Valley School artists in changing exhibits. There are interesting gift items and a frame shop. Owners Tony and Barry are welcoming to those from out of the area and are knowledgeable about art and antiques.

ANTIQUES AND FLEA MARKETS

The search for treasures in the county will take you to a dusty little shop on a side road, or into full-fledged auction barns where prices are steep and sales move fast. Many antiques shops are open all year, but some serve only the vacation crowds; call before you go to avoid disappointment. There are dozens of shops throughout the county; the following is only a sampling of the ones I would recommend and have visited.

The Antique Palace Emporium (845-292-2270), 300 Chestnut Street, Liberty, has more than two floors of restored furniture and original collectibles. Open year-round, but call for hours which can be erratic.

Ferndale Antiques Marketplace (845-292-8701), 52 Ferndale Road, Ferndale. Open July through Labor Day, Friday through Sunday 10-5. Call for hours at other times of the year. Here you will find several dealers under one roof, with vintage costume jewelry, furniture, lamps, and a wide array of pieces representing several periods and styles.

Fiddlers Flea Market (845-583-6375), 1080 Route 17B, Bethel. Open May through Labor Day, Saturday and Sunday, 9-5. This outdoor country market offers flowers, plants, antiques, household items, and more. There are occasionally special events on holiday weekends.

In2Retro (845-583-3126), 1163 Route 17B, Mongaup Valley. Open daily 11-5:30. There is quality art deco, midcentury, and modern furniture, lighting mirrors, glass, porcelain, ceramics, and decorative items. There is also costume jewelry, clothing handbags, and other fashion accessories. For bargain items there's a backyard "tent sale;" make sure to check that area out as well.

Liberty is filled with antiques shops. If you stop there and feel so inclined, check out: **Kraus Farm Antiques & Vintage** (845-295-9278), 110 Mill Street, open by appointment only. They have oak, mahogany, pine, and walnut furniture, as well as china, artwork, crystal, glassware and pottery. **Town & Country Antiques** (845-292-1363), 1 North Main Street, is open September through June, Thursday through Sunday 10-5; July and August, daily, 10-5. This multi-dealer shop in the heart of the downtown historic district is housed in a wonderful building dating from the late 1800s. A sign for Gold Medal flour was discovered and restored on the north side of the building. Wander around and find loads of interesting items. **Treasure Box Antiques** (845-292-8585/6566), 342 Chestnut Street (Route 52 West), is open all year round with hours varying, so call ahead. There are fine porcelains, glass, linens, dolls, and more here, as well as stained glass. Antiques lovers will thoroughly enjoy this stop.

SPECIAL EVENTS

January: **Winter Carnival** (845-434-5877) Morningside Park, 11 Morningside Road, Hurleyville. Ice skating, ice fishing, snowman decorating, relay races and more; call for date. **Trout Town Winterfest** (607-290-5002), 145 Rockland Road, Roscoe. Held at the Roscoe NY Beer Company, there's live music, horse-drawn carriage rides, snowshoeing and release of winter specialty brews. Large bonfire too!

April: **Opening Day of Trout Season**. April First is the day trout season opens throughout the county and throughout the region.

May: **Wild Ramp Fest** (607-290-5002), 145 Rockland Road, Roscoe. Live music, vendors, craft beer, food with local farmers selling ramps and other products.

June: **Trout Parade** (845-436-4227), Downtown, Livingston Manor. The annual fish-themed street fair and parade with children's entertainment, food vendors, live music and a huge parade with floats and fishy fun for the entire family.

July: The **River Run**, River Road Callicoon. A 5K and 10K race down River Road, a flat course along the scenic Delaware River. Walkers welcome too!

August: **Shandelee Music Festival** (845-439-3277), Young Road, Livingston Manor. Features internationally acclaimed performers who sing classical solo pieces; chamber concert artists perform in an outdoor pavilion.

December: **Handmade for the Holidays** (607-498-5207), Duke Pottery, 855 County Route 93, Roscoe. This holiday shopping paradise features the artwork of over 30 artists, crafters, and local producers for three weekends, Saturday & Sunday from late November to mid-December, 11-5.

Entrance to the Catskill Fly-Fishing Center & Museum in Roscoe.

A local farm in Gardiner.

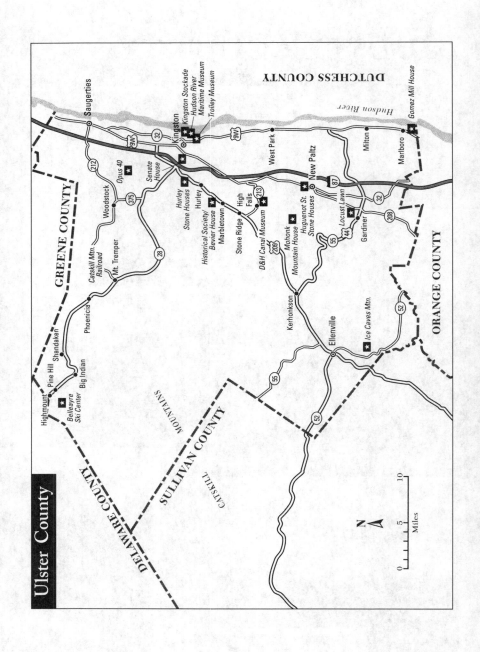

Ulster County

DUTCHESS COUNTY

GREENE COUNTY

DELAWARE COUNTY

SULLIVAN COUNTY

ORANGE COUNTY

Saugerties

Kingston Stockade
Hudson River
Maritime Museum
Trolley Museum
Kingston

Hudson River

Gomez Mill House

West Park

Milton

Marlboro

Opus 40

Senate
House

New Paltz

Woodstock

Hurley
Stone Houses

Hurley

Historical Society/
Bevier House

Marbletown

Stone Ridge

High
Falls

D&H Canal Museum

Mohonk
Mountain House

Huguenot St.
Stone Houses

Locust Lawn

Gardiner

Catskill Mtn.
Railroad

Mt. Tremper

Phoenicia

Kerhonkson

Ice Caves Mtn.

Shandaken

Pine Hill

Big Indian

Ellenville

Highmount

Belleayre
Ski Center

CATSKILL MOUNTAINS

212

9W

32

9W

87

32

208

375

28

213

205

55

44

208

52

55

52

N

0   5   10
Miles

ULSTER COUNTY

Both the Dutch and the English settled in Ulster County, drawn by the lush farmlands along the Hudson. Snug, well-built homes were constructed of stone, brick, and wood; many still stand and are open to the public. Ulster County was not always blessed with peace and prosperity, however; it was the scene of conflict during the American Revolution. Burned by the British, the city of Kingston was leveled and spies were hanged in the outlying orchards. But the area rebuilt itself through the years, and today Ulster is a study in contrasts. Businesses have settled alongside farms, and artist colonies thrive among boutiques. Dutch names of towns and lanes recall the past, while a thriving community of second-home owners, immigrants, and vacationers has brought different cultures to the region.

The county is mountainous, flat, river-lined, and forested by turns, and the outdoors offers excellent fishing, skiing, and hiking. There's enough here to keep visitors busy for weeks. The region is easy to travel, with several major roads and enough byways to please all travelers. The seasonal changes in the county are dramatic, with spring giving way to summer overnight and winter making guest appearances with storms as late as April. And in recent years, the county seat and only city in Ulster, Kingston, has become a "hipster capital," with many transplanted Brooklynites moving in and following them have been burgeoning businesses: boutiques, cafes, restaurants and galleries....as well as a vape lounge or two!

VISITOR INFORMATION

Kingston Heritage Area Visitors Center (845-331-7517; kingston-ny.gov), 20 Broadway, Kingston. Open year-round, Monday through Friday 9-5; May through October, also open Saturday and Sunday 11-5. Free. New York State has designated Urban Cultural Parks as the interpreters of urban settings of particular historic interest. Kingston is known for its importance in the history of transportation. Located in the historic Rondout section of the city, the center offers dozens of brochures and information about Kingston and Ulster County.

Ulster County Tourism, (845-340-3566; 800-342-5826), 20 Broadway, Kingston 12401; ulstercountyalive.com.

Ulster County Chamber of Commerce (845-338-5100), 214 Fair Street, Kingston 12401; ulsterchamber.org.

GETTING THERE

By car: Ulster County is accessible from the New York State Thruway exits 18, 19, and 20, and in the southern section of the county from Routes 17 and 9W.

By bus: Adirondack/Pine Hill Trailways (845-331-0744; 800-858-8555; trailwaysny.com), 400 Washington Avenue, Kingston, offers frequent daily service between the Port Authority in Manhattan and New Paltz, Kingston, Woodstock, and Phoenicia, as well as points north and west.

By train: **Amtrak** (800-872-7245; Amtrak.com) operates trains between Manhattan and Rhinecliff which is a 10-minute drive over the Kingston-Rhinecliff Bridge to Ulster County. **Metro-North Railroad—the Hudson Line** (800-METRO-INFO; mta.info/mnr) operates train service from Grand Central Station to Poughkeepsie. There are trains every two hours; and more frequently during rush hours. There are reduced fares during off-peak hours. Ulster County runs bus service to and from the train station in Poughkeepsie to Kingston and points in between. For a complete bus schedule, call **UCAT--Ulster County Area Transit** (845-340-3333), 1 Danny Circle, Kingston 12401.

By air: **Albany International Airport** (518-242-2200; albanyairport.com), 737 Albany Shaker Road, Loudonville, is the closest major airport to the northern part of the county.

River Aviation (845-336-8400), 1161 Flatbush Road, Kingston, operates Kingston Airport, near the Kingston-Rhinecliff Bridge.

Stewart International Airport (845-838-8200), 1180 First Street, New Windsor, is the closest major airport to the southern part of the county.

MEDICAL EMERGENCY

If you dial 911 anywhere in the county, you will receive emergency assistance.

Ellenville Regional Hospital (845-647-6400), 10 Healthy Way, Ellenville.

Emergency One Urgent Care and Diagnostic Center (845-338-5600), 40 Hurley Avenue, Kingston.

Health Alliance of the Hudson Valley Hospital--Broadway Campus (845-331-3131), 396 Broadway, Kingston.

Health Alliance of the Hudson Valley Hospital—Mary's Avenue Campus (845-338-2500), 105 Mary's Avenue, Kingston.

VILLAGES

There are several beautiful villages in Ulster County. In addition to the City of Kingston, my three favorite places to walk and take self-guided tours are Hurley, Saugerties, and Woodstock, located near exits 19 and 20 off the NYS Thruway.

HURLEY

Take Route 209 south to Hurley and follow signs. Every second Saturday in July, for one day only, the historic stone houses here are open to the public. The day is called Hurley Stone House Day and admission is charged for house tours. The village of Hurley was established in 1651 by Dutch and Huguenot settlers who built wooden homes along the Esopus Creek. After a short war with the Esopus Indians, which resulted in the burning of much of the settlement, the homes were replaced with stone structures, 25 of which are still standing. Hurley was a hotbed of activity during the Revolution, serving as the state capital when Kingston was burned, a resting place for troops, and a meeting place for spies. Later Hurley was a stop on the Underground Railroad, the escape route for slaves fleeing to Canada, as well as the home of abolitionist Sojourner Truth. Visitors can still walk around the town and see the largest group of stone houses still in use in the United States. Although the homes are open only one day each year, Hurley is worth a walk anytime, and many of the buildings have historic markers that tell something of their history and lore. Along Main Street look for the **Polly Crispell Cottage** (built in 1735), which was once used as a blacksmith shop. This house was also equipped with a "witch catcher"—a set of iron spikes set into the chimney, presumably to discourage witches (and birds) from flying in! The **Jan Van Deusen House** became the temporary seat of New York's government in 1777, and a secret room was used to store important documents. The outer door is set off by the work of an early Hurley blacksmith, and a date stone is visible. Also on Main Street is the **Dumond House**, which was to confine a convicted British spy before he was hanged from an apple tree across the road; the **Parsonage**, built in 1790; and the **Elmendorf House** (once the Half Moon Tavern), built in the late 1600s. A burial ground can be found between the Crispell and Elmendorf buildings. If you drive west on Main Street, follow the Hurley Avenue Extension, and you will see several more stone buildings.

SAUGERTIES

Once a prosperous river town, a center of the bluestone and tanning industries, Saugerties has had its ups and downs over the past 200 years. During the 1830s, the town was well situated on the Hudson River so that bluestone could be floated down to Manhattan from the docks for use in city sidewalks and streets. Today travelers will be treated to a renaissance in Saugerties---just walk up and down Main Street and Partition Street and visit the bookstores, antiques shops, cafes and boutiques. There are even two chocolate shops, **Lucky Chocolates** and **Krause's**! One of my favorite gift shops is **Light House** (845-246-1000), 86 Partition Street. Owner Shari Weingarten has created an amazing array of fine decorative items, soaps, lovely linens, baby gifts and more, in this wonderful emporium. Make sure to stop in there as well as the fine bookstore, **Inquiring Mind** (200 Main Street), while walking through Saugerties. If you are in need of caffeine, **Bluestone Coffee Roasting Company**, a cozy café located at 138 Partition Street, has excellent coffee and an enormous selection of teas as well as some of the best waffles I've ever had (made entirely from scratch).

A strong commitment to revitalizing the community through civic projects and commercial ventures has yielded excellent results. The **Saugerties Lighthouse**, with its wonderful Hudson River Views located at 168 Lighthouse Drive, is now a bed & breakfast. On Saturday (May through October) from 10am-2pm there is a **farmers' market** in town (115 Main Street). The best way to see everything is to wander and enjoy!

WOODSTOCK

The town of Woodstock has long attracted creative people. Home to farmers and quarrymen for two centuries, the hamlet saw new changes in the spring 1902, when Ralph Radcliffe Whitehead, an Englishman schooled in the theories of John Ruskin, was searching for a place where an arts colony could be organized. With two friends as partners, Whitehead bought seven lush farms and formed a community called Byrdcliffe (a combination of his and his wife's names). Workshops for metalworkers, potters, and weavers were soon built, and over the years the colony has continued to attract artists and craftspeople. Today the Byrdcliffe Arts Colony, America's first utopian arts and crafts colony, situated on 300 wooded acres with 30 picturesque buildings and listed on the National Register of Historic Places, is worth a short walking tour.

During the 1930s, folksingers discovered Woodstock; later the town became a haven for talents like Peter Seeger; Bob Dylan; Joan Baez; Peter, Paul and Mary; and other musicians of the 1960s who discovered inspiration there. In 1969 an eponymous concert, actually held over 50 miles away on a farm in Bethel (Sullivan County), made Woodstock a legend in the world of rock music—and the world at large. The promoters/organizers of the event lived in Woodstock, hence the name.

Legends of Woodstock is a fun place for visitors to buy a souvenir.

Today the somewhat eccentric, but never dull, town is still a gathering place for talent of all types. The surrounding mountains, and the shadow of Overlook Mountain, create a dramatic backdrop for colorful galleries and boutiques. Woodstock's main thoroughfare is Mill Hill Road, which becomes Tinker Street (according to legend, a tinker's wagon sank into the spring mud here). Most shops in town are reached by walking along Tinker Street, so enjoy a leisurely exploration. Of special interest (and my favorite places in the town where I have lived for over 35 years) are: the wonderful spacious gift emporium in the center of town, **Jean Turmo; H. Houst & Son**, the **Gilded Carriage**, the **Center for Photography** and **Mirabai Bookstore**. There's also a tiny cupcake eatery, **Peace Love and Cupcakes**, open on weekends only.

Mower's Saturday/Sunday Market (845-679-6744), Maple Lane, in the center of town has been a tradition in Woodstock since 1977. A large flea market offering antiques, crafts, collectibles, and an array of eclectic items, Mower's is a must for weekend shoppers in the village. Open mid-May through November, weekends, 9-5; July through Labor Day, and Wednesday 1-8 in conjunction with the Woodstock Farm Festival market. There are parking lots off Rock City Road or Tannery Brook Road. There is also a municipal lot near the town offices. Off Tinker Street, across the street from the old firehouse, is Comeau Drive, where you will find the **Woodstock Historical Society Museum** (845-679-2256), which will be of interest to history buffs. **The Colony** (845-679-7625), is the historic Colony Arts building dating back to 1929, 22 Rock City Road, and offers an eclectic mix of music Thursday through Monday. There's a wonderful atmosphere here, so make sure to stop in for a drink even if you don't have time to take in the music. A drive up Rock City Road is a must to the **KTD Tibetan Buddhist Monastery**. There are tours of this rare jewel in Woodstock on weekend afternoons at 1pm. Across the road from KTD is the trailhead to the relatively short, but steep, trail up Overlook Mountain where stunning panoramic views of three states may be enjoyed on a clear day.

And later, if you need a rest, sit on the village green and watch the colorful parade of people pass by.

The town of Woodstock is filled with tony bars where you can drink and relax. There's **A&P Bar** (845-679-5395), 83 Mill Hill Road, on the side of Bank of America with an amazing array of cocktails and excellent food; **Station Bar & Curio** (845-810-0203), 101 Tinker Street, in an old train depot; **R&R (Reynolds & Reynolds) Tap Room** (845-217-7921), 104 Mill Hill Road, with an array of craft beers and quite decent fare; and in Bearsville, two miles west of town, at 297 Tinker Street, is the busy **Commune Saloon** (845-684-0367), where the music rarely stops on summer weekends on the outdoor patio. A recent addition to the music/bar scene in town is **The Lodge** (845-679-2814), 20 Country Club Lane, off Route 375, near the Woodstock Elementary School, where the music and food are fine and new owners have created a great atmosphere.

DO-NOT-MISS ATTRACTIONS

KTD Tibetan Buddhist Monastery (845-679-5906; Kagyu.org), 335 Meads Mountain Road, Woodstock. Located 2.6 miles from town, group tours are offered by appointment. Free monastery tours for individuals leave the bookstore Saturday and Sunday 1:30-3pm. The grounds are open free to the public from 8:30am-5:30pm daily, unless there are restrictions due to practice. Karma Triyana Dharmachakra Monastery is one of the highest centers of Tibetan Buddhism in the world and is worth a detour any time of year. Founded in 1978, the monastery combines traditional Tibetan architecture and design with Western construction. The monastery has undergone a significant expansion in recent years and all weekend visitors to Woodstock should drive up the mountain. The main shrine room is 2400 square feet and features one of the largest statues of Buddha in North America, while smaller shrines are decorated with traditional art. Be sure to stop at the bookstore/ gift shop with its wide assortment of imported items from the Himalayas. A stop here will provide a great change of pace from the crowded streets of Woodstock on weekend afternoons!

Mohonk Mountain House (845-255-1000; mohonk.com), 1000 Mountain Rest Road, New Paltz. Open year-round; call ahead of check the website for full-service spa appointments, ice-skating, cross-country skiing, and hiking information and special events weekends. Admission. When Alfred and Albert Smiley built this resort in 1869, they were determined to preserve the surrounding environment and offer gracious accommodations to visitors from the city. Guests here could hike the nearby Shawangunks, take a carriage ride around the manicured grounds or enjoy the carefully tended flower gardens. There was a lake for ice-skating as well as croquet lawns. The hotel itself was furnished with

The KTD Buddhist Monastery in Woodstock is one of the most interesting sights to see in town and tours are given on weekends.

the best of the Victorian era: acres of polished oak paneling and floors, hidden conversation nooks, and homey, overstuffed furniture. Mohonk has endured the last century with timeless grace, and today visitors will find many aspects of the hotel unchanged. They are still dedicated to preserving the natural world, and the gardens have won awards for their beauty. Mohonk sits next to a trout-stocked lake that becomes the focus of special winter carnival weekends. The stone tower atop the mountain offers a six-state view on sunny days. Hikers, birders, horseback riders, and cross-country skiers will find Mohonk unequaled. Day visitors are welcome, but it takes more than a day to sample all of the surprises at Mohonk. Note that on holiday weekends the hotel is often closed to day visitors, so call in advance to check.

Old Dutch Church (845-338-6759; olddutchchurch.org), 272 Wall Street, Kingston. Open year-round, Monday through Friday 10-3; guided tours by appointment. Free. Organized in 1659, the Reformed Protestant Dutch Church of Kingston has served the people of the area continuously ever since. The present building was constructed in 1852; its bluestone exterior is in the Renaissance Revival style, and the windows were made in the Tiffany studios. Local tradition once held the bell was cast from silver and copper items donated by the congregation. Inside there are bronze statues as well as artifacts from the

1600s onward. Take some time to wander through the churchyard and view the fine examples of early gravestone art (Governor DeWitt Clinton's gravesite is here). In the spring, thousands of yellow and red tulips planted in honor of the Netherlands line the church walks. In addition to wonderful Christmas concerts, there are musical performances by local artists, usually during the spring, summer and fall. The church is a magnificent place to hear music any time of year.

Opus 40 & The Quarryman's Museum (845-246-3400; opus 40.org), 50 Fite Road, Saugerties. Open Memorial Day weekend through Columbus Day, Friday through Sunday, holidays, and Monday 11:30-5. Admission. In 1938 artist Harvey Fite's bluestone quarry outside Saugerties was merely the source of material for his sculpture. But as work on the individual pieces progressed, Fite realized the terraces and steps he had created as a backdrop for the sculpture had themselves become the focus of his work. Naming the site Opus 40 because he believed it would take 40 years to complete, Fite set about creating a vast environmental work that would eventually contain six acres of steps, levels, fountains, pools, and paths. Each of the hundreds of thousands of bluestone pieces was hand-cut and fitted, and the nine-ton central monolith was lifted into place with a boom and winches. Today Opus 40 is open to the public as an environmental sculpture and concert site. Fite, who had studied theology and law and worked as an actor and teacher, also built a museum to house his collection of quarrymen's tools and artifacts. The museum offers a rare glimpse into a lost way of life.

Saugerties Lighthouse (845-247-0656; saugertieslighthouse.com), 168 Lighthouse Drive, Saugerties. From the center of town, follow Main Street to the end, heading north and make a right onto Mynderse Street, which becomes Lighthouse Drive. There are no signs; just keep bearing to the left. This site is also accessible by boat from the Route 9W boat-launch area. Open Memorial Day weekend to Labor Day; tours given on weekends and holidays noon-3. Enjoy a walk through the Ruth Glunt Nature Preserve, and at low tide walk out to the historic lighthouse, which contains a museum with artifacts from the commercial heyday of the Saugerties waterfront. Overnight accommodations are available and a live-in lighthouse keeper resides on the premises. I spent a night here in the month of June 20 years ago, and it was truly a memorable experience!

Overlook Observatory (845-679-0785), 141 Silver Hollow Road, Willow. Hours by appointment; fee charged for classes. Both home and scientific workshop to nationally know astronomer Bob Berman, the observatory offers visitors a guided tour of the night sky, with all its mysteries, quirks, wonders, and outstanding instruments for viewing the heavens. Bob is a knowledgeable and enthusiastic guide, as well as the author of several popular astronomy books that have been featured in national media.

FOR FAMILIES

Catskill Animal Sanctuary (845-336-8447; casanctuary.org), 316 Old Stage Road, Saugerties. Open April through October, Saturday and Sunday 11am–4pm. Last tour begins at 2:30. Admission. Tours are available every half-hour along with vegan food demonstrations and tastings at the Visitors Center. This amazing sanctuary is located on 150 acres of land dedicated as a haven for abused and abandoned farm animals. Stories of rescue and rehabilitation of these animals as well as their remarkably individual "personalities" will endear them to all who visit. Children will be particularly delighted to get "up close and personal" with horses, cows, pigs, goats, turkeys, sheep, donkeys and more in a bucolic atmosphere. This is a place where they will enjoy nature, make friends, and learn new things, not only about nature, but about how our lifestyle choices impact them. Special event days include hayrides, children's activities, and workshops and speakers on a variety of issues. Since 2001 this sanctuary has provided refuge for more than 4000 needy animals. This is a wonderful stop for families traveling with youngsters. The sanctuary has its own fully restored 1813 inn, *The Homestead*, with three rooms and an apartment, for those who would like to extend their visit. (See *Lodging*).

Catskill Mountain Railroad (845-688-7400; cmrrevents.com), 149 Aaron Court, Kingston. Open Memorial Day weekend through December, weekends and holidays only; trains leave from Kingston Plaza in Kingston. Admission, but children under the age of four ride for free. This six-mile round-trip from Kingston to Hurley and back takes about 45 minutes. In November and December on weekends, there is a train called "The Polar Express" that travels through the city. Check website for the schedule. This is a relaxing way to take in the countryside if you are traveling with children; besides, just about everyone loves a train ride!

Fiber Flame (845-679-6132), 1776 Route 212, Saugerties, open Tuesday through Sunday 10-5, is a make-your-own mixed-media art space where everyone is an artist. It's a great place for both adults and children to be creative. Whether you enjoy painting your own pottery, making collages, beading, or any array of fun endeavors, you are welcome to walk in and do your own thing. In addition, there are parties, after-school classes, and other activities by special arrangement. It's a wonderful stop for après-ski fun as well.

Forsyth Nature Center (845-339-3053; forsythnaturecenter.org), 167 Lucas Avenue, Kingston. Open September through April, Monday through Friday 7-5, weekends and holidays 9-1; May through August, Monday through Friday 7-7, weekends and holidays 9-5. Free. There are several species of mammals in this small zoo that includes llamas, deer, bulls, pygmy goats, and sheep. An aviary on the premises is filled with a variety of birds. There is a large playground in the park, and the two activities make a nice outing for those with young children. A number of special programs are offered here year-round, including bird walks, estuary studies, and arts and crafts sessions. Check the website for a schedule.

Kaleidoworld (845-688-5800; emersonresort.com), 5340 Route 28, Mount Tremper. Open year-round, daily 10-5; extended hours in the summer. The Emerson Resort and Spa is one of the county's premier family destinations for fine lodging, dining, and shopping. Kaleidoworld, is the Guinness Book of World Records-certified world's largest kaleidoscope. Visitors walk into a 60-foot-high, silo-shaped room, where they experience a color and sound show unlike any other: as if you are inside a kaleidoscope. After the show, step into the shops; one of them offers a large selection of kaleidoscopes for sale. Other boutiques feature regional books, fine clothing, antiques, furniture, and unique gifts. This is an unusual stop for families traveling in western Ulster County. The Emerson is just a 15-minute drive west of Woodstock.

Skate Time 209 (845-626-7971; skatetime209.com), 5164 Route 209, Accord. Open year-round, Thursday through Sunday; check times of sessions on website. This indoor skate park and roller rink offers "wheelie" fun for children and their parents. Skate and helmet rentals are available; no skateboard rentals. This is a good place for families to visit on weekends during the winter months when outdoor activities are limited.

Trolley Museum (845-331-3399; tmny.org), 89 East Strand, Kingston. Open Memorial Day weekend through Columbus Day, weekends and holidays noon-5. Admission. Housed in an old trolley shed along the Rondout, this small museum will interest anyone who remembers the ring of a trolley bell or the rolling ride of a self-propelled car. The displays offer a nostalgic trip through the past and children will enjoy a short ride on a restored trolley car.

Wooden Wheel (845-331-9680; woodnwheel.com), 365 Route 9W, Ulster Park. Open Friday 7-10pm; Saturday 1-4:30 and 7-10; Sunday 12:30-4. Tyke Time for those age six and under, Saturday 10am-12:30pm. The public roller blade sessions on weekends attract a wide variety of enthusiasts. There are other activities here so check the website for a full list of what's happening and when!

HISTORIC HOMES

Bevier House/Ulster County Historical Society (845-338-5614; ulstercountyhs. org), 2682 Route 209, Kingston (six miles south of the uptown area on the right side of Route 209). Open May through October, Saturday and Sunday 11-5. Admission. Built in the late 1680s, this stone house now serves as headquarters of the county historical society, and it is a treasure trove of odd collections and memorabilia. The house was once a single-story Dutch Farmhouse, and much of the present structure was added during the last three centuries. Throughout the house you will see fine Hudson Valley Dutch Victorian furniture in addition to the tool and kitchenware collections, ceramic pottery from an early factory in Poughkeepsie, portraits, and decorative accessories. The Bevier House is not a formal museum and has a great old-fashioned feel about it. The website lists special events, including holiday candlelight tours, local history lectures, and craft workshops.

Century House Historical Society and A. J. Snyder Estate (845-658-9900; centuryhouse.org), 668 Route 213, Rosendale (watch for signs). Tours are given from mid-May through Labor Day on Sunday 1-4 and by appointment. Admission. This estate sits directly across from the Delaware & Hudson Canal. The house is open for tours, and the carriage house, with its fine collection of more than 20 antique sleighs and carriages—some dating from the 1820s—is a must-see. Phaetons, wagons, and cutters are all here and in beautiful condition. There are also the ruins of old cement kilns on the property, the canal slip, and the Widow Jane Mine, a cave often used for special events, including concerts and plays.

Gomez Mill House (845-236-3126; gomez.org), 11 Mill House Road, Marlboro. Open mid-April through mid-November, Wednesday through Sunday 10:30-4 with tours at 10:30am, 1:15pm and 2:45pm. You must take a tour to see the inside of this home. Open off-season by appointment. Admission. (NOTE: This site lies in both Orange and Ulster counties but I chose to include it in Ulster County.) Visitors will see the oldest surviving Jewish homestead in North America here, as well as a unique cultural landmark. Built in 1714 as a sawmill and trading post, the site was named after the Gomez family, who supplied traders roving the upstate New York wilderness. Later owners were farmers, boatmen and soldiers in the Continental Army. William Joseph "Dard" Hunter (who owned the place from 1913 to 1919) was a paper mill owner whose mill is still in working condition (you can buy handmade paper in the gift shop). The site has also served as a home, inn, and school, and the buildings reflect the many personalities of those who have lived and worked here.

Huguenot Street Stone Houses (845-255-1889; huguenotstreet.org), 81 Hugeuenot Street, New Paltz. The area is open year-round; weekends only in May, November and December. Tours are offered June through October, daily except Wednesday, 10-5. Admission. The tours last 1½ hours, but those with younger children may choose to leave after an hour. The last half hour delves into more detailed history of the stone houses.

In 1677 a group of 12 Huguenot men purchased land from the Esopus Indians and began the settlement that was referred to as "die Pfalz," after an area in the Rhineland Palatinate. By 1692 their original dwellings were being replaced by stone houses, several of which still stand today as a result of the efforts of the Huguenot Historical Society. A trip to New Paltz offers a unique chance to see what life was like three centuries ago in upper-middle-class homes. The walking tour begins at the Dubois Fort on Huguenot Street, near the gift shop. All the buildings are owned by the society, and many still have their original furnishings. At the Abraham Hasbrouck house (1721), the dark rooms include a cellar-kitchen, which was the heart of village social life, and a built-in Dutch bed. Other houses of the period include the **Bevier-Elting House**, distinguished by a long well sweep and covered walk for the convenience of the ladies, the **Freer House,** with its mow door, which made it easier to move provisions into the attic and the **Dubois Fort**, reputed to be haunted by a headless woman. Possibly the most interesting house is the **Jean Hasbrouck House** (1678), which once served as a store and tavern. Downstairs is a bar as well as a jamb-less fireplace with its curtain-like decorations; upstairs is a massive brick chimney, the only one of its type in the United States. Several other buildings are also open to the public, including the reconstructed **French Church**, the Federal-style **LeFevre House**, and the **Deyo House**, a remodeled 17th-century home. Special programs are offered at this site year-round. The website has a complete schedule of events. NOTE: The **Huguenot Path** (845-255-0100) is a self-guided walking tour through the Harcourt Nature Sanctuary spanning Huguenot Street and the Wallkill River trail.

Matthewis Persen House (845-340-3040), 74 John Street, Kingston. Open Memorial Day weekend through mid-November, Tuesday through Saturday 9-4. Free. This house is named after its longest resident, Matthewis Persen (1739-1819), and some parts of the structure date back to 1661. The house was burnt twice over the centuries and has been home to doctors, tailors,grocers, druggists, and innkeepers. There are four landmark buildings on each corner of John and Crown streets, and it is the only intersection in the U.S. with 18th-century stone houses on all four corners! The house was purchased by Ulster County in 1994. Restoration began in 1999, and artifacts discovered in the process are on display. The house was opened to the public in the spring of 2011.

MUSEUMS

Delaware & Hudson Canal Historical Society & Museum (845-687-2000; canalmuseum.org), 23 Mohonk Road, High Falls. Open May through October, Saturday and Sunday 10-4:30. Admission. This small museum is dedicated to the history and lore of the great Delaware & Hudson Canal. Built in the early 19th century, the canal was used to ship coal from the mines in Pennsylvania to the factories of New York. Later cement was produced here and was used for bridges, locks, basins, and dams: the engineering wonders of their era. Visitors will find a miniature setup of the canal and its workings, offering a sense of what life was like on the canal boats used for the six-day trips. After you tour the museum, make sure to take the self-guided walk along the locks across the road. On this path, you will see examples of stonework, snubbing posts, weirs, locks, and loading slips. To me, the walk is more interesting than the museum!

Empire State Railway Museum (845-688-7501; esrm.com), 70 Lower High Street, Phoenicia. Open Memorial Day weekend through October, weekends and holidays 11-4. Donation. This very small museum is for railroad aficionados and offers exhibits about railroads and life in the Catskill Mountains. There are photographs and artifacts related to the building of the reservoirs, tourism history, and railroads in the Catskills. The volunteer guides love trains and they usually make a tour of the museum fun for everyone.

Hudson River Maritime Museum (845-338-0071; hrmm.org), 50 Rondout Landing (at the foot of Broadway), Kingston. Open May through October, daily, 11-5. Admission. This museum is dedicated to preserving the maritime heritage of the Hudson River. For almost 200 years the Hudson was a major water highway between New York City and Albany. One of the ports along the way was the Rondout Landing in Kingston, once a bustling area of boat yards and rigging lofts that echoed with steam whistles and brass ships' bells. But when shipping on the Hudson fell into decline, so did the fortunes of the Rondout. In 1980 the museum was opened and it has since restored several riverside buildings and historic vessels; visitors can now see a working part of the Hudson's legacy. An exhibit hall features shows on marine history. Outside there is an ever-changing display of river vessels, including the 1899 steam tug *Mathilda* and the cruise boat *Indy 7*. Visitors to the landing have also included the presidential yacht *Sequoia* and the sailing ships *Clearwater* and *Woody Guthrie*. Special weekend festivals are held throughout the year, including a Harvest Festival in October. There are an array of children's programs and lectures listed on the website.

Klyne Esopus Museum (845-338-8109; klyneesopusmuseum.org), 764 Route 9W, Ulster Park. Open June through mid-November, Friday through Tuesday, 1-4. Free. This museum is located in a Dutch country church built in 1827 and features exhibits concerning the culture, business, and history of the town of Esopus. The website has a schedule of free Saturday speakers; topics include subjects like the stone houses of the Hudson Valley and tugboats on the Hudson River.

Samuel Dorsky Museum of Art (845-257-3844; newpaltz.edu/museum), SUNY New Paltz, 75 South Manheim Boulevard, New Paltz. Open year-round, Wednesday through Sunday 11-5. Closed Monday, Tuesday and holidays. Donation. Opened in 2002, this is the only art museum between Manhattan and Albany on the west side of the Hudson River. There are six galleries with a total of more than 9000 square feet of exhibit space. There are changing displays of contemporary art, which complement exhibits from the museum's permanent collection that spans more than 4000 years. The focus includes American and European works on paper, regional paintings, prints, sculpture, photographs, and metalwork. There is an emphasis on the cultural heritage of the Hudson Valley and Catskills as well as diverse world cultures.

Senate House State Historic Site (845-338-2786; nysparks.com), 296 Fair Street, Kingston. Open April through October, Wednesday through Saturday10-5; Sunday and holiday Mondays 1-5. Group tours by appointment year-round. Admission. When the New York State government was forced to leave New York City during the Revolution, it sought safety upstate. The house

Stone House Day, a Saturday in July, is when the historic houses on Hurley's main street are open to the public.

in which the committee met was built in the 17th century by a Dutch settler, Wessel Ten Broeck, and was partially burned by the British in 1777. After numerous additions and changes to the building, the house has been restored to reflect its part in history. Visitors will see several rooms, including the kitchen with its kitchenware and huge fireplace. There is a meeting room where the first state senate deliberated. The colonial gardens are beautiful, particularly in June, when the roses are in full bloom. A second Colonial Revival-style building on the site, added in 1927, houses a museum with historic displays and changing exhibits that reflect the story of Kingston. One room is given over to the works of John Vanderlyn, a Kingston native, who was considered one of the finest painters in 19th-century America. The Italianate Loughran House (1873) is used for offices. This historic site/museum offers a variety of special events, including concerts and lectures throughout the year. Evening candlelight tours are given during the month of December.

Volunteer Firemen's Hall and Museum (845-331-0866; kingstonvolunteer firemensmuseum.weebly.com), 265 Fair Street, Kingston. Open May through October, Friday 11-3; Saturday 10-4. Check website for hours during the rest of the year. The museum is housed in an old firehouse where antique fire apparatus, memorabilia, and period furniture are on display.

SCENIC DRIVES

Ulster County has hundreds of miles of well-maintained roads coupled with some of the most spectacular views in the Hudson Valley. It doesn't matter if you travel in autumn, with all the riotous color, or in winter, with its stark beauty— Ulster County is filled with striking scenery.

For a drive that combines history and scenery, start at Kingston (exit 19 off the NYS Thruway) and head south along Route 209. This is one of the oldest roads in America: the Old Mine Road, which was a trading route between upstate New York and Pennsylvania in the 17th century. As you pass by Hurley, Marbletown, and Stone Ridge, you will see acres of fields planted with sweet corn, the area's largest agricultural crop, and there are dozens of farm stands in summer and autumn. The architectural styles of the homes range from Dutch stone to late Victorian. At Route 213, head east through High Falls, along the old Delaware & Hudson Canal. Stop in at the High Falls Food Co-op if you enjoy natural foods, or just continue down the road that follows the canal into Rosendale. At Route 32 you can head south into New Paltz and explore the old stone houses or head north back to Kingston.

For a second scenic route from Kingston, take Route 9W south along the Hudson River. At West Park you may want to follow the signs to Slabsides, once the writing retreat of naturalist John Burroughs; it's on your right across the railroad tracks. Park at the bottom of the hill and walk up. Back on Route 9W, continue south and take Route 299 west through New Paltz, then follow Route 44/55 west for some of the finest views and overlook sites in the Shawangunks. At Route 209 head back north past old Dutch farms and stone houses to Kingston.

From Kingston you can also follow Route 28 to Route 28A around the Ashokan Reservoir, a special treat in the autumn months. Follow the signs to the pump station, and walk around the fountain or have a picnic—it's a fairly quiet undiscovered area, except on weekends. However, since New York City watches its watershed area carefully, be wary of where you park, hike or stop. The NO PARKING and NO STOPPING signs are clearly marked and violators are often fined.

For an unusual drive, take the Hudson Valley Pottery Trail to studios in Accord, High Falls, and Stone Ridge. A detailed map and list of craftspeople opening their studios to visitors is on potterytrail.com.

WINERIES, BREWERIES, CIDERIES AND DISTILLERIES

The Hudson Valley has been an important center of wine production in New York State for some time, and Ulster County wineries range in size from tiny "boutique" operations to full-size vineyards complete with restaurants, bottling plants, and cellars. Wherever you go, you will find people who love their work and are more than willing to share their expertise and wines with you. Some vintners offer formal guided tours; others have a showroom and tasting area only. There are special events, concerts and festivals throughout the season. Note that hours may change when harvest time begins, so always give a call before you go!

(NOTE: The **Shawangunk Wine Trail** is an 80-mile route that runs between the Shawangunk Mountains and the Hudson River directing travelers to wineries along the way. Check out the website, gunkswine.com.)

The following vineyards offer their own distinctive experience. If you only have time to visit one of them, Whitecliff Vineyard & Winery is my favorite!

Baldwin Vineyards (845-744-2226), 176 Hardenburgh Road, Pine Bush, is located on a 200-year-old estate where more than 40 acres of pastures, vineyards, and woodlands are great for strolling. Open April through December, Thursday through Sunday, noon-5. Their wines include chardonnay, merlot, Riesling, brut champagne, and a strawberry-flavored selection.

Benmarl Winery (845-236-4265), 156 Highland Avenue, Marlboro. Open April through December, daily, noon-6; January through March, Friday through Sunday or by appointment. Situated high on a hill overlooking the orchards, with magnificent views of the Hudson River and surrounding countryside, this location has to be the most scenic of the region's wineries.

Brimstone Hill Vineyard (845-744-2231). 61 Brimstone Hill Road, Pine Bush. Open Memorial Day through Columbus Day, Friday through Monday;

the rest of the year, Saturday and Sunday 11:30-5:30. French-style wines are the specialty here, especially dry reds and sweet whites.

Cereghino Smith (845- 334-8282), 2583 Route 32, Bloomington. Open year-round by appointment only. This winery began in a Manhattan apartment in the late 1990s with traditional Italian blends inspired by the grandfather of owner, Paula Cereghino. Paula and her husband, Fred Smith, now produce fine red wines (*Eaten by Bears* is my favorite) using New York State and Sangiovese grapes, as well as some California varieties. This is an interesting recent addition to the Ulster County wineries with an old-world approach. There are five blends that will interest oenophiles.

Robibero Winery (845-255-WINE), 714 Albany Post Road, New Paltz. Open year-round Thursday through Monday 11-6. This small family-owned and operated winery has an excellent Reisling.

Stoutridge Vineyard (845-236-7620), 10 Ann Kaley Lane, Marlboro. Open year-round for tastings and tours, Friday through Sunday 11-6. This winery/distillery was built on the site of a historic farm and has had vineyards on the property since the early 19th century. Stephen Osborn and his wife, Kimberly Wagner, have restored the farmhouse and constructed a state-of-the-art winery using gravity-feed design built on the original winery site. There is a 15,000-case annual capacity here, and they specialize in German-style whites from Riesling and pinot blanc varieties, as well as Northern Italian-style reds from Sangiovese, pinot noir, and Teroldego grapes. One of the first distilleries in the county, the vodkas are derived from apples and pears grown on local farms. Stoutridge is worth a visit to see sustainable practices employed in the winemaking process.

Whitecliff Vineyard & Winery (845-255-4613), 331 McKinstry Road, Gardiner. Open June through October, daily 11:30-5:30; February through May, November and December, Thursday through Monday 11:30-5:30; January, weekends only, 11:30-5:30. This 75-acre stunning farm grows chardonnay, merlot, cabernet franc, and pinot noir grapes. There are phenomenal views of the Shawangunks from the winery. Whitecliff has one of the largest vineyards in the region, and

Yancey Migliore, owner of Whitecliff Winery in Gardiner.

they are known for complex dry wines. Owners Yancey and Michael Migliore make their award-winning wines both from their own grapes and those of other New York State growers. There is an art gallery on the premises featuring work by an array of fine Hudson Valley artists.

In recent years, a number of breweries, microbreweries, cideries and distilleries have emerged in Ulster County, just as they have in other areas of the Hudson Valley.

These breweries and microbreweries are worth a visit if you enjoy beer; almost all are located in the New Paltz area:

Arrowood Farms (845-253-0389), 236 Lower Whitfield Road, Accord. Open Friday 5-9; Saturday 1-9; Sunday 1-8. This craft beer business creates small batches of beer with organic hops and grain grown on their farm. Those interested in organics will enjoy a visit and tasting here.

Keegan Ales (845-331-BREW), 20 St. James Street, Kingston. Open year-round for beer, light fare and music on Thursday through Sunday: Tuesday and Wednesday 4-10; Thursday 4-11:30; Friday and Saturday 11:30-midnight; Sunday 1-8. Closed Monday. This microbrewery features several different beers: a golden ale, a pale ale, and a milk stout called Jo Mama's Milk: brown sugar and Monkey Joe Roasting Company's coffee extract are added to the mix, creating an unusual flavor. Beer lovers will enjoy relaxing in the pub atmosphere. At one time, this was the only brewery in the Hudson Valley! It's definitely a happening place in Kingston and a "pioneer" in the region: they opened in 2003.

New Paltz Brewing Company–Pfalzerbrau (845-419-3040), 7174 Route 209, Wawarsing. Open Thursday and Friday 3-8; Saturday noon-8; Sunday 1-6. Nestled in the Shawangunks, and easily accessed on Route 209, this brewery uses natural ingredients and employs traditional methods in their eight excellent beers.

Woodstock Brewing (845-688-0054), 5581 Route 28, Phoenicia ($) Open Thursday 2-8; Friday 2-10; Saturday noon-10; Sunday noon-8 and holiday Mondays. This 8500-square-foot brewery is a happening place, located 15 miles west of Woodstock. There are 16 taps including Parabolic (American Pale Ale) brewed with oats and crystal malt and Between Two Points, a blend of five grains. These were the two beers I sampled when I visited on opening weekend in January 2018. Both were excellent. There are plans in the offing to serve food and feature live music. The place is spacious and the owners are interested in creating an inviting atmosphere; a great stop for weekend travelers heading east or west on Route 28.

Yard Owl Craft Brewery (845-633-8576), 19 Osprey Lane, Gardiner. Open Friday through Sunday 3-7pm. Two brew masters have created a European-style beer using only top shelf ingredients. There is a tasting room and fine light fare is available to accompany the craft brews.

CIDERIES

Bad Seed (845-236-0956), 43 Baileys Gap Road, Highland. Open April through December, Saturday and Sunday noon-6; January through March Saturday noon-6. The Wilkows are a sixth-generation family farm and they are now making hand crafted hard cider from 100 percent fresh-pressed apples. There is a taproom and tours are available.

Brooklyn Cider House at Twin Star Orchards (845-633-8657), 155 North Ohioville Road, New Paltz. Open Wednesday through Sunday 11-6. There's cider, a tasting room and restaurant here. It's a sizable operation with another outlet in Brooklyn.

Kettleborough Cider House (845-255-7727), 277 Route 208, New Paltz. Open Saturday and Sunday noon-5:30. The Dressel family has been growing apples in New Paltz for almost a century. All the apples used in their cider are grown on their farm within a few miles of where they are pressed.

Stone Ridge Orchard (845-687-2587), 3120 Route 213, Stone Ridge. Open daily 9-6. Freshly-pressed cider from fruit grown on the orchard is served up here. The owner has a commitment to ecological growing practices and production of highly flavored fruit. The tasting room is open daily, not just on weekends!

Westwind Orchard (845-626-0659), 215 Lower Whitfield Road, Accord. Open Memorial Day weekend through Columbus Day, Saturday 11-8; Sunday 11-6. The cider here is certified organic: it is unfiltered and contains no added sulfites, carbon dioxide or sugar. This is my personal favorite. You may also enjoy wood-fired pizza here with your drinks.

DISTILLERIES

Coppersea Distilling (845-444-1044), 239 Springtown Road, New Paltz. Open Saturday noon-5; Sunday noon-4. This award-winning farm distillery crafts fine whiskey from locally sourced grain and fruit. They offer tours at 11am on weekends by advance reservation. While I don't imbibe whiskey, I found the tour extremely interesting.

Tuthilltown Spirits Distillery (845-255-1527), 14 Gristmill Lane, Gardiner. Open year-round, Monday through Saturday 11-6; Sunday noon-6. The Tuthilltown gristmill is a landmark listed on the National Register of Historic

Places. In 2001 the mill was converted to a distillery and now produces whiskey, vodka, gin, and brandy using local fruit and grain. This is the only whiskey distillery in New York State and the first to open in the state since Prohibition.

ACTIVITIES

BICYCLING

Ashokan Reservoir (800-575-5263; nyc.gov/dep). Located off Route 28 west; turn onto Reservoir Road at Winchell's Corners, then make a left onto Route 28A where there is a public parking sign on your right. Just after the sign make a left turn onto a short road that will lead to this special place. Open year-round, daily, dawn to dusk. This is a wonderful place to bike, walk, run, or rollerblade; the 1.25-mile stretch of pavement that runs along part of the Ashokan Reservoir here is a must-see for visitors to the area. There are breathtaking views of the mountains, and the area is renowned as a place where eagles nest. If you are lucky, you may see one fly by or get a glimpse of an eagle perched in a tree. There is no vehicular traffic and dogs are not permitted.

Ashokan Reservoir.

Hudson Valley Rail Trail (845-691-6313; hudsonvalleyrailtrail.net), 101 New Paltz Road, Highland. Open daily dawn to dusk. This 3.6-mile nature trail extends from the Mid-Hudson Bridge through the town of Lloyd. There is a two-mile paved portion of the trail that makes for a good family bicycle outing. The trail is part of a network of rail trails that cover 10,000 miles across America. Turnoffs along the way run to overlooks and down to the banks of the river---great places to get off your bike for a picnic and take in the scenery. This trail is also pet-friendly.

Minnewaska State Park Preserve (845-255-0752; nysparks.state.ny.us), 5281 Route 44/55, New Paltz. Open year-round, daily from 9am (closing time is posted each day at the entrance). Admission. This preserve is located atop the dramatic Shawangunk Mountain Ridge, more than 2000 feet above sea level, and offers miles of trails and carriage roads for bicyclists of all abilities.

Mohonk Preserve (845-255-00919; mohonkpreserve.org), 3197 Route 44, Gardiner. Open daily from sunrise to sunset; a day use fee is charged for non-members. There are more than 100 miles of trails and carriage roads here for use by bicyclists. The visitor center is open daily from 9-5 and offers excellent exhibits about the geology of the region, free of charge.

Shawangunk Mountains Scenic Byway (845-255-4281;mtnscenicbyway.org). This 88-mile route encircles the northern Shawangunk Mountains through the Rondout and Wallkill Valley, with scenic mountains, forests, farms, rivers and streams.

Wallkill Valley Rail Trail (wvrt.org). Open daily dawn to dusk. This 24-mile multi-use trail is great for biking—and walking. It passes through countryside and downtown areas. There was once a busy railroad line that existed in the late 19th century. In 1977 the railroad took its last freight run; in 1983, all the ties and rails were removed and volunteers cleared the trail. It officially opened to the public in 1993.

The Mohonk Preserve in Gardiner offers some great trails for biking.

The following Ulster County shops rent both mountain bikes and road bikes:

Bicycle Depot (845-255-3859), 15 Main Street, New Paltz.

Kingston Bike Rentals (kingstonbikerentals.com), 25 Broadway, Kingston.

Overlook Mountain Bicycles (845-679-2122), 93 Tinker Street, Woodstock.

Bike Friendly Kingston (bikfriendlykingston.org) sponsors events in the Kingston area and is a great resource for those looking for fellow bicyclists in the Ulster County area. They meet twice each month to advocate for better bicycle infrastructure and to promote local bike events. The website lists current group rides and other activities.

TRT Bicycles (845-658-7832), 1066 Route 32, Rosendale.

There is an indoor cycling center at **The Bicycle Rack** (845-255-1770), 13 North Front Street, in New Paltz. This is a place to ride a bike from November through March; they are conveniently located by the entrance to the Wallkill Valley Rail Trail.

BOAT CRUISES

The Hudson River runs the length of Ulster County, and visitors can select from a few companies that cruise the river. It can be very breezy and cool, yet sunny, out on the river; bring a hat, scarf, sweater, and sunscreen.

Black Swan Sailing (845-542-SAIL; blackswansailing.com), Abeel Street, Kingston. From May through October, daily, weekday evening sails and weekends at all hours. The U.S. Coast Guard-licensed Captain Robert Henderson and crew sail the Black Swan, a 36-foot Catalina sailboat, on the Hudson River. Up to six people are welcome on a cruise that departs from both Kingston and Saugerties on the Hudson River.

Hudson River Cruises (845-340-4700; 800-843-7472; hudsonrivercruises. com), 36 Broadway, Kingston. This is the best Hudson River tour and it's reasonably priced. Two-hour cruises head south of Kingston for one hour toward the Hyde Park area, passing both the Kingston and Esopus Meadows lighthouses. Enjoy the spacious ship *Rip Van Winkle*, which features plenty of seating, restrooms, and a snack bar. The ride is smooth and pleasant and there's often live music on Friday evenings. Dinner and holiday cruises and special events listed on the website. (In May, weekends only, departs at 2:30pm from dock at 1 East Strand Street, Kingston; June, September and October, Tuesday through Sunday, departs 2:30pm; July through August, Tuesday through Sunday, departs at 11:30am & 2:30pm).

Hudson Sailing (845-687-2440; hudsonsailing.com), 1 Broadway, Kingston. Departs from the Rondout Creek in Kingston, May through November, daily,

9am-10pm. Excursions on the *Cirrus*. This Corsair F-28R is a fast, comfortable sailing vessel that accommodates a maximum of six people and is operated by owner Dan Feldman, a U.S. Coast Guard-licensed captain. Memorable trips are by appointment only; they are well worth making the arrangements.

CANOEING AND KAYAKING

Atlantic Kayak Tours (845-246-2187; atlantickayaktours.com), 320 West Saugerties Road, Saugerties. Open April through November, 9-6. They offer kayak trips on the Hudson River Esopus Creek and other local waterways. This outfitter will make an excursion fun; this is a particularly good choice for first-time kayakers. They have a few dozen different tours to choose from.

City of Kingston Kayak Tours and Lessons (845-481-7336; kingstonparksandrec.org), 53 Delaware Avenue, Kingston. Open May through September, Friday and Saturday. They offer guided nature-oriented kayak tours on the Hudson River and Rondout Creek. Sightings include bald eagles, osprey, turtles, and other birds and wildlife.

I Paddle New York (845-532-77797; ipaddlenewyork.com), 61 South Partition Street, Saugerties. Open May through October, by appointment. There are guided kayak tours offered to Canine Falls, the Saugerties Lighthouse, Esopus Bend Nature Preserve and other places on the Hudson. Beginners, children and groups will feel welcome here. Gail Porter, ACA Certified Kayak Instructor, is your guide.

NOTE: **KENCO** (845-340-0552; atkenco.com), 1000 Hurley Mountain Road, Kingston, rents kayaks, canoes, paddles, life jackets and car-top carriers from May through September. The store is open year-round, daily, 9am-7pm; Sunday 11-5.

FARMERS' MARKETS AND PICK-YOUR-OWN FARMS

Since the earliest colonists arrived, fruit farming has been important to Ulster County's economy. The first commercial orchard in America was established here in 1820. At that time, Robert Pell of Esopus began growing Newton Pippin apples for export to England. Apples are still the leading fruit crop, with more than 8000 acres planted and about three million bushels produced annually. Notice that many orchards are located on the sides or top of hills, which reduces the likelihood of crop losses due to late-spring frost.

Some Ulster County farms are still owned by the families that founded them; others have been cultivating the same site for centuries. The harvest season here stretches from early-summer strawberries to late-fall pumpkins and holiday greenery. Some farm stands offer freshly baked pies and cakes, while others have recipes for you to take home, along with food and other local goodies. Pick-your-own farms let you do the work as well as give you the choice of what you want in the basket. Most growers provide containers, but if you bring your own, the price is usually lower. However, if you decide to gather in the harvest, the following is just a sampling of places to try. Because weather conditions make it difficult to predict exact harvest dates, do call ahead for information about the crops available when you intend to go.

FARMERS' MARKETS

The Kingston Farmers' Market (347-721-7386), Wall Street between Main and John streets (May through November, 9-2); Old Dutch Church, Wall Street (December through April, first and third Saturdays of the month, 10-2), Kingston. This is the largest farmers' market in the county and I think it's the best. You will find fruits, vegetables, fresh-cut flowers, cheeses, breads, smoked meats, organic chicken, game, honey, pies and more.

New Paltz Farmers' Market, Church Street between Main and Academy streets, New Paltz. Open mid-June through mid-November, Sunday 10-3. There is an array of local produce, fruit, meats, cheese, baked goods, coffee and more.

Rosendale Farmers' Market (845-658-8348), 1055 Route 32, Rosendale

The farmers' market held on Saturdays on Wall Street in Kingston is the largest one in the county.

(Community Center parking lot, rain or shine). Open late June through October, Sunday 10-2; December through April, second and fourth Sunday, 10-2. There is live acoustic folk music along with traditional and organic vegetables, potted plants, apples, berries, flowers, cookies, pies, breads, cheeses, wine, honey, pickles, and maple syrup.

Saugerties Farmers' Market (845-750-0626), 115 Main Street, Saugerties. Memorial Day weekend through October, Saturday, 10-2. Fresh local seasonal fruits, vegetables, meats, fish, eggs, cheeses, baked goods and specialty products.

Woodstock Farm Festival (845-594-1946), Maple Lane, Woodstock. Open June through mid-October, Wednesday 3:30pm-dusk, rain or shine.

PICK-YOUR-OWN & FARM STANDS

Adams Fairacre Farms (845-336-6300), 1560 Ulster Avenue (Route 9W), Lake Katrine.

This is one of the largest farm markets in the county and they carry fresh produce from several local farms as well as meats, fish, cheeses and groceries. A family business, this is one of my favorite places to do shopping. And on Wednesday after 5pm, everyone receives 10% off their tab!

Davenport Farms (845-687-0051), 3411 Route 209, Stone Ridge. Open daily March through December. An extensive selection of local produce, including raspberries, grapes, corn, apples, pumpkins, and melons.

Dressel Farms (845-255-0693), 271 Route 208, New Paltz. Open daily, except Sunday, June through October. You can pick your own strawberries, apples, and pumpkins here in season, surrounded by magnificent views of the Shawangunk Mountains.

Four Winds Farm (845-255-3088), 158 Marabac Road, Gardiner, has certified organic vegetables; grass-fed lamb and beef, poultry (including turkey), and pork; as well as eggs and herbs. Call ahead to make sure someone will be there and stock up!

Two other organic farms are the **Phillies Bridge Farm Project** (845-256-9108), 45 Phillies Bridge Road, and **Taliaferro Farms** (845-256-1592), 187 Plains Road, both located in New Paltz. They offer a variety of fresh products in season.

Jenkins-Leuken Orchards (845-255-0999), 69 Yankee Folly Road, New Paltz. Open August through May, daily 9-6. Pick apples and pumpkins here. They have a large variety of apples, including Macouns, pears, peaches, tomatoes, and vegetables are available in season. Honey and cider are produced on this farm as well.

Liberty View Farm (845-883-7004), 340 Crescent Avenue, Highland. Open May through October, this delightful farm, with spectacular views of the Shawangunks, is one of the best places in the region to pick apples. Absolutely no chemical pesticides are used on the crops and their Cortlands are among the best I've ever tasted. The free range chickens are beautiful to look at and are fed organically, as are the goats. Make sure to check out the historic chicken coop and get some eggs before leaving the farm. These heirloom chickens produce fantastic tasting eggs. Owner Billiam van Roestenberg has a variety of seasonal festivals at the farm. There is also a Lease-an-Apple-Tree program!

Migliorelli Farm (845-757-3276), 5150 Route 28, Mount Tremper, offers a dazzling array of local produce. They are open May through November.

Saunderskill Farms (845-626-2676), 5100 Route 209, Accord, is one of my favorite places to pick strawberries, blueberries, and pumpkins in Ulster County. They are open April through December, daily, except Monday, 9-6. This beautiful family-owned and family-operated farm and store, named for the tributary of the Rondout Creek that flows through the farm, offers home-grown vegetables (excellent corn and tomatoes), fruits, flowering annuals, perennials, and herbs. The on-site bakery makes fine fruit pies, cookies, brownies, and cider doughnuts. There is local maple syrup, honey and jams for sale. In autumn the children will enjoy horse-drawn hayrides. Originally granted to Hendrick Schoonmaker by Peter Stuyvesant in 1663, the family's original 300 acres have been continuously farmed since 1680, making this farm the second-oldest family farm in the country. (There are now over 800 acres.) The stone manor house, built in 1787, still stands on the property. And Jack, Dan Dave, and Cathy Schoonmaker are on the premises every day.

Sunfrost in Woodstock is a great place to have breakfast or lunch, but Halloween is when they go all out.

Stone Ridge Orchard (845-687-0447), 3012 Route 213, High Falls. Open from July through October, daily 9-6 for picking apples, pumpkins, and raspberries. They have more than a dozen varieties of apples and the orchard is surrounded by hundreds of acres of forest and farmland. This spot is easy to find, right on Route 213, off Route 209, and it's a beautiful place to spend a couple of hours on an autumn afternoon.

Wallkill View Farm Market (845-255-8050), Route 299, just outside New Paltz. The produce and baked goods here are first-rate. You can also pick your own pumpkins in season. And the sunflowers in summer are stunningly beautiful.

Wilklow Orchards (845-691-2339), 341 Pancake Hollow Road, Highland. This is one of the oldest family-run pick-your-own farms and has been in business for over a century. They are open daily Labor Day through October for pick-your-own apples (there are 10 varieties here) and pumpkins. The stand sells home-grown vegetables and fruits as well as cider. Children will enjoy the farm animals on the property.

MAPLE SYRUP FARMS

The time for maple syrup tastings and tours is mid-February to mid-April. The following places will be glad to show you around and sell you their fine syrup, maple cream and honey. It's a good idea to call before you go, since erratic weather affects the season. **Arrowhead Farm** (845-626-7293), 5941 Route 209, Kerhonkson, has tours during the season. **Lyonsville Sugarhouse** (845-687-2518), 591 County Route 2, Accord, offers tours. **Oliverea School House Maple Syrup** (845-254-5296), 609 Oliverea Road, is open year-round by appointment only. They have over 4000 taps in the Catskills. **Sugar Brook Maple Farm** (845-594-2843), 351 Samsonville Road, Kerhonkson, has wonderful tours March through mid-April and is open year-round for sales (always call first).

FISHING

Ulster County offers fishing enthusiasts a chance to try their luck in scores of streams, a reservoir, and the great Hudson River. The waters are well stocked with a variety of fish—trout, bass, pike, pickerel, and perch are just some of the more popular catches. Fishing areas are well marked, and New York State licenses are required, as are reservoir permits. Call the Department of Environmental Conservation Department of Fisheries (845-256-3161), New Paltz.

There are only a few fishing guide services since the Esopus Creek and other waterways are accessible. Just about anyone can get to many excellent fishing spots in the county with ease. Some of the better-known fishing streams include the renowned Esopus Creek (access points along Route 28, west of Kingston), Rondout Creek (access points on Route 209, south of Kingston), Plattekill Creek (access near Route 32 in Saugerties), and the Sawkill Creek (access along Route 212 in Woodstock). Major access points are indicated by signs and some have designated parking areas. If you are uncertain about the stream, ask; otherwise, you may find yourself on the receiving end of a heavy fine. Holders of reservoir permits will want to try the Ashokan Reservoir (Route 28A, west of Kingston), with 40 miles of shoreline, and trout, walleye, and bass lurking beneath the surface. The Kingston City Reservoir requires a city permit for fishing, but it's worth the extra effort to obtain.

GOLF

Ulster County golf courses can be by turns dramatic, relaxing and colorful, and the areas that offer golf cater to a wide range of skills and interests. Hotel courses are usually open to the public, like Mohonk, but it's recommended you call in advance since they schedule special events and competitions that may preclude the usual schedule.

Woodstock golf club is close to the shops and restaurants in the village.

IN THE KINGSTON/SAUGERTIES AREA

Alapaha Golf Links (845-331-2334), 180 Sawkill Road, Kingston. Open daily 7-dusk. Note the hours vary with the season. This nine-hole course, par 30, 1800 yards long, is a great place for novices. There is a driving range and putting green.

Green Acres Golf Club (845-331-2283), 250 Harwich Street, Kingston. Open daily 7-dusk. This nine-hole, par 36 course is 2774 yards long. A driving range is also available and this is a popular place with local residents.

Lazy Swan Golf & Country Club Village (845-247-0075), 1754 Old Kingston Highway, Saugerties. Open 8-dusk. There are nine holes and a par 35 at this 3100 yard-long course. There is a clubhouse restaurant on the premises; pro shop and lessons available. Award-winning architect, Les Walker of Woodstock, designed the seven-building village, which includes the clubhouse, restaurant and a Pilates facility.

IN THE NEW PALTZ AREA

Apple Greens Golf Course (845-883-5500), 161 South Street, Highland. Open weekdays 7-dusk; weekends 6-dusk. This 18-hole course, par 71, is 6500 yards in length, and there is a driving range, putting green, clubhouse restaurant, pro shop, and lessons, as well as a twilight rate.

Mohonk Mountain House Golf Course (845-256-2154), 1000 Mountain Rest Road, New Paltz. Open daily dawn to dusk. There are nine holes, par 35, on this scenic Scottish-style course. There is also a driving range, putting green, and lessons are available.

New Paltz Golf Course (845-255-8282), 215 Huguenot Street, New Paltz. Open March through November, daily, dawn to dusk. There are nine holes at this par-36 course with all the amenities: driving range, putting green, restaurant, pro shop and lessons.

IN ACCORD, KERHONKSON, AND ELLENVILLE

Fallsview Golf Course at the Honor's Haven Resort & Spa (845-210-3106), 1195 Arrowhead Road, Ellenville. Open daily 7-dusk. There is a nine-hole championship course here designed by Robert Trent Jones Sr. There is also a driving range and golf school.

Hudson Valley Resort & Spa Golf Course (845-626-8888), 400 Granite Road, Kerhonkson. Open daily 7-6. This 18-hole, par-71, 6700-yard course is beautiful; it is on the grounds of a full-service resort and there is a driving range, putting green, pro shop, lessons, golf school and group packages.

Rondout Golf Club (845-626-2513), 10 Bank Street, Accord. Open daily 6am-7pm. This 18-hole, par-72 course has a driving range, putting green, restaurant, pro shop, lessons, golf packages, and twilight rate.

Shawangunk Country Club (845-647-6090), 38 Country Club Road, Ellenville. Open March through November, daily 7-6. This nine-hole, par-34 course has a putting green, pro shop and restaurant.

Stone Dock Golf Course (845-687-7107), 12 Stone Dock Road, High Falls. Open April through October, daily, 7-5. This nine-hole, par-36, 3315-yard course is pleasant to play. There is a driving range and a restaurant on the premises. There are group packages and a twilight rate.

Turtle Creek Golf Course at the Garden Cathay (845-564-3220), 219 Plattekill Ardonia Road, Wallkill. Open daily, April through November, 7 to dusk. This nine-hole course has a tight design that will challenge even the most experienced golfers. There are sand traps, grass bunkers, and water hazards on five holes. There is a restaurant on the premises.

HIKING

Ulster County is home to the Catskill Forest Preserve. This state-owned and maintained land within the Catskill Park---300,000 acres of forests, lakes, springs, cliffs, teeming with birds and wildlife—serves as a watershed, recreational area, and ecological reserve. There are seven mountainous areas, each with hiking trails ranging from easy to difficult. The county has some of the best hiking in the Hudson Valley with views that go on for miles and trails that range from an easy walk to a hard day's climb. There are several pending rail trail projects including the Ashokan Rail Trail and Kingston Rail Trail. Hopefully, both will open to the public in the spring 2019, as scheduled.

In the meantime, the following suggestions for afternoon or day hikes provide magnificent vistas. Remember to dress appropriately: Lyme disease is prevalent in many areas and it is advised to follow trails rather than bushwack to avoid ticks.

Belleayre Mountain (845-254-5600), Bellayre Mountain Road, Pine Hill, offers excellent hiking in the Catskill Forest Preserve. There are marked cross-

country ski trails that provide a nice walk in the woods and a hike to the summit of Belleayre reveals sweeping views of the mountains below. Elevations range from 600 to 4200 feet, and much of the area is rugged, steep terrain. A more moderate walk is the hike to Pine Hill Lake, which is part of the state preserve. In the summer months you can stop for a swim there after hiking.

Black Creek Forest Preserve (845-473-4440), intersection of Route 9W and Winding Brook Road, Esopus. This 13-acre forest preserve

Reese Park follows various trails along the Hudson River under the Mid-Hudson Bridge.

lies along a major Hudson River tributary. Walkers will cross a suspension footbridge over the Black Creek and pass through forest woodlands with vernal pools on the three hiking trails (a total of 2.5 miles) that have direct access to the Hudson River. This is the perfect place for a short hike and it is a good choice on a hot day, since it always seems a bit cooler with much of the trail area being shaded.

Esopus Meadows Point Preserve (845-473-4440), 257 River Road (County Route 24), Ulster Park. This 100-acre site offers great views of the Esopus Meadows Lighthouse, three trails, and an environmental center. The trails go through beautiful woodlands and in some places along the Hudson River. This is a good place to take a hike for an hour or two on gently sloping terrain.

Falling Waters Preserve (845-473-4440), 996 Dominican Lane, Glasco. This park features 150 acres with over two miles of trails leading to views of the Hudson River and Catskills, meadows and waterfalls. In some areas the trail reaches the shores of the Hudson. It's an easy walk for those with families looking for a nice outing.

Five Locks Walk (845-687-2000), 23 Mohonk Road, High Falls. This walk along the towpath of the Delaware and Hudson Canal from locks 16 to 20 is easily accessible and is a pleasant stroll along a national historic landmark. The path is located across the street from the D&H Canal Museum.

Franny Reese State Park (845- 473-4440), 129 Macks Lane, Highland. Open year-round dawn to dusk. This stunning riverside park is a tribute to Frances Reese who spent 40 years of her life making the Hudson Valley a better place to live. Scenic Hudson manages this 251-acre park which has 2.5 miles of trails that pass the ruins of a 19th-century estate while offering fantastic views of the Mid-Hudson Bridge, Walkway Over the Hudson and the City of Poughkeepsie. (Drive down Haviland Drive in Highland and follow down to a parking area before descending the steep staircase to the entrance of the park, literally under the Mid-Hudson Bridge!)

John Burroughs' Slabsides and Nature Sanctuary (845-384-6556), 261 Floyd Ackert Road, off Route 9W, West Park. The retreat of naturalist John Burroughs is located on 200 acres filled with hiking trails, waterfalls and forest. The trails on the property are open year-round from dawn to dusk. Burroughs' writing cabin is open the third Saturday in May, the first Saturday in October and the second and fourth Saturdays in June, July, August and September, or by appointment.

Hurley O & W Rail Trail, Route 209, Hurley. You can see some of this six-mile trail when driving on Route 209. It connects High Falls and Hurley and

Lake Mohonk is a beautiful place that attracts visitors from throughout the world.

passes through dense woodlands. There is a parking lot off Route 209, about one mile south of Route 28, at the intersection of Route 209 and Russell Road. I prefer walking here on dry days since it can get quite buggy in the summer months, particularly after it rains.

Maurice D. Hinchey Catskill Interpretive Center (845-688-3369), 5096 Route 28, Mount Tremper. Opened in 2014, in honor of the retired Congressman who initiated and supported the development of this interpretive center for over 30 years, this is a great place to stop and get oriented to the Catskills. Located on a 62-acre site, this "gateway" for both travelers and residents alike, provides information on recreation, cultural activities and natural history in the Catskill Park. There is a half-mile nature trail to a picnic area here with views of Mount Pleasant. There is also an excellent selection of local books for sale on all aspects of the Catskills.

Minnewaska State Park Preserve (845-255-0752), 5281 Route 44/55, New Paltz. Open year-round, daily, 9am to dusk. Hours may change seasonally and are posted daily at the entrance. Located on the dramatic Shawangunk Mountain Ridge, this park offers spectacular mountain views, waterfalls, and meadows. Lake Minnewaska is surrounded by a network of woodland trails and carriageways; all are excellent for hiking, horseback riding, and cross-country skiing. The paved carriageways make for fine biking. You can take a leisurely two-mile walk around Lake Awosting, a good way to get oriented in this large park. Swimming is permitted at the sandy beach area, and there is a lifeguard on duty. The lake is about a three-mile walk from the entrance if you decide to hike in. Minnewaska is a day-use area only; no camping is permitted. There are several places to picnic.

Mohonk Mountain House (845-255-1000), 1000 Mountain Rest Road, New Paltz. Open year-round, daily, dawn to dusk. Admission. This 2000-acre natural paradise surrounding the Mohonk Mountain House resort is filled with miles of hiking trails and carriage roads stretching out in all directions. The trails are ideal for cross-country skiing in winter as well as walking. From the tower at Sky Top, the highest point along the trails, 1500 feet above sea level, you can see six states on a clear day (New York, New Jersey, Pennsylvania, Connecticut, Massachusetts, and Vermont). Sky Top was built in 1920 as a memorial to Albert Smiley, one of the founders of Mohonk Mountain House, which opened in 1870. The panoramic vistas from some of the trails here are some of the most scenic views in the Hudson Valley.

Mohonk Preserve (845- 255-0919; mohonkpreserve.org), 3197 Route 44/55, Gardiner. The visitor center is open daily 9-5; the preserve and trails are open from dawn to dusk. There is a day-use fee for nonmembers. Over 100 miles of trails and carriage roads in this 3000-acre preserve provide some of the best hiking in the county. They offer an array of children's nature programs and special events for all ages, so check the website to see what is happening before you head up there to hike. The visitor center has a wealth of information on the area, including excellent maps.

Overlook Mountain, Meads Mountain Road, Woodstock, is a moderately difficult walk up a graded roadbed. From Tinker Street at the village green, take Rock City Road to Meads Mountain Road which leads straight to the trailhead across from KTD Tibetan monastery. The summit takes about an hour to reach, depending on how fast you travel the two-mile ascent. You will pass the ruins of the Overlook Mountain House on the way up; a lookout tower and picnic tables are at the top. The panoramic view of the valley and Ashokan Reservoir makes this ascent worthwhile!

Sam's Point Area of Minnewaska Preserve (845-647-7989), 400 Sam's Point Road, Cragsmoor (off Route 52, near Ellenville). This 5000-acre section of the Minnewaska Preserve is open year-round, from dawn to dusk. One of the best examples of ridge top dwarf-pine barrens in the world may be found here. The views are magnificent, and the hiking trails are excellent, leading to Sam's Point, Verkeerderkill Falls, the Ice Caves, and Indian Rock. This is an environmentally sensitive area, and it's important visitors stay on the marked trails. To reduce damaging impact to the delicate mosses, hike in early spring when there is still a protective snowpack. Sam's Point supposedly got its name from a trapper who, seeing a Native American war party, jumped over the edge and landed safely in some trees. Nature trails lead to dwarf-pine barren. Trails are well marked, and tours are self-guided with signs. A walk will take you past chasms and tunnels and around incredible balanced rocks.

Shaupeneak Ridge (845-473-4440), 143 Popletown Road, Esopus. There are about four miles of trails here that wend their way through this 560-acre wildlife conservation area owned by Scenic Hudson. You will see wetlands and

Louisa Pond, which was carved out by glaciers thousands of years ago. This is a good place to go for a hike of moderate difficulty and it is easily accessible from a main road. This site is also used for environmental education programs.

Trolley Route to Kingston Point (845-877-5263), East Strand, Kingston. Walk from Lower Broadway in Kingston along East Strand and follow the trolley tracks by the Hudson River for about two miles to Kingston Point and further on to the pavilion at Hutton Brickyards. Also known as the Kingston Point Rail Trail, part of the Kingston Greenline, a multi-phase program to expand hiking and biking trails throughout the city and connect them.

Vernooy Kill Falls, Lundy Road, Kerhonkson. The trail may be reached by taking Route 209 to Lower Cherrytown Road, bearing right and continuing five miles to Upper Cherrytown Road. After three miles there is a parking lot on the right and the trailhead on the left. The trail is approximately 3.5 miles up and back.

Wallkill Valley Rail Trail (wvrta.org), New Paltz. This 24-mile multi-use trail is popular for walking and biking. The trail passes through the countryside as well as downtown areas and connects Gardiner and New Paltz. You can pick up the trail in the Huguenot Street area or downtown across from the Water Street Market.

Wilson State Park (845-679-7020), 857 Wittenberg Road, Mount Tremper. Open year-round; Memorial Day weekend through Labor Day, daily 9-6; limited winter hours. This park is surrounded by mountains and is only a short distance from the center of Woodstock. It's a great place to stop for those traveling with young children. There are places to picnic and walking trails on paths through the woods along the stream. Campsites are available for overnight stays, and there are cross-country ski trails in the winter (no services, however, and it's ski at your own risk).

HORSEBACK RIDING/HORSE SHOWS

Ulster County offers only a small number of places for visitors to go horseback riding on a trail through the woods. The following are a few privately owned establishments that still provide this pastime:

Braden Brook (845-647-7556), 19 Mountaindale Road, Greenfield Park. Open year-round, daily 10-6. There are trail rides and pony rides here: something for all ages and abilities.

Mohonk Mountain House (845-255-1000), 1000 Mountain Rest Road, New Paltz. Open year-round, daily. Enjoy the trails and carriage rides through 7500 historic acres by advance reservation only. Those who are not guests of the hotel must purchase a day pass in addition to the charge for horseback riding.

Payne Farm (845-255-0177), 125 Dubois Road, New Paltz. Open year-round, daily, 10-6. There are trail rides here for all levels of ability, along with great views of the Shawangunk and Catskill mountains. There are both indoor and outdoor arenas.

NOTE: **HITS Horse Shows** (845-246-8833; hitsshows.com), 454 Washington Avenue Extension, Saugerties. Open Memorial Day weekend through Labor Day, Wednesday through Sunday 8-5. Admission is charged on weekends only. Horse lovers will enjoy seeing a show at this nearly 300-acre facility. There are ten permanent all-weather hunter, jumper, and equitation rings; two amphitheaters; and hundreds of stalls on the show grounds. There are also dozens of retail shops and food concessions on the premises. Check website for show schedule.

ROCK CLIMBING

The Shawangunk mountain range in Ulster County is renowned nationally for rock climbing. Those who want to learn should contact an outfitter that specializes in instruction.

Alpine Endeavors (877-486-5769), Rosendale. Open year-round by appointment only. This is a place to go if you are considering professional instruction or a guided trip either rock or ice climbing.

Eastern Mountain Sports Climbing School (845-255-3280), 3124 Route 44/55, Gardiner. Open year-round, daily 8:30-5. This rock and ice climbing school and guide service, provides instruction at all levels.

High Xposure Adventures (800-777-2546), 3197 Route 44/55, Gardiner. Rock climbing specialists since 1974, this guide service and school offers climbing lessons from beginner to advanced.

The Inner Wall (845-255-ROCK), 234 Main Street, New Paltz. This indoor rock climbing gym is open year-round and provides a great place to practice, even in the pouring rain or a snowstorm!

SWIMMING

Many of the best places to swim in Ulster County are reservoirs; naturally, they strictly forbid swimming. However, there are rivers and creeks with access in several places along main roads that are not on private property. They are good places to stop and cool off on a hot day.

The following are some scenic places to swim; all have lifeguards, a beach and picnic areas:

Belleayre Beach at Pine Hill Lake (845-254-5202), 33 Friendship Manor Road, Pine Hill. Open Memorial Day weekend through Labor Day, Monday through Friday, 10-6; weekends until 7. Admission. This tranquil lake offers boating and fishing with a beach area, picnic pavilions and snack bar, in addition to swimming. Bring your own canoe, or rent a kayak, or rowboat. Admission is charged per car. The beach is roped off into different sections; one area is for toddlers.

Kingston Point Beach (845-331-1682), Delaware Avenue, Kingston. Take Broadway to the end, turn left, and follow East Strand which becomes North Street for one mile to the park. Open year-round, daily, dawn to dusk. Free. Open mid June through Labor Day for swimming. This small beach on the Hudson River is run by the city of Kingston. There are no services, and it isn't advisable to swim in the Hudson even now, but it is a beautiful spot to sunbathe and enjoy river views. And children will love the sandy beach and small playground as well as watching the boats pass by.

Minnewaska State Park Preserve (845-255-0752), 5281 Route 44/55, New Paltz. Admission. Open mid-June through Labor Day, daily, noon-5 for swimming in Lake Awosting at the designated beach area only. There is also great hiking in the park here. Keep in mind that being high up in the Shawangunks, the weather is always a few degrees cooler than in the towns below.

Saugerties Village Beach (845-246-2321), Partition Street, Saugerties. Free. On the Esopus Creek, this sandy beach with swimming dock, playground and picnic areas, is a popular summer spot with local residents.

Sojourner Truth Ulster Landing County Park (845-336-8484), 916 Ulster Landing Road, Kingston. Open May through September for swimming, daily, 11-7. This county-owned and operated park offers a small, quiet sandy beach area just north of the Rhinecliff Bridge, with swimming in the Hudson River. There are restrooms and a picnic pavilion. This spot is usually less crowded since it is somewhat off the beaten track.

TUBING

Tubing is a popular Ulster County pastime. It doesn't take any special skills and can be done by just about anyone. All you do is rent a huge, black inner tube, put it in the water, and hop on for rides that last anywhere from one to three hours. Maneuvering can be done with your hands, and proper tubing attire consists of shorts and a T-shirt, or a bathing suit. Make sure to wear a pair of old sneakers. A life jacket is a necessity. Although most waters are not very deep, they are cold, and the currents can be swift. The tubing season runs from the first warm weather until the last—somewhere between late May and late September—but the best time to go is the dog days of August. You will have to leave a security deposit for the tube, and rental does not include extras like a life jacket or "tube seat," which keeps you from bumping along the rocky stream bottom.

Tubes and gear, including helmets, can be rented at **Town Tinker Tube Rental** (845-688-5553), 10 Bridge Street, Phoenicia, the grandfather of tubing services, with a well-stocked headquarters, having been in business for many years. They are open from Memorial Day weekend through September 9am-6pm. (The last tube rentals go out at 4pm.)

WINTER SPORTS

CROSS-COUNTRY SKIING

Belleayre Mountain (845-254-5600; belleayre.com), 181 Galli Curci Road, Highmount, has several marked, groomed trails that cover about six miles.. They follow the old Ulster and Delaware Turnpike, and even pass an old family cemetery. Some are mogul trails, for those who want a particularly challenging experience. Lessons are available, but call in advance to schedule; rentals are offered across the road from the trails. There is no fee for skiing, and no charge for parking or use of the lodges on the premises.

Frost Valley YMCA (845-985-2291), 2000 Frost Valley Road, Claryville. There are 20 miles of groomed trails that wind in and out of the forest and alongside streams here. The trails are all color coded, and there is a warming hut. A small use feel is charged; call for lesson and rental information.

Minnewaska State Park Preserve (845-255-0752), 5281 Route 44/55, New Paltz. Free. There are 150 miles of cross-country trails to suit everyone here, from novice to advanced. Open daily from 9am.

Mohonk Mountain House (845-255-1000), 1000 Mountain Rest Road, New Paltz. Admission. The hotel offers 35 miles of carriage-road trails opening onto views of distant mountain ridges, glens, and valleys. The trails are color coded and mapped. Rentals and refreshment sites are available.

Mohonk Preserve (845-255-0919) 3197 Route 44/55, Gardiner. Admission. There are many miles of cross-country ski trails here. A map is available at the visitor center; all trails are color-coded.

Wilson State Park (845-256-3099), 958 Wittenberg Road, Mount Tremper. Free. Enjoy approximately five miles of color-coded trails that wind through woodland forest, wetlands, and along a lake. This is a good place for beginners. There are no services and you must have your own equipment. I taught my son to cross-country ski here and have always enjoyed the fact it's close to Woodstock and I could head out for an hour or so without much planning!

DOWNHILL SKIING

Downhill skiing in Ulster County offers the best of all worlds: country surroundings and challenging slopes convenient to several cities, including Albany and New York.

Belleayre Mountain (845-254-5600; belleayre.com), 181 Galli Curci Road, Highmount. This is the largest downhill ski area in Ulster County, with the longest ski trail in the Catskills (the Deer Trail at 12,042 feet). Open mid-November through mid-April, daily 9-4. There are over 50 trails here with a top elevation of nearly 3500 feet, the highest base elevation of any Catskill ski area This is also the only ski area with a natural division: The upper mountain is for intermediate and expert skiers; the lower mountain is for beginners and novices. There is plenty of free parking, and a courtesy shuttle bus runs throughout the parking area all day. At the upper mountain the trails are serviced by snowmaking equipment. There are several lifts: two quads as well as double and triple chairlifts. New in 2018 is the **Catskill Thunder** gondola with 60 "cabins" that will transport up to eight adults at a maximum speed of 1000 feet per minute. Runs range from novice and intermediate to extreme expert. For those who want more of a challenge, there is a complete racing program for both adults and children. The ski school at Belleayre is outstanding, with patient, capable instructors who can teach the youngest beginner or help advanced skiers polish their skills. Snowboards are allowed and there is a terrain park and rail park. The Overlook Lodge (upper lodge) is a large welcoming log building with a fieldstone fireplace, bar, ski shop, cafeteria, lounge area, and outside deck. The Discovery Lodge (lower lodge) has a cafeteria and ski shop. Both have restrooms and locker areas. Belleayre has great children's programs, including the KidsCamp, and minimal-cost untimed beginner lessons for skiers and snowboarders. Beginners should check out the "Learn to Ski programs. This ski area is family and service oriented. The old-fashioned feeling reminds me of the place I learned to ski in the 1960s. It's a favorite of many local residents, offering good value for the money and a variety of package deals. I shouldn't neglect to mention you get to ski for half price on your birthday!

Sawkill Family Ski Center (845-336-6977), 167 Hill Road, Kingston. Open from late December through mid-March on weekends and holidays only, 10-4. This is the smallest ski area in the East, with one magic carpet lift and a snow tubing run with its own lift. There are three trails for skiing and snowboarding. They make lots of snow here and keep the area in great condition. This is an ideal place for families with young children. Lift tickets are relatively inexpensive. There are ski and snowboard rentals available.

ICE SKATING

Kiwanis Ice Arena (845-247-2590; kiwanisicearena.com), Washington Avenue Extension, Suagerties. Open daily late August through March. Check the website for public skating schedule. This fully enclosed, refrigerated ice rink, while not heated, is a great place to skate any day from approximately 10am until 3:30pm. There is a series of one-and-a-half-hour sessions, and the cost is minimal. Children under the age of five skate free and seniors receive discounts as well. Skate rentals are available. There are restrooms and a snack bar. I've been skating here regularly since 1999, before the rink was enclosed, and it's a wonderful venue. There are plans in the works to make this a year-round ice skating facility in 2019.

Mohonk Mountain House Ice Rink (845-255-1000), 1000 Mountain Rest Road, New Paltz. Open November through March. Those who are not guests of the hotel may purchase a day pass as well as admission to the rink. (This makes skating here rather pricey, btw.) The setting, in a Victorian open-air pavilion, is quite beautiful. It's unusual to find an outdoor rink anywhere these days. Keep in mind this rink is not regulation size and is for recreational purposes.

The Kiwanis Ice Arena in Saugerties is a great place to enjoy ice skating: public sessions are held daily and the rink is closed only a few months of the year.

LODGING

Many of the bed & breakfasts in Ulster County are tucked away down private roads or are off the beaten path. The following list is what I consider the best places in their class and I've organized them by location in the county since Ulster is so large (1161 square miles).

Northeastern Ulster County
(Hurley, Kingston, Saugerties, Woodstock)

Best Western Plus Kingston Hotel & Conference Center (845-338-0400), 503 Washington Avenue, Kingston 12401. ($$)

This is a privately owned and operated hotel. Although it is part of the Best Western hotel group, it has been owned and operated by the same Kingston family for decades. Conveniently located less than a half-mile off the NYS Thruway at exit 19, this full-service hotel is only a short walk from the historic uptown area of Kingston. Woodstock, Rhinebeck, and Stone Ridge are a short drive away. There are 212 rooms and five suites, and the indoor garden courtyard has a large heated swimming pool, whirlpool, sauna, and game room, a great place to relax if the weather isn't ideal. There is a fitness center and restaurant on the premises as well. This hotel is a great choice if you are traveling with children since there is always something to keep them occupied; the hotel also offers all the modern amenities. *(NOTE: If you don't stay here, you can pay a reasonable fee for use of the pool, hot tub and sauna; I spent many a rainy weekend afternoon here with my son!)*

Chateau and Tudor Rooms, Saugerties Bed & Breakfast (845-246-4058), 122 Burt Street, Saugerties 12477. ($$) This architectural treasure, an English Tudor estate, offers two luxurious spacious rooms with private baths, fireplace, and views of the Catskill Mountains and Esopus Creek. Guests may enjoy the beautiful gardens, reflecting pool, and pond on the property. Open year-round. Children and pets are welcome.

Diamond Mills Hotel (845-247-0700), 25 South Partition Street, Saugerties 12477. ($$$) The 30 rooms in this hotel, opened in 2011, all have private balconies overlooking the waterfalls of the Esopus Creek. There is a choice of double queen, king, or two king suites; the latter offer more space and a fireplace. Included in the amenities here are sumptuous towels and bathrobes, fine linens, flat-screen TV, gourmet minibar, and high speed Internet access. There is a restaurant on the premises. Open year-round. Children are welcome.

Emerson Resort & Spa (845-688-2828), 5340 Route 28, Mount Tremper 12457. ($$$) Located minutes from Belleayre Mountain and the town of

Woodstock, this luxurious hotel, with 25 individually and lavishly decorated suites, has an exotic feeling about it, combining both Asian and Indian design. The resort first opened in 2006 and it is set along the Esopus Creek. Every suite has a view of the stream, a fireplace, and whirlpool tub. There is a full-treatment spa, the largest in the Catskills, which offers facials, massages, body wraps and *ayurvedic* treatments. Guests may enjoy a sauna, indoor pool, and fitness facilities. The Lodge, features contemporary Adirondack-style décor in 27 rooms. The spacious private suites here offer a wet bar, refrigerator, and whirlpool bath; all have air-conditioning and cable TV. Many rooms have decks overlooking the scenic Esopus Creek. These accommodations are best for families; children and pets are welcome. The restaurant, ***Woodnotes***, is open daily for breakfast and dinner. The resort is open year-round.

Enchanted Manor of Woodstock (845-679-9012), 23 Rowe Road, Woodstock 12498. ($$) There are four rooms with private baths, cable TV and fireplaces on this eight-acre secluded property owned by hosts Claudia and Rolan. Guests may enjoy a heated outdoor pool and hot tub, and large pond with a waterfall during the summer months. Open year-round.

The Forsyth B&B (845-481-9148), 85 Abeel Street, Kingston. ($$) All four newly renovated guest rooms feature a mix of modern and vintage furniture, as well as beautifully appointed private baths. This is an excellent place to stay in the historic Rondout section of the city and the gourmet breakfast is top-notch. Not recommended for children. Open year-round.

The Homestead at Catskill Animal Sanctuary (845-706-3533), 316 Old Stage Road, Saugerties. ($$) The building housing this guest house dates back to the 1800s and is located on a 110-acre farm animal sanctuary. A vegan breakfast is offered but be aware three bedrooms share one bathroom. This is a good option for a family traveling with children. Open year-round.

Kate's Lazy Meadow (845-688-7200), 5191 Route 28, Mount Tremper 12457. ($$) Sleep creekside in a vintage Airstream trailer, enjoy listening to the rushing stream and kick back under the stars in a hammock. This unusual motel (co-owned by Kate Pierson of the B-52s) is located on nine acres along the scenic Esopus Creek. There are also 10 efficiency units with high-speed Internet service, cable TV, and private baths. Open year-round.

Onteora: The Mountain House (845-657-6233), 96 Piney Point Road, Boiceville 12412. ($$) Onteora has the most spectacular mountain views of any B&B in the Catskills. Located just one mile off Route 28, it was the estate of Richard Hellmann, the mayonnaise mogul. There are five bedrooms, all with cathedral ceilings and private baths. A separate luxurious two-room cottage, each room with its own bath, is available. A full gourmet breakfast is served to all guests. Children over the age of 12 are welcome. Open year-round.

Renwick Clifton House B&B (845-246-0552), 27 Barclay Street, Saugerties 12477. ($$$) This beautifully renovated 1812 Southern-style mansion has four guest rooms, all with private baths, views of the Hudson River, air-conditioning, cable TV, and WiFi, within 6000 square feet. Luxurious details include fresh-cut flowers and truffles upon arrival, and marble-tiled bathrooms. Guest rooms are named after the old steamships that plied the Hudson River. A four-course gourmet breakfast is served. Open mid-April through November.

Saugerties B&B at Tamayo (845-246-9371), 91 Partition Street, Saugerties 12477. ($$) There are four rooms in the village with queen-size beds; the two-bedroom suite sleeps four in an historic 1864 building. Open May through October.

Saugerties Lighthouse B&B (845-247-0656), 168 Lighthouse Drive, Saugerties 12477. ($$) Treat yourself to a unique, romantic experience: Sleep in a renovated lighthouse. Watch the boats pass by, and see the stars from the bedroom window. The lighthouse keeper will prepare a hearty breakfast in the morning. Two upstairs rooms share a bathroom downstairs. Travel light since it's a 10-minute walk from the parking area on a nature trail; and don't forget to check the tide schedule online! Open year-round.

Twin Gables of Woodstock (845-679-9479), 73 Tinker Street, Woodstock 12498. ($$) The architecture and furnishings of the 1930s create a relaxed, easy ambience at this guesthouse: its service and hospitality have earned it a reputation for comfort and affordability. There are 10 guest rooms, and a living room and refrigerator are available to visitors. Twin Gables is only a short walk from restaurants, shopping, galleries, and entertainment. The New York bus line stops nearby, so it's a great spot for those traveling to Woodstock without a car. Rooms are all air-conditioned; four have private baths; six share three baths. Children over the age of 12 are welcome. Open year-round.

Twin Lakes (845-338-2400), 198 Walton Lane, Hurley 12443. ($$) There are 12 cabins and two efficiencies here. The honeymoon suites have heart-shaped Jacuzzi tubs. This is a good venue for families, with boating, hiking and trails on the property, as well as an outdoor pool and stocked fishing lake. The restaurant serves breakfast, lunch, and dinner in a dining room with scenic views. Open year-round.

The Villa at Saugerties (845-246-5440), 159 Fawn Road, Saugerties 12477. ($$$) This phenomenally renovated four-bedroom retreat in the Catskills gives one a feeling of being in Tuscany. The owners, Amanda and Joe, a couple who pay attention to every detail, have created a fantastic getaway. A stay here is pricey, but it is definitely a place to go for a special memorable occasion. The meals are prepared to order with local sustainable ingredients and they will dazzle too! Open year-round. This venue is not appropriate for children.

A stay at The Villa at Saugerties is like being transported to a Mediterranean villa.

The Warehouse (845- 594-5659), Partition Street, Saugerties 12477. ($$) Sherri and Frank Cruz have converted this 800-square-foot warehouse into an industrial chic loft for nightly and weekly rentals in the middle of historic Saugerties. One can step out the door and be in the middle of shops and restaurants. The roomy open space has a deep soaking tub, repurposed plumbing pipe fixtures throughout and ambient lighting. A quiet location, it is still within a few steps of all the action. Open year-round.

Woodstock Country Inn (845-679-9380), 185 Cooper Lake Road, Woodstock 12498. ($$) This quiet, elegant inn is located in the countryside outside the village of Woodstock, yet it is near enough that a short drive will bring you to all the cultural action the town is famous for. The inn—which once belonged to artist Jo Cantine, whose work is in the permanent collection of the Metropolitan Museum of Art—has been restored and is filled with antiques. There are charming nooks throughout the place to relax or dream in. Several of Cantine's paintings and some of her hand-painted furniture are displayed in the common room. There are five rooms, all with private bath, air-conditioning, and private deck or porch; there is a heated in-ground pool with magnificent mountain views. There are special mid-season rates and the inn is open year-round.

Woodstock Inn on the Millstream (845-679-8211), 38 Tannery Brook Road, Woodstock 12498. ($$) This motel-like accommodation has its own special charm. Located on a brook, there are 18 separate rooms, and the innkeeper gives you the option of enjoying an elaborate continental breakfast buffet waterside, or in the sunroom. A short walk brings you to the village green in town. All rooms are air-conditioned with cable TV. Children are welcome; open year-round.

Southeastern Ulster County
(New Paltz, Gardiner, Stone Ridge)

Audrey's Farmhouse Bed & Breakfast (845-895-3440), 2188 Brunswyck Road, Wallkill 12589. ($$) This pastoral spot offers visitors a relaxing getaway. There are five guest rooms (three with private bath and two share a bath), each with air-conditioning and magnificent mountain views. Guests may use the in-ground pool and enjoy an outdoor Jacuzzi and fireplace in the main room. A gourmet breakfast is served. Pets are welcome here. Open year-round.

Captain Schoonmaker's Bed & Breakfast (845-687-7946), 913 Route 213, High Falls 12440. ($$) A fine place for antiques lovers, this 18th century house will make you feel as if you are stepping back into an earlier era. Schoonmaker's has been featured in many publications, and the host serves a hearty breakfast. All five rooms have private bath. Open year-round.

Country and Farm Bed & Breakfast (845-626-4596), 71 Stonykill Road, Accord 12404. ($$) Beth and Tim are your hosts on this 27-acre horse farm. Enjoy the privacy of a spacious apartment stocked with fresh baked goods, juices, coffee, and organic teas. There is a swimming hole on the property and plenty of space to walk or cross-country ski, so there is a lot to do here in every season. Conveniently located to several local attractions. Open year-round.

1850 House & Tavern (845-658-7800), 435 Main Street, Rosendale 12472. ($$) This charming boutique 12-room hotel is housed in a structure built in 1850. In fact, the building has had eight previous incarnations as a hotel. Reopened in 2012, this is a great place to stay for those who want to be within steps of the shops and restaurants in Rosendale, as well as those traveling the area without a car. The completely renovated rooms have private baths, fine linens, air-conditioning, flat-screen TVs, and wireless Internet access. Continental breakfast is served on the river-view porch in the warm weather months. The Tavern on the premises is a nice place to relax and enjoy drinks. There is a wonderful wrap around deck in the rear of the hotel that overlooks the Rondout Creek. No children under the age of 17. Open year-round.

Elm Rock Inn (845-687-4492), 4496 Route 209, Stone Ridge 12484. ($$) This renovated brick Colonial, originally a 1770 farmhouse features five unique air-conditioned guest rooms, all with private bath. A full gourmet breakfast is served fireside in the dining room or on the outdoor patio. Enjoy afternoon tea in the spacious great room. The accommodations in the carriage house are both pet and child friendly. Rooms in the main house require children be age 12 or over. Open year-round.

Fox Hill Bed & Breakfast (845-691-8151), 55 South Chodikee Lake Road, Highland 12528. ($$) This B&B is located about five miles from exit 18 off the NYS Thruway. Wander through the woods, sit by the garden pool and feed the colorful koi, or just relax in your room. There are three suites, all with private bath, air-conditioning, TV; one with a fireplace. There is a whirlpool spa, fitness center, and heated in-ground pool. Open year-round.

Gatehouse Gardens Bed and Breakfast (845-255-8817), 5 Gatehouse Road, New Paltz. ($$) Just a mile from the village of New Paltz and bordering the Mohonk Preserve, there are a few options here: two B&B rooms, an efficiency apartment that sleeps four and a three-room suite (the latter two choices are available May through October only). Although there is no TV, rooms are air-conditioned and a hot tub awaits you after hiking. Guests will enjoy a peaceful private setting at a reasonable price.

Hasbrouck House (845-687-0736), 3805 Route 209, Stone Ridge 12484. ($$$) For a romantic getaway, this gem is a wonderful place to go year-round, but particularly in spring, when the flowers around the stone swimming pool are in bloom. The Hasbrouck House is an 18th century stone mansion set on 40 acres amid magnificent gardens. There are six beautifully renovated suites and a two-bedroom carriage house. Listed on the National Register of Historic Places, the inn is open all year round and a restaurant is on the premises.

Inn at Kettleboro (914-213-2487), 321 Route 208, New Paltz 12561. ($$) Located on a 12-acre orchard over looking the Shawangunks, there are four rooms, all with private baths, near the village of New Paltz. The inn is perfect for a romantic getaway and is not recommended for children. Open year-round.

Inn at Twaalfskill (845-691-3605), 144 Vineyard Avenue, Highland 12528. ($$) This spacious, renovated Victorian built in 1902 was once the home of a local businessman and congressional representative. The name of the inn comes from the creek that runs in front of the property. The three guest rooms have private bath, central air-conditioning, and TV. Located just outside the village of Highland, the inn is open year-round and a continental breakfast is served to guests. No children under the age of 12 are permitted.

Minnewaska Lodge (845-255-1110), 3116 Route 44/55, Gardiner 12525. ($$$) This contemporary 26-room mountain lodge is nestled on 17 acres at the base of the spectacular Shawangunk Ridge. The lodge successfully combines the ambience of a bed & breakfast with the conveniences of a fine hotel. Half the rooms have private decks and mountain views. Guests may enjoy the fitness center on the premises as well as hiking in the nearby Mohonk Preserve and Minnewaska State Park Preserve. A full buffet breakfast is served. Children are welcome. Open year-round.

Mohonk Mountain House (845-255-1000), 1000 Mountain Rest Road, New Paltz 12561. ($$$) This National Historic Landmark is a mountaintop Victorian castle that stands in the heart of 22,000 unspoiled acres. Dazzling views are everywhere, and serene Mohonk Lake adds to the dramatic setting. Although the hotel offers a full-service spa, museum, golf, boating, tennis, horseback riding, a modern sports facility and wonderful hiking and mountain biking on 85 miles of trails and carriage roads, the place is still very much the way it was more than 100 years ago. And Mohonk is still managed by the Smiley family, who founded the hotel. During the winter trails become a cross-country skier's paradise. There is an ice rink in a Victorian open-air pavilion and snowshoeing with equipment available for guests. The spa includes a solarium, stone fireplace, outdoor heated mineral pool, indoor heated swimming pool, and fitness center. Of the 251 rooms, more than 100 have working fireplaces and nearly 200 have a balcony. Rates include three meals daily. Open year-round.

Mountain Meadows B&B (845-255-6144), 542 Albany Post Road, New Paltz 12561. ($$) This country home nestled in the foothills of the Catskills is a fine place for people who enjoy a casual atmosphere lounging by an in-ground pool, relaxing by a fireplace, or playing a game in a recreation room. The spacious landscaped grounds offer croquet, badminton, and horseshoes. All four rooms have private bath, central air-conditioning, and a king-or queen-size bed. Located less than five miles from the NYS Thruway, exit 18. Open year-round.

Rocking Horse Ranch (845-691-2927; 800-647-2624), 600 Route 44/55, Highland 12528. ($$) There are 120 rooms at this well-maintained ranch resort with full facilities and evening entertainment. Guests may enjoy boating on the lake, indoor/outdoor pools, waterslides, tennis, exercise room, and sauna. There is snow tubing and ice skating during the winter months. Children's programs and babysitting are available. This is a great family getaway any time of year.

The 1712 House (845-687-7167), 93 Mill Dam Road, Stone Ridge 12484. ($$$) When the King of England and a local Native American chieftain granted the Hardenburgh family a tract of land that encompassed about 250 square miles, the 1712 House was part of their original farm. Built in the style of the 1700s, its features include custom-made colonial furniture (all crafted from trees cut on the land and all pieces replicas of 18th-century items). Set on 80 acres, this majestic bluestone-and-wood structure offers guests a six-acre front lawn, winding streams, sprawling hills, mountains, and meadows---as well as all the modern amenities. The spacious living and dining rooms are complete with an enormous fireplace, wide-board floors, and beamed ceilings. The six bedroom suites each offer private bath with whirlpool or claw-foot bathtub, air-conditioning, telephone, cable TV and high-speed Internet access. Each one has a beautiful view of the grounds, sitting chairs, and table and chairs for in-room dining. A full gourmet breakfast will be made to your order. Enjoy it on the deck, the bluestone patio, or in your room. This is a good place to celebrate a special occasion. Not recommended for children. Open year-round.

Northwestern Ulster County
(Big Indian, Highmount, Pine Hill)

Alpine Osteria B&B (845-254-9851), 32 Galli Curci Road, Highmount 12441. ($$) The seven rooms here have private baths and are comfortable and cozy. There is a dining room, lounge, fireplace, and game room. For those who want to be within walking distance to Belleayre Mountain, this is a good choice. A full breakfast is served by the owner, a Culinary Institute graduate. Open year-round.

Beaverkill Valley Inn (845-439-4844), 1532 Beaverkill Valley Road, Lew Beach 12753. ($$$) This National Historic Site, built in 1893 and restored by Laurance Rockefeller, offers a perfect retreat for those who love the outdoors. Located within the Catskill Forest Preserve, near hiking trails and some of the best fishing anywhere, the inn also has tennis courts and a great indoor pool. During the summer guests can bike, hike, swim, and fish; in winter cross-country skiing and swimming are popular pastimes. There are a total of 20 rooms, all with private bath. Children are welcome. Open year-round.

Blue Hill Lodge & Café (845-985-0247), 1471 Denning Road, Claryville 12725. ($$) Nestled in the Catskill mountain hamlet of Claryville, this quiet, simply furnished motel has a good restaurant and bakery on the premises.

There is also a cabin and three-bedroom house on the property for rent by guests. Located near several hiking trails, fishing streams and 30 miles from Bethel Woods, it is an oasis in the nether reaches of Ulster County! Children are welcome. Open year-round.

Pine Hill Arms (845-254-4012), 288 Main Street, Pine Hill 12465. ($$) Completely renovated and re-opened in 2017, this cozy comfortable 20-room inn makes for a delightful rural getaway. There is a cocktail lounge, sauna and game room; they are located a mile from Belleayre ski center and close to dozens of excellent hiking trails. Children are welcome. Open year-round.

Starlite Motel (845-254-4449), 8722 Route 28, Big Indian. I stayed overnight here and enjoyed the experience: Starlite is an old-fashioned motel with modern conveniences. Amenities include full kitchen, cable TV, picnic area and continental breakfast. There's nothing fancy, but it's close to Belleayre Mountain, lake swimming and hiking. This is a fun place that will take you back several decades. Children welcome. Open year-round.

Southwestern Ulster County
(Ellenville, Kerhonkson)

Honor's Haven Resort and Spa (845-210-1600), 1195 Arrowhead Road, Ellenville 12428. ($$) The setting here is magnificent. Situated on 250 acres with gorgeous mountain views, this 232-room full-service resort offers a championship golf course, indoor and outdoor pools, tennis, lake fishing and boating, sauna, fitness center, and spa. Meals are decent and are included in the room rate. Children are welcome. Open year-round.

WHERE TO EAT

DINING OUT

Northeastern Ulster County

Armadillo (845-339-1550), 97 Abeel Street, Kingston. ($$) Open for dinner Tuesday through Sunday 5-10. Tex-Mex Southwest cuisine from an enormous menu includes great ribs, fajitas, and fish specialties; make sure you try the grilled tuna with lime marinade and wasabi mustard. Outdoor dining in the warm weather months in a charming patio area. Crayons are provided so you or the kids can draw on the paper tablecloths! Children's menu.

Bear Café (845-679-5555), 295 Tinker Street, Woodstock. ($$) Open daily, except Tuesday, for dinner from 5. This is a French American bistro that serves a range of imaginative entrees, from grilled fish and chicken to steaks and unusual pasta dishes. The appetizers, salads, and daily specals are consistently excellent. There is a nice view of the Sawkill Creek from the dining area. Be sure to make a reservation on weekends, and any evening during the summer months. This is a busy restaurant year-round and for good reason!

The Bear Cafe is one of the most popular and consistently excellent restaurants in Woodstock.

Christina's (845-339-7400), 812 Ulster Avenue, Kingston. ($$) Open daily, except Tuesday, 11-9; Sunday noon-8. All the Italian favorites prepared to order at reasonable prices. I love the house salad, eggplant parmigiana and seafood Cioppino. Nestled in a busy shopping district, this is a place favored by local residents. Children are welcome.

Chops Grille (845-339-1111), 33 John Street, Kingston. ($$) Open Monday through Thursday 4:30-9:30; Friday 11:30-10; Saturday 4-10; Sunday 4-9. Steaks, salads and seafood are served in generous portions here. Monday is $12 burger night with half price on select bottles of wine. Tuesday through Thursday evenings a three-course fixed price menu is offered. There is something here to please every taste. Not recommended for children.

Cucina (845-679-9800), 109 Mill Hill Road, Woodstock. ($$) Open for dinner daily 5-9; Saturday and Sunday brunch 11-3. *Cucina* means "kitchen" in Italian; this one is headed up by Gianni Scappin, from the Culinary Institute's Caterina de Medici restaurant. The building has been renovated with a distinctly modern feel and offers up fine Northern Italian cuisine. There are thin-crust pizzas, fresh vegetables, and fish, several imaginative pasta selections, rib eye steak and crisp calamari. Children are welcome.

Diamond Mills—The Tavern (845-247-0700), 25 South Partition Street, Saugerties. ($$) Open for dinner Wednesday through Sunday 4-10; Saturday 10am-10pm. The atmosphere here is delightful, and one can enjoy a meal alfresco in the warm weather months overlooking the waterfalls, or in a booth by the fireplace in the main dining room. The menu includes appetizers like lobster corn chowder and beef carpaccio, and entrees like cedar plank-roasted wild steelhead trout and beef burger. The emphasis is on fresh local ingredients, and the menu changes seasonally.

Downtown Café (914-466-9800), 91 Broadway, Kingston. ($$) Open Wednesday through Friday 5-9; Saturday 10-9; Sunday 10-3. Chef Graziano Tecchio is back in his own restaurant on the Rondout. Since the Fall 2017, he has created a wonderful informal Italian restaurant with exceedingly reasonable prices. The gnocchi, chicken, steak and sole entrees were all excellent; and each was $15 or less (surprising, considering the high quality of the fare). Leave room for dessert. The night I was there, the blueberry tiramisu was amazing. Enjoy outdoor dining in the warm weather months.

Duo's (845-383-1198), 299 Wall Street, Kingston. ($$) Open daily, except Wednesday, for lunch 11-3:30; dinner 5:30-9 (except Sunday), Friday and Saturday open until 10. Art lines the walls of this cozy café known for innovative preparations of New American cuisine. Everything is prepared to order and while it's somewhat pricey for Kingston, the fare is consistently excellent. This is one of my favorite Kingston restaurants, especially for lunch.

Emiliani Ristorante (845-246-6169), 147 Ulster Avenue, Saugerties. ($$) Open for dinner Tuesday through Saturday, 4-9. Some of the finest Italian cuisine you will find anywhere in the Catskills is served in this informal yet elegant establishment. The pastas are made on the premises and all dishes are made to order. Children are welcome.

Golden Ginza (845-339-8132), 24 Broadway, Kingston. ($$) Open daily 11am-10pm; Sunday 1-10. Enjoy all types of Japanese cuisine, including tempura, teriyaki, sushi and sashimi. However, the specialty here is the hibachi "theater." Children (and most adults) will love watching the flames rising from the grill at the center of the table if you order hibachi dinners; they are prepared Benihana style. There is a sushi bar too and everything is created fresh from scratch. A fun family restaurant!

Joshua's Restaurant (845-679-5533), 51 Tinker Street, Woodstock. ($$) Open daily, except Wednesday, 11am-10pm; Saturday and Sunday 10-10. This family-owned and operated restaurant has been a mainstay in Woodstock for decades. They are known for their enormous menu, featuring an array of international favorites as well as Middle Eastern and Greek specialties. Whether you prefer traditional favorites like steak, pasta, and chicken, or enjoy falafel, baba ghanoush, and Mediterranean salads, it's all here in the center of town. There is often music upstairs in the evenings as well. For a quiet Sunday breakfast, this place is a well-kept secret!

Kyoto Sushi (845-339-1128), 337 Washington Avenue, Kingston. ($$) Open daily 11:30-9:30; Sunday 4-9:30. Enjoy the artistry of Chef Chun Chao Chen from Manhattan, now in uptown Kingston, and dine on meticulously prepared sushi and sashimi. For those who prefer cooked cuisine, there is chicken or beef teriyaki on the bill of fare.

Le Canard-Enchaine (845-339-2003), 276 Fair Street, Kingston. ($$) Open daily, except Wednesday 11:30-9:30; Sunday 1-9. Enjoy a classic French meal in a casual bistro atmosphere: a touch of Paris in Kingston. A variety of fresh fish is available daily. There are classic duck entrees and the freshly baked pastries are excellent. This is a good choice for lunch since there is a fixed-price option daily.

Little Bear Chinese Restaurant (845-679-8899), 295 Tinker Street, Woodstock. ($) Open daily for lunch and dinner noon-10:30. Sit along the Sawkill Creek in the warm weather months and enjoy Chinese cuisine. They offer an array of vegetarian dishes here, as well as imaginative entrees that are quite different from the usual Chinese restaurant fare. They will prepare any dish to your specifications, so tell them what you would like! The setting is great and this is a good place for take-out, as well. Children are always welcome.

Molé Molé (845-338-4765), 23 Broadway, Kingston. ($$) Open Tuesday through Thursday 4-9:30; Friday and Saturday noon-10; Sunday noon-8:30. This is my favorite place to eat when I'm in the Rondout area of Kingston. The Mexican fare is fresh, meticulously prepared, and portions are generous. I love the black bean and tortilla soups as well as all the standard favorites. They can make every dish for vegans and note that Margaritas are $3.00 every Wednesday!

New World Home Cooking (845-246-0900), 1411 Route 212, Saugerties. ($$) Open daily for dinner 5-9:30; Friday and Saturday until 10:30; Sunday 4-9. Lunch is served during the summer months; call for hours. Eating here is like taking a tour of America's funkiest restaurants. The house specialties are Jamaican jerk chicken, Thai mussel stew, and black-sesame-seared salmon (my favorite). Try the phenomenal blackened string beans with remoulade appetizer. According to chef-owner Ric Orlando (a finalist of the TV show, *Chopped*), the emphasis is on peasant flavors, and the colorful, casual ambience reflects the many cultures represented on the menu. This is a fun place to eat, and there is often live music on weekends after 9pm, so call ahead to see what is happening. Children are welcome.

The Red Onion Restaurant & Bar (845-679-1223), 1654 Route 212, Saugerties. ($$) Open for dinner daily 5-9; Friday and Saturday until 10. This was one of the only places in Ulster County with a smoke-free bar long before it was required by law. As someone who has never smoked a cigarette, this was much appreciated! The creative international bistro cuisine is first-rate, and so is the service. Enjoy appetizers like spicy shrimp ragout with garlic chilies and lemon. Entrees include wild striped bass on herbed risotto with lobster mushrooms. Desserts range from crème caramel with fresh berries to tricolor chocolate mousse. Children are welcome.

Reginato Ristorante (845-336-6968), 34 Leggs Mill Road, Lake Katrine. ($$) Open for lunch Tuesday through Friday 11:30-2; dinner Tuesday through Saturday 4-9 and Friday and Saturday until 10; Sunday 1-8. Enjoy homemade Northern Italian specialties in a relaxed atmosphere. Children are welcome.

Stella's (845-331-2210), 44 North Front Street, Kingston. ($) Open for dinner Monday 5-9; lunch and dinner Tuesday through Sunday noon-10. For some of the best traditional Italian home cooking, including baked lasagna, eggplant parmigiana, or spaghetti and meatballs, this is the place to go. The casual atmosphere and good-size portions make this a local favorite. Stella's has been open for decades and is popular with local residents: they offer a child-friendly menu.

Sushi Makio (845-853-8078), 1088 Morton Boulevard, Kingston. ($$) Open Tuesday through Saturday 4-9; Friday and Saturday until 10. I cannot recommend

this restaurant highly enough for fans of sushi and sashimi. There is always meticulous attention to detail and the chef/owner is ALWAYS on the premises creating wonderful meals and overseeing every aspect of the operation. Even if Chef Makio hadn't been chef to the premier of Japan, he runs a first-rate place and I feel lucky to have Sushi Makio so close to my home! Not recommended for children.

SushiMakio in Kingston has first-rate sushi and sashimi prepared by master chef Makio.

Southeastern Ulster County
(High Falls, Highland, New Paltz, Stone Ridge)

A Tavola (845-255-1426), 46 Main Street, New Paltz. ($$$) Open Thursday through Monday for dinner 5:30-10:30. This fine restaurant melds the recipes of the Italian countryside and the freshest Hudson Valley ingredients. The chef had two decades of experience in Manhattan restaurants before opening his own trattoria. There are imaginative pasta dishes as well as osso bucco, duck, and bronzino. Everything is prepared to perfection; make sure not to skip the dolci!

The Country Inn (845-657-8956), 1380 County Route 2, Krumville. ($$) Open for dinner Thursday through Sunday 5-9:30. The road twists and turns as you approach this rustic oasis in the woods of Ulster County, and it has been a renowned local spot for decades. There are still 350 types of beer available, with 10 on tap, but the food has undergone a transformation. There is calamari with roasted red pepper sauce for dipping as well as duck, steak and homemade fries. There is a unique ambience here. Keep in mind credit cards are not accepted.

The Egg's Nest (845-687-7255), 1300 Route 213, High Falls. ($$) Open Thursday through Monday 11-9. Completely renovated and re-opened in 2017 by Eric and Christina Silver, this renowned restaurant has taken the fare at this High Falls mainstay up a notch or two. They have also improved on the festive décor without losing the original spirit of the place. All ingredients here are sourced locally and the house-made nacho chips with seasoned black beans, cheddar cheese, lettuce, tomatoes, roasted beet sour cream & guacamole were the best I've had anywhere. Also first-rate are the steak quesadillas and hearty soups. I look forward to returning soon to try the crab cake stuffed trout, the poke bowl, and eggplant parmagiana. Prices here are exceedingly reasonable for the high-quality fare.

Global Palate (845-384-6590), 1746 Route 9W, West Park. ($$) Open for dinner Wednesday through Sunday 5-9; Sunday brunch 10-2. The motto here is "where local ingredients greet the world". This is a favorite restaurant of mine— consistently good, with healthful international creations that are truly first-rate. Chef Jessica Winchell uses hormone-free meats and local produce to turn out some phenomenal dishes influenced by global cuisine. The atmosphere is casual and relaxed; there is a decent wine and beer list.

Mountain Brauhaus (845-255-9766), 3123 Route 44/55, Gardiner. ($$) Open Wednesday through Sunday 11:30-9. After hiking in the Mohonk Preserve or Minnewaska State Park Preserve, this is my go-to restaurant. It's also a favorite of local residents and is always bustling. The lunches and dinners are excellent: portions are huge and one of my favorite items on the menu is their house made turkey sandwich on

The Egg's Nest restaurant in High Falls was completely renovated in 2017, yet retains the colorful ambiance that has made it an Ulster County landmark.

fresh rye with hand-cut fries....accompanied by one of the dozens of beers on tap! If you love spaetzle, theirs is great and so are the burgers and wursts. Children are welcome and it's always fun to sit at the bar. Service is consistently first-rate.

Ship Lantern Inn (845-795-5400), 1725 Route 9W, Milton. ($$) Open Tuesday through Saturday 4-9:30; Sunday 1-8. This charming restaurant has nautical décor and serves fine Continental cuisine. The food and service are consistently excellent. House specialties include fresh fish, mignonette of beef bordelaise, and saltimbocca Romana. Children are welcome.

The Would Restaurant (845-691-9883), 120 North Road, Highland. ($$) Open Tuesday through Saturday 5-11. A former gin mill once known as the Applewood Bar, this informal restaurant is becoming renowned for its high-quality creative cooking. There is a mix of international and New American cuisine, with several unique touches. The menu includes grilled lamb chops on roasted walnut-mint pesto with Mediterranean vegetable compote. The pastry chef bakes focaccia and pesto bread as well as terrific desserts. Try the flaky apple pie spiced with cinnamon, or the raspberry-chocolate brulee.

Northwestern Ulster County

Peekamoose Restaurant & Tap Room (845-254-6500). 8373 Route 28, Big Indian. ($$) Open for dinner Thursday through Monday 5-10 (hours may vary seasonally). Chef Devin Mills and his wife, Marybeth, have created a consistently fine restaurant close to Belleayre. A graduate of Hyde Park's Culinary Institute, Devin worked for Waldy Malouf at the Hudson River Club, Le Bernardin, and the Gramercy Park Tavern. Peekamoose specializes in American cuisine with fresh seasonal ingredients. It's a great place to stop for drinks and a small meal; the taproom is cozy, classy, and comfortable, like the restaurant. There is also a first-rate wine list.

The Phoenician Steakhouse (845-688-9800), 10 Main Street, Phoenicia. ($$) Open for dinner Wednesday through Sunday 5-9:30. Steaks are the specialty here although there are a number of seafood selections as well. The portions are large and the service is consistently excellent. Children are welcome.

Woodnotes Grille at the Emerson Resort & Spa (845-688-2828), 5340 Route 28, Mount Tremper. ($$) Open for breakfast daily 7am-noon; dinner daily 5-9; Sunday 4-8. Happy hours weekdays with bargain drink prices. Enjoy American favorites featuring local ingredients (burgers, steaks, grilled fish, pasta, and more). Children are welcome.

Southwestern Ulster County

Aroma Thyme Bistro (845-647-3000), 165 Canal Street, Ellenville. ($$) Open Monday, Tuesday and Thursday, 5-10; Friday 3-11; Saturday noon-11; Sunday 11-10. Closed Wednesday. There is something for everyone at this certified green restaurant! There are steaks, seafood, pizza, vegan and gluten-free selections. The wine and beer list is excellent. There is Kobe beef meat loaf, sesame-crusted albacore tuna, tempeh chili, and grilled New York strip steak. This is definitely the hub of Ellenville! Children are welcome.

White Wolf Restaurant & Lounge (845-647-4200), 7400 Route 209, Napanoch. ($$) Open for dinner Wednesday through Sunday 4:30-10. This is a good place to stop for a drink and snack when traveling on Route 209, if only to take in the opulent décor that includes the granite-top zigzag bar and deluxe dining rooms with mahogany and cherry woods, and etched glass with wolf motifs on the mirrors. The food is straightforward American fare with a good selection and ranges from bar food to prime rib, chicken, ribs and pastas. Children are welcome.

EATING OUT (BARS INCLUDED)

Northeastern Ulster County

A&P Bar (845-684-5395), 83 Mill Hill Road, Woodstock. ($$) Open daily 5-midnight; Sunday 11-midnight. This recent addition to the Woodstock bar scene (they opened in the summer 2017) is the place to go for fancy cocktails. The food happens to be quite good too. I enjoy the locally sourced burgers, thin-crust pizza and chicken Kiev. The décor is quite unusual and reminds me of the San Francisco bars I've visited!

Beverly Lounge (845-514-2570), 224 Foxhall Avenue, Kingston. ($) Open daily 5-10; Saturday until 11. **Make sure to call before going!** (*I went there on a Monday night in October and they were closed!*) This restaurant serves burgers, salads and decent bar food in an authentic old city atmosphere. There is happy hour with bargain drinks from 5 to 7pm; it's located in the midtown area of the city, off the tourist trail!

Blue Mountain Bistro To Go (845-340-9800), 948 Route 28, Kingston. ($$) Open Monday through Thursday 9-7; Friday 9-8; Saturday and Sunday 11-5. Mary Anne and Richard Erickson of Blue Mountain Bistro Catering Company opened this wonderful gourmet take-out shop with a small restaurant on the premises. There are paninis, sandwiches, salads and hearty soups. The house-roasted turkey with pesto mayo makes an excellent sandwich. All ingredients are fresh and many are organic. The Mediterranean treats change continually. If you are planning a picnic lunch, make sure to stock up here before heading into the Catskill Park. And don't leave without sampling one of the marvelous desserts in the adjoining bakery!

Bread Alone (845-679-2108), 22 Mill Hill Road, Woodstock; also 2015 Ulster Avenue, Kingston. ($) Open daily 7-5 at both locations. This bakery is renowned for its variety of excellent breads—Norwegian farm, mixed grain, Swiss peasant, sour dough rye, and others—all baked in a wood-fired oven. Enjoy a latte or cup of tea and satisfy your craving for something sweet and rich from the array of tempting desserts beautifully displayed. The soups and chili are quite good too and are served with your choice of bread or a roll.

Cheese Louise! (845-853-8207), 940 Route 28, Kingston. ($) Open Tuesday through Friday 11:30-7; until 9 on Friday; Saturday 10-5; Sunday noon-5. Take home some of the world's best cheeses featured here. Also available for take-out are artisanal breads, whitefish salad, fresh turkey, stuffed grape leaves, and more. The lunch specials include soups, sandwiches, and tasty salads. Everything here is of high quality and freshly prepared.

Cub Market and Deli (845-679-6569), 3203 Route 212, Bearsville. ($) Open year-round, daily 7-7; until 5pm on Sunday. This is a great place to get a breakfast wrap, hot soup, club sandwich, or garden salad. Everything is super fresh, and organic ingredients are used. The coffee is excellent and the tea selections are extensive. There's a counter for eating in along with a couple of tables outside.

Deising's Bakery & Coffee Shop (845-338-7503), 111 North Front Street, Kingston. ($) Open Monday through Saturday 6-5:30; Sunday until 3. The array of pastries, breads, and other baked items (like napoleons and butter cookies) are renowned by a faithful local clientele who have been patronizing Deising's for decades. The coffee shop offers large, overstuffed sandwiches, fresh soups and breakfast is a bargain. Children are welcome.

Dutch Ale House (845-247-2337), 253 Main Street, Saugerties. ($) Open daily 11-9; Friday and Saturday until 10. Hearty American favorites in a tavern atmosphere are served here. Try the stuffed garlic cheeseburger, a specialty of the house or the Pilgrim (thinly sliced turkey breast, homemade stuffing, and provolone sandwiches between two slice of fresh rye bread and grilled). The salads, soups, and chili are good and the portions are generous. Along with carnivorous fare, there's veggie bean chili, veggie pitas and of course, 15 craft beers on tap.

Hudson Valley Dessert Company (845-246-1545), 264 Main Street, Saugerties. ($) Open daily 8-6. Enjoy high-quality desserts (cakes, cookies, pies, muffins, biscotti, and more), as well as potpies and quiche. A clean, contemporary, pleasant place to stop for afternoon tea and a sweet snack while sitting at a table looking out on Saugerties' Main Street. Children will love this place, especially at the holidays.

Kovo Rotisserie (845-338-5686), 43 North Front Street, Kingston. ($) Open daily 11:30-9. This Greek inspired casual restaurant emphasizes rotisserie meats and fresh, seasonal salads. I love the big "make your own" salad bowls here. This is where I go for fast food….because it's so much better tasting—and healthier! Children are welcome.

La Florentina (845-339-2455), 604 Ulster Avenue, Kingston. ($$) Open weekdays 11:30-10; weekends 4-10. Enjoy excellent wood-fired pizza, calzones, and other baked specialties. A traditional wood-fired oven is the centerpiece of the open kitchen here. The cheeses are all homemade and there are great Sicilian desserts, including cannoli, ices, and layer cake. Children are welcome.

The Lodge (845-679-2814), 20 Country Club Lane, Woodstock. ($$) Open for dinner Thursday through Saturday 5pm to midnight. Bar open daily from 4pm; Saturday from 1pm. There are burgers, salads, wings and flatbreads here: a nice selection of bar fare. Enjoy karaoke and live music at this recently (2017) renovated venue in Woodstock. The new owners are gradually transforming the place and it has been a nice addition to the entertainment scene in town.

Love Bites Café (845-246-1795), 85 Partition Street, Saugerties. ($) Open daily 8:30-4; Friday through Sunday dinner also served 5-9. Breakfast is served all day in this tiny cozy eatery with an open kitchen. The organically produced foods are reasonably priced and made to order. There's carrot-coconut French toast, smoked chicken panini with cheddar, roasted red peppers, avocado aoli and greens on

Mary Anne Erickson, owner of Blue Mountain Bistro To Go on Route 28 between Kingston and Woodstock.

peasant bread, and excellent coffee. Don't bring the kids here, please...unless they can sit quietly and enjoy the fare!

Monkey Joe's Roasting Company & Coffee Bar (845-331-4598), 478 Broadway, Kingston. ($) Open Monday through Friday 6:30-6; Saturday 7:30-4. This café is housed in the Hutton building (1906), formerly an oyster house. The original tin ceiling, tile floor, lights, wainscoting, and fireplace make this charming renovated space relatively unchanged for over a century. It's a nice spot to enjoy organic coffee. For those who prefer tea or hot chocolate, there are other options. Children are welcome.

Nancy's of Woodstock Artisanal Creamery (917-605-4477), 105 Tinker Street, Woodstock. ($$) Ice cream, sorbet, sundaes and ice cream sandwiches, made from locally sourced ingredients. Yes, it's pricey, but it's excellent (a single scoop is $3.75; a double is $5.50; seven layer ice cream cakes go for $40; pints are $9). There's a nice patio for relaxing and it's next door to the *Station Bar & Curio*.

Oriole 9 (845-679-5783), 17 Tinker Street, Woodstock. ($$) Open for breakfast and lunch daily, except Thursday 9-4. Enjoy omelets, crepes, hearty soups, salads; all are served until late afternoon in a European café atmosphere. The place is filled with changing art exhibits featuring the work of Woodstock artists. Take note: the coffee here is the best in town. Keep in mind, however: on summer weekends the restaurant is exceedingly busy and noisy.

PAKT (845-331-2400), 608 Broadway, Kingston. ($) Open Thursday through Monday 10-4. The motto here is smartly sourced and packed with flavor. This eclectic Southern eatery offers all kinds of omelets, mac & cheese, catfish club sandwich, chicken & biscuit. Portions are generous and everything is prepared to order. Good food at reasonable prices. It can get crowded here on weekends so leave the kids at home!

R&R (Reynolds & Reynolds) Taproom (845-217-7921), 104 Mill Hill Road, Woodstock. ($) Monday & Thursday 4-10; Friday 4-midnight; Saturday 1pm-midnight; Sunday 1-10. This wine bar with several beers on tap—and in bottles—is a great place to relax and listen to live music (often on weekends). The menu has

Oriole 9 on Tinker Street in Woodstock, serves up some of the best coffee you can find in the county.

vegan and gluten free options and the food is quite good (snacks, sandwiches, small plates).

Shindig (845-684-7091), 1 Tinker Street, Woodstock. ($) Open Tuesday through Thursday 10-10; Friday, Saturday and Sunday 9am-10pm. Comfort food with local organic ingredients in an informal café atmosphere. Salads, burgers, mac & cheese with an imaginative twist. It's a small place so leave the kids home, please!

Sissy's Café (845-514-2336), 324 Wall Street, Kingston. ($) Open Monday through Friday 8-4; Saturday and Sunday 9-3. This is one of the best places in Kingston to get breakfast or lunch. The sandwiches, salads, and paninis are fresh, and the portions are generous. Their fakin' bacon tastes like the real thing, and there are several selections for vegans and vegetarians. I enjoy the Hot Bird Panini (turkey, bacon, avocado, red onion, and chipotle mayo with cheddar), which was tasty and satisfying. Children are welcome.

Station Bar & Curio (845-810-0203), 101 Tinker Street, Woodstock. ($) Open weekdays 4pm-2am; Friday through Sunday noon-2am. This renovated 1900 vintage Delaware & Ulster railroad station is now an old-fashioned pub with eight beers on tap and 30 others in bottles. Food selections are quite limited: grilled cheese, hummus, and perhaps another choice of a small plate or two.

Stockade Tavern (845-514-2649), 313 Fair Street, Kingston. ($$) Open daily 4pm-midnight; Friday and Saturday 4pm-2am. Closed Sunday. If you are in Kingston and have a hankering for excellent unusual cocktails served in contemporary surroundings, head for this bar. There are a few high-back booths and a pressed tin ceiling, and the building has been completely renovated. The pretzels, pickled eggs, and other savory snacks accompanying the imaginative drinks are particularly tasty. The bar is named for the Stockade District in Kingston, a part of uptown that dates back to the mid-17th century.

Stone Soup Food Company Cafe (845-340-0470), 470 Broadway, Kingston. ($) Open Monday through Friday 8-6. There are a few tables here, but this cozy spot is really just a wonderful take-out place featuring soups, chili, salads, sandwiches, and wraps. Curried chicken salad is one of my favorite choices; the grilled vegetable panini with pesto, fresh mozzarella and baby spinach, is excellent too. There are daily specials and tasty homemade baked goods for dessert.

Sunfrost (845-679-6690), 217 Tinker Street, Woodstock. ($) Open daily 8:30-6. In addition to a market with first-rate fruits and vegetables and a gourmet take-out deli, there is an adjoining juice bar/eatery with patio dining in the warm weather months. They serve several varieties of smoothies, burritos, overstuffed sandwiches, salads, and paninis. Everything is fresh, and much of the produce is organic. This is a great stop for a quick healthful snack or lunch. Local Woodstockers come here regularly for breakfast and lunch. My favorite soup is their three-bean chili.

Tony's Pizzeria (845-338-3978), 582 Broadway, Kingston. ($) Open Tuesday through Saturday 4-10; Sunday 1-9. For real home-style Italian thin-crust pizza, pasta, salads, calzones and stromboli, Tony's can't be beat. This is a great family place so if you have a large party, ask for the back room. Children welcome.

Two Ravens Tavern (845-383-1462), 316 Wall Street, Kingston. ($) Open daily noon-4am; Wednesday 4pm-4am. The Russian chef creates homemade dishes that are always interesting: the mushroom and potato dish and kasha salad are my favorites.

Southeastern Ulster County

Anatolia (845-255-1424), 76 Main Street, New Paltz. ($) Open daily 11-10. Turkish cuisine is one of my favorites and this restaurant has terrific kebabs, baba ghanoush and other traditional Turkish dishes. There is a pleasant relaxed setting where tables are far apart from one another….a nice change! The salads, lentil soup and enormous menu offers something to please every taste.

The Bakery (845-255-8840), 13A North Front Street, New Paltz. ($) Open daily 7-7. The bagels, butter cookies and overstuffed sandwiches, salads and paninis are first-rate here. The outdoor café is surrounded by gardens and is a good place to relax and enjoy a treat, a satisfying breakfast sandwich or lunch. Locals and travelers alike love this place. Children are welcome.

Café Mio (845-255-4949), 2356 Route 44/55, Gardiner. ($) Open daily, except Tuesday 8:30-4:30. This is a great place to stop for a hearty breakfast before setting out on a hike in the Shawangunks. They have a smoked salmon omelet that is wonderful. There are tofu scrambles, organic yogurt with granola and baked apple French toast. For lunch you can design your own burger. Cappuccino and lattés of all types are available, and a wide variety of teas are served. If you don't have time to relax and eat, they will prepare whatever you like to go. Children are welcome.

The Cheese Plate (845-255-2444), 10 Main Street, New Paltz. ($) Open daily 11-6. This oasis in the Water Street Market complex is a delightful place to stop for a snack. Enjoy a cheese plate, ice cream, gourmet coffee or tea here. There are several interesting gift items throughout, so take some time and look around after enjoying refreshments.

1850 House Inn & Tavern (845-658-7800), 435 Main Street, Rosendale. ($) Open Wednesday through Sunday 4-10. Pub fare and drinks (10 beers on tap) are served in this beautifully renovated tavern. Diners may enjoy burgers, sandwiches and salads. This is a delightful place to relax after strolling through Rosendale or hiking in the area.

El Paso Deli (845-691-7621), 78 Vineyard Avenue, Highland. ($) Open Monday through Friday 6am-5pm; Saturday 8-4. Closed Sunday. This casual family-run restaurant is a great spot to grab a quick taco ($1.50 each). It's a hole in the wall place, but the food is authentic Mexican and well prepared. The menu is quite large (quesadillas, nachos, fried chicken, burritos and enchiladas are available), and there is something here to please anyone who enjoys Mexican fare. Children are welcome.

Duo Restaurant on Wall Street in Kingston has an adjoining gourmet store stocked with great gifts and take-out items.

Gadaleto's Seafood Market & Restaurant (845-255-1717), 246 Main Street, Cherry Hill Shopping Center, New Paltz. ($$) Open daily, except Tuesday, 11-9. Enjoy fresh fish, shrimp, clams, crabs or lobster in this informal eatery adjoining a fish market. This is a great place to get take-out. Children are welcome.

Gilded Otter Restaurant & Brewery (845-256-1700), 3 Main Street, New Paltz. ($$) Open daily 11:30-10; Sunday noon-9. The dining room and pub here overlook the Wallkill River and offer views of the Shawangunks. This is a place beer lovers should try as the brew-master has created some award-winning beers.

Gomen Kudasai Noodle Shop (845-255-8811), 232 Main Street, New Paltz. ($$) Open daily, except Wednesday, for dinner 4:30-9:30; lunch served Saturday and Sunday 11:30-3. Gomen Kudasai means "welcome" in Japanese and this restaurant is a great place to enjoy the non-sushi cuisine of Japan. There are several soba noodle dishes, udon soups, tempuras and an array of vegan choices. Prices are reasonable and the service is excellent.

Karma Road (845-255-1099), 11 Main Street, New Paltz. ($) Open daily 8-8; Sunday until 6. The fresh organic ingredients change with the season but this is an oasis for those seeking healthful, fresh fast food to take out or eat at one of the few tables in the restaurant. The juices, smoothies, soups and sandwiches are excellent and include roasted chickpea and tempeh paella, sautéed greens, Thai rolls with peanut-chili sauce, and karma pesto pasta. If you are vegan or vegetarian, you will enjoy this place.

Lola's Café (845-255-6555), 49 Main Street, New Paltz. Open Monday through Thursday 11-9; Friday and Saturday 11-10; Sunday 11-8. Quick casual healthy food is served up here; sandwiches, wraps, salads of all kinds. Several bottled craft beers are also available.

Main Course (845-255-2600), 175 Main Street, New Paltz. ($) Open daily, except Monday, 11-9. Sunday 9-9. Fresh, delicious sandwiches and salads featuring contemporary American dishes with grilled fish specials and homemade pasta. This casual relaxing eatery with al fresco dining on a small patio in the warm weather, offers an array of healthful—and tasty—choices. Children are welcome.

Main Street Bistro (845-255-7766), 59 Main Street, New Paltz. ($) Open daily 8-4; Saturday and Sunday 7-5. This informal bistro serves hearty American breakfasts, lunches and weekend brunches in a casual atmosphere. The warm flour tortilla wrapped around scrambled eggs, bacon and cheddar is my favorite breakfast here. There are frittatas, pancakes and French toast. For lunch the hearty soups, wraps and sandwiches never disappoint. Children are welcome.

Pure City (845-744-8888), 100 Main Street, Pine Bush. ($) Open Tuesday through Saturday 11-10; Friday and Saturday until 11. Closed Sunday and Monday. This vegan Chinese restaurant provides an interesting variation on traditional Asian cuisine, with offerings like barbecued veggie ribs, sesame Spanish roll, and steamed mushrooms. The menu also includes veggie burgers, salads, noodle dishes, and intriguing desserts like green tea ice cream and tofu cheesecake. They do a big take-out business, and there are about 10 tables for eating in. Children are welcome.

Raccoon Saloon (845-236-7872), 1330 Route 9W, Marlboro. ($$) Open daily 11:30-10:30; Sunday until 9. Some of the best burgers in the region, along with excellent fries, chicken, ribs, soups, and salads, have been prepared here for decades. A renowned local eatery, it is a popular casual stop for lunch or dinner. There is also a cozy bar with great views of the Hudson River. Children are welcome.

Rosendale Café (845-658-9048), 434 Main Street, Rosendale. ($) Open daily 11-10. This vegetarian restaurant offers a variety of soups, salads, sandwiches, and pasta dishes. Try the Fakin' Bacon FLT. The nachos and burritos are quite

The Rosendale Cafe is known for hearty comfort food and also as a venue for fine musical performances on weekends.

good. Their meatless black-bean chili over brown rice is excellent. Organic coffees and homemade desserts are served. There is music on most weekends, and it is usually quality entertainment.

Village Tea Room (845-255-3434), 10 Plattekill Avenue, New Paltz. ($) Open Wednesday through Saturday 8am-9pm; Sunday 8-8. Enjoy home-baked muffins, scones, and other treats, as well as light lunches and country suppers here. The emphasis is on fresh local products. All eggs used are organic, and so is the oatmeal. The Murray's Natural Chicken and roasted pepper sandwich with cilantro almond relish on seven-grain health bread is delicious. The tearoom is located in a 200-year-old building with exposed hand-hewn beams. Afternoon tea is available all day and includes sandwiches, a scone with fresh jam and clotted cream, a plate of cookies and pot of tea. There is outdoor dining in the warm weather. A children's tea is offered with kids' tastes considered!

Northwestern Ulster County

Belladiel Pizzeria & Restaurant (845-663-3680), 3187 Route 28, Shokan. ($) Open daily, except Tuesday, 11:30-9. They serve pizza as well as Guatemalan, Mexican and Peruvian cuisine in this informal eclectic eatery. Empañadas, tacos and many more selections are available on a large menu. The pizza is particularly good and local residents line up for it on weekends. The location is quite convenient, at Winchell's Corners. Children are welcome.

Brio's (845-688-5370), 68 Main Street, Phoenicia. ($) Open daily 7am-11pm. This luncheonette is a good place to stop for pizza or hearty chili. The breakfasts are terrific featuring 10 kinds of pancakes. A popular place with local residents, kids will love the spaghetti and meatballs.

Fruition Chocolate (845-657-6717), 3091 Route 28, Shokan. ($$) Open Tuesday through Sunday 11-5. A retail store at 17 Tinker Street in Woodstock is open noon to 6 daily, except Tuesday. Chocoholics take note: This handcrafted bean to bar chocolate workshop and retail store, owned and operated by Ulster County native, Bryan Graham, is open to the public. The chocolate here has won international awards and it is made from fair trade organically grown cocoa beans. If you have a craving for some of the world's finest chocolate, make sure to stop here and indulge!

Marty's Mercantile (845-657-4159), 4075 Route 28A, West Shokan. ($) Open Monday through Friday 7-3; Saturday and Sunday 9-5. Breakfast and lunch are prepared beautifully in this delightful eatery. The menu is limited, but delicious. My favorite sandwich is the spiced, breaded organic chicken breast topped with melted Havarti, horseradish aioli, red onion, lettuce and tomato on bread of your choice. Breakfast includes several egg dishes. Local gourmet products are available for sale and, lest I forget, the coffee is first-rate. Children are welcome.

Phoenicia Diner (845-688-9957), 5681 Route 28, Phoenicia. ($) Open daily 7-5. (Closed Tuesday and Wednesday during the winter months.) Opened in the autumn of 2012, this has become a popular destination, with its soda fountain, Formica counters, and retro barstools. The owner, Michael Cioffi, uses the products of several local purveyors. French toast and waffles are served all day long, along with excellent egg dishes. Comfort food is featured for lunch and includes corned beef hash, meat loaf and hearty soups. There are plenty of vegetarian selections as well. Children are welcome.

Pine View Bakery (845-657-8925), 3374 Route 28, Shokan. ($) Open daily 7-3; Saturday and Sunday 6-4. This eatery offers simple, straightforward fare at amazingly reasonable prices. It's an old-fashioned place with a counter and six or seven tables at most. The place has a large loyal customer base, almost all locals. I enjoy having breakfast on the terrace during the summer and always order the egg sandwich on their fresh eight-grain brad. Children are welcome, but it's a small place, so they can't run around here without getting underfoot.

Sweet Sue's (845-688-7852), Open Friday through Monday 8-1. This is a renowned breakfast and lunch place, with more than a dozen types of spectacular pancakes and French toast (my favorite is walnut crunch). Everything, from muffins to soups and all desserts, is homemade. This is a casual café with a good reputation, so make sure to arrive early on weekend mornings: there can be a line out the door. Children will love the fare here.

ENTERTAINMENT

PERFORMING ARTS

Backstage Studio Productions (845-481-5158; bspkingston.com), 323 Wall Street, Kingston. An early 1900s building featuring live music concerts, dance classes, and an art gallery with changing exhibits. There are 75,000 square feet of space and a 2000-seat concert hall. The website lists the full schedule.

Bearsville Theater (845-679-4406; bearsvilletheater.com), 291 Tinker Street, Woodstock. There are nationally renowned musicians who perform here throughout the year. For updated concert and events listings, check the website.

Belleayre Music Festival (845-254-6094; belleayre.com), 181 Galli Curci Road, Highmount. On Saturday nights during the summer there are jazz concerts under a tent as well as lawn seating at reduced prices. The evening concerts offer cool summer's night entertainment.

Colony Woodstock (845-679-7625; colonywoodstock.com), 22 Rock City Road, Woodstock. Open Thursday through Monday, 7pm to close, this music

venue/bar is located in a fascinating building that dates back to 1929. A cross between an American diner and British pub, it's a great place to hear live music in Woodstock. Reopened and renovated in 2017, this intimate venue features terrific entertainment. I saw Maria Muldaur and John Sebastian perform here, as well as Darlene Love.

Commune Saloon (845-684-0367), 297 Tinker Street, Woodstock. Open daily 5-11; Friday and Saturday until midnight. This 65-seat bar/restaurant has an adjoining billiards room and a large stone patio around a circular fire pit for outdoor dining in the warm weather

The Colony Cafe on Meads Mountain Road in Woodstock attracts excellent performers year-round.

months. There is usually live music on weekends and the food is simple bar fare: burgers, wings, pizza and salads. This is a fun place to go on summer weekends and families will be comfortable in the outdoor venue.

Kleinert/James Arts Center of the Woodstock Guild (845-679-2079; woodstockguild.org), 34 Tinker Street, Woodstock, offers a series of musical performances year-round.

Levon Helm Studios (845-679-2744; levonhelm.com), 160 Plochmann Lane, Woodstock. Although legendary musician Helm passed away in 2012, the barn on his property is still open for weekend performances, usually held once a month, known as "rambles." Woodstock is home to several well-know rock musicians who enjoy performing in this unusual venue, at one time Helm's recording studio. Amy Helm, daughter of Levon, also a musician, has kept her father's spirit alive here!

Live at the Falcon (845-236-7970; liveatthefalcon.com), 1348 Route 9W, Marlboro. Open year-round, with performances Thursday through Sunday nights, usually beginning around 10pm. Sunday jazz brunch 10-2. This bustling live-music venue offers a potpourri of world-class blues and jazz performers. There are no tickets, no cover charge, and no minimum here. The place overlooks the Hudson and there's dining on the deck overlooking a gorge in the warm weather months. There's also a pub under the club, *The Falcon Underground*, a beer garden and taproom featuring spirits produced in New York State.

Maverick Concerts (845-679-8217; maverickconcerts.org), 120 Maverick Road, Woodstock. Chamber music concerts on Sunday afternoons in July and August. Admission. Founded in 1916 by author Hervey White, the Maverick Concerts were to be a blend of the best that chamber music and the natural world had to offer. White wanted to encourage other "maverick" artists, and he attracted some of the premier string and wind players of the time to this glass and wood concert hall. The building seats about 400, but many people enjoy hearing the concerts from the surrounding hillside, a setting that was White's idea of perfection. The concerts are the oldest chamber music series in the country and they are still attracting the best groups in the world, among them the Tokyo, Shanghai, Miami and Emerson string quartets. They also offer children's concerts on Saturday mornings in July and August at 11am.

Mount Tremper Arts (845-688-9893; mounttremperarts.org), 647 South Plank Road, Mount Tremper. Mid-July through August. This world-class performance and visual arts venue is housed in a post-and-beam studio between Woodstock and Phoenicia. There are dance, opera, and music performances during the summer months, as well as art and photography exhibits.

Phoenicia International Festival of the Voice (845-688-1344; phoeniciavoicefest.org), Parish Field, Ursula Drive, Phoenicia, features world-class performances. From opera to gospel, world music to Broadway favorites, this venue celebrates the human voice in all its multifaceted glory. The summer season is when performances are held outdoors.

Ulster Performing Arts Center (845-331-1613; upac.org), 601 Broadway, Kingston, is on the National Register of Historic Places. The renovated Broadway theatre is the largest arts showcase in the county, offering a variety of theater productions and concerts year-round.

Unison Arts and Learning Center (845-255-1559; unisonarts.org), 68 Mountain Rest Road, New Paltz, is a multi-arts center with performances of jazz, folk, world music, and dance. There are also poetry readings, children's theater, workshops, and monthly art exhibits and an outdoor sculpture garden. Open year-round, Monday through Friday 10-5 and during performances.

Woodstock Film Festival (845-679-4265; woodstockfilmfestival.com), at various venues throughout the town, as well as in Rhinebeck and Rosendale. Separate admission is charged at each film or seminar. Since 2000 the five-day (Wednesday through Sunday) annual program features over 100 films along with seminars, workshops and an awards ceremony. The festival is held in late September or during the month of October; the date varies from year to year.

THEATER

Bird-On-A-Cliff Theatre Company (845-247-4007; birdonacliff.org) produces a Shakespeare festival on the grounds of the Comeau property (by the town offices) in Woodstock every July and August, Friday through Sunday. They also feature dramatic productions. This is a good place to enjoy a picnic dinner and take in some theater at the right price ($5 suggested donation per person). Performances begin at 5pm; the website lists the schedule.

Coach House Players (845-331-2476; coachhouseplayers.org), 12 Augusta Street, Kingston. This community theater group performs four times a year in its venue, an original coach house.

Community Playback Theatre (845-691-4118; playbackcentre.org), 150 Kisor Road, Highland. An improvisational theater company that weaves the stories told by audience members into scenes that are then "played back" on the spot.

Piano Summer at New Paltz and the School of Fine & Performing Arts at SUNY New Paltz (845-257-3860;newpaltz.edu/piano), 1 Hawk Drive,

New Paltz. This program, under the aegis of internationally acclaimed pianist Vladimir Feltsman, offers master classes (some may be audited by the public), as well as concerts during the month of July. SUNY New Paltz offers workshops and lectures by visiting artists and composers that are open to the public.

Performing Arts of Woodstock (845-679-7900; performingartsofwoodstock. org), Woodstock Town Hall, 76 Tinker Street, Woodstock. For nearly 50 years this company has been offering high-quality new and classic theater productions in the community. There are usually three plays presented each year. The price is reasonable and the quality is high.

Shadowland Stages (845-647-5511; shadowlandstages.org), 157 Canal Street, Ellenville. This is the county's only professional nonprofit theater company, featuring a five-play main-stage season from May through September. Offerings include contemporary dramas, comedies, classics, and new plays. The theater first opened in 1920 as an art deco movie and vaudeville house. Renovations have rebuilt the interior retaining the charm of the past and creating a 148-seat intimate venue for the theater. All seats are within 25 feet of the stage.

Shandaken Theatrical Society (845-688-2279; stsplayhouse.com), 10 Church Street, Phoenicia, is a community-theater organization that produces a musical in the spring, a drama or comedy in the fall, and a summer production. There are several films shown here as well.

SELECTIVE SHOPPING

Ulster County has a number of interesting villages and Kingston, the county seat: all are filled with boutiques, galleries, bookstores and places that sell everything from teapots and hand-blown glass, to soaps and chocolates.

NOTE: In the city of Kingston, and the villages of New Paltz and Saugerties, you need to pay careful attention to the parking meters. The attendants in Kingston and New Paltz are particularly strict. If you are only moments late, count on receiving a minimum of a $20 ticket. This does not make for a relaxing shopping experience hence many locals shop elsewhere. In Saugerties there are two large parking lots conveniently located. However, in Kingston and New Paltz, decent parking remains an ongoing problem.

The following stores are my favorite places to shop in the county:

Bop to Tottom (845-338-8100), 334 Wall Street, Kingston, is open Monday through Saturday, 10-6. Karen Clark Adin, one of the people responsible for the amazing renaissance in uptown, owns this fantastic bazaar. It is filled with the latest fashions in handbags, scarves, costume jewelry, an array of novelty items, and gifts, all at incredibly reasonable prices. The name of the store is difficult to forget. You will usually find something you love, but did not know you were looking for!

Clouds (845-679-8155), 1 Mill Hill Road, Woodstock, is open daily 11-6 (closed Tuesday & Wednesday during part of the winter). To see top-of-the-line American crafts, including porcelain, glassware, woodwork, and jewelry, this is the place to go. Even if you are window-shopping, don't pass this store by: they have an amazing selection of fine gifts.

Clove and Creek, 73 Broadway, Kingston. Open daily, except Tuesday, 11-6. This hip, eclectic store has an interesting array of accessories for home and hearth. Owner Scott Nield serves Parlor coffee and home baked treats that enhance the welcoming atmosphere here. If you are looking for a gift of any kind, this is a store that will make shopping for that special something fun!

Duo Pantry (845- 340-1237), 297 Wall Street, Kingston. Open daily, except Monday, 10-6. If you're looking for a gourmet gift item produced in the Hudson Valley, an autographed local book, or crave some fine take-out, make sure to stop here. Adjoining the excellent restaurant, Duo, the "pantry" is a must stop after lunch.

Emerson Country Stores (845-688-5800), 5340 Route 28, Mount Tremper. Open daily 9-5. The Emerson Resort & Spa includes several wonderful gift shops adjoining the hotel. In addition to a kitchen/gourmet shop, antique market, clothing, and toy stores, there is one shop that specializes in kaleidoscopes of all kinds. The selection of local books is excellent. Do stop in at their café for coffee and a snack after shopping! There's plenty to see here.

Fed On Lights (845-246-8444), 34 Market Street, Saugerties is open Friday through Monday, noon-5:30. This is an amazing shop, and the two floors here are worth browsing for anyone passing through Saugerties. It is packed with 19th and 20th century lamps and plumbing fixtures, claw-foot tubs, marble-top sinks, and all kinds of items you might have given up on ever finding.

Fruition Chocolate (845-657-6717), 3091 Route 28, Shokan & 17 Tinker Street, Woodstock (845-684-5874). Open Tuesday through Sunday 11-5 in Shokan and Wednesday through Monday noon-6 in Woodstock. This small-batch, bean-to-bar workshop in Shokan has won international awards for its distinctive dark chocolate, made without milk. Local resident Bryan Graham's chocolate bars are expensive, but worth trying if you're a chocoholic. The best seller in both locations is still the 100 percent dark chocolate bar, but there are several varieties to enjoy.

Green Cottage (845-687-4810), 1204 Route 213, High Falls, is open daily, except Tuesday, 10-5. Both a florist and fine gift shop, there are a number of unusual items if you are looking for something special (jewelry, scarves, bags, and beautiful accessories).

Handmade and More (845-255-6277), 6 North Front Street, New Paltz, is open daily 10-7 (until 6 on Sunday). This wonderful gift shop features the work of local craftspeople: clothing, jewelry, glass, pottery and toys.

H. Houst & Son (845-679-2115), 4 Mill Hill Road, Woodstock, is open daily, 8-6. While this is one of the best old-fashioned hardware stores you will find in the Hudson Valley, it is also chock-full of basic necessities along with books, magazines, kitchen items and all kinds of interesting gifts. The prices are excellent too, so I rarely have to head to any box stores in Kingston! They can order anything and match the discounts of the chains.

Hurley Country Store (845-338-4843), 2 Wamsley Place, next to the Hurley Town Hall, is one of the most eclectic shops you will find anywhere, with a variety of unusual toys, regional books, model trains and accessories, gourmet foods, and much much more. Owner Glenn Carlberg is an interesting character and he is at the store daily. If you are in the Hurley area, make a stop here!

Inquiring Mind Bookstore (845-246-5775), 65 Partition Street, Saugerties, is open daily 10-9; Sunday until 6. Here you will find an excellent selection of new releases, best sellers and literary gems. There's even a cozy café in this spacious store. The New Paltz "branch" is called **Inquiring Minds** (845-255-8300), 6 Church Street. This bookstore is also worth a stop for bibliophiles!

Jean Turmo Ltd. (845-679-7491), 11 Tinker Street, Woodstock, is open daily 10:30-5:30, and this spacious, inviting shop has something for everyone. It's

housed in a lavender building in the center of town, across from the village green. Owner Rebecca Turmo will create your own shampoo and moisturizer depending upon what fragrance you select from the numerous choices. She carries all kinds of fine soaps and creams for both men and women, as well as a variety of teas, teapots, cards, books, nightlights, handbags, and the best selection of sexy reading glasses you will find anywhere. This is a wonderful place to browse, and the owners aim to please. There IS a Jean Turmo....and she is at the store part-time!

For over 40 years, Jean Turmo, in the center of Woodstock, has been stocking unusual gifts and personal care items.

Kenco Outfitters (845-340-0552), 1000 Hurley Mountain Road, Kingston is open Monday through Friday 9-7; Saturday 9-6; Sunday 11-5. This locally owned and operated family business has been around for over 35 years selling quality clothing, footwear, and kayaks, as well as camping & hiking gear of all kinds. They are known as "the work and play outfitter" and that is exactly what they are. Watch for their semi-annual sales since you can find some excellent bargains at those times!

Light House (845-246-1000), 86 Partition Street, Saugerties, is open daily 11-6 (limited hours in the winter months). I love this store with its array of unusual gift items for the bedroom, kitchen and bath, as well as soaps, perfume, and baby gifts. Do not miss this shop if you are in Saugerties. Owner Shari Weingarten has filled it with beautiful things; you will always find something for yourself, even when looking for a gift for someone else!

Morne Imports (845-688-7738), 52 Main Street, Phoenicia, is open every day 7-6. This is the place to go for fishing, camping, hiking, and hunting gear, as well as newspapers, magazines and local books. The store is also the bus stop in town with service to New York City.

Rough Draft Bar & Books (609-351-2035), 82 John Street, Kingston. Open Tuesday through Sunday 11am-11pm. Enjoy craft beer, Hudson Valley wines, cider, coffee and espresso drinks, while perusing an array of books and magazines. Also, meet a variety of fascinating authors at this welcome addition to Uptown Kingston (as of November 2017), a popular gathering place for the local literati thanks to owners, Amanda and Anthony Stromoski.

Rough Draft Bar & Books, a welcome addition to Uptown Kingston in 2017.

Scandinavian Grace (845-657-2759), 2866 Route 28, Shokan, open Friday through Sunday 11-6, is a fantastic fun space with 5000 square feet of furniture, rugs, glassware, and dozens of items for the kitchen and bedroom, all made in Denmark, Norway and Sweden. There are Marimekko pillows and kitchen towels at reasonable prices, as well as soaps, gourmet food items, and even shoes. Owner Fredrik Larsson will be glad to answer any questions you may have about the merchandise. A café on the premises serves gourmet coffees, teas, pastries, and Scandinavian cakes and cookies. The shop is truly an oasis not to be missed by travelers heading east or west on Route 28. You will see the colorful flags of all the Scandinavian countries prominently displayed outside as you approach the store.

The Tender Land Home (845-688-7213), 64 Main Street, Phoenicia, is open daily, except Wednesday, 10-6; Saturday until 8. The fine kitchenware and tasteful home accessories here make it one of the best places in the county to find an unusual gift. High-quality merchandise at reasonable prices is what shoppers will be delighted to find. Once I went in looking for a small gift for a friend and came out with two hand-painted pillows for my bedroom! Dave Pillard, the owner, is always there with helpful suggestions too.

Water Street Market (845-255-1403), 10 Main Street, a village within the village of New Paltz, with more than 30 shops, cafes, and galleries, is a great place to wander and relax. And there's plenty of free parking. The market is located across the street from an entrance to the Wallkill Valley Rail Trail.

ANTIQUES

Ever since the 17th century, people in Ulster County have been accumulating things, which now turn up as valuable antiques. But even if you don't collect rare furniture, you can enjoy hunting down that special collectible vase or colorful quilt. Auctions are listed in the local papers, and yard sales pop up every weekend during the spring and summer. There are numerous antiques shops throughout the county. The following places include antiques centers with several dealers under one roof and give browsers a wide selection. Since no listing of a center's stock is ever comprehensive, visitors will never know what treasures they may find while exploring on their own! Call for hours before heading out.

Craftsmen's Gallery (845-688-2100), 48 Route 214, Phoenicia, has mission and mission-style collectibles and antiques. In nearby Shandaken, the **Blue Barn Market Place** (845-688-2161), 7053 Route 28 (5000 square-feet) is where to shop for a variety of furniture and decorative accessories, as well as clothing and knick-knacks.

In High Falls, **Barking Dog Antiques** (845-6874834), 7 Second Avenue and Route 213, has an eclectic assortment of items emphasizing Americana. They are open year-round on weekends only, noon-5. In Pine Bush, the **Country Heritage Antiques Center** (845-744-3792), has a large collection of 18th and 19th century furniture and accessories. In New Paltz, check out **Water Street Antiques Center** (845-255-1043), 10 Main Street, at the Water Street Market, and **Jenkinstown Antiques** (845-255-4876), 520 Route 32, south of town. Both have interesting selections of furniture, jewelry and collectibles.

Van Deusen House Antiques (845-331-8852), 59 Main Street, Hurley, has a nice selection of furniture and collectibles. **Skillypot Antiques Center** (845-338-6779), 41 Broadway, in the Rondout section of Kingston, is a co-op of several dealers with lamps, glassware and collectibles. One of my favorite relatively new shops is **Exit Nineteen** (845-514-2485), 309 Wall Street, in the uptown area of Kingston. They specialize in mid-century antiques and home furnishings and have some truly fine pieces.

The **Saugerties Antiques Center** (845-246-8234), 220 Main Street, is located in the middle of town. There are smaller shops in Saugerties on both Main and Partition streets that carry antiques as well.

If you are in Woodstock on a weekend in May through November, stop by **Mower's Flea Market** (845-679-6744), 11 Maple Lane, where there are antiques, collectibles, clothing, organic produce, plants and much more.

If you are interested in attending an auction, **JMW Auction Service** (845-389-1933; jmwauction.com), 612 Washington Avenue in Kingston specializes in fun sales. The website lists a schedule.

ART GALLERIES

Anyone interested in the arts should leave a couple of hours free in the afternoon since most are closed in the morning, to drive to the following galleries and points of interest in Kingston and Woodstock. Both towns are filled with wonderful paintings, photography, and sculpture in an array of places, some off the beaten path. The Arts Society of Kingston coordinates the First Saturday Art Openings at galleries throughout the city on the first Saturday of the month. Check the website, askforarts.org, for a full schedule of events. The Art Trolley runs from 5 to 9pm that evening taking visitors to different venues throughout the city.

ARTBAR Gallery (845-338-2789), 674 Broadway, Kingston is open year-round, Thursday through Saturday, 2-9pm, and has First Saturday openings. This is a comfortable place to share art with family and friends. Nearby is **Arts**

Society of Kingston (A.S. K.) Gallery (845-338-0331), 97 Broadway. They feature changing shows of the work of local artists (open Tuesday through Saturday 1-6pm; First Saturday 5-8pm).

In Woodstock, the perpetual art colony, don't miss the **Center for Photography at Woodstock** (845-679-9957), 59 Tinker Street, open year round, Wednesday through Sunday, noon-5, with its changing selection of photography exhibits throughout the year. There are workshops, lectures, a library, and archives here as well. **The Historical Society of Woodstock** (845-679-2256), 20 Comeau Drive, is open Memorial Day weekend through Labor Day, Saturday and Sunday 1-5pm. Founded in 1929 by a group of artists and local citizens, visitors will enjoy art exhibits in the historic Eames House. An extensive archive with paintings, photos, books, documents and recordings, may be accessed by appointment only. The **Woodstock Guild** (845-679-2079), 34 Tinker Street, is open year-round, Friday through Sunday 10-5, featuring art exhibits, readings, classes and concerts. A few doors away is the **Woodstock Artists' Association** (845-679-2940), 28 Tinker Street, open year-round, Thursday through Monday, noon-5, where visitors will see a variety of work by local artists along with the work of the original Woodstock Art Colony artists of days long gone. **Woodstock Framing Gallery** (845-679-6003), 31 Mill Hill Road, is open daily, except Wednesday, 11-5. The emphasis is on contemporary art, and the majority of exhibitors are Hudson Valley artists. Nationally renowned painter Richard Segalman, whose work is in several museums in Manhattan and Naples, Florida, shows his work in this gallery. Diagonally across the street is the **Fletcher Gallery** (845-679-4411), 40 Mill Hill Road, with its focus on 20th-century American artists, including Peter Max. They are open Thursday through Sunday noon-5, and by appointment.

Take a drive out of town west on Route 212 toward Phoenicia, and you will come to the **Elena Zang Gallery** (845-679-5432), 3671 Route 212, Shady, just four miles from the center of Woodstock. They are open year-round, daily 11-5. This on-site pottery/gallery features handmade porcelain and stoneware along with contemporary painting and the sculpture of many internationally known artists, including Mary Frank, Joan Snyder, and Judy Pfaff. There is an outdoor sculpture show year-round in a beautiful garden setting. Visitors are invited to walk around the grounds and enjoy the stream that runs through the property. Children will feel comfortable here; this is one of my favorite art venues and Elena is welcoming and knowledgeable!

If you continue west on Route 212 to Willow, you will come to the **James Cox Gallery** (845-679-7608), 4666 Route 212, which is open year-round Tuesday through Sunday 10-5. Cox is a veteran art dealer who relocated to Woodstock from Manhattan in 1990, and his gallery has changing exhibits of painting and sculpture in a beautiful garden setting. Mary Anna Goetz, his wife, exhibits her beautiful paintings here as well.

In New Paltz, the **Mark Gruber Gallery** (845-255-1241), 17 New Paltz Plaza, near NYS Thruway exit 18, specializes in Hudson Valley artists, primarily painters and photographers, with changing exhibits every six weeks. They are open year-round, daily, except Sunday.

POTTERY & CERAMICS

Ulster County is home to the studios of several nationally renowned potters. For those interested in visiting the artists' studios, many potteries are open to the public. They are located in High Falls, Stone Ridge, Accord, West Park, Bloomington, and West Hurley. The website, potterytrail.com, contains detailed directions and photos of the work.

SPECIAL EVENTS

February: Maple tours take place in late winter when the sap begins to run. There is nothing to match the fragrance of steamy maple syrup. At **Arrowhead Maple Syrup Farm** (845-626-7293), 5941 Route 209, Kerhonkson, tours are offered daily, noon-5; but call before you go to confirm hours. **Lyonsville Sugarhouse and Farm** (845-687-2518), 591 Route 2, Accord, also offers tours, but call before going as everything is weather dependent. Annual **Chili Bowl Fiesta** (845-658-9133), Ulster County Community College, 491 Cottekill Road, Stone Ridge. Over 700 bowls and tumblers handmade in the Women's Studio Workshop's ceramic studio are on sale on this late February afternoon. The bowls are filled with chili donated by local chefs.

March: **St. Patrick's Day Parade** (845-331-7517), Broadway, Kingston. Numerous bands and floats celebrate the wearing of the green with this annual colorful celebration in the county seat.

April: **Annual Pasta Primo Vino** (845-256-8456). Experience the region's fine wines paired with sample pasta dishes at all 15 wineries along the Shawangunk Wine Trail. Two day tickets, one day tickets and designated driver tickets are options.

May: **Woodstock/New Paltz Art and Crafts Fair** (845-679-8087), Ulster County Fairgrounds, 249 Libertyville Road, New Paltz. Shows are held Memorial Day weekend and Labor Day weekend, Saturday and Sunday 10-5:30; Monday 10-4. Admission. This huge fair offers more than just booths of crafts; some of the region's finest artisans are on hand each year to exhibit their works. The craftspeople demonstrate their skills, which include quilting, scrimshaw, weaving, pottery and broom making. There is a children's tent with art projects for young fairgoers; face painting is a popular activity. Furniture and architectural crafts, regionally produced foods, entertainment, wine, and dozens of food vendors are all there. The large tents will shield you from the sun, but dress appropriately for the weather—it can get hot, both inside and outside the tents (and, if it rains, make sure to wear heavy shoes... it does get muddy). On a beautiful day, this is a great place to go with the family or friends!

June: **Independence Day Celebration in Kingston** (845-331-7517), Rondout waterfront. Kingston occasionally celebrates the nation's birthday the weekend before July 4th. Enjoy music, food, games, and fireworks after sunset.

July: There are **4th of July Celebrations** in **Highland** (845-691-2144), over the **Walkway (**845-454-9649), in **Saugerties** (845-246-9701) and **Ellenville** (845-647-4620). In Saugerites there is a parade at 11am and bands and vendors during the day. Fireworks begin at 9pm. Call for up-to-date happenings!

Annual Hurley Stone House Day (845-331-7728), Main Street, Hurley. Tour America's older private homes in a National Historic Landmark hamlet. Costumed guides craft demonstrations, children's activities, historic reenactors and more. Admission. Rain or shine.

August: **Ulster County Fair** (845-255-1380), Ulster County Fairgrounds, 249 Libertyville Road, New Paltz. One price admission includes all rides, shows, parking and exhibits. Tuesday through Sunday, the first weekend of the month. The kids will love this fair.

Annual Phoenicia International Festival of the Voice (845-688-6900). Offering a diverse range of world-class vocal artists including opera, Broadway musicals, plays, and children's programs. Each summer has a different theme (in 2017 it was all things French) and the entertainment takes place at several venues throughout the town.

Annual Artists' Soapbox Derby (845-339-2996), Lower Broadway in the Rondout area, Kingston. Free. The carlike creations that ride down lower Broadway are something to behold. If you are in town at this time, make sure to stop by. The cars start to roll at noon.

Saugerties Artists Studio Tour (845-246-7493). Free and open to the public. Discover the work of painters, sculptors, printmakers, potters and mixed media artists while driving to their studios with help from a map. Held on a weekend in mid-August from 10am to 6pm, this experience provides an enjoyable way to meet some amazing people while learning about the Hudson Valley's artistic heritage.

Wild Blueberry & Huckleberry Festival (845-647-4620), Canal Street, Ellenville. This is a street fair celebrating the Shawangunk Mountains, with folk music, barbecue, all-blueberry bake sale, pie-judging contest, crafts, children's activities, and exhibits. Nearly 200 vendors participate from 9am-4pm; pancake breakfast 7:30-11 at Norbury Hall, Center Street. Free.

September: **Hooley on the Hudson** (845-338-6622), T.R. Gallo Park, 1 Broadway, Kingston. This Irish festival sponsored by the Ancient Order of Hibernians in Ulster County takes place each year on the Sunday of Labor Day weekend. Free. There's Celtic music, Irish step dancing, pipes and drums, crafts, and food vendors. This event is fun for the entire family.

Headless Horseman Hayrides (845-339-2666), 778 Broadway (Route 9W), Ulster Park. Named the Number 1 Haunted Attraction in the U.S., this hayride, six haunted houses, and corn maze runs from the last two weekends in September and every Friday, Saturday and Sunday in October, evenings from dusk to 11pm. Reservations are required. Admission. There are illusions, special effects, acres of thrills and chills, and a cast of more than 100 performers to entertain you on this 35-minute hayride.

Hudson Valley Garlic Festival (845-246-3090), Cantine Field, Saugerties, last weekend of the month. Admission. Visitors don't need a map to find this festival: the nutty fragrance of garlic attracts tens of thousands to this

The Woodstock/New Paltz Art & Craft Fair every Memorial Day and Labor Day weekend is an Ulster County tradition.

weekend celebration, where garlic-flavored foods, from pizza to ice cream, await the connoisseur. Craftspeople and entertainment enliven the daily activities, and there are dozens of garlic vendors.

Woodstock Comedy Festival, Bearsville Theater, Woodstock. There are big names in stand-up comedy here every year for a weekend in mid-September and they perform at various venues throughout town. Past comedians participating include Mario Cantone, Susie Essman, Gilbert Gottfried and Eddie Brill. Enjoy panels, performances and parties: and leave the kids home.

October: **Burning of Kingston** (845-331-7517). In 1777 the British invaded and burned the city of Kingston. Now the city reenacts the battle, complete with British and American troops and period music, crafts, food, and entertainment. The battle takes place the second weekend in October, but call for specific times and events. Free.

Family of New Paltz Turkey Trot (845-481-3534), Water Street Market, 10 Main Street, New Paltz. This three-mile run/walk is fun for the entire family. The races are 9-11am.

Mum Festival (845-246-2809), Seamon Park, 5 Malden Avenue, south of the village of Saugerties. Open dawn to dusk. Free. For the entire month of October, Seamon Park is one big chrysanthemum celebration. Thousands of mums bloom throughout the 17-acre park at this time, and the display of yellow, lavender, and rust-colored flowers in shaped beds is breathtaking. The actual festival is held the first Sunday in October, with music, entertainment and a parade, but the park is open to visitors throughout the year.

O+ Festival, Kingston. Every October internationally known artists come to Kingston and make large-scale permanent murals that reflect the history and culture of the city and its diverse population. These creative individuals receive complimentary health care from local medical personnel in exchange for their work. The weekend festival includes live music, film screenings, dance parties and more, at various venues throughout the city.

Woodstock Invitational Luthiers Showcase (845-679-4406), Bearsville Theater, 291 Tinker Street, Woodstock. Admission. Friday, Saturday and Sunday, 11-6. Celebrating the art and craft of lutherie, and the music inspired by and made on these instruments, this annual weekend gathering displays the best acoustic guitars ever made. Meet the artisans who make them. There are nearly 100 exhibitors from as far away as Japan, Italy, France and Sweden; Baker Rorick, a Woodstock resident, organizes a fascinating show.

November: **Greek Festival** (845-331-3522), St. George Greek Orthodox Church, 294 Greenkill Avenue, Kingston. Free. Enjoy all the Greek culinary specialties here, along with a holiday boutique. Held the weekend before Thanksgiving on Friday, Saturday and Sunday.

International Pickle Festival (845-204-8827), Community Center, 1055 Route 32, Rosendale. This unusual, fun festival is held the Sunday before Thanksgiving. There are dozens of food booths with wares from Germany, Romania, and Japan, as well as throughout the United States. Enjoy free samples, listen to live music, and discover great holiday gifts. You can enter your pickled goods in the contests. There is even a pickle toss and pickle juice drinking contest.

Kingston Model Railroad Club Train Show (845-334-8233), 99 Susan Street, Kingston. Admission. A complete 'O' Scale Railroad system in Action may be seen here along with scale models of steam and diesel locomotives. The complete villages and scenery are modeled after Hudson Valley towns. The kids will love these displays, but so will everyone else!

The Woodstock Invitational Luthiers Showcase is an annual October event that attracts exhibitors from throughout the world.

Sinterklaas! (845-514-3998/339-4280), A festive celebration with open houses, musical performances and workshops creating crowns and branches, a blessing of the animals ceremony and maritime parade on lower Broadway. Kingston celebrates its Dutch heritage with the story of Sinterklaas's arrival in the Hudson Valley the Saturday of Thanksgiving weekend.

December: **Frozendale in Rosendale** (845-658-3131), Main Street, Rosendale. This annual December tradition celebrates the coming of winter with events held both indoors and out. There is hot chocolate, live music, gifts for sale, and open houses at the art galleries and shops. The event is held the first weekend in December.

Holiday in the Village of Saugerties (845-246-1337), Market, Main and Partition Streets. There are horse-drawn wagon rides; crafts, entertainment and Santa will delight the kids at the historic Kiersted House. Enjoy carolers singing on Main Street and the Christmas tree lighting. Merchants remain open late with free refreshments for shoppers. The festivities are held the first Saturday in December.

Polar Express Train Ride (845-688-7400), 149 Aaron Court, Kingston. The Catskill Mountain Railroad created this wonderful ride where kids of all ages will discover the magic of Christmas aboard this train inspired by the book and film, "The Polar Express." The train leaves from an area adjacent to Kingston Plaza in the city.

Woodstock Open House (845-679-6234), Tinker Street, Woodstock. Held on the first Saturday in December from 5-9pm, this celebration includes all shops in the village staying open late and offering treats including cookies and hot cider to holiday shoppers. Windows are decorated, and there's a festive air throughout the town.

Wreath Fineries at the Wineries (845-256-8456). Follow the Shawangunk Wine Trail and receive a handmade grapevine wreath at the first winery on the itinerary. At each of the dozen wineries, receive an ornament to decorate your wreath, along with tastings of special holiday wines and foods. One ticket admission price admits you to all participating wineries. Oenophiles will not want to miss this seasonal event!

The promenade on the Rondout in Kingston is named in honor of Congressman Maurice D. Hinchey who served the people of Ulster County for over 40 years.

DELAWARE COUNTY

5

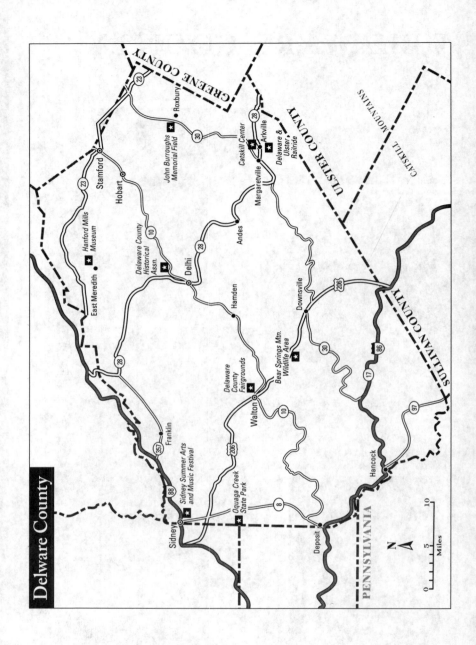

Delware County

DELAWARE COUNTY

One of the largest counties in New York, 1500 square miles (about the size of Rhode Island), Delaware County is a region of tranquil meadows, curious cows, wilderness, and small villages that look as if they were plucked from a 19th-century picture book. Much of the land, including several reservoirs, is state-owned and has been proclaimed "forever wild." This foresight has resulted in an area that is a paradise for anglers, canoeists, kayakers, hikers, bikers, walkers, and those who just enjoy rural charm and an old-fashioned way of life an easy drive away from home.

VISITOR INFORMATION

Great Western Catskills Tourism/Delaware County Chamber of Commerce (607-746-2281; 866-775-4425), 5½ Main Street, Delhi 13753; Delawarecounty.org.

TO GET THERE

By car: Delaware County is most easily reached by taking the New York State Thruway to exit 19 (Kingston), then following Route 28 west toward Pine Hill. Route 30 intersects with Route 28 in Margaretville.

By bus: **Adirondack Trailways** (800-858-8555; trailwaysny.com) operates daily bus service from New York City to several towns in Delaware County. There are also tours and charters through this company.

MEDICAL EMERGENCY

Be aware that public telephones are scarce in the county and cellular service may be spotty. In the event of an emergency, call 911 or the **Delaware County Sheriff** (607-832-5555/746-2336).

Delaware Valley Hospital has three family health centers in the county with 24-hour emergency care: Walton (607-865-2100), 1 Titus Place; Downsville (607-363-2517), 15205 Route 30; Roscoe (607-498-4800), 1982 East Main Street.

Margaretville Memorial Hospital (845-586-2631), 42084 Route 28 Margaretville.

O' Connor Hospital (607-746-0300), 460 Andes Road, Delhi.

TO SEE – TOWNS & HISTORIC SITES

Andes. This delightful village is filled with fine eateries, antiques shops, gift emporiums, and wonderful architecture. Sidewalks were built in 2007, making a walk through town a true pleasure, especially during the winter months and mud season! The best way to explore the village is by walking. The town got its name due to its surrounding hills, including Mount Pisgah, the highest point in Delaware County at 3,400 feet. Originally called Trempersville due to its location along the Tremperskill Stream, it was a milling and lumbering outpost first settled in the late 18th century and became a town in 1819. The hamlet is certainly worth a day trip; it is listed on both the State and National Registers of Historic Places.

Franklin Walking Tour. Main Street in historic Franklin is only one mile long, but it is filled with buildings of architectural interest. The town was first settled in 1784 and was named after the eldest son of Benjamin Franklin, who owned land in the area. The Delaware Literary Institute, the cultural center of the village, was a school that opened in 1835 in town. Architectural styles range from early Federal and Greek Revival to Gothic Revival and Italianate. Some buildings of note are the Franklin Central

The Andes Rail Trail combines a variety of terrain with woodland paths that are easily hiked by people of all ages.

School, Chapel Hall, St. Paul's Episcopal Church, and several homes along Main and Center streets. The Ouleout Valley Cemetery, at the edge of the village is where James McCall, founder of McCalls magazine and Reverend Willard Parsons, founder of the Fresh Air Fund, are buried. In 1983 the entire village was placed on the National Register of Historic Places. The **Franklin Railroad and Community Museum** (607-829-2692), 572 Main Street, has a restored 1889 railroad car, "The Warwick," a tool display, and several items from local life over a century ago. Call for hours.

Gideon Frisbee Homestead at the Delaware County Historical Association (607-746-3849; dcha-ny.org), 46549 Route 10, two miles north of Delhi. Open May through October, Tuesday through Sunday 11-4. Admission. A fascinating site comprised of historic buildings that have been donated, purchased, or just rescued from neglect, where visitors can get a taste of life in rural America during the 19th century. The main building houses a library and exhibit hall, where changing displays of farm tools, household goods, folk art, and crafts are offered each season. Additional interpretive exhibits focus on different aspects of farm life in several of the other buildings. The Gideon Frisbee House, a 1797 example of Federal architecture, once served as a tavern, county meeting room, post office, and the private home of a local judge. The interior has been restored to reflect the changes in life from pioneer days to the period just before World War 1. Decorative arts and furniture collections include Belter chairs, woven rugs, glassware, and a chair that tradition holds was used at the Constitutional Convention in Philadelphia. The Frisbee barn houses a collection of farm implements and a permanent exhibit titled "It's a Fine Growing Time," which guides the visitor through the joys and hard work of a farmer's year. Other buildings include the gunsmith's and blacksmith's shops, the schoolhouse, a tollhouse, and a family cemetery.

Hanford Mills Museum (607-278-5744; hanfordmills.org), 51 County Route 12, East Meredith. Take Route 28 to the intersection of Routes 10 and 12 in East Meredith; follow the signs. Open Memorial Day weekend through October 15, Wednesday through Sunday 10-5. Admission. Once the industrial center of the surrounding farm country, the mill has today been restored to its clanking and chugging past. Flour, lumber, wooden goods (like butter tubs and porch posts), and electricity (courtesy of nearby Kortright Creek) were all produced at Hanford Mills, one of the few remaining industrial mills of the 19th century still in use. Visitors will see lathes, jigsaws, and other machines used to produce woodenware, along with the pulleys and belts that were once the staples of manufacturing. Inside the mill itself, a series of catwalks and walkways wind through the workrooms, where museum interpreters are hard at work. Downstairs, the enormous metal reconstruction of the original wooden waterwheel is turned by the millpond waters. Throughout the site, water-generated electricity powers light bulbs and machines, a reminder of the time when light didn't come with the simple flick of a switch. Also on the site is Gray Barn, in which there are agricultural and farm equipment displays, a shingle mill, the millpond, and the mill store, where local crafts are sold. Hanford Mills hosts several special events each year, including blacksmithing workshops; Independence Day, complete with ice cream and speeches; and late winter's Ice Harvest Day (when the ice is cut and stored for the summer ice-cream social). There are several educational programs for children's groups visiting the museum.

Hobart Book Village (607-538-9788; hobartbookvillage.com), Main Street, Hobart. There are several eclectic bookshops on the main street in town here. They are all wonderful for browsing, particularly for those interested in rare and used books, and include a sizable collection of fiction, nonfiction, history, biography, mysteries, and children's books. The website lists special events

Blenheim Books on Main Street in Hobart's "book village" is just one of the wonderful shops to explore in this unusual town in Delaware County.

that include lectures, book signings and art walks. This is a must-see for bibliophiles. I have spent several delightful hours in this unusual, delightful village of books!

Hunting Tavern Museum (845-676-3775; andessociety.org), 288 Main Street, Andes. Open Memorial Day weekend through Columbus Day weekend, Saturday only 10-3; or by advance appointment. This beautifully restored building is filled with exhibits detailing local history, particularly the Anti-Rent Wars. Those interested in Delaware County's past should not miss this small museum. There are workshops and programs held during the summer months. This is a good place to begin a Saturday morning walking tour of Andes!

Covered Bridges. Delaware County has three historic covered bridges, and visitors are welcome to enjoy them. The Downsville Covered Bridge (1854), Route 206, is in the center of the village. Other bridges include

Fitches Bridge (1870), on Route 10 north of Delhi at the Delaware County Historical Association, and Hamden Covered Bridge (1859), on Route 10 northwest of the village. Additionally the Tappan or Kittle Bridge in Arkville is southeast of town off Dry Brook Road. A 43-foot-long singe span bridge, the Tappan was built in 1906 as a king truss, but was rebuilt in 1985 without the functional truss.

Delaware and Ulster Railroad (845-586-DURR; durr.org), 43510 Route 28, Arkville. Open July-October, Saturday and Sunday, with two train rides daily, 11am & 2pm. Trains depart from Roxbury and Arkville depots. The entrance to the site and depot is free but admission is charged for the ride. The Catskill Mountains were once a daily stop for tourist and milk trains from New York City, but when the service stopped in the 1960s, many believed the echo of a train whistle was gone forever from the valleys. The railroad has resurrected some of the favorite trains that rattled along the tracks, and there is no better way to sample the fun of old-time travel than to hop aboard any of the vintage propelled trains still at work. Or take some photos of the farms and homes; many tell a tale or two about train history. Special events, held through the summer and fall, include a costumed train robbery, Halloween ghost trains, foliage runs and more. At the Arkville Depot there is a snack caboose and restrooms. Wheelchair accessible.

John Burroughs Memorial State Historic Site (518-827-6111/6782; woodchucklodge.org), 1633 Burroughs Memorial Road, Roxbury. Take Route 30 north through Roxbury and follow signs. Open May through September, the first weekend of the month, Saturday and Sunday, 11-3 or by appointment. Free. Although this is not an active site, the former summer retreat/writing studio and grave of nature writer John Burroughs is worth a stop. A friend of Teddy Roosevelt, Henry Ford, and Thomas Edison, Burroughs is a respected American writer whose many essays spoke of Delaware County, the Catskills, and the Hudson Valley. Today his writing nook, Woodchuck Lodge, is maintained by his descendants and dedicated to his legacy. Just up the road is Memorial Field where Boyhood Rock is located. Here is where Burroughs spent many hours observing the natural world; and the Burroughs gravesite is also in this area. A quiet spot with a breathtaking view of the Catskills, it is a lovely place to sit and enjoy the same scene that inspired a great author. Check the website for lectures and tour schedule.

SCENIC DRIVES

Delaware County offers many lovely views and well-maintained roads, but as in any other rural area, some of the back roads can be difficult to navigate in bad weather, four-wheel drive or not. Snow and ice can make the steeper stretches of both paved and dirt roads treacherous. And once off state or county routes, there are often no signs with road names, and it's easy to get lost without GPS. Deer and other wildlife are also a problem, particularly at night, so be aware and don't speed.

If you want to see dairy farms, cornfields, the county seat, and the Pepacton Reservoir, start in **Margaretville** and follow Route 28 to Delhi. The town square in Delhi was painted by Norman Rockwell about 50 years ago and appeared on the cover of the *Saturday Evening Post*. The town square still looks very much as it did back then, and the gazebo was restored in recent years. Pick up Route 10 and take it south to **Walton**; pick up Route 206 and head east to **Downsville**. Then take Route 30 back to Margaretville. The roads are well marked, and you will pass two covered bridges along the way, one near Hamden, the other outside of Downsville. This drive also takes you past farm stands, including Octagon Farms near Walton, where you will see an eight-sided brick house, a remnant of a mid-19th-century fad for building such houses across the nation. Legend has it that the ghost of a young woman killed in a carriage accident roams the road at night!

If you have extra time, take a detour through **Delhi** and follow the signs west to **Franklin** on the Franklin Turnpike, a winding road that offers beautiful vistas in summer.

A second county drive follows part of the old turnpike, once a major stagecoach route through the area. From Margaretville, follow Route 28 west to **Andes** and then to Delhi. From there, take Route 10 north to **Stamford**, make a right onto Route 23 and drive to **Grand Gorge**, and finally, turn right onto Route 30 and head south back to Margaretville. If you can, stop in Stamford and look at some of the grand homes that made this village a popular turn-of-the-20th-century resort area and gave it the name "Queen of the Catskills."

If you wish to drive up Mount Utsayantha (3214 feet), follow Route 23 east to Mountain Avenue; the twisty road is accessible in all seasons except winter. The views are great, especially if you climb the fire tower. The headwaters of the Delaware River's East Branch rise alongside Route 30 between Grand Gorge and Roxbury, and the road back to Margaretville passes through farm country.

The Catskill (Susquehanna) Turnpike once ran from the village of Catskill in Greene County to the village of Unadilla on the Susquehanna River. In Delaware County, the turnpike is now followed by town roads from Stamford west to Franklin, then along Route 357 to Unadilla. Some of the original stone mileage markers for the turmpike can still be seen along this route. There are hilltop views for miles along the turnpike near where it crosses Route 28.

A lovely drive follows along the shores of the two reservoirs: Pepacton and Cannonsville. From Margaretville head southwest along Route 30, which follows the Pepacton Reservoir to Downsville; then go northwest to Walton on Route 206, and head southwest again along Route 10 to Deposit. There are a few crossings over the reservoirs, and both dams are in view.

ACTIVITIES

AUCTIONS

It may seem everything is auctioned off in Delaware County: don't be surprised, it is! Cows, puppies, cabbages, eggs, Shaker chairs, Irish pewter, even antique coffins have all shown up in the hands of auctioneers. Some auctions are weekly institutions attended by locals and weekenders alike. Others are specialty sales for real estate or farm equipment. Country auctions are fun, but make sure to get there early and examine the goods before the sale. Bring a chair for outdoor auctions, plus a hat or umbrella, depending on the weather. Don't buy anything you can't take with you, unless you plan to make shipping arrangements. And finally, know what you're bidding on; don't get stuck with the overstuffed armchair because you thought you were getting the Tiffany lamp!

McIntosh Auction Service (607-832-4829; mcintoshauction.com), 213 Fair Street, Margaretville, has auctions year-round. There is plenty of parking and seats go fast. The auctioneer, Chuck McIntosh, keeps the sales moving and has a good sense of humor. For over 40 years this business has been selling everything from fine furniture to an array of antiques. Several on-site auctions are conducted during the summer months.

Roberts Auction (845-586-6070; robertsauctiononline.com), 820 Main Street, Fleischmanns, conducts auctions year-round, usually on Saturday evening. Auctioneer Ed Roberts Jr. is in charge here and you will never be bored. The crowd is a lively mix of locals and visitors. There are restrooms and a snack bar. Arrive early since some seats are reserved.

BICYCLING

Delaware County offers a range of terrain that will appeal to downhill racers as well as those seeking a scenic tour by bike. For off-road trips, there is the **Catskill Scenic Trail** (607-652-2281; durr.org), a 19-mile Rails-to-Trails corridor from Grand Gorge to Bloomville. The CST can be accessed at various points and there are designated parking areas: one is at the historic

Stamford Depot at the intersection of Railroad Avenue and South Street in the village. There is also a parking lot north of Route 10, just east of the village of Bloomville. The CST is marked with octagonal signs that show the distance to the trailhead in the direction you are facing. There is only a 400-foot change in elevation over the entire 19 miles. Stamford is the peak, and it's downhill in both directions from that point, so I suggest you begin your trip there!

Bike Plattekill Mountain Resort (607-326-3500; plattekill.com), 469 Plattekill Mountain Road, Roxbury. Open April through November on weekends and holidays. Admission. This outstanding mountain bike area offers equipment rentals, a chairlift ride to the summit, and more than 60 miles of trails. Beginners who are wary of trying mountain biking here may try Greenhorn, a new "starter trail" for beginners; package deals provide a bike, lift ticket, helmet and lesson with a guide.

CANOEING & KAYAKING

The East and West branches of the Delaware River, as well as the Susquehanna, offer spectacular opportunities for canoeists and kayakers. Some of the best canoeing may be found along the western border of the county with Pennsylvania. A word of caution: as with all water sports, don't attempt to canoe or kayak unless you are familiar with the rivers. Both the Delaware and the Susquehanna can be treacherous, especially in spring or after a heavy rain. If you are a beginner, it is best to use one of the canoe outfitting services. They provide the right equipment, maps and often a shuttle service.

Al's Sport Store (607-363-7740), 6964 River Road, Downsville, is a clearinghouse for canoe, kayak, and fishing information. They rent equipment and have tours in season.

Catskill Outfitters (800-631-0105), 97 Townsend Street, Walton, can supply kayaks, canoes, and tubes. They are open daily 10-4.

Hawk Mountain Guide Service (607-865-7830), Trout Creek, will put together a complete package based on your ability and desires.

FARMS & FARM STANDS

When the harvest begins in early summer with strawberries and flowers, farm stands begin to blossom along the roadsides as well. In Delaware County there are dozens of farm stands where you can pick out the produce, bag it and leave the money for the owner. Other stands are a bit more formal, but the hours of operation vary widely with the season and some crops, including strawberries, seem to disappear after only a few days. The best way to find local produce is to watch for these roadside stands. This is also savvy farm country: in the past few years county agriculture has grown to include specialty crops like blue potatoes and garlic, which often turn up in Manhattan's trendiest restaurants.

The largest and best produce market in the county is the **Pakatakan Farmers' Market** (845-586-3326), 46676 Route 30, Halcottsville (just north of Margaretville at the Round Barn). Open May through October, Saturday 9-3. Vendors offer everything from fresh trout, organic produce, and bouquets of wildflowers to fine crafts and home-baked pies. The selection changes with the season, and there's plenty of food to sample, so have a light breakfast before heading out there!

Other county farmers' markets include **Andes Farmers' Market**, 72 Main Street, Andes, open Memorial Day weekend through Columbus Day weekend, Saturday 10-2; **Delhi Farmers' Market**, Courthouse Square, Main Street, Delhi; open June through September, Wednesday 9-2. **Koo Koose Farmers' Market**, 171 Second Street, Deposit, June through October, Saturday 8:30-1.

Betty Acres Organic Farm Stand (607-746-9581), 21529 Route 28, Delhi; open May through October, daily 9-6. Farm-raised organic vegetables and meats, as well as local cheeses, jams, honey and maple syrup are sold here. Farm tours by appointment. The **Brovetto Dairy and Cheese House** (607-278-6622), 1677 Route 29, Jefferson, has a farm store open daily 11-4. Learn about the cheese-making process here and make sure to visit the cave, with its 600 wheels of Harpersfield cheese! Visitors may taste a variety of cheeses in the farm store. **Byebrook Farm** (607-538-9796), 7531 Route 18, Bloomville, is open daily year-round. A Holstein dairy, the farm has been in the same family for eight generations. They make raw milk Gouda that is aged a minimum of 60 days. Bottled raw milk and free-range eggs, along with Gouda cheese, are for sale at the farm stand. Honey lovers may want to stop at **Ballard's** (607-326-7100), 53996 Route 30, Roxbury, which stocks honey from its own hives. Make sure to call before going, however. **Hillhaven Farms** (607-652-2274), 2 Hobart Road, Stamford (corner of Routes 23 and 10), is open May through December for blueberries as well as other fruits and vegetables. There are also handcrafted wreaths and trees for Christmas. **Maple Shade Farm** (607-746-8866), 2066 County Route 18, Delhi, is open from mid-September through early November, Saturday and Sunday 10-5. Explore the barn, pick a pumpkin, make a scarecrow, see the farm animals or enjoy the corn maze and wagon rides in autumn at this 200-acre historic family farm. Open for group and school tours by appointment. Overnight stays may be arranged. **Octagon Farm Market** (607-865-7416), 34055 Route 10, Walton, sells its own fruits and vegetables along with many other local offerings. Open daily, July through October 10-5.

Stone & Thistle Farm and Kortright Creek Creamery (607-278-5800), 1211 Kelso Road, East Meredith, is open daily, year-round, 9-6. Farm tours are available Memorial Day weekend through Columbus Day on weekends or by appointment. Visitors can tour the farm, pet the animals, and milk a goat, as well as enjoy free tastings of grass-fed meat or milk. The specialty here is organic beef, pork, lamb, goat, chicken, turkey, rabbit and eggs. Kids will enjoy this farm. For those who would like to spend a night on the farm, inquire about the one-bedroom suite with adjoining library that can accommodate a family. There are prix-fixe dinners by reservation in the warm weather months on Saturday nights in the 1860 Greek Revival farmhouse. Call for details.

Stony Creek Farmstead (607-865-7965), 1738 Freer Hollow Road, Walton. Open daily year-round. The Marsiglio family sells beef, pork, lamb, chicken, eggs, and vegetables in season. They adhere to rigorous free-range pasturing practices for all the animals and supplement their grazing diet with local organic grains. Farm tours are offered at 11am Saturday mornings.

FISHING

Delaware County is home to the East and West branches of the Delaware River, the Susquehanna River, and Beaverkill Creek. The county is served by the Cannonsville, Pepacton, and Schoharie reservoirs, making fishing a popular sport in the region. The Beaverkill is the most famous trout fishing stream in America, the birthplace of fly-fishing. So if you want to try the sport, this is one of the best places anywhere to begin. New York State fishing licenses are required. They are easy to purchase in most towns; check with the town clerk or at the village offices. For reservoir fishing, special permits are required. The DEC regional office (607-652-7366) has information on permits and maps. Stream fishing areas open to the public are indicated by brown and yellow wooden signs along the rivers. Most areas offer off-road parking areas. Detailed maps are available where you purchase a fishing license and at town offices. Riverfront property may be posted off-limits as part of the New York City watershed, so maps should be consulted as heavy fines can result from illegal fishing.

GOLF

Golf enthusiasts will appreciate the courses in Delaware County where the lush greens of summer and the blazing trees of autumn provide everyone a beautiful setting in which to play. Greens fees vary depending on the season, so call for information before going.

College Golf Course at Delhi (607-746-GOLF), 85 Scotch Mountain Road (off Route 28), Delhi, has a course that is used as a training area for students in golf management. It's a small gem, though it's a full 18 holes, and rarely is crowded. There's a driving range, practice green, pro shop, and café.

French Woods Golf & Country Club (607-637-1800), 17440 Route 97, East Newman Road, Hancock. This 18-hole, par-72 course is a challenging one in a beautiful country setting.

Hanah Mountain Resort & Country Club (845-586-4849), 576 Hubbell Hill Road, Margaretville, has an 18-hole course, practice greens, and a driving range. There is also a golf school and restaurant on the premises.

Hardwood Hills Golf Course (607-467-1031), 11160 Route 8, Masonville, is an 18-hole course in a mountain setting.

Meadows Golf Center (845-586-4104), 42565 Route 28, Margaretville, has a nine-hole, par-27 course, miniature golf, lessons, night golf, and a driving range. Those who want to practice their techniques should head here and young golfers will enjoy this place as well.

Shephard Hills Golf Club (607-326-7121), 185 Golf Course Road, Roxbury. There is a 9-hole public course on challenging terrain with great views along with a pro shop, and restaurant.

Tennanah Lake Golf & Tennis Club (888-561-3935), 100 Fairway View Drive, Roscoe. This 18-hole championship golf course offers panoramic views of the countryside. There are practice greens, a driving range, restaurant and inn on the premises.

HIKING

A large part of Delaware County is part of the "forever wild" park system in New York State. A number of the existing hiking trails are for experienced hikers only, and some require overnight stays in simple trail huts; those who would like detailed trail information should contact the Catskill Forest Preserve regional office (607-652-7365), 65561 Route 10, Stamford. The preserve contains more than 300 miles of trails varying in length from a half mile to almost 100 miles so even novice hikers will find something they are comfortable taking on, whether for a day of walking or an overnight hike.

The Catskill Center for Conservation and Development (845-586-2611; catskillcenter.org), 43355 Route 28, Arkville, has lectures and special events, including guided hikes, bird walks, and snowshoe excursions. The website has a full schedule and encourages membership in this worthy organization. The office is open Monday through Friday, 9:30-4:30; Saturday 10-2.

The trailhead of Palmer Hill Trail outside of Andes.

Catskill Outdoor Education Corps (607-746-4112), 4112 Route 28, Delhi, offers woods walks, educational excursions, and a nature preserve with marked trails. This is a good place to introduce young children to hiking.

Catskill Scenic Trail (CST) (607-652-2821; catskillscenic trail.org), Railroad Avenue, Stamford, has a marked 19-mile Rails-to-Trails area with a hard-packed surface and gentle grade perfect for hiking, biking, horseback riding, and cross-country skiing. An excellent choice for families with young children.

Oquaga Creek State Park (607-467-4160), 5995 Route 20, Bainbridge. Open year-round. There are 6.5 miles of marked hiking trails that will delight people of all abilities. The park spans three counties: Delaware, Broome, and Chenango.

Utsayantha Trail System (607-652-2821), Stamford. This marked trail system takes hikers through scenic mountaintops and serene valleys. From Stamford, follow signs on Route 10 to Archibald Field. The trail begins there and is marked.

West Branch Preserve (518-690-7850), County Road 26, Hamden. This 446-acre preserve features a .7 mile moderate trail and a strenuous two-mile mountainside trail for experienced hikers.

HORSEBACK RIDING

There are miles of trails to ride on in Delaware County, as well as private stables where beginners can go on a guided ride or take lessons.

Bear Spring Mountain State Park (607-865-6989), 512 East Trout Brook Road, Walton. This is the only campground in New York State specifically designed for use by horseback riders. There are campsites that accommodate horse trailers and provide lodging facilities for the animals. There are 24 miles of trails that will delight those who like to travel with their horses.

Broken Spoke Stables (607-538-9651), 874 Narrow Notch Road, Hobart. Open year-round. There are trail rides here and lessons in both English and Western riding. There is also a children's summer camp.

Catskill Scenic Trail (607-652-2821). The CST may be picked up in Bloomville, Stamford, Grand Gorge, or Hobart by those who are looking for wooded trails. There are 19 miles of gently graded trails.

Grey Goose Farm (607-746-3645), 83 Maggie Hoag Road, Delancey. Call before going if you are interested in heading out on a trail. Their specialty is English-style riding.

HORSE FARMS

Mountain Breeze Miniature Horse Farm (607-588-6208), Route 23, Grand Gorge, breeds little horses as well as larger minis. The owners, Glenda and Earl Krom, offer a variety of horses for sale year-round. The animals are handled regularly and they are friendly. You are welcome to stop by this farm if you are considering a miniature horse as a pet. Kids will love petting the miniature donkeys and newborn horses. Call for directions.

The Night Pasture Horse Farm (607-588-6926), 35146 Route 23, two miles west of the center of Grand Gorge. This 56-acre horse farm boasts a large indoor arena, tack room, lessons, and quality horses for sale at reasonable prices. The Horseplay Tack Shop offers the horse enthusiast everything from bridles and saddles to a variety of gifts. New and used equipment are for sale and the Catskill Scenic Trail may be accessed from the parking area.

SKIING

DOWNHILL

Ski Plattekill (607-326-3500), 469 Plattekill Mountain Road, Roxbury. Open December through March, Friday through Sunday and during the week on school holidays 9-4. There is a vertical drop of 1100 feet, 35 trails, and four lifts, including the Northface Express double chairlift. They make snow and snowboarders and skiers will find excellent conditions. There is a snow tubing park, rentals, lessons and snack bar. In 2012 there were several improvements made at the ski center. A Snowkidding Children's Learning Center opened. This area caters to the youngest skiers. The Powder Puff Beginner's Trail, a popular run, was substantially widened, and the outdoor deck at the base lodge was expanded. Food service offerings incorporate locally grown produce and meats.

CROSS-COUNTRY

Andes Rail Trail, County Route 2, Andes. The trail is four miles round trip. The first mile is flat, traveling on an old rail bed. The second mile climbs up

Hemlock Knoll with a switchback. There are stone steps in places. This part is a moderate climb; track ties can be felt under foot in several areas. There may be muddy areas during rainy or snowy spells.

Catskill Outdoor Education Center (607-746-4112), 4112 Route 28, Delhi. There are marked trails here for cross-country skiing, and guided snowshoe walks for groups by advance reservation.

Kirkside Park (607-326-3722), Main Street (Kirkside Driveway), Roxbury. This historic 14-acre treasure was formerly the estate of Helen Gould-Shepard, daughter of railroad magnate and Roxbury native son, Jay Gould. Rich in natural beauty and history, and restored to its glorious splendor, Kirkside has rustic Adirondack-style bridges, graceful paths along the East Branch of the Delaware River, and lush plantings to admire in the warm-weather months. During the winter, however, this is a wonderful place to cross-country ski. A good bet for those with young children. Several special events are held here year-round.

Ski Plattekill Mountain Resort (607-326-3500), 469 Plattekill Mountain Road, Roxbury. There are over twelve miles of cross-country ski trails (beginning to advanced; open to the public for a fee). There are also lessons and guided snowshoe tours by reservation.

DISTILLERIES, CIDERIES

Beverage makers in Delaware County are all fairly new and this exciting addition to the region is one to explore while enjoying a drive through the beautiful scenery.

Delaware Phoenix Distillery (607-865-5056), 144 Delaware Street, Walton. Call for hours since they vary with the season. Owner-operator Cheryl Lins has earned international recognition for her handcrafted absinthes. She sources wormwood from local farmers to make this unusual liquor and now creates bourbon as well. The distillery is in the middle of Walton and is well worth a visit.

Union Grove Distillery (845-586-6300), 43311 Route 28, Arkville. Open Wednesday through Sunday noon-7; Sunday until 5. First opened in 2016 with the launch of Vly Creek vodka, the owners are planning to feature bourbon and whiskey spirits as well. There's a delightful cocktail lounge and tasting room with a fireplace, copper-topped bar and even a playroom for young children.

Wayside Cider (845-676-6002), 55 Redden Lane, Andes. Open Thursday & Friday 5-10; Saturday noon-10; Sunday noon-8. Taste cider from foraged apples in a converted barn after walking through town.

LODGING

Bed & breakfasts are a great way to spend time in Delaware County, and most are moderately priced. The establishments I have chosen have been providing excellent service and accommodations for several years. Their focus is not on the wedding business! Let me know if standards are not to your liking. You may also want to check out the **Delaware County B&B Association** (bnblodgings.com). Delaware County is the second-largest county in New York State, and entries are listed by both village and desired amenities. (Keep in mind: those listed pay membership in the organization!)

ARKVILLE, HALCOTTSVILLE, MARGARETVILLE, ROXBURY

Bed & Eggs (607-326-6184), 43 Montgomery Hollow Road, Roxbury 12474. ($$) There is one cozy suite here with kitchenette and all the comforts of home. Your hosts are ex-Brooklynites, Frieda and Matt, and they will supply you with at least a half dozen eggs each day to create your own farm-fresh breakfast from their chickens. The price is exceedingly reasonable, the place is immaculate, and great hiking is just outside the door. Open year-round.

Margaretville Mountain Inn (845-586-3933), 1478 Margaretville Mountain Road, Margaretville 12455. ($$) This restored Victorian home was originally built as a boardinghouse and functioned as a working farm. There are six rooms, all with private bath. Guests may enjoy spectacular views of the New Kingston Valley from the veranda and the inn is less than two miles from town. A full breakfast is served in an elegant dining room; outdoors on the veranda, in summer. Children are welcome. Open year-round.

Meadowood Inn (845-586-5199), 50 Hornbeck Street, Arkville 12406 ($$) This turn-of-the-20th-century Victorian operated as an inn a century ago. Located on an acre of land on a quiet country road, it's within walking distance of Arkville and Margaretville. There are five spacious two-room suites and two single rooms, all with private bath (two have Jacuzzi tubs): all have cable TV and are furnished with antiques. There is one pet-friendly room, separate from the main part of the inn, with a separate entrance. A country breakfast is served in the dining room, or outside on the wraparound porch in the warm weather. Located near Union Grove Distillery and the Delaware-Ulster Railroad, innkeeper Tanya Minteer runs a cozy place with reasonable rates. Included in a stay here are discounts on lift tickets and ski rentals at Belleayre Mountain and Plattekill. Breakfast is fantastic: the pancakes are the tastiest I've eaten in years; Tanya will accommodate all special dietary requirements.

The Roxbury (607-326-7200), 2258 Route 41, Roxbury 12474. ($$) Gregory Henderson and his partner, Joe Massa, have furnished every room here in a unique imaginative manner. Some feature bold colors and are filled with interesting, yet tasteful, touches. The owners genuinely care about the comfort of guests and make sure they enjoy their stay. There is a variety of accommodations at a range of prices. Some rooms have king-size bed and flat-screen TV. A spa is available on the premises with hot tub, steam room, and sauna, for an additional charge. Open year-round.

BOVINA

The Carriage House Inn (607-832-4209), 471 Jim Lane Road, Bovina Center 13740. ($) This family-friendly place surrounded by 150 acres of farmland is like having your own one-or two-bedroom apartment in the country (complete with spacious living room, full kitchen, and bedroom).

The Roxbury Hotel is nestled in a quiet corner of town with beautiful views of the Catskill Mountains.

If you are traveling with children or a pet, you will find any of the three units here ideal. In the summer, enjoy boating or fishing on the pond. During the winter there are trails nearby for cross-country skiing.

Highlander's View Bed & Breakfast (607-832-4805), Crescent Valley Road, Bovina 13740. ($) The views at this 2-room plus one suite B&B are absolutely spectacular. The place borders the Plattekill Forest and hiking, swimming and birding are only a short walk away. Patty and Liam, your hosts, prepare a full country breakfast for guests. The place is kept beautifully. Children are welcome. Open year-round.

The Mountain Brook Inn (877-692-7665), 5333 Route 6, Bovina Center 13740. ($$) This 36-acre paradise with an 18th-century stone bridge will be particularly appreciated by those who love seclusion. Eight suites, all with private bath, living room, and kitchen, create a feeling of having your own place in the country, with acres of hiking trails and places to fish (there are two waterways on the property). Enjoy playing croquet and horseshoes on the lawn. Continental breakfast, custom made to order, arrives at your door at 8am. It's a 15-minute drive to Margaretville, Andes and Delhi. Open year-round.

DELHI

West Branch House Bed and Breakfast (607-746-3378), 28 Franklin Street, Delhi 13753. ($$) This lovely mid-19th-century village house has been completely renovated and includes two rooms, each with its own bath, one with a whirlpool tub. The owners make a full breakfast using local, seasonal ingredients. A short walk from the B&B takes you into town where there are a few fine eateries. Open year-round.

DEPOSIT

Dream Catcher Lodge (877-275-1165), 393 River Road, Deposit 13754. ($$) Built in 1854 and fully renovated in recent years, this lodge, decorated in Southwestern décor has five rooms with two baths and a lodge that sleeps eight. There are also six private cabins along the river. Rates are reasonable. Furnishings are simple and comfortable. Excellent fly-fishing is nearby as well as fine hiking and bicycling. Children welcome. Open year-round.

Scotts Family Resort at Oquaga Lake (607-467-3094) Oquaga Lake, Deposit 13754. ($$) This family vacation resort on 1100 acres offers evening entertainment as well as an array of daytime activities, including golf, tennis, waterskiing, fishing, biking and hiking. Three meals daily are included in the price. Good value. Open year-round.

DOWNSVILLE

Victoria Rose B&B (607-363-7838), 15146 Bridge Street, Downsville 13755. ($$) A lovely Queen Anne home, filled with antiques and country touches, where guests will enjoy breakfast, tea and evening snacks. There are four rooms, each with private bath. Open year-round.

Old Schoolhouse Inn (607-363-7814), 28218 Route 206, Downsville 13755. ($$) This newly renovated inn features four beautiful rooms and a honeymoon suite with air-conditioning, WiFi, and flat screen TVs. There is a fine restaurant on the premises serving lunch and dinner. Children welcome: they stay free with parents in the same room. Open year-round.

EAST MEREDITH

Harmony Hill Lodging (607-278-6609), 694 McKee Hill Road, East Meredith 13757. ($$) Located on 70 pristine, secluded acres, yet less than 15 miles from Delhi, the two yurts here provide a wonderfully different kind of getaway. Both are equipped with fine bathrooms, kitchens, and king-size beds, all in a circular structure reminiscent of a luxurious cabin in the woods. Harmony Hill is a special place with a natural stone labyrinth, a few miles of groomed nature trails in the surrounding woods, and phenomenal sunsets. Host Chris Rosenthal creates a first-class getaway at amazingly reasonable rates. There is a cozy mountain chalet/lodge available—a perfect getaway for a family or small group. The chalet is open most of the year; the yurts are closed in the winter season.

FISHS EDDY

River View Estate (607-651-6980), 1650 Bodoit Road, Fishs Eddy 13783. ($$) Ideal for a large group-stay like a family reunion, this gorgeous estate in a magnificent forest setting has all the amenities you could want: swimming pool, air-conditioning, flat screen TV, pool table, workout area, fire pit, and amazing views everywhere. Children welcome. Open year-round.

HANCOCK

Hancock House (607-637-7100), 137 East Front Street, Hancock 13783. ($$) There are 29 rooms and suites decorated in mission-style at this small hotel just a short walk away from the best trout fishing in America. The East and West branches of the Delaware River converge right here. The owners, Lynn and Russell Bass, are local residents who have renovated every room with care and attention to detail. Children welcome. Open year-round.

West Branch Angler Resort (607-467-5525), 150 Faulkener Road, Hancock 13783. ($$) This wonderful new addition to the Delaware County accommodations scene is a place offering rental of a luxury cabin on the banks of the Delaware River. There are one, two and three-bedroom options. All have private decks, gas grills, cathedral stone fireplaces, full kitchen, central air-conditioning and WiFi. Children welcome. Open year-round.

SIDNEY

Keepers of the Flag B&B (607-563-2554), 474 Thorpe Road, Sidney 13838. Located conveniently off exit 9 of I-88, this cozy spot up the mountain offers a full-breakfast, tranquility, and fabulous views. Two rooms share a bath; both have satellite TV, WiFi, and air-conditioning. A family suite with full bath is also available. Children welcome. Open year-round.

WALTON

D'Angelo's Bed & Breakfast (607-865-6285), 24 Griswold Street, Walton 13856. ($$) This Victorian is in the town of Walton, next to a park with a gazebo. There are three guest rooms: one has a private bath, and two share a bathroom. The rooms are air-conditioned for summer comfort; in the winter electric blankets are offered. Children welcome. Open year-round.

Stony Creek Farmstead (607-865-7965), 1738 Freer Hollow Road, Walton. 13856. ($$) A fabulous place for a farm stay there are platform tents here with canopied ceilings, canvas walls and wooden floors, to keep you cozy and private, but close to the natural world. There's a small water closet with a flush toilet in each "room." A short stroll across a footbridge takes you to the shower house. A second-generation farm, you can pick up freshly-laid eggs for breakfast, gather fresh herbs and vegetables from the gardens, pick up warm bread from the oven at the farmhouse, and just enjoy a slower pace and the exquisite scenery. Children are welcome. Closed during winter months.

WHERE TO EAT

Casual is the operative word for Delaware County restaurants, where moderate prices and comfort food are the rule. Hours and days of operation may vary with the seasons, so it's recommended to call ahead if you are making a long trip. Reservations aren't necessary, except on busy holiday weekends.

DINING OUT

Andes/Delhi

Andes Hotel (845-676-3980), 110 Main Street, Andes. ($$) Open for lunch and dinner daily 11:30-9; Sunday brunch served 10-4:30. Housed in a historic building, this bustling restaurant and tavern features mouthwatering American favorites at reasonable prices. An imaginative menu from a Culinary Institute-trained chef. Children are welcome; dine alfresco on the terrace in the warm weather.

Two Old Tarts Restaurant and Bakery (845-676-3300), 22 Lee Lane, Andes. ($$) Open Thursday through Monday, 10-9. There is a wonderful selection of comfort food here along with fresh baked cakes, muffins, croissants and, of course, tarts. Local ingredients are featured and you won't go wrong here. Informal atmosphere; children welcome.

Arkville, Margaretville, Fleischmanns, Pine Hill

La Cabana (845-254-4966), 966 Main Street, Fleischmanns. ($$) Open daily 4-10. There is pretty decent Mexican food here with specialties like mole poblano or carnitas Yucatan, as well as an array of burritos, tacos, and enchiladas. Children welcome.

Zephyr (845-254-8024), 302 Main Street, Pine Hill. ($$) Open Thursday through Monday for dinner 4-9. Delightful eatery featuring farm to table dining at reasonable prices. Although somewhat out of the way, this is a wonderful new (2017) addition to the Delaware County dining scene. Just about all the entrées and produce are organic. I love their wild salmon!

Bloomville

Table on Ten (607-643-6509), 52030 Main Street, Bloomville. ($$) Open Thursday through Sunday 10-3; Friday and Saturday dinner served 6-9. There are frittatas, granola, and egg wraps for breakfast, with an array of soups and sandwiches for lunch. The coffee and espresso drinks are excellent. There are pizza nights featuring wood fired-oven pizza. The café is truly a gathering place for locals and visitors alike.

Bovina

Brushland Eating House (607-832-4861), 1927 County Route 6, Bovina. ($$) Open Wednesday through Sunday 5:30-10. Located in a two-story frame structure in a sleepy village, this New American bistro with an open kitchen and terrific bar is one to travel to from wherever you are in the Catskills. Flavorful, imaginative twists on a range of standard favorites including hand-rolled pasta, pork schnitzel, burgers and more. Loved this recent addition to Bovina's Main Street!

Delhi

Meredith Inn (607-464-5029), 4206 Turnpike Road, Delhi. ($$) Open Wednesday through Friday 4-9; Saturday and Sunday 8-8. This is a family place with large portions and attention to detail in preparing a variety of sandwiches, salads, pasta and pizza dishes.

For first-rate sandwiches, burgers and salads at reasonable prices, Cassie's is the place to go in Roxbury.

East Meredith

Fable (607-278-5800), 1211 Kelso Road. ($$) Open for Sunday brunch and Saturday dinner by reservation only. The prix-fixe menu features the farm's organic grass-fed meats, milk, yogurt, and produce. There's a relaxed atmosphere in a beautifully renovated open-kitchen/dining room with two large tables. Twelve people are seated at each. The outdoor patio is used during the warm weather months. Menus change seasonally and reflect what is raised at the farm. The Kortright Creek Creamery on the premises produces milk products, including yogurt, used in meals. This is an unusual dining experience and may interest those who want to know more about local farms.

Franklin

The Tulip and The Rose Cafe (607-829-4040), 435 Main Street. Open Tuesday through Thursday 11-3; Tuesday, Friday, Saturday & Sunday 5-8; Saturday & Sunday 8-3. Monday closed. Offering a menu of omelettes, pancakes and their renowned gyros they feature an eclectic mix of international specialties including Mediterranean, Indian, French, Thai and Russian choices. An informal atmosphere; children welcome. An unlikely find in the recesses of the Catskills!

Meridale

Greenane Farms (607-746-8878), 196 Route 10. Open Thursday 5-10; Friday and Saturday noon-10. Closed Sunday through Wednesday. Authentic farm fresh Mexican fare at reasonable prices. Do try the Molcajete chicken and steak selections, for something excellent—and different.

Stamford

Mama Maria's (607-652-2372), 26817 Route 23. ($) Open Tuesday through Sunday noon-10. Eat lunch or dinner at this authentic Southern Italian restaurant in a country setting. Enjoy home-cooked favorites like lasagna and manicotti as well as steaks, chops, fresh fish and salads. A great family place and Mama Maria does all the cooking! Children welcome.

Walton

Feather & Stone (607-510-4027), 38 West Street, Walton. ($) American fare including sandwiches, burgers, salads, tacos and seafood; there's often live music in this colorful, contemporary café.

Rainbow Lodge (607-865-7534), 440 Rainbow Lodge Road, Walton. ($$) Open Thursday and Friday 4-9; Saturday noon-9; Sunday noon-7. The setting here is the reason to go. The restaurant overlooks a small lake and is surrounded by forest. The food is passable...mostly bar fare (wings, burgers, steaks and salads). Deck dining in the warm weather; children welcome.

EATING OUT

Andes/Delhi

Blue Bee (607-746-8060), 114 Main Street, Delhi. ($) Open daily 10-4. This lively café serves fresh coffee, tea cappuccino, espresso, and cold drinks, along with paninis, salads, soups, croissants, and cookies. Everything is fresh and delicious. I always stop in when I'm in Delhi!

Cross Roads Café (607-746-7007), 80 Main Street, Delhi. ($) Open daily, except Sunday, 7-2. Healthful, great-tasting fare is what you will find here.

Everything is made fresh on the premises: salads, desserts, breads, and an array of smoothies. Vegetarian and vegan dishes are noted on the menu. The coffee bar features gourmet coffees.

Delhi Diner (845-746-2207), 95 Main Street, Delhi. ($) Open Tuesday through Friday 6-3; Saturday 6-1:30; Sunday 7-1:30. The best items on the menu are the egg dishes, waffles and pancakes. The usual diner fare is available and the menu is huge. Try the daily specials. Children welcome.

General Store (845-676-6091), 103 Main Street, Andes. ($) Open daily 6am-8pm. This is a wonderful old-fashioned general store, recently renovated, serving fresh salads and sandwiches for take-out. Local products, maps and books are featured here and owner Lauren Atcher is usually around: she will be happy to answer any questions about the area you may have!

Woody's Country Kitchen (845-656-4500), 85 Main Street, Andes. ($) Open for breakfast and lunch daily 7-2. Dinner is served Wednesday from 4-8. Bacon and eggs, waffles, French toast, grilled chicken sandwich, salads, homemade pies and hearty soups are served here. The early Wednesday dinners are a bargain!

Arkville, Margaretville, Fleischmanns, Pine Hill

Arkville Bread & Breakfast (845-586-1122), 43285 Route 28, Arkville. ($) Open daily 7-2. This roadside restaurant is an ideal stop for a casual breakfast or lunch and the food is hearty. The egg sandwiches and stuffed French toast with fruit is made with their delicious breads. Children welcome.

The Andes General Store has great coffee, sandwiches, local food products and gifts.

The Cheese Barrel (845-586-4666), 798 Main Street, Margaretville. ($) Open daily 8-5. An excellent selection of snacks and cheese is found in this shop and the dishes are great for take-out and picnics. I have enjoyed their homemade soups. There is a small, close dining area, but if you want quiet and privacy, or are traveling with children, this isn't the place to go!

Goatie White (845-254-3005), 46 Depot Street, Fleischmanns. ($) Open Monday, Tuesday and Thursday 4-9; Friday through Sunday noon-9. Closed Wednesday. This is a terrific place to stop for an informal lunch or have a snack when you're traveling with kids. There's pizza, chili, Reuben sandwiches, barbecue and ice cream. Local farm products are the mainstay.

Maine Black Bear Seafood Company (845-586-4004), 13 Riverside Drive— just off Route 28, Arkville. ($$) Open late May through October, Friday through Sunday, 6am-9pm. This is a fish shack like those in coastal Maine, only it's in the Catskills. There's a retail fish market as well as a restaurant here and understand there's a very rustic ambience. For nearly 30 years owner Bruce Beddoe has been serving up the freshest seafood. The lobster dinners are renowned locally and have attracted local celebrities with weekend homes in the area. Dine alfresco on the outdoor deck and arrive early since the place is quite small and fills up quickly. Children welcome.

Picnic! (845-586-1919), 75 Bridge Street, Margaretville. ($) Open daily 7-2; closed Monday. There are excellent bagels, egg sandwiches and six different kinds of burritos, all prepared to order and freshly prepared with local ingredients. This is a wonderful bakery featuring hearty soups, muffins of all kinds, and fabulous cookies. A welcome addition (2017) to the eatery scene in Margaretville!

Bovina

Russell's Store (607-832-4242), 2099 Route 6 (Main Street), Bovina Center. ($) Open daily, except Tuesday, 7-6; Saturday and Sunday 9-4. The breakfasts here are not to be missed. Enjoy French toast and first-rate pancakes. For lunch there are wraps, soups and overstuffed sandwiches at the counter or tables. This is a marvelous general store so don't forget to pick up some treats before departing!

Downsville

Downsville Diner (607-363-7678), 18 Main Street. ($) Open daily 7am-7pm. All the diner favorites are served here, along with daily specials and pizza. Baking is done on the premises, and there is even a full line of sugar-free desserts!

Hamden

Lucky Dog Café (607-746-8383), 35796 Route 10. ($) Open for breakfast and lunch daily, except Monday, 10-3. This café has enjoyed an excellent reputation in Hamden. They are known for their farm fresh salads, homemade soups, and hearty sandwiches. The emphasis is on seasonal ingredients from local purveyors. Don't skip the heavenly desserts! Children welcome.

Walton/Masonville

Crescent Wrench Café at the Masonville General Store (607- 265-3808), 2095 Route 206, Masonville. ($) Open Thursday through Monday, 10-6. This beautifully renovated building has been a general store since 1849. The emphasis in the store is on local and regional products as well as organic and natural food items. The café serves light fare—soups, croissants, tea and coffee. If you want to relax and have a drink or snack, this is a delightful place to stop.

Penguin Café (607-510-4173), 38 West Street, Walton. ($) Open Thursday through Monday 11-8. This is definitely my favorite place to eat healthy comfort food in Walton. There are wonderful vegetarian soups, paninis of all types, crisp sweet potato fries, and an array of ice cream flavors. The coffee is even served in large porcelain mugs! Children welcome.

Molto Espresso (607-865-7375), 147 Delaware Avenue, Walton. ($) Open daily, except Sunday, 7am-8pm. The egg dishes, pancakes, fresh sandwiches, paninis, and coffee are terrific here. The service is friendly and efficient. If you're traveling with children, this is a fine choice. I loved the pesto grilled cheese— a new experience....and a good one!

T.A.'s Place (607-865-7745), 249 Delaware Avenue, Walton. ($) Open daily for breakfast, lunch and early supper 6am-8pm. Old-fashioned American favorites like meat loaf and mashed potatoes, grilled pork chops, and marinated chicken breasts are the specialties here. Everything is homemade.

ENTERTAINMENT

Franklin Stage Company (607-829-3700;franklinstagecompany.org), 25 Institute Street, Franklin. Founded in 1996 and dedicated to the production of classic and new plays that provoke and entertain, this is one of the only free professional theaters in the country. The venue, Chapel Hall, is a majestic Greek Revival structure that dominates the town of Franklin. If you are in the area during the summer months, make an effort to see one of their fine productions. Nationally acclaimed guest artists and exhibits are also featured in the admission-free program.

Open Eye Theater (845-586-1660;theopeneyetheater.org), 960 Main Street, Margaretville. Enjoy new plays and classics, including Shakespeare, by the company that has been performing in town for over 45 years. Monthly Open Mic nights give everyone a chance to perform!

Roxbury Arts Group (607-326-7908; roxburyartsgroup.org), 5025 Vega Mountain Road, Roxbury. There is a full range of performances here—concerts, theater, film and children's events—year-round at various venues. Check the website for programming schedule.

Tri-Town Theatre (607-563-1924), 55 Union Street, Sidney. This is a community theatre celebrating over 50 years of family-friendly plays and musical performances. Call or go to Facebook for a schedule of events.

Walton Theatre (607-865-6688; waltontheatre.org), 31 Gardiner Place, Walton. In the historic district of Walton, this theater, built in 1914, now features live theater, first-run movies, and concerts.

West Kortright Centre (607-278-5454; westkc.org), 49 East Kortright Church Road, West Kortright. Performance schedules vary but are usually Memorial Day weekend through October. Nestled in a hidden valley, the Centre is housed in a charming white-clapboard 1850s church that was rescued from neglect by dedicated volunteers. Stained-glass windows and kerosene chandeliers glow in the twilight. The center offers unique performances throughout the summer with concerts and special events held both outdoors in the green fields and inside where guests are seated in unique rounded pews; the lawn is often dotted with preconcert picnickers. The intimate setting makes all events a delight and you may see the evening's featured performer as he or she warms up in the churchyard!

SELECTIVE SHOPPING

Delaware County has several unique craft and antiques shops. Villages like Andes, Bovina, Margaretville and Walton are fun to explore. There are a variety of stores, antiques emporiums, and the best way to see things is to wander. Although you can find interesting shopping in just about every village, Arkville is home to **The Miracle Mile Flea Market**, on Drybrook Road, off Route 28. It's held every Saturday and Sunday, mid-May through October, weather permitting, 8-5. There are all kinds of vendors: approximately two dozen in total, but the number varies.

The following shops are some of my favorites. Enjoy walking around on your own discovering new places!

ANDES

Andes Art & Antiques (845-676-3420), 173 Main Street. Open year-round, daily 11-5. Closed Tuesday and Thursday. If you are looking for rare prints, old photos, books, or jewels, both real and fake, stop here.

Hudson Made (845-676-6010), 72 Main Street. Open April through December, Wednesday through Sunday 11-5. You will find high-quality soaps, oils, brushes and shaving kits all made in Delaware County.

BLOOMVILLE/BOVINA

Turquoise Barn (607-538-1235), 8052 County Route 18, Bloomville. Open June through December, Thursday through Sunday 11-5. This gem is chock-full of artwork in the gallery section. There is also a variety of wood products, jewelry, and unusual gifts.

Russell's Store (607-832-4242), 2099 County Route 6 (Main Street), Bovina Center, is a don't-miss experience. They still tie up packages with string from a dispenser, the old-fashioned way! There's delicious comfort food, groceries, gifts, local crafts, homemade baked goods, produce, and more. Open weekdays, except Tuesday, 7-6; Saturday and Sunday 9-4.

DELHI

Dee Tiques Gift and Train Shop (607-746-6900), 1260 Peaks Brook Road, a short distance off Route 10. This is one of the region's most complete trains stores with accessories, paint, tools, books, and parts. Open Wednesday through Sunday 10-5.

Stone and Sawyer (888-502-2800), 76 Main Street. Beautiful handmade ceramic lamps are made here. There are other local crafters' products as well, including candles, pillows, blankets and more.

Tay Tea (607-746-6086), 159 Main Street. Open May through December, Saturday and Sunday, 10-5. This amazing teashop offers a range of handcrafted teas. The owner is a colorful character who opened her store in Andes originally and loves to serve samples of her eclectic tea collection to visitors. If you are lucky, you will find the teas in select restaurants as you travel the county.

DEPOSIT

Axtell Antiques (607-467-2353), 1 River Street, specializes in early Americana. They have been in business since 1968 and are located in the oldest building in town, a historic brick structure that dates back to 1799. Hours of operation are Thursday through Saturday and Monday 10-4; Sunday noon-4.

FRANKLIN

Blue Farm Antiques & Letterpress Printing (718-781-5487), 322 Main Street. Open Saturday and Sunday noon-5. This is one of the few places left anywhere that does letterpress printing. The antiques are quite interesting as well.

HANCOCK

Delaware Delicacies Smokehouse (607-637-4443), 420 Rhodes Road, is open daily 9-5. They have all kinds of smoked delicacies—trout, salmon, turkey, even shrimp—and they will mail them anywhere.

Ultimate Fly-Fishing Store (607-637-4296), 159 East Front Street, will delight anglers, but I enjoyed poking around there myself, although I'm not into fishing! Call for hours.

Karcher's Country Kottage (607-637-2555), 156 Leonard Street and **City Mouse, Country Mouse** (607-637-2951), 67 Apex Road (Route 268), both have a good selection of antiques and collectibles. Call first, since both are open more or less by chance or by appointment.

MARGARETVILE/ROXBURY

Catskill Mountain Artisans Guild (845-586-3443), 785 Main Street, Margaretville. Open daily 10-5; Friday and Saturday until 6. They carry a wide selection of handmade items by local craftspeople and offer several workshops. They are located in the Commons, which houses a number of specialty shops. **Home Goods** (845-586-4177), 784 Main Street, Margaretville. Is one of the best kitchenware shops in the Catskills, open daily 10-6; Sunday 11-4.

Antiques at Rick's Barn (607-326-7700), 50061 Route 30, Roxbury, is the place to find an enormous inventory of American and fine European furniture. They have a large inventory and are open year-round, Saturday and Sunday 10-5.

Roxbury General Store is a must-stop when visiting this beautiful Catskill town.

MASONVILLE

Masonville General Store (607-265-3808) 2095 Route 206, is one of the most unusual general stores you will find anywhere. They carry a variety of distinctive items for the kitchen, pantry, bath, and home. The emphasis is on local products from the Catskills. Don't miss this store if you are traveling through the area; it's also a nice place to stop for a drink (see Eating Out).

WALTON

Full Circle Antiques (607-865-5810) 147 and 164 Delaware Street, offers two stores, both multi-dealer locations, chock-full of furniture, glassware, old postcards, and vintage items. There are several hidden treasures here! Open year-round, daily 10-5.

Hidden Antiques (607-510-4245), 6 Townsend Street, is a consortium of 10 antiques and collectibles dealers, and offers furniture, glassware, and an array of small items. Open Friday through Monday 10-6; extended hours during the summer.

SPECIAL EVENTS

Since Delaware County is still a largely rural area, the events listed here tend to take place during the "better weather" months, from late spring through early October.

February: **Ice Harvest at Hanford Mills** (607-278-5744), 73 Route 12, East Meredith. This event is held annually on the first Saturday in February from 10am to 4pm. Admission. Children will enjoy the hands-on ice cutting and adults will appreciate the vintage films about ice harvesting in days of yore. Walk out on the frozen millpond, weather permitting, and help cut the ice using vintage tools. The ice is then hauled by sled to a traditional icehouse. There are hot drinks and food on hand, horse-drawn sleigh rides, and ice-sculpting demonstrations. This is a wonderful winter celebration if you have young children; it's both fun and educational.

July: The week of July Fourth ushers in the **Fire Department Field Days** at the village park in Margaretville, where a week-long carnival with music, rides, entertainment, games of skill and chance, and food concessions keep everyone busy.

The **Deposit Lumberjack Festival**, Riverside Park, includes fireworks, antique cars, a parade and demonstrations of lumberjack skills. The **Sidney Arts and Music Festival** features handmade arts and craft items along with music, games, bands and dance performances. Free. This celebration is usually held in mid-July on a Saturday from 10am-7pm.

August: The **Delaware County Fair**, at the fairgrounds off Route 10 in Walton, runs the second week of August with six days of activity from 9am-10pm. Admission. Part of the agricultural and social life of Delaware County for more than a century, this is one of the last of the truly agricultural county fairs in New York State. Each year hundreds of 4-H members show their prize goods including sheep, pigs, cows and horses. Local produce is displayed and sold in one building and another bursts with colors of hundreds of quilts. You may not bid on the livestock, but you'll enjoy the tractor pulls, horse shows and more. There are pancake and pie tents, sausage sandwiches, and an antique popcorn wagon, listed on the National Register of Historic Places!

September: **Roxbury Revelry**, is celebrated on the Sunday of Labor Day weekend, a daylong event with fireworks, live music and family fun and games in Kirkside Park.

The Cauliflower Festival is held the last Saturday in September from 10am to 4pm. Fields of cauliflower were once a big crop in Delaware County and this festival in Margaretville celebrates the vegetable with food vendors, crafts, a history tent, cooking demos, music and a tractor parade before noon.

October: **Taste of the Catskills**, 2066 Route 18, Delhi, is held at Maple Shade Farm on the Saturday and Sunday of Columbus Day weekend, from 10am-6pm. This is a family-friendly event featuring the fall harvest crops, beer, and wine of the Catskills, and children's activities (hayrides, a corn maze and pumpkin patch). Experience the rich agricultural heritage of the region; meet local farmers and food purveyors. What better way to enjoy the pleasures of Delaware County?

Rondout Creek Marina in Kingston

Slopes of Hunter Mountain.

GREENE COUNTY

6

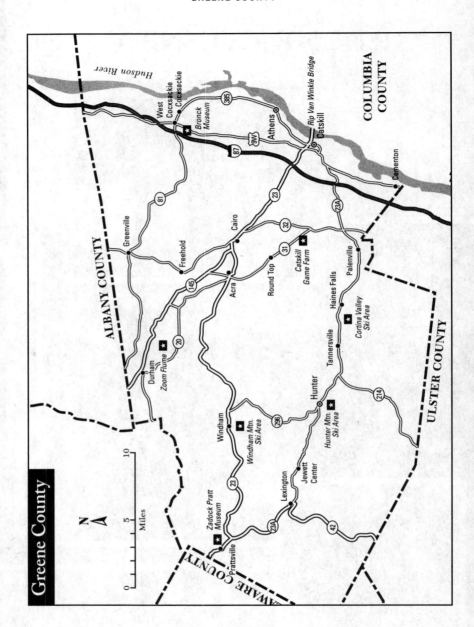

Greene County

GREENE COUNTY

Greene County offers the perfect outdoor experience any time of year. In winter dramatic, snow-filled gorges yield to gray and white fields, and cross-country skiers may come across bear tracks; others can fly down the slopes at Hunter or Windham Mountain, which provide some of the best downhill skiing in the East. In spring, wildflowers cling to wind-scraped rocks, and visitors to the county can watch or join in hiking, biking and canoeing. Each June a tour of homes, farms and estates is held to benefit the county historical society. Summer celebrates with the gifts of icy brooks for tired feet and a flood of cultural festivals. This is a fine time of year to visit North and South lakes and Kaaterskill Falls. Autumn is a season to wonder at the colors that transform the hills and villages into paint pots full of orange and red—the magic that drew Rip Van Winkle to Catskill still enchants visitors today. Or stop by Thomas Cole's house, the place where the Hudson River School of landscape painting began. There are also hiking trails, museums, country auctions, breathtaking waterfalls, quaint villages, festivals, and fine restaurants to enjoy.

VISITOR INFORMATION

Greene County Promotion Department (518-943-3223; 800-355-CATS), 700 Route 23B, Leeds 12451; greatnortherncatskills.com.

GETTING THERE

By car: Greene County is off exit 21 of the NYS Thruway. Routes 23 and 23A run east-west across the county; Route 32 runs north-south. Almost all sites in this chapter can be accessed from these three roads.

By bus: **Adirondack Trailways** (800-858-8555; trailwaysny.com) has daily bus service from Port Authority Terminal in New York City to Catskills, Hunter, Palenville and Windham. *By train:* There are frequent daily **Amtrak** trains between New York City and Hudson (8 miles from Catskill across the Rip Van Winkle Bridge). Check the website, Amtrak.com, for schedules.

By air: **Albany International Airport** (518-242-2222; albanyairport.com) is about 40 miles north of the city of Catskill.

MEDICAL EMERGENCY

Dial 911 in the event of an emergency. The **Greene County Sheriff's office** (518-943-3300) and **New York State Police** (518-622-8600) may also be called directly.

Columbia Memorial Hospital (518-828-7601), 71 Prospect Avenue, Hudson (8 miles from the city of Catskill, across the Rip Van Winkle Bridge).

HISTORIC SITES

Bronck Museum and Greene County Historical Society (518-731-6490; gchistory.org), 90 Route 42, Coxsackie. Open Memorial Day weekend through October 15, Wednesday through Friday noon-4; Saturday and holidays 10-4; Sunday 1-4. Admission. The Vedder Research Library (518-731-1033) is open Tuesday and Wednesday 10-4; Saturday 9-noon.

Once home to nine generations of the Bronck family (which also gave its name to the Bronx), the museum collection traces the history of the Upper Hudson Valley. Visitors should begin with the original structure, a 1663 stone house containing an Indian lookout loft—from a time when settlers were not welcome. The house was remodeled in the late 18th century, when a wing was added, along with fine paneling and fireplaces. Displays include an impressive exhibit of local textiles, looms, and spinning wheels that chronicle the production of Bronck cloth and clothing. The 1738 brick house was connected to the stone house through the hyphen hall. This part of the home is now used to display a fine collection of paintings by 18th- and 19th-century artists, including Ammi Phillips, John Frederick Kensett, Nehamiah Partridge, Ezra Ames, Benjamin Stone, and Thomas Cole. Outside is a kitchen, a charming tiny house itself, set apart from the main house in the style of plantations. The displays here include furniture and kitchen tools. Farm buffs will enjoy the three barns at the complex, each representing a different era. The Dutch barn, with its huge beams; the center-pole-supported, 13-sided Liberty Barn, once the storage area for the wheat harvest, now the oldest documented multisided barn in New York State; and the Victorian horse barn, called the Antiquarium. Each offers visitors a look at the tolls, carriages, and wagons of the day. A walk through the family and slave cemeteries will bring you even closer to the people who made the Bronck complex a working and living farm. The Bronck Museum sponsors a Greene County house tour each June when a different area of the county offers a look into the region's many historic homes. Researchers into local history and genealogy will want to stop at the Vedder Research Library, with its extensive collections of Greene County and New York State records.

Hudson-Athens Lighthouse (518-828-5294; hudsonathenslighthouse.org). Built in 1874, this architectural gem visible from Riverfront Park in Athens, was designed in the Second Empire style. If you are interested in taking a tour, they are held July through October, on the second Saturday of the month, at 11:30, 12:30, 1:30 and 2:30; or by appointment. The tours depart from the Athens Riverfront Park.

The main house at the Thomas Cole National Historic Site in Catskill.

Thomas Cole National Historic Site (also known as Cedar Grove) (518-943-7465; thomascole.org), 218 Spring Street, Catskill. Open May through October, Thursday through Sunday 10-4. Groups may visit by special appointment. Admission.

The grounds are open at no charge daily 8-sunset. Thomas Cole, a painter, poet and essayist, played a significant role in determining how America viewed its landscapes and vistas; his 19th century paintings helped inspire the land conservation movement, and tourism became an industry as visitors trooped to the Catskills in search of the sites Cole depicted. His family home, Cedar Grove, is open to the public and presents an unusual look into the daily life of a Hudson River painter. Cole is credited with founding the Hudson River School of landscape art. The graceful Federal-style house and gardens still look off to the Catskill Mountains, and a locust tree that Cole mentioned in his writings remains outside the front entrance. Inside, interpretive exhibits introduce the visitor to Cole and his family, the Catskills region, artists such as Asher B. Durand and Frederic Church and the Hudson River School. Several small oils and sketches by Cole are on display here, along with family heirlooms, including his Aeolian harp, sketching stool, paint box, and Bible. There are leaves from his journal and traveling trunk. Outside on the grounds, you can stop and see the recently opened (2016) new studio that was torn down in 1973 due to disrepair and has been beautifully reconstructed. The family's Greek Revival privy (with a front door for family and a back door for servants) and Cole's "old studio," which once served as slave quarters. There are lectures and events throughout the summer months, usually on Sunday afternoons, and visitors can take a short walk to the Cole family gravesite. The gift shop has an excellent selection of regional books so make sure to stop there (at the Visitors Center) before leaving the site.

Zadock Pratt Museum and Pratt's Rocks (518-299-3258; zadockprattmuseum. com), 14540 Main Street (Route 23), Prattsville. Open Memorial Day weekend through Columbus Day, Friday through Monday, 10-5. Guided tours are given each hour. School and group tours year-round by appointment. Admission.

Born in 1790, genius businessman Zadock Pratt started out as a harness maker and soon went into the leather-tanning business. He became such a prominent community leader that the town of Prattsville was named in his honor. His tanning facilities were among the largest in the state, and he built many of Prattsville's homes for his workers. In later years Pratt served in both the state and federal governments. Today his home is a museum that shows what life in New York State was like in the 1850s. Exhibits focus on the tanning industry as well as the story of Greene County, with rooms displaying period furniture and decorative arts. In a separate gallery the work of local artists is shown, and special events are held. When your visit to the museum is completed, you can stop outside Prattsville on Route 23 (there's a sign) at Pratt's Rocks, a memorial carved by an itinerant stonemason. Free and open year-round, the huge stone reliefs show Pratt's son, a favorite horse, and Pratt himself. A small picnic area overlooks Schoharie Creek, and there are great views from the summit.

FOR FAMILIES

Round Top Raptor Center (518-622-0118; roundtopraptorcenter.com), 733 Bald Hill Road, Round Top. Open Memorial Day weekend through Labor Day, Friday through Sunday 1-4. Admission. Falconing is one of the oldest sports known to man. Enjoy the sights and sounds of falcons and hawks presented by master falconer Gino Altimari. There are demonstrations of lure flying, one of the best ways to exercise falcons that doesn't require a large field, along with fascinating facts about these remarkable creatures!

Zoom Flume Water Park (518-2394559; zoomflume.com), 20 Shady Glen Road, East Durham. Open daily Father's Day weekend (mid-June) through Labor Day, Monday through Friday 10-6; Saturday and Sunday 10-7. Admission. This aqua-amusement park is set into the Shady Glen canyon, a natural formation of steep walls and running water, so the site itself is beautiful, even if you are going to observe rather than participate in the array of water activities. The Raging River Ride and Zoom Flume let you slosh and slide your way down the canyon; the Rip Tide Wave Pool is a fun addition to the park. There's an enormous activity pool and several slides of all sizes, a game area, and a Toddler Section for one-and two-year-olds. The Black Vortex Speed Slide takes three people at a time through an exciting water adventure older kids will love. There are nature trails, scenic overlooks and waterfalls, and a restaurant with an observation deck for drying out in addition to a good-size outdoor food court and picnic area. A wonderfully unique scenic water park that is sure to make everyone in the family happy.

SCENIC DRIVES

Mountains, deep gorges, valleys, and waterfalls can all be seen during a leisurely drive through Greene County and a tour can take all day or only a few hours, depending on the number of stops you want to make. Some of the roads are narrow and winding, though, so use the designated parking areas to take in scenic views. And be careful to check out driving conditions if you take a ride in the winter months or even early spring.

Some lovely parts of the county can be seen by taking Route 42 north over the **Deep Notch**, which is cool even on the hottest days. At Route 23A head east through Hunter, Haines Falls, and Palenville. Along the road you will see **Hunter Mountain**, breathtaking waterfalls, winding streams and the **Amphitheatre,** a natural, bowl-shaped rock formation. Follow Route 23 into the city of Catskill, where you can pick up the NYS Thruway at exit 21.

Another tour starts at the junction of Routes 23A and 23C; follow 23C east to **Jewett**. The large elegant homes lining the roads tucked into the hills were part of Onteora Park, a "cottage" colony where many wealthy families summered during the 19th century. The junction of Route 25 and 23C shelters the **Old Stone Church**, in which there are some lovely murals. The church is closed during the winter months. At County Route 17 head south to Route 23A, where you can pick up the aforementioned scenic drive into Catskill.

To see some exceptional churches, begin the drive on Route 23A in **Jewett Center**. Here you will see **St. John the Baptist Ukrainian Church** and **the Grazhda**, which were constructed in the traditional style, suing large beams and wooden pins instead of nails. The interior of the church is decorated with wood carvings and panels, and the education building has displays relating to Ukrainian history. Concerts and art shows are held in the **Grazhda** (518-263-3862). On Route 23A in Hunter you will find **Our Lady of the Snow**, one of the oldest Catholic churches in the Mountaintop region. Continue on Route 23A to Haines Falls, where you will see the **Grotto of Our Lady of the Mountain**. This shrine was constructed in the 1920s and recalls the miracle of Lourdes. The grotto is open to the public. Continue on 23A to Palenville, where the **Gloria Dei Episcopal Church** is open for tours Saturdays. Then take Route 23A to Route 32 north into Cairo, then Route 24 to South Cairo. There you will find the **Mahayana Buddhist Temple** (518-622-3619), a retreat complex complete with Chinese temple, dragon decorations, and fine artwork. The walkways are open to the public year-round. From South Cairo, you can take Route 23B east to the NYS Thruway.

Crossroads Brewery on Water Street in Catskill.

WINERIES AND BREWERIES

Cave Mountain Brewing Company (518-734-9222), 5359 Main Street, Windham. Open Thursday, Friday and Monday 4:30-10; Saturday noon-11; Sunday noon-9. This brewery/eatery featuring pub fare is decorated with beer cans from throughout the world. In addition to the sampler of 12 beers brewed here, there's live music on Thursdays and Saturdays. The food is what would be expected (burgers, wings, sandwiches), all served on paper plates. The place is packed during ski season and service is somewhat slow at that time. Hours vary with the season, so call ahead.

Crossroads Brewing Company (518-945-BEER), 21 Second Street, Athens. Open Monday, Wednesday and Thursday 4-9; Friday 4-midnight; Saturday 1-midnight; Sunday 1-9. Closed Tuesday. Located in the historic village of Athens, this brewery offers award-winning ales along with fresh, locally sourced fare in a spacious, informal setting. Ten of their own craft beers are on tap; and six New York State wines are served, along with their own root beer. Enjoy live music most Saturday nights. There is another location (518-444-8277), 201 Water Street, Catskill. The space is large and there's also a "beer garden" to drink alfresco.

Windham Vineyard & Winery (518-734-5214), 11 Mount View Estates Road, Windham. Open year-round, Saturday 1-6; Sunday 1-4. This small, family-owned vineyard is located off County Route 10, between Windham and Ashland. There are handmade chocolate truffle tastings here and they feature an un-oaked chardonnay as well as a gold-medal winning ice-wine. In season visitors can pick their own grapes. In the winter months it's a wonderful place to stop after skiing.

ACTIVITIES

BICYCLING

Elm Ridge Mountain Bike Trail Network (518-734-4700; windhamarf.org), Route 23, Windham. There are over 25 miles of marked mountain biking trails: some are suited for short family outings and others provide adventures for the most advanced bikers.

Huckleberry Multi-Use Trail/Tannersville Bike Path (518-589-5850), County Route 25, Tannersville. This 2.7 mile gentle path runs from Clum Hill Road across from Cortina Valley, down around Tannersville Lake, to Bloomer Road. It is ideal for walkers, hikers and cross-country skiers as well as bikers. The path is well marked and welcomes all activities.

Round Top Trail Network (518-965-0487; rtmba.com), 43 Ravine Drive, Round Top. Five family resorts in Round Top have organized over 25 miles of single and double-track trails that pass waterfalls and bridges in this particularly scenic part of Greene County. There are sections of the network experienced bikers will find extremely challenging.

Windham Path (518-734-4700), Route 23 (entrance behind Windham Pharmacy, Route 296, Windham). This 1.5 mile loop, a multi-use path for walking, biking or snow-shoeing and cross-country skiing in the winter, offers great views and foot bridges. Ideal for the youngest athletes!

Windham Mountain Bike Park (518-734-4300; windhammountain.com), 19 Resort Drive, Windham. Take a scenic quad-chairlift ride to begin your bike tour. The ski center maintains a large network of trails for bikers of all ages and abilities. The lift operates July through October, weekends 11-3 and there are rentals, lessons, guided tours and a restaurant on the premises.

The bike shop at **Windham Mountain Outfitters** (518-734-4700), 61 Route 296, Windham, is where you can hire a guide or purchase trail maps and rent a mountain bike to ride the trails on your own. They have guided group mountain bike rides, and there are excursions for all abilities.

BOAT CRUISES & BOATING

The Spirit of the Hudson (518-822-1014; hudsoncruises.com) departs from the waterfront in Hudson and offers sightseeing cruises on the river from June through September Wednesday, Saturday and Sunday at 1pm. There are also ferry rides for $12 on Saturday and Sunday from Hudson to Athens and back; 5:30pm-10pm. Charter boats are available for rent. Check the website for latest schedules.

North-South Lake State Park (518-589-5058), County Route 18, Haines Falls. This is a great place to go if you want to rent a canoe, kayak, or rowboat and relax on two of the most beautiful lakes in the county.

Riverview Marine Services, Inc. (518-943-5311), 103 Main Street, Catskill, is a full-service marine facility with a store, motorboat service and accessories. They rent kayaks, canoes, and motorboats. If you are interested in motoring on the Hudson River, this is one of the only places that offers rentals.

FARMS, FARMS STANDS & PICK-YOUR-OWN FARMS

Greene County is filled with farm stands that carry everything from mushrooms to maple syrup. The **Catskill Farmers' Market** (518-719-8244), at Catskill Point (the end of Main Street), Catskill, is held June through October, every Friday 4-7pm. This is a great place to see what farmers throughout the county are offering. This riverside market, on the banks of the Hudson River, usually has several different activities going on, in addition to the market. For those who want to explore on their own, the following are some of my favorite places to discover the bounty of the county.

Black Horse Farms (518-943-9324), 10094 Route 9W, Athens, is open March through December, daily 9-6, and stocks everything from vegetables, herbs, eggs, plants and pumpkins to maple products, flowers, Christmas trees, and honey. This is a terrific market located in a renovated barn that dates back to 1864. Local residents have been shopping here for years and the place is definitely worth a detour!

Boehm Farm (518-731-6196), 233 County Route 26, Climax, is open mid-August to mid-December, daily 9-5. Here you can pick your owns apples (several varieties are available) and peaches. They sell sweet cider, plums, jams and jellies. While in Climax, another lovely farm is **Schnare's Sunset Orchard** (518-731-8846), 1008, Route 81, Climax. They are open daily in September and October for apple picking. The location is beautiful and kids love to watch the cider doughnuts being made here.

Catskill Mountain Country Store has two locations: one at 6014 Main Street, Tannersville (518-589-6777), and one at 5510 Route 23, Windham (518-734-3387). Both stores are open Thursday through Monday 8-3 (Tannersville) and 9-5 (Windham). These terrific general stores/country markets have a bakery, café and gift shop specializing in organic produce in season, local maple syrup and other regional products including honey, plants, Christmas trees, and more. There are lots of books about hiking the Catskills and interesting toys for the kids. Make sure to stop and look around here.

Dines Farms (518-239-4206), 176 Dingman Road (off Route 81), Oak Hill. Open year round, but call for hours, as they change with the season. Buy natural and pasture-raised meats here (chicken, duck, pork, rabbit, and lamb), directly from the farmer. No hormones or antibiotics are used on this farm! The chicken sausage is excellent.

Hull-O Farms (518-239-6950), 3739 County Route 20, Durham. Open year-round; call for hours. Kids will love the corn maze, as well as pumpkins to be picked in season at this eight generation working dairy farm. Families can stay overnight in private guesthouses and have a chance to milk cows, feed baby calves, and collect eggs from the chickens. So if you enjoy picking pumpkins, you might want to stay overnight and experience life on a working farm. This is a great stop for families with young children.

Maple Hill Farms (518-299-3604), 135 County Route 2, Prattsville (9 miles west of Hunter), is open daily. They are a sixth generation family-owned and operated farm specializing in maple products. Enjoy maple cream, maple sugar and, of course, fabulous syrup. They also sell pure honey and farm-fresh preserves. Call for hours since they change with the season.

Pathfinder Farms (518-943-7096), 2433 Old Kings Road, Catskill. The Bulich Family sells organically grown products: vegetables, fruit, beef, pork, chicken, herbs, and honey on their 400-acre farm. Call before heading there: they love people to stop by, but want to make sure they are around to greet you….and not plowing the land far from the entrance of the farm!

Traphagen's Honey (518-263-4150), 8350 Main Street, Hunter, is open year-round, Friday through Monday 9-5, selling all kinds of honey and maple-related products, as well as gourmet foods.

FISHING

Fishing in Greene County can mean a lazy day spent pond-side or an exciting, nerve-ripping hour fighting a sturgeon in the Hudson. There are more than 58 streams that shelter wild trout here, as well as lakes, and, of course, the Hudson River. A state fishing license is required in Greene County, and town permits are also needed for the Potuck Reservoir in Catskill and the Medway Reservoir in Coxsackie. Permits and licenses can be obtained at many bait & tackle and sports shops, as well as in town clerks' offices and through the county clerk in Catskill. Seasons and limits vary with the species of fish; check with the **Department of Environmental Conservation** (845-256-3000) for specifics.

Public fishing areas are marked by yellow signs: parking spaces are available, although sometimes limited. If you want to catch one of the more than 150 species of fish found in the Hudson River—shad, perch, herring, and sturgeon among them—you may want to use the public boat ramps in Athens, Coxsackie or Catskill. Route 23A will take you past Rip Van Winkle Lake in Tannersville, Schoharie Creek, and the Schoharie Reservoir, all of which are great fishing areas. Route 145 leads to Lower Catskill Creek, Upper Catskill Creek, and Ten Mile Creek; while Route 296 provides access to the Batavia Kill boat launch and the East Kill Trout Preserve. BASSmaster invitational fishing tournaments have been held in Greene County; information may be obtained by calling the **Greene County Promotion Department** (518-943-3223).

Guide Services: **Finns and Grins** (518-929-1888), Catskill. Bob Lewis runs charters for striped bass on the Hudson River during April and May. He is fully licensed and insured and supplies all necessary equipment. **Judd Weisberg NYS Licensed Guide** (518-989-6583; fishwithjudd.com), provides full-service guiding and instruction in fly-fishing. He also offers wade and float trips in the Catskills. **Upstate Adventure Guides** (845-399-9948; upstateadventureguides.com) offers hiking, paddling, camping and backpacking trips throughout the Catskills. They will customize a trip to fit your needs and can do this for all ages and abilities.

GOLF

The greens of Greene County require widely varying levels of skill, but no one who picks up a club will leave the region disappointed. The following establishments are open to the public. It is suggested you call before going to determine hours of operation and available tee times.

Blackhead Mountain Lodge and Country Club (518-622-3157), 50 Crows Nest Road, Round Top, has an 18-hole par-72 championship course that is quite challenging. There is a pro shop, lessons, restaurant, and bar on the premises.

Catskill Golf Resort (518-943-0302), 27 Brooks Lane, Catskill, has an 18-hole, 6382-yard course. There is a pro shop, club rentals, and restaurant, all in a beautiful country atmosphere.

Christman's Windham House Country Inn and Golf Resort (518-734-6990, 888-294-4053), 5742 Route 23, Windham, one of the oldest inns in the region, offers an 18-hole, 7072-yard Mountain Course. With five sets of tees, this forest links layout is fun to play at any skill level. There is also a nine-hole Valley Course that will please walkers and beginners. Cart and club rentals, pro shop, snack bar, driving range. There is a Ben Sutton Golf School that offers lessons, and overnight packages are available for golfers.

Colonial Golf Club (518-589-5310), Route 23A, Tannersville, has a nine-hole course, par 35, 2718 yards. There are carts, a pro shop, snack bar, club rentals, and lessons. This is a good place for novices and there are many gorgeous views.

Rainbow Golf Club (518-966-5343), 3822 Route 26, Greenville, offers an 18-hole, USGA-regulation championship course. There is a driving range and carts; a restaurant and bar as well as rentals are available. The club offers golf packages and vacation apartments just off the course.

Rip Van Winkle Country Club (518-678-9779), 3200 Route 23A, Palenville, has a nine-hole Donald Ross-designed course with alternate tees, par 36, 3120 yards. A restaurant and bar are on the premises. This is a nice course for beginners.

Sunny Hill Resort & Golf Course (518-634-7642), 352 Sunny Hill Road, Greenville, has a challenging 18-hole, par 66 course that overlooks a beautiful lake; clubhouse with pro shop and snack bar. Gas and handcart rentals are available.

Thunderhart Golf Club (518-634-7816), 2740 County Route 67, Freehold, offers an 18-hole championship course, par 74, 6863 yards; driving range and pavilion for outings. An informal atmosphere prevails here.

Windham Country Club (518-734-9910), 36 South Street (Route 296), Windham, has an 18-hole, par 71, 6024-yard championship course. There is a pro shop, lessons, and driving range. They were awarded three and a half stars by *Golf Digest* magazine. A restaurant and bar are on the premises.

HIKING

Greene County provides some of the best hiking and views in the Catskills. You don't have to be a seasoned hiker to enjoy a day walking on the clearly marked trails. The magnificent vistas have inspired Thomas Cole and other Hudson River School painters. These are my favorite hiking places in the county; most are easy to moderate difficulty and will be enjoyed by experienced hikers and novices alike.

Cohotate Preserve is located just off Route 385 in Athens. It's a nature preserve with a self-guide tour on easy trails that run along the banks of the Hudson River. You will see the sign for the preserve on the right side of the highway if you are heading from Catskill toward Athens. This is definitely an easy walk and is a good choice for anyone traveling with children. I like walking here on holiday weekends since it is always quiet and there are no crowds.

Coxsackie Riverside Park & Four-Mile Point Preserve. The park is located at Betke Boulevard on the Hudson River in town; the preserve is on Four Mile Point Road and is a 7.6-mile riverfront preserve that may be explored by walking or biking.

Devil's Path will appeal to more adventurous hikers: it's steep and relatively

The trail along the Hudson River in Four Mile Point Preserve outside of the village of Coxsackie.

isolated. The path passes over much rugged terrain, particularly Indian Head Mountain, and includes the Hunter Mountain Trail and West Kill Mountain Range Trail. To reach this trailhead, turn south off Route 23A at the only light in Tannersville. Go 1.5 miles to the road's intersection with Bloomer Road. Make a left and soon after bear left onto Platte Clove Mountain Road. Stay on this road for one mile to Prediger Road; then go about a half-mile farther to find the trail. Each mountain on the Devil's Path can be hiked in a day or less.

Diamond Notch/West Kill Falls are reached by a pleasant day hike. Five miles north of Phoenicia, right off Route 214, it's easy to find the entrance to the trail. From Route 214 take Diamond Notch Road one mile to a bridge. Cross it and park. The hike is about 4.5 miles round trip and should take approximately three and a half to four hours at a moderate pace. There are beautiful waterfalls along the way.

The Escarpment Trail runs from Kaaterskill Creek on Route 23A to East Windham on Route 23 (24 miles in all). There are several short hikes along the path to Kaaterskill High Peak, North Point, and Mary's Glen. The trails in the North Lake area are renowned for their waterfalls and fantastic views of the entire Hudson Valley. **Kaaterskill Falls** and the **Catskill Mountain House** are particularly notworthy sites. The easy-to-find entry point for these trails is at the junction of Route 23A and Kaaterskill Creek on the north side of the highway. These hikes are usually very popular on summer weekends, so you might want to go during the week to avoid the crowds. North Lake and decent campgrounds are nearby for those who want to take a swim....or stay overnight.

Four-Mile Point Preserve in Coxsackie is reached by taking Route 385; it is eight miles from the Rip Van Winkle Bridge. This 7.6-acre riverfront preserve offers picturesque shoreline vistas and a tranquil inland pond. There are nature trails, and it's a wonderful place to observe all kinds of birds.

Hunter Mountain is the second highest peak in the Catskills at 4040 feet and it is best hiked on the trail that begins on Spruceton Road. To get there, take Route 42 north from Lexington and go four miles to Spruceton Road. The trailhead and trail are well defined.

Rams Horn-Livingston Sanctuary in Catskill may be reached by following Route 9W south from the Rip Van Winkle Bridge for 2.5 miles. Make a left onto Grandview Avenue and follow the road for a half-mile to a parking area. There are 480 acres of the Hudson's largest tidal swamp forest here, a breeding ground for American shad and bass, and more than three miles of trails. Following a half-mile walk, you can canoe from the tidal marsh out to the Hudson River.

Shinglekill Falls, on the eastern fringe of the Catskills, are only a few hundred feet from the road. From Cairo, head south, then west on County Route 24. After passing South Road, the falls are about 500 feet farther along on the right side. Shinglekill Grist Mill, a small store, once an old mill, provides access to the falls. For those who want to enjoy a few hours by a cool stream or are looking for an easy walk to a waterfall, this is the perfect spot!

HORSEBACK RIDING

Catskill Equestrian Center (518-925-0095), 118 Castle Road (take Route 32 to Game Farm Road and follow signs to the center), Catskill. Open year-round, daily 10-6. A family business for more than 40 years, this equestrian center at Bailiwick Ranch offers riding for all ages and abilities. Scenic mountain trail rides are available: riders must be over the age of seven to participate. For those who want something more intensive, there are all-day mountain trips and overnight camping excursions. The pony rides and a petting zoo will enchant the youngest children. For those interested in lessons, both English and Western riding instruction are offered in both indoor and outdoor riding arenas.

Hidden Meadow Farm (518-928-0939), 352 Brown Road, Durham. Open year-round by appointment. If you are an experienced rider, you will enjoy going out on acres of private trails at this establishment. Owner Erika Rose gives lessons as well.

K&K Equestrian Center (518-966-4829), 5203 Route 67, East Durham. Open May through October. This business has been owned and operated by the Phillips family for more than 35 years. They offer guided scenic trail rides, pony rides, and lessons in an informal pleasant atmosphere.

ZIP LINES AND CANOPY TOUR

Hunter Mountain Zipline Adventure (518-263-4388; ziplinenewyork.com), 64 Klein Avenue (off Route 23A), Hunter.

Open daily year-round, 8-4. Make sure to check the website for necessary clothing in both cold and warm weather, as well as age restrictions. And make sure to wear closed-toe shoes that can sustain high winds: no sandals are permitted. There are two experiences offered:

The Mid-Mountain Tour is family friendly and takes participants into the canopy with six zip lines, four rope bridges, nine aerial tree platforms, and a rappel. The longest zip line on this excursion is about 650 feet and nearly 60 feet above ground. The tour lasts three hours and is the best option for first-timers.

The Skyrider Tour is the second-largest zip line in the world and is classed as an extreme activity. There are about 5 miles of zip lines, including five side-by-side racing zip lines, and one reaches a speed of 50 mph. This tour lasts about three hours and is recommended for those who have experience with this sport and enjoy a difficult challenge.

For those who decide the zip line adventure isn't for them, they can still enjoy the **Hunter Mountain Sky Ride**, the longest and highest in the Catskills, and the only six-passenger chairlift in the state. It takes riders to a height of 3200 feet and offers panoramic views. The sky ride is open on weekends only, July through October, weather permitting.

Windham Mountain Adventure Park Zip Line (518-734-6974; windhammountain.com), South Street, Windham; ¼ mile west of Windham Mountain. Open during winter ski season only; daily 8-4. This zip line consists of two racing zip lines 40 feet high and both travel 500 feet. A midpoint station landing connects to another zip line and rope bridge. Participants must weigh at least 80 and not more than 270 pounds. This is a great zip line for first-timers to try.

WINTER SPORTS

The slopes at Windham Mountain.

CROSS-COUNTRY SKIING & SNOWSHOEING

Greene County is home to some of the best cross-country skiing to be found in New York State. More than 1000 acres of groomed and un-groomed trails snake their way through the county's forests and fields. Many of these areas are patrolled by Nordic Ski Patrol members.

Cross-Country Ski and Snowshoe Center at Windham Country Club (518-734-9910; windhammountain.com), 36 South Street, Windham. Open 8-4 on weekends and holiday weeks. There are several miles of marked groomed trails at the Windham Country Club golf course for both cross-country skiing and snowshoeing. The views are spectacular. Rentals are available.

Mountain Trails X-Country Ski and Snowshoe Center (518-589-5361; mtntrails.com), 6198 Route 23A, Tannersville. Open on weekends and holiday weeks. There are over 20 miles of woodland trails here that are groomed, marked and track-set. After skiing, enjoy hot chocolate in the snack bar or warming hut which has an enormous fireplace. There are ski and snowshoe rentals available as well as lessons.

North-South Lake (518-357-2289; dec.ny.gov) County Route 18, Haines Falls. While there are no services here, only open trails on old carriage roads, the scenic overlooks are magnificent and rentals are available at a nearby general store. This is a great spot for more experienced cross-country skiers and snowshoe enthusiasts.

DOWNHILL SKIING

Skiers from beginner to expert will enjoy excellent snow conditions, modern facilities and some of the best skiing and amazing views anywhere in Greene County, which lies in New York's snow belt. Here, sudden storms can dump several inches of powder in an hour, and the ski season may last six months. In addition to specialty offerings, both Hunter and Windham have equipment rentals, child-care services, dining facilities, picnic areas, ski shops, and overnight accommodations.

Hunter Mountain (518-263-4223 or 888-486-8376; huntermtn.com), 64 Klein Avenue (off 23A), Hunter. From exit 21, NYS Thruway, the trip is approximately 24 miles taking Route 23 east to Route 9W south, then 23A west; or 18 miles from exit 20, taking Route 32 north to 32A north to 23A west. Open daily 9-4; Saturday, Sunday & holidays from 8:30; Hunter West 9:30-3:30. Hunter Mountain's reputation as the snowmaking capital of the East is well deserved. The three different mountains—Hunter One, Hunter West and Hunter Mountain—offer skiers of all skill levels a chance to test themselves on 58 trails spread out on 240 skiable acres serviced by twelve lifts. Runs at Hunter can extend more than two miles, with a 3200-foot summit elevation and vertical drops of 1600 feet. There are some extremely difficult trails, even for expert skiers. Hunter Mountain has New York State's first six-passenger high-speed detachable lift. The double, triple and quadruple chairlifts cut the lines down to size, but in such a popular area you should be prepared for crowds on holidays, weekends and special promotion days. During the week there are rarely lift lines and, of course, it's less expensive.

Hunter offers ski and snowboard lessons for all levels, and a wide variety of amateur and professional races are held during the season, including one for chefs, fire fighters, and nurses. There are two Terrain Parks for snowboarders with a 1000-watt stereo system blasting motivational music. Two slopes wide, the Terrain Park offers a dozen features and several rails for jibbing, jumping and pumping action. There are also snowshoeing and snow tubing areas, with nine 1000-fott long chutes. Hunter offers 100 percent snowmaking capability, so the season sometimes begins before Thanksgiving and lasts well into April. There are complete facilities here, including a full-service hotel, restaurant, cafeterias, lodge, museum, ski shop, and plenty of parking. There is also zip lining if you want to experience the slopes from a different perspective!

Apres ski relaxation at Hunter Mountain on a gorgeous winter day.

Windham Mountain (518-734-4300; 800-754-9463; windhammountain. com), 19 Resort Drive, Windham. Open Monday through Friday 9-4; Saturday, Sunday and holidays 8-4 and 4-8 for night skiing. The hours for the Advenure Park, including the ice rink there, are Friday 4-8; Saturday and holoidays 10-8; Sunday 10-4. This is a wonderful place to ski in the Catskills and I still like it the best. Windham Mountain has one of the nicest lounge areas and bar with a panoramic view of the mountain. The atmosphere is friendly and relaxed. Diversity is a hallmark of Windham Mountain: It's a great place for either a family excursion or a romantic escape. There are 54 trails on 285 skiable acres and elevations of 1600 feet at the base and 3100 feet at the summit. Trail difficulty ranges from easy to expert, and the longest trail is more than two miles long. The Advenure Park near the mountain has several snowtubing lifts and dozens of tubes for sliding. The mountain is renowned for the high quality of its private lessons and employs over 200 ski instructors. A conveyor lift on the beginner slope makes learning to ski and snowboard easier than ever. The Children's Learning Center offers fun for young nonskiers or tired kids. Windham has won awards for its courtesy services, including valet parking and decent dining facilities, along with a senior-skier development program and lessons in racing, freestyle sking and snowboarding. The area is well-known for remarkable work with disabled skiers. For those who prefer ice skating to schussing down the slopes, there is a 60-foot by 120-foot ice rink lighted for night use, as well as a timber frame warming and rental center, within the Adventure Park. There are also kid snowmobiles and a 500-foot zip line in the park. Fees at the Adventure Park are charged by activity.

PARKS

Mountaintop Arboretum (518-589-3903; mtarboretum.org), 4 Maude Adams Road (off Route 23C), Tannersville. Free. Open year-round, 7am-7pm, but call in advance for a guided tour (by appointment only). This public garden in the Catskills, run by a nonprofit organization, features a living collection of both exotic and native trees and shrubs. Some plants on this 193-acre site are indigenous to the Catskills, but not all. Each season brings delights, from the flowering height of spring to the brightly colored autumn foliage. Many have identification markers. There are workshops throughout the year and horticulturalists or those who just want to know "What is that tree?" will enjoy this stop and should check the schedule of educational programs. This center also serves as a botanical research facility and will delight amateur gardeners.

North Lake and South Lake (518-589-5058; 518-943-4030), Take Route 23A to County Route 18, Haines Falls. Route 18 leads to the entrance. Open late May through November, daily 9-dusk. Admission; extra fee for campsite rental. This recreational area offers breathtaking scenery and a multitude of activities. Visitors can swim in a mountain lake with a clean, sandy beach. Boat rentals and fishing are also available. This is an ideal place for a family outing.

A short hike from North Lake is **Kaaterskill Falls** (518-935-3735), one of the highest falls on the East Coast and a popular subject for Hudson River School artists. A viewing platform opened in 2016 so make sure to drive to 103 Laurel House Road, where there is a short trail to the platform and a steep trail goes down to the falls. Do not park along Route 23A, but rather continue driving to County Route 18 and there is plenty of parking and only a short walk to the trail. (The North-South Lake area also has a multiuse campground with hookups for recreational vehicles; it is advisable to make reservations early in the season since this is a popular site, and it gets very crowded on summer weekends.)

A true oasis in the wilderness (selling soft drinks, toys, T-shirts, and groceries) is the **Twilight General Store** (518-589-6480), North Lake Road, Haines Falls, on the left side of the road, two miles before you get to the entrance of the park. They stock all kinds of camping supplies in case you forgot something. The gift shop is also filled with dozens of regional books and guides to the Catskills. Open mid-May through mid-October, 8-6

LODGING

Greene County is an extremely popular resort area, especially during the summer, and there are hundreds of B&Bs, inns, motels, and campgrounds. Some establishments once catered to lovers of Irish, Italian, or Scandinavian heritage. Today many offer a full range of facilities on lakes and rivers. The following list is only a sampling of what can be discovered throughout the county.

Catskill Area
(Leeds, Purling, Round Top)

The Bavarian Manor Country Inn (518-622-3261), 866 Mountain Avenue, Purling 12470. ($$) This historic Civil War-era inn has been operating for over a century. The third-generation-owned property offers 18 lovely rooms, all with private baths, cable TV, and air-conditioning. Some have fireplaces. There is a full bar and decent restaurant featuring German specialties; a hearty breakfast is served to guests. The inn offers plenty of old-world charm and is located on 100 acres of wooded property. There are plenty of trails for those who enjoy walking and hiking. Children welcome. Open year-round.

Caleb Street's Inn (518-943-0246), 251 Main Street, Catskill 12414. ($$) This beautiful, elegant home is filled with antiques and has a large veranda that overlooks the Catskill Marina. There are four rooms here: two share a bath, and two large suites have private baths. It's a nice place to stay for those who want to walk to shops and restaurants and prefer to stay in town. Open year-round.

The Kaaterskill (518-678-0026), 424 High Falls Extension, Catskill 12414. ($$) This 100-year-old farm, set on 32 acres with panoramic views of the Catskills, is now an inn with six private suites, each with a Jacuzzi, kitchenette, fine linens, stone fireplace, and wireless Internet access. Guests will enjoy the private hiking trails as well as access to the Kaaterskill Creek. The inn welcomes pets and is open year-round.

Post Cottage (518-719-0747), 174 Spring Street, Catskill 12414. ($$) There are four rooms here: all have king-size beds, private baths with Jacuzzi tubs, gas log fireplaces and air-conditioning. There is a tennis court on the premises for use by guests. Open year-round.

Shinglekill Falls B&B (518-216-2587), 508 Mountain Avenue, Purling. ($$) There are four cozy rooms with private baths in this former miller's house situated above a 32-foot waterfall. A full breakfast is served and they are open year-round.

Tumblin' Falls House (518-622-3981), 44 Falls View Lane, Cairo 12413. ($$) There are four guest rooms and most have gorgeous views. The Falls View Suite makes for an especially romantic experience. Wander the gardens and trails here or relax listening to the sound of "tumblin'"water on the multilevel deck with spa overlooking Shinglekill Falls. Open year-round.

Winter Clove Inn (518-622-3267), 557 Winter Clove Road, Round Top 12473. ($$) Located on 400 acres adjoining the Catskill Forest Preserve, this inn opened in 1830 and is still run by the same family, the Whitcombs. There are swimming pools, tennis courts, a golf course, cross-country ski trails, hayrides in autumn, and even a bowling alley. All baked goods are homemade, and many of the recipes have been passed down in the family for generations. Children are welcome and this is an ideal getaway for families. All meals are included in the rates, unless special arrangements are made in advance. The 51 rooms all have private baths. Open year-round.

Coxsackie

Mansion & Reed Guesthouse (646-691-8598), 45 Reed Street, Coxsackie 12051 ($$) This renovated historic building houses a beautiful retail store with four suites upstairs. Located in the charming village of Coxsackie, each room is beautifully decorated and has stunning views of the Hudson River or the village. Open year-round.

Hunter Area
(Palenville, Tannersville)

Clark House Bed & Breakfast (518-678-5649), 3292 Route 23A, Palenville 12463. ($$) This turn-of-the-20th century Victorian guesthouse offers five rooms, all with private bath, as well as his and hers bathrobes. Guest rooms are decorated in a range of styles: The Lodge has a wood-burning stove; the Sea Room, a gas fireplace; and the French Quarter Room offers a canopy bed and claw-foot bathtub. The Asian Room is simple, yet chic, with antique furnishings, and the American Room has stunning mountain views. They are open year-round—and so is their 10-person hot tub!

Deer Mountain Inn (518-589-6268), 790 County Route 25, Tannersville 12485. ($$$) This gracious, elegant country estate has seven beautiful guest rooms. All have private bath and TV; some have working fireplaces and sitting areas. There is a fine restaurant on the premises. Open year-round.

Fairlawn Inn (518-263-5025), 7872 Main Street, Hunter 12442. ($$) This inn is the epitome of Victorian charm, from the three-story corner turret and wraparound porches to the elaborately designed wallpapered ceilings and cozy brass beds. A stunning grand staircase and antiques-filled lobby are only a preview for the inn's several large common rooms, which provide a variety of settings for quiet contemplation or socializing. Each of the nine bedrooms has a queen-size bed and private bath. A breakfast feast here may include spinach quiche or stuffed French toast. Special midweek rates. Open year-round.

Rosehaven Inn (518-589-5636), 147 Sunset Park Road, Haines Falls ($$) Four beautiful rooms with Jacuzzi tubs and fireplaces in this restored building surrounded by pastoral views, are just minutes away from Hunter Mountain. A full breakfast is served by hosts Kelly and Sean and this lovely bed & breakfast is a nice alternative to the numerous motel accommodations in the area.

Windham Area
(Durham, East Windham)

Albergo Allegria Bed & Breakfast (518-734-5560), 43 Route 296, Windham 12496. ($$$) Step up on the wicker-furnished porch, and feel the grace and beauty of days gone by. The Victorian theme is continued throughout this bed & breakfast with antique furnishings and period wallpaper and décor. A full breakfast of fresh, fruit, home-baked muffins, croissants, omelets, and local honey is served. The main lounge with overstuffed couches and fireplace, as well as a library, are warm and inviting. There are 14 rooms, and 7 suites with Jacuzzis. Several fine Windham restaurants are within walking distance. Open year-round.

Bed on Clouds B&B (518-734-4692), 5320 Main Street, Windham. ($$) There are five rooms, all with private baths, located in the village of Windham and two off-premise studios. The Main Street Victorian inn dates back to 1854. In summer enjoy breakfast with items from their organic garden: vegan and gluten-free friendly. Pets often permitted but only by advance arrangement. Open year-round.

Christman's Windham House Country Inn and Golf Resort (518-734-4230), 5742 Route 23, Windham 12496. ($$) There are 49 rooms, all with private bath, at this beautifully located inn, with two golf courses, an outdoor heated pool, fishing, tennis courts, hiking, a library, and a restaurant. Children welcome at this family-oriented resort. Open year-round, except the months of April and November.

Hull-O Farms (518-239-6950), 3739 County Route 20, Durham 12422. ($) For those traveling with children, this is a homespun experience that will be long remembered. You can live the country life on this 300-acre working dairy farm in the same family for seven generations. Milk a cow, collect chicken eggs, feed pigs and calves, fish, or go on a nature walk. The hands-on experience is unusual and fun for everyone. Hayrides and barbecues are part of the summer activities. There are three extremely comfortable guesthouses with home-cooked meals served in the homestead, a short walk away. Rates include daily breakfast and dinner Thursday through Saturday. Children under the age of two are free; ages 2-12 are discounted. Open year-round.

The Thompson House (518-734-4510), 19 Route 296, Windham 12496. ($$) Since 1880 the Thompson family has provided gracious hospitality and a vacation destination with spectacular views for guests in the lovely Catskills. There's a golf course across the street, a large heated outdoor swimming pool, and a variety of entertainment daily. The exercise room and recreation room with video games and a Ping Pong table are on the premises, making this an ideal getaway for families. Special package rates include breakfast and dinner during the summer months when rooms without air-conditioning are available at reduced rates. Children under the age of four stay free. Open year-round, except for the months of November and April.

Winwood the Mountain Inn (518-734-3000), 5220 Route 23, Windham 12496. ($$) Only a half mile from Windham Mountain, and the ski center's own hotel and condominium complex, this establishment combines a country setting with comfortable rooms and spectacular mountain views. It is ideal for families, with a dining room, tennis court, indoor recreation center, and outdoor pool. Winwood combines the conveniences of a hotel with the warmth of a country inn. There 47 rooms range from standard doubles to deluxe suites and all have private baths, TV and a restaurant, Rock'n Mexicana Cantina & Grill (6am-10pm), on the premises. Inquire about the Kids-Stay-Free policy for children under the age of 12 staying in parents' room. Open year-round.

WHERE TO EAT

DINING OUT

The Basement Bistro (518-634-2338), 776 County Route 45, Earlton. ($$$) Open for dinner Wednesday through Sunday 5-9. This unique restaurant gives diners the opportunity to sample everything offered on the menu (prix-fixe and made up of a dozen courses that change seasonally). Located on a pastoral country road in the basement of a house hand-built by the chef-owner who lives with his family upstairs, the restaurant seats only

26. Reservations MUST be made several weeks in advance. The kitchen specializes in healthful, imaginative cuisine using purees and infused oils instead of butter and cream. The chef makes his own aged cheeses and prosciutto, and grows much of the produce used in the restaurant. Since 1989 when it opened, almost all fruits and vegetables on the menu have been organically grown.

Main Street in Coxsackie.

Bavarian Manor (518-622-3261), 866 Mountain Road, Purling. ($$) Open for dinner Thursday through Saturday 5-9; Sunday 1-8.. Located in a historic building that has been operating as an inn and/or restaurant since 1865, the manor's specialties are sauerbraten, Wiener schnitzel, spaetzle, dumplings, and bratwurst. Those who don't care for German cuisine will find fresh seafood entrees and hand-cut steaks on the menu. The German beer on draft is excellent, and diners may enjoy marvelous black forest cake and apple strudel for dessert. Children are welcome.

Bistro Brie & Bordeaux (518-734-4911), 5386 Route 23, Windham. ($$) Open for dinner Thursday through Sunday 5-10. This French-country restaurant, owned and operated by a native-born French chef, offers wonderful prix-fixe dinners on select evenings. The cuisine is absolutely first-rate. Dine Alfresco in the warm weather months. Children are welcome.

Brandywine (518-734-3838) 11157 Route 23, Windham. ($$) Open for dinner daily, except Monday, from 4-10; Saturday and Sunday 1-10. An excellent informal dining spot with Italian specialties including fettuccine Alfredo, shrimp Brandywine and chicken Scarpariello. Desserts include fantastic cheesecake. There's a bright greenhouse room for dining and cozy booths in the main area. Children are welcome.

Chalet Fondue (518-734-4650), 55 Route 296, Windham. ($$) Open for dinner Thursday through Monday 4-10. The Swiss Austrian, and German dishes are excellent, and the atmosphere is elegant yet relaxed. Specialties include veal entrees and a full line of fondues. There are early bird specials between 4 and 6pm that are excellent value. (A recent addition is an adjacent pizza parlor open daily 11-10.)

Chateau Belleview (518-589-5525), 65f89 Route 23A, Tannersville. ($$) Open for dinner Thursday through Sunday 5-10. Fine Continental cuisine served with candlelight amid spectacular mountain views: lovely romantic atmosphere. Do not bring the kids! This restaurant has been consistently good over the decades.

Deer Mountain Inn (518-589-6268), 790 County Road 25, Tannersville. ($$) Open Thursday through Monday for dinner 5-10; Sunday Brunch 11-3. Enjoy eclectic international cuisine in a romantic, tranquil atmosphere where steaks, seafood, duck and lamb (a specialty of the house) are popular with diners. Not recommended for children. (There are also seven rooms in the adjoining inn, all with private bath, *see Lodging*).

La Conca D'Oro (518-943-3549), 440 Main Street, Catskill. ($$) Open Saturday through Monday 4-9; Wednesday through Friday 11:30-10. The name means "the golden bay," and this unpretentious Italian restaurant serves fine food at reasonable prices. The veal entrees, chicken dishes, and homemade mozzarella are house specialties. For dessert, there are excellent cannoli. Children are welcome.

Messina's La Griglia Ristorante (518-734-4499), 5658 Route 23, Windham. ($$) Open daily, except Tuesday and Sunday, for dinner 4-10. Ed Messina worked at *La Griglia* for many years; he now has his own restaurant. A graduate of the Culinary Institute of America, he serves excellent Northern Italian cuisine, featuring some of the best fresh seafood around. House specialties include osso buco Milanese, roast, duck, several fresh fish entrees, and pasta made on the premises. Children welcome. Reservations suggested.

Millrock Restaurant (518-734-9719), 5398 Main Street, Windham. ($$) Open Thursday through Monday 5-10 for dinner. This Italian American family restaurant features an open kitchen and wood-burning oven that turns out an array of gourmet pizzas. A specialty of the house is seafood and there's a Seafood Lovers for Two entrée that includes a mix of mussels, clams, calamari, and shrimp topped with a zesty red sauce over pasta. Most desserts are homemade and all are first-rate. Children welcome.

New York Restaurant (518-943-5500), 353 Main Street, Catskill. ($$) Open daily, except Wednesday noon-9 for lunch and dinner. A restaurant dating back to 1922, the latest incarnation is now owned by a Polish-American, Natasha Witka, who has created a local hub for Hudson Valley music, food and spirits. The menu includes in-house cured meats, pierogi, flatbreads, seared salmon and a brie-burger with arugula, as well as vegan and vegetarian options. I have enjoyed the varied beers here as well as the hearty fare. This place is a wonderful addition to Catskill's Main Street!

Rive Gauche Bistro (518-945-1009), 7 Second Street, Athens. ($$) Open Monday through Friday 4-10; Saturday noon-11-10; Sunday noon-9. This wonderful French bistro is a fairly new addition (2017) to the Greene County dining scene. Enjoy French favorites perfectly prepared. The service is excellent and you won't be disappointed. Make sure not to skip dessert! Prices are reasonable; leave the kids home.

Rock'n Mexicana Cantina & Grille (518-734-4055), 5220 Route 23, Windham. ($$) Open daily 6am-10pm. Just minutes from the ski slopes, enjoy a relaxed atmosphere with an open-hearth fireplace and reasonable prices. They serve up all the Mexican favorites—burritos, quesadillas, tacos—as well as burgers, salads and sandwiches. This is a good place to go après-ski in winter and for an informal summer supper. Children welcome.

Ruby's Hotel (518-634-7790), 3689 Route 67, Freehold. ($$) Open for dinner Thursday through Saturday 5-9; during the winter Friday and Saturday 5-9. Housed in a renovated 19th-century hotel converted into a terrific restaurant, Ruby's serves seasonal American fare with a French accent. Entrees include salmon, rib eye steak and seafood, served in a cozy bistro atmosphere. There's an art deco bar here, as well as a gallery on the second floor of the building featuring the work of local artists. Chef Ana Sporer serves fresh, simple flavorful dishes; do not pass up the dessert course. Ana teaches at the Culinary Institute and worked as a chef at the Pierre Hotel in Manhattan before opening this restaurant. Many of the vegetables and herbs are grown in the giant garden behind the restaurant. Open year-round, but call before heading out on winter weekends. (Note: There are two guest rooms above the restaurant, both with private baths.)

EATING OUT

394 Main (518-947-4774), 394 Main Street, Catskill. ($) Open Tuesday through Friday 7am-1pm & 4-10pm. A great place to get coffee.

Catskill Mountain Country Store & Restaurant (518-734-3387), 5510 Route 23, Windham. Store is open daily 9-5; Saturday and Sunday 8-6; the restaurant stops serving at 3pm. This charming country store/café is family-owned and operated by Natasha and Drew Shuster, former championship skiers. There is a bakery, a small "looking zoo," where children are free to watch the animals, and an array of produce, gourmet items, plants, and toys on the premises. Enjoy fantastic muffins, breads, pastries, pancakes, omelets, wraps, hearty soups, and all kinds of wonderful treats. I love their chocolate-cherry French toast. The kids will thoroughly enjoy this bustling eatery, and if they get impatient for the food to arrive, you can always walk around with them and visit the animals!

NOTE: The **Catskill Mountain Country Store & Restaurant** also has a location at 6014 Main Street, Tannersville (518-589-6777). The restaurant is open Thursday through Monday, 9-3; the store remains open until 5pm. It's a delightful place and not to be missed if you are in Tannersville.

Circle W General Store (518-678-3250), 3328 Route 23A, Palenville. ($) Open daily 7:30-5; 8am on weekends. This beautifully restored general store is a wonderful place for breakfast or lunch—or to pick up gourmet picnic fare. A few of the sandwich choices include fresh turkey BLT, roast beef with smoked Gouda and caramelized onions, or prosciutto with goat cheese

and figs. There are hearty soups, quiche, and fresh coffee to savor. Organic and local products like fine chocolate, maple syrup, cereals, and jams abound. There is also an impressive selection of regional books. So if you are heading up to Hunter or Windham on Route 23A, make sure not to miss this gem. You will find something to buy even if you aren't in the mood to shop!

The Catskill Mountain Country Store in Tannersville.

Crossroads Brewing Company (518-945-BEER), 21 Second Street, Athens. ($$) Open Monday, Wednesday and Thursday 4-9; Friday

4-midnight. Saturday 1-midnight; Sunday 1-9. Enjoy wings, nachos, salads, burgers and pizza accompanied by your choice of several beers. This is a fun place to stop and if you check the website you'll discover all kinds of specials and evening entertainment. Check out their location at 201 Water Street, Catskill. There is an enorous space and outdoor dining (518-444-8277).

Frank Guido's Port of Call (518-943-5088), 7 Main Street, Catskill ($$) Open daily, except Monday, 11:30-10. Located on the Hudson River, this is a great spot to enjoy drinks outdoors in warm weather before lunch or dinner. Basic American fare is served. However, DO NOT dine here. If you're in Catskill, simply head down Main Street to the New York Restaurant (see *Dining Out* section) or 394 Main (see listing above).

Higher Grounds Coffee Company (518-734-4120), 61 Route 296, Windham. ($) Open daily 7am-9pm. The Big Hollow Blend (South American) and Black Dome Dark (Indonesian) are both excellent but there is more than coffee here. The sandwiches and salads are renowned by local residents. I love the Veggie Wrap and the Turkey Reuben. Desserts are baked fresh daily and include their famous chocolate chip and peanut butter cookies! Smoothies, frappes and Italian sodas are among the summer refreshers.

Last Chance Antiques and Cheese Café (518-589-6424), 6009 Main Street, Tannersville. ($) Open daily 11-9, but hours vary in spring and fall when they open on weekends only. This retail gourmet store, antiques shop and café all in one offers up some great homemade soups and sandwiches. There are cheeses, chocolates, and candy of all kinds that make this a wonderful place to go for a meal or take-out. Children welcome.

The Yellow Deli (518-239-4240), 18 South River Street, Coxsackie. ($) Open daily, except Saturday, 9-2; Wednesday until 9; Sunday 11-9. I stumbled upon this cozy eatery on my travels and look

The Yellow Deli is a great stop for a snack or sandwich in Coxsackie.

forward to returning soon. The prices are exceedingly reasonable for the high quality fare, much of it organic. I enjoyed the Long Island Rancher hot sandwich (fresh-cooked turkey, cheddar cheese, tomatoes and ranch dressing with the house sweet garlic mayo on an egg roll) for $7.50. Their latte drinks were quite good ($3.00) and the breakfast sandwiches are delicious. Lest I forget: the service was friendly and fast too!

Mama's Boy Burgers (518-589-6667), 6067 Main Street, Tannersville. ($) Open daily 11:30-9; until 10 Friday and Saturday. This is a fun informal place to stop when you're in the mood for a burger with ice cream for dessert. In addition to an array of choices, you can "build" a hamburger to suit your taste. Vegetarians take note: there are falafel burgers along with other options. Hot dogs and grilled cheese are served along with shakes, floats, sundaes and other summer delights. Bring the kids.

ENTERTAINMENT

Altamura Center for Arts and Culture (518-622-0070; altocanto.org), 404 Winter Clove Road, Round Top. Open Memorial Day weekend through October. The charismatic founder of this philanthropic center offers amazing theater (including Shakespeare), opera, jazz, dance and a variety of cultural events. Carmela Bucceri Altamura, a former child musical prodigy, organizes a voice competition during the summer. Website has a full schedule of events.

Catskill Mountain Foundation Venues This nonprofit organization has done a great deal to revitalize the town of Hunter. CMF is a great place to find out what's happening culturally in the mountain top region at their two performance centers.

DCA—Doctorow Center for the Arts (518-263-2063; catskillmtn.org), 7971 Main Street, Hunter. This performance center has a theater that seats 160 as well as three film auditoriums. In addition to showcasing films, it is a venue for children's theater, dance and music performances. Open year-round.

OPAC—Orpheum Film & Performing Arts Center (518-263-2063; catskillmtn.org). 6050 Main Street, Tannersville. The Orpheum offers music performances, including jazz, folk and classical concerts. Open year-round.

Dutchman's Landing (518-943-3830), Catskill Point, end of Main Street, Catskill. This area once served as a boat landing for Hudson River craft, and today visitors can enjoy spectacular views of the river and eastern shore. There's a farmers' market on weekends from summer through fall, displays of the river and cultural history of the Catskills, travel information, a picnic area and entertainment. This is a nice place to begin a tour of Greene County, and one of the easiest access areas to the Hudson River for non-boaters who just want to enjoy being by the water's edge.

Hi-Way Drive-In (518-731-8672), 10769 Route 9W, Coxsackie. Open March through October, daily 6pm-midnight. Located between Catskill and Coxsackie, this drive-in has good quality sound and shows first-run films. It's a fun way to watch a movie in the warm weather months, especially if you have kids. There are four screens with four different options. The snack bar offers popcorn, hot dogs and other expected treats!

Lumberyard (518-943-1912; thelumberyard.org), 62 Water Street, Catskill. Besides providing studios and housing for artists, this renovated four-building complex will include a state-of-the-art performing arts venue with dance performances (American Dance Institute) as well as a children's dance program. The site has been evolving since opening in 2017, so check the website for the most recent developments.

Windham Chamber Music Festival (518-734-3868; windhammusic. com), 3379 Route 23, Windham. This 250-seat concert hall is recognized for its natural acoustics and historic interior, the perfect venue for a series of chamber music performances. The directors of this festival were both musicians with the Metropolitan Opera for many years. The festival features top-notch soloists and ticket prices are reasonable. Performances usually take place May through September.

SELECTIVE SHOPPING

Greene County's towns and villages have some interesting gift shops. The following are a few of my favorite places to find unusual items for the home and garden, as well as the kids and grandchildren.

Catskill Mountain Country Store (518-734-3387), 5510 Route 23, Windham Open Monday through Friday 9-5; Saturday and Sunday 8-6. In addition to the eatery and looking zoo this busy hub in town sells candy, toys, maple syrup, baked goods, books, and other local products. There are mugs, metal art, wooden signs, and all kinds of interesting items. (NOTE: Their other location, 6014 Main Street, Tannersville, open Thursday through Monday 9-3, has similar merchandise and is chock-full of interesting gifts: there's also a terrific local book section.)

Gavin's Irish Tea Shop (518-634-2582), 2460 Route 145, East Durham. Open Thursday through Sunday, 10-2. For tea-lovers like myself, this is an oasis in Greene County! Authentic imported Irish teas abound along with freshly baked scones; it's a nice stop as well as a place to stock up on your favorite Irish teas.

Magpie Bookshop (518-303-6035), 392 Main Street, Catskill. Open daily, except Sunday, 10:30-5:30. I love this bookshop with its fine selection of "nearly used" books, many practically new, at reduced prices. They have an excellent section of biography and fiction and have expanded to two floors as of 2017. Enjoy browsing, but I guarantee you'll find something to buy.... no matter how determined you are not to buy yet another hardcover book!

ANTIQUES & AUCTIONS

Greene County offers the antiques lover everything from the funky to the fabulous, although with a small range of shops, auctions, and flea markets. Some places are open year-round, but most tend to have limited hours in the off-season, so call before you go.

Barn Antiques @ the Country Suite (518-734-4079), 11365 Route 23, Windham. Open year-round daily, except Sunday, 10-5. This restored barn that dates back 200 years houses a large collection of antiques, collectibles and decorative items.

Coxsackie Antiques Center (518-731-8888), 12400 Route 9W, West Coxsackie. Open year-round, daily, 10-8. Enjoy browsing through the wares of over 100 dealers of fine antiques and collectibles under one roof. The goods range from glass, china and lamps to books, clothing and postcards.

Lincoln Auction Services (518-731-8444/ 258-3108; lincolnauctions.us/home), 81 Water Street, Catskill. Auctions are held twice each month selling estate items acquired throughout the region. The website has a full schedule.

Tannersville Antique & Artisan Center (518-589-5600), 6045 Main Street, Tannersville. Open year-round daily 10-6. There are over 35 select artisans and antique dealers from the county exhibiting their wares in a spacious, renovated 19th-century building.

Town House Antiques & Bob Barnes Toys and Ephemera (518-943-7400), 375 Main Street, Catskill. Open year round, Wednesday through Saturday noon-5. There are antiques, toys, and a plethora of collectibles here.

Twigz-N-Thingz (518-734-5877), 5449 Route 23, Windham. Open year-round Saturday 10-5; Sunday 10-2, or by appointment. Fine rustic furniture, décor, antiques and wood creations.

ART GALLERIES

Greene County has a wealth of artists and galleries, but some places are open only by chance or by appointment. For further information on their offerings, contact the **Greene County Council on the Arts** (518-943-3400), 398 Main Street, Catskill. The council also operates two crafts galleries that represent regional artists; for a calendar of exhibits and events go to their website (greenearts.org).

Two of my favorite galleries in the county are **Stanley Maltzman's Four Corners Art Gallery** (518-634-7386), 3392 Gayhead Road, Freehold. Stanley is a nationally renowned, award-winning artist who works in the Hudson River Valley tradition. He has drawings, pastels, watercolors, and lithographs for sale at his studio, but call for an appointment. The other is **Windham Fine Arts** (518-734-6850), 5380 Main Street, Windham. This traditional fine-arts gallery has exhibits of local artists that change monthly. They are open Friday through Sunday noon-7; until 4 on Sunday.

SPECIAL EVENTS

From spring through autumn, fairs and festivals abound throughout the county. The following are some of my favorite celebrations held annually in the county.

February: **Tannersville Ice Sculpture Festival** (newyorkstatefestivals.com), Main Street, Tannersville. Free. This is a great winter family outing, so bring your tools and make your own ice sculpture!

April: **Tap New York Craft-Beer & Food Festival** (518-263-4223), Hunter Mountain, Route 23A, Hunter. Admission. This festival is usually held the last weekend in April; Saturday 1-5; Sunday noon-4. No one under the age of 21 will be admitted. Fine beers produced by dozens of New York State's craft breweries may be sampled, along with all kinds of food. The event is a huge draw and it gets extremely crowded as the afternoon progresses. To avoid long lines for tasting, make sure to arrive early!

May: **East Durham Irish Festival** (518-634-2286/2319; eastdurhamirishfestival. com). Concerts are scheduled at various venues in the East Durham area for two days in late May. Enjoy Irish musical entertainment and activities that will appeal to all ages. Website has the full schedule.

May through September: **Cat'n Around Catskill** (518-943-0989), Main Street, Catskill. Free. This summer-long celebration showcases the talent of local artisans who create imaginative fiberglass cat sculptures displayed throughout

Main Street. In the fall these cats are auctioned off at a town fund-raiser, with a percentage of the proceeds going to the artist and the remainder to the town. Make sure to walk up and down Main Street to see dozens of these amazing creations on both sides of the street.

June: **Radio Woodstock Mountain Jam at Hunter Mountain** (855-821-9209; mountainjam.com), Hunter Mountain, Hunter. This annual three-day rock n' roll festival features over 50 artists on multiple stages.

Bavarian Summer Fest in Round Top (518-622-9584), Riedlbauer's Resort, 43 Ravine Drive, Round Top. This annual festival has been taking place since 1992 and is usually held the third weekend in June (both Saturday and Sunday noon-10). Enjoy Bavarian bands and German American fare as well as lots of fine beer. **Greene County Historical Society Tour of Homes** (518-756-8805; 518-731-6490). The location changes every year, so call ahead. Picnic lunches are offered for sale and tickets usually cost about $25. It's a wonderful opportunity to visit a dozen or so historic homes and support the county historical society.

July: **Grey Fox Bluegrass Festival** (888-946-8495; greyfoxbluegrass.com), Walsh Farm, 141 Route 22, Oak Hill. This four-day outdoor music festival features award-winning bluegrass and acoustic music with performances on four stages. There are food and craft vendors as well as music workshops. On-site camping available, as well as day tickets. The festival begins at noon on a Wednesday in mid-July and runs through the weekend. Check the website for a schedule of performances.

Greene County Youth Fair (518-3313-9333; greencountyyouthfair.com), Cairo. Thursday through Sunday; hours vary. Kids will love this fair that is full of competitions, live animals, rides, food vendors, and more. **Athens Street Festival** (518-945-1551), Riverfront Park, Athens. This daylong festival (10am-11pm) on the Hudson River includes vendors, food, and entertainment; it's a great family outing.

October: **Oktoberfest** (888-486-8376), Hunter Mountain, Route 23A, Hunter. The mountains are magnificent in autumn and provide a colorful backdrop for musical entertainment from Germany, craftspeople selling their

Main Street, Catskill.

wares, hayrides and an array of children's activities.

December: **Athens Victorian Stroll** (518-945-2136), 24 Second Street, Athens. This lovely holiday gathering features hayrides, crafts, ice sculptures, face painting, museum displays, and more. It's a nice way to get outdoors and walk around with the family in the winter!

Thomas Cole National Historic Site in Catskill.

New York State Capitol.

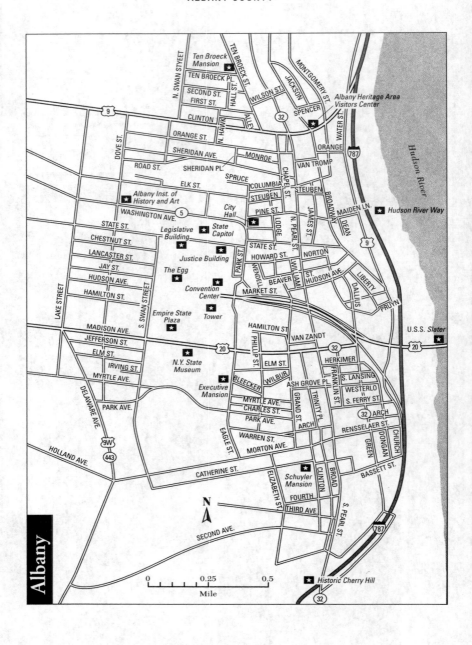

Albany

Ten Broeck Mansion
N. SWAN STYEET
TEN BROECK ST.
TEN BROECK PL.
SECOND ST.
FIRST ST.
HALL ST.
WILSON ST.
JACKSON
MONTGOMERY ST.
SPENCER
Albany Heritage Area Visitors Center
9
CLINTON
N. HAWK
ALLEY
32
WATER ST.
DOVE ST.
ORANGE ST.
SHERIDAN AVE.
MONROE
ORANGE
787
ROAD ST.
SHERIDAN PL.
VAN TROMP
Hudson River
ELK ST.
SPRUCE
COLUMBIA
CHAPEL ST.
STEUBEN
STEUBEN
Albany Inst. of History and Art
WASHINGTON AVE.
5
City Hall
PINE ST.
N. PEARL ST.
LODGE
JAMES ST.
BROADWAY
MAIDEN LN.
DEAN
Hudson River Way
STATE ST.
Legislative Building
State Capitol
STATE ST.
HOWARD ST.
WILLIAM
NORTON
9
CHESTNUT ST.
LANCASTER ST.
JAY ST.
Justice Building
PARK ST.
WENDELL
BEAVER
ST.
HUDSON AVE.
LIBERTY
DALLIUS
HUDSON AVE.
HAMILTON ST.
The Egg
MARKET ST.
PRUYN
Convention Center
Empire State Plaza
Tower
HAMILTON ST
VAN ZANDT
LAKE STREET
S. SWAN STREET
MADISON AVE.
20
PHILIP ST.
32
U.S.S. Slater
20
JEFFERSON ST.
ELM ST.
IRVING ST.
MYRTLE AVE.
N.Y. State Museum
ELM ST.
WILBUR
HERKIMER
FRANKLIN ST.
S. LANSING
WESTERLO
S. FERRY ST.
DELAWARE AVE.
PARK AVE.
Executive Mansion
BLEECKER
ASH GROVE PL.
MYRTLE AVE.
CHARLES ST.
PARK AVE.
GRAND ST.
TRINITY PL.
ARCH
32 ARCH
RENSSELAER ST.
9W
443
HOLLAND AVE.
EAGLE ST.
WARREN ST.
MORTON AVE.
GREEN
DONGAN
CHURCH
CATHERINE ST.
ELIZABETH ST.
Schuyler Mansion
CLINTON
BROAD
BASSETT ST.
S. PEARL ST.
FOURTH
THIRD AVE.
787
SECOND AVE.

N

0   0.25   0.5
Mile

Historic Cherry Hill
32

ALBANY

Albany is the oldest chartered city in the United States and the second oldest continually inhabited settlement in the country. One of the best things about the city today is it is home to Northeast Public Radio (800-632-9262), 318 Central Avenue, and its performance venue, the Linda, that offers amazing live entertainment, political debates, concerts and more. So tune in to 90.3 FM while driving through the area and enjoy the intelligent exchange of ideas that is truly the Spirit of Albany! Check the website, wamc.org, for a full program schedule and event listings at the Linda.

Long before Albany received its city charter, granted July 22, 1686, by Governor Thomas Duggan, the settlement was an important river stop and trading center. After Henry Hudson visited the region in 1609, Albany's fertile valleys and abundant game attracted Dutch settlers. Albany was to become a city of tremendous contrast—stagecoaches and steamboats, muddy roads and medical colleges, farmers and politicians. But through a combination of pride, pluck, and foresight, Albany has made the best of it all. A visit to the city today can focus on many things—history, politics, art, and architecture—and can be made at any time of year. Spring brings the blossoming of thousands of tulips, pools of color that reflect Albany's Dutch origins. The Pinksterfest, a weekend celebration in May, welcomes the warm weather in the Dutch tradition, and the city parks come alive with fairs and shows. In summer the great Empire State Plaza becomes a unique combination of outdoor park, art gallery, and seat of government, and autumn turns out to be a perfect time to explore the city on foot and discover the tiny side streets that still remain from three centuries ago. Winter ushers in Victorian greenery displays, snow festivals, and the lighting of the state Christmas tree. Whatever the season, be prepared to discover an area where the past and future coexist.

VISITOR INFORMATION

Albany County Convention and Visitors Bureau (518-434-1217, 800-258-3582), 25 Quackenbush Square, Albany 12207; Albany.org.

GETTING THERE

By car: The city is located off exits 23 and 24 of I-87 (NYS Thruway/Northway); watch for signs.

By bus: **Adirondack Trailways** (800-858-8555; trailwaysny.com) runs several buses daily to the city of Albany from the Port Authority Bus Terminal in Manhattan.

By train: **Amtrak** (518-462-5763; 800-872-7245; Amtrak.com) service is available to 525 East Street in Rensselaer, just across the river from Albany. Trains leave from Penn Station in Manhattan.

By air: **Albany International Airport** (518-242-2222; Albany airport.com), 737 Albany Shaker Road, is located at exit 4 off the Northway (take the NYS Thruway to exit 24; pick up the Northway there at exit 1N just after passing through the tollbooth; stay to the right!).

MEDICAL EMERGENCY

Albany Medical Center (518-262-3125), 43 New Scotland Avenue.

Albany Memorial Hospital (518-471-3221), 600 Northern Boulevard.

St. Peter's Hospital (518-525-1550), 315 South Manning Boulevard.

Urgent Care Center (518-783-3110), Capital Region Health Park, 711 Troy-Schenectady Road, Latham. Open Monday through Friday 5pm-midnight, Saturday and Sunday 10-8. This facility sees patients in the evening hours and weekends.

MUSEUMS & POINTS OF INTEREST

Albany Heritage Area Visitors Center and Henry Hudson Planetarium (518-434-0405; 800-258-3582; Albany .org), 25 Quackenbush Square. Open year-round, Monday to Friday, 9-4; Saturday 10-3; Sunday 11-3. Free. This site offers guests a series of changing exhibits, interactive displays that highlight history and culture in the capital city and provide an overview of the region. The planetarium features star shows on the third Saturday of the month at 11am for young children and at 1pm for older children and adults. A permanent exhibit highlighting Albany's role in the Underground Railroad is open to the public at the visitor center. It is the only permanent exhibit in the capital and offers a glimpse into local and state connections to the Underground Railroad. If you are interested in seeing downtown Albany on foot, download a free walking tour on your smartphone for a personally guided tour. (Go to Albany.org for instructions). There is also a printed brochure guiding walkers through four centuries of Albany history by way of its buildings and streets. This self-guided tour begins at the visitor center where an exhibit features highlights from the city's past.

The Albany Institute of History and Art (518-463-4478; albanyinstitute.org), 125 Washington Avenue. Admission. Open year-round, Wednesday through Saturday 10-5; until 8 on Thursday and admission is free from 5-8pm; Sunday noon-5. Founded in 1791, this exceptional museum is one of the oldest in the country, yet still provides visitors with a chance to see varied, changing exhibits focusing on the Hudson Valley's rich cultural history. The

An exhibit at The Albany Institute of History & Art.

building is a graceful collection of individual galleries and sweeping staircases, and there is even a small display area in the entrance hall. The institute's collections include fine European porcelain and glass; Dutch furniture, paintings, and decorative arts from the early settlement period in Albany; pewter and silver produced by local smiths in the 18th century; and breathtaking examples of Hudson River School painting. The Dutch Room offers an interesting look into early Albany family life. Be sure to see the Egyptian Room on the lower level, where human and animal mummies rest along with some of their prized belongings. Changing exhibits are featured throughout the year.

Albany Pine Bush Discovery Center (518-456-0655; albanypinebush.org), 195 New Karner Road, Albany. Free. Open year-round, daily Monday through Friday 9-4; Saturday, Sunday and holiday Mondays 10-4. Constructed in 1987, the building was once a local bank. New York State acquired the facility and added solar panels, a composting toilet system, native landscape restoration, a discovery trail, and various exhibits. There are several hands-on activities for children, but the center is dedicated to educating everyone about the natural and cultural history of the Albany pine bush. The center received a LEED gold rating, making it one of the nation's most advanced in design, construction, and operation of high-performance green buildings.

Irish American Heritage Museum (518-427-1916; irish-us.org), 370 Broadway, Albany. Open year-round, Wednesday through Friday 11-4; Saturday and Sunday noon-4. Tours may be arranged at other times by appointment. Admission. The exhibits here reveal the impact of Irish heritage in America. There are also videos, lectures, educational programs, and special events throughout the year, so check the website for a schedule. (NOTE: For those who would like to take a horse-drawn trolley tour of the city, they leave from the museum at 11am in the summer months (clayhavencarriage.com) and pass historic points of interest downtown with commentary by a local historian.)

New York State Museum (518-474-5877; nysm.nysed.gov), Empire State Plaza (Madison Avenue). Take exit 23 off the NYS Thruway. Pick up I-787, and get off at the Empire State Plaza exit. Open year-round, except national holidays, Tuesday through Sunday 9:30-5. Closed Monday. Free. Today it anchors one end of Empire State Plaza, but the museum has been part of the state's history since 1836, making it one of the oldest state museums in America. It is not, however, a dusty old repository with outdated displays of rocks and bones. The museum is alive with multimedia presentations that allow visitors to experience everything from a thunderstorm to a Lower East Side pushcart alley of the 1920s. The permanent exhibits include "Adirondack Wilderness," which explores the natural history of that region; "New York Metropolis," which focuses on New York City and the surrounding counties (here you will find a Duke Ellington-era A train and a set from the TV show Sesame Street); and displays that focus on Native American life and the ice age in the Empire State. A moving September 11th exhibit was installed in 2002. A second-floor exhibit has a large carousel and old-fashioned soda fountain, depicting life in an era long past. Changing exhibits feature folk art, dinosaurs, giant insects, or contemporary art and fine crafts, and shows are given in the museum's theater. Special events are scheduled year-round.

Also check out the **Corning Tower Observation Deck** (518-474-2418), the viewing area on the 42nd floor of the tower (entrance at Concourse Level of Plaza). Open Monday through Friday, except holidays, 10-3:45. There are 270-degree views of the Taconics and Berkshires. A great stop on a clear day for an above-the-clouds view of the entire mall! (NOTE: Anyone over the age of 16 must present a photo ID before being allowed to enter the elevator.)

U.S.S. Slater Destroyer Escort-766 (518-431-1943; ussslater.org), Broadway and Quay, at the foot of Madison Avenue. Take exit 3B off I-787 South. Open April through November, Wednesday through Sunday 10-4. Admission. This is the only remaining WWII Destroyer Escort afloat in the country. See how the crew lived and carried out its mission of antisubmarine warfare. Armament, combat-information and radio rooms, pilot house, galley, mess, officers' quarters, and sleeping area are authentically restored. Military-history buffs will enjoy this stop.

HISTORIC HOMES

Historic Cherry Hill (518-434-4791; historiccherryhill.org), 523 ½ South Pearl Street. Open April through December, Wednesday and Saturday. Tours are given those days at noon, 1, 2, and 3pm. Admission. Built in 1787 by Philip Van Rensselaer to replace what was called the Old Mansion, this Georgian-style house was the centerpiece of a 900-acre farm. Cherry Hill remained in the family for five generations, until 1963, and provides the visitor with a rare picture of the growth and care of a home over a 200-year period. The farm has, of course, disappeared. The view across the road is now of oil tanks instead of orchards. But the house itself still offers a sense of grace and elegance. A visit begins in the basement orientation center, where a wall chart untangles the complicated series of marriages and relationships that kept Cherry Hill in the family. Upstairs many of the over 30 rooms have not been restored to match one particular period, but contain the designs, belongings, and personal touches of their former inhabitants. The collections found here are a record of America's social history. There are dozens of chairs and tables as well as thousands of decorative objects, which include 18th-century paintings, 19th-century Oriental export ware, and early 20th-century clothing. Although modernized over the years, Cherry Hill is chock-full of New York history and spirit and will be greatly appreciated by history buffs.

Schuyler Mansion State Historic Site (518-269-4099; schuylerfriends.org), 32 Catherine Street. Open year-round for tours by appointment only. Admission. Once home to Philip Schuyler, a U.S. Senator and general in the Revolutionary War, the Schuyler Mansion was completed in 1764 on a rolling plot of land known as the Dutch Church Pasture. Many well-known statesmen, including George Washington, Benjamin Franklin, and the defeated English general John Burgoyne, visited the mansion over the years. During the war, Schuyler's daughter married Alexander Hamilton here. A kidnap attempt by the Tories was later made against her and a gash on the wooden banister is supposed to have been made by a kidnapper's tomahawk. The house did not remain in the family after Schuyler's death, but passed through a succession of owners before being purchased by New York State in 1912. Although numerous changes have been made to the exterior of the house over the years, including removal of all outbuildings, visitors can still see examples of 18th-century furniture, glassware, pottery, and art, as well as Schuyler family possessions.

Ten Broeck Mansion (518-436-9826; tenbroeckmansion.org), 9 Ten Broeck Place. Open May through October, Thursday and Friday 10-4; Saturday and Sunday 1-4. Tours are given on the hour. Admission. Home of the Albany County Historical Association, this Federal mansion was built in 1798 for General Abraham Ten Broeck, a member of the Continental Congress who fought in the battle of Saratoga. Once called Arbor Hill, the house now offers a look at the lifestyle of Albany's upper class during the last two centuries.

Exhibits include period furniture and decorative items, and the house also contains a wine cellar, which when rediscovered during renovations was found to have a valuable collection of very aged wines!

STATE GOVERNMENT SITES

NYS Executive Mansion (518-473-7521), 138 Eagle Street. One hour tours are offered on Thursday only 10-2, on the hour. Call two weeks in advance for reservations. Closed July and August. This mansion is tucked down a side street just around the block from the Empire State Plaza. Built in 1850 as a private home, it now serves as the governor's residence. The tour covers the public rooms, which are filled with art from the 18th through the 20th centuries.

NYS Capitol (518-474-2418; ogs.ny.gov), located at the State Street end of the Empire State Plaza. Open for tours year-round, Monday through Friday at 10, noon, 2 and 3. Tours leave from the Empire State Plaza visitor center on the concourse of the Plaza. This fairy-tale building, with its red towers and hundreds of arched windows, is one of the few state capitols not topped by a dome. Construction, completed in 1899, took more than 30 years and cost the then-unheard-of sum of $25 million. This is where the state senate and assembly

Known as the Million Dollar Staircase, this is an amazing piece of architecture within the Capitol.

meet, and where you will find the governor's offices once used by Theodore Roosevelt, Nelson Rockefeller, and Franklin D. Roosevelt. Throughout the building are thousands of fine stone carvings, a tradition that can be traced back to the great churches of the Middle Ages. Many were caricatures of famous politicians and writers; others were of the families and relatives of the artisans; still others were self-portraits of the stone carvers themselves. But the most compelling carvings are the ones that form the **Million Dollar Staircase**, which took years to complete and is the best known of all the capitol's embellishments. Another unusual architectural feature is the senate fireplaces: The huge chimneys did not draw well, so the fireplaces' original function was abandoned in favor of using them as private "discussion nooks." And if you enjoy military history, don't miss the small military museum here; it traces the history of the state militia and National Guard. Flower lovers should make a special point of visiting the Capitol Park in spring, when thousands of tulips blaze into red and yellow bloom.

WALKING TOURS

There is so much to see in this historic city that a walk down just about any street will give you a glimpse into Albany's colorful past.

The **Hudson River Way** opened for all to enjoy on August 10, 2002, extending from Broadway at Maiden Lane, over I-787, to the **Corning Riverfront Park** and amphitheater. This magnificent pedestrian walkway was designed to connect downtown Albany to the shores of the historic Hudson River, and also to tell the story of Albany through a series of paintings depicting historical artifacts.

Created by mural principal artist Jan-Marie Spanard and her talented crew, the paintings adorn the two staircase landings and the 30 lampposts that line both sides of the bridge. The story begins hundreds of millions of years ago when Albany was at the bottom of a prehistoric sea. As you progress over the bridge, the story continues through time and includes the early Dutch merchants and other scenes of historic importance. There are two large murals on the landings that divide the three flights of the grand staircase. The paintings are done in a permanent liquid stone paint called "keim" that will not fade, peel, or change for decades. Although this isn't a tour for people with young children, I recommend a walk over the pedestrian bridge for visitors who can walk stairs and don't mind the river breezes (they can be quite brisk in the cold weather months).

The following are not specific city tours, but rather suggestions for starting points on an Albany exploration on foot:

An example of a 19th-century row-house community, the **Pastures Historic District** is bounded roughly by Morton and Second avenues and Elizabeth and Pearl streets. Here you will find the Schuyler Mansion as well as many impressive private homes. The **Mansion Historic District**, bounded by Eagle, Dongan, Hamilton, and Ferry streets, is a kaleidoscope of building styles: Italianate, Federal, and Greek Revival being only a few. Although the area became run-down earlier in the 20th century, people have been rediscovering the richness of the district, and there is a sense of renewal here. The **Center Square-Hudson Park Historic District**, bounded by South Swan Street, Madison Avenue, South Lake Street, and Spring Street, is the largest historic district. Its centerpiece is **Washington Park**, a 90-acre area that once served as parade grounds and cemetery. Throughout the park you will find statues, lovely flower beds, and a lake. The district itself has scores of restored houses and commercial buildings.

For walking tours of **Underground Railroad sites** in the downtown area, call 518-432-4432. There are some fascinating ones, and they are located throughout the city. The **Stephen and Harriet Myers Residence**, 194 Livingston Avenue, was home to Albany abolitionists, the Myers. There are tours available of the home by appointment only.

ACTIVITIES

BICYCLING

The Mohawk-Hudson Bike Trail (800-258-3582;mhbht.org). This 41-mile bike path is one of the area's most popular recreational features, traveling along the Hudson and Mohawk rivers and connecting Albany, Schenectady, and Troy. For those who prefer other means of travel, rollerblading is also permitted here. To access the bikeway, head to the **Corning Preserve**, along the west bank of the Hudson River. (Take exit 23 off the NYS Thruway and pick up I-787 north to exit 4. Follow the signs for Colonie Street.) This bike trail also includes the **Colonie Riverfront Bike-Hike Trail** (518-783-2760), a 5.5-mile trail that runs along the Mohawk River; the **Niskayuna Riverfront Bike-Hike Trail**, a 7-mile paved path built on an old railroad bed along the Mohawk River; and the **Rotterdam Riverfront Hike-Bike Trail** (518-386-2225), a 7-mile paved path.

BOAT CRUISES

Dutch Apple Cruises & Tours (518-463-0220; dutchapplecruises.com), 141 Broadway. Open April through October, river tours daily. The boat holds 145 people; cash bar, light refreshments, and discounts for seniors and children. Check website for full schedule.

FARM MARKETS

Empire State Plaza Farmers' Market (518-473-2982), Empire State Plaza. Open May through October, Wednesday and Friday, 10-2. Approximately 20 vendors gather on the Plaza to sell fruits, vegetables, baked goods, honey, maple syrup, and other local produce in season. During winter months the market moves indoors to the concourse of the Plaza and is open on Wednesday 10-2.

Goold Orchards: Farm Store, Bakery, Apple Orchard, Cider Mill & Winery (518-732-7317), 1297 Brookview Station Road, Castleton. Open daily, except Sunday, 10-4:30. Head across the Route 9 and Route 20 Bridge into Rensselaer County and down Route 9 (follow signs to the orchard) for pick-your-own apples and raspberries in September. There are homemade cider doughnuts and fresh-pressed cider, and an array of fruit pies and cookies, all made fresh on the premises. The store is open year-round for apples and cider. Their Brookview Station Winery produces five white wines, including seyval blanc, a blush, and four reds. There are also semidry pear and peach wines. There is lots going on here to interest just about anyone!

Lansing Farm Market & Greenhouse (518-464-0889), 204 Lishakill Road, Colonie. Open daily 9-6. (Take NYS Thruway to exit 24, then pick up Route 5 west to Lishakill Road.) Pick your own strawberries here in June. Other goodies on sale in the market include tomatoes, corn, peppers, squash, and all other fruits and vegetables grown on the Lansing farm in season. This eighth-generation family farm was founded in 1788, and their doughnuts, breads, and homemade pies are first-rate.

Shaker Shed Farm Market & Greenhouse (518-869-3662), 945 Watervliet Shaker Road, Colonie. (Take NYS Thruway to exit 24; pick up the Northway to exit 4 and make a left off the exit and another left onto Albany-Shaker Road. Pass the airport and at the stop sign, make another left. The market is over the hill on the left side of the road.). Open Easter through Christmas, daily 9-6. Pick your own tomatoes here in late August. The market offers home-grown produce, crafts, candles, and fresh pies. Enjoy a drink and dessert in the café. During the spring months there are plants galore; at the holidays, a nice selection of wreaths and trees.

GOLF

Capital Hills at Albany (518-438-2208), 65 O'Neil Road, Albany. This 18-hole, par-71 public course, owned by the city of Albany, is the only place to golf in the capital. For walkers who accompany golfers to this course, there is a 2.6 mile trail that wends its way through wooded areas. Open mid-March to mid-November, weather permitting. Call in advance for tee time. There is a restaurant with a full bar and driving range on the premises.

Mill Road Acres (518-785-4653), 30 Mill Road, Latham. This 18-hole, par-58 public course is open daily April through October, 7am-7pm. There is equipment rental and senior discounts. A restaurant and snack bar are on the premises.

Town of Colonie Golf Course (518-374-4181), 418 Consaul Road, Colonie. This 36-hole, par-72 course is open daily April through October, 7am-7pm. Call two days ahead to ensure a tee time if you are a resident of Colonie; otherwise, there are no reservations. There is equipment rental, driving range, a restaurant with a full bar, and snack bar on the premises.

ICE SKATING

Albany County Hockey Training Facility (518-452-7396; albanycounty. com), 830 Albany-Shaker Road, Albany. Open year-round, except the months of May and June, for both figure skating and hockey. There are public sessions for figure skating. Snack bar and rentals are on the premises.

Empire "Skate" Plaza Ice Rink (518-474-4759; empirestateplaza.org). Open daily, December through March, 11-8, weather permitting. Closed daily for maintenance from 3 to 4pm. Skating is free and there are rentals available.

Swinburne Skating Rink (518-438-2406), 810 Clinton Avenue, below Manning Boulevard, Albany. This is an outdoor rink, so call before you go for the time of the sessions since they change with the season and are often weather-dependent.

SPECTATOR SPORTS

Albany Devils—Ice Hockey (518-487-2000; thealbanydevils.com), Times-Union Center, 51 South Pearl Street, Albany. The season runs from October through April for hockey, and the website lists a full schedule. The team is an American Hockey League-New Jersey Devils affiliate.

Siena Saints Basketball (518-487-2000; sienasaints.com), Times-Union Center, 51 South Pearl Street, Albany. The website has a full schedule of basketball games for the season.

GREEN SPACE

Corning Riverfront Park (800-258-3582). This section of the Corning Preserve lies along the west bank of the Hudson River. To get there, take exit 23 off the NYS Thruway; pick up I-787, and get off at exit 4. Follow signs for

Colonie Street. This is a delightful park where strollers will enjoy walking along the river. Those who prefer roller skating and biking can pick up the Mohawk-Hudson Bike Trail here and enjoy miles of paths.

Empire State Plaza & Art Collection (518-474-2418; ogs.ny.gov), located off exit 23 of the NYS Thruway. Go through tollbooth to I-787 and take Empire State Plaza exit. Open daily year-round. Free. Popularly called the Plaza, this is really a government complex. It includes office buildings, a convention center and performing arts venue known as **The Egg**. There is also a concourse and the state museum. Built at a cost of more than two billion dollars and completed in 1978, the Plaza has fulfilled then-governor Nelson Rockefeller's dream of a government center that would draw visitors and allow them to feel in touch with their state government. Tours of the Plaza are offered several times a day, but you may enjoy walking it yourself. The esplanade area is wonderful to explore, with tranquil reflecting pools, plantings, modern sculpture by such artists as David Smith and even a play area known as the Children's Place. An environmental sculpture called The Labyrinth offers benches to the weary. Lining the interior halls of the concourse are fine examples of modern art on permanent display—the largest publicly owned and displayed art collection in the country, and they are all the work of New York artists. More than 92 sculptures, tapestries, paintings, and constructions are on display, among them works by such artists as Calder, Nevelson, Frankenthaler, and Noguchi.

A series of **12 memorial statues and sculptures** provides an interesting walking tour through the Plaza. In addition to the New York State Vietnam Veterans Memorial, there are memorials honoring fallen firefighters, George Washington, General Philip Henry Sheridan, police officers, women war veterans, those from New York State who fought in World War II and the Korean War, Dr. Martin Luther King Jr., children who died at the hands of abusers, parole officers who were killed in the line of duty, and crime victims.

Washington Park (518-434-2032), State and Willett streets, Madison and Lake avenues. This 90-acre park in the center of Albany is the site of several interesting and enjoyable special events throughout the year. It is a great place to relax and take a stroll after sightseeing in the city.

LODGING

The Albany area is filled with dozens of motels and hotels, but few inns and bed & breakfasts: most are located outside the city itself. The lodging section here emphasizes establishments within the city proper. Several "corporate alternatives" abound and if you opt for one of them, I recommend the **Hampton Inn & Suites** (518-432-7000), 25 Chapel Street; or the **Albany Hilton** (518-462-6611/800-227-6963), 40 Lodge Street.

Albany Mansion Hill Inn (518-465-2038), 115 Phillip Street, Albany 12202. ($$) This bed & breakfast is within walking distance of the state capitol and the downtown business district. Winner of a preservation award, the inn has eight rooms, each with private bath. Choose from a wide variety of choices on the breakfast menu. Children welcome. This is one of the few inns in the city that is pet friendly. There is a restaurant on the premises. Open year-round.

Angel's Bed & Breakfast (518-426-4104), 96 Madison Avenue. Albany 12202 ($$) A historic urban inn built in the early 19th century; a great place to stay for those who want to be within walking distance of downtown Albany's major museums and restaurants. Governor Joseph Yates rented the house in 1822 and hosted several prominent people here. Each of the three small cozy guest rooms has a private bath and is located on the second floor. There is a café on the first floor, and the innkeeper lives on the third floor. Open year-round.

Hotel Indigo (518-869-9100), 254 Old Wolf Road, Latham 12110. ($$) There are 107 guest rooms here, and the décor has been selected for its calming affect. The unique design and serenity here are different from the usual chain hotels. Guests may enjoy plush bedding, spa-style bathrooms, and large murals on the walls. There is a restaurant, the Blu Stone Bistro, on the premises and their breakfasts are first-rate. Open year-round.

The Inn on South Lake (518-438-7646), 145 South Lake Avenue, Albany 12208 ($) This cozy bed & breakfast is housed in an 1890s Victorian home that combines mission-style influences with modern amenities. It is within easy walking distance of the capitol and Empire State Plaza. The main floor features a library, fireplace, wood-beamed ceilings, and leaded glass doors. The five guest rooms are on the second floor; three have private baths, and two share a bathroom. Guests may enjoy the enclosed front and rear porches as well as a backyard. Continental breakfast is served. Parking is available in the rear of the inn. Air-conditioning, laundry facilities, Internet access, and a lounge with cable TV. Open year-round.

Morgan State House Inn (518-427-6063), 393 State Street, Albany 121210. ($$$) This luxury inn on Washington Park offers 16 rooms, all with private bath; 6 rooms are located in the 19th-century main house, and 10 are in the condominium suites that date from the early 20th century. A full breakfast is served on weekends. Only children over the age of 16 are welcome. Open year-round.

State Street Mansion Bed & Breakfast (518-462-6780/800-673-5750), 281 State Street, Albany 12210. ($$) This bed & breakfast is located in the center of the city's Center Square Historic District, only one block from the Empire State Plaza. One of the oldest B&Bs in Albany, in business for over 30 years, it offers easy access to cultural activities, entertainment, and dining, making it a popular stop with businesspeople. The brownstone dates from 1889; the seven rooms all have private bath. A continental breakfast is served to guests. Parking is available and is included in the room charge.

WHERE TO EAT

Albany offers a wealth of restaurants to choose from, and they offer a range of culinary traditions—from fusion cuisine to Indonesian—for both the adventurous and the less daring diner alike. The following establishments were selected for their particularly high quality fare— or interesting offerings and atmosphere.

DINING OUT

Ama Cocina (518-776-4550), 4 Sheridan Avenue. ($$) Open daily, except Sunday, 11-10. Enjoy modern Mexican street food with a bar containing an enormous selection of tequilas. A fresh and funky twist on Mexican favorites in an informal fun atmosphere, this is a terrific addition to Albany's downtown area. Bring the kids and enjoy!

Angelo's 677 Prime (518-427-7463), 677 Broadway. ($$$) Open daily, except Sunday, 11:30-10; Saturday 5-10. Enjoy fine dining at this New York City-style steakhouse, where you can choose from over a half dozen types of aged, hand-cut steaks. There are several tempting fish and seafood entrees as well, including seared ahi tuna. Glass-enclosed wine lockers display the extensive wine list. Desserts are made fresh daily at the restaurant's bakery. The crème brulee and homemade ice creams are excellent. For the carnivorous, this restaurant is a must!

Athos Restaurant (518-608-6400), 1814 Western Avenue. ($$) Open for dinner daily 4-9; Friday and Saturday until 9:30. The classic Greek cuisine here is a rarity in the capital. The wide spectrum of offerings includes lamb, veal, *pastitsio*, and *moussaka*, as well as several fish entrees. I recommend the fixed price dinner that includes three hearty courses. Everything here is prepared with attention to detail.

This is my favorite restaurant in Albany!

black & blue (518-313-7388), 1470 Western Avenue. ($$$) Open Monday through Friday 11:30-10; Saturday 4-11; Sunday 4-9. Steak and crab in a fabulous setting. I enjoyed a memorable repast here—one of the best steaks I've had in decades, cooked perfectly, while my friend ordered halibut....also excellent. I cannot say more about this recent addition to Albany's dining scene: go and experience "black & blue" for yourself. Not recommended for children.

Bongiorno's (518-462-9176), 23 Dove Street. ($$) Open for lunch Monday through Friday 11:30-2; dinner 5-9. Closed Sunday. The home-style Southern Italian cooking features veal and seafood. I enjoy the clams marinara and seafood fra diavolo here. There are always lunch specials. *Mangia,* and feel like you escaped to Italy for a repast!

Caffe Italia (518-459-8029), 662 Central Avenue. ($$$) Open for dinner daily, except Sunday, 5-10. This family-run Italian restaurant is a popular place with members of the state legislature (a dish or two are even named after lawmakers). Everything is prepared to order and the veal and pasta specialties are worth the trip. Reservations are required. Not recommended for children.

Jack's Oyster House (518-465-8854), 42 State Street. ($$) Open for dinner daily 5-10. This is Albany's oldest restaurant, and for close to a century the place has been owned and operated by the same family. Steak and seafood are the traditional fare to order here, and the daily specials are consistently good. Reservations are suggested; children are welcome.

Mezza Notte Ristorante (518-689-4433), 2026 Western Avenue. ($$) Open daily, except Sunday, 5-9. This classic Northern Italian restaurant has fine food, a decent wine list, and excellent service. Everything is well prepared and diners won't be disappointed, whether ordering pasta, calamari, veal, chicken or seafood. Don't skip dessert here; the tiramisu is wonderful.

Mio Posto (518-542-7581), 200 Lark Street. ($$) Open Monday through Saturday 4:30-9; until 9:30 Friday and Saturday. This Italian osteria specializes in excellent grilled fish, osso bucco, potato gnocchi with beef brasato, to name just a few of the imaginative entrees served in a cozy atmosphere. Not recommended for children.

My Linh (518-465-8899), 272 Delaware Avenue. ($$) Open for dinner Friday through Sunday 5-9:30. Albany's first Vietnamese restaurant, opened in 1993, and still popular among local residents. Dinner is served in a casual, comfortable atmosphere. One of my favorite items on the menu are the shrimp summer rolls. The crispy pan-fried boneless duck is tender and served perfectly. And the crepes filled with chicken or sliced beef sauté in spicy curry sauce are delicious. Vegetarians have an array of items to choose from, like grilled tofu topped with spicy bean curd sauce. Children are welcome.

New World Bistro & Bar (518-694-0520), 300 Delaware Avenue. ($$) Open for dinner daily 5-9:30; Friday and Saturday until 10. Sunday brunch 11-3. A fun place to dine, New World has its own unique style of "global neighborhood cuisine," including lustily spiced dishes of the American melting pot. Chef/owner Ric Orlando garnered national attention when he appeared on the Food Channel show Chopped in 2011. He operates another restaurant, New World Home Cooking in Saugerties and divides his time between the two places. There are the Cajun pan-blackened string beans, Jamaican jerk chicken, and purple haze shrimp, but a bistro bar menu includes yeast-free pizzas, burgers, and pot roast sandwich. It's a great place to have a bite before heading to the nearby Spectrum Theater. The menu changes seasonally to reflect what's freshest.

Van's Vietnamese (518-436-1868), 307 Central Avenue. ($$) Open daily, except Monday, noon-9. Chef-owner Hung Van Nguyen serves some of the best spring rolls you will find any where in this spacious cheerful restaurant. The noodle dishes are first-rate too. The whole crispy duck is my favorite entrée, but there are many tempting Vietnamese specialties from which to choose. Children are welcome.

Yono's (518-436-7747), 25 Chapel Street. ($$$) Open for dinner daily 5:30-10. An intriguing blend of French technique and Indonesian influence is found here, along with Continental specialties. Excellent steaks, chicken and vegetarian selections coexist on the eclectic menu with Far Eastern dishes. Relocated in 2006 to the Hampton Inn & Suites, Yono's now has the rich warm atmosphere of an elegant bi-level dining room highlighted by bronzed mirrors, a marble fireplace, and a crystal chandelier. Reservations are strongly suggested; this is a popular restaurant.

EATING OUT

Albany Pump Station & C.H. Evans Brewing Company (518-447-9000), 19 Quackenbush Square. ($) Open daily 11:30-10; Sunday noon-8. This downtown city brewpub offers a wide variety of American favorites. The menu includes meat loaf, burgers, and calamari, mango salmon, dinner salads, and overstuffed sandwiches. There's a full bar, and the place is a popular spot for the younger crowd to grab drinks and a light dinner after the workday. Not recommended for children.

Bellini's Counter (518-608-1146), 624 New Loudon Road, Latham. ($) Open daily 11-9. Wraps, salads, pasta dishes and build-your-own bowls with a protein, starch and vegetable. Who could ask for more if you're looking for a healthful, quick meal? I love this place and always stop when I'm passing through Latham.

Berben & Wolff's Vegan Delicatessen (518-599-5306), 227 Lark Street. ($) Open daily 10-8; Sunday until 3; Closed Monday. Even if you are an omnivore, this fantastic eatery with its imaginative vegan cuisine is a great place to enjoy a tasty, healthful lunch or supper. There are soups, salads, wraps and sandwiches to eat-in or take-out. Bring the kids!

Bountiful Bread (518-438-3540), 1475 Western Avenue. ($) Open Monday through Friday 7am-8pm; Saturday 7-6; Sunday 10-5. Enjoy hearty soups, sandwiches and salads, in a large airy café.

Daily Grind (518-427-0464). 204 Lark Street. ($) Open daily 7am-8pm. Since 1976, this "coffee shop" has been serving a lot more than coffee. Upstairs is a retail shop specializing in fresh-roasted coffee beans, while downstairs a European-style café offers an eclectic variety of light fare (soups, sandwiches, wraps, cookies and more). There is even a decent selection of teas for those who don't indulge in coffee.

Druthers Brewing Company (518-650-7996), 1053 Broadway. ($) Open 11:30-9; until 10 Friday & Saturday. Housed in a renovated warehouse, they pair a rotating menu of beers with tasty comfort food offerings. The beer is drawn directly from the serving tanks here—no bottles or packaging—from kettle to fermenter to serving tank to your glass. The fresh taste is terrific!

El Loco Café (518-436-1855), 465 Madison Avenue. ($) Open daily, except Monday, 11:30-9; Sunday 4-9. This lively eatery specializes in Tex-Mex fare and is located in a restored 19ᵗʰ-century building. El Loco is well known for its chili (the heat is up to you) and a large selection of Mexican beer. Children are welcome.

Galleria 7 Market (518-785-1082), 1214 Troy Schenectady Road, Latham. ($) Open daily 11-8; Friday until 9. This open-air food market with an array of fabulous eateries, all under one roof, offers something to please every palate: pizza, salads, sandwiches… with a gourmet twist.

Honest Weight Food Co-op Café (518-482-2667), 100 Watervliet Avenue. ($) Open daily 8am-10pm. The organic café at this large, full-stocked food co-op has a hot bar filled with an array of offerings including falafel, noodle dishes and soups. There are sandwiches and salads as well. You don't have to be a member of the co-op to shop here. Their cheese section is enormous and free samples are regularly given away. This is a good place to stop for a quick nutritious lunch. Vegan and gluten-free options abound, and there's a coffee bar.

Iron Gate Café (518-445-3555), 182 Washington Avenue. ($) Open daily 8-3; Saturday and Sunday 9-3. A gated, serene garden seating area fronts this American breakfast/lunch eatery located in a sandstone mansion. The delightful setting is a serene spot to enjoy soups, sandwiches, salads or omelets…and escape the bustle of the city for a while.

Mamoun's Mideast Café (518-434-3901), 206 Washington Avenue. ($) Open daily 11:30-10; Sunday 12:30-9. In addition to the vegetarian fare at this eatery, enjoy a variety of chicken and lamb dishes. The shish kebab, a house specialty, is my favorite dish here. The food is prepared to order and will appeal to just about everyone. Mamoun's is a family-run business. Once when I arrived with a friend, the restaurant was closed. However, someone came to the door, invited us in, and within minutes we were seated and someone was taking our order!

Peaches Café (518-482-3677), 1475 Western Avenue (Stuyvesant Plaza). ($) Open 8am-9:30 pm every day; Sunday until 8pm. This is the go-to place for breakfast all day, every day, in a relaxing atmosphere. Belgian waffles and specialty omelets are what they are known for here. Although lunch is served, breakfast is the meal to order here.

Tipsy Moose Tap & Tavern (518-631-4444), 185 Old Loudon Road, Latham. ($) Open daily 11:30am-1am; Saturday and Sunday 10am-1am. Several beers on tap along with garlic knots, pulled pork nachos, "moose sticks," house made pretzel sticks with moosehead cheddar ale sauce, are few of the of the choices here. A fun informal place for lovers of beer and comfort food.

ENTERTAINMENT

Albany Civic Theater (518-462-1297; albanycivictheater.org), 235 Second Avenue. Admission. Musicals and dramas are offered throughout the year. There is a playwright's showcase, an annual spring event.

Albany Symphony Orchestra (518-465-4755; albanysymphony.com), 19 Clinton Avenue. Admission. The season runs from October through May, and performances are given at the Palace Theatre in the city as well as the acoustically renowned Troy Savings Bank Music Hall across the Hudson River. There is a mix of concerts, as well as a series of children's musical performances.

Capital Repertory Theatre (518-445-7469; 5158-445-SHOW; capitalrep.org), 111 North Pearl Street. Admission. Theater lovers will enjoy the year-round performances here. Capital Rep has offered first-rate entertainment in the city for over 35 years. The company employs professional equity actors and designers from Manhattan. Productions include musicals, comedies, dramas and family-oriented productions.

Eba/Center for Dance & Fitness (518-465-9916; eba-arts.org), 351 Hudson Avenue. Once known as electronic body arts, this company offers dance performances throughout the year with an emphasis on modern dance.

The Egg (518-473-1845; the egg.org), 1 Empire State Plaza. This marvelous venue includes year-round ballet, modern dance, theater, rock concerts, and other musical performances. There is a cornucopia of entertainment and the website has a full schedule.

The Linda: WAMC's Performing Arts Studio (518-465-5233; the linda. org), 339 Central Avenue. This is a fantastic venue, truly a hub of the community, just like Northeast Public Radio itself. In addition to concerts and entertainment by renowned Hudson Valley residents, there are talks on critical issues affecting the city and political debates at election time. There's an intimate setting here that lends itself to a variety of events. Check the website for a full schedule.

The Egg, a performing arts venue in Albany, with the New York State Museum in the background.

Massry Center for the Arts (518-337-4871; strose.edu), 1002

Madison Avenue. The Picotte Recital Hall is state-of-the-art with the latest environmentally sound heating and cooling systems, in addition to first-rate acoustics. During the school year there are several concerts, art exhibits and lectures. The website has a full schedule.

Palace Theatre (518-465-3334; palacealbany.org), 19 Clinton Avenue. The Palace Theatre, a cultural entertainment facility in the heart of the city, first opened in 1931. Today this renovated landmark theater offers a diverse calendar year-round filled with popular musical acts, cultural events, and classic movies.

Park Playhouse (518-434-0776; parkplayhouse.com), Washington Park. Free. There are several musicals and plays performed in an outdoor setting during the warm weather months. This is a terrific family-friendly venue and a good way to expose young children to music and theater.

Spectrum Theater (518-449-8995; landmarktheatres.com), 290 Delaware Avenue. There are eight theaters at this locally owned, independent movie theater, which is committed to showing the best first-run independent and foreign films. It's rare to find this kind of theater anywhere these days; the owner installed 216 photovoltaic solar panels on the roof in 2011 to conserve energy. This is definitely a special place!

Times Union Center (518-487-2000; timesunioncenter-albany.com), 51 South Pearl Street. This enormous sports and entertainment complex is home to two athletic teams and is also where you can see a range of entertainment including acts like Cher, *Stars on Ice* and Bon Jovi. I heard Bob Dylan perform here as well as comedian Jim Gaffigan. Additionally, there are car shows, regional basketball playoffs, and more, as you will see on the website.

UAlbany Performing Arts Centers (518-442-3995; albany.edu/pac), 1400 Washington Avenue. This venue offers musicals, dramatic productions and more at reasonable prices from September through May (the school year). The website has a detailed calendar of performances.

SHOPPING

Lark Street in Albany is known as "the village in the city." There are dozens of restaurants and boutiques, and several fine-art venues on this one street. The best way to experience this area is to walk up and down the street and wander into places that interest you. Throughout the year there are festivals on **Lark Street,** so make sure to check artonlark.net to see what's happening when you visit. The Albany area is renowned for its excellent shopping and the majority of shops may be found in the city's malls.

A couple of my favorite stops in Albany are **Trader Joe's** (518-482-4538), 79 Wolf Road, Albany and **Whole Foods** (518-621-5300), 1425 Central Avenue, Albany.

The following three shopping districts are each distinctive in style and provide enough variety for just about anyone.

Colonie Center (518-459-9020; shopatcoloniecenter.com), 131 Colonie Center, Albany. Macy's and Sears are the anchor stores at this huge mall filled with dozens of shops.

Crossgates Mall (518-869-9565; shopcrossgatesmall.com), 1 Crossgates Mall Road, Albany. This enormous mall has 180 stores, as well as a 12-theater Cineplex.

Stuyvesant Plaza (518-482-8986; stuyvesantplaza.com), 1475 Western Avenue, Albany. What I love about this shopping area is the upscale, privately owned shops are not enclosed in a mall: the setup is rather old fashioned. You must walk outdoors along a sidewalk from store to store. There's plenty of parking and the restaurants are first-rate. Unless it's raining, I head here first, especially if you are looking for something a little different. *Pearl Grant Richman* and *TaDa* with its plethora of novelty gifts, as well as *Ten Thousand Villages*, a fair trade retailer, are a few of my favorite stores in the Albany area.

RAD Soap Company in Stuyvesant Plaza is owned by an Albany family who produce their array of products in the capital.

SPECIAL EVENTS

Seasonal events abound in the capital city and will enhance any vacation stay. **1st Friday Citywide Art Exhibits** are held throughout Albany on the first Friday of the month. If you are planning a trip to Albany, check albany.org for what's happening when you will be in the city.

February: **New York in Bloom** (518-474-5877; nysed.gov), New York State Museum, Empire State Plaza, is the capital's "flower show," a terrific outing for the entire family—and the perfect antidote for over 25 years to the winter blues! **Bridge Jazz Fest**

(518-337-4871), Massry Center for the Arts, College of St. Rose, 1002 Madison Avenue. Enjoy two nights of world-class jazz on the last weekend in February.

March: **The Capital District Garden & Flower Show** (518-631-2288), deemed one of the top 100 events in America by a national organization, it is held across the Hudson River at Hudson Valley Community College in Troy. There are gardening workshops, lectures, dozens of booths with floral designers, and much more to delight those who love flowers!

Display at Albany Institute of History & Art.

May: **The Annual Tulip Festival**, also known as Pinksterfest (518-434-2032), is usually held the second weekend in May and includes outdoor crafts and food fairs in Washington Park, entertainment, the crowning of the Tulip Queen, scrubbing down State Street, and a dance. The celebrations are colorful and peopled with costumed performers—and, of course, more than 100,000 tulips! Mother's Day Art & Craft Show (518-786-1529), Empire State Plaza, Albany. Free. This annual juried show is a nice place to go on Mother's Day weekend. It's held on both Saturday and Sunday 10-6.

June: **Art on Lark** (518-248-9770; artonlark.net) held on Lark Street in the city, is a fantastic display of painting, sculpture, jewelry, and more. Food vendors from local restaurants are there along with live music. Arts mingle with the public at this festive spring event. The **Father's Day Concert** (518-434-2032), an annual tradition in Riverfront Park, makes for a wonderful outing with Dad.

July: **Fabulous 4th on the Plaza** (518-473-0559), Empire State Plaza, Albany. Free. There is a dazzling display of fireworks at sundown. There are food vendors, crafts, and live music. It's a great place to enjoy the holiday festivities.

August: **Latin Fest** (518-434-2032), Washington Park, offers the best in Latin music, food and crafts. Children's rides will delight the young ones and make this a festive family outing. It's been going on in the city for over 20 years.

September: **JazzFest** (518-434-2032) is held in Riverfront Park by the waterfront. Listen to jazz in the Amphitheater and it's free to all. **LARKfest** (518-248-9770; larkfest.net), held on Lark Street, is the capital's end of summer open-air street festival. There are several stages showcasing live music and entertainment, craft and food vendors and family activities. **Capital District Scottish Games** (518-

785-0507), Altamont Fairgrounds, 129 Grand Street, Altamont. Admission. Held every year on Saturday and Sunday of Labor Day weekend, this Celtic festival of culture and arts features pipe bands, Highland dancing, athletic events, and Celtic folk music, to name just some of the attractions.

October: **Goold Apple Festival & Craft Show** (518-732-7317), Goold Orchards, 1297 Brookview Station Road, Castleton-on-Hudson. Free. This celebration of the arts and agriculture of the capital region has been held for over 25 years on Saturday and Sunday of Columbus Day weekend, 9-5. There are several activities for kids, and it's a family-friendly event.

Path Through History Weekend (518-473-3835; iloveny.com), State-wide celebration of New York's unique role in shaping America with lectures, tours and re-enactments on Columbus Day weekend.

November: **Capital Holiday Lights in Washington Park** (518-435-0392), is a dazzling drive-through holiday light display with more than 40 illuminated scenes and characters. At the end, there are surprises and holiday treats in the Lakehouse. Thanksgiving through December, Sunday through Thursday 6-9pm; Saturday & Sunday until 10. Admission charged per vehicle.

December: **Holiday Tree Lighting & Fireworks Festival** (518-473-0559), Empire State Plaza, Albany. Free. A spectacular fireworks display is part of the festivities as the official New York State holiday tree is lit, ushering in the holiday season. Kids will be thrilled to watch this celebration. The **Annual Holiday House Tour** (518-465-0876), throughout Albany's historic neighborhoods. Admission. Usually a dozen private homes participate and visitors will see them beautifully decorated for the holidays. **Winter WonderLARK** (518-248-9770), Lark Street, Albany. Free. Usually held on the second Saturday in December, this festival includes a Santa Speedo Spring, family–friendly activities, a holiday market, and window display contest.

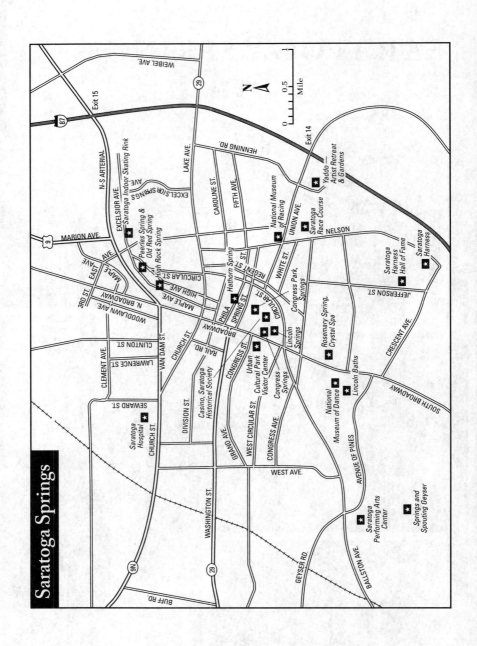

Saratoga Springs

Saratoga Hospital ✦

Saratoga Indoor Skating Rink ✦

Peerles Spring & Old Red Spring ✦

High Rock Spring ✦

National Museum of Racing ✦

Saratoga Race Course ✦

Yaddo — Artist Retreat & Gardens ✦

Saratoga Harness Hall of Fame ✦

Saratoga Harness ✦

Congress Park, Springs ✦

Rosemary Spring, Crystal Spa ✦

Casino, Saratoga Historical Society ✦

Urban Cultural Park Visitor Center ✦

Congress Springs ✦

Lincoln Springs ✦

National Museum of Dance ✦

Lincoln Baths ✦

Saratoga Performing Arts Center ✦

Springs and Spouting Geyser ✦

N

0   0.5   1
Mile

SARATOGA SPRINGS

When one thinks about Saratoga Springs, the words elegant, gracious, exciting and eccentric are some of the words that come to mind. Since the 18th century the city has played host to visitors from around the world. Parks and nature preserves abound for hiking and biking. There are several outstanding public golf courses in the area. Saratoga Lake is often referred to as the Bass Capital of the World. Museums and specialty boutiques abound and when you are tired of exploring, the springs and spas will revive you. Dance enthusiasts can enjoy a picnic dinner while ballets are performed under the stars. Lovers of Victorian architecture can stroll down a side street or two where they will spot grand old mansions and exquisite gardens. With all of this, Saratoga Springs also offers the best thoroughbred horse racing in the world. Each summer this quiet city pulses with the color, crowds, and excitement of the racecourse, where the best jockeys and horses vie for enormous winnings. In addition there are horse auctions and polo matches, and the public is invited. After a week or two in Saratoga Springs, it is likely you will not experience all it has to offer... and will plan to return.

VISITOR INFORMATION

Saratoga County Chamber of Commerce (518-584-3255; 800-526-8970), 28 Clinton Street, Saratoga Springs 12866; Saratoga.org.

Saratoga Springs Heritage Area Visitor Center (518-587-3241), 297 Broadway (Drink Hall), across the street from Congress Park, open Memorial Day weekend to mid-November, Monday through Saturday 9-6; Sunday 10-3; closed Sunday mid-November through late May. This well-located information center is a good place for summer visitors to find out what's happening in town upon arrival.

GETTING THERE

By car: Saratoga Springs, approximately 200 miles from New York City and Boston and 30 miles from Albany, is located north of Albany on I-87 (the Northway), exits 13N through 15.

By bus: **Adirondack Trailways** (518-583-7490; 800-858-8555); trailwaysny.com), 135 South Broadway, Saratoga Springs, provides service to Albany, Boston, and New York City, as well as other destinations.

By air: **Albany International Airport** (518-242-2222; albany airport.com) is less than a half-hour drive from Saratoga.

MEDICAL EMERGENCY

Saratoga Hospital (518-587-3222), 211 Church Street, Saratoga Springs.

CITY MUSEUMS

Children's Museum at Saratoga (518-584-5540; cmssny.org), 69 Caroline Street. Open Labor Day through June, Tuesday through Saturday 9:30-4:30; Sunday noon-4:30. July through Labor Day weekend also open Monday. Admission. This unique museum offers children ages one to nine a chance to explore the world, from the local community to international locations. Interactive exhibits allow kids to run a general store, make giant bubbles, and "freeze" their shadows. A tree house, fire-truck, science section, movie theater, and two toddler areas are also popular with young visitors. The museum is centrally located and a visit can be combined with shopping or stops at the Canfield Casino Museum and park.

Nearby is **Congress Park** (Broadway and Circular Street). Open daily from dawn to dusk. Part of the daily life of Saratoga Spring a century ago was "taking the waters," and Congress Park was a popular watering hole. Wealthy urban dwellers came to Saratoga Springs each summer to escape the plagues and stink of industrial cities. They would stay at the area's fine hotels and stroll along the park's pathways to various fountains. Today the park has lovely plantings, places to sit and ponder the past, and some interesting decorative offerings. Daniel Chester French's statue *The Spirit of Life* greets visitors near the entrance (he also created the

Broadway, the Main Street in Saratoga Springs, has stunning architecture and wonderful boutiques and restaurants.

renowned seated president's statue in the Lincoln Memorial), and two huge lovely urns called "Day" and "Night" bloom with flowers each summer. Tucked in the back of the park is a small reflecting pool with the most popular of the park's denizens: a pair of Triton figurines that shoot out streams of water and are nicknamed Spit and Spat. Enjoy walking among the columns in the Italian Gardens. Both young and old visitors to the park will enjoy the antique carousel that operates from May through October, Friday through Sunday noon-6. Also located in the park is **Canfield Casino** (518-587-3550), which was once one of the most famous gambling establishments in the country. Today it is home to a museum and art gallery.

Saratoga Springs History Museum (518-584-6920; saratogahistory.org), 1 East Congress Street. Open year-round, Wednesday through Sunday 10-4. Admission. The museum maintains a lovely series of rooms that offer vignettes of life in Saratoga Springs during the Gilded Age of the late 19th century, when Lillian Russell, Diamond Jim Brady, and a host of others sparkled each night over the gaming tables. Downstairs in the museum's art gallery there are changing exhibits of works by local and regional artists. The museum also hosts a crafts show in summer and fall.

National Bottle Museum (518-885-7589; nationalbottlemuseum.org), 76 Milton Avenue (Route 50), Ballston Spa (7 miles south of Saratoga Springs). Donations appreciated. Open year-round June through September Tuesday through Saturday 10-4; Closed Sunday through Wednesday at other times of the year, so call before going. This museum focuses on the history of the handmade bottle. Until 1903 bottles were handmade, not manufactured. The permanent collection consists of approximately 2000 bottles, but there are also changing exhibits that borrow from collections throughout the nation. When I visited, there was an exhibit of blue-decorated stoneware bottles, a bottle-dating exhibit that explained how to recognize various marks made on the glass by hand tools, and a cross-section of a privy dig (many bottles are often found in old privies since during winter they had to be stored in a place where a hole had been dug in the ground).

Make sure to stop at the working glass studio across the street, owned by the museum; classes in glassblowing and workshops with internationally renowned guest artisans are offered. And every June the museum has a bottle show and sale, featuring antique-bottle dealers from throughout the East Coast.

National Museum of Dance (518-584-2225; dancemuseum.org), 99 South Broadway. Open March through November, Tuesday through Saturday 10-4; Sunday noon-4. Admission. This is the only museum in the country

The National Museum of Dance in Saratoga Springs.

dedicated to preserving the history and art of dance in America, and it does an excellent job. Changing exhibits feature costumes, artwork, personalities, and choreography of American dance. Videos help place various dances in their historical settings, and it is one of the few places where dance enthusiasts may get up close to the costumes and accessories of their favorite dance "characters." Special events include talks and films; check the website for a complete schedule of events.

National Museum of Racing and Hall of Fame (518-584-0400; racingmuseum. org), 191 Union Avenue. Open year-round, Monday through Saturday 10-4; Sunday noon-4. During racing season, hours are extended: 9-5. Closed holidays. Admission. This museum is one of the most modern sports exhibits in the world, and is a must-see for anyone who ever enjoyed the sight of a racehorse blasting out of a starting gate. The film shown, entitled Race America, is an introduction to the racetrack, and throughout the various galleries video and audio exhibits let visitors experience the sounds and sights of a horse race. Silks, fine paintings, furniture, and historic items all tell the story of the thoroughbred in America: the museum covers photography from contemporary artists. Even if you've never placed a bet in your life, the gift shop will immediately turn you into a horse fan. Make sure not to miss the steeplechase gallery dedicated to the sport, featuring several interactive exhibits.

Saratoga Harness Hall of Fame & Museum (518-587-4210; museumsusa. org), 352 Jefferson Street, at the Saratoga Harness Raceway. Harness racing fans will want to visit this museum with memorabilia and artwork depicting the history of harness racing. Free.

New York State Military Museum and Veterans Research Center (518-581-5100; nysmm.org), 61 Lake Avenue. Open year-round, Tuesday through Saturday 10-4. (The research center is closed on Saturday; only the museum is open.) Admission. Some 10,000 military artifacts—weapons, artillery, flags, and more—from New York State's participation in military conflicts, dating from the War of 1812 to Desert Storm, are displayed in this armory, built in 1898. Visitors will see the largest battle flag collection in the world, with more than 1700; most of the flags are from the Civil War, but they range from the War of 1812 to the Gulf War. The Veterans Research Center contains 2000 volumes and 6000 photographs (half are from the Civil War era). This is a great stop for Civil War buffs, particularly those interested in New York State involvement. Note there are no federal records in the research center, just those from the state of New York.

Saratoga Automobile Museum (518-587-1935; saratogaautomuseum.org), 110 Avenue of the Pines (Spa State Park). Open year-round, Tuesday through Sunday 10-5; January through March, Wednesday through Sunday 10-5. This museum is housed in a restored 1930s Saratoga Water Bottling Plant in the park. Dozens of classic cars are on display, including a 1928 sedan once owned by Charles Lindbergh and a 1931 Duesenberg Model J Roadster.

Tang Teaching Museum and Art Gallery (518-580-8080; tang.skidmore. edu), Skidmore College, 815 North Broadway. Open Tuesday through Sunday noon-5. Suggested donation. The two-story building housing this relatively new museum (opened in 2000) was designed by Antoine Predock. Paid for by a gift from the Chinese-born American businessman Oscar Tang, whose daughter and wife both graduated from Skidmore, the museum covers post World War II art, giving preference to visual work with an aural component. In addition to fine art, the Tang has a few peripheral exhibits (films, performances) in progress and some intriguing auditory treats, including collaborative exhibits with Skidmore's science and history departments.

HISTORIC SITE

Saratoga National Historical Park (518-664-9821; nps.gov/sara), 648 Route 32, Still water. Open year-round, daily 9-5; closed holidays. Park road for bikers open seasonally. The **Philip Schuyler House** is open daily Memorial Day weekend through Labor Day. Admission. The Battle of Saratoga turned the tide of the American Revolution, and history buffs will enjoy spending a day here. The British hoped to cut New York into sections with a three-pronged attack and destroy communications among the areas. At Saratoga the supposedly untrained, undisciplined American troops won the field, and history was changed. Your tour should begin at the battlefield visitors center, where dioramas, maps, and explanatory exhibits show how the battle was fought and won. Weapons, uniforms, and other items are on display, and because the battle was such a large one, it is necessary to read the material before you set out on the 10-mile self-guided driving tour. Markers at each stop explain what went on during the battle. At the Schuyler House, memorabilia of General Philip Schuyler and his wife show what life was like for people who lived through the battle and the days after. There is even a monument on the field to a leg: Benedict Arnold was wounded in the leg during the battle and became a hero, until he later turned traitor. Special events include military encampments. They are held at the park throughout the year. Saratoga Monument, a 155-foot obelisk commemorating the American victory in the Battle of Saratoga, is open to visitors from late June through Labor Day, Wednesday through Sunday 9-5.

Saratoga Spa State Park is 2400 acres of grounds, trails, a theater, a hotel, and, of course, mineral springs.

SPRINGS & SPAS

Saratoga is famous for its springs, many of which are still open. A spring-tasting guide is available from the **Heritage Area Visitor Center** opposite Congress Park. The center is only open in July and August, but it has small exhibits on the history of Saratoga Springs and its commerce. The springs in Saratoga each have their own chemical makeup up and characteristics; there are explanatory signs at each spring and usually, paper drinking cups. Just remember too much spring water might not sit well with your digestive system; try no more than a sip or two to start. You can also find lots of bottled spring water at shops in Saratoga or at the spas.

Congress Park, on Broadway, houses Congress Spring, located underneath an elaborate pavilion. Its waters were some of the first to be bottled and sold commercially in the early 19th century. Also in the park, along the path, are the Columbian Spring, Congress 3, and, in the northeast corner, freshwater Spring. Across from the park, on Spring Street, the Hathorn No. 2 Spring is a popular stop on a hot summer's day; it has a small seating area, and lovely plantings surround it.

The Crystal Spa, 120 South Broadway (diagonally across from Saratoga Spa State Park), has been in business since 1988. Built on the same property where you will find the Rosemary Spring, the Crystal Spa once offered a luxurious pampering experience. That isn't true any longer and I strongly suggest you go elsewhere in Saratoga if you are interested in visiting a spa while in town.

High Rock Park (go north on Broadway, make a right onto Lake Avenue, then a left onto High Avenue). Here you can sample water from Old Red, the Peerless, and the Governor springs. These were the original public springs of Saratoga, and each one has its own distinctive taste; Old Red, so called because of its high iron content, was considered good for the complexion. Others were purported to have health and curative benefits. There are still 21 public mineral springs in the city. Most are naturally carbonated and no two taste alike. The city visitor center distributes a brochure with a self-guided tour to all the springs, if you are interested in visiting a number of them.

Saratoga Spa State Park (from the center of town, take Route 9 south to the Avenue of Pines, on the right, and follow that road into the park; the site is well marked, and it isn't far from the highway). There are springs here and bathing facilities. Drinking springs throughout the park include Island Spouter (the only spouting geyser east of the Mississippi), Hayes Well (with an inhaling hole), Orenda Spring, Coesa, and Ferndale. A marked walking path leads to many of the springs—a lovely stroll on a summer afternoon. There is no charge for tasting the springs.

The Roosevelt Baths & Spa (800-452-7275; gideonputnam.com), 39 Roosevelt Drive Extension. This facility is just a 10-minute walk across the park from the Gideon Putnam Hotel and is now part of the resort. The building housing the baths and spa was renovated and reopened in the summer of 2004; it was originally opened in 1935 as a bathhouse. The mineral springs like those here have been used for centuries as a health treatment. Today the spa offers a full menu of services including herbal mineral baths, as well as massages, facials, scrubs, body wraps, waxing, manicures, pedicures, and hair styling. This is the place to go when you want to treat yourself to a special relaxing experience and de-stress.

WALKING TOUR

A walk through Saratoga Springs gives visitors a chance to see the great variety of architectural styles in vogue during the 19th and early 20th centuries, but it would be impossible to list all the houses worth looking at. A self-guided tour brochure is usually available at the information booth near Congress Park, or from the Saratoga Chamber of Commerce, 28 Clinton Street. Scores of homes offer a look at Italianate, Gothic Revival, Queen Anne, Romanesque, and other styles popular with the upper middle class and wealthy residents of the city.

The Adelphi Hotel has been serving guests in Saratoga Springs since 1877.

The **Batcheller Mansion**, at the corner of Whitney and West Circular streets, is a fantasy of French Renaissance and Eastern influence. The **Jumel Mansion**, 129 Circular Street, was the summer home of the infamous Madam Jumel, one-time wife of Aaron Burr. The **Adelphi Hotel**, 365 Broadway, recalls the hotels of the past with tall columns and many arched windows.

Several streets and areas you may want to enjoy for their architectural gems include Broadway, Circular Street, Franklin Square, Clinton Street, Lake Avenue, and Union Avenue. All the homes are private, but their beauty can easily be appreciated from the sidewalk or the window of a car if you are tired of walking and prefer driving.

Saratoga's main thoroughfare is Broadway, which has won numerous awards for its main-street restoration. There are dozens of shops, galleries, and places of interest to check out—an Irish specialty store, fantastic bookshop, clothing boutiques, fine glass and porcelain, jewelry, and more—both fashionable and funky. Don't forget to wander the side streets off Broadway (Phila, Spring and Caroline, are a few), where many other surprises await the curious walker. One of my favorite bookstores anywhere is the **Lyrical Ballad** (518-584-8779), 7 Phila Street, just off Broadway, an enormous emporium housed in an old bank. You can wander through room after room (the old vaults and inner recesses of the building) and discover thousands of used and rare books, maps, and literary treasures that will surprise and delight. On a hot summer day, this is the perfect escape from the crowds and the sizzling sidewalks! And don't miss **Northshire Bookstore** (518-682-4200), 424 Broadway, open daily 10am-7pm. It is one of the best bookstores in the region.

WINERIES AND BREWERIES

Druthers (518-306-5275), 381 Broadway. Open year-round daily, 11:30-9. This is a somewhat new addition to the brewery scene in upstate New York. There's a restaurant on the premises along with a brewery and some of the specialties are sumptuous burgers, mac and cheese, along with over a dozen beers to choose from.

Saratoga Winery (518-584-9463) 462 Route 29. Open daily 11-7. Located only four miles from downtown, this Adirondack-style tasting room and vineyard showcases several wines made largely from grapes of the Finger Lakes region. The offerings include Rielsings, chardonnay, merlot, and cabernet sauvignon. Their signature wine, Melomel, is made of grapes and honey fermented in Kentucky bourbon barrels with no additives whatsoever. Visitors may enjoy live music and barbecue dinners some Friday nights from 6 to 9. Check the website, saratogawinery.com, for current schedule.

Swedish Hill Winery (518-450-1200), 379 Broadway. Open year-round, Thursday through Monday noon-5; Saturday until 6. This tasting room, opened in 2011, offers about 30 different Swedish Hill wines, including sparkling selections. The vineyard is located in the Finger Lakes, but visitors can enjoy tasting their wines here.

ACTIVITIES

BICYCLING

Blue Sky Bicycles (518-583-0600), 71 Church Street, rents hybrid bikes for recreational touring and riding. Open April through September, Tuesday through Friday 10-7; Saturday 9-5; October through March, Tuesday through Saturday 10-5

Clock Tower Bikeworks (518-587-0071), 20 Prospect Street, Ballston Spa, does not rent bicycles. However, if you need any equipment for your bike, they are a full-service shop, just outside of the city.

BOATING

Fish Creek Marina (518-584-1901), 251 Route 67, on Saratoga Lake. From town, take Route 29 east, and make a right on Staffords Bridge Road (about two miles out of town). Go another 1.5 miles over the bridge, and you will see the marina. Open May through September daily 9-7. Rent kayaks here and learn how to kayak, but call in advance to arrange a lesson. There's a large pavilion available for barbecues and campfires. The most dramatic sunset can be seen from this spot on the lake—people come from all over Saratoga to watch it! At the same marina **Mountainman Paddlesports** (518-584-0600), rents canoes, kayaks and paddleboards. They are open daily during the season, 10-6.

Point Breeze Marina (518-587-3397), 1459 Route 9P, on Saratoga Lake. Open April through November, daily 9-6. This is a place to rent rowboats, pontoon boats, speedboats and fishing boats.

Saratoga Boat Works (518-584-BOAT), 549 Union Avenue, Saratoga Springs. Open Monday through Saturday 8-5; Sunday by appointment. At the north end of the lake, near the bridge, just past the racetrack, is where this full-service marina is located. It's a good place to rent power boats or pontoon boats. If you want to water-ski, this is where to rent the necessary equipment.

FARM STANDS & PICK-YOUR-OWN FARMS

Among the many things Saratoga is famous for is melon: specifically, Hand melons, named after the family that first grew them.

The Hand Melon Farm (518-692-2376) is located 13 miles east of Saratoga Springs on Route 29; the melons are usually ready to go from late July through mid-September. They are sweet and resemble cantaloupes; you will see signs for them at many farm stands. You can also pick your own strawberries in June; raspberries may be picked in September. The farm stand is open May through September.

A great deal of excellent produce is raised on local farms. At **Ariel's Vegetable Farm** (518-584-2189), 194 Northern Pines Road, Gansevoort, five miles north of Saratoga Springs, permits visitors to pick their own berries, buy fruit and vegetables off the stand, or take a tour of the farm. Open April through December daily 9-6.

Bowman Orchards and Farm Store (518-371-2042), 141 Sugar Hill Road, Rexford, has pick-your-own berries and apples. Try the farm store's apple pie ice cream. They also sell more than 20 varieties of fudge. There's even a "play land" for the kids. Open June through October, Wednesday through Saturday 9-5; Sunday noon-5.

Riverview Orchards (518-371-2174), 660 Riverview Road, Rexford, has pick-your-own apples (September and October) and farm tours. Open year-round, Thursday through Sunday 9-5.

Saratoga Farmers' Market (518-747-9492), 105 High Rock Avenue, is held May through October, Wednesday evening 3-6 and Saturday 9-1. You can sample the famous local waters there. The winter market is held November through April, Saturday 9-1, at Lincoln Baths building, Saratoga Spa State Park, 65 South Broadway.

FISHING

Head out to **Saratoga Lake** early in the morning, and stop at one of the marinas or bait and tackle shops you'll see around the lake for information on the local fishing scene (also see *Boating* for suggested marinas with rentals). The **Kayaderosseras Creek** offers decent trout fishing during the season (April 1st through October 15th).

GOLF

Eagle Crest Golf Club (518-877-7082), 1004 Route 146A, Clifton Park. Open April through October, 6am-8pm. The 18-hole, par-72 championship course is fairly open—a good bet for novices. Also on the premises: a driving range, par-3 course, miniature golf course, restaurant, and snack bar.

Pioneer Hills Golf Course (518-885-7000), 3230 Galway Road, Ballston Spa. Open mid-April through October, weather permitting. This 18-hole, par-70 championship course has a restaurant and bar on the premises. In summer, golfers will enjoy the large outdoor patio (canopy covered), a nice place to enjoy refreshments after playing.

Saratoga Lake Golf Club (518-581-6616), 35 Grace Moore Road. Open April through October 6:30am-8:30pm. This 18-hole, par-72 course was designed in what was once the middle of a forest. Although not a championship course, it is quite challenging. The course has shorter distances for each hole, but there are many elevation changes. Accuracy will help you do well here. There is a snack bar, a pleasant place to enjoy a drink after golfing.

Saratoga National Golf Club (518-583-GOLF), 458 Union Avenue. Next to Longfellow's restaurant. Open late April through mid-November, depending on the weather, daily 7am-sunset. This beautifully maintained 18-hole, par-72 championship course has 24 bridges and several wetland areas, and is reminiscent of courses in South Carolina. The club opened in 2001, and *Golf Digest* magazine rated it the fifth best new course in the country at the time. Call to reserve a tee time over the phone with a credit card 30 days in advance during the summer months, or a week or two before you intend to go at other times of the year.

Saratoga Spa Golf Course (518-584-2006), 60 Roosevelt Drive, Saratoga Spa State Park. Open April through October, weekdays 6am-dusk; weekends from 5am. This beautifully maintained 18-hole, par-72 championship course boasts that no two holes touch each other. The towering pine trees make the surroundings special, and the prices are reasonable. There is also a driving range, restaurant, and complete facilities. The Victoria Pool is adjacent to the golf course. They will take reservations a week in advance if you call to reserve a tee time. This is necessary, particularly in the summer months.

NOTE: **Saratoga Mini Golf** (518-581-0852), 3071 Route 50, next to the Wilton Mall. This is the place to go for family fun; they are open mid-April through mid-October, daily 11am-9pm. Located a short ride from downtown Saratoga Springs, there are plenty of after-game treats from the snack bar at this 18-hole course the kids will especially appreciate.

HORSEBACK RIDING

Muddy Acres Farm (518-581-0264), 95 Middle Grove Road, Greenfield Center. Open during the summer months daily, except Wednesday, 10-dusk; the rest of the year, Saturday and Sunday, 10-dusk, weather permitting. There are one-hour trail rides and pony rides at reasonable rates here. Wagon and sleigh rides are available seasonally. For those who want Western riding lessons, there is a certified instructor on staff.

Schauber Stables (518-281-0088), 428 Schauber Road, Ballston Spa. Open daily, spring through autumn, weather permitting, 9am-9pm; Saturday and Sunday until 7pm. This family-owned and operated stables offers trail rides combined with a trail lesson. There is a minimum age requirement of seven, and a weight limit of 220 pounds. Mini trail rides are also available.

HORSE RACING

Saratoga Casino and Raceway (518-584-2110; 800-727-2990), 342 Jefferson Street. Open year-round, daily 9am-5am. Admission.

Formerly a plain harness track, the raceway was often overshadowed by its sassier cousin, the Saratoga Race Course. But the venue has expanded to include gaming (slot machines, electronic table games, etc.) in a 55,000-square-foot facility and now offers lots of excitement around the clock. This is the first video gaming property to open in New York State. Visitors can enjoy watching horses vie for purses on the world's fastest half-mile trotting and pacing track, which, unlike the "flats," is open year-round. The backstretch area contains the only pool in the state located on the grounds of a racetrack and is reserved solely for the use of horses. There are two polo fields and an outdoor arena with more than 200 acres and 1100 stalls for the equine patrons. Several restaurants are in a large food court. In order to enter the casino, you must be at least 18 years old.

Saratoga Horse Racing.

Saratoga Race Course (518-584-6200 in season; 718-641-4700 off-seasonnyra. com), 267 Union Avenue. Open for six weeks from late July through Labor Day. Dates change each season. Closed Tuesday. Admission. The Saratoga racetrack is a hub of activity for a month and a half and it's busy from early morning until late afternoon. Rub shoulders with celebrities, rail birds, and just plain folks; dress in jeans and T-shirts or elegant suits and hats; the choice is yours. You may begin with Breakfast at Saratoga (7-9:30am; get there early; free admission), a popular way for people to enjoy the horses and jockeys close up. An announcer keeps things lively as the horses and their riders breeze by. Handicapping seminars, very useful for novice bettors, are held at the track and are announced at breakfast. Seminar times are also posted throughout the track. Breakfast is also served daily in the clubhouse dining room, in an outdoor tent, and buffet-style in the box seats. Outside, a continental breakfast is served near the clubhouse. Visitors can enjoy a tour of the backstretch area where the horses board during the racing season. The tour is guided and the area is viewed from an observation "train"; sign up for the tour early during breakfast.

The track opens to the racing crowd at 11am weekdays and 10:30am weekends. Although there is lots of parking and seating available, remember: the crowds can be quite large, and the track is smaller than many modern racetracks. So get there early for good viewing. You can park in an official track lot or at a private lot. The latter cost more, but the former fill up quickly. Bring your own chair, if possible, and remember both restaurant food and snacks, though usually decent, can be very expensive. You are allowed to bring coolers to the track. Both steeplechases and flat races are held throughout the season. Check the daily racing forms to see exactly who is racing when. The races begin (post time) at 1pm weekdays and 12:30pm on weekends, rain or shine.

POLO

You can't play polo unless you have your own string of ponies, but you can watch in season at Saratoga. The players come from all over the world and are the best in their sport. Matches are held July through Labor Day, Friday and Sunday at 5:30pm, at Whitney Field, out Seward Street. Go north on Broadway and turn left onto Church Street. After a half-mile, make a right onto Seward Street and travel one mile to the railroad overpass. Turn right. The polo field is on the left. For a complete schedule, call 518-584-8108 or go to saratogapolo.com.

SCENIC RAILROAD RIDE

Saratoga and North Creek Railway (877-726-7245; sncrr.com), 26 Station Lane. Open Memorial Day weekend through Columbus Day, Thursday through Monday. There are three trips daily starting from North Creek down to Saratoga in vintage rail cars. A nice excursion is to leave Saratoga for North Creek at 10am and arrive at 12:15pm. There are several places to have lunch in North Creek, and the village is filled with interesting shops. A train leaves at 3:45pm and arrives back in Saratoga at 6pm. It is possible also to return later at night, and those who go fishing or rafting may choose to do so, or perhaps stay overnight. Check website for latest schedule.

SWIMMING

Saratoga Spa State Park (518-584-2000), 65 South Broadway. There are two pools in the park, and both are open to the public. The Victoria Pool opens Memorial Day weekend and remains open until Labor Day, daily 10-6. Admission. There is a smaller pool here for young children in addition to the larger pool. The Peerless Pool is open from late June through Labor Day, also daily 10-6. Admission and a parking fee are charged. This Olympic-size pool is a great place to cool off after a day at the races or walking the streets of the city. If you have small children, however, the Victoria Pool is probably a better choice.

YMCA (518-583-9622), 262 Broadway. Indoor pool only. Open year-round. Call for information on public swimming sessions, which change daily. There are family swim times, as well. The pool is 25 yards long and five lengths wide; temperature is usually about 84 degrees.

WINTER SPORTS

CROSS COUNTRY SKIING

Saratoga Spa State Park (518-584-2535). A network of marvelous groomed trails here will delight cross-country skiers of all abilities.

ICE SKATING

Saratoga Spa State Park (518-584-2535), 65 South Broadway. There is an outdoor rink here in season, weather permitting. Call for hours which change depending on the weather. There is also open adult hockey at this rink.

Saratoga Springs Ice Rinks (518-583-3462), 30 Weibel Avenue. There are two rinks here, and they accommodate both hockey and figure skating. They are open year-round, except from mid-April to late June for maintenance. Call for a schedule, which varies from week to week. The Weibel rink is Olympic size, and the Vernon rink is smaller. Both offer public skates and family skating, open adult figure, and hockey sessions.

PARKS AND NATURE TRAILS

Bog Meadow Nature Trail (518-587-5554). Open year-round, daily dawn to dusk. Free. (From Broadway make a right onto Route 29 east. Go through the traffic light at Weibel Avenue. The trail entrance is about 500 feet farther on the right.) This two-mile nature trail is ideal for people traveling with children or those who want to take a short walk away from town. It's fairly flat and goes through the wetlands just outside of the city. You can run or walk in the warm-weather months and cross-country ski or snowshoe in winter. There is a parking area too.

Congress Park (518-587-3550). Open year-round. This lovely city park is great for a stroll, particularly after shopping on Broadway.

East Side Recreation Field (518-587-3550), 226 Lake Avenue. (Make a right on Lake Avenue and go about 1.5 miles. The field is on the right, just after the East Avenue light.) Open year-round. This 20-acre park is free. There is an excellent skateboard park that is open May through October and a small fee is charged for this activity only. A spray fountain and playground will appeal to small children, while tennis and basketball courts, and a quarter-mile paved circular track, are great for rollerblading and running.

Saratoga Spa State Park (518-584-2535; saratogaspastatepark.org), 65 South Broadway (one mile south of the city on Route 9). Open year-round. Free. There is a small charge for swimming and use of the bathhouses. This 2000-

acre park is a gem: it's clean, wide open, full of activities to keep visitors busy, and it is located only minutes away from downtown Saratoga Springs. Listed on the National Register of Historic Places, the park is home to SPAC (Saratoga Performing Arts Center) and the Gideon Putnam hotel. Recreation opportunities abound.. There are two pools, tennis courts, streamside trails for walking, and two golf courses (reservations are required) open during the summer months. In the winter, cross-country skiing and ice-skating are available. Special film evenings, nature walks, tours, and other events are held throughout the year.

Yaddo (518-584-0746; yaddo.org), 312 Union Avenue (Route 9P). Open year-round, but the gardens are at their peak from June through September. Free. The plantings here are superb, and visitors are welcome to walk among the paths and enjoy the fountains, roses and peaceful seating areas. Yaddo, once a private home, is now an artists' retreat offering residencies to professional creative artists working in virtually all media and used by both the famous and the someday-to-be famous. The site offers a respite from the summer frenzy of racing and the society scene. *Note:* Mid-June through Labor Day, Saturday and Sunday at 11am (also Tuesday during racing season), a guided garden tour is given. A fee of $10 per person is charged. From mid-September through October, "ghost tours" are given on Friday and Sunday at 5:30pm.

LODGING

A note on staying overnight and dining in Saratoga Springs: During racing season, late July through Labor Day, prices are sky-high and accommodations are difficult to obtain. Some places are booked solid as early as April. Restaurants can be crowded, expensive and difficult to obtain reservations for...unless you know someone. So be prepared to pay top price for your stay at this time of year. I prefer to visit the city in May and October, when things are calmer and the weather is still beautiful. The accommodations I recommend here are organized by type: hotel, motel or inn/bed & breakfast. All are top-notch.

HOTELS

Adelphi Hotel (518- 678-6000), 365 Broadway. ($$) This renovated grand Victorian hotel, originally constructed in 1877, is located in the heart of Saratoga, and it exudes elegance and charm, transporting visitors back to another era. In the summer of 2017 the hotel underwent an extensive renovation. There are now 32 rooms and guests can dine at the beautiful Blue Hen restaurant downstairs.

The bar at the recently renovated Adelphi Hotel on Broadway in Saratoga Springs.

Gideon Putnam Resort and Spa (866-890-1171), Saratoga Spa State Park, 24 Gideon Putnam Road. ($$$) This historic Georgian-style resort hotel is set in the 2200-acre park only a few minutes walk from the Saratoga Performing Arts Center and minutes away from the track and downtown area. The resort is named after one of Saratoga's first settlers, Gideon Putnam, founder of the hotel business in Saratoga. Born in Massachusetts in 1763, Putnam arrived in Saratoga with his wife in 1789 and set up a sawmill. He then invested in another business, the Putnam Tavern and Boarding House; a bathhouse followed later. Today referred to as the Jewel of Saratoga, the hotel stands as a reminder of the city's rich history. Make sure to see the murals by renowned artist James Reynolds in the dining room, depicting scenes from Saratoga society and the Adirondacks. Several celebrities have stayed at the hotel, including Robert Redford in 1997, when he filmed The Horse Whisperer. A scene from the Dustin Hoffman film Billy Bathgate was shot in the hotel lobby in 1991. The place blends the ambience of the past with all the modern conveniences. In addition to over 100 double rooms, 18 parlor and porch suites are available. The service is quite good, and guests may choose to have meals included in the rate. Several packages are available, so inquire about them especially if you will be staying midweek or off-season. Children are welcome. Open year-round.

Hampton Inn & Suites (518-584-2100), 25 Lake Avenue. ($$$) This 2008 addition to the hotel scene in Saratoga has 123 rooms in the heart of the downtown area. There is an indoor pool, fitness center, and all the modern conveniences. Children welcome.

Saratoga Arms (518-584-1775), 497 Broadway. ($$) This concierge hotel, with 31 rooms, in the middle of the downtown area, is perfect for those who want to be within walking distance of shops, restaurants, and cultural activities. It is housed in a brick building that dates from 1870 and is filled with grand staircases, ornate moldings and ceiling medallions. Every room is beautifully restored and custom decorated with period pieces and antiques; the rooms also have TVs and wireless Internet access. Some have working fireplaces. The antique wicker furniture on the wraparound porch overlooking Broadway is a great place to relax after sightseeing. A full breakfast is served; there is a fitness room and small spa on the premises. Children over the age of 12 are welcome. Open year-round.

Saratoga Casino Hotel (518-584-2110; 800-727-2990), 342 Jefferson Street. ($$$) If you are interested in being near a casino, this hotel has one with 1700 slots and electronic table games in the lobby. There are 117 modern rooms and suites with a small pool and 24-hour fitness center on the premises. Three dining options, including the renowned Morton's Steakhouse, live entertainment and harness racing are in the hotel as well. Children are welcome. Open year-round.

Saratoga Hilton (518-584-4000), 534 Broadway. ($$$) This full-service hotel in the heart of Saratoga's downtown is only a short walk down Broadway to shops and restaurants. Management here is first-rate. The 212 renovated guest rooms and 30 spacious suites are decorated in vibrant colors; all are comfortable and immaculate. Facilities include an indoor heated pool and fitness center with sauna. All rooms have cable TV, wireless Internet access, and air-conditioning. Open year-round. This is a great choice for familiess.

MOTELS

Carriage House Inn (518-584-4220), 198 Broadway. ($$) There are 14 spacious Victorian-and Adirondack-style suites here, all with private bath. Some have canopy beds and a fireplace; others have a kitchenette and Jacuzzi tub. All have air-conditioning and TV. Guests will enjoy the atmosphere of an inn and the privacy and convenience of a hotel. Enjoy coffee or tea in the morning on the lovely porch during the warm-weather months. Open year-round.

Springs Motel (518-584-6336), 189 Broadway. ($) This clean, comfortable standard motel is a short walk from the racecourse and the state park. There are 28 rooms: all with air-conditioning and cable TV. An outdoor pool makes this a good place to stop if you are traveling with young children. Open year-round.

INNS/BED & BREAKFASTS

Anne's Washington Inn (518-584-9807), 111 South Broadway. ($$) Owner Joe Bokan, makes a stay at this beautiful inn extremely comfortable. The building, once a birthing center, was in the same family for generations. The location is excellent and one can walk both to the downtown area as well as the Saratoga Performing Arts Center (SPAC). Bicycles may be borrowed free of charge. In the evening guests may sit by the fire pit and enjoy a glass of wine. Continental breakfast is served all morning. Open year-round.

Batcheller Mansion (800-616-7012), 20 Circular Street. ($$$) Built in 1873 by George Sherman Batcheller, an attorney and judge, this magnificent structure is resplendent with beautiful gardens and architectural details that will delight history buffs. President Ulysses S. Grant slept here shortly after the house was built. They still host guests in the timeless tradition of grace and ease reminiscent of a time long past. The nine graciously appointed rooms, four with fireplaces, offer a warm and inviting reprieve from the outside world. This is the perfect spot for a romantic getaway. The luxurious surroundings include a plush sitting room and a library where you can recline on a red-velvet sofa. The formal dining room breakfast offers a glorious start to the day with freshly baked breads and pastries of your choice. No children. Open year-round.

Brunswick Bed & Breakfast (518-584-6751), 143 Union Avenue. ($$) This is one of the oldest continuously operating lodging facilities in Saratoga Springs. They have been serving guests since 1886 and the building has been continually renovated. Currently there are 10 private rooms; two of them are suites. All are centrally air-conditioned with a good deal of variety. One room has a gas fireplace and two other rooms have Jacuzzis. There is also a suite with a kitchenette. All rooms have cable TV and wireless Internet access. The value for money is excellent. Children welcome. Open year-round.

Circular Manor (518-583-6393), 120 Circular Street. ($$) This 6000-square-foot Victorian home was built in 1903 by Newton Breeze, a well-known Saratoga architect at the turn of the 20th century. There are five beautifully decorated guest rooms, all with private bath, central air-conditioning, claw-foot tubs, and marble floors. This is a place where you will feel pampered yet comfortable. All details have been attended to here: There are beautiful duvets, cotton sheets, and luxurious Egyptian-cotton towels. The full gourmet breakfast (a few choices are available daily) features freshly baked breads, fruit, and wonderful egg creations. Enjoy relaxing on the huge wraparound porch in the heart of the city's historic district, a quiet section of town surrounded by lovely Victorian homes, yet only a few blocks from shops and restaurants. No children. Open year-round.

Geyser Lodge Bed & Breakfast (518-584-0389), 182 Ballston Avenue ($$) A comfortable Queen Anne-style Victorian dating from 1896, this spacious 16-room B&B was once referred to as a "cottage" by the wealthy New York City family who used it as a summer residence. Located near Skidmore College, there are four guest rooms, all with private bath and air-conditioning. Full breakfast served on weekends; continental during the week. An in-ground pool in the back yard is open to guests. Children over the age of 12 are welcome. The policy is flexible with younger ones, so be sure to inquire. Open year-round, except the month of January.

The Mansion (888-996-9977), 801 Route 29, Rock City Falls 12863. ($$$) Located 7 miles west of town on Route 29. This inn was built in 1866 as the summer home of a prominent industrialist, George West, across the street from his Excelsior Mill. He also invented the folded paper bag and became known as the Paper Bag King. The inn has had only seven owners and is a dream come true for lovers of Victoriana. The mansion has been featured in several major publications. Designed to suggest a Venetian villa, the building retains its original mirrored fireplaces and elaborate chandeliers. The rooms are furnished with Victorian antiques, and Mamie Eisenhower's piano is the striking centerpiece of the downstairs library. A full breakfast is served. This is a special spot and will appeal to those who want a respite from the summer crowds. The old mill and lovely waterfall across the street from the inn are perfect for taking a short stroll I enjoyed running on a beautiful road that follows a stream on the grounds of a state fishing preserve close to the B&B. All nine rooms are beautifully decorated, air-conditioned and have cable TV. Adults only. Open year-round, except the month of January.

Saratoga Farmstead Bed & Breakfast (518-587-2074), 41 Locust Grove Road. ($$) Located two miles from downtown Saratoga Springs this restored 18th-century farmhouse has seven air-conditioned rooms, all with private bath. A gourmet breakfast is served and many items in season come from the organic garden on the premises. This is a casual farm setting, a nice change from the bustle of downtown. Bring your binoculars: there are a few acres of walking trails filled with all kinds of birds and wildflowers. Children welcome. Open year-round.

Saratoga Sleigh (518-584-4534), 203 Union Avenue. ($$) The location is attractive to those who want to be near the action: This moderately priced B&B overlooks the racecourse. Housed in a historic 1887 Queen Anne Victorian, the B&B's four rooms, all with private bath, are filled with antiques. Each room is air-conditioned and has a TV. A full breakfast is served. Children must be over the age of 12. Open year-round.

Springwater Bed & Breakfast (518-583-3661), 94 George Street. ($$) This establishment is run by two women, a mother and daughter team; they attend to every detail making it a first-rate accommodation. The place combines the charm of Old Saratoga with all the modern conveniences and will appeal to the sophisticated traveler. It is also a "green" property with Energy Star Certification. There are five beautifully appointed guest rooms with cable TV and air-conditioning. The breakfast is excellent and this B&B is highly recommended. Children welcome. Open year-round.

Union Gables Inn (518-584-1558), 55 Union Avenue. ($$) This restored Queen Anne Victorian, circa 1901, is a family-owned and occupied bed & breakfast. Each of the 10 guest rooms has a private bath, cable TV and air-conditioning and all are exquisitely decorated to reflect the style of Old Saratoga. Conveniently located near the downtown area and only one block from the thoroughbred racetrack. Children and pets are welcome. Open year-round.

WHERE TO EAT

There is a wealth of wonderful restaurants in the Spa City. Some are popular with both travelers and local residents. I've included my favorite places whether you're seeking a leisurely gourmet dinner or a quick informal meal. All are first-rate. Please note all restaurants are within the city limits unless otherwise indicated.

Some restaurants cut back their hours during the winter months, January through March. If you visit at that time, especially on a Monday or Tuesday, call to make sure the restaurant of your choice is open. Days and hours of operation listed here are for *most* months of the year.

DINING OUT

Chianti Il Ristorante (518-580-0025), 18 Division Street. ($$$) Open for dinner daily 4:30-9:30; Friday and Saturday until 10:30. Savor Northern Italian cuisine in an elegant atmosphere with impeccable service. There is penne pasta with cannellini beans and sausage, stuffed quail, risotto with porcini mushrooms and filetto al Gorgonzola. I sampled one of the salmon dishes and it was superb. The portions are generous and there is an extensive wine list. Makes sure to leave room for dessert; the tiramisu and chocolate soufflé are excellent. No reservations are taken so it's best to arrive before 6 or after 9 during the summer season. Not recommended for young children.

Duo Modern Japanese Cuisine (518-580-8881), 175 South Broadway. ($$) Open daily 11:30-10:30. Enjoy contemporary Japanese fare in a clean crisp ambience. The sushi and sashimi are excellent. Lunch specials are offered daily and are quite reasonable. This is a nice place to relax and have a couple of rolls with a pot of green tea after shopping downtown. Not recommended for children.

15 Church (518-587-1515), 15 Church Street. ($$$) Open for dinner daily 5-9:30; Friday and Saturday until 10. Located in a beautiful restored building, this elegant restaurant is relatively new on the Saratoga dining scene. The "Patio" menu includes a raw bar, oysters on the half shell, clams, wings and fish and chips. Seafood is flown in fresh daily and is the specialty here along with aged beef. Not recommended for children.

Forno Bistro (518-581-2401), 541 Broadway. ($$) Open for dinner daily 4:30-9:30. The casual yet sophisticated ambience here is inviting and romantic. An enclosed terrace is a fine place to dine in the warm weather. The Tuscan cuisine is "rustic Italian," and the imaginative pastas created by the chef-owner who comes from Tuscany are superior. The wood-fired pizzas and calamari are excellent as well. Children welcome.

Jacob and Anthony's American Grille (518-871-1600), 38 High Rock Avenue ($$) Open daily 11:30-9:30. They serve up classic American favorites here—soups, salads, burgers, wraps, steaks and seafood—with interesting variations on the usual fare. There is an enormous menu with something for everyone. Children welcome.

One of my favorite Italian restaurants in Saratoga Springs is Forno Bistro across the street (Broadway) from City Center.

Lake Local (518-886-1373), 550 Union Avenue. ($$) Open daily 11-10. This waterfront restaurant with adjacent marina is open in the summer daily for both lunch and dinner. Known for their fish tacos and craft cocktail and beer selections, keep in mind service can be lacking during racing season. Outdoor dining during the warm weather months is the big draw here. Children are welcome.

Lake Ridge Restaurant (518-899-6000), 35 Burlington Avenue, Round Lake (exit 11 off the Northway). ($$) Open Tuesday through Sunday 11:30-9. Fine Continental dining at reasonable prices is served; the menu includes steaks, seafood, and pasta entrees. It's worth the short drive south of the city if you want to escape the summer crowds! Children welcome.

Longfellow's Restaurant (518-587-0108), 500 Union Avenue. ($$$) Open for dinner daily 5-10; Sunday 4-9. Located in an old country estate dating from the late 1800s, this establishment prides itself on its warm, relaxing ambience. The restaurant is unusual in that it has a waterfall and pond inside. The American cuisine includes several mesquite offerings. In addition to prime rib, rack of lamb, seafood and pasta, there are some imaginative creations. Bourbon-glazed salmon or pan-roasted garlic shrimp are my favorites. There is something on the menu to please every taste; children are welcome.

Mouzon House (518-226-0014), 1 York Street. ($$$) Open daily 5-10. Enjoy sustainable meats, seafood and produce at a restaurant that supports local farms. The menu is somewhat limited and changes daily depending on what is fresh, local and available. Not recommended for children.

Max London's (518-587-3535), 466 Broadway. ($$) Open Monday through Thursday 3-9; Friday through Sunday 10-9. Mrs. London's son, Max, has created a wonderful contemporary restaurant serving pizzas, pastas, and small plates of treats like Copper River salmon tartare or grilled quail salad. Big plates include grilled pork porterhouse chops and Painted Hills hanger steak. Don't skip dessert. In addition to the black bottom butterscotch budino with soft caramel I sampled (truly ambrosia-like), there is Chocolate Maximus with pistachio ice cream, along with a sizeable selection of after-dinner drinks.

One Caroline Street Bistro (518-587-2026), 1 Caroline Street ($$) Open daily, except Tuesday, 5-midnight. This family-owned and operated bistro-style restaurant has live music most nights of the week. The cuisine is an international mix featuring Cajun, Italian, and Asian dishes. The chef tells me the jambalaya and filet mignon are popular entrees, but adventurous diners won't want to pass up the tasty Thai-style bouillabaisse.

Panza's on the Lake (518-584-6882), 510 Route 9P, Saratoga Lake. ($$) Open for dinner daily, except Tuesday, 5-9; Friday and Saturday until 10. Solid Italian American cuisine with a Continental flair is what you can enjoy, along with beautiful views of the lake. There is a full bar with an extensive wine list and this is a good place to have cocktails before moving on elsewhere. Known for his veal dishes, the chef suggests the veal martone (with shrimp, artichoke hearts, and mushrooms). The shrimp sorentino (topped with eggplant, prosciutto, and fresh mozzarella) is another popular entrée. All desserts are homemade on the premises. Children welcome. Reservations suggested.

Prime at Saratoga National Golf Club (518-583-4653), 458 Union Avenue ($$$) (Located off exit 14 of I-87; take Route 9P south one mile.) Open daily 11:30-10; Sunday 10-9. If you are a major carnivore and enjoy prime steak, this is the place to go. You will be paying handsomely for the meal, however. From USDA prime to steak au *poivre* as well as fish and seafood selections, the offerings here are excellent. The restaurant is a satellite operation of Angelo's 677 Prime in Albany. There is a full-time pastry chef, so save room for the mouthwatering desserts. Dine alfresco on the outdoor terrace during the summer. There's an extensive wine list and reservations are strongly suggested.

Salt & Char (518-450-7500), 353 Broadway. ($$$) Open daily 11:30-10. Locally sourced ingredients at this fine (and pricey) steakhouse. I haven't dined here yet but would recommend stopping for lunch rather than dinner judging from the prices. The Wagyu of the Woods burger is $36 on the lunch menu; onion soup, $13. Not recommended for children.

Siro's (518-584-4030), 168 Lincoln Avenue. ($$$) Open daily for dinner during racing season only (late July through Labor Day). Call for hours, which may vary. This is probably the most popular dinner spot with race-goers. Reservations are required, although the bar area is open and crowded. The food here is Continental, with steak and seafood the specialties. Recommended if you want to continue enjoying the horsey atmosphere —and the crowds—during the evening hours. Not recommended for children.

Sperry's (518-584-9618), 30 Caroline Street. ($$) Open for dinner daily 5-9: Friday and Saturday until 10. This American bistro-style restaurant offers grilled seafood and steak specials, fresh pasta, and sautéed soft-shell crabs in season. The homemade pastries and desserts are first rate. The crème caramel was featured in the New York Times. They butcher their own meats and there is a pastry chef on the premises. The bar is a favorite of jockeys and trainers. This is one of Saratoga's most reliable year-round gems. Reservations are recommended, especially on weekends and during racing season.

Sushi Thai Garden (518-580-0900), 44-46 Phila Street. ($$) Open daily 11:30-10. Step off the busy streets of Saratoga Springs into the Far East for a taste of fine, exotic Thai cuisine. Every dish is made to order, with the freshest of ingredients. Japanese entrees like chicken teriyaki are available, as well as several vegetarian selections. The sushi bar is excellent. Children are welcome.

The Wine Bar (518-584-8777), 417 Broadway. ($$) Open daily, except Sunday, 2pm-midnight. Live piano music here most weekends during the summer. Oenophiles rejoice: There are nearly 50 different wines that may be ordered by the glass here. The eclectic American menu complements the large wine list with entrees like rack of lamb, panko-crusted ahi tuna, and Cuban spiced pork tenderloin. There is a cheese sampler featuring both European and American offerings. Dine outdoors during the summer months. This is also one of the few places with a separate smoking lounge for those who still indulge in cigarettes and cigars. It is completely set off from the dining area with a state-of-the-art ventilation system, however; no smoke enters the restaurant.

EATING OUT

Caffe Lena (518-583-0022; caffelena.org), 47 Phila Street. ($$) Open Wednesday through Sunday, but hours change depending on the entertainment. Almost all major folk, jazz and blues artists have appeared at this well-known coffee house/nightspot over the decades. The food is secondary to the performances, although the coffee, including specialties like iced mocha java, is excellent. This is worth a stop, no matter who is on the bill. Not recommended for children in the evening. Check the website for the performance schedule.

Cantina (518-587-5577), 430 Broadway. ($) Open daily 11:30-9; Friday and Saturday until 10. The hearty Mexican cuisine with international influences is served in a casual atmosphere, with alfresco dining on the patio in the warm weather. Portions are generous, and the margaritas are first-rate. Children welcome.

Country Corner Café (518-583-7889), 25 Church Street. ($) Open daily 7-2. One of the best breakfasts I've had in Saratoga is served until closing time in the cozy eatery. Try the home-baked breads and muffins with preserves or the fresh fruit pancakes with maple syrup. The hearty soups and sandwiches make this a popular lunch spot with local residents who have been patronizing the place for many years. Children are welcome.

Dango Fitzgerald's Irish Pub, Steakhouse & Sports Bar (518-587-2022), 38 Caroline Street. ($$) Open daily 3pm-4am; Saturday and Sunday noon-4am. All the basic pub fare will be found here—salads, sandwiches, burgers, wraps, steaks, seafood and pizza. The Irish chowder is a house specialty.

Druthers Brewpub (518-306-5275), 381 Broadway. ($$) Open daily 11:30-9. This brewpub, which opened in the summer of 2012, is one where you can actually enjoy a conversation! The floors, tables and bar were made from wood taken from an 1840s-era Columbia County barn. The brew-master, George de Piro, from the Albany Pump Station, explains the name of the place comes from the saying, "given our druthers, we would brew beer." There are over a dozen different beers on tap and the menu offers steaks, fish, ribs, burgers, pasta, sandwiches and salads.

Esperanto (518-587-4236), 4 Caroline Street. ($) Open daily 11am-2am. International cuisine is served here and they use fresh ingredients for soups, salads, pizza, and sandwiches. Enjoy falafel, jambalaya, Mexican specialties, and a few imaginative daily specials, as well. Children welcome.

Falafel Den (518-886-9192), 6 Phila Street ($) Open daily 11-9. This eatery has few seats and is best suited for takeout of falafel and stuffed grape leaves (two choices I think they do best here). Healthful, inexpensive fare in the Spa City.... and a good place to get the kids to eat healthy!

Four Seasons Natural Foods Store & Café (518-584-4670), 33 Phila Street. ($) Open daily 9am-8pm. This vegan/vegetarian café offers daily specials in addition to a buffet lunch. The fare is basic and desserts are wonderful. Children will feel comfortable here.

Gaffney's (518-587-7359), 16 Caroline Street ($) Open daily 11am-4am. Yes, they are part of the Saratoga bar scene, but the menu is huge and offers a range of selections including steak, seafood, burgers, soups, omelets, and salads.

Hattie's (518-584-4790), 45 Phila Street. ($) Open daily for dinner 5-9pm. Saratogians go here for Southern-style fried foods: chicken, fish, potatoes, and more. For lovers of the lost art of the deep fry, this is a place to check out. Children are welcome.

The Local Pub & Teahouse (518-587-7256), 142 Grand Avenue. ($) Open Monday through Friday 11:30-midnight; Saturday and Sunday brunch 9:30-midnight. There is decent basic fare here—soups, salads, burgers, tea sandwiches. Prices are inexpensive and the place is known for their fish-and-chips. It's a good stop for afternoon tea, a welcome break from shopping. And, of course, there's a separate tea and sweets menu!

Mexican Connection (518-584-4466), 41 Nelson Avenue. Open daily 4-9; Saturday and Sunday 11:30-9. For over 30 years this restaurant has been serving down home Tex-Mex favorites. All dishes are prepared to order and there is a full bar featuring over 100 different tequilas. This is a fun place to go after the races; it's close to the track. Children welcome.

Mrs. London's (518-851-8100), 464 Broadway. ($$) Open daily 7-6. The homemade soups, sandwiches, and wraps are first-rate, and the baked goods are the best in Saratoga Springs. Don't miss this spot for a simple, yet elegant, lunch.

Nunzio's Pizza (518-584-3840), 119 Clinton Street. ($) Open daily 11-9; Friday and Saturday until 11. This place doesn't look like much from the outside, but those who venture in will be treated to wonderfully tasty gluten-free pizza, as well as the usual Italian specialties. They offer a few gluten-free entrees and rolls, so make sure to ask if you don't see any listed on the menu.

It isn't easy to find an inexpensive, pizzeria in Saratoga; this is also a great stop when traveling with young children.

Olde Bryan Inn (518-587-2990), 123 Maple Avenue. ($) Open daily 11am-10pm. There's one menu all day and all night in this unpretentious country inn. It's a good stop for hearty burgers and fries, fresh salads, grilled steaks or pasta. Try the hot spinach salad or deep-fried cheese sticks with raspberry sauce. Children are welcome.

The Parting Glass (518-583-1916), 40 Lake Avenue. ($) Open daily 10am-2am. This Irish pub-style bar/restaurant features entertainment on weekends and the place is a favorite with the racetrack crowd It's great fun if you enjoy pubs. There's a vast selection of beers and even a serious dart league on Tuesday nights. Try the Guinness and black bean soup served with home-baked bread for a hearty meal. Not recommended for children.

PJ's BAR-B-QSA. (518-583-RIBS), 1 Kaydeross Avenue. ($) Open year-round, daily 11-8. You will smell this restaurant before you see it, and the aroma will be irresistible to barbecue aficionados. There are huge barbecue pits behind the place, and they're smoking with racks of chicken, ribs, beef brisket, and pulled pork. Sides include homemade coleslaw, macaroni salad, barbecue beans, and corn on the cob. This is the home of the unique "wick" sandwich and old-fashioned custard ice cream. Also enjoy their Loganberry fruit beverages to accompany the thick, smoky ribs and chicken. Spicy and satisfying for either take-out or eating at one of the outdoor picnic tables. There are hot dogs and burgers for those who don't or won't indulge! Children love the place.

The Putnam Market (518-587-FOOD), 431 Broadway. ($$) Open daily 9-7; Sunday 10-5. This gourmet eatery with an open deli and bakery specializes in picnic take-out items. If you are heading to SPAC or the racetrack, this is a convenient stop. About a dozen tables are available if you choose to eat at the market and it's a great place to pick up soup, a sandwich or a salad. The side dishes, like green beans and hazelnuts topped with lemon dressing are what I enjoy here. One can easily make a

A weekday winter afternoon at Mrs. London's, a cozy spot to enjoy coffee and a sweet treat after walking on Broadway.

meal of a few fresh seasonal salad creations, all in full view when you enter the store. Sandwiches include boneless free-range turkey breast with cheddar cheese and cranberry mayo, and the salmon en croute is baked to perfection. Brownies, cookies and other dessert treats are not to be missed. Children can't run around here; space is tight.

Saratoga City Tavern (518-581-3230), 19-21 Caroline Street. ($$) Open daily noon-4am. This is the only rooftop bar in the city, and it's a delightful place to have drinks in the warm weather months.

The "cheese room" at one of my favorite places to get take-out in Saratoga is the Putnam Market on Broadway.

The building (circa 1903) was renovated about 15 years ago and there's a mahogany bar and comfortable atmosphere.

Scallions (518-584-0192), 44 Lake Avenue ($) Open daily 11-9; Sunday 9-3; Monday 11-3. A gourmet eatery with a cheerful café atmosphere, there are unique sandwich combinations, homemade soups, and specialty pasta dishes. Desserts are first-rate: The carrot cake is the best around. This is a good place to get take-out items for a picnic if you are heading to SPAC or the racecourse.

Shirley's Restaurant (518-584-4532), 74 West Avenue. ($) Open daily 6:30am-2pm. There are exceedingly reasonable prices here and the service is efficient and friendly. The usual diner standards, including dinner specials like roast turkey breast, plus all kinds of overstuffed sandwiches, are the fare most often enjoyed by patrons. All pies are homemade on the premises. This is a great place to stop if you are traveling with young children.

ENTERTAINMENT

PERFORMING ARTS

Home Made Theater (518-587-4427; homemadetheater.org), at the Spa Little Theater, Saratoga Spa State Park, 19 Roosevelt Drive. Open October through April. This theater offers performances during a calmer time of year in the city. Visitors may enjoy comedy, drama, or children's theater in this venue that caters largely to local residents.

Opera Saratoga (518-584-6018; operasaratoga.org). Operas are performed in repertory from Memorial Day weekend through mid-July at various local venues. Tickets are sold through SPAC and can be purchased online.

Saratoga Film Forum (518-584-FILM; saratogafilmforum.org), 110 Spring Street. Films are shown year-round at the Spring Street Gallery and in summer at the Spa Little Theater in the Saratoga Spa State Park. Advance tickets may be purchased online by going to the website.

Saratoga Performing Arts Center—SPAC (518-587-3330; spac.org), 108 Avenue of the Pines, Saratoga Spa State Park. Open from May through September; schedules, performances and ticket prices vary. There are seasonal performances by the New York City Ballet, top names in jazz, rock, and folk music. Both matinee and evening shows are offered and attendees may bring a picnic, select items from the gourmet food carts, or stop at one of the restaurants in town and arrange for an elegant take-out dinner. There is a covered, open-air seating area and lawn seats under the stars. SPAC is only a few minutes' drive from the center of town. Beware: A popular concert can create traffic tie-ups and bottlenecks throughout the area. Arrive early; there's plenty of parking. Lawn tickets may be purchased the night of most performances, but call in advance to be sure.

VENUES TO HEAR MUSIC

There are several cafes and restaurants in town that offer wonderful blues, jazz, tango and dance bands. The schedules vary with the time of the year. If you want to hear live music, give these places a call:

Caffe Lena (518-583-0022), 47 Phila Street.

Gaffney's (518-587-7359), 16 Caroline Street.

One Caroline Street (518-587-2026), 1 Caroline Street.

The Parting Glass (518-583-1916), 40 Lake Avenue.

The Wishing Well Restaurant (518-584-7640), 745 Saratoga Road, Wilton. They may be out of town a little way, but there is usually excellent piano playing and jazz here, featuring local musicians. Open for dinner daily, except Monday, 4-10.

SPECIAL EVENTS

The following events are held annually during the month listed. If you know you will be in Saratoga Springs at a particular time, call to find out exact date during the month an event will take place. Many will enhance your stay!

Year-round: **Beekman Street Artists Exhibits**. Galleries are open to the public on the first Saturday of each month from 5-8pm. Free.

April: **Woodworkers Showcase** (518-584-0027), See fine woodworkers creating an array of pieces and displaying their fine crafts.

May: **Saratoga Springs Horse Show** (518-490-1214; saratogaspringshorseshow. com), Yaddo Show Grounds, Union Avenue. Hunter and jumper competitions held throughout the month and open free to the public. **Historic Homes Tour** (saratogapreservation.org). Visitors may see privately-owned historic homes throughout the city.

June: **Skidmore Classic Horse Show** (518-580-5633), 28 Brickhouse Road, Stillwater. Free. This world-class hunter/jumper horse show features over 500 top horses and riders from all over North America. **Saratoga Balloon and Craft Festival** (balloonandcraft.com). Saratoga Fairgrounds, 162 Prospect Street, Ballston Spa. Watch beautiful balloons glow at dusk and perhaps enjoy a tethered balloon ride. Enjoy the work of artisans, entertainment and specialty foods. There's a "kids zone" and craft beers. Admission. **Saratoga Jazz Festival** (518-584-9330; spac.org), There are two stages at SPAC and over 20 musical acts, some of the biggest names in jazz from throughout the country, performing continually from noon to 10pm. I've gone several times: bring a blanket and a picnic; the lawn seats are the best way to experience this unusual venue. Admission.

July: **Concerts in the Park**, Congress Park, Tuesday and Sunday evenings at 7pm. **All American Celebration** (518-587-3550; saratogajuly4th.com), Entertainment, fireworks, history and more in downtown Saratoga. **British MotorFest Summer Lawn Show** (518-587-1935; saratogaautomuseum.org), Saratoga Automobile Museum, Spa State Park, 110 Avenue of the Pines. Free. Enjoy the display of antique cars at this unusual small museum in the park. **Hats Off to Saratoga Music Festival** (518-584-3255; Saratoga.org). Various venues in downtown Saratoga Springs. Enjoy an array of music: jazz, bluegrass, classical, folk, country, Latin, Cajun and more during this weekend festival. Friday and Saturday nights 7-11pm. **Saratoga County Fair** (518-885-9701), Saratoga County Fairgrounds, 162 Prospect Street, Ballston Spa. Admission. From 9am to midnight Tuesday through Sunday, enjoy exhibits, food rides, shows, animals and live entertainment.

August: **Annual Saratoga Arts Celebration** (saratogaartscelebration.org), National Museum of Dance, 99 South Broadway. Free. This is a beautiful tribute to artists and their work and a great way to introduce young people to the arts.

Travers Stakes Festival Week (518-584-6200; nyra.com), Saratoga Race Course, Union Avenue. This weeklong celebration centers on the racecourse's midsummer derby, the Travers Stakes, the oldest stakes race in America. Gates at the racecourse open at 7am and post time is 11:35am. There are numerous events at various locales so check the website for a complete schedule.

September: **Battle of Saratoga Anniversary and Encampment** (518-664-9821), Saratoga National Historical Park, 648 Route 32, Stillwater. Admission. Enjoy a comedic portrayal of British general Burgoyne. Everyone is in period costumes. There's a festive atmosphere yet the event is also educational. This is a great place to take the kids who will love the musket drill, cannon firings, and open-fire cooking. **Saratoga Giant PumpkinFest** (saratogagiantpumpkinfest.com), Sunnyside Gardens, Church Street. Free. The pumpkin weighing begins at 10am and noon; children of all ages will enjoy this fun event.

October: **Yaddo Garden Ghost Tours** (518-584-0746; yaddo.org), 312 Union Avenue. Experience the Spirits of the Gardens! Tours are given on Friday and Sunday at 5pm. **Saratoga International Flavorfeast** (518-365-3459; saratogaflavorfeast.com), downtown Saratoga. Free. Festivities celebrating the city's international cuisines begin at 11am.

November: **Victorian Street Walk** (518-587-8635; saratogadowntown.com). Enjoy strolling musicians, horse-drawn trolley rides, theater and more. Santa is on hand and most retail stores have an open house with refreshments. Broadway is closed to traffic 5-10pm.

December: **First Night Saratoga** (518-584-4132), downtown Saratoga. Enjoy holiday music, jazz, carols, dance performances and theater. This alcohol-free celebration of the arts and the community is held from 6pm to midnight. Free. There are fireworks at midnight to ring in the New Year.

The historic Gideon Putnam Hotel in Saratoga Spa State Park.

Old Chatham Country Store is a gathering place in town.

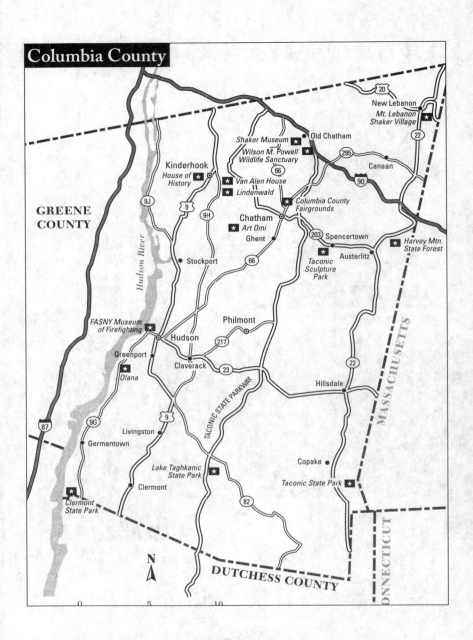

Columbia County

GREENE COUNTY

New Lebanon
Mt. Lebanon
Shaker Village
20
22

Shaker Museum
Old Chatham
Wilson M. Powell
Wildlife Sanctuary
295
Canaan
66
90

Kinderhook
House of
History
Van Alen House
Lindenwald
Columbia County
Fairgrounds

Chatham
Art Omi
Ghent
203
Spencertown
Austerlitz
Harvey Mtn.
State Forest

Taconic
Sculpture
Park

Stockport

66

Hudson River

Philmont

FASNY Museum
of Firefighting
Hudson
217

Greenport
Claverack
23
22

Olana

Hillsdale

87
9G

Livingston

Germantown

9

Copake

TACONIC STATE PARKWAY

Lake Taghkanic
State Park
Clermont

Taconic State Park

Clermont
State Park

82

MASSACHUSETTS

CONNECTICUT

N

DUTCHESS COUNTY

0   5   10

COLUMBIA COUNTY

F irst the home of the Native Americans who greeted Henry Hudson, Columbia County later attracted Dutch, German, and New England settlers with its river and fertile farmland. Whaling became a major industry, with ships moving up the Hudson River unloading their international cargo at Hudson in the 1830s. The city echoed with the noises of trading, rope making...and prostitution. Fine homes resembling the wood-and-brick extravaganzas of Maine and Massachusetts were built. The unusual became the rule in Hudson: a colorful museum filled with firemen's equipment and a library that was once an asylum for the mentally ill. The Shakers built settlements in the area and led their sober lives, which were also filled with song, dance and fine craftsmanship. Across the county antiques glow in the windows of well-appointed shops, while the simplicity of Shaker furniture offers its own comment on what life should be like. Martin Van Buren lived in Columbia County (in fact, the term OK is thought to have originated from Van Buren's nickname, Old Kinderhook). Thoroughbred racehorses are bred, raised, and trained in the county. Every Labor Day weekend the state's oldest county fair brings together people of all ages in celebration of the harvest's best at the county fairgrounds in Chatham.

VISITOR INFORMATION

Columbia County Tourism (518-828-3375; 800-724-1846), 401 State Street, Hudson 12534; columbiacountytourism.org.

Columbia County Council on the Arts (518-671-6213), 209 Warren Street, Hudson 12534; artscolumbia.org.

Columbia County Chamber of Commerce (518-828-4417), 1 North Front Street, Hudson 12534; columbiachamber-ny.com.

GETTING THERE

By car: Columbia County may be reached from the **Taconic State Parkway** and by Routes 9, 9H, and 22, all of which run north to south; I-90 (the Mass Pike in Massachusetts) cuts east-west across the county.

By train: **Amtrak** (800-872-7245) runs regular service between Penn Station in New York City and Hudson. The station is located at 69 South Front Street (518-828-3379).

By air: **Albany International Airport** (518-242-2200), 737 Albany Shaker Road (exit 4 on the Northway), is less than 30 miles from most parts of Columbia County. **Columbia County Airport** (518-828-9461), 1142 Route 9H, West Ghent.

MEDICAL EMERGENCY

Columbia Memorial Hospital (518-828-8500), 71 Prospect Avenue, Hudson.

ATTRACTIONS OF INTEREST TO FAMILIES (AND OTHERS TOO!)

One of the outdoor sculptures at Art Omi in Ghent.

Art Omi (518-392-4747; artomi.org), 1405 Route 22, Ghent. Open daily sunrise to sunset. Free. Founded in 1988 as public grounds for viewing contemporary sculpture, as part of the Art Omi International Arts Center, the park features over 70 sculptures with works by Liberman, Lipski, Pepper Highstine, Knowlton, Venet, and others. The Charles Benenson Visitor Center (and café) is open May through October, Thursday through Sunday 11-5; Saturday and Sunday the rest of the year. It is best to stop there upon arrival to find out what is being exhibited in the art gallery. Temporary exhibits change throughout the year and are made possible with the assistance of independent curators. This arts center is located on over 150 acres, of which 90 are dedicated to the sculpture park that stretches through rolling fields, wooded knolls, and wetlands. Allow an hour to tour the entire park and make sure to wear comfortable walking shoes. There are a limited number of golf carts for those who are handicapped. Guided tours are provided for groups of six or more people, but reservations must be made in advance. This is a great place to expose children to art; it is definitely an unusual attraction.

Catamount Adventure Park (518-325-3200; catamounttrees.com), 3290 Route 23, Hillsdale. Open May through October, daily 9:30-5:30, weather permitting. After Labor Day through October, Saturday and Sunday only. Admission. (The charge, $53 for adults and children over the age of 12; $47 for children 10-11 and $39 for ages 7-9, is good for a three-hour stay. Note that children must be a minimum of seven years of age to be admitted. The 5-acre wooded setting near the base of the Catamount ski area is now an aerial forest challenge park with 150 platforms in trees connected by cable, wood, rope, and two 2000-foot zip lines to form a series of bridges. The courses are designed from easy to expert and are designated with colors to denote the degree of difficulty. All participants must wear a harness attached to a lifeline at all times. There are no rides here, but the park provides a fun adventure that will be long remembered.

FASNY (Farmers' Association of the State of New York) American Museum of Firefighting (518-822-1875; fasnyfiremuseum.com), 117 Harry Howard Avenue, Hudson. Open year-round, daily 10-4:30, except national holidays. Admission. Take a step back in time to the glory days of firefighting at this fascinating museum. You will discover the oldest and broadest collection of firefighting gear and memorabilia in the country. Scores of horse-drawn and steam-and gas-powered pieces of equipment are on display, some dating from the 18th century. Greeting you as you enter the museum is a wooden statue of a volunteer fire chief dressed in patriotic red, white, and blue, complete with stars and golden trumpet. The museum is divided into five halls that house firefighting pumps, mobile apparatus, and engines, as well as paintings, clothing, banners, photographs, and other items. A Newsham engine, built in 1725, was used to quench flames in Manhattan houses and saw more than 150 years of use. A delicate silver parade carriage from Kingston, New York, is topped by the figure of a fireman holding a rescued baby. Throughout the museum you will see lots of gleaming brass, bright-red paint, and an oddity or two, like ornate firemen's parade trumpets, hand-grenade-style fire extinguishers, and brass fire markers that indicated which fire company had the right to fight a particularly fire. There are even modern fire clothes that show the difference in firefighting techniques through the years. A September 11th memorial display filled with photographs lists the names of all the firefighters who lost their lives and exhibits that will intrigue older children and just about anyone interested in the history of firefighting in New York State. Most children between the ages of 3 and 8 will find the museum of interest as well.

Mud Creek Environmental Learning Center (518-828-4386; ccswcd.org), 1024 Route 66, Ghent. The center, located behind the USDA building, is open year-round, daily 8-4:30, but the nature trail is open all the time to visitors. Free. The trail wends its way through wetlands with two loops: one is a mile long, and a shorter loop is about a half-mile long. A number of kiosks along the way provide information about the flora and fauna on the trail. Special programs for groups are available by advance reservation. A full-time educator is on staff to assist visitors from schools and private groups. This is an interesting stop for families traveling with children between the ages of 3 and 12.

Pleshakov Piano Musem (518-263-3333; plesakov.com), 337 Warren Street, Hudson. Open year-round BY APPOINTMENT ONLY. Admission. This impressive collection of five pianos includes an 1826 Tischner, which was built for Russian royalty, and a Longman and Broderip built in London in 1789. The collection will interest those studying piano. There is an 1863 Steinway concert grand, formerly the piano of the Vienna Philharmonic. Several decades ago Vladimir Pleshakov and Elena Winther began this collection of instruments, books, and historical recordings pertaining to classical music. Today the collection is open to the public to educate both students of music and visitors to the region.

Taconic Sculputre Park and Gallery (518-392-5757; taconicnet/kanwit), 221 Stever Hill Road, Spencertown. Open Saturday and Sunday 9-5. Free. Roy Kanwit, a working sculptor, has 40 works exhibited on his grounds. His home/studio is an enormous stone castle-like structure. Here is also a chance to witness the sunset through solar disks. The park attracts a few thousand visitors each year. Older children will love this stop...and so will their parents!

HISTORIC HOMES

Columbia County Historical Society Museum & Library (518-758-9265; cchsny.org), 5 Albany Avenue, Kinderhook. This museum and library, owned and operated by the county historical society, which is also headquartered here, is open May through November. Hours and days vary by season; check the website for days/hours of your visit. Admission. Children, students and members admitted free of charge. The exhibits here include paintings, textiles, and other items from the permanent collection that tell the story of Columbia

County. The historical society also administers the **Luykas Van Alen House**, the **Ichabod Crane Schoolhouse** and the **James Vanderpoel House**. Entries for these historic sites are listed in this section.

Clermont State Historic Site (518-537-4240; friendsofclermont.org), 1 Clermont Avenue, Germantown. Open mid-April through October, Wednesday through Sunday 11-4; weekends only November and December, 11-3. The grounds are open year-round from 8:30am until sunset. Admission. (NOTE: There is a vehicle charge on weekends and holidays.) Standing on land that was awarded to the Livingston family in 1686, this Georgian mansion remained in the family for nearly 300 years. The family's illustrious history— Judge Robert Livingston wrote the letter of protest to King George just before the Revolutionary War, and Chancellor Robert R. Livingston helped draft the Declaration of Independence—is evident throughout the house. Clermont was burned by the British during the war but was later rebuilt around the old walls and foundation. Alterations and additions were made into the late 19th century, so the house today reflects changes wrought by several generations. Clermont's 46 rooms are furnished with family heirlooms and fine examples of period furniture and decorative accessories. A crystal chandelier brought from France in 1802 hangs above the drawing room, where you will also find a French balloon clock made to commemorate the first hydrogen balloon in Paris in 1783. Family portraits decorate the hallways and help visitors sort out the confusing Livingston family tree, and there are exquisite examples of cabinetmaking throughout the mansion. The visitor center presents an informative video about Clermont and I suggest watching it before taking the house tour.

As lovely as Clermont is, the setting makes it more so. The first steamboat, the *Clermont*, made its way up the Hudson River here in August 1807, over 200 years ago. The views of the Catskill Mountains across the river are magnificent and the family purchased as much land as possible to preserve this idyllic setting. Tradition holds the black locust trees flanking the house were planted by many generations of the Livingston family. The roses in the Italian walled garden transform the month of June into an enchanting time at Clermont. Several special events are held here, including a July Fourth celebration, a Halloween event, and a December holiday open house. There is a small gift shop and the house tour begins in the visitor center. The tour is not recommended for young children but the grounds are a wonderful place for them to explore. (NOTE: Be especially careful of ticks here since the land extends close to the banks of the Hudson River.)

James Vanderpoel House (518-758-9265; cchsny.org), 16 Broad Street, Kinderhook. Open year-round, but hours vary by season. Check website for hours when you intend to visit. Admission but children, students and members are admitted free. This site is also known as the House of History. Built in 1819 for attorney and politician James Vanderpoel, the Federal-style house is characterized by delicate ornamentation, including plasterwork ceilings, graceful mantelpieces, and a floating staircase. An exhibit from the permanent collection: the work of several New York State cabinetmakers who created a blend of American pride and European style is displayed throughout the rooms. A fine selection of paintings, including many by county artists, depicts life in the area during a time gone by.

Luykas Van Alen House (518-758-9265; cchsny.org), 2589 Route 9H, Kinderhook. Open July Fourth weekend through October. Days and hours vary, so check the website for current information. After visiting Lindenwald, home of Martin Van Buren, you may want to stop here. Operated by the Columbia County Historical Society, a National Historic Landmark brick Colonial Dutch farmhouse of the early 18th century, it has been beautifully restored to reflect its heritage. At the same location is the **Ichabod Crane Schoolhouse**, a restored single-room schoolhouse, named after the character in Washington Irving's tale. In fact, Irving was a friend of the local schoolteacher who taught in the original Log-Cabin Schoolhouse here, and later based his character on the Kinderhook schoolteacher. Exhibits reflect the relationship between Washington Irving, Jesse Merwin, and Martin Van Buren set in the context of an outfitted schoolhouse.

Martin Van Buren National Historic Site (518-758-9689; nps.gove/mava), 1013 Old Post Road (off Route 9H), Kinderhook. Open late May through October, daily 9-4:30. Admission. Grounds are open year-round, 7am to dusk; free. Known as **Lindenwald**, the house was the home and farm of Martin Van Buren, eighth president of the United States. Built in 1797 and renovated in 1849, the resulting structure is a blend of Federal, Italianate, and Victorian styles. Van Buren was born in Kinderhook (Dutch for "children's corner), the son of a tavern keeper. He studied law and from Kinderhook embarked on a 30-year political career. At Lindenwald, visitors will see the house to which Van Buren returned to look back on three tumultuous decades of public service. Named after the linden trees on the property, the graceful building—complete with shutters, double chimneys, and arched windows—was renovated in recent years to remove or lessen the impact of certain Victorian "improvements." The grounds offer an escape to the peace of rural 19th-century America, but inside the renovations are more evident. A center stairway winds upward through the house, with hundreds of turned spindles so polished they gleam. The old wallpaper was stripped and replaced with paper appropriate to the era, and furniture and decorative objects finally look as if they belong to the home. The house contains a fine collection of Van Buren memorabilia, and a visit is an excellent way to become acquainted with the president known as the Little Magician because of both his size and his political acumen.

Olana (518-828-0135; olana.org), 5720 Route 9G, Greenport (one mile south of the Rip Van Winkle Bridge). Open mid-May through October, Tuesday through Sunday 10-5; November through March, Friday through Sunday 10-4. Admission. The house may be viewed by guided tour only, and group size is limited. Call for reservations before you go. The grounds may be explored from 8am to sunset without a guide and free. *(This is one of my favorite sites in the Hudson Valley: it is truly unique and should be visited even if you have only a short time to spend in the region!)*

Frederic Edwin Church was one of America's foremost artists, a painter who captured the grandeur and mystery of the nation in the 19th century. Church first gained acclaim for his vision of Niagara Falls, a painting that won a medal at the 1867 Paris International Exposition. In 1870 Church and his wife, Isabel, returned from their travels in the Middle East and Europe to their farm in Hudson and began the planning and building of the Persian fantasy that would become known as Olana. Hand-painted tiles on the roof and turrets of the 37-room mansion, situated 460 feet above the Hudson River, add touches of pink and green to the sky. Church called his style "personal Persia," and inside you will discover hand-carved, room-size screens; rich Persian rugs; delicate paintings; decorative pottery and china; and even a pair of gilded crane lamps that look as if they stepped out of an Egyptian wall painting. Olana is also rich in examples of Church's paintings, including Autumn in North America and Sunset in Jamaica. His studio is still set up as it was in his time. During the holiday season, the house is decorated with elaborate greenery, and Yuletide confections grace the tables. Visitors can hike year-round along the carriage paths and roadways that wind

Olana State Historic Site.

through the property or take in the Hudson River views; just across the river is Cedar Grove, Thomas Cole's home, and the place where Church apprenticed as a young artist. The house tour is not recommended for young children. The visitor center contains an excellent museum shop and offers a short video about Frederic Church and the site. An extensive schedule of art and nature programs is held at the Wagon House Education Center on the premises. An array of activities is featured, and many are oriented toward families. Check the website for up-to-date listings. Olana is truly a treasure and you will understand why after visiting this unique site.

Shaker Museum (518-794-9100;shakermuseumandlibrary.org), 202 Shaker Road, New Lebanon. Open mid-June through mid-October, Friday through Monday 10-4. On the site of a former Shaker settlement is a walking tour through several buildings, including the stone dairy barn; the tour takes a little over an hour and is offered at 11, 12 and 2pm. The journals, letters, and drawings here are considered one of the foremost study collections of Shaker cultural materials in the United States.

In the late 18th century a group of English people immigrated to the colonies with the hope of being allowed to practice their communal religion. Called Shakers because they danced and moved around during worship services, the group established settlements throughout their new country and became as well known for their fine crafts and innovations as for their unusual celibate lifestyle. Industry, thrift, and simplicity were their bywords. In their workshops, chairs, seed packets and tin milk pails, were made with equal skill and care, and today Shaker-made items are still valued for their beauty and grace. The Shakers are credited with inventing the circular saw and the revolving bake oven, although they rarely took out a patent, preferring the world to benefit from their hard work.

Steepletop: House & Gardens of Edna St. Vincent Millay (518-392-3362; millay.org), 440 East Hill Road, Austerlitz. Open for tours of the house and garden Memorial Day weekend through October, Friday through Monday 10:30-4:30. Admission. Only six people are permitted on each tour, so call ahead to reserve space, particularly on weekends. Each tour takes approximately one hour. A tour of the farmhouse also includes the writing cabin and icehouse.

Edna St. Vincent Millay was a Pulitzer-Prize winning poet born in Maine in 1892. She lived in Manhattan in the 1920s and was in the forefront of the American literary movement of that time. The line of poetry she is best known for is: "My candle burns at both ends." In 1925 Millay and her husband purchased the 19th-century farmhouse at Steepletop, and it became a social gathering place for other writers and artists. Millay died in 1950, and her gravesite is also on the property. There is a half-mile, narrow country road known as the Poetry Trail marked with a dozen of Millay's favorite nature poems. The trail ends at the family cemetery and is open year-round free of charge.

SCENIC DRIVES

It is difficult to *avoid* taking a scenic drive in Columbia County—wherever you look, you can see rolling green meadows, misty ponds, and quiet villages that look much the same as they did a century ago. You may find yourself on a bluff overlooking the Hudson River or in a city that recalls the glory of the whaling industry. The roads are well maintained, and you won't get lost for long.

For a sampling of the county's charms, both Routes 9 and 9H will take you through Hudson, Kinderhook, and Valatie, with plenty of museums, shops and historic sites to explore. Other routes worth a drive include north-south Route 7 and Route 22, in the eastern part of the county, and Route 82, which runs northwest from the county line at Ancram to near Hudson. Route 11 between Routes 23 and 27, in the town of Taghkanic, has actually received an award for its scenic beauty, having been declared a National Beauty Award Highway (you will see the sign marking this road when you pass by).

One marvelous driving tour through Stuyvesant offers a chance to see many old barns in varied styles, reflecting the agricultural heritage of the town. With more than 12,000 acres of tillable land bordering the Hudson River and Kinderhook Creek, the agricultural area of the town of Stuyvesant dates back centuries. You will see "historical roots" barns, with their distinct architectural features; "English roots" barns, which are rectangular in shape; the large square "Dutch roots" barns with their H shape; and the "German roots" barns, which are rectangular with doors on the long side and rooflines higher than the Dutch barns. Begin the tour in the town of Kinderhook south of the Martin Van Buren National Historic Site on Route 9H and bear to the right onto County Route 25. At the intersection of County Routes 25 and 25A, turn left. Go for about two miles to County Route 46, where you will see three silos across a field on the right. At the T- junction with Route 9J, make a right and go for a half mile to Sharptown Road. Turn right onto Sharptown, where you will see a barn practically in the road; this is a side-hill barn with a lower floor built into the hill, and it is now used as a woodworking shop. Farther along this road you will see the Gleason Farm barns.

WALKING TOUR – CITY OF HUDSON

Hudson, located roughly between Routes 9 and 9G, is rich with the traditions and cultural heritage of its settlers: first the Dutch, then seafarers from Massachusetts and Rhode Island, and later, Quakers and whalers. Carefully designed in the 1780s as a shipping center, with straight streets and "gangway" alleys, ropewalks, wharves, and a warehouse, Hudson was the first city to receive a charter after the Declaration of Independence. Soon whaling and industry took over as the mainstays of the economy, and although Hudson has had its ups and downs since, the city is now in the full flower of a renaissance. On a walking tour, you will see dozens of architectural styles and hundreds of commercial buildings and homes that have been maintained or restored to their earlier glory.

A walk around several main streets will reveal the architectural heritage of the area. Visitors to Hudson who enjoy antiques will discover excellent shopping here. Many of the shops are located along Warren Street and range in selection from fine European and 18th-century American furniture, glassware, and fine arts to 1950s lamps, textiles, and ephemera. Many stores are open by chance or appointment, although Thursday through the weekend is a good bet for browsers.

Coming from the south, from Route 9G, follow Warren Street west to Front Street (by the river), and park. At Front Street you will see the Parade, an 18th-century park that was kept open for use by the city's inhabitants. From the park, also called **Promenade Hill Park,** you will have a dazzling view of the Hudson River and the Catskill Mountains, plus the **Hudson-Athens Lighthouse,** built in 1874 and used to warn ships off the Hudson Middle Ground Flats. Inside the park you will find a statue of St. Winifred, donated to the city by a man who felt Hudson needed a patron saint.

If you walk downhill from there toward the train station and continue on a short distance, you will see **Basilica Hudson**, an enormous concert and event venue.

The easiest walk in Hudson is up **Warren Street**, the aforementioned antiques and boutiques mecca. The architectural styles to be found include Greek Revival, Federal, Queen Anne, and Victorian. Today Warren Street is filled with restaurants, cafes, boutiques and gift shops of all kinds and a walk up the street with a stop for a meal or refreshments can easily take a couple of hours. On your stroll there are a few structures that may be of interest, particularly to history and architecture buffs. Many of the fine 18th and 19th century buildings are undergoing restoration.

At the **Curtiss House**, 32 Warren Street, look up at the widow's walk, built by the owner, a whaler, in the 1830s to provide a sweeping view of the river.

Olde Hudson on Warren Street in the city of Hudson is a gourmet grocery that carries all kinds of local products; a wonderful coffee bar adjoins the food emporium.

Some of the houses here sport "eyebrow" windows—narrow ones tucked under the eaves that are often at floor level within the houses. The building at 116 Warren Street is considered a rare remnant from the early 19th century and boasts an enclosed private garden.

The 1811 **Robert Jenkins House** (518-828-9764;hudsondar.org), 113 Warren Street, is open for group tours and to the public by appointment. The house serves as the headquarters of the local chapter of the Daughters of the American Revolution and was built by an early mayor of Hudson. The exhibits here offer a look at the city over the past 200 years and contain material on whaling and genealogy, paintings by Hudson River School artists, and other items of historic interest.

At Warren and Fourth streets is the former Register Star newspaper building, with its tiny park. Like many other buildings in the city, it has served several purposes: It was a dance hall, an opera house, a county jail, and an assembly hall.

North on Fourth Street to 400 State Street is the **Hudson Area Library Association**, an 1818 stone building guarded by stone lions. The structure has served as an almshouse, an asylum for the mentally ill, a women's seminary, and a private home. If the building is open, stop in at the second-floor History Room, which has local memorabilia, prints, and books.

Other walking areas with interesting architecture include Union Street, East and West Court streets—appropriately, by the courthouse, and East Allen Street.

WINERIES, DISTILLERIES, BREWERIES AND CIDERIES

Chatham Brewing (518-697-0202), 59 Main Street, Chatham. Open Wednesday and Thursday 4-9; Friday and Saturday noon-9; Sunday noon-8. There are 14 varieties of ales and lagers on tap in the tasting room as well as seasonal offerings. There's outdoor seating and live music on weekends during the summer months.

Harvest Spirits (518-253-5917), 3074 Route 9, Valatie. Open daily noon-5. Located at Golden Harvest Farms, this micro-distillery creates alcoholic drinks from apples grown at their farm. The fruit is pressed, fermented, distilled, and bottled in the same place. The result is a wonderful vodka, applejack, and brandy, all available for tasting. Their latest creation is pear brandy made from locally sourced fruit.

Hillrock Estate Distillery (518-329-1023), 408 Pooles Hill Road, Ancram. Open for tours by reservation only. One of the few places in the country where hand crafted single malt whiskey is created on site from estate-grown grain. Visitors will see a beautiful Georgian house overlooking the distillery and 100 acres of farmland for growing several heirloom varieties of rye and barley used in the process. There's a malt-house, granary and distillery with a tasting room that includes a 250-gallon copper pot still. David Pickerell, who spent 14 years at Maker's Mark, is the master distiller. Owner Jeffrey Baker opened this distillery in 2012 and it will be a fascinating stop for those who love single-malt!

Hudson-Chatham Winery (518-392-WINE), 1900 Route 66, Ghent. Open year-round, Wednesday through Sunday noon-5. This is Columbia County's first winery (2007), and it's conveniently located between Hudson and Chatham. Situated on the former Brisklea Farms Ayrshire Dairy, with views of the Berkshires and Catskills, the winery features a full selection of wines, regional cheeses, and local maple products. Their award-winning wines are made from New York State fruits; some are handcrafted classic, dry wines, and there are also sweeter dessert choices.

Hudson-Chatham Winery is open year-round for tastings; it's located midway between Hudson and Chatham.

Hudson Valley Distillers (518-537-6820), 1727 Route 9, Germantown. Open Friday through Sunday noon-6; other times by appointment. A family business creating spirits from ingredients sourced from their farm and those of their neighbors, this distillery is housed in a 150 year-old barn. Relax on the patio overlooking the orchard and sample the offerings.

Old Klaverack Brewery (518-965-1437), 150 Thielman Road, Claverack. Open Friday 3-8; Saturday 2-8; Sunday noon-6. They brew small batches on a 1.5 barrel system, which allows them to brew high quality beer. All ingredients used are locally sourced. A new addition to the brewery scene in Columbia County, it's definitely an interesting one!

Sundog Cider (518-392-4000), 343B Route 295, Chatham. Open Monday through Friday 10-4. Sundog hard cider is made from locally harvested apples in a 100% solar-powered mill. Hard cider is made from a combination of sweet and tart apples, fresh pressed, and combined with champagne yeast to gently ferment the mixture. The cider is then bottled here.

Tousey Winery (518-567-5462), 1774 Route 9, Germantown. Open year-round Friday noon-7; Saturday and Sunday noon-5. Overlooking the Hudson River, this winery produces mostly chardonnay, Riesling and pinot noir grapes on 15 acres. Owners Kimberly and Ben Peacock describe Tousey as a "drier winery," and their cabernet franc is not to be missed. It's one of my favorite local wines.

ACTIVITIES

AIRPLANE RIDES

Columbia County Airport (518-828-9461), 1142 Route 9H, Ghent. Richmor Aviation provides scenic flights, either for a half-hour or for an hour, by special appointment. If you want to experience the views airborne, give them a call and make arrangements for a flight.

BALLOON RIDES

Russ Barber Hot Air Balloon Rides (518-828-3735), 73 Route 25, Stockport. The flights are about one hour long and cost approximately $250 per person. The length of the balloon flight is subject to weather conditions, fuel, and availability of landing sites. Call in advance for an appointment.

BICYCLING

Harlem Valley Rail Trail (518-789-9591; hvrt.org). This 12.2-mile paved bicycle/pedestrian path built on the old railroad line that connected New York City, the Harlem Valley and Chatham, has a few places where it can be accessed: In Ancram, off Route 22, at Undermountain Road; in Copake, take Valley View Road; and the Taconic State Park entrance (not to be confused with Lake Taghkanic State Park) near Depot Deli in Copake Falls (see Hiking section).

The following parks in Columbia County have excellent paved roadways for bicycling:

Lake Taghkanic State Park (518-851-3631), 1528 Route 82, Taghkanic.

Martin Van Buren Park (518-758-9689), 1013 Old Post Road (across from the President Martin Van Buren home), Kinderhook. There are three trails here, and the longest will take about one hour to walk at a leisurely pace and a half hour to bike. A good choice if you are traveling with children.

Taconic State Park (518-329-3993), 253 Route 344, off Route 22, Copake Falls.For those who want to explore the countryside with an organized bike tour, there are a couple of places to contact: **Gotham Bicycle Tours** (917-748-1119; gothambiketours.com) and **Great Freedom Adventures** (877-545-1864; greatfreedomadventures.com). Both provide bike rentals and accommodate those without cars who are arriving via rail or bus.

BOAT CRUISES

Hudson Cruises (518-822-1014; hudsoncruises.com), Waterfront Park, Front Street, Hudson. Enjoy dining, dancing and scenic cruises. There is a Hudson Athens ferry service that operates between 5 and 10:30pm on Friday and Saturday evenings.

CANOEING AND KAYAKING

Columbia County doesn't have an array of outfitters where visitors can rent canoes or kayaks, like in Sullivan County. The state parks are the best places to rent a canoe or rowboat on a lake. If you have a canoe or kayak, you might enjoy Copake Lake, Kinderhook Lake and Queechy Lake. Those who want to explore the Hudson River may find these places of interest:

Rogers Island (under the Rip Van Winkle Bridge). Row or paddle out to this paradise for bird watching. There are eagles, waterfowl, and an amazing array of birds inhabiting this intriguing island, in the Hudson River between Greene and Columbia counties.

Stockport Flats (Station Road, Greenport). If you are traveling north on Route 9, look for Station Road on the left, just after you cross the Columbiaville Bridge. This state land offers the perfect place to explore by canoe. There are 250 acres here. I paddled a canoe in this area and remember the waters of these flats being easy to navigate; a good place for beginners to practice.

There are a few places in the county where there is decent access to the Hudson River for boaters. The **boat launch in the city of Hudson** is located on Front Street, at the end of Warren Street. The **town of Germantown has a boat launch** on County Route 35A (Northern Boulevard), off Route 9G. In the **town of Stockport**, off Station Road in Columbiaville, there is a small boat launch, and use is recommended at high tide only.

FARMERS' MARKETS, FARM STANDS AND PICK-YOUR-OWN FARMS

The rolling farmlands of Columbia County are fun to visit and you will find a remarkably large variety of farms here. Along with the traditional apple orchards, the county has melon patches, cherry orchards, cornfields, heirloom tomatoes, and more. Don't forget to bring a hat and long-sleeved shirt to protect you from insect bites, sunburn and scratches.

Chatham Farmers' Market (518-392-3353), 15 Church Street (Route 203). Open June through mid-October, Friday 4-7.

Copake/Hillsdale Farmers' Market (518-851-7518), 9140 Route 22 (Roeliff Jansen Park), Hillsdale. Open Late May through October, Saturday 9-1.

Hudson Farmers' Market (518-851-7515), 6th & Columbia Streets. Open May through mid-November, Saturday 9-1.

Kinderhook Farmers' Market (518-755-9293), Route 9 at the village square. Open early May through mid-October, Saturday 8:30-12:30.

In Ancram, stop at **Thompson-Finch Farm** (518-329-7578), 750 Wiltsie Bridge Road, open daily 8-5, if you love to pick your own organically grown strawberries, blueberries and raspberries. Theirs are some of the best you will ever taste—all grown without synthetic fertilizers or pesticides on compost-fed soil. Just give a call before going to make sure the berries are ripe for picking.

The Berry Farm (518-392-4609), 2309 Route 203, Chatham, is a haven for berry lovers and they're open year-round, 9-6. They raise blueberries, strawberries and raspberries here but call to find out if the crops are ready to pick.

A truly special farm is found in Ghent, north of Hudson: **Loveapple Farm** (518-828-5048), 1421 Route 9H, open mid-June through November. You can pick all types of fruit here and can buy pears, prunes, cherries, and more. The pies and doughnuts are excellent; they are created at the bakery on the premises. Kids will enjoy the petting zoo, with llamas, goats, pigs and lambs, as well as a small playground. This is definitely a fun lunch stop for families.

In Hillsdale, **Cool Whisper Farm** (518-672-6939), 1101 Route 21 specializes in natural grass-fed meats and poultry. They are open Wednesday through Saturday 10-7, Sunday 10-5. **Hawk Dance Farm** (518-325-1430), 362 Rodman Road, is open daily 9-5; call for winter hours. They are on three acres of land and use no chemicals, pesticides or herbicides in raising their large variety of heirloom vegetables, herbs and flowers.

Kinderhook is home to **Samascott Orchard** (518-758-7224), 5 Sunset Avenue, open June through November, which has more than a dozen pick-your-own harvests including grapes, pears, plums, and strawberries, and several types of apples. **Samascott's Garden Market** is located at 5 Chatham Street (Route 9) and they are open year-round with locally sourced fruits, vegetables, eggs, beef, chicken and an on-site bakery.

Near Claverack you will find **Philip Orchards** (518-851-6351), 270 Route 9H, with pick-your-own apples and pears from Labor Day weekend through October, daily 8:30-5:30; **Holmquest Farm** (518-851-9629) 516 Spook Rock Road (Route 29), has fruits and vegetables; and **Bryant Farms** (518-851-2777), 5498 Route 9H, is strictly a roadside market, but offers a good selection of local products and produce.

The region around the city of Hudson is filled with seasonal farm stands, including **Taconic Orchards** (518-851-7477), 591 Route 82, open daily, year-round, 9-5, where you can pick berries and buy everything else imaginable; **Don Baker Farm** (518-828-9542), 183 Route 14, with more than a half-dozen varieties of apples, both standard and heritage varieties, on their 100-acre farm. They're open daily 9-5, year-round.

Valatie is home to **Golden Harvest Farms** (518-758-7683), 3074 Route 9, just outside town. They are open daily year-round 9-5 with a retail market featuring local products as well as a micro-distillery producing Apple Jack and other spirits from the farm's crops. Tastings are held Saturday and Sunday from noon-5. They offer pick-your-own apples in season and have a large roadside stand. **Yonder Farms** (518-758-7011), 37 Maple Lane, just north of Valatie, has apples, berries, tomatoes, vegetables and pumpkins for picking.

FISHING

Columbia County is filled with deep lakes, clear streams, and stocked ponds and creeks. Keep in mind a New York State fishing license is required for anyone over the age of 16 partaking of the sport.

The following creeks are stocked by the DEC (Department of Environmental Conservation):

Claverack Creek. At Roxbury Road, off Route 217, a bridge crosses the creek at Hess Farm; there is access from the bridge. There is also access on Route 23 at Red Mills, off the south side of the bridge only (not where the falls are); at the bridge on Webb Road, off Route 29; and on Route 29 halfway between Webb and Hiscox roads.

Kinderhook Creek. From the county line in New Lebanon at Adams Crossing Road to the county line at Route 20 behind the Lebanon Valley Speedway. Access can be obtained from Route 66 in the town of Chatham at Bachus Road. There is also access to the creek at the bridge in Malden Bridge.

Roeliff Jansen Creek. Access this area from Route 2 between Elizaville and the Taconic State Parkway; at the junction of Routes 2 and 19, at Turkey Hill Road; at Buckwheat Road (off Route 9 between Routes 8 and 6, at the bridge known as Oars Bridge); or about two miles south of Hillsdale on Black Grocery Road, off Route 22.

There is also fishing at other places in the county:

Lake Taghkanic State Park, off Route 82, three miles south of the Taconic State Parkway exit. Here you will find year-round fishing for sport fish such as chain pickerel; largemouth, smallmouth, and rock bass; bluegill; pumpkinseed sunfish; yellow perch; brown bullhead; and the occasional cisco in deeper waters.

Taconic State Park, Route 344 off Route 22, Copake Falls, has *Ore Pond*, where there is stocked trout and other fish native to ponds.

Oakdale Pond, at Clinton Street and Glenwood Boulevard in Hudson, is stocked annually with trout, and it's a nice family fishing spot.

Queechey Lake, at the intersection of Route 22 and Route 30, Canaan, is heavily stocked with trout.

GOLF

Copake Country Club (518-325-4338), 44 Golf Course Road, off Route 11, Copake. Open March through November, daily 7-7. This 18-hole, par-72 course offers a variety of facilities, including riding cart and pull cart rentals, pro shop, lessons, and seasonal memberships. Senior citizen and group rates are available. There is a fine restaurant, **The Greens**, on the premises.

Meadowgreens Golf Course (518-828-0663), Route 9H, Ghent. Open daily, April through October 7-5:30. This nine-hole, par-36 course has both pull cart and riding cart rentals, lessons, and a pro shop. The restaurant/bar offers outdoor dining in the warm weather months.

Undermountain Golf Course (518-329-4444), 274 Undermountain Road (off Route 22), Ancram. Open April through November daily 7-7. This 18-hole, par-65 executive course offers, club, pull cart, and riding cart rentals. There is a pro shop, lessons, snack bar and practice green. Group rates are available.

Winding Brook Country Club (518-758-7054/9117), 2839 Route 203, Valatie. Open April through October, daily, 8-7. This 18-hole, par-70 course is 6400 yards long. There are lessons available as well as cart and club rentals. Pro shop and restaurant on the premises; group discounts available.

The following places offer driving ranges, not full golf courses and facilities:

Campbell's Hillside Driving Range (518-325-6651), 61 Bloody Hill Road, Craryville.

Hillsdale Driving Range/Miniature Golf and Go Carts (518-325-9689), 2816 Route 23, Hillsdale.

Stony Kill Disc Golf Course (discgolfscene.com), 488 Route 295, behind the Chatham Town Hall, Chatham. This 9-hole disc golf course is free and open to the public year-round.

HIKING

Make sure to take precautions when walking through wooded and grassy areas: **Lyme disease**, transmitted by deer ticks that come from mice, is EXTREMELY prevalent in this county, particularly in recent years. Ticks are found in grassy areas as well as in brush, shrubbery, and woodland habitats. Wear long-sleeved clothing, long pants, use insect repellant, and be careful to check your body thoroughly at the end of your outing if you must wander off marked trails for any reason.

The trails across Old Post Road from the Martin Van Buren National Historic Site.

Raccoon **rabies**, while rare, may be present in this part of New York State. Do not approach, feed or even touch any wild animals you see while walking. In an animal is behaving strangely, report this to a member of the park staff.

NOTE: In an effort to reduce operating costs, trash receptacles have been removed from many day-use areas. Plastic disposal bags are available for the transport of trash from the park. Dispose of waste responsibly, which will keep user fees low.

The **Columbia Land Conservancy** (clctrust.org) maintains 2000 acres in the county with 20 miles of trails open to the public for hiking and outdoor education. This private land trust manages several sites, and their website has a complete listing of these conservation areas. If you visit the county, go to their website for a schedule of year-round free public programs; many are designed for families visiting these preserves.

Beebe Hill State Forest (alltrails.com), Route 5, Austerlitz. Open year-round. There is a great network of trails here. Most are of moderate difficulty. In addition to use by hikers and bicyclists, horses, and snowmobiles are permitted on the trails. No ATVs are allowed. A six-mile trail runs from the top of Beebe Hill to Harvey Mountain, with a lean-to along the way for overnight camping. Otherwise, there are no facilities.

Borden's Pond Preserve (clctrust.org), 1628 Route 203, just outside the village of Chatham. Open year-round, daily dawn to dusk, this 62-acre preserve provides a nice change of pace after shopping or grabbing a bite to eat in town, and it is within walking distance of the main village streets. This is a fairly new area, with an old woodland millpond surrounded by forest. There is a parking area.

Drowned Lands Swamp (clctrust.org), 654 Route 3, Ancram. Open year-round, daily dawn to dusk. This wetland, consisting of 110 acres, is one of the largest in southeastern New York. Home to bog turtles and several species of rare plants, it offers a half-mile steep walk to the summit. Old Croken (the old English word for "crooked"), the path, twists and turns. The views of the Taconic Hills and Catskill Mountains from this point, 800 feet above sea level, are wonderful. You can see the entire Drowned Lands Swamp. There is also a lower swamp trail that makes for an easier walk.

Greenport Conservation Area (alltrails.com), 319 Joslen Boulevard, Greenport (off Route 9). There is a parking area and information kiosk with interpretive brochures detailing the 3.5 miles of trails marked in red, blue, and green. This is a good place for those who want to take a short hike and are traveling with children; the trails wend their way through meadows, woodlands, and wetlands along the Hudson River. A hand-hewn cedar gazebo overlooking the Hudson is a great spot to rest and enjoy the view.

Hand Hollow State Forest (dec.ny.gov/lands), Route 34 (Hand Hollow Road) near intersection of Route 9 and Schoolhouse Road, New Lebanon. This is the county's newest state forest: 518 acres of wooded property, open brush land, and a ten-acre lake available for hiking, biking, paddling and kayaking. There are no official trails on the property at this time but there will be in the near future.

Harlem Valley Rail Trail (hvrt.org), Undermountain Road, off Route 22, Ancram; Valley View Road, Copake; Taconic State Park entrance near Depot Deli, Copake Falls. When completed this paved bicycle/pedestrian path will stretch from Wassaic in Dutchess County to Chatham in Columbia County and run some 46 miles. It was built on the old railroad bed that connected New York City, the Harlem Valley, and Chatham. Trains stopped running on the Harlem Line north of Dover Plains in 1976. The State of New York has purchased several miles of land to build this linear park, about half of which lies in southern Columbia County.

The area is ideal for hiking, biking and cross-country skiing. Those who travel the trail may see many birds, deer, coyotes, foxes, hawks, turtles and beavers (or at least their dams), to name just some of the wildlife flourishing here. The trail passes through the hamlets of Amenia and Millerton in Dutchess County to Copake Falls, so hikers can explore these towns along the way.

Harvey Mountain State Forest (alltrails.com), East Hill Road, off Route 22, near I-90, B-3 exit, Austerlitz. Open year-round. Walk either the former logging road or hike through the woods on a marked trail (look for the red blazes) to the top of Harvey Mountain, with a spectacular view (and picnic table) at the summit. It's about 1.5 miles long and not too difficult. A good choice for those with older children, but keep in mind there are no facilities here.

Lake Taghkanic State Park (nysparks.com), 1528 Route 82, Taghkanic, off Taconic State Parkway. Open year-round. Admission. This 1569-acre park was donated to the state in 1929 by a descendant of the Livingston family. There is a large number of hiking and fitness trails here and there is a map you can get at the entrance of the park. Overnight camping is available from May through October. Facilities include a cabin and cottage area, two bathing beaches, picnic areas, boat rentals, playgrounds, and a ball field. During the winter you can cross-country ski, ice fish, snowmobile and ice skate here.

New Forge State Forest (alltrails. com), New Forge Road, off Route 82, Taghkanic. Open year-round. This state forest consists of 655 acres. An easy two-mile hike on an old logging road goes through the park.

Pachaquack Preserve (518-758-9806; veravalatie.com), 4106 Elm Street, off Route 203, Valatie. A 43-acre preserve operated by the town of Valatie, enjoy an easy walk here in any season. There are two miles of trails, picnic tables, and a gazebo. The trails follow Kinderhook Creek where there is excellent fishing. *Pachaquack* is a Native American word meaning "cleared meadow and meeting place."

Taconic State Park (518-329-3993; nysparks.com), 253 Route 344, off Route 22, Copake Falls. Open year-round. Parking fee. A 25-mile network of hiking trails here range from very easy to quite difficult in this 5000-acre park,

Olana State Historic Site, just outside the city of Hudson, has hiking trails open daily, free of charge.

one of the largest in the Hudson Valley, spanning two counties (Dutchess and Columbia) and bordering Massachusetts and Connecticut. The park runs for 16 miles along the Taconic Ridge, offering spectacular views in several places. This is a good stop for families; there's a small nature center with a few displays, and camping areas are open May through October. There is winter camping here in small cabins that may be rented year-round. The historical section of the park includes the Copake Iron Works, which dates from 1845, when iron making was the main industry in town. For more than 60 years, iron ore, limestone, and hardwood were taken from local deposits with water power from Bash Bish Creek; 2500 tons of blast iron, much of which was used for making car wheels, was taken out of the "park." In the 1920s the owner of the foundry sold the site to the state. The cabins that once housed laborers are now rented out as overnight lodging for park visitors.

Wilson M. Powell Wildlife Sanctuary (clctrust.org), Hunt Club Road, off Route 13, Old Chatham. Open year-round, daily, dawn to dusk. This 145-acre sanctuary offers a variety of walks with lovely views of the mountains; some meander around a pond. A marked trail leads you on a half-mile walk to the observation area called Dorson Rock. At the pond, one can observe waterfowl. This is also a good place to cross-country ski in the winter.

HORSEBACK RIDING

A Horse Drawn Affair-Broe Farm (518-329-5249; ahorsedrawnaffair.com), 258 Crest Lane, Ancramdale. The focus here is on breeding, training and showing horses, but you may want to get in touch with them if this is your interest.

Cricket Hill Farm (518-329-6166; crickethillfarm.org), 115 Snyder Road, Ancramdale. Located in the Columbia Land Conservancy, there are trail rides available for experienced riders. Contact them for information.

Liberty Farms (518-653-9343; libertyfarmsny.com), 114 Ostrander Road, Ghent. Boarding and dressage training are available at this beautiful equestrian facility. No trail rides here!

SWIMMING

Knickerbocker Lake (518-758-9754), 23 Knickerbocker Lake Road (off Route 9), Valatie. Open late June through August. This large lake, operated by the town of Kinderhook, has a nice beach, making it a popular place to swim, especially for those with young children. It is open to the public and there is a charge per car.

Lake Taghkanic State Park (518-851-3631), 1528 Route 82, Taghkanic. Open Memorial Day weekend through Labor Day. Parking fee. This

156-acre lake has two beaches. The west beach is larger, with boat rentals (rowboats and paddleboats) and volley ball courts; the east beach is good for those traveling with young children. Both beaches have snack-bar concession stands and restrooms.

Taconic State Park (518-329-3993), 253 Route 344, off Route 22, Copake Falls. Open Memorial Day weekend through Labor Day. Free. This flooded iron ore mine/quarry with a dock allows swimmers to swim in water eight feet deep. There is no beach, and it is not recommended for those with small children. However, there is an adjacent small pond for kids with two feet of water; do come prepared, since there is no snack bar or any services, just restrooms.

WINTER SPORTS

CROSS COUNTRY SKIING

Cross-country skiing in Columbia County is centered in the state parks, where well-marked trails aren't crowded—and they're free. The natural surroundings are quite beautiful and you must have your own equipment, of course!

These are my favorite places to cross-country ski in the county:

Clermont State Historic Site (518-537-4240), 1 Clermont Avenue, Germantown.

Taconic State Park (518-329-3993), 253 Route 344, east of Route 22, Copake.

Harlem Valley Rail Trail (hvrt.org), Route 22, off Undermountain Road, Ancram.

Lake Taghkanic State Park (518-851-3631), 1528 Route 82, 11 miles south of Hudson at the Taconic Parkway, Taghkanic. In addition to cross-country skiing, they also have ice skating, weather permitting.

DOWNHILL SKIING

Catamount Ski Area (518-325-3200; catamountski.com), 78 Catamount Road, Hillsdale. This location straddles the borders of New York State and Massachusetts. Open Monday through Friday 9-4; Saturday and Sunday 8:30-4; night skiing Wednesday through Saturday 3-9. This is a popular ski area with all ages and abilities, beginner to expert. First opened in 1939, Catamount is one of the oldest ski areas in the state. It is still privately owned and operated and the atmosphere reflects a down-home warmth that is nice for young skiers and families. There are 32 slopes and seven lifts, as well as a terrain park for snowboarding. There are lessons available as well as day care. Trail expansions and improvements include runs like Sidewinder and Catapult (the steepest run in the Berkshires). Upper Promenade gives beginners a mile-long run, and more experienced skiers can take a 2.5-mile route to the base lodge from the summit. Catamount offers 98 percent snowmaking, rentals, and camping facilities. In the off-season, visitors will enjoy the adventure park here.

ICE FISHING

Ice fishing is only allowed when the ice is tested and known to be thick enough for people to venture out safely. Make sure to call in advance at these locations where the sport is permitted:

Lake Taghkanic State Park (518-851-3631), 1528 Route 82 at the Taconic State Parkway, 11 miles south of Hudson.

Queechy Lake (518-367-2069), Queechy Lake Drive, off Route 30, Canaan. You will find some of the best ice fishing in the county here.

Rudd Pond (518-789-3059), 59 Rudd Pond Road, Millerton, is also a popular place to ice fish.

LODGING

The following fine establishments welcome visitors and are my favorite places to stay in Columbia County. If you need further information about any place listed, contact the **Columbia County Lodging Association** (800-558-8218; columbiacountylodging.com). PO Box 383, Copake, NY 12516.

Most visitors to the area stay in the city of Hudson and set out from there, so I have included more options in the "county seat!"

CLAVERACK/CRARYVILLE

1805 House (518-929-5923), 775 Snydertown Road, Craryville. ($) Set on 100 acres, six miles from the city of Hudson, this historic home offers a quiet getaway on a pastoral stream. There are three guest rooms, each with a private bath and air-conditioning. Antiques decorate the rooms and some have fireplaces. Not recommended for children. Open all year.

Thyme in the Country B&B (518-672-6166), 671 Fish & Game Road, Claverack. ($) This lovely B&B is situated on five rural acres. In the summer the organic garden supplies many of the ingredients for the farm to table breakfast served here. There are three rooms and one suite, all decorated tastefully with antiques. Open year-round.

EAST CHATHAM

Inn at Silver Maple Farm (518-781-3600), 1871 Route 295, East Chatham. ($$) This elegant Shaker-inspired inn is just minutes from the Berkshires. There are 11 rooms and suites with all the modern amenities. The location is stunning and a full country breakfast is served. Children are welcome. Open year-round

HILLSDALE AREA

Honored Guest Bed & Breakfast (518-325-9100), 20 Hunt Road, Hillsdale 12529. ($$) Located two miles from the Catamount ski area, this 4000-square-foot house (a Frank Lloyd Wright design built in 1910) is a delightful, comfortable establishment run by an innkeeper who loves her work. Originally the building was a guesthouse on the 68-acre estate of the architect who built St. Patrick's Cathedral. There are four guest rooms, all with private bath, and they are all on one floor of the three-story structure. A gourmet breakfast is served, complete with home-baked muffins and the banana-pecan pancakes are amazing. Afternoon tea is offered at 4:30pm with wonderful baked treats; during winter guests may gather around the fireplace. Expect turndown service at night, complete with romantic lighting in the room and chocolates on your pillow. Children welcome with advance notice. Open year-round.

Inn at Green River (518-325-7248), 9 Nobletown Road, Hillsdale 12429. ($$) Set on an acre of lawn and gardens above a meadow where Crane Creek flows into the Green River, this 1830 Federal house is a truly special place for a relaxing weekend. The Green River is a good spot to fish or cool off in the summer months. A full breakfast is served in the dining room or on the screened-in porch. The lemon-ricotta pancakes and honey-spice French toast are house specialties. The seven rooms, all with private bath; some with gas fireplaces, two with Jacuzzis; a good place for an anniversary weekend or special occasion. Children over the age of 12 only on weekends; the policy is flexible on weekday nights. Open year-round.

HUDSON

26 Warren B&B (661-927-7362), 26 Warren Street, Hudson 12534. ($$) Built in 1810, this is one of the few original homes in historic Hudson. The five rooms are spacious and TV free....but with excellent WiFi. Enjoy the historic ambiance and the enormous gourmet breakfast. Children must be over the age of 12. Open year-round.

Country Squire Bed & Breakfast (518-822-9229), 251 Allen Street, Hudson 12534. ($$) This restored 1900 Victorian home has many of its original details intact and décor that is sophisticated yet cozy. The five guest rooms offer private bathrooms (they're large with claw-foot tubs), cable TV, air-conditioning, and wireless Internet access; parking is free. The continental breakfast will keep you going throughout the morning. Walk to the Amtrak train station. Children welcome Open year-round.

The Croff House (518-828-1688), 5 Willard Place, Hudson 12534. ($$) Just a few minutes walk from Warren Street, the main thoroughfare in town, this B&B combines historic charm and modern amenities. The five rooms have private baths with multi-jet spa showers. The rooms are named after the original homeowners of Willard Place, once a gated community dating back to 1872. A three-course gourmet breakfast is served at 9am (the double raspberry muffins are renowned) and guests may enjoy luxury bedding and plasma TV. Not recommended for children. Open year-round.

Hudson B&B (518-929-6199), 136 Union Street, Hudson 12534. ($$) A renovated Federal-style house offering three spacious rooms each with private bath, cable TV and a full breakfast. Within easy walking distance of the train station as well as shopping and dining spots on Warren Street. Children over the age of 10 are welcome. Open year-round.

Warren Street, Hudson.

Hudson City B&B (518-822-8044), 326 Allen Street, Hudson 12534. ($$) This three-story building dates back to 1865 and is filled with period antiques. Located in the Historic Hudson district, it's in a quiet area of the city only a short distance from the bustle of Warren Street. Guests will enjoy the deluxe rooms as well as those that are not! Attention to detail is respected here and everyone leaves happy with the experience. Not recommended for children. Open year-round.

The Inn at Hudson (518-828-1321), 317 Allen Street, Hudson 12534. ($$) The architecturally elegant Morgan Jones House, built circa 1906, has been beautifully restored and is now a majestic inn. Four spacious rooms with separate bathrooms each have a queen-size bed, cable TV, air-conditioning, and wireless

Internet access. Two rooms share a bath and are available at a reduced rate. The inn is within walking distance to the city's shops and restaurants. Children and well-behaved dogs are welcome. Open year-round.

Mount Merino Manor (518-828-5583), 4317 Route 23, Hudson 12534. ($$$) This beautifully renovated and decorated historic home across from Olana was built by Frederic Church's physician. Guests may enjoy reading on the lovely wraparound porch or walking on the trails around the manor, which is situated on a 100-acre estate overlooking the Hudson River. Although presiding over an elegant Victorian mansion, innkeepers Rita and Patrick Birmingham make visitors feel completely relaxed. Many of the seven guest rooms have wonderful river views, and all have large, luxurious private bathrooms with whirlpool tubs and spa showers. Most rooms also have fireplaces and king-size beds. While guests will feel transported back in time to another era (yet with all the modern amenities), the manor is conveniently located only a few minutes away from the shops and restaurants in the city of Hudson. This is a perfect place to celebrate a special occasion. Children over the age of 10 are welcome. Open year-round.

Wm. Farmer and Sons Boarding & Barroom (518-828-1635), 20 South Front Street, Hudson 12534. ($$) This beautifully renovated building houses a 10-room hotel and restaurant across the street from the historic Hudson train station. Two suites set off families traveling with children from the remaining 8 rooms. Open year-round.

KINDERHOOK

Farm Stay at Kinderhook Farm (518-929-3075), 1958 Route 21, Valatie 12184. ($$) Open late May through October, this is a wonderful way for families to experience rural living in Columbia County. The large renovated red barn, beautifully furnished and with all the modern amenities, sleeps 4 adults and 2 children. Wake up with the crow of a rooster, collect eggs from chickens and enjoy the amazing views.

Mile Hill B&B (518-691-8757), 2461 Route 21, Valatie 12184. ($$) Guests will enjoy an 1852 colonial farmhouse on seven acres in rural Kinderhook with two cozy guest rooms and all the modern amenities. There's a beautiful swimming pool where guests will enjoy relaxing during the summer months. Marat, the innkeeper, serves a superb breakfast and pays attention to detail. You will thoroughly enjoy a stay here. Children over the age of 12 are welcome. Open year-round.

Van Schaack House (518-758-6118), 20 Broad Street, Kinderhook 12106. ($$$) This Georgian-style historic house was built in 1785 and has had only six owners. In 1865 Victorian touches were added, including a slate mansard roof;

the porches were built on in the early 20th century. This grand old mansion, decorated with antiques and fine paintings, was once the home of Peter Van Schaack, a prominent 18th-century attorney and close friend of John Jay. His sister married into the Roosevelt family. There are four guest rooms, all with private bath, air-conditioning, and cable TV. You will find a plush bathrobe and bottle of Old Kinderhook water in your room upon arrival. There's an extensive library here for guest use, as well as a gym and computer room. The gourmet breakfast includes terrific breads and a different egg dish every day. No children. Open year-round; advance reservations always required.

NEW LEBANON

Red Robin Song Guesthouse (518-794-0186), 94 Schoolhouse Road, West Lebanon 12195. ($) Set on over 80 acres here, with several hiking trails (snowshoeing in winter), this is a good choice for those who like to be in the woods, yet close to the attractions of the Berkshires. There are three cozy rooms: one with private bath and two share a bath. A vegan breakfast is served with a variety of health choices like tofu scramble or banana French toast. Snacks are provided in the afternoon. One room is pet friendly. Children are welcome. Open year-round.

Shaker Meadows Bed & Breakfast (518-794-9385), 14209 Route 22, New Lebanon 12125. ($) This 1821 farmhouse, located on 50 scenic acres of meadows and hills, overlooks a pond. The centrally air-conditioned farmhouse has three large rooms (each with private bath) and three small bedrooms (each with private bath outside the room). This is an ideal place for a family reunion as the farmhouse sleeps 12. A second adjacent building has three guest suites, all with private deck. A dining room, separate from the farmhouse, is where guests are served a hearty full breakfast. During the summer, make sure to get a pass to the private town beach on Queechy Lake; the innkeepers will provide towels and beach chairs. Children welcome. Open year-round.

Spencer House Bed & Breakfast (518-794-6500), 466 Route 20, New Lebanon 12125. ($$) Originally the home of Colonel Allen Spencer, who served in the War of 1812, this classic Shaker-style structure is located in a pastoral country setting. You will find plenty of peace and quiet here yet still be conveniently located near a few good restaurants. The extended continental breakfast includes muffins, bagels, fruit and cereal. The six rooms (four with private bath and queen size beds; two share a bath) are cozy, comfortable and nicely decorated. Children over the age of 12 are welcome. The bed & breakfast is located next door to Mario's restaurant and is owned by the same family. Open year-round.

STOCKPORT

Balloon Bed & Breakfast (518-828-3735), 73 Route 25, Stockport. ($$) This 1869 Victorian structure houses three beautiful guestrooms. Each has a private bath and the b&b is located in Stockport, only two miles north of Hudson. Those who want to take a hot-air balloon ride should book the trip well in advance. Children are welcome. Open year-round.

WHERE TO EAT

DINING OUT

Chatham

Blue Plate (518-392-7711), 1 Kinderhook Street, Chatham. ($$) Open for dinner daily, except Monday, 5:30-9. This American bistro housed in a Victorian building serves a variety of pastas, steaks, seafood, and salads with international touches. The antique copper bar downstairs has wonderful murals. The restaurant has earned a fine reputation with local residents as well as weekenders and travelers. Children welcome.

Chatham Grill (518-392-1471), 34 Hudson Avenue, Chatham. Open daily 11-9:30. This is one of my favorite restaurants in the region for basic comfort food that's healthful and well prepared. I've had their veggie burgers, Tex-Mex salad and soups, and never been disappointed. Those traveling with children will feel comfortable here and the bar has quite a good selection of spirits.

Destino Cocina Mexicano and Margarita Bar (518-392-6663), 112 Hudson Avenue, Chatham. ($$) Open for dinner daily 5-9; Friday and Saturday until 9:30. Excellent authentic Mexican food is served here along with homemade chips and salsa. There are a dozen different types of margaritas and a good selection of beers. The large menu offers a range of burritos, fajitas, and enchiladas, but there are burgers and steaks and vegetarian options as well. The pozole, a traditional Mexican pork soup, is delicious. Outdoor seating on the patio is available during the warm weather months.

Germantown

Gaskins (518-537-2107) 2 Church Avenue, Germantown. ($$) Open Thursday through Monday 5-10. The husband and wife who own and operate this farm to table restaurant have both worked at some fine establishments in Manhattan before opening this bright, airy, yet tavern-like restaurant. The menu isn't large, but there are interesting twists on the classic American favorites (burgers, duck, steak, pasta).

Hillsdale

Crossroads (518-325-1461), 2642 Route 23, Hillsdale. ($$) Open Wednesday through Sunday 8:30-2:30. Locally sourced products are the mainstay here; there are always interesting daily specials. Not inexpensive, but imaginative and healthy! Children welcome.

Swiss Hutte (518-325-3333), 3290 Route 23, Hillsdale. ($$) Open Wednesday through Friday 5:30-9; Saturday and Sunday noon-9. Hours vary with the season. Overlooking the slopes at the Catamount Ski Area, this dining room, housed in a 19th-century farmhouse with wood paneled dining rooms and three fireplaces, make for a warm, cozy atmosphere. The Swiss chef-owner is both a master in the kitchen and on the ski slopes (a racer). The menu features French-Swiss dishes and excellent home-baked pastries. Children welcome.

Hudson & Environs

Ca'Mea (518-822-0005), 333 Warren Street, Hudson. ($$) Open Tuesday through Sunday noon-10; Sunday until 9. Winter hours vary, so call first. Enjoy Tuscan and Northern Italian specialties in casual elegance. Soft colors complement the mahogany ceilings, hardwood cherry floors, and granite bar. The paninis and homemade pastas are popular at lunch. The gnocchi and calamari casserole with fresh squid, capers, black olives and fresh tomatoes is a popular dinner entrée. The buffalo mozzarella and gelato are imported from Italy. There is also homemade tiramisu for dessert. Outdoor dining in the summer may be enjoyed in a charming courtyard garden that seats about 40. There is also a four room inn adjacent to the restaurant connected by a courtyard.

The Greens at Copake Country Club (518-325-0019), 44 Golf Course Road, Copake. ($$) Open April through October, daily 11-9 for lunch and dinner. Call for limited winter hours, November through March. Enjoy American cuisine—steaks, seafood, chicken and pasta—while overlooking the beautiful golf course here. The porterhouse steak, saffron fettuccine with scallops and Herondale Farm beef are a few of the popular entrees. There are also burgers, nachos, quesadillas and salads for both lunch and dinner. There's an informal atmosphere and a children's menu is offered.

Local 111 (518-672-7801), 111 Main Street, Philmont. ($$) Open Wednesday through Sunday 5:30-9, Sunday brunch 10-2. This former garage on Main Street is now an eatery serving full breakfasts, organic egg sandwiches, and an array of freshly baked muffins, scones, and breads. At dinnertime, the eclectic American cuisine, using local ingredients, ranges from burgers and salads to grilled fish and steaks. The restaurant has the best fare in town and it's a local hub.

Red Dot Bar & Restaurant (518-828-3657), 321 Warren Street, Hudson. ($$) Open for dinner Monday through Friday 5:30-10; Saturday and Sunday 11-9. Eclectic Continental cuisine is served in this bistro: There are burgers, steaks, pasta, duck, and roast chicken. Diners will find the standard favorites done with a slight twist. Located in a former butcher shop, now completely renovated with a bright red door, the atmosphere is casual. The low-key bar is even a nice place to enjoy dinner, even if you're traveling alone. Not recommended for children.

Swoon (518-822-8938), 340 Warren Street, Hudson. ($$) Open for dinner daily 5-10; Saturday and Sunday lunch served noon-3:30. Enjoy a taste of SoHo in Hudson at reasonable prices. The freshest ingredients are used in a menu that changes seasonally. The owners have a passion for fine wine and this is reflected in the wide variety of wines served by the glass. The menu features contemporary American cuisine; desserts are noteworthy and are made on the premises.

William Farmer & Sons (518-828-1635), 20 South Front Street, Hudson. ($$) Open Wednesday through Sunday for lunch 11-2; dinner 5-9. Tuesday dinner only 5-9. This is a relatively new addition to the Hudson restaurant scene and the service and food are both first-rate. The menu changes seasonally and the bar is terrific. Whether you want a drink, a snack or dinner, this restaurant is consistently good....enjoy! Not recommended for children.

Kinderhook

Carolina House (518-758-1669), 59 Broad Street. ($$) Open for dinner daily, except Monday, 5-9:30. All the Southern specialties—baby back ribs, Caribbean chicken, catfish and more—are served up here in generous portions. From Memorial Day weekend through Labor Day there is outdoor dining. Children welcome.

Dyad Wine Bar (518-610-8511), 16 Hudson Street. ($$) Open Monday through Thursday 5-9; Friday and Saturday until 5-11. This family run charming wine bar has terrific fare and excellent service. I've enjoyed their marvelous seafood chowder and there are tapas, Caesar salad and beef tenderloin, among the choices. Not recommended for children.

New Lebanon

Mario's (518-794-9495), 458 Route 20, New Lebanon. ($$) Open daily, except Tuesday, 4-9. ($$) The Italian American cuisine here is very good, and the prices are reasonable. There's linguine with white clam sauce, osso buco Milanese, veal parmigiana, tournedos of beef, and shrimp scampi. Desserts are all made on the premises and include fried ice cream, tiramisu, chocolate raspberry mousse cake, and a variety of homemade gelatos. Those with young children will feel comfortable here.

Stuyvesant

Riverview Café (518-758-8950), 48 Riverview Street. ($$) Open Thursday through Saturday 9-9; Sunday 10-3. This farm to table café offers creative American fare and comfort food made from scratch. The views are terrific too: diners look out at the Hudson River and Catskills in the background. The brunches are first-rate, lest I neglect to mention their wonderful egg dishes!

Valatie

Magdalena's (518-758-1127). 3018 Main Street. ($) Open Tuesday through Sunday 11-8.($$) Authentic Mexican fare at reasonable prices. The tacos, burritos, and chiles rellenos are excellent, but check out the specials too. The homemade chips and salsa are wonderful. And don't skip the fabulous flan for dessert! Children welcome.

n Main Street, Valatie, has wonderful enchiladas and an array of homemade ılties. It's the best place to dine if you're in the Kinderhook area.

EATING OUT

Ancramdale

The Farmer's Wife (518-329-5431), 3 Route 8, Ancramdale. ($$) Open Monday through Saturday 7-5; Sunday 7-3. High-quality gourmet prepared foods and baked goods to eat in or take out are available in this cozy eatery next door to the local post office. It's truly at oasis in the midst of Columbia County's pastoral countryside. They own and operate another eatery in Mabbettsville, outside Millbrook in Dutchess County (2017).

Chatham/Old Chatham

Ben Gable Savories (518-392-0205), 17 Central Square, Chatham. ($$) Open Tuesday through Sunday 8-3. The crème fraiche biscuits here topped with sweet butter and jam, are reminiscent of an English scone with clotted cream! Attention to detail is the norm; breakfast and lunch are fabulous. Owners Ben and Michael left Manhattan, but didn't abandon their high standards when they decided to open an upstate bakery. Despite the fact they had no experience in the food business, they created a fine eatery with European flair in the center of Chatham. Children welcome.

Old Chatham Country Store (518-794-6227), 639 Albany Turnpike Road, Old Chatham. ($$) Open daily, except Wednesday, 8-3; Friday, Saturday and Sunday 7-3. A landmark building houses this eatery and the fine fare reflects the attention to detail of the owners. The homemade chips and salsa are the best I've had anywhere and I always stock up when passing through the area. The soups, salads, sandwiches, and quesadillas are excellent. Local products are sold including cheeses, ice cream, maple syrup and other gourmet items. Four Fat Fowl, a local cheese from Stephentown in Columbia County is sold here; it is superb. They sell Jeni's Splendid Ice Cream from Columbus, Ohio, a rare treat in the Hudson Valley! An adjoining dining room to the deli area is a great place to enjoy breakfast or lunch. Open year-round. Children welcome.

Our Daily Bread (518-392-9852), 54 Main Street, Chatham. ($) Open Wednesday through Sunday 8-5. Enjoy breakfast and lunch at this vegetarian restaurant where soups, salads, sandwiches, and quiche are the mainstay. All breads, cookies, cakes and pies are baked on the premises. Beer and wine are available and there's outdoor dining in the summer months. Children are welcome.

Our Daily Bread Deli (518-392-2233), 116 Hudson Avenue, Chatham. ($) Open Wednesday through Sunday 8-5. This is a fantastic place to get Mediterranean specialties in addition to enormous high-quality meat and veggie sandwiches.

A favorite lunch stop of mine when traveling in northern Columbia County, is Our Daily Bread Deli on Hudson Avenue in Chatham, just south of the center of the village.

The breakfasts are first-rate too. And there's an informal, cozy atmosphere with excellent service. Can't recommend this place highly enough for breakfast and lunch. Children welcome.

Elizaville

Elizaville Diner (518-756-3559), 573 Kerleys Corners Road, Elizaville. ($) Open daily 7am-9pm. An old-fashioned diner with juke boxes in each booth overlooking a goose pond. The breakfasts are terrific, whether you order an egg dish, French toast or pancakes. Children welcome.

Germantown

Otto's Market (518-537-7200), 215 Main Street, Germantown. ($) Open Monday through Saturday 7-7; until 3 on Sunday. This delightful grocery/café has an amazing selection of products in a well-organized small space. It is also an ideal spot to have a tasty breakfast burrito or bagel with eggs and cheese. Their hearty soups, salads, and hot and cold sandwiches are first-rate, employing ingredients from local purveyors. Last, but not least, prices are extremely reasonable.

Hudson

For those who enjoy grabbing something quick to eat, the City of Hudson has ~~~~~ trucks, most of them on Warren Street, between Third and Fourth. ~~~~~ em from April through October, and they are usually open 11-7.

Tortillaville is my favorite, and they serve up phenomenally delicious Mexican treats. Truck Pizza serves first rate wood-fired Neapolitan-style pizza with a crispy crust and lots of cheese. Winnie's Jerk Chicken & Fish serves shrimp and curried goat, as well as jerk chicken and fish; orders come with rice, beans, and steamed vegetables.

Baba Louie (518-751-2155), 517 Warren Street, Hudson. ($) Open daily, except Wednesday, for lunch 11:30-3; dinner 5-9:30, until 10 Friday and Saturday. They create some of the best thin-crust pizza you will find anywhere, and the selections are incredibly imaginative. I love the one with roasted Portobello mushrooms, garlic, tomatoes, and goat cheese. There is a vegetarian pizza with spelt (wheat-free) crust filled with an array of veggies and soy mozzarella cheese. The barbecued chicken pizza is one of the more ordinary choices! For those who aren't pizza aficionados, there are pasta specials and fresh salads for lunch and dinner. The soup du jour is always vegetarian based. I enjoy the veggie paninis here as well as the chicken salad for lunch. Children welcome.

Café Le Perche (518-822-1850), 230 Warren Street, Hudson. ($$) Open daily, except Monday, 7-4; Friday and Saturday 5-9. This popular café/bar/bakery turns out croissants, walnut sourdough loaves of bread, and pesto rolls that are amazing. Luckily, they keep up with demand: the 17-ton wood-fired oven imported from France bakes 200 baguettes per hour. Owner Allan Chapin, inspired by the cuisine of the Le Perche region of France, is a great great-grandson of Herman Melville; interestingly, he chose Hudson, once a whaling port, as the place to open his bakery. Make sure to sample a taste of France. This is a good stop for refreshments after walking on Warren Street. My favorite treat here is the *pain au chocolat*. I've also enjoyed the roasted vegetable grilled sandwich with roasted red peppers, zucchini, eggplant, and goat cheese. Children welcome.

The Cascades (518-822-9146), 407 Warren Street, Hudson. ($) Open daily, except Sunday, 8-4. This café/gourmet deli has just about every type of fresh bagel imaginable. It's a terrific stop for a simple, healthful breakfast or lunch and features homemade soups, salads, and sandwiches. The desserts are sumptuous (try the chocolate silk pie). I love their signature sandwiches: my favorite is the Mount McKinley: fresh turkey with bacon, Monterey Jack cheese, tomato, sprouts and mayo on whole grain bread. Children welcome.

Grazin' (518-822-9323), 717 Warren Street, Hudson. ($) Open daily noon-8; Friday, until 9; Saturday 9am until 9:30pm; Sunday noon-6. Dan Gibson, owner of Grazin' Angus farm in Ghent, now offers his grass-fed, hormone-free beef in this landmark diner. And you can purchase some to take home from the display freezer in the restaurant. The beef is not only grass-fed, it's grass-finished; and you

Grazin' in Hudson is one of my favorite places in the region to get a grass fed (AND grass finished) burger.

can taste the difference! The beef here is definitely one of my favorite red meats: it's high quality and locally sourced like everything served here. In addition to all types of burgers, there's smoked pork sirloin, pulled short rib sandwich, steaks, and omelets. They even make their own soda! Children welcome.

Lick (518-828-7254), 253 Warren Street, Hudson. ($) Open May through Columbus Day, noon-9. If you have never tried exotic-flavored ice creams like lavender, prune, Armagnac, or Thai coconut chili, this is the place to splurge. My favorite treat is the made-to-order ice cream sandwich on a choice of oatmeal, chocolate chip, or ginger cookies with the flavor of your choice. The ice cream here isn't cheap, but it's a worthwhile indulgence—and memorable! Children of all ages will be delighted.

Olde Hudson (518-828-6923), 434 Warren Street, Hudson. ($) Open daily 10:30-6. The European cheeses, coffee and gourmet fare in this spacious renovated building are absolutely wonderful. There are meats, salads and other provisions and this is a lovely place to sit outside in the café after walking around town. Enjoy a home baked pastry with a latte; after relaxing, pick up some items for a gourmet picnic in the Columbia County countryside! Children welcome.

Park Falafel & Pizza (518-828-5500), 11 North Seventh Street, Hudson. ($) Open daily 11:30-8. This is the place to find healthful, tasty, inexpensive fare (and it's even kosher). All baking is done on the premises. For breakfast there are omelets and hot oatmeal. Lunch offerings include homemade soups, salads, falafel, carrot salad, and pita sandwiches stuffed with fantastic fillings and fresh vegetables. This is a wonderful unusual addition to the Hudson dining scene...the city's first kosher restaurant in over 75 years! Children welcome.

Tanzy's (518-828-5165), 223 Warren Street, Hudson. ($) Open daily, except Wednesday, 8-2. Enjoy breakfast, lunch or afternoon tea in a delightful atmosphere. There are omelets, egg sandwiches, and cinnamon French toast for breakfast. Lunch offerings include turkey pesto melt (they roast their own turkey here), Angus burger, buffalo chicken salad with blue cheese dressing, and homemade soups. The hot fudge sundae is one of their signature desserts; feel free to indulge; you won't be disappointed!

Wunderbar & Bistro (518-828-0555), 744 Warren Street, Hudson. ($) Open for lunch and dinner daily 11:30-midnight. Lunch specials include entrees like grilled chicken breast over salad, meat loaf and mashed potatoes, linguine with sausage, and fish-and-chips. The dinner menu offers a range of comfort food including pork chops, pasta primavera, bratwurst, and burgers. This isn't a place for vegetarians or those seeking gourmet touches! Children are welcome.

Vertigris Tea & Chocolate Bar (518-828-3139), 135 Warren Street, Hudson. ($) Open daily, except Monday, 10-6. Chocoholics rejoice! Owner Kim Bach offers a variety of drinking chocolates, pastries, tea, and coffee drinks, as well as exotic chocolate bars from around the world. This is a great place to indulge and satisfy all those cravings for sweets! Children welcome.

New Lebanon

Blueberry Hill Market (518-794-2011), 515 Route 20. ($) Open daily 7-4. While this market/café may not look like much from the outside, don't be deceived: it's got farm fresh, delicious food at decent prices and everything is prepared to order. You cannot go wrong here with breakfast or lunch and the coffee is excellent too. Sit outdoors in the warm weather months. Children are welcome and will feel comfortable in the informal atmosphere.

ENTERTAINMENT

Basilica Hudson (518-822-1050; basilicahudson.com), 110 South Front Street, Hudson. This historic structure is where a variety of special events, including concerts and art fairs, take place year-round. There are exhibits featuring the work of emerging Hudson Valley artists and various performances. If you are planning a trip to Hudson, check the website to see what's happening in this enormous event space.

Club Helsinki Hudson (518-828-4800; helsinkihudson.com), 405 Columbia Street, Hudson. There are two performance spaces here, a full service restaurant, gallery space, recording facilities, and office space. The calendar is packed year-round with various kinds of entertainment, including musical and comedy acts. The restaurant/bar serves dinner daily from 5-10.

The Crandall Theater on Main Street in Chatham offers excellent films year-round—both matinees and evening showings.

Crandell Theatre (518-392-3445; crandelltheatre.org), 48 Main Street, Chatham. This is one of the few remaining independently owned movie theaters showing first-run films. The single screen, lantern lights, and a balcony with wooden seats make the 1930s theater a landmark. Tickets are inexpensive and a box of popcorn (they even have it unbuttered!) is a bargain.

Ghent Playhouse (518-392-6264; ghentplayhouse.org), 6 Town Hall Place, Ghent. The season runs from October to early June. Offerings range from comedy and musicals to drama. The website lists current productions.

Hudson Hall Center for the Arts (518-822-1438; hudsonoperahouse.org), 327 Warren Street, Hudson. Hudson Hall is now a cultural center for the city, with lectures, performances, readings and more. If you are walking on Warren Street, stop in to see what's going on. There may not be the sound of arias coming from this former opera house, but Hudson Hall is in transition. A new director is now at the helm (2017) and she is bringing great energy and exciting changes to this vibrant city resource.

Mac-Haydn Theatre (518-392-9292; machaydntheatre.org), 1925 Route 203, Chatham, specializes in summer-stock musical productions. The intimate theater is the perfect venue for all-time favorites like *Oliver*,

Oklahoma, Fiddler on the Roof, and other entertainment that will appeal to the entire family. I have great memories of taking my son here each year to see musical performances when he was in grade school!

Spencertown Academy Arts Center (518-392-3693; spencertownacademy. org), 790 Route 203, Spencertown. Open April through early December. Built in 1847 as a private school, this structure is now a cultural arts center where visitors may enjoy films, dance, theater, lectures, book fairs, concerts and a variety of cultural events. The arts center has a reputation as a leading venue for great folk music and jazz. Groups of local, regional, and national renown entertain in an intimate setting here. Two art galleries feature changing art and crafts exhibits.

Stageworks/Hudson (518-828-7843; stageworkshudson.org), 41 Cross Street, Hudson (opposite the Amtrak train station). This is the home of the only professional equity theater in Columbia County. There are a variety of theatrical performances but the focus of the dramas is on the work of playwrights who have a statement to make about the contemporary world. This is one of the best regional theaters in the Hudson Valley, with exciting productions from May through November.

Tannery Pond Concerts (888-820-1696; tannerypondconcerts.org), 110 Darrow Road (off Route 20), New Lebanon. On weekends June through mid-September, chamber-music concerts are held in an original Shaker tannery on the campus of the Darrow School and Mount Lebanon Shaker Village. The 300-seat performance space is an unusual and interesting venue and featured performers have included the Tokyo String Quartet, Earl Wild, and the Emerson String Quartet.

The Theater Barn (518-794-8989; theaterbarn.com), 654 Route 20, New Lebanon. This professional theater offers the best of Broadway and off-Broadway, July through September. Productions range from musicals to dramatic offerings. The plays are usually performed Thursday through Sunday, with matinees on the weekends.

Time & Space Limited—TSL (518-822-8448; timeandspace.org), 434 Columbia Street, Hudson. Open year-round, this is one of the most interesting venues to emerge anywhere in the Hudson Valley. Housed in a converted bakery with 8800 square feet, it is now a performance space offering independent films with talks by filmmakers, musical productions, readings and open forums dealing with community issues. An interdisciplinary arts organization, run by two transplanted New Yorkers, TSL was described in the *New York Times* as "making unusual statements in the area ever since they packed up their Manhattan theater company (in 1991) and handed back a $10,000 check to the politically charged National Endowment for the Arts." This is the kind of independent, dynamic programming needed now more than ever in America today.

SELECTIVE SHOPPING

ANTIQUES

When searching for antiques in Columbia County, expect to discover rare items at shops that are often as well stocked as many museums. Quality antiques and shops are located throughout the county, but you will have to search for bargains. Many dealers carry only the best, with prices to match. Several sellers have relocated from New York City and are savvy about their goods.

A holiday window at The Bee's Knees children's store on Warren Street in Hudson.

In the city of Hudson, an antiques hub, Warren Street is filled with shops. In fact, 50 shops fill seven blocks here. The best way to enjoy antiquing here is to spend a day wandering and looking around. If you require specific information about any stores (days & hours of operation), check the **Hudson Antique Dealers Association** website; hudsonantiques.net.

After wandering through the shops of Hudson, make sure to stop at **Vasilow's** (518-828-2717), 741 Columbia Street, for take-out truffles, chocolates, licorice, and dozens of kinds of candy, all made with natural ingredients by the Vasilow family since 1923. They are open Tuesday through Saturday 10-5; Sunday 11-4.

Chatham Center's **The White Goose** (518-766-3909), 317 Reed Road, is open March through November, daily 9-4, and has a wide variety of antiques and collectibles. **Pitkin Company Refinishers & Antiques** (518-392-3162), 14 River Street on Central Square in the village of Chatham, specializes in antique furniture of all kinds. The shop is open Monday through Friday 8-5; Saturday 8-noon.

Hillsdale Barn Antiques (518-325-1357), 10394 Route 22, is open May through November, Saturday and Sunday 11-5. They have an excellent collection of American country furniture, folk art, rugs, quilts, stoneware and baskets from the 18th through the 20th centuries.

Rodgers Book Barn (518-325-3610), 467 Rodman Road, Hillsdale, is one of the best used-book stores, with more than 50,000 volumes in a huge barn. Bibliophiles rejoice! They're open year-round, Thursday through Monday 11-5. (September through May; closed Thursday).

AUCTIONS

Copake Auction, Inc. (518-329-1142; copakeauction.com), 266 County Route 7A, Copake, handles Americana and conducts specialty auctions only: one will feature all types of antique bicycles, etc. The auctions are usually held once every month, May through September, on Saturday at 5pm, but check the website for details.

Meissner's Auctions (518-766-5002; meissnersauction.com), 438 Route 20, New Lebanon, holds auctions year-round on Saturday starting at 5pm.

Stair Galleries (518-751-1000; stairgalleries.com), 549 Warren Street, Hudson, specializes in estate sales of fine and decorative art, antiques, furniture, and décor. There are monthly auctions and the website has dates and times.

SPECIAL EVENTS

May: **Hudson Children's Book Festival** (hudsonchildrensbookfestival.com), 215 Harry Howard Avenue, Hudson. Free. In addition to dozens of children's book authors signing their books, there are workshops and talks. A great way to introduce children to books and reading, it's truly a family destination.

July: **Independence Day Celebration** (518-537-4240), Clermont State Historic Site, 1 Clermont Avenue, Germantown. Free. This celebration complete with fireworks, all kinds of food and drinks, activities for the kids, is a great place for a picnic, at one of the most scenic spots on the Hudson River. Make sure to take insect repellant and beware of ticks!

August: **Falcon Ridge Folk Festival** (860-364-2138; falconridgefolk.com), 44 County Route 7D, North Hillsdale. Admission. This three-day festival of folk music and dance with more than 40 acts on four stages includes concerts, dancing, workshops, ethnic food, and activities for the kids. You may attend for a day or camp all weekend. Schedule of performances is posted on the website.

September: **Columbia County Fair** (518-392-2121; Columbia fair.com), 182 Hudson Avenue, Chatham. Labor Day weekend. Admission. This is the oldest continuously held fair in the country, now over 175 years old. A three-day celebration, it's less raucous and somewhat smaller than many other county fairs, but just as much fun. Horses, sheep, cows and other livestock are displayed by 4-H members, while prizewinning vegetables and fruits are shown off in the Grange buildings. There is much more than exhibits—there is also entertainment in the best country tradition. Bluegrass bands, folksingers, and country-and-western stars perform in the evening. Of course there are midway games and fair food!

October: **CCCA Artswalk** (artscolumbia.org). This early October tradition showcases the work of Columbia County's visual artists. There are over 100 art exhibits, demonstrations, concerts, dance performances and poetry readings. A full schedule is posted on the website. Many events are free. **Film Columbia Film Festival** (518-392-1162; filmcolumbia.com), Crandell Theatre, 48 Main Street, Chatham. Admission. This film festival is a small one, but will be of interest to film buffs. The theater is a landmark in town and you can pick and choose the films and talks they want to attend.

November: **Basilica Farm and Flea Holiday Market** (basilicahudson.com), 110 South Front Street, Hudson. Held on Friday through Sunday of Thanksgiving weekend, there are dozens of vendors here selling an array of of items for holiday gift giving. This venue is enormous. The market is a perfect family outing with lots of walking around after indulging in heaps of turkey and rich desserts!

December: **Winter Walk on Warren Street** (518-822-1438; hudsonoperahouse. org), Warren Street, Hudson. Free. Held the first Saturday in December, 5-8pm. Holiday revelers may ride in horse-drawn carriages on Warren Street. Carolers will be dressed in Victorian costumes singing songs of the season. The shops are decorated beautifully and most will be serving refreshments. Music and dance performances abound making for an old-fashioned, family-friendly holiday celebration.

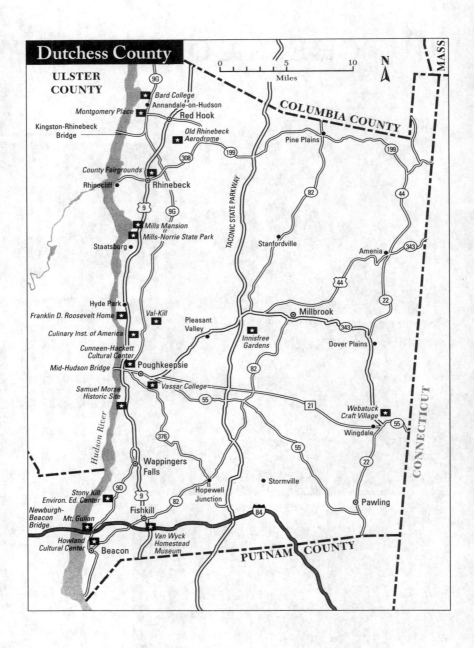

Dutchess County

ULSTER
COUNTY

MASS

COLUMBIA COUNTY

0   5   10
Miles

N

9G

Bard College
Annandale-on-Hudson
Montgomery Place
Red Hook

Kingston-Rhinebeck
Bridge

Old Rhinebeck
Aerodrome

Pine Plains

199

199

308

199

County Fairgrounds
Rhinecliff
Rhinebeck

44

9

9G

82

Mills Mansion
Mills-Norrie State Park
Staatsburg

Stanfordville

Amenia

343

TACONIC STATE PARKWAY

44

22

Hyde Park
Franklin D. Roosevelt Home
Val-Kill

Pleasant
Valley

Millbrook

343

Culinary Inst. of America

Innisfree
Gardens

Dover Plains

Cunneen-Hackett
Cultural Center
Mid-Hudson Bridge
Poughkeepsie

82

Samuel Morse
Historic Site

Vassar College

55

21

Webatuck
Craft Village
Wingdale

55

Hudson River

376

55

CONNECTICUT

Wappingers
Falls

Stormville

Pawling

Stony Kill
Environ. Ed. Center

9D

Hopewell
Junction

22

Newburgh-
Beacon
Bridge

9

82

84

Mt. Gulian
Fishkill

Howland
Cultural Center
Beacon

Van Wyck
Homestead
Museum

PUTNAM COUNTY

DUTCHESS COUNTY

When Henry Hudson sailed up the river that bears his name, one of his crew described the region known today as Dutchess County as "as pleasant a land as one can tread upon." With an area of 800 square miles, Dutchess boasts more than 30 miles of Hudson River shoreline and thousands of acres of farms and fields. The generous forests, impressive mountains, and abundance of wildlife attracted the Dutch first, but the county was named for the Duchess of York, and later, Queen Mary of England. Powerful families controlled local industries like farming, lumbering and mining, and built elegant stone and wood manors overlooking the river and mountains. Today much of the county's past is still visible in the grand homes perched over the Hudson River, the gracious villages, and the historic restorations that dot the county. The Fisher Center for the Performing Arts at Bard College and Dia: Beacon arts museum draw thousands of visitors to Dutchess County from around the world.

VISITOR INFORMATION

Dutchess County Tourism Promotion Agency (845-463-4000; 800-445-3131), 3 Neptune Road, Poughkeepsie 12601; dutchesstourism.com.

Dutchess County Regional Chamber of Commerce (845-454 1700), One Civic Center Plaza, Suite 400, Poughkeepsie 12601; dutchesscountyregionalchamber.org.

Rhinebeck Chamber of Commerce (845-876-5904), 23 East Market Street, Rhinebeck 12572; rhinebeckchamber.com.

GETTING THERE

By car: Dutchess County can be reached via I-84, the Taconic State Parkway, or Route 9.

By bus: **Coach USA/Short Line** (800-631-8405; coachusa.com/shortline), has daily service from Port Authority to Poughkeepsie.

By train: **Amtrak** (800-872-7245; Amtrak.com) has daily service to both Poughkeepsie and Rhinecliff from Penn Station in New York City. **Metro North** (212-532-4900; mta.info) offers daily service to Poughkeepsie and Beacon from Grand Central Station. It is substantially less expensive than

Amtrak and offers generous senior discounts on tickets for those over the age of 65 who may purchase their tickets on the train without penalty. *NOTE:* The **Roosevelt Ride** (845-229-5320) is a free shuttle that runs daily, May through October. The bus meets the 8:45am train from Grand Central in Poughkeepsie and returns travelers in time to make the 5:40pm train to New York City. The shuttle bus runs throughout the day between the Roosevelt Home, Vanderbilt Mansion, Valkill, and Top Cottage, and visitors may tour all four sites, or only one or two. This is a great way for those who live in the metropolitan area to enjoy several history sites without having to drive. Reservations are strongly suggested, particularly on weekends.

By air: **Stewart International Airport** (845-838-8200), 1035 First Street, New Windsor. Located in Orange County, across the Newburgh-Beacon Bridge, there is connecting service to and from the Hudson Valley throughout the country. **Dutchess County Airport** (845-463-6000), 263 New Hackensack Road, Wappingers Falls. **Sky Acres Airport** (845-677-5010), 30 Airway Drive, LaGrangeville.

MEDICAL EMERGENCY

Mid-Hudson Regional Hospital (845-483-5000), 241 North Road, Poughkeepsie.

Northern Dutchess Hospital 9845-876-3001), 6511 Springbrook Avenue, Rhinebeck.

Vassar Brothers Medical Center (845-454-8500), 45 Reade Place, Poughkeepsie.

MAJOR SITES TO SEE

HISTORIC HYDE PARK

Any visit to Dutchess County should include a stop at FDR's home, Eleanor Roosevelt's Val-Kill, and the Vanderbilt Mansion. So begin your travels in Hyde Park at the **Henry A. Wallace Visitor and Education Center** (845-486-7770), 4079 Albany Post Road, Hyde Park. Open year-round, daily, 9-5. Visitors may choose to tour any or all of four National Historic Sites and information and tickets may be obtained here to: the Franklin Delano Roosevelt Home, the Vanderbilt Mansion, Val-Kill, Eleanor Roosevelt's retreat and Top-Cottage, FDR's hilltop house. Ask about the tickets being valid for two days, as most are.

There is also an excellent orientation film, so take the time to view it. Make sure to include the FDR Museum in your tour. It is truly an amazing journey through the World War II era of American history. (The café in the visitor center is open April through October 10-4.)

Franklin Delano Roosevelt Home (845-229-9115; nps.gov/hofr), 4097 Albany Post Road (Route 9), Hyde Park. Open year-round, daily 9-5. Admission. The Victorian house, embellished with Georgian touches, was the boyhood home of FDR. Here Eleanor and Franklin raised their family, entertained heads of state, and shaped world history. The site includes the house, the first presidential library, rose garden and the Roosevelts' graves. In the house itself, once jokingly called the Summer White House by Roosevelt, family memorabilia, including photos, antiques, and the possessions of Franklin's iron-willed mother, Sara, are displayed. Don't forget to stop at the gravesite and rose garden (exquisite in June).

Franklin D. Roosevelt Presidential Library & Museum (877-444-6777; fdrlibrary.org), 4079 Albany Post Road (Route 9), Hyde Park. Open April through October, daily 9-6; November through March, daily 9-5; research library year-round, Monday through Friday 9-5. Admission. The museum has both permanent and changing exhibits reflecting the impact the Roosevelts had on their times and world events. Visitors will enjoy detailed displays on the lives and careers of the Roosevelts, as well as an array of interactive exhibits. Walking through this museum is like taking a historic tour of the first 50 years of the 20th century. The site is a must-visit for World War II buffs!

Top Cottage (845-229-9115), 7097 Albany Post Road (Route 9), Hyde Park. Open year-round, daily 9-4. (Note that shuttle buses leave from the visitor center where tickets must be purchased for access to this site.) Tours are given throughout the day. This hilltop retreat FDR designed for himself, provided a tranquil place for him to get away after he left office. During his third and fourth terms, the cottage was used as a private meetinghouse for political purposes: forging essential relationships with Winston Churchill and King George VI of Great Britain, among others. It's interesting to see how the cottage was designed to accommodate a wheelchair and meet Roosevelt's physical needs. First opened to the public in 2001, the cottage has been restored to its original appearance during Roosevelt's time. Displays of memorabilia and photographs may be seen throughout the site.

Val-Kill, Eleanor Roosevelt National Historic Site (845-229-9422; ervk. org), 106 Val-Kill Park Road, Hyde Park. Open daily May through October 9-4. November through April, Thursday through Monday, tours at 1pm and 3pm only. Admission. This is the only national historic site dedicated to the memory of a first lady. Val-Kill was a favorite spot for Roosevelt family picnics. In 1924 FDR deeded the land to Eleanor for a personal retreat. A Dutch-style stone cottage was built (it is now a conference center), and an existing building was converted into a factory, in keeping with Eleanor's efforts to encourage rural economic development. The factory was later remodeled into a house, which now holds the museum. The small furniture factory was adjacent to the cottage shared with Eleanor Roosevelt's friends, Nancy Cook and Marion Dickerman. The three women met in the early 1920s working for the League of Women Voters. They shared a dedication to politics, education, and progressive reform that motivated their interest in creating Val-Kill Industries, a social experiment that embraced the revival of handicraft traditions to supplement income in an agricultural economy. In this way, young people might choose to remain in the area instead of seeking work in the cities. The economic strains of the Depression put an end to the business in 1937. Visitors can learn more about this experiment, tour the cottage, and enjoy a film biography about Eleanor Roosevelt: First Lady of the World, as well as walk the trails on the 180-acre site. Ongoing seminars and community programs centering on Eleanor Roosevelt's concerns, including solutions to social problems and exploring contemporary values, are conducted here year-round.

Vanderbilt Mansion National Historic Site (845-229-7770), 119 Vanderbilt Park Road, Hyde Park. Open year-round, daily 9-5. The house is open by tour only, although the grounds, gardens, and excellent gift shop are open free of charge to travelers. I suggest stopping here even if you don't have time to spare for the house tour. The views of the Hudson River are spectacular. Admission. This imposing Beaux Arts mansion was used by Frederick Vanderbilt and family as a spring and fall residence. A fine example of Gilded Age living in the 19th century, the mansion was the focus of a large Hudson River estate and was built at a cost of $600,000, a fortune at that time. Lavish furnishings, fine art, and decorative items from around the world are on view throughout the spacious rooms. The living room alone is 30 by 50 feet. The restored formal Italian gardens feature a reflecting pool, terraces, and a pergola and loggia with three levels of annuals, perennials, and roses. The wonderful gift shop on the premises is filled with a terrific selection of books and souvenirs.

After exploring Hyde Park's historic residences, make a stop at The Culinary Institute, just a few miles south on Route 9 from the FDR Home and Museum. There are several fine restaurants here (See Dining Out), but for "foodies," this is a must-see.

Culinary Institute of America (845-452-9600; ciachef.edu), 1946 Campus Drive, Hyde Park. Open year-round, except for vacation periods: late July through last August, Thanksgiving week and the last two weeks in December (exact dates are shown on the website). Free. Founded in 1946 as a place where returning veterans could learn useful culinary job skills, the school is regarded today as a premier training institute for those in the food-service and hospitality industries. The 170-acre property, once a former Jesuit seminary, provides visitors with a sweeping view of the Hudson River. Public tours are offered on Monday at 10am and 4pm; Tuesday through Friday at 4pm only. Reservations are required (call 845-451-1588), and the cost is $6 per person. Visitors will be able to watch the chefs at work. The courtyard has a fine display of carved pumpkins at Halloween time and ice sculptures in winter. After breakfast or lunch in the Apple Pie Bakery Café (no reservations necessary), take time to walk around the campus, which overlooks the Hudson River.

OTHER SPECIAL HISTORIC HOMES

Locust Grove Estate (845-454-4500; lgny.org), 2683 South Road (Route 9), Poughkeepsie. Open year-round daily 10-5; November through March guided tours are given only on Saturday and Sunday; the rest of the year they are given every day continuously. Grounds are open 8am to dusk. Situated along an old stagecoach route, this 150-acre estate known as Locust Grove was the summer home of Samuel Morse. An artist and scientist who changed the way the world communicates (he invented the telegraph and Morse code), he purchased the country residence in 1847 and under the tutelage of architect Alexander Jackson Davis began to transform the house into an Italianate villa with extensive gardens. The house boasts a four-story tower, a billiard room with skylights, and a false stone exterior. Throughout the house decorative items (including china and a then-elegant and new fabric known as denim), furniture, art, and paintings by John James Audubon, may be enjoyed. The formal gardens, walking trails, and wildlife sanctuary offer a great setting in which to spend an afternoon. The site includes a network of trails that cover three miles through a diverse habitat teeming with wildlife as well as a variety of trees and wildflowers. If you have the time, take a walk on one of the many trails formerly used by wagons and horse-drawn carriages that have been restored. The visitor center, where tours begin with a ten-minute orientation film, distributes a trail guide. Most of the paths are fairly flat and easy to walk. The visitor center contains the Morse Gallery with paintings and sculptures by Morse, as well as his patent model for the telegraph and a display on telegraphic communication.

The Staatsburgh State Historic Site, formerly the country home of Ogden Mills and his wife, Ruth Livingston Mills, was designed by McKim, Mead, and White and has been beautifully restored with its Beaux-Arts details.

Staatsburgh State Historic Site (845-889-8851; nysparks.com), 75 Mills Mansion Road, Staatsburg. Open late April through October, Thursday through Sunday 11-5. Call for hours in November and December. Open by appointment only for group tours January through mid-April. Admission. One of the grand old Hudson River estates, the Mills Mansion has it origins in the 18th century, when Morgan and Gertrude Lewis built a home on the site. The house was destroyed by fire in 1832 and was rebuilt by Ruth Livingston Mills in 1896. Rooms were gilded and plastered, with ornamental balustrades, ceilings, and pilasters. The size of the rooms is overwhelming as are the furnishings: dining tables that take 20 leaves; carved, gilded, and floral furniture in the style of Louis XIV, XV, and XVI; and many fine paintings and elaborate tapestries. Incredibly, the house was used primarily as an autumn retreat and then infrequently the remainder of the year. There is a fine museum store on-site, and popular annual events include outdoor summer concerts and an antique car show. This is one historic site where access to the Hudson River is only a short walk away. It's an easy stroll, so make sure to go down to the water after a house tour. There are also several miles of walking trails on the land surrounding this site.

Wilderstein (845-876-4818; wilderstein.org), 330 Morton Road, Rhinebeck. May through October, Thursday through Sunday noon-4; December, weekends only 1-4. Admission. The history of this country seat begins in 1852, when Thomas Suckley purchased this riverfront site and commissioned an architect to build an Italianate villa. He named the property Wilderstein (wild man's stone) in reference to a Native American petroglyph by a cove on the property. For over 150 years and three generations, the Suckley family owned Wilderstein. It is filled with their furniture, paintings, antiques, and other effects, which attest to the lively social history of the estate and family's relationship to the Hudson Valley. The main floor features rooms designed by J. B. Tiffany. Calvert Vaux was responsible for the landscape design. An intricate network of drives, walks, and trails winds throughout the property, so make sure to explore a few of them when you visit. This site is listed on the National Register of Historic Places; it's a gem and it will intrigue both scholars and those interesting in 19th-century Hudson Valley life.

TWO OTHER HOMES IN BEACON...
(OF POSSIBLE INTEREST TO HISTORY BUFFS)

Madam Brett Homestead (845-831-6533), 50 Van Nydeck Avenue, Beacon. Open April through December, the second Saturday of the month, noon-4pm. Group tours by appointment only. Admission. One of the oldest homes in Dutchess County, this homestead was once the center of a 28,000-acre estate built in 1708 by Catheryna and Roger Brett. The house remained in the family until 1954 when the Daughters of the American Revolution purchased it. Today there are 17 rooms of furnishings, porcelain, paintings, books, and tools that offer visitors a look back to a time when there were lodgings on the property for slaves. The herb and formal gardens add to the property during the summer months.

Mount Gulian Historic Site (845-831-8172; mountgulian.org), 145 Sterling Street, Beacon. Open May through October, Wednesday through Friday and Sunday 1-5. Admission. This 44-acre Dutch homestead was the family seat of the Verplancks, a prominent Hudson Valley family of farmers. Today it is a place to learn about agricultural life in the 18th and 19th centuries along the Hudson River. There is a Dutch barn that dates from the 1740s. Mount Gulian was built between 1730 and 1740. During the American Revolution it was the headquarters of general von Steuben. The house was also where the Society of the Cincinnati was formed in 1783, a fraternal organization for officers still in existence. The English formal gardens have been restored to their former glory. Interestingly, the history of these gardens has been recorded by James Brown (an escaped slave who worked them from 1829 to 1868).

FOR FAMILIES

Beacon Institute for Rivers and Estuaries (845-838-1600; bire.org), 195 Main Street, Beacon. An evolving global center for research and education, this institute is dedicated to rivers, estuaries, and their connection to the world. Those traveling with children will find the activities and continually changing exhibits offered here of particular interest. The Center for Environmental Innovation and Education (CEIE) is the primary education facility at the institute, and it is equipped with surround-sound video conferencing and broadcasting capabilities. The building has solar panels, composting toilets, and a green roof filled with plants that act as natural insulation. The website contains up-to-date information about special events at this site. The visitor center at Denning's Point provides public access to the Hudson River and a network of walking trails that may be navigated by the youngest travelers. (*NOTE:* There are two short trails with wonderful views of the Hudson River. The Denning Point State Park Trail is an easy loop of less than two miles in length. The Riverside Trail connects this area to the Beacon train station and is less than a mile walk.

Hyde Park Railroad Station (845-297-0901; hydeparkstation.com), 34 River Road, Hyde Park. Open year-round, Saturday and Sunday noon-5. This railroad station, built in 1914, was based on a design shown at the Pam American World Exposition of 1898. The building was nearly demolished in 1975, but the Hudson Valley Railroad Society acquired the station and restored it. Over four decades later, the station is now listed on the National Register of Historic Places and houses exhibits of trains that tell the story of the area's railroads and their history. Model trains run throughout the building and this is a good stop along historic Route 9 for railroad aficionados.

Hyde Park Roller Magic (845-229-6666), 4178 Albany Post Road (Route 9), Hyde Park. Hours vary with the season; call before going. This is the indoor place to go for roller-skating and roller blading; it's a great choice on a cold dreary weekend, if your children enjoy the sport.

Institute of Ecosystem Studies (845-677-5343; caryinstitute.org), 2801 Sharon Turnpike, Millbrook. Open April through October, Monday through Saturday 9-6; Sunday 1-6. There are nearly 2000 acres of nature trails and plant collections at this educational and research facility. Public ecology programs, perennial gardens, and a greenhouse are highlights. The grounds are a good stop if you are traveling with children. Check the website for special programs.

Mid-Hudson Children's Museum (845-471-0589; mhcm.org), 75 North Water Street (at the waterfront, near the train station), Poughkeepsie. Open Tuesday through Saturday 9:30-5; Sunday 11-5; Monday in July and August and on holidays weekends. This hands-on museum features permanent and changing exhibits that focus on the sciences and the arts. Children ages 2 to 12 will enjoy these educational displays, some of which include a horizontal rock climbing wall, a huge play structure of the heart and lungs, and science on wheels that includes a bicycle gyroscope and giant bubble machine. There is a Star Lab planetarium and Hudson River tides water-play table.

Old Rhinebeck Aerodrome (845-752-3200; oldrhinebeck.org), 9 Norton Road, Red Hook. Open May through October, daily 10-5; mid-June through mid-October, Saturday and Sunday air shows at 2pm. Admission. Viewing stands for the air show are outside, so dress appropriately. This is one of the most unusual history museums around. The aerodrome is the site for air shows, displays and demonstrations of aeronautic history. The finely restored planes or copies with original engines are not earthbound. They are frequently taken for a spin over the Hudson Valley. Fokkers, Sopwiths, and Curtiss airplanes are found in the museum, which offers guided tours. During the air shows, daring men and women reenact flights from the pioneer and Lindbergh eras, completely with nefarious villains, beautiful damsels, and brave fighter pilots. Open cockpit biplane rides in a 1929 craft are available during the week by appointment only. Picnic tables, snack bar, and gift shop.

Poughkidsie (845-243-3750), 50 Springside Avenue, Poughkeepsie. Open every day 10-5; Saturday and Sunday, open at 9. This 5000-square-foot interactive site for children offers crafts and interactive projects, as well as classes and birthday parties (in two spacious private rooms). Walk-ins are always welcome; this is a great place to go on a rainy day.

Splash Down Beach (845-897-9600; splashdownbeach.com), 16 Old Route 9, Fishkill. Open May through Labor Day, daily 10-6; until 7 on weekends. This multi-activity water park includes a wave pool, bullet bowl, half-pipe, water slides, a shipwreck island, and a 700-foot river for the adventurous. A Bob the Builder splash works will delight the youngest visitors. There are plenty of indoor amusements here, including an arcade, so this is a good place to go with children on a sweltering summer day!

Stony Kill Farm Environmental Education Center (845-831-1617; stonykill. org), 79 Farmstead Lane, Wappingers Falls. The grounds are open year-round, daily, sunrise to sunset for fishing, hiking, birding and snowshoeing. This 700-acre farm was once part of a 17th century estate owned by Gulian Verplanck.

Today Stony Kill provides agricultural and natural history programs to the public. There are five major trails and all are relatively short (the longest is two miles). Along the way, there are places to study pond life, deciduous forests, swamps, and fields. The bird observation area is a good place to view migrating and native birds, and special events and family-oriented workshops are held throughout the year.

Trevor Zoo (845-677-3704; trevorzoo.org), 282 Millbrook School Road, Millbrook. Open daily 9-5. Admission. Started as a teaching zoo in 1936 with the hope children would better appreciate wildlife if they were familiar with it, the zoo is now a four-acre site accredited by the American Zoological Association, offering close-up views of more than 80 types of animals, both exotic and indigenous. Red-tailed hawks, coatis, otters, red pandas, wolves, and alpacas, are some of the zoo's residents. There is a self-guided nature walk visitors may take through the zoo.

Wing's Castle (845-677-9085; wingscastle.com), 717 Bangall Road, Millbrook. Open Memorial Day weekend through Labor Day, Wednesday through Sunday noon-4:30. After Labor Day through October, weekends only noon-4:30. Admission. An intriguing site, the "castle" has been under construction for nearly 50 years. Salvaged materials went into the towers, crenellations, cupolas, and arches. Don't be surprised if a Victorian birdbath turns up as a sink or a cauldron as a bathtub. Toni Wing operates a bed and breakfast here and this is a must-see for travelers interested in architecture and anomalies!

MUSEUMS

Dia: Beacon (845-440-0100; diaart.org), 3 Beekman Street, Beacon. Open year-round mid-April through Columbus Day, Thursday through Monday 11-6; the rest of the year, Friday through Monday 11-4. The museum is off I-84 and Route 9D, just beyond the Beacon railroad station. Admission (children under 12 free). In 2003 this 240,000-square-foot museum, on a 31-acre site along the banks of the Hudson River (adjacent to 90 acres of riverfront parkland and the railroad station) opened its doors to the public. Housed in a restored printing facility built in 1929 by Nabisco, the expansive light-filled galleries are illuminated almost entirely by natural light, displaying the large-scale works in Dia's renowned collection of American art of the 1960s and 1970s. Since 1974 Dia Art Foundation has become internationally recognized as one of the world's most influential contemporary-art institutions. The name "Dia," taken from the Greek word meaning "through," was chosen to suggest the role of the foundation in enabling the extraordinary artistic projects that might not be realized without financial assistance. Dia's permanent works include art by Joseph Beuys, Dan Flavin, Agnes Martin, Richard Serra, and Andy Warhol. The art of this period often represented a radical departure in practice from conventional work, and much of it was large-scale. In addition to holding one of the world's foremost collections of work by artists who came of age in the 1960s and 1970s. Dia maintains long-term site-specific projects in the American West, Manhattan and elsewhere. Modern-art aficionados will particularly enjoy this museum; most people will enjoy the structure itself, which is as interesting as the art within its walls!

Hessel Art Museum of Bard College (845-758-7598; bard.edu/ccs), 33 Garden Road (off Route 9G), Annandale-on-Hudson. Open year-round, Wednesday through Sunday 1-5. Free.

Founded in 1860 as a men's school, today Bard College is a coeducational institution known for its emphasis on the creative arts. In 1992, this 9500-square-foot exhibition space opened at Bard to house the college's permanent collection, the core of which is the Marieluise Hessel Collection, with 1000 works of painting sculpture, photographs, and video from the 1960s to the present. Hessel founded the center with a generous gift to the college, and the building contains a museum and research library as well as the college's master's program in curatorial studies. Student shows are presented in the winter and spring; museum shows in the summer and fall. After visiting the museum, take a stroll to two lovely centerpieces of the campus: the Hudson River estate houses Blithewood and Ward Manor. There are gardens and a Victorian gatehouse nearby, as well as the Fisher Center for the Performing Arts. These attractions make Bard College a nice stop any time of year. Even if you cannot make it to a music or dance event at the **Richard B. Fisher Center for the Performing Arts** (845-758-7900; fishercenter.bard.edu), 60 Manor Avenue, Annandale-on-Hudson, if you are at the Bard campus, be sure to stop at the East Coast's only Frank Gehry-designed performing arts center, which opened in 2003. This unique and controversial venue, an architectural wonder, is worth a visit for all travelers to Dutchess County, even just to see the exterior. There are two theaters: one has 900 seats (the Sosnoff Theater) and the other has 200 seats (Theater Two) and is used by students in Bard's dance and theater programs. This facility celebrates Bard College's advocacy of the arts. With this remarkable space (the acoustics are phenomenal), the building is a statement of the college's mission that the arts are essential to our lives. (*NOTE:* For seven weeks every July through mid-August, **Bard Summerscape** presents continual performances of opera, music, theater, dance, films and cabaret, making the summer an ideal time to visit!)

Van Wyck Homestead Museum (845-896-9560), 504 Route 9, Fishkill. Open June through October, Saturday and Sunday, 1-4. The grounds are open daily from dawn to dusk at no charge, but there is an admission fee for the house tour. If you are interested in early American history and are in the Fishkill area on a weekend afternoon, you may want to make a stop at this small site. Built in 1732 by Cornelius Van Wyck and untouched by any changes after a 1757 addition, guides in period costume escort visitors through this Dutch Colonial house. During the Revolution, the homestead served as a depot and courtroom, and it is also believed to have been the inspiration for the setting of James Fenimore Cooper's novel, *The Spy*. Furnished with 18th-century pieces, visitors can examine artifacts recovered from surrounding archaeological sites and see changing exhibits.

Vassar College Francis Lehman Loeb Art Center (845-437-5632; fllac.vassar. edu), 124 Raymond Avenue, Poughkeepsie. Open Tuesday through Saturday 10-5; Sunday 1-5. Free. When Matthew Vassar founded the college in 1861, he not only broke new ground by making it a women's college, but he also made it the first college to have an art gallery and museum. The gallery's permanent collection consists of more than 16,500 pieces, including Hudson River School landscapes, Whistler prints, a large photography collection, European coins, armor, and sculpture; it spans the history of art from ancient Egypt to contemporary America. Shows and exhibits change on a regular basis.

After enjoying the art, visitors can walk around the Vassar campus, with its lakes, gardens, amphitheater, and rare trees. Docent-led tours are available by appointment only (call 845-437-7745). Stop in at the chapel to see the Tiffany windows. Also on campus is the **A. Scott Warthin Museum of Geology and Natural History** (845-437-5540; Ely Hall, open Monday through Friday 9-5, when the college is in session), which houses a large collection of mineral, gem and fossil exhibits.

Poughkeepsie. After visiting Vassar, a drive through the city, with its several historic districts, is worthwhile. At 185 Academy Street you will discover **Springside National Historic Site** (845-454-2060; springsidelandmark. org) with tours by appointment only. However, you may walk the 20 acres of carriage roads on this site, the creation of America's first native-born landscape architect, Andrew Jackson Downing, and the last surviving example of his work. Go south off Montgomery Street to reach Garfield Place, one of the most beautiful streets in the city. It was a residential area in the 1850s, and the huge homes have been kept up ever since. The houses, which span several periods, boast turrets, towers, cupolas, and characteristic Hudson River decorative bracketing. Academy Street from Montgomery to Holmes

Street is still a gracious residential area with ornate Victorian houses, as is the Union Street Historic District (cross Market Street and continue down Union to Grand Street). In the 1760s Union was a path to the river, and later it was the German-Irish area of town. Notice the cast-iron details on the brick and clapboard buildings. This area is now the Little Italy of Poughkeepsie. (Two of my favorite eateries are here: **La Deliziosa** (Mount Carmel Place) for homemade cannoli and **Rossi's Deli** (45 South Clover Street) for fantastic Italian subs and salads. Lower Mansion Avenue, off North Bridge Street, has fine examples of 19th-century architecture, although there are many modern buildings here as well.

SCENIC DRIVES

In Dutchess County almost any drive is a scenic one. Even the Taconic Parkway, on which construction began in 1931, offers more a country drive than a trip on a major highway. There are commanding views of the mountains along its length. The roads of this county are well marked, both with direction and historic-site signs. Feel free to follow the back roads: these are a few suggestions that will take you through farmland, villages and along the Hudson River. Route 9 is the old stagecoach route, once the main road to Manhattan; there are many restorations and historic sites along this road, but it can be clogged with traffic, particularly during rush hours and on Saturday. Route 9G takes you past old homes and gracious stone walls. Route 44/55 hooks up with the Taconic, which is, despite being a parkway, quite scenic. Route 199 runs from east to west toward Connecticut, and the views are more like New England than New York. My favorite is County Route 60; it's on the left, off Route 199, a shortcut into the village of Millerton, about five miles after passing through the village of Pine Plains coming from the west. And Millerton is a great town to spend time in with an entrance to the rail trail on Main Street for biking or hiking, excellent eateries and boutiques; and Oblong Books, one of the best independent bookstores you will find anywhere.

WALKING TOURS

BEACON

Nestled between the majestic Hudson Highlands and the Hudson River, the city of Beacon has been reborn in recent years. This renaissance includes the opening of Dia: Beacon museum, the renovation of the Riverfront Park and Beacon Landing, and an explosion of shops, galleries, and restaurants springing up on Main Street. At one time the city was accessible by rail, steamboat, ferry,

Franklin Avenue in Millbrook, the main street, is filled with interesting shops.

and trolley, and Beacon became a hot spot for people from the city looking for an escape. In 1900 a group of local businesspeople formed the Incline Railway Association to erect a cable railway to the top of Mount Beacon. The railway, a monument to the ingenuity of the engineers of the day, was built on a steep grade of 65 percent and transported passengers to the summit at 1150 feet. Opened in 1902, the railway carried 60,000 passengers during its first season. At the top, the Beacon Crest Hotel and a casino offered breathtaking views. Both were destroyed by fire in 1932 and were never rebuilt. Mount Beacon was the most popular day-trip destination in the Hudson Valley at the turn of the 20th century, and more than three million people rode the rail in its 75 years of operation. Today, Mount Beacon park is again welcoming visitors. During the post-World War II years, the economy of the city went into decline, but in the early 1990s restoration efforts began. Artists have settled in the city and with the arrival of Dia: Beacon, the community has new energy and life as a creative center that attracts visitors from throughout the world.

Walk up and down Main Street, anchored by historic districts featuring numerous architectural treasures that are home to antiques shops, clothing stores and interesting eateries. Try to visit on a **Second Saturday** of the month, when there are art openings, reading and music performances throughout the city. **Riverfront Park** offers picnic areas and fishing access; the **Beacon Landing** is the 23-acre waterfront property managed by Scenic Hudson . A former city library, designed by Richard Morris Hunt, the **Howland Cultural Center** (845-831-4988; howlandculturalcenter.org), 477 Main Street, features decorative exterior, brickwork, and a grand interior crowned by ornate wood vaulting. It's open Friday through Monday, 1-5. **Hudson Beach Glass**, 162 Main Street, is a three-story firehouse converted into a gallery complete with its own glassblowing studio: they are open daily 11-6.

After walking around town on a hot summer day, it's imperative to make your last stop **Zora Dora's Micro Batch Ice Cream & Paletas,** a Mexican term for gourmet ice pops. Located at 201 Main Street, there are amazingly imaginative popsicles. The ice cream is made with organic milk from a local farm; the fruits used are from Dutchess County orchards and berry patches. Usually there are at least 35 flavors of "paletas" from which to choose, and all are refreshing and delicious. If you crave something with sugar and aren't in the mood for a cold treat, visit the **Alps Sweet Shop**, 269 Main Street, where they have been making chocolate candy since 1922. Kahlua truffles, chocolate-covered Oreos, and butter crunch are just a few of the handcrafted confections offered here to satisfy any sweet tooth.

MILLERTON

An idyllic Victorian village with sophisticated shops in a beautiful rural setting, this hamlet is best explored on foot. **Oblong Books** (518-789-3797), 26 Main Street, an oasis in the heart of town since 1975 and renowned for its eclectic selection of books and music, is a great place to begin your walking tour. There are several vintage shops, a glassworks, and an array of interesting places to explore. Millerton is one of my favorite places in the Hudson Valley and I strongly suggest travelers visit the village and wander along Main Street, as well as bike or walk along the rail trail, with an access point in the middle of town. Some of the shops I love are **Terni's** (518-789-3474) and **Little Gates Company Wine Merchants** (518-789-3899). After shopping stop in at **Irving Farm Coffee House** (518-789-6540) or **Harney & Sons Fine Teas & Tea Room** (518-789-2100) for whichever drink you prefer. Both serve high-quality products. Millerton also has one of the most interesting department stores in the Hudson Valley—and one of the oldest. **Saperstein's Department Store** (518-789-3365), where you will find a huge selection of casual clothing for the entire family at exceedingly reasonable prices. Don't pass by without going in. The store is reminiscent of a bygone era, perhaps because it has been in the same family for three generations—since 1946.

RED HOOK

The town was possibly named when Henry Hudson anchored off its shore in October 1609, and the crew noted the brilliant red sumac and Virginia creeper that covered the hook-like peninsula of Cruger's Island. Another theory is that the name became attached to the town from the re-painted barns at Tivoli, formerly called Hoffmans' Mills, once part of Rhinebeck. The early population of the area was concentrated in Red Hook, once known as Hardscrabble, and Tivoli. The location contributed to the growth of water-powered mills, wool processing factories, fishing, and river transport in the 18th century. The 19th century was when dairy and fruit farms sprang up, tool and tin making burgeoned, and tobacco processing thrived. The railroad was built in the 1850s, and freight and tourists traveled largely by train until the early 20th century. The population has more than doubled from 4500 in 1955 to about 10,000 at the start of the 21st century, when an influx of people was drawn by the technology and electronics industries.

Make sure to visit **Mansion Row**; the old **Fraleigh Store** (now the **Lyceum Theater)** built in 1875; and the **Tobacco Factory**, at the corner of Tobacco Lane and Broadway (the main street). At the intersection of Cherry Street and North Broadway is the **Elmendorph Inn** (circa 1760), listed on the National Register of Historic Places, a Federal-style structure with a Dutch gambrel roof. One of the two earliest buildings in the village, it was a former stagecoach stop and tavern as well as the site of the town's first kindergarten. Saved from the wrecking ball through a community effort, the inn has a working kitchen fireplace and a reconstructed beehive oven. The building is open by appointment only for tours: call 845-758-1920.

RHINEBECK

A village rich in architectural and cultural delights, a walk through town can make the history of families like the Roosevelts, Livingstons, and Beekmans come alive. **The Beekman Arms**, in the center of town is one of the oldest inns in the United States. Across the street, the corner department store is housed in a Civil War-era building. The post office was reconstructed in 1938 under the direction of Franklin Delano Roosevelt; it is a replica of a 1700 Dutch house and contains murals by local artists. If you amble down Route 9 and along the side streets, you will discover Gothic Revival homes, Georgian-style churches, and houses with mansard roofs, arched windows, and Second Empire touches. Make sure not to miss Montgomery Row on your walk. There are stores, restaurants, and interesting places in this section of Rhinebeck's historic downtown, in an alleyway, just off East Market Street, where you'll find a number of small shops and eateries and a terrace area, a great place to enjoy a drink after exploring town.

If you are interested in learning more about Rhinebeck's past, make sure to stop at **The Museum of Rhinebeck History** (845-554-6331), 7015 Route 9 (Quitman House). The museum is open from late June through September, Saturdays, 1-4. The collection of gifts to this museum includes letters, books, clothing, furniture and other artifacts that tell the story of daily life in the community through the centuries.

TIVOLI

This lovely, tranquil town is filled with historic buildings. The **Watts De Peyster Hall** (Fireman's Hall) in the center of town was built in 1898 and given to the village by a local landowner, John de Peyster, who was a fireman in New York City while he attended Columbia College in the 1840s. At one time the hall contained a courtrooms; today it houses the Tivoli Free Library and village offices. The town got its name from a Frenchman, Peter de Labigarre, who bought land on the waterfront in the 1790s. He wanted to design the town with a central square in the European style, but the project went bankrupt, and he had to abandon the plan. A plaque on the brick wall at the end of Friendship Street marks the location of his home, name Le Chateau de Tivoli; he had envisioned an ideal community named after Tivoli in Italy.

WINERIES, BREWERIES, DISTILLERIES & MAPLE SYRUP

Blue Collar Brewery (845-454-2739), 40 Cottage Street, Poughkeepsie Open Monday through Thursday 3-10; Friday and Saturday noon-midnight; Sunday noon -10. Kevin and Randall Marquis (father and son) have created a "blue collar" atmosphere where their American craft beer may be enjoyed in a restored former factory building. Randall is a professional brewer with credentials from University of California (Davis). There are five choices that will please just about every beer drinker. I love this place!

Cascade Mountain Winery & Restaurant (845-373-9021), 835 Cascade Mountain Road (off Route 82A—watch for signs), Amenia. Open Saturday and Sunday 11-5, or by appointment. This respected winery, which offers tours and tastings, has won accolades from both oenophiles and connoisseurs of fine food. There is a wonderful restaurant on the premises that serves lunch May through November, from noon to 3, using organic produce. Owner Charlie Wetmore is extremely knowledgeable about his wine—and welcoming to all!

Clinton Vineyards & Winery (845-266-5372), 450 Schultzville Road, Clinton Corners. Open for tours and tastings April through December, Friday through Sunday, 1-5:30. There are limited hours during November and December, so call ahead. This small, picturesque, family–run winery specializes in award-winning seyval blanc, champagne, and dessert wines.

Crown Maple (845-877-0640; crownmaple.com), 47 McCourt Road, Dover Plains. Open year-round, Saturday and Sunday 10-5, with tours during maple season. Admission. This maple syrup processing business opened in 2012. Madava Farm is located on 800 acres filled with sugar and red maple trees in the wilds of Dutchess County. The wood and stone building is stunning and there is lots more here than just maple syrup. Several miles

The shipping room at Crown Maple is adorned by a mural by a local artist.

of beautiful hiking trails on the property are open to the public. The owners have a long connection to the area and are involved in all aspects of creation of their products. The public is invited to sample the maple treats and taste the difference in Crown Maple syrup when compared with other similar products. February and March bring pancake breakfasts, of course! The café on the premises serves a fantastic brunch on weekends thanks to a Culinary Institute-trained chef. Some of the tempting choices include Crown Maple's signature pancakes, chicken and waffles, roasted vegetable omelet, *huevos rancheros* and more. This is a good place to introduce older children to food production; Crown Maple is a first-rate operation, a perfect choice for a family outing.

Denning's Point Distillery (845-476-8413), 10 North Chestnut Street, Beacon. Open Friday and Saturday 2-8pm; Sunday 2-6, for tours and tastings. The product here is bourbon.

Dutch's Spirits at Harvest Homestead Farm (518-398-1022), 98 Ryan Road, Pine Plains. This distillery, located on a 400-acre farm, was raided by prohibition agents in 1932. Interestingly, Dutch's Spirits was once home to an illegal liquor-producing operation! Today visitors may take a tour of the new tasting barn and sample some moonshine!

Millbrook Vineyards & Winery (845-677-8383; 800-662-WINE; millbrookwine.com), 26 Wing Road, Millbrook. Open for tours and tastings,

September through May, daily noon-5; June through August, daily 11-6. They have the largest 100 percent vinifera vineyard in the Hudson Valley. Production follows French techniques. They offer chardonnay, pinot noir, and cabernet wines. There are summer concerts, special events, and art exhibits here, so check the website to see what's happening if you are planning to visit. There is also a delightful café, the **Vineyard Grille**, serving lunch overlooking a tranquil lake from June through October.

North River Hops & Brewery (845- 297-2190), 1571 Route 9, Wappingers Falls. Open Thursday through Monday 3-8; Sunday noon-6. There are freshly crafted ales produced here and visitors may enjoy a flight, a pint or fill a growler to go.

Taconic Distillery (845-393-4583; taconicdistillery.com), 179 Bowen Road, Stanfordville. This family operation specializes in high quality bourbon; if you enjoy drinking that spirit, this is the place to go. They're open Saturday from 10-6; Sunday 10-5.

ACTIVITIES

BALLOONING

The primary season for a hot-air balloon trip is April through October, but flights are available year-round, weather conditions permitting.

Blue Sky Balloons (845-831-6917), 34 Lauer Road, Poughkeepsie, organizes balloon festivals as well as flights and lessons. Flights are always within two hours after sunrise or two hours before sunset. The company uses only FAA-certified pilots and balloons, and has more than 30 years of experience.

BICYCLING

Dutchess Rail Trail (845-486-2925). This 12-mile bike path runs from Hopewell Junction north to the city of Poughkeepsie.

The Harlem Valley Rail Trail (518-789-9591; hvrt.org). Two paved sections of this 20-mile rail trail are open, and the Dutchess County section, about 8 miles, runs from Amenia to Millerton. There is access to the bike trail in the center of both towns: in Millerton, Railroad Plaza, across from the gazebo; in Amenia, at the Mechanic Street parking lot. The Copake Falls South section of the rail trail (8 miles round trip) begins along Route 22 (Undermountain Road at the south end).

Hyde Park Trail (845-229-8086), Route 9, Hyde Park. Open daily dawn to dusk. Part of the Hudson River Greenway, this 14-mile trail runs from Mills Mansion to Norrie Point, and between the Vanderbilt Mansion, the FDR Home, and

Val-Kill. Bicycling is permitted on the **Roosevelt Farm Lane Trail**, the 1.8 miles (3.6 miles round trip) between the FDR Home and Val-Kill only.

Mills-Norrie State Park (845-889-4646), just off Route 9, Staatsburg. Open daily dawn to dusk. This 1000-acre state park offers several bicycle paths and all are easily accessed from the entrance to the park off Route 9 (watch for signs).

Walkway Over the Hudson (845-454-9649), 61 Parker Avenue, Poughkeepsie. Open 7am to dusk. This 1.5 mile paved walkway over the river is great for people biking with small children. It opened in October 2009 and is a popular attraction in the city.

Wilbur Boulevard Trailway (845-451-4100), Poughkeepsie. This trailway runs along Wilbur Boulevard in the city and town of Poughkeepsie. The paved length is 1.2 miles.

The following state highway corridors in Dutchess County have been designated as part of a regional system of state bike routes: **Route 9D, Route 52, Route 82, Route 199, and Route 308**. While this system of state bike routes is intended to provide safe bicycling, it is imperative to be extra cautious when bicycling on these roads. For further information on the best bicycling in the county, contact **Mid-Hudson Bicycle Club** (midhudsonbicycle.org) in Poughkeepsie. They have a wealth of information about both road and mountain biking. **Gotham Bike Tours** (917-748-1119; gothambiktours.com) and **Great Freedom Adventures** (877-545-1864; greatfreedomadventures. com) both offer organized bicycle tours in summer and fall.

If you want to rent a mountain bike or road bike, here are some places in Dutchess County to contact:

Bikeway (845-463-7433), 1581 Route 376, Wappingers Falls.

Peoples Bicycle (845-765-2487), 430 Main Street, Beacon.

Rhinebeck Bicycle Shop (845-876-4025), 10 Garden Street, Rhinebeck.

Wheel and Heel (845-632-3050), 2568 East Main Street, Wappingers Falls.

BOAT CRUISES

If you want to spend an afternoon on a tour boat, passing elegant estates, and being dazzled by autumn's painted trees, head across the river to Newburgh or Kingston (see Boat Cruises in Orange County and Ulster County). However, there are a couple of options to explore in Dutchess County.

Black Swan Sailing (845-542-7245; blackswansailing.com), Rhinecliff. Excursions on the Hudson River depart from the Rhinecliff dock. There are sunset cruises for up to six passengers as well as day sails of varying lengths. Arrangements must be made in advance.

Shadows Marina Water Taxi (845-986-9500; shadowsmarina.com), 176 Rinaldi Boulevard, Poughkeepsie. Open Memorial Day weekend through mid-October, Friday through Sunday, every hour from 3pm to midnight. The schedule may vary depending on weather conditions. A Coast Guard licensed crew operates this water taxi, taking travelers on a 20-minute trip to the Newburgh waterfront at a speed of 60mph. The round-trip fare is about $30 per person; $15 one-way.

FARMERS' MARKETS, FARM STANDS, AND PICK-YOUR-OWN FARMS

June's ripe strawberries, summer blueberries, and jewel-like raspberries are a few of the most popular crops in Dutchess County. But the harvest doesn't end with the berries. There are apples and big-bellied pumpkins later in the season. Farm stands sprout like corn along the back roads. Many are small, homey places where fresh cider and doughnuts lure you inside. Harvest times vary with the weather and temperature, so call before you head out.

NOTE: If you are driving north to the Hudson Valley along the Taconic, don't miss the **Taste New York Market at Todd Hill** (845-849-0247), 4640 Taconic State Parkway, Lagrangeville. Open daily year-round, except Tuesday, 8-6; Friday until 8pm; Sunday 9-7. This market is chock full of regional products, local books and information, and shouldn't be missed by travelers. The store is located in the Todd Hill Rest Area on the parkway and a farmers' market is held there in season.

FARMERS' MARKETS

Arlington (845-559-0023), Vassar College Campus, 49 Raymond Avenue, Poughkeepsie. Open June through October, Thursday 3-7.

Beacon (845-234-9325), 1 Ferry Plaza, Beacon. Open May through mid-November, Sunday 10-4. A winter market is held December through April, indoors in the same location, Monday 10-2.

Fishkill (845-897-4430), Main Street Plaza (Route 52). Open May through October, Thursday 9-3.

Hyde Park (845-229-9336), Hyde Park Drive-In, 4390 Route 9. Open June through October, Saturday 9-2.

Millbrook (914-419-7621), 3263 Franklin Avenue. Open May through October, Saturday 9-1.

Poughkeepsie Waterfront Market (845-471-0589, ext. 12), 75 North Water Street. Open June through October, Monday 4-7:30.

Rhinebeck. 61 East Market Street. Open May through mid-November, Sunday 10-2.

ORGANIC PRODUCE

Community Supported Agriculture (CSA) brings fresh produce—often organic—directly to consumers. Shareholders pay in advance for a portion of the farm's seasonal production to cover the farmer's costs. In return, they get a weekly portion of the farm's produce. A few such farms:

Poughkeepsie Farm Project (845-516-1100), 51 Vassar Farm Lane, Poughkeepsie.

Sisters Hill Farm (845-868-7048), 127 Sister Hill Road, Stanfordville.

Sprout Creek Farm (845-485-9885), 34 Lauer Road, Poughkeepsie.

Two excellent places where travelers can pick up organic produce:

McEnroe Organic Farm Market (518-789-4191), 5409 Route 22, Millerton, is open daily year-round. They have a café and an enormous selection of produce.

Green Horizons Organic Farm (845-855-5555), 6 South Dingle Road, Pawling, is open April through September for pick-your-own fruits and vegetables and pumpkins in season.

PICK-YOUR-OWN & FARM STORES

Greig Farm (845-758-1234), 223 Pitcher Lane, Red Hook. Open daily, May through October. There are acres of fields available for self-harvesting here, as well as a wonderful farm market and year-round farmer's market on Saturday. Berries, beans, apples, pumpkins, and peaches are only some of the seasonal treats here. This is one of the largest and most popular stops for pick-your-own in the county, and visiting all the farm has to offer may take a couple of hours if you spend time in the fields.

Montgomery Place Orchards Farm Market (845-758-6338), 4330 Route 9G, Red Hook. Open June through October, Tuesday through Sunday 9-6. There is a good selection of fruits and vegetables in season at this stand at the junction of Routes 9G and 199.

Migliorelli Farm Market (845-758-3273), junction of River Road and Route 199, Red Hook. Open May through December 9-6. Homemade products in addition to apples, berries, pumpkins, squash, and other vegetables, will be found here, depending on the time of year.

Secor Farms (845-452-6883), 63 Robinson Lane, open June through August and the month of October, has pick-your-own strawberries, which they are known for, as well as apples, berries, and pumpkins in autumn. The kids will enjoy the hayrides here too!

Wonderland Farms (845-876-6760), 191 White Schoolhouse Road, has pumpkins for picking in late September and October, and Christmas trees in November and December.

Adams Fairacre Farms 765 Dutchess Turnpike, Poughkeepsie (845-454-4330) & 160 Old Post Road, Wappingers Falls (845-632-9955). Open 8am-9pm; Sunday until 7pm. This is a fantastic farm market/supermarket with a great gift shop and garden center. There are four locations in the Hudson Valley and the business is family-owned and operated. I have been shopping at the Kingston store for decades!

Wigsten's Farm Market (845-235-7469), 1096 Salt Point Turnpike, which is open June through October for picking your own fruits and vegetables, depending on the season. They have an array of home-baked goods and local gourmet products too.

The Greig Farm Market on Pitcher Lane in Red Hook is renowned for quality produce and an array of local products.

Hahn Farm's store in Salt Point sells their meat, poultry, fresh eggs and vegetables in a delightful roadside store.

Arch River Farm (845-988-6468), 515 Woodstock Road, Millbrook, is open daily 10-5. They sell pasture raised, farm fresh meats and poultry….an omnivore's delight.

Barton Orchards (845-227-2306), 63 Apple Tree Lane, off County Route 7 in Poughquag, is open June through December for pick-your-own crops and Christmas trees in season. This is a great place to visit, especially with children. They have autumn hayrides and special events throughout the season.

Battenfeld & Son (845-758-8018), 856 Route 199, Red Hook, has been renowned for decades as the place to go for those colorful anemones and Christmas trees in season. A family operation for several generations, they are open to the public daily 9-6 for flowers.

Hahn Farm (845-266-3680), 1697 Salt Point Turnpike, Salt Point, has a store on the premises where they sell meat, chicken eggs, and other products from the farm. Call for hours since they vary with the seasons. Make sure to attend the Hahn Farm Harvest Festival on October weekends!

Terhune Orchards (845-266-5382), 761 North Avenue, Salt Point, is one of the oldest apple farms in the county. Visitors may enjoy picking their own fruit after a hayride up to the orchard during the autumn months.

Ronnybrook (518-398-6455), Prospect Hill Road, Pine Plains, has their own store at the farm, open daily 9-5, selling their well-known yogurt, butter, and chocolate milk, as well as other products from their dairy farm. Ronny is usually there overseeing the operation, and you'll see his contented cows grazing as you drive up the pastoral road to the farm!

GOLF

Several courses are open to the public in Dutchess County. Most are open from April through mid-November. There is sometimes a waiting list during the summer months Call ahead to reserve a tee time, particularly on weekends. Just about all courses open at 6am on weekends and 7am on weekdays.

Beekman Country Club (845-226-7700), 11 Country Club Road, Hopewell Junction. This 27-hole championship course has first-rate facilities that include a clubhouse, driving range, putting green, pro shop, cart rental, and restaurant. There are special rates for junior golfers.

Casperkill Golf Club (845-463-0900), 110 Golf Club Lane (off Route 9), Poughkeepsie. This 18-hole championship golf course was designed by Robert Trent Jones Sr. There is a clubhouse s well as a driving range, putting greens, pro shop, lessons, cart and club rental, and snack bar.

College Hill Golf Course (845-486-9112), 149 North Clinton Street, Poughkeepsie. This nine-hole course is inexpensive and has junior rates; it's good for novice golfers.

Dinsmore Golf Course (845-889-4071), 5371 Albany Post Road (Route 9), Staatsburg. This 18-hole course is the second-oldest golf course in the country. There is a clubhouse, pro shop, putting green, and restaurant. The views of the Hudson River and Catskill Mountains are wonderful here, especially when the leaves are off the trees!

Dutcher Golf Course (845-855-9845), 135 East Main Street, Pawling. This nine-hole course is the oldest public course in America. There is a pro shop, putting green, and snack bar; cart and club rentals are available.

Fishkill Golf Course (845-896-5220), 387 Route 9, Fishkill. There is a nine-hole course, driving range, and miniature golf course here, as well as a pro shop, practice greens, and restaurant. Club rentals are available.

Harlem Valley Golf Club (845-832-9957), 109 Wheeler Road, Wingdale. This nine-hole course is a good place for novice golfers.

James Baird State Park Golf Course (845-473-6200), 280 Club House Road, Pleasant Valley. This 18-hole championship course designed by Robert Trent Jones Sr. has a clubhouse, driving range, putting green, pro shop, lessons—and reasonable prices.

The Links at Union Vale (845-223-1000), 153 North Parliman Road, Union Vale. This 18-hole links-style course is quite challenging. There is a clubhouse, driving range, putting green, pro shop, and restaurant on the premises. Lessons and cart rental available.

McCann Memorial Golf Course (845-454-1968), 155 Wilbur Boulevard, Poughkeepsie. This 18-hole championship course also has a driving range, putting greens, pro shop, snack bar, and restaurant on the premises. Lessons and cart rentals available.

Red Hook Golf Club (845-758-8651), 650 Route 199, Red Hook. This 18-hole championship course, with clubhouse, putting and chipping greens, driving range, pro shop and restaurant on the premises, also offers lessons and cart and club rentals. Soft spikes required.

Vassar Golf Course (845-473-9838), Vassar College Campus, 124 Raymond

Avenue, Poughkeepsie. This nine-hole course is inexpensive and great for beginners. There are junior and senior rates; club and cart rentals available.

GARDENS AND PARKS

Innisfree Garden (845-677-8000), 362 Tyrrel Road, Millbrook. Open May through October, Wednesday through Friday 10-4; Saturday, Sunday and holidays 11-5. Admission. Inspired by the Eastern cup garden, or three-dimensional image composed of natural elements, these individual "garden pictures" draw the attention to a particular object, setting it apart by establishing an enclosure around it. Following the tradition of Asian artists, garden founder Walter Beck used natural formations as well as terraces, walls, and paths, to keep specific areas in "tension," believing that moving rocks or plants only an inch or so would destroy the effect. Visitors can stroll these public gardens and enjoy this visual laboratory and garden notebook. There is a picnic area for use by visitors; no pets are permitted and note there is limited handicapped access here.

Peach Hill Park (845-298-4600), 34 Edgewood Road, Poughkeepsie. Open year-round, daily dawn to dusk. It's a beautiful park located off Salt Point Turnpike near the town of Hyde Park. There are 157 acres here with several marked trails. It's also the highest elevation in the town of Poughkeepsie.

Poet's Walk Romantic Landscape Park (845-473-4400), 776 River Road (County Route 103), Red Hook. This 120-acre park offers magnificent views of the Hudson River, Kingston-Rhinecliff Bridge, and Catskill Mountains. There are two miles of paths, along with rustic cedar pavilions and benches when you want to rest and take in the scenery. This is a good place to stop and take a walk while touring the county by car. It's located only a few miles from the bridge and even young children will be able to manage walking the rather flat terrain here.

Quiet Cove Riverfront Park (845-298-4600), 1 Clear Water Drive (off Route 9), Poughkeepsie. This 27-acre riverfront park is a favorite spot among local residents. It's open to the public year-round daily 9am-9pm.

Wethersfield Estate and Gardens (845-373-8037), 214 Pugsley Hill Road (off County Route 86), Amenia. The formal gardens are open June through September, Wednesday, Friday and Saturday noon-5; house by appointment only. This 10-acre formal garden created by Chauncey D. Stillman (1907-1989) is arranged in the classical style, like the Italian villas of the 17th century. It is a garden of scenic views and statues, bursting with colorful flowers. There is an east garden, cupid fountain, arbor vitae arch, as well as cutting, water and inner gardens; a knot garden south terrace; pine terrace; peacock walk; belvedere; and rune stone (designed from a ninth-century Swedish original). Stillman's house is a Georgian-style Colonial, with the highest point on the property offering panoramic views of the Catskills to the west and Berkshires to the north. It is filled with his antiques, paintings, sculptures and fine furniture. Stillman, an early conservationist, ran one of the first estates in Dutchess County to use soil and water conservation farming techniques. He constructed 12 ponds for irrigations, rotated crops, reforested, and employed organic farming methods. Today the farm carries on the tradition of conservation. Stillman also had a large stable on the property and acquired 22 carriages he restored. Most of them date from 1850 to 1910 and can be seen by appointment, along with the interior of the house. Although the gardens here are only open limited days and hours, they are worth seeing if you enjoy horticulture.

HIKING

Appalachian Trail (appalachialtrail.org/newyork). Thirty miles of the AT pass through southeastern Dutchess County. Within the county there are 4000 acres of protected parkland with hiking, backpacking, snowshoeing, cross-country skiing, and five overnight use areas. Look for trailheads, marked by AT trail crossing signs, at the following locations: Route 52, four miles east of the Taconic Parkway, with parking on the north side of the road; Route 55, west of Pawling, near the Route 292 intersection, with parking west of the trail crossing; Route 22 north of Pawling, between Route 68 and the DOT parking area, north of Route 68 and Hurds Corners Road. Free. Open year-round.

Buttercup Farm Audubon Sanctuary (518-325-5203), 6862 Route 82, Stanfordville. Open daily dawn to dusk, there are 640 acres of diverse habitats with rolling fields and open grasslands. Although there are only six miles of trails, there are over 80 species of birds that have been observed here, including great blue herons, wood ducks, and bobolinks. This is an excellent place for young hikers and families since the trails are fairly flat and there is lots to observe.

Dutchess Rail Trail Park (845-298-4600; dutchessrailtrail.com). This is a 13-mile rail trail that stretches from the former Hopewell Junction train depot, north to the Poughkeepsie

The Buttercup Farm Audubon Sanctuary, just south of Pine Plains on Route 82, contains 641 acres of diverse habitats including grasslands, woodlands and marsh with several walking trails.

entrance of the Walkway over the Hudson. It is a shared use rail trail and the park is ideal for walking, biking, running, and rollerblading. Open year-round.

Edward R. Murrow Park (845-855-1131), 142 Lakeside Drive, Pawling. Open May through August, daily 10-7. Admission. There are several hiking trails on this 86-acre site, which also has a lake with a small beach for swimming, a restaurant, and picnic pavilions.

Ferncliff Forest (845-876-1559), 68 Mount Rutsen Road, Rhinebeck. This 200-acre forest preserve and game refuge has a pond for fishing as well as hiking trails and a fire tower offering excellent panoramic views. This is a good choice for those who want to hike with children. It is well located; only a few miles from the Kingston-Rhinecliff Bridge and village of Rhinebeck.

Fishkill Ridge Conservation Area (845-473-4440), 32 Sunnyside Road, Beacon. This 1900-acre area of the ridge, the northern gateway to the Hudson Highlands is filled with wildlife and offers stunning views of the Hudson River. There are over 11 miles of hiking trails that connect to the Hudson Highlands State Park and Mount Beacon.

Harlem Valley Rail Trail (518-789-9591; hvrt.org). There are 20 miles of scenic paved trail, linking villages and parks on the rail bed from Amenia and Millerton to Copake Falls in Columbia County. There is access to the trail at Railroad Plaza in Millerton and on Mechanic Street in Amenia. Free. Open year-round.

Tivoli Bays Wildlife Management Area (845-889-4745), Cruger Island Road, Tivoli. Located on the Bard College campus, this preserve has 1700 acres that can be hiked (there are six trails) or enjoyed as part of the public programs offered during the year (guided canoe trips, organized walks, etc.). Stop at the Tivoli Free Library on Broadway in the village between 10am and 2pm on Saturday. Be aware hunting, fishing and trapping are permitted in season in this wildlife management area. From May through October there is canoe and kayak access here to Tivoli North Bay.

Hyde Park Trail (845-229-8086). The Hyde Park Trail system is a community trail that includes 28 miles of trails through public and private lands, connecting parks, preserves and historic sites. There are entrances to the trail at the FDR Home, Val-Kill, Vanderbilt Mansion, Mills-Norrie State Park and the Winnakee Nature Preserve. All trails are open free to the public year-round from sunrise to sunset, weather permitting.

Mills-Norrie State Park (845-889-4646), 9 Old Post Road, Staatsburg. There are 1000 acres of woodlands with hiking trails, a marina, picnic areas, and a golf course. Free. Open year-round.

Montgomery Place (845-752-5000), 26 Gardener Way, Red Hook. In 2016 this amazing property became part of Bard College. It is now the Montgomery Place Campus, near Barrytown, an early 19th-century Livingston family estate that has been designated a National Historic Landmark. There are nearly 400 acres and several trails on the property available to the public year-round free of charge, from dawn to dusk. Visitors may enjoy watching ships pass along the Hudson River and seeing the variety of trees on the property. There are waterfalls, footbridges, gardens and Catskill Mountains views. The magnificent Classical Revival-style mansion is open June through late October on Saturday only for tours given throughout the day.

Mount Beacon Park (845-473-4440). Both the parking area and trailhead are located at the intersection of Route 9D and Howland Avenue in the city of Beacon. The short hike to the top of Mount Beacon offers fantastic views of the highlands and Hudson River. This is considered the northern gateway to the Hudson Highlands. Visitors will also see remnants of the world-famous incline railway once the steepest of its kind anywhere; it operated from 1902 until the late 1970s. Free. Open year-round, daily dawn to dusk.

Pawling Nature Reserve (518-690-7878), Quaker Lake Road, Pawling. This 1000-acre reserve with miles of hiking trails amid mountains, fields, woods, and ponds is seemingly undiscovered, and its trails are underutilized. It's a wonderful destination for birders. Nearly 80 species use the area's diverse habitat for nesting or foraging. Free. Open year-round.

Stissing Mountain Fire Tower (518-398-5069), 532 Hicks Hill Road, Stanford, has an elevation of 1492 feet. The 90-foot lookout tower is reached by following a hiking trail from the base of the mountain, the second-oldest mountain in the Western Hemisphere. There are incredible views of three states, along with an interesting piece of local history: the fire tower, a structure that has nearly disappeared from the face of the Hudson Valley. Enjoy watching eagles, hawks, and vultures in flight. Open year-round. Free.

Thompson Pond Preserve (518-690-7850), Lake Road, Pine Plains. Open year-round; free. After climbing Stissing

The Walkway Over the Hudson State Historic Park is a pedestrian and bike path over the River – walkers, joggers, bicyclists and people with disabilities are welcome.

Mountain, check out this multi-acre reserve with its fields, woods and pond areas.

Walkway Over the Hudson (845-454-9649; walkway.org), between Highland (87 Haviland Road) in Ulster County and Poughkeepsie (61 Parker Avenue) in Dutchess County. A landmark railroad bridge has been transformed into a 1.25-mile linear park and trail. There is now public access to the Hudson River's scenic landscape for pedestrians, hikers, joggers, and bicyclists. The walkway will eventually connect with a network of rail trails, parks and communities. The cost of removing the bridge would have been over twice the cost of preserving it! The website has information about special events on the walkway.

Wilcox Memorial Park (845-758-6100), 1639 Route 199, Stanfordville. Open year-round, this 615-acre site has the amenities of a larger park, along with hiking trails suitable for a family outing. Free park entry.

HORSEBACK RIDING

Calypso Farm (845-474-2514), 25 Seelbach Lane, Staatsburg. This equestrian center offers lessons, training, and a children's summer riding program. They are open year-round by appointment only.

Cedar Crest Farm Equestrian Center (518-398-1034), 2054 Route 83, Pine Plains. Open year-round, Tuesday through Sunday 9-5. This equestrian center offers lessons in show jumping, cross-country, and dressage to riders of all abilities.

Netherwood Acres (845-266-3774), 883 Netherwood Road, Hyde Park. Lessons are available here for riders of all abilities.

Southern Dutchess Equestrian Center (845-226-1256), 187 Robinson Lane, Wappingers Falls. Lessons, training, boarding and summer camp are offered here.

The Southlands Foundation (845-876-4862), 5771 Route 9, Rhinebeck. Open year-round, but call in advance to schedule lessons. There is a summer riding program and camp as well as after-school programs, but no trail rides. This equestrian farm is located on 200 acres overlooking the Hudson River. Horses are boarded here, but acres of trails are open to the public daily from 8 to 4 for hiking, cross-country skiing and snowshoeing. Use of these trails is free but visitors are asked to check-in at the office before heading out.

KAYAKING

There are some excellent places to launch kayaks in Dutchess County. A few of them are: **Mills-Norrie State Park**, off Route 9, in Staatsburg, **Tivoli Bays**,

Kidd Lane, off Route 9G, less than a mile south of Tivoli, and **Rudd Pond**, 59 Rudd Pond Road, off Route 62, Millerton, two miles north of town.

If you are a beginner and have no equipment, consider these excellent outfitters:

Atlantic Kayak Tours (845-246-2187), 1 Norrie Way, Staatsburg. Available mid-May through mid-September, Saturday and Sunday 10-4 or by appointment. They rent kayaks and organize excursions at the Norrie Point Paddle Sport Center. This is a great way for beginners to get out on the Hudson River.

Mountain Tops Outfitters (845-831-1997), 144 Main Street, Beacon. This company is the official outfitter at Scenic Hudson's Long Dock Park kayak launch on the Hudson River in Beacon. They rent kayaks by the hour and provide guided tours for groups of four or more. Metro North has partnered with Scenic Hudson: NYC residents may take one-day all–inclusive kayaking getaways by going to Grand Central Station, riding the train to Beacon, then walking to he nearby river center kayak launch.

The River Connection (845-229-0595), 9 West Market Street, Hyde Park. This is an excellent place to go if you are new to kayaking and don't have equipment. They organize outings on the Hudson River and offer classes for beginners as well as advanced students. I went on one of their trips and found it to be an amazing experience, particularly just before sunset—a new, delightful way to experience the Hudson!

SWIMMING

Bard College Stevenson Gymnasium (845-758-7531), 32 Woods Avenue, Annandale-on-Hudson. Open daily 7:30am-10:30pm; until 9pm on Saturday and Sunday. Admission. This indoor, six-lane, 75-foot-long swimming pool is a great place to go for those who enjoy doing laps. It is open to the public for day use, but memberships are also available. There are locker rooms with saunas, a fitness center, squash course, and outdoor tennis courts.

Beekman Recreation Park (845-227-5783), 29 Recreation Center Road, Hopewell Junction. Open daily late June through Labor Day, 9-5. There is a pool here as well as a summer camp.

Edward R. Murrow Park (845-855-1131), Lakeside Drive and Old Route 55, Pawling. Open May through August, daily 10-7. Admission. This 86-acre park has a wonderful lake with a small beach making it a good choice for those with young children.

Lakeside Park (845-855-1131), 2 Lakeside Drive. Pawling. Open mid-June through Labor Day, daily 8:30-4. There's a lake here with a sandy beach and it's a good choice for those with young children.

Taconic State Park (*Rudd Pond Area & Copake Falls Area*) (518-789-3059), 59 Rudd Pond Road, Millerton & 253 Route 344, Copake Falls (518-329-3993). The Rudd Pond Area is open Memorial Day weekend through Labor Day, daily 11-6. Admission is charged per vehicle. There is a small beach area, a good place for young children. The pond is eight feet deep in the swimming area. There is fishing, rowboat rentals, a picnic area, and bicycling. Ore Pit Pond in the Copake Falls Area has a small swimming area with a separate wading pool. This area would be of interest to those with young children.

Wilcox Memorial Park (845-758-6100), 1639 Route 199, Stanfordville. Open Memorial Day weekend through Labor Day, weekends 10-7. Admission fee per vehicle is charged for non-Dutchess County residents. This man-made lake (between six and seven feet deep) offers a good-size beach where you can relax with lots of shade nearby. Hiking trails surrounding the lake provide an easy walk after your swim. The park is great for bicycling, as well.

WINTER SPORTS

CROSS COUNTRY SKIING

Dutchess County was made for cross-country skiing, with low hills that slope down toward the river, open meadows turned liquid silver by moonlight, and secret paths that cross streams and disappear into the pines. Most are quiet. The **Harlem Valley Rail Trail** and **Hyde Park Trail** are excellent places to cross-country ski. The following parks also offer fine cross-country skiing during the winter months. Since the weather is changeable, call ahead to check conditions.

Ferncliff Forest (845-876-1559), 68 Mount Rutsen Road, Rhinebeck. Open daily dawn to dusk. Free. This 200-acre park is a gem and is less crowded than some of the other parks in the county.

James Baird State Park (845-452-1489), 14 Maintenance Lane, Pleasant Valley. Open daily, dawn to dusk. Free. There are about 600 acres here, including several miles of scenic wooded trails. The park offers several wooded trails for skiing, some of which have Hudson River views. The park also has picnic and sledding areas.

Taconic State Park, Rudd Pond Area (518-789-3059), 59 Rudd Pond Road, Millerton. Open daily 8-6. Parking fee. There are 225 acres here with several trails for cross-country skiing.

Wilcox Memorial Park (845-758-6100), 1639 Route 199, Stanfordville. Open daily 9-4. Free. This is a wonderful place for winter hiking and walking as well as cross-country skiing. There are 615 acres with trails that go around the lake. They are not marked, however.

ICE SKATING

NOTE: *After skating for 22 years at the Poughkeepsie Civic Center's McCann Ice Arena, I am heartbroken to report this news: this sports facility is woefully mismanaged. I prefer not to catalog any of the ill-advised decisions that have been made here in 2017 and the complete non-responsiveness by management since the former manager resigned in early 2017. This is a tragic loss for both the city of Poughkeepsie and Dutchess County. In addition to the mismanagement of the ice rink, the Civic Center concert venue has deteriorated. All of us who have skated here for decades and supported this facility are hoping the Dutchess County business community will "rescue" what used to be a fantastic county resource.*

Bontecou Ice Rink (845-677-8261), 131 Millbrook School Road, Millbrook. Open mid-December through mid-February, Sunday only, 2:15pm-4:15pm. Call to confirm schedule before going.

LODGING

Northwestern Dutchess County
(Red Hook, Rhinebeck, Rhinecliff, Staatsburg, Hyde Park, Tivoli)

The Barn in Tivoli (845-757-2312), 33 Broadway, Tivoli 12583 ($$) This cozy two-bedroom home is located on over four acres of woods with a creek and pond within walking distance of the center of town. The set-up is ideal for a couple with one or two children.

Beekman Arms (845-876-7077), 24 West Market Street, Rhinebeck 12572. ($$) The oldest continuously operating inn in America, a beautiful hotel, has a fascinating history. Located in the center of one of my favorite Hudson Valley towns, Rhinebeck, there are interesting shops and an array of restaurants just outside the door. The 23 rooms all have private baths and air-conditioning; and there's a restaurant and cozy tavern downstairs. Children are welcome. Open year-round. (If you want a quieter place, ask for accommodations in the nearby Townsend, also operated by the hotel, with its four modern deluxe rooms, each with a king-size bed and gas fireplace. Additionally, the renovated Old Firehouse, has exposed brick walls and high ceilings, and is also available to guests.)

Hideaway Suites (845-266-5676), 439 Lake Drive, Rhinebeck. 12572 ($$) Enjoy secluded elegance in the middle of a forest. The three suites and three guest rooms all have private bath, king-size beds, air-conditioning, and TV; most have a fireplace, Jacuzzi, wet bar, and private deck. Located one mile from the Omega Institute. Open year-round.

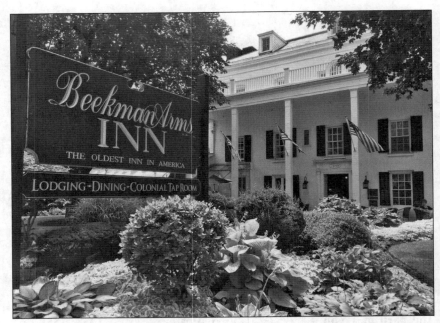

The Beekman Arms in Rhinebeck is the oldest continuously operating inn in the U.S. and dates back to 1766.

Journey Inn Bed & Breakfast (845-229-8972), One Sherwood Place, Hyde Park 12538. (\$\$) Situated directly across from the entrance to the Vanderbilt Mansion and grounds (where guests can take a beautiful morning walk or run), this comfortable B&B is chock-full of fascinating memorabilia from the travels of the owners. There are two master suites, one with a king-size bed, and five bedrooms, all with private bath. Children over the age of nine are welcome. Open year-round.

Hotel Tivoli (845-757-2100), 53 Broadway, Tivoli 12583. (\$\$) The nine-rooms here were renovated with striking colorful art; there's definitely an eclectic contemporary ambience here. Be aware that it's an historic building and the walls are thin, so if there's excessive noise next door you will hear it! *The Corner,* the restaurant on the main floor, is quite good and guests may dine alfresco in the warm weather months on the wraparound porch. Open year-round.

Olde Rhinebeck Inn (845-871-1745), 340 Wurtemburg Road, Rhinebeck 12572. (\$\$\$) Listed on the National Register of Historic Places, this early American farmhouse, built before the Revolutionary War by Dutch Palatine settlers, retains many of its original architectural details, including hand-hewn chestnut beams and wide-plank floors. The four rooms, each with its own charm, combine authentic touches with modern amenities. One room offers a Jacuzzi and private balcony overlooking the spring-fed pond. The large suite has a queen-size canopied bed with adjoining sitting room. All rooms have private bath, satellite TV, air-conditioning, refrigerator, plus terry-cloth robes, and fresh-cut flowers. A full gourmet breakfast is served. There is a two-night minimum stay required on weekends. Children are not permitted. Open year-round.

Red Hook Country Inn (845-758-8445), 7460 South Broadway, Red Hook 12571. ($$) There are eight rooms with private bath, and a carriage house, in this 160-year-old Federal-style house, converted to a charming inn. A few rooms have fireplaces and whirlpool baths. Guests are welcome to enjoy the movie library, in-room coffee service, bathrobes, chocolates, and fresh flowers. The owners, Nabil and Pat, are genuinely warm and hospitable, and go out of their way to make everyone comfortable. A full breakfast is served and children are welcome. Open year-round.

The Rhinecliff Hotel (845-876-0590), 4 Grinnell Street, Rhinecliff 12574. ($$) There are nine rooms with beautiful river views in this country hotel, adjacent to the Amtrak railroad station. All have private baths and balconies, whirlpool tubs, air-conditioning and cable TV. There is a bar/restaurant downstairs. Recommended for heavy sleepers, as the trains do pass by throughout the night!

Whistlewood Farm (845-876-6838), 52 Pells Road, Rhinebeck 12572. ($$) This distinctive B&B is also a working horse farm, located on 40 acres with miles of walking trails through beautiful woodlands. Animals abound here. The living room has a stone fireplace and a view of the paddock area, and there are antiques, including a player piano, throughout the house. A hearty farm breakfast with home-baked muffins and jams is served daily. The four bedrooms have private bath with Jacuzzi, and private patio; two cottages have fireplaces, and one has a hot tub. Guests may use the entire house. The owner offers discounted rates during the week to single travelers. Children and pets are welcome. Open year-round.

Southwestern Dutchess County
(Beacon, Fishkill, Hopewell Junction, Poughkeepsie)

Botsford Briar B&B (845-831-6099), 19 High Street, Beacon 12508. ($$) There are five rooms, all with private bath, in this beautifully restored 1889 Queen Anne Victorian; the design is by the same architect who redesigned Wilderstein in Rhinebeck. This B&B was also used as a set location for the film *Nobody's Fool*, starring Paul Newman. A deck, built in 2008 by the innkeeper, offers panoramic views of the Hudson River. Since the location is close to both Main Street and the Metro North train station, this is a good choice for those who don't have a car and plan on exploring Beacon on foot. A continental breakfast is served in your room; TV, air-conditioning, and high-speed Internet service round out the amenities. Open year-round.

Bykenhulle House Bed & Breakfast (845-592-0255), 21 Bykenhulle Road, Hopewell Junction 12533. ($$) This 15-room Greek Revival-style manor house was built by Peter Adriance, a prominent silversmith, in the early 1800s. There have been several interesting residents, including the current owners, William and Florence Beausoleil, who purchased the house in 1972. In 1991 the house was listed in the National Register of Historic Places. There is a beautiful sunroom, ballroom and patios and the linens and furnishings are first-rate in all six rooms here. Older children are welcome. Open year-round.

Chrystie House Bed & Breakfast (845-765-0251), 300 South Avenue, Beacon 12508. ($$)There are four renovated rooms on four acres of landscaped gardens and woods here. The hosts are welcoming and provide a gourmet breakfast. Children are welcome. Open year-round.

Courtyard by Marriott (845-485-6336), 2641 South Road, Poughkeepsie 12601. ($$) There are 149 spacious rooms in this moderately priced hotel, located in the heart of the city's largest shopping area. Enjoy all the modern amenities, including an indoor pool and exercise room. A breakfast buffet is available every morning. This is a good choice of accommodations for families. The hotel is next door to Locust Grove Estate, which has wonderful walking paths for those who enjoy morning exercise outdoors!

Hilton Garden Inn (845-896-7100), 25 Westage Drive, Fishkill 12524. ($$) There are 111 rooms in this hotel, at the junction of Route 9 and I-84. All have high-speed Internet access, refrigerator, microwave, and coffeemaker, in addition to the usual hotel amenities. There is an indoor pool and fitness center; children are welcome. Open year-round.

Hyatt House (845-897-5757), 100 Westage Business Center Drive, Fishkill 12524 ($$) This recently renovated hotel has 86 suites and 49 rooms. There is a full kitchen in all suites; indoor pool, complimentary hot breakfast buffet, and fitness center make this a great place for families. The central location in Dutchess County is nice too!

The Inn and Spa at Beacon (845-205-2900), 151 Main Street, Beacon 12508 ($$) These 12 beautiful rooms are a good choice for those arriving in Beacon by train and don't intend to rent a car. The roof gardens offer views of the mountains and Hudson River. Therapeutic spa treatments are available and you should book appointments in advance. Not recommended for children. Open year-round.

Mount Beacon Bed & Breakfast (845-831-0737), 829 Wolcott Avenue, Beacon 12508. ($$) This beautiful B&B is everything a fine establishment should be. Wolcott Manor is a 1911 Colonial Revival home at the foot of Mount Beacon. High ceilings, period furniture, four fireplaces and stunning hardwood floors all contribute to a feeling of stepping back into another era. This is a special spot and the breakfast is excellent. Not recommended for children. Open year-round.

The Residence Inn (845-896-5210), 15 Schuyler Boulevard, Fishkill 12524. ($$) Part of the Marriott hotel chain, there are 139 suites here, each with the usual modern amenities, as well as fireplace and kitchen. A continental breakfast is served. There is an outdoor pool, whirlpool, and exercise room on the premises. Children are welcome. Open year-round.

Swann Inn (845-831-6346), 120 Howland Avenue, Beacon 12508. ($$) Originally built in 1866, this cozy B&B is located at the base of Mount Beacon. There are five rooms, each with its own distinctive character; four have private bath. A full breakfast is served to guests. Innkeepers Neil Caplan and his wife, Darlene, offer a wealth of knowledge about the area. Open year-round.

Willow Lake Cottages (914-475-5254), 4 Willow Lake Drive, Fishkill 12524. ($$$) There are four different types of houses on a five-acre lake. Each house sleeps six, is fully furnished, and has a kitchen; all are air-conditioned. This is a good choice for families or groups who enjoy hiking, boating, fishing, and swimming. This is also an ideal place for a family reunion. Children and pets are welcome.

Central Dutchess County
(Pine Plains, Millbrook, Dover Plains)

Blue Barn Bed n Breakfast (845-750-2669), 62 Old Route 82, Millbrook 12545. ($$) There are three simple rooms here, each with private bath, in a 1830 restored home. The place is within easy walking distance to the village of Millbrook. Guests will enjoy a three-course gourmet breakfast; it's served overlooking the colorful gardens on the premises in the summer months. Open year-round.

Inn at Pine Plains (518-771-3117), 3036 East Church Street, Pine Plains 12567. ($$) There are four standard rooms here as well as four suites, a great option for families. All have private bath, TV, and air-conditioning. A full breakfast is served to guests and local products are featured. Open year-round.

Millbrook Country House (845- 677-9570), 3244 Sharon Turnpike, Millbrook 12545. ($$) The four guest rooms in this delightful 1808 center-hall Colonial, all with private bath and central air-conditioning, are decorated with several 18th-century Italian antiques and paintings. Imported linens are featured on all the beds and guests can spend time around any of the several fireplaces. The wonderful gardens here, both flower and herb, are filled with modern sculptures. Guests will enjoy a full gourmet breakfast with homemade jams and omelets with herbs from the garden during the summer months. Breakfast is served any time at your convenience between 7 and 10. Afternoon tea is available between 4 and 5. Those interested in art and antiques will particularly appreciate a stay here. Children over the age of 10 are welcome. Open year-round.

Old Drovers Inn—Preston Barn (845-832-9311), 196 East Duncan Hill Road, Dover Plains 12522. ($$$) There are six beautifully decorated rooms with private baths. Although built in 1750, this completely renovated inn specializes in fine service. I highly recommend a stay here and am delighted the place has new owners who have beautifully restored this historic property. There is cable TV, farm-to-table breakfast, central air-conditioning and a fabulous barn on the premises. The young innkeepers are knowledgeable and will assist you in planning your stay.

Eastern Dutchess County
(Amenia, Millerton, Pawling)

Pawling House Bed & Breakfast (845-855-3851), 105 West Main Street, Pawling 12564. ($$) Set back from West Main Street, in a pastoral woodland setting, this five-room B&B dating back to 1799 is only a ten-minute walk into the center of town. All rooms have fine linens, TV, air-conditioning and are furnished with fine antiques. Your host, Rosalinda Archibold Weiner, will point you in the right direction and happily answer all your travel concerns! Not recommended for children. Open year-round.

Troutbeck Inn & Conference Center (845-789-1555), 515 Leedsville Road, Amenia 12501. ($$$) This English country estate on 600 acres is an executive retreat during the week, but on weekends it's a relaxed getaway. Fronted by sycamores and a brook, the slate-roofed estate has leaded-glass windows, walled gardens, antiques throughout, and an outdoor pool and tennis courts. The 42 rooms and 6 suites, all with private bath and nine with fireplaces, are beautifully decorated. There are no television sets in any of the guest rooms. Not recommended for children. Open year-round.

WHERE TO EAT

DINING OUT

Northwestern Dutchess County
(Tivoli, Red Hook, Rhinebeck, Staatsburg, Hyde Park)

Aroi Thai Restaurant (845-876-1114), 55 East Market Street, Rhinebeck. ($$) Open for lunch Thursday through Monday 11:30-4; dinner daily 5-9. This Thai restaurant serves well-prepared curry and noodle dishes as well as daily specials, in charming surroundings. Outdoor patio dining is available in the warm weather months. Desserts include homemade ice cream flavors: lychee, ginger and Thai iced tea. Children welcome.

Cinnamon Indian Bistro (845-876-7510, 51 East Market Street, Rhinebeck. ($$) Open for lunch Wednesday through Monday 11:30-2:30: dinner 5-9:30. The flavors of India's many regions are now available in the Hudson Valley. There are several small plates—healthful interesting dishes—that combine Indian spices with contemporary American ingredients. Most offerings are sourced from local farms. Located in the center of Rhinebeck, there is an excellent buffet available on Sundays. Not recommended for children.

Culinary Institute of America (800-CULINARY; ciachef.edu), 1946 Campus Drive, Hyde Park. ($$) Hours vary; call or check the website for current information. There are four restaurants at this world-famous culinary institution, where the food is prepared and served by the students under the guidance of world-class chefs. Reservations are essential (although not necessary at the **Apple Pie Bakery Café**—see *Eating Out*), and should be made several weeks in advance. The wait is usually well worth it. Note that all CIA restaurants are closed Sunday, for three weeks during the summer, and the week between Christmas and New Year's Day. Menus change seasonally and the freshest ingredients available are used.

American Bounty Restaurant (845-451-1011) offers the best in American regional cuisine. There is smoked turkey with black-pepper pasta and cream and a Mississippi Riverboat for dessert. **Ristorante Caterina d'Medici** (845-451-1013) is located in the Colavita Center for Italian Food and Wine, which specializes in Northern Italian cuisine like tricolor pasta diamonds with prosciutto. The menu features the culinary traditions of various regions of Italy and the décor is reminiscent of the landscape of Tuscany. Most of the year it is possible to have lunch here without a reservation between 1 and 6pm. The **Bocuse Restaurant** (845-451-1012) features contemporary international cuisine; this is the newest of the dining options here (opened in 2013).

The Bocuse Restaurant at the Culinary Institute of America in Hyde Park specializes in modern French fare made by students at the school.

Hana Sushi (845-758-4333), 7270 South Broadway, Red Hook. ($) Open for lunch Friday 11:30-2:30; dinner Tuesday through Thursday 5-9; Friday and Saturday until 10. This is a small, unpretentious eatery in a tiny strip mall. The rolls, tempura, and other Japanese specialties are consistently fresh and well prepared. The service is always friendly, and prices are less than those at other sushi restaurants in the area.

Le Petit Bistro (845-876-7400), 8 East Market Street, Rhinebeck. ($$$) Open Wednesday through Monday for dinner 5-8:30; Friday and Saturday until 9:30. This charming, intimate French bistro is a great place to enjoy dinner on a special occasion; the food and service are consistently excellent, and everything is prepared to order. There is a great wine list. Not recommended for children.

Liberty Public House (845-876-1760), 6417 Montgomery Street, Rhinebeck. ($$) Open 11-10; Friday and Saturday until 2am. Located in the historic Starr Building, next door to Upstate Films, this restaurant has two dining areas, a cozy sports bar, and a nightclub downstairs with live entertainment on weekends. One dining room is decorated with a 48-star American flag and engravings from the Civil War. In the warm weather food is served on the patio where the outdoor bar is a 23-foot sailboat surrounded by bar stools and picnic tables. The surroundings are unusual, and the hearty, eclectic American fare includes something for everyone: grass-fed beef burgers with freedom fries, matzo ball soup, and crispy duck, are just a few of the popular dishes here. Desserts are all homemade an delicious.

The Local (845-876-2214), 38 West Market Street, Rhinebeck. ($$) Open Tuesday through Saturday 5:30-10; Friday and Saturday until 11. Enjoy international cuisine in an informal yet elegant renovated farmhouse. The name sums up most of the fare here, including an array of healthy, interesting dishes prepared with an imaginative flair by a Culinary Institute-trained chef. Some entrees include grilled sea scallops, cedar planked wild king salmon, duck "two ways," and pork scallopini. There are small plates like phyllo-wrapped goat cheese, Asian chicken dumplings, and pretzel-crusted crab-claw cakes. This is also a wonderful place to have a drink at the bar with a snack like pickled quail eggs or Japanese-style popcorn! Not recommended for children.

Market Street (845-876-7200), 19 West Market Street, Rhinebeck. ($$) Open Monday through Thursday 5-9:30; Saturday and Sunday 11-9:30. Gianni Scappin has created a terrific venue where you can enjoy a dozen types of tasty Neapolitan-style pizzas at the pizza bar, have a drink and appetizer at another bar, or sit in the main room and dine on baked salmon, local aged sirloin or Berkshire pork chop. There is also an array of interesting sides and pasta dishes. I love the lasagna with green noodles. Service is first-rate and all dishes are prepared to order. Children welcome.

Mercato (845-758-5879), 61 East Market Street, Red Hook. ($$) Open for dinner Wednesday through Sunday 5-9:30; Friday and Saturday until 10. This Italian restaurant serves rustic fare in a simple atmosphere with a busy bar. The imaginative pasta selections are recommended, but there are also grilled fish, poultry, and meat entrees.

Osaka (845-876-7338), 22 Garden Street, Rhinebeck. ($$) Closed Tuesday. Open for lunch Monday through Friday 11:30-2:30; dinner served daily 4:30-9:30; Sunday 3-9:30. Eat in or take out from this informal Japanese restaurant. The sushi is excellent and there is usually a grilled fish daily special. The chicken teriyaki is a good choice if you aren't a sushi aficionado. Dinners are reasonably priced and are accompanied by soup or salad. A seat at the bar offers a great view of the sushi chefs at work. Children welcome.

Panzur Restaurant & Wine Bar (845-757-1071), 69 Broadway, Tivoli. ($$) Open for dinner Tuesday through Saturday 5:30-10; Friday and Saturday until 11. Named after chef-owner Rei Peraza's late grandfather, Panzur's contemporary Spanish cuisine is very good. This is the kind of place to go for a light dinner and a bottle of wine. They cure their own sausages, and the produce is sourced from local farms. Larger plates include hanger steak, lamb shank and rainbow trout. Be prepared for something different here. Not recommended for children.

Rhinecliff Hotel Restaurant & Bar (845-876-0590), 4 Grinnell Street, Rhinecliff. ($$) Open for dinner Wednesday through Sunday 5:30-9; Sunday brunch 10-3. Extended hours in the summer months include Saturday brunch

10-3. This restaurant/hotel is housed in a renovated 1850 building, and the restaurant boasts a mahogany bar and 90-foot wraparound porch. The pine and hemlock floors have been refinished, and the brasserie restaurant serves local, seasonal produce and regional American cuisine. It's only a short walk from the Amtrak train station. The wine list is impressive, and the hotel's restaurant is a good place to stop for a drink, particularly in the warm-weather months when you can dine alfresco overlooking the Hudson River. There is live jazz during brunch. Children welcome.

Santa Fe (845-757-4100), 52 Broadway, Tivoli. ($$) Open for dinner daily, except Monday, 5-10. Enjoy traditional Mexican favorites including tacos and enchiladas in a festive atmosphere. The goat cheese in the quesadillas is locally made. Children welcome. Great margaritas with a number of tequilas from which to choose.

Terrapin (845-876-3330), 6242 Montgomery Street, Rhinebeck. ($$) Bistro open for lunch and dinner daily 11:30-midnight. A former Baptist church that dates from the 18th century, the cathedral-ceilinged structure has been completely renovated. The New American cuisine featured in the dining room fuses Asian, Southwestern, and Italian flavors. For those who prefer lighter fare, try the innovative bistro menu with organic-beef burgers, free-range chicken wings, fresh salads, and a create-your-own sandwich option. Children welcome.

Tavern at the Beekman Arms (845-876-1766), 6387 Mill Street (Route 9), Rhinebeck. ($$) Open daily for lunch and dinner: Monday through Thursday 10:30-9; Friday and Saturday 11:30-10; Sunday brunch 10:30-3:30; dinner 3:30-9. This Hudson Valley institution is housed in the oldest continuously operating inn in America and dates from 1766. I love their weekend brunch. The colonial atmosphere is wonderfully refreshing—and rare. Make sure to stop for a drink or enjoy their wonderful onion soup at the welcoming bar. Children are welcome.

Southwestern Dutchess County
(Poughkeepsie, Beacon, Fishkill, Hopewell Junction, Wappingers Falls)

Aloy's (845-473-8400), 157 Garden Street, Poughkeepsie. ($$) Open Wednesday & Thursday 3-9; Friday noon-10; Saturday and Sunday 2-9. This is one of my favorite Italian restaurants in the Hudson Valley. Everything is prepared with care and all the Italian specialties are done as they have been for generations. The atmosphere is similar to Italian restaurants I remember from childhood: big booths, spacious and cozy with excellent service. You won't go wrong here and children are welcome.

Aroma Osteria (845-298-6790), 114 Old Post Road, off Route 9, Wappingers Falls. ($$) Open for dinner daily, except Monday, 5-10, until 11 Friday and Saturday; Sunday 4-9. Lunch served Tuesday through Saturday noon-2:30. The rustic Italian cuisine is served in a cozy country setting. There is an extensive wine list and many wines by the glass. The meal begins with rustic bread and olive oil. The antipasti of bruschetta al pomodoro and steaming Price Edward Island mussels in a broth of extra-virgin olive oil, garlic, and fresh herbs are fine appetizers. Everything is prepared to order. Children welcome.

Artist's Palate (845-483-8074), 307 Main Street, Poughkeepsie. ($$) Open for lunch Monday through Friday 11-2:30 and dinner 5-9; dinner only Saturday 5-10; closed Sunday. This contemporary bistro is housed in an enormous renovated space with a high ceiling, exposed brick walls, dark-wood floors, soft lighting, and an open kitchen. The restaurant is also an art gallery with a bar featuring an affordable wine list and about 25 wines by the glass. The fresh fare is wonderful at dinner and a bargain for what you are served at lunch. An enormous grilled chicken salad is a favorite of mine here along with the Kobe burger on onion brioche. Make sure to sample the lobster mac and cheese (available as an appetizer and entree). This place is reason enough to venture into downtown Poughkeepsie after strolling on the Walkway Over the Hudson!

The Blue Fountain (845-226-3570), 940 Route 376, Hopewell Junction ($$) Open Tuesday through Friday 11am-10; Saturday 4-11; Sunday 1-9. Closed Monday. The Italian American cuisine here includes the standard steaks, seafood, chicken, and veal dishes. The zuppa di pesce, an enormous platter of shrimp, mussels, clams, scallops, sole, and calamari over linguine is excellent. The dining room tables all have a view of a huge fountain. There is a children's menu and families are welcome. Good value.

Brasserie 292 (845-473-0292), 292 Main Street, Poughkeepsie. ($$) Open Tuesday through Friday 11-9:30; Saturday 2-10:30; Sunday 11-8. Enjoy steak tartare, steamed mussels, crispy duck confit and a full raw bar in this delightful brasserie. The décor includes oversized mirrors, a tin ceiling, red leather booths, and lots of white tile.

Brothers Trattoria (845-838-3300), 4654 Main Street, Beacon. ($) Open daily 11-10. A tradition in Beacon for the past 20 years, this is a good place to go for pizza and pasta as well as standard Italian favorites, particularly if you are traveling with children.

Canvas Restaurant (845-483-9463), 305 Main Street, Poughkeepsie. Open daily 9am-9pm. The owners of The Artist's Palate opened this place next door and it serves excellent American fare for breakfast, lunch and light dinner. There are several options for vegetarians and it's a great place for a large group to dine.

Crave (845-452-3501), 129 Washington Street, Poughkeepsie. ($$$) Open for dinner Tuesday through Saturday 4-10; Sunday 11:30-3; Closed Monday. Three Culinary Institute graduates opened this restaurant in 2009, bringing a touch of Manhattan to Poughkeepsie. They are located just under the Walkway Over the Hudson. The contemporary American cuisine is excellent; in the warm weather months, enjoy patio dining. This is a great place for a special occasion: entrees include coffee ancho rubbed filet mignon and rabbit gnocchi; the honey lavender crème brulee is phenomenal. Not recommended for children.

Crew (845-462-8900), 2290 South Road, Poughkeepsie. ($$) Open Monday through Thursday 11-10; Friday and Saturday noon-midnight; Sunday noon-9. The Culinary Institute-trained chef specializes in local organic fare at this popular restaurant that opened in 2009. Enjoy international favorites like blackened chicken sandwich and Chinese chicken wrap for lunch or grilled salmon and filet mignon for dinner. The menu is large and varied and there's something here for everyone.

Il Barilotto Enoteca (845-897-4300), 1113 Main Street, Fishkill. ($$) Open daily, except Sunday, for lunch 11-2:30; dinner 5-10, until 11 Friday and Saturday. Enjoy Italian cuisine with a contemporary flair in this trattoria and wine bar, housed in a historic 1870 brick building with a romantic ambience and old-world charm.

Ice House on the Hudson (845-232-5783), 1 Main Street, Poughkeepsie. ($$) Open daily 11:30-9; until 10 on Friday and Saturday. Only a short walk from the train station the historic Ice House is now a beautifully restored restaurant on the Hudson River. The lunch and dinner fare includes wraps, paninis, chili, an array of salads, grilled chicken BLT, and much more. Enjoy watching the boats go by while dining alfresco in the summer months. Since opening in 2012, this has become a popular place to have a drink or light meal after exploring the Walkway Over the Hudson. Children welcome.

Longobardi's Restaurant & Pizzeria (845-297-1498), 1574 Route 9 (in Imperial Plaza mall), Wappingers Falls. ($) Open Tuesday through Sunday 11:30-9:30; until 10:30 Friday and Saturday. Closed Monday. This informal restaurant is a perfect stop for lunch or dinner when shopping on Route 9. One of my favorite dishes here is the grilled chicken salad; I also love their pasta e fagioli (soup). They offer the full range of Italian favorites including pizza, pasta, and calzones, as well as seafood, veal, and eggplant dishes. Everything is prepared to order. There is also a children's menu.

Meyer's Olde Dutch Food & Such (845-440-6900), 184 Main Street, Beacon. ($$) Open Wednesday through Sunday noon-9; Friday and Saturday until midnight. A modern interpretation of a classic burger joint, the kind of place every town should have! The crispy chicken sandwich is an excellent choice and my vegetarian friends love the mushroom veggie burger here. Bring the kids and enjoy decent fare at a reasonable price.

Mill House (845-485-2739), 289 Mill Street, Poughkeepsie. ($$) Open daily 11:30-9; until 10:30 Friday and Saturday. Sunday brunch 11:30-3. Located in a restored mill house, the basic fare here is always good (burgers, salads, etc.) although the service can be spotty on busy weekends. Beer lovers will be delighted with their selection; the atmosphere is cozy and inviting. Not recommended for children.

Northeastern Dutchess County
(Millerton, Pine Plains, Millbrook, Amenia)

Aurelia (845-677-4720), 3299 Franklin Avenue, Millbrook. ($$) Open daily, except Tuesday, noon-9; until 10 Friday and Saturday.

This charming Mediterranean restaurant offers a full menu of paninis, burgers, BLTs, salads, and pasta for lunch. Dinner includes grilled fish, short ribs, lamb chops, risotto, and several specials. During the summer, dine alfresco on the large patio.

Canoe Hill (845-605-1570), 3264 Franklin Avenue, Millbrook. ($$) Open Thursday and Sunday 5-10; Friday and Saturday 5-11. This restaurant opened in 2017 and has become extremely popular serving salads, small plates, roast chicken, grilled fish and burgers at reasonable prices. The imaginative dishes are served beautifully and will satisfy just about every taste. Children are welcome.

Charlotte's (845-677-5888), 4258 Route 44, Millbrook. ($$$) Open Wednesday through Friday 5-8:30; Saturday 11:30-10:30; Sunday 11:30-8:30. Call for winter hours (November through April). Housed in a 200-year-old converted church, this restaurant changed hands in 2006. Enjoy American cuisine with a French accent served in two dining rooms—one is elegant, the other more informal. The emphasis is on fresh local fare as well as game in season. There is outdoor dining in the warm weather months in a charming patio area.

52 Main (518-789-0252), 52 Main Street, Millerton. ($$) Open Tuesday through Friday 4-10; Saturday noon-11; Sunday noon-10. This casual tapas and wine bar specializes in small plates that use local products. Two of my favorite dishes here are the spinach and garlic chick pea puree with pita chips and the Kobe beef sliders with red onion confit and Cabrales cheese. You can order flights of wine and enjoy a number of small drinks with the variety of tastes here.

La Puerta Azul (845-677-AZUL), 2510 Route 44, Millbrook. ($$) Open daily noon-9; until 10:30 Friday and Saturday. Enjoy fine authentic Mexican cuisine in a colorful festive atmosphere. Everything here is homemade, including all the sauces, chips, and tortillas. The diverse menu features tacos, enchiladas and lighter fare. The tableside guacamole is excellent. There are 80 different wines to choose from here as well as dozens of beers; 12 are on tap. There is even a tequila humidor serving 60 varieties of this Mexican specialty.

Les Baux (845-677-8166), 152 Church Street Millbrook. ($$) Open Wednesday 5-9; Thursday through Monday for lunch noon-2:30; dinner 5-9. Named after Les Baux, a picturesque, medieval village in France, with narrow streets filled with ruins and stone houses, this cozy bistro is run by a Frenchman who worked at a fine restaurant in Les Baux. For lunch or light dinner, there is a variety of wonderful salads; the onion soup and steamed mussels are superb. For dinner there is grilled sirloin, rack of lamb, salmon fillet and pork tenderloin.

Manna Dew (518-789-3570), 54 Main Street, Millerton. ($$) Open for dinner Thursday through Monday 5-10. The excellent modern American cuisine here is sprinkled with international favorites. Only the freshest local ingredients are used: there is even a large garden in back of the restaurant and they use their own vegetables in the summer months. This is a delightful restaurant with an informal atmosphere—and one of my favorites.

The Millerton Inn (518-592-1900), 53 Main Street, Millerton. ($$) Open daily 11-9. A beautiful venue, both inside and outside, the specialty here is farm-to-table local American favorites including burgers, Caesar salad, squash risotto, and New York strip steak. The service is friendly and the food is consistently decent. The owner also operates Four Brothers pizza eateries all over Dutchess County.

Serevan (845-373-9800), 6 Autumn Lane (off Route 44), Amenia ($$) Open for dinner Thursday through Monday 5-10. This is the place to savor the exotic flavors of the Middle East and Mediterranean cuisine in a relaxing atmosphere with an open kitchen and fireplace. The name comes from Lake

Serevan in Armenia. A signature dish is the pan-seared branzino with cumin-scented hummus, lemon, and fresh dill. The lamb with apples, cardamom, and steamed couscous is a house specialty.

Stissing House (518-398-8800), 7801 South Main Street, Pine Plains. ($$) Open for dinner Thursday through Sunday 5:30-9; until 10 Friday and Saturday. Housed in a historic structure that has been a tavern for over 100 years, this establishment offers American regional cuisine in an informal, relaxed atmosphere. Their thin-crust wood-fired oven pizza is first-rate. I loved the one with truffle oil, something I had never had on pizza. Children welcome.

Max's on Main in Beacon serves up BLT Bloody Marys—crispy bacon and lettuce with grape tomatoes on a toothpick—as well as hearty burgers, salads and wraps.

Southeastern Dutchess County
(Pawling, Wingdale, Poughquag)

McKinney and Doyle Fine Foods Café (845-855-3875), 10 Charles Colman Boulevard, Pawling. ($$) Open Tuesday through Friday 6:30am-9pm; Saturday and Sunday, 7am-9:30 pm. This old-fashioned, high-ceilinged storefront café has exposed brick walls, a mix of booths and tables, and lots of local memorabilia as part of the décor. The eclectic cuisine includes such unusual treats as grilled shrimp with Thai peanut sauce over angel-hair pasta, and breast of duck with peppercorns and applejack soaked figs. The bakery that operates out of the café is quite good so don't skip dessert! Children welcome.

EATING OUT

Northwestern Dutchess County

Bread Alone Bakery & Café (845-876-3108), 45 East Market Street, Rhinebeck. ($) Café is open daily 7am-6pm; dining room open daily 8-4. The homemade soups, sandwiches and breads offered here make this informal eatery a renowned stop among locals for breakfast, lunch, or take-out. The desserts are excellent. Children are welcome.

Bubby's Take Away Kitchen (845-758-TACO/8226), 19 West Market Street, Red Hook. ($) Open Tuesday through Saturday 11-8. I love this eatery with salads, quesadillas, burritos, soups, pita sandwiches and fantastic carrot cupcakes and brownies. Home cooking at its best! A perfect pre-picnic stop.

Buns Burgers (845-516-5197), 20 Garden Street, Rhinebeck. ($) Open Tuesday through Saturday 11-8; Sunday 11-6. I absolutely love this simple informal eatery. Where else in Rhinebeck can you have a satisfying meal for $10? The menu is small: grass-fed local burgers (lamb or beef), the "yardbird" (grilled chicken sandwich), veggie burger (Portobello mushroom), and a couple of other choices. The fries are thin and crispy: always perfectly done. The kids will love the open kitchen. Eat outside in the warm weather months.

Calico Restaurant & Patisserie (845-876-2749), 6384 Mill Street, Rhinebeck. ($$) Open Wednesday through Friday 10-8; Saturday 8-8; Sunday 8-1. This cozy spot is great for an elegant lunch. The smoked salmon with capers and chicken-salad sandwich are first-rate….and this is definitely the place to enjoy a pastry for dessert.

Cancun's Family Mexican Restaurant (845-835-8207), 7483 South Broadway, Red Hook. ($) Open daily 11-10; until 11 on Friday and Saturday. This restaurant serves up tasty Mexican treats at reasonable prices. Their tacos, enchiladas and mole sauce are excellent and the service is quick and efficient. A children's menu is available.

Grand Cru (845-876-6992), 6384 Mill Street (Route 9), Rhinebeck. ($) Open daily Monday through Thursday noon-9; Friday and Saturday noon-11; Sunday noon-7. Enjoy a craft beer or glass of wine along with a cheese plate at this market also serving a variety of brews. Owner Rod Johnson offers live music quite often in the evening; this is a lively place where something is always "brewing."

Holy Cow (845-758-5959), 7270 South Broadway, Red Hook. ($) Open year-round, Monday through Saturday 11-10; Sunday until 9. The line can be long here on hot summer nights for a good reason: They have some of the best soft-serve ice cream in the Hudson Valley. The prices are very inexpensive, too. If you have a craving for a sundae, shake, or cone, this is the place to go. There are myriad toppings to choose from. My favorite is the chocolate "flying saucer," the circular ice cream sandwich I loved as a child with chocolate ice cream inside!

J & J'S Gourmet Café (845-758-9030), 1 East Market Street, Red Hook ($). Open Monday through Friday 7:30-5; Saturday 8-4; Sunday 9-4. ($) I love this place for hearty soups, wraps, sandwiches and salads. There's an informal atmosphere in the center of town and Julianne, the new owner (2017) has added some interesting choices to the standards, like a tasty quinoa bowl salad, one of my favorites. This eatery is good for both take-out and dining in. Children are welcome.

Samuel's (845-876-5312), 42 East Market Street, Rhinebeck. ($) Open daily 8-6. In July and August there are extended hours. This small confectionery and coffee shop is the perfect place to enjoy a cup of high-quality coffee, tea, or hot chocolate after browsing the stores in town. The cookies and biscotti are delicious. Children will be delighted by the attractively displayed penny candy and gourmet jellybeans. Although there is a variety of truffles, hand-dipped chocolates, and sugar-free sweets, the place is quite small, so take-out is the way to go here!

Taste Budd's Chocolate and Coffee Café (845-758-6500), 40 Market Street, Red Hook. ($) Open daily 7am-9pm. The fare here includes sandwiches, soups, wraps, veggie burgers, and vegan options. Capital City Coffee Roasters coffee is served here, and there is a list of dozens of teas. The baked goods are created on the premises and some of the pastries are obtained locally. This is a gathering place for Bard students, with an atmosphere reminiscent of a 1960s coffeehouse. Children are welcome and will feel comfortable here.

Southwestern Dutchess County
(Poughkeepsie, Fishkill, Beacon)

Antonella's (845-229-1200), 4246 Albany Post Road (Route 9; in a strip mall), Hyde Park. Open Tuesday through Sunday 11-10. Good thin-crust and Sicilian pizza are served up here, as well as all the Italian specialties. This is a family restaurant with authentic home cooking. Service can be spotty, so beware. Children welcome.

Apple Pie Bakery Café at the Culinary Institute (845-905-4500), 1946 Campus Drive (off Route 9), Hyde Park. ($) Open Monday through Friday 7:30-5. Enjoy fine, fresh soups, salads, sandwiches, and pizzas at reasonable prices in this eatery, where students in baking and pastry arts programs run the show. The cookies, brownies and other dessert creations are first-rate. This is a great stop for breakfast or lunch, as well as take-out. Children are welcome.

BC Kitchen (845-485-8411), 1-3 Collegeview Avenue, Poughkeepsie. ($$) Open Tuesday through Saturday 8am-9pm; until 10 on Friday and Saturday; Sunday 8-4. Closed Monday. Located near Vassar College, this popular eatery gets busy at lunchtime. They are known for their salads, signature sandwiches, and burgers. Breakfasts are served all day. Children welcome.

Beacon Falls Café (845-765-0172), 472 Main Street, Beacon. ($) Open Monday, Tuesday and Thursday 11:30-4; Friday 11:30-9; Saturday 10-9; Sunday 10-4. Closed Tuesday and Wednesday. This informal American bistro serves a particularly good brunch. The pancakes, fritatas, and bananas Foster French toast are recommended. There are salads, Reubens, and Panini for lunch; the back blue burger is delicious. Generous portions; children welcome.

Coffee Bean Café (845-452-4400), 35 Main Street (by the train station), Poughkeepsie. ($) There are paninis, sandwiches, salads and soups as well as breakfast specials—and good coffee. Make this a stop before heading to Manhattan on the train.

Deliziosa Pastry Shoppe (845-471-3636), 10 Mount Carmel Place, Poughkeepsie. ($) Open Monday 9-5; Tuesday through Saturday 8-7; Sunday 8-6. This wonderful shop is a throwback to another era, so make sure to stop in for dessert if you are in the area. They have been in business for decades and the cannolis and butter cookies are the best!

Cup and Saucer Tea Room (845-831-6287), 165 Main Street, Beacon. ($) Open Monday and Wednesday 11-3; Thursday through Sunday 11-5; Closed Tuesday. There are seasonal high teas, and reservations must be made in advance. A Victorian tearoom, decorated with teatime accessories throughout, serves up hot grilled sandwiches, veggie and grilled chicken salads, quiche, soups, and desserts. A specialty of the house is the Portobello club sandwich. Not recommended for those with young children.

Ella's Bellas Gluten-Free Bakery (845-765-8502), 418 Main Street, Beacon. ($) Open daily, except Tuesday, 8-6. The treats here are both healthy and delicious and you won't be able to tell what is gluten-free, so indulge!

Eveready Diner (845-229-8100), 4184 Albany Post Road (Route 9), Hyde Park. ($) Open Sunday through Thursday 7am-1am; Friday and Saturday 24 hours. This retro 1950s-style diner is difficult to miss when traveling along Route 9. The Food Network featured their delicious pancakes, my favorite menu item here, but this community oasis is known locally for comfort food like meat loaf and macaroni and cheese. The apple pie is made on the premises with fruit fresh from the owner's orchard. A children's menu is available.

Gino's Pizza and Restaurant (845-297-8061), 1671 Route 9, Wappingers Falls (Lafayette Plaza). ($) Open daily, except Monday, 11:30-9; until 10 on Friday and Saturday. Enjoy Italian-style home cooking in this family-owned and operated casual dining spot. They offer a range of pizzas, pasta dishes, heros, and sandwiches in addition to lasagna, veal parmigiana, calamari, and much more. Children are welcome.

Homespun Foods (845-831-5096), 232 Main Street, Beacon. ($) Open daily 8-5. This is a great laid-back spot for breakfast or lunch. I've had the pulled pork

Jeanie Bean's, an eclectic eatery serving breakfast and lunch in Clinton Corners, also sells food products imported from England and Ireland.

quesadilla, shrimp and sweet potato muffaletta, smoked trout salad, and black bean burger. This is one of my favorite eateries in Beacon.

Hyde Park Brewery (845-229-8277), 4076 Albany Post Road, Hyde Park. ($) Open Wednesday through Saturday 11-10; Sunday noon-9; Monday and Tuesday 4-10. They brew their own beer here (about 1000 barrels per year), and there are several different kinds to choose from, both light and dark varieties. The fare includes creative international specials at reasonable prices. I enjoy the vegetarian pita sandwich: grilled Portobello mushrooms layered with mozzarella, roasted red peppers, and pesto mayo. This is a good stop for lunch; it is conveniently located across the road from the FDR Home. Children are welcome.

Julie's Restaurant (845-452-6078), 49 Raymond Avenue, Poughkeepsie. ($) Open Monday, Tuesday, Wednesday and Friday 7-3; Thursday 7am-8pm; Saturday and Sunday 8-2. Julie and her husband serve great breakfast wraps (try the Vassar or Greek wraps, my favorites) along with pancakes, omelets, and great oatmeal. Lunches include burgers, salads, sandwiches and soups. This is a popular local eatery with a loyal following. Children are welcome.

Lola's Café (845-471-8555), 131 Washington Street, Poughkeepsie. ($) Open Monday through Saturday 10-5. There are some wonderful variations on the usual sandwich selections here. Tropical curried-chicken wrap and marinated Portobello-mushroom Panini are just a couple of the intriguing selections offered at lunch time. This is a great stop if you're planning to pick up take-out for a picnic or just want to grab something and go.

Maya Café & Cantina (845-896-4042), 448 Route 9, Fishkill. ($$) Open daily 11am-10pm; Friday and Saturday until 11. Authentic Mayan cuisine from Guatemala and the Yucatan region of Mexico served in a colorful, upbeat atmosphere. Adorning the walls are striking murals hand-painted by local artists. In addition to tacos, enchiladas, and quesadillas, there is always a variety of interesting specials. Save room for the chimi banana dessert (cheesecake and banana wrapped in a tortilla, deep-fried, then drizzled with caramel, chocolate syrup, and whipped cream). Children are welcome here.

Palace Diner (845-473-1576), 294 Washington Street, Poughkeepsie. ($) Open daily 24 hours. This well-established gathering place near Marist College, just off Route 9, has been a mainstay of the community. It is a popular place for lunch among county attorneys and politicians. In addition to the usual diner fare, there are Greek and international dishes, as well as several daily specials. Children are welcome.

Rossi & Sons (845-471-0654), 45 South Clover Street, Poughkeepsie. ($) Open Monday through Friday 7:30-6; Saturday 8-5; closed Sunday. This is a wonderful Italian deli/eatery with both hot and cold goodies, gourmet imported products, and some of the best sandwiches in the county. Everything is made fresh before you, and there's outdoor seating in the warm weather. Avoid lunch hours if you don't want to wait on line!

Taco Gol (845-471-3223), 553 Main Street, Poughkeepsie. ($) Open daily, except Tuesday, 8am-10pm. They close at 9pm on Sunday. This informal Mexican restaurant features excellent fare at rock-bottom prices. There are tacos, enchiladas, and several Mexican specialties, as well as tortas for dessert. The daily specials are a good value. Children are welcome.

Tiramisu (845-227-8707), 810 Route 82, Hopewell Junction. ($) Open daily 11-10; until 11 on Saturday. This family-oriented eatery in a strip mall features brick over-baked pizzas of all kinds: there are an array of pasta dishes, and Chicken Tiramisu, a dish that includes chicken breast, roasted red peppers, onions, and artichokes over pasta in a light marinara sauce. Children are welcome and the reasonable prices here make it a popular place with local residents.

Tomato Café (845-896-7779), 1123 Main Street, Fishkill. ($) Open daily 11-9; until 10 Friday and Saturday; Sunday 9-3. This café has an enormous menu with imaginative creations to please just about any taste. There are eggplant cakes, a specialty of the house, wings, salads, sandwiches, pizzas and pastas.

Everything is prepared to order and portions are generous. This is a great family dining place favored by Fishkill residents.

Northeastern Dutchess County
(Millbrook, Millerton)

Babette's Kitchen (845-677-8602), 3293 Franklin Avenue, Millbrook. ($) Open daily, except Tuesday, 7-5; until 6 Friday and Saturday; Sunday 8-4. This eatery has some of the best healthful gourmet sandwiches, salads, soups, wraps, coffee and baked goods in Millbrook. It's a favorite of mine and the owner, Beth, prepares everything to order. Children are welcome and prices are reasonable for the high quality.

Harney's Tea Room (518-789-2121), 13 Main Street, Millerton. ($) Open daily 10-5; Sunday 11-4. This charming eatery, part of the delightful store where you can purchase hundreds of fantastic loose teas, serves fine lunches. There are salads, soups, and an array of intriguing sandwich selections served on whole wheat bread or baguettes baked fresh daily. Although it's a small dining area off the restaurant, this is a cozy place to enjoy brunch or lunch and relax after shopping in Millerton.

Irving Farm Coffee House (518-789-2020), 44 Main Street, Millerton. ($) Open daily 7-5. Diners may enjoy breakfast sandwiches, waffles, fresh baked muffins, scones and pastries at this spacious informal eatery. For lunch, curried chicken salad sandwich, roast turkey, and several panini, quiche, soup and salad selections are offered. They brew some of the best coffee you will find in the Hudson Valley. The eatery is definitely a hub of Millerton.

Millbrook Diner (845-677-5319), 3266 Franklin Avenue, Millbrook. ($) Open daily 6am-9pm. This small diner is a local hangout renowned for their club sandwiches, Reubens, burgers, and wraps. The fare is simple yet hearty. Kids will be comfortable here.

Taro's Pizzeria and Restaurant (518-789-6630), 18 Main Street, Millerton. ($) Open for lunch and dinner Tuesday through Sunday 11:30-9; dinner Monday 4:30-9. First opened in 1989, this basic, informal Italian eatery serves grinders (subs), calzones, eggplant Florentine, pastas of all kinds and pizza (Sicilian, white, and New York style). There are 23 types of gourmet pizzas and over a dozen kinds of fresh salads. The portions are generous and the prices are reasonable. They accept cash and checks only—no credit cards. Children are welcome.

Southeastern Dutchess County

Beekman Square Restaurant (845-223-3401), 2515 Route 55, Poughquag. ($) Open daily 8am -10pm; Sunday 7:30-9. Early in the day enjoy three-egg omelets, chocolate-chip or banana-walnut pancakes, cinnamon-raisin French toast, or Belgian waffles at this neighborhood eatery specializing in international favorites. They offer French onion soup, grilled chicken Caesar salad, quesadillas and make their own breads. The Beekman Square burger includes bacon, onion, mushrooms, and cheese. Bourbon Street ribs are marinated in homemade light barbecue sauce. There is an extensive children's menu here.

ENTERTAINMENT

THEATER & DANCE

Bardavon 1869 Opera House (845-473-2072; bardavon.org), 35 Market Street, Poughkeepsie. Open year-round. First named the Collingwood Opera House, this elegant concert hall was constructed in 1869 and is the oldest continuously operating theater in New York State. The dramatic dome ceiling has sheltered everything from movies and rock concerts to ballet and dramatic theater. Mark Twain, Frank Sinatra, Sarah Bernhardt, John Phillip Sousa, and Al Pacino are among the entertainers who have performed on the 816-square-foot stage. After being added to the National Register of Historic Places in 1978, the Bardavon has undergone more than $3 million worth of renovations. It is the perfect place to enjoy a symphony, rock concert or comedian. Check the website to see what's happening during your time in Dutchess County.

Center for Performing Arts at Rhinebeck (845-876-3080; centerforperformingarts.org), 661 Route 308, Rhinebeck. Open year-round. This multipurpose cultural and education center features dramatic plays, musicals, dance, concerts, lectures and workshops. There are also children's shows.

Cocoon Theatre (845-452-7870; cocoontheatre.org), 9 Vassar Street, Cunneen-Hackett Art Center Poughkeepsie. This non-profit educational arts organization presents drama and dance performances for all ages year-round.

County Players Falls Theatre (845-298-1491; countyplayers.org), 2681 West Main Street, Wappingers Falls. Four or five productions are offered annually by this community-theater group. The work usually consists of traditional Broadway fare. The theater is large, the seats are comfortable, and the productions I have attended were light entertainment well done.

Cunneen-Hackett Arts Center (845-486-4571; cunneen-hackett.org), 9 Vassar Street, Poughkeepsie. They host dance, music, drama, lectures, films, and plays here. There is a 200-seat theater.

Fisher Center for the Performing Arts (845-758-7900;fishercenter.bard.edu), 30 Campus Road, Annandale-on-Hudson. Internationally distinguished performing arts center, designed by renowned architect Frank Gehry, has two theaters offering music, opera, drama, and dance performances. There are tours of the Sosnoff Theater Monday through Friday from 10am to 4:30pm.

Howland Cultural Center (845-831-4988; howlandculturalcenter.org), 477 Main Street, Beacon, sponsors exhibits, concerts, and workshops year-round in a late-19th-century building designed by famed architect Richard Morris Hunt.

Kaatsbaan International Dance Center (845-757-5106; kaatsbaan.org), 120 Broadway, Tivoli. Open year-round. This performance center for all types of dance, as well as a working retreat center, is dedicated to the growth, advancement, and preservation of professional dance. Located in a renovated space on a spectacularly scenic 153-acre setting (a former horse farm) overlooking the Hudson River, Kaatsbaan is Dutch for "playing field". They present an array of multi-ethnic dance companies. The former Callendar House farm developed by the Livingston family in the 18th century and turned into a horse farm by the Osborne family is now home to three dance studios, one of which serves as a 160-seat public theater. The historic barns and cottage were designed at the turn of the 20th century in the shingled Arts and Crafts style. There are open rehearsals here in addition to workshops, world premieres, and performances. The website lists a complete schedule.

Powerhouse Theater at Vassar College (845-437-5599; 437-5902; powerhouse. vassar.edu), Summer Theater at Vassar College, 124 Raymond Avenue, Poughkeepsie. Dramatic performances are offered in June and July only, Tuesday through Saturday at 8pm; Saturday and Sunday at 2 and 8. Admission. Each summer since 1985, New York Stage and Film, in conjunction with Vassar, has presented new plays premiered in a professional-theater venue. The name is derived from the actual powerhouse on the Vassar campus,

Flamenco dancers performing at Kaatsbaan International Dance Center in Tivoli.

built in 1912 to accommodate the college's changeover from gas to electric power. In 1973 the original structure was reinvented as a black-box theater and renamed the Hallie Flanagan Davis Powerhouse Theater, in memory of the legendary dramatist who created the Experimental Theater at Vassar College. Productions have been consistently of excellent quality and have featured the likes of Juliana Margulies, Kyra Sedgwick, David Strathairn, Jill Clayburgh, and John Heard, to name some of the actors who have been part of this dynamic venue.

MISCELLANEOUS VENUES

Art Along the Hudson (845-454-3222; artalongtheHudson.com) There are monthly arts celebrations, openings and exhibits in 13 communities along the Hudson River. There are Second Saturdays in Beacon, Third Saturday in Rhinebeck (Art Walk), Poughkeepsie and Hyde Park. Check the website for current information.

Carmine's Comedy Club at Umberto's (845-464-1572), 2245 South Road (Route 9), Poughkeepsie. On weekend evenings this club presents some top-notch comedy stars.

The Chance (845-471-1966; the chancetheater.com), 6 Crannell Street, Poughkeepsie. This downtown nightclub showcases national musical acts, including rock'n'roll, R&B, and blues. The club is housed in a building constructed in 1912 for vaudeville acts.

Hyde Park Drive-In (845-229-4738; hydeparkdrivein.com), 4114 Albany Post Road (Route 9), Hyde Park. This theater has been open since 1949 and is located on 12 acres with a full-service snack bar and radio sound. They are open every night, April through September, and Tuesday is bargain day with reduced rates.

Moviehouse (518-789-0022; themoviehouse.net), 48 Main Street, Millerton. This terrific independent cinema screens mainstream Hollywood movies as well as art films and documentaries. There are three theaters and usually there are films to please all tastes. Check the website for a schedule.

Overlook Drive-In (845-452-3445; hydeparkdrivein.com), 126 DeGarmo Road, Poughkeepsie, is owned by the same company as the Hyde Park Drive-In; it is open every night from April through September.

Towne Crier Café (845-855-1300; townecrier.com), 379 Main Street, Beacon. Open Wednesday through Sunday evenings, this club presents live folk, jazz, blues and zydeco artists with an array of performers. They are renowned for excellent entertainment throughout the Hudson Valley. The website has a current list of entertainment.

Upstate Films (845-876-2515; upstatefilms.org), 6415 Montgomery Street (Route 9), Rhinebeck. Open year-round. There are two to three films daily in the two theaters here (matinees on holidays, weekends, and Fridays), and you won't find the usual mall offerings. Provocative international cinema is featured, including foreign, independent, documentary, and animated films. Guest speakers appear regularly—filmmakers and critics—often to discuss their work after it is screened. This theater a local treasure, especially in these days of mostly meaningless commercial movies. Upstate has a large local following, so get there early and enjoy their wonderful popcorn made to your liking and home-baked goods, coffee and tea for sale in the lobby. This is one of my favorite winter haunts!

SELECTIVE SHOPPING

ARTS & CRAFTS/BOOKS/GALLERIES

Albert Shahinian Fine Art (845-876-7578), 22 East Market Street (third floor), Rhinebeck. This gallery has changing exhibitions and specializes in the work of Hudson Valley artists. Open Thursday through Saturday 11-6; Sunday noon-5, and by appointment or chance.

Arrowsmith (845-677-5687), 3788 Route 44, Millbrook. Open Wednesday through Saturday 10-5. This is one of the few remaining places to purchase custom steel furniture, lamps, and other accessories made at their own forge. They also operate a gift shop at 3275 Franklin Street in Millbrook.

Barrett Art Center (845-471-2550), 55 Noxon Street, Poughkeepsie, is open Wednesday through Friday 10-3; Saturday noon-3. You will find exhibits of distinguished Hudson River School and other American artists here.

Beacon Artist Union-BAU (845-440-7584), 506 Main Street, Beacon. Open Friday 3-8; Saturday and Sunday noon-6, or by appointment. This cooperative gallery features the works of local artists.

Betsy Jacaruso Studio and Gallery (845-516-4435), The Courtyard, 43 East Market Street, Rhinebeck. Open Thursday through Saturday 11-5; Sunday 11-4, or by appointment. Enjoy luminous landscape in watercolor as well as works by regional artists.

Country Thistle (845-635-8642), Key Food Plaza, 1600 Main Street (Route 44), Pleasant Valley. Open Monday through Saturday 10:30-5:30; Thursday until 7. Closed Sunday. There are terrific cards and gifts in this emporium that combines traditional and contemporary items. Owner Susan Holland took over this shop ten years ago and has created a great place to find just the right unusual gift. No need to go to the mall!

Gilmor Glass (518-789-8000), 2 Main Street, Millerton, is open Monday through Friday 11-5; Saturday 10-5; Sunday 11-4. Their hand-blown glass has been made at this working studio since 1977. Enjoy watching the bowls, ornaments, vases and special pieces being created before your eyes.

Hammertown (845-876-1450), 6240 Montgomery Street, Rhinebeck, and 3201 Route 199, Pine Plains (518-398-7075), has country wares, folk art, and primitives. Both stores are filled with terrific gift items, fine linens, coffee table books, and more. Make sure to stop in when you are in Rhinebeck or Pine Plains!

Hudson Beach Glass (845-831-3116), 162 Main Street, Beacon. Open Monday through Saturday 10-6; Sunday 11-6. There are four artists whose hand-cast glass, using an ancient process, is exhibited here. Both sculptural and functional objects are on display and for sale.

Hyde Park Oriental Market (845-452-7940), 419 Violet Avenue (Route 9G), Poughkeepsie. This amazing emporium sells an array of Filipino and Asian food items. Those who love to cook and enjoy creating Asian dishes should definitely stop here. The place is exotic, immaculate and owned by a family who are exceedingly pleasant and helpful.

Merritt Bookstore & Toystore (845-677-5857), 55-57 Front Street, Millbrook. Open daily 9-6; Sunday 10-5. Kira Wizner took over this bookstore in recent years and created a cultural hub of the community as well as the eastern part of Dutchess County. In addition to a wide range of fiction and nonfiction, there are terrific toys and children's books. The spacious room upstairs hosts several author talks and other activities.

Oblong Books and Music—26 Main Street, Millerton (518-789-3797) & 6422 Montgomery Street (Route 9), Rhinebeck (845-876-0500). The Millerton store is open daily 10-6; Rhinebeck 10-8; Friday and Saturday until 9; Sunday 10-6. Dick and Suzanna Hermans have owned and operated this fantastic bookstore

for decades. I cross the Hudson River to attend several amazing events they host (book signings and talks)—as well as to purchase books in these wonderful community resources. In recent years, I have heard Hillary Clinton, Ralph Nader, Joan Juliet Buck, and many other authors and celebrities discussing their latest books. Bibliophiles take note!

Saperstein's in Millerton has been in the same family for three generations carrying all kinds of quality clothing at exceedingly reasonable prices.

Paper Trail (845-876-8050), 6423 Montgomery Street (Route 9), Rhinebeck. Open daily 11-6; closing Sunday at 5. Serine Hastings and Maureen Missner have the best cards you will find anywhere in the region. In addition, there are beautiful invitations, wrapping paper, gift books, and dozens of unique items that will delight just about anyone. This is a must-stop in the busy village of Rhinebeck!

Periwinkles (845-876-4014), 24 East Market Street, Rhinebeck. Open Monday through Friday 11-5; Saturday 10-6; Sunday 10-5. This is definitely an eclectic gift shop carrying everything from fabulous soaps and colognes to books, clothing and ceramics. Located in the center of town, make sure to pop in and look around when you visit Rhinebeck.

Millerton is renowned for its wonderful shops on Main Street, including Terni's, an old-fashioned store with fishing tackle, outdoor clothing, retro candy and more.

RiverWinds Gallery (845-838-2880), 172 Main Street, Beacon. Open Wednesday through Monday noon-6; Second Saturday of the month noon-9. This art space features the work of over 50 Hudson Valley artists. There is photography, crafts, clothing, and fine art. This is definitely worth a stop when you are in Beacon.

Sugar Plum Boutique (845-876-6729), 71 East Market Street, Rhinebeck, is open daily 10-6, with unique sterling and gemstone jewelry as well as clothing from England and California, all at reasonable prices.

Tivoli Artists Gallery (845-757-2667), 60 Broadway, Tivoli. Open Friday 5-9; Saturday 1-9; Sunday 1-5. There are over 30 artists represented in this gallery that includes painting, sculpture, jewelry, photographs, ceramics and digital art. Exhibits change monthly.

Winter Sun & Summer Moon (845-876-3555), 12 East Market Street, Rhinebeck. Open Monday through Saturday 10-5; Sunday 11- 4. They carry distinctive shoes, women's clothing, jewelry, craft items, and natural makeup and skin care products in these two adjoining shops on the main shopping street in town. While there are several places to visit in Rhinebeck, don't pass up this one.

AUCTIONS AND ANTIQUES

Lovers of antiques and collectibles will have a field day in Dutchess County, where it seems every village boasts a selection of fine antiques shops. Clocks, vintage clothing, fine china, and Hudson River School paintings are all waiting for a home. It's easy to spend an afternoon looking for that one-of-a-kind treasure. The search is made easier at antiques centers that offer a cluster of dealers in one building and regular hours year-round.

Annex Antiques Center (845-758-2843), 7578 North Broadway, Red Hook, is filled with Victorian and country furniture, jewelry, collectibles, and Americana. **George Cole Auctions** (845-758-9114; georgecoleauctions.com), at the same location, holds auctions every Saturday beginning at 5pm.

Beekman Arms Antique Market and Gallery (845-876-3477), 6387 Mill Street (behind the Beekman Arms), is a multidealer antiques emporium open daily 11-5.

Hopewell Antiques Center (845-221-3055), 2 Church Street, Hopewell Junction has over 20 dealers in one place; all are open year-round, daily 11-5.

Hudson Valley Auctioneers (845-831-6800; hudsonvalleyauctioneers.com), 432 Main Street, Beacon, conducts auctions of fine European and American antiques year-round. The website has a schedule.

Hyde Park Antiques Center (845-229-8200), 4192 Route 9, Hyde Park, has over 50 dealers and a large range of specialty collectibles and antiques. Open daily 10-5.

Millbrook Antique Center (845-677-3921), 3283 Franklin Avenue, has nearly 50 different mini shops under one roof. Open daily 11-5; Sunday open at noon.

Millbrook Antiques Mall (845-677-9311), 3301 Franklin Avenue, specializes in dealers of 18th-century furniture. Open daily 11-5; Sunday open at noon.

Millerton Antiques Center (518-789-6004), 25 Main Street, Millerton, has over 30 dealers under one roof. Open daily, except Wednesday, 10-5; extended hours on weekends.

Ole Carousel Antiques Center (845-702-7622), 6208 Route 82, Stanfordville, offers a large collection of books, records, and home décor items.

Red Hook Antique Center (845-758-2223)), 7531 North Broadway (Route 9), Red Hook, features several dealers. They are open daily, except Tuesday, 11-5.

Rhinebeck Antique Emporium (845-876-8168), 5229 Albany Post Road (Route 9), Staatsburg, is open daily 10-5. They are south of the village of Rhinebeck and offer an array of vintage items, china, lamps, furniture and more.

The Stormville Airport Antique Show & Flea Market (845-221-6561; stormvilleairportfleamarket.com), 428 Route 216, Stormville. Open one weekend each month from late April through October. There are over 600 vendors here offering apparel, jewelry, tools, housewares, antiques, art, gourmet food and more. Free admission and free parking, but no pets are allowed. The show goes on rain or shine. One Saturday and Sunday per month 8-4. Check website for exact dates.

SPECIAL EVENTS

May: **Rhinebeck Antique Car Show & Swap** (845-876-4001), Dutchess County Fairgrounds, 6550 Spring Brook Avenue, Rhinebeck. This is one of the largest weekend car shows in the Northeast, including hot rods and custom vehicles and pre-1977 unmodified antique classic cars. There is also a car corral and swap meet, handcrafts building and food court.

Music in the Parks (845-229-8086; dutchesstourism.com), at both the Vanderbilt National Historic Site in Hyde Park and the Staatsburgh State Historic Site in Staatsburg. From Memorial Day weekend, through August, there is a series of free outdoor concerts. This is the time to get the blankets and lawn chairs, pack a picnic, and enjoy the evening overlooking the Hudson River with the sounds of the area's fine bands. The website lists the summer offerings.

June: **Country Living Fair** (845-876-4001), Dutchess County Fairgrounds, 6550 Spring Brook Avenue, Rhinebeck. Sponsored by *Country Living* magazine, this is a popular spring weekend event with dozens of booths and a large food court.

Rhinebeck Crafts Festival (845-876-4001), Dutchess County Fairgrounds, 6550 Spring Brook Avenue, Rhinebeck. The fine contemporary crafts and fine art at this juried weekend show are first-rate.

July: **Bard Summerscape** (845-758-7900; fishercenter.bard.edu), Bard College campus, Annandale-on-Hudson. This performing-arts festival includes music, dance, opera, and film. It runs from early July through mid-August and events are held on the campus in various venues, including the Spiegeltent which is renowned for theater, comedy and wonderful professional entertainment.

Hudson Valley Hot Air Balloon Festival at Barton Orchards (845-454-1700), Barton Orchards, 63 Apple Tree Lane, Poughquag.

Film director, John Waters, performing at the Spiegeltent at Bard College, part of the annual Summerscape entertainment.

Sponsored by the Dutchess County Regional Chamber of Commerce, hot air balloon rides are offered in the morning and evening, weather permitting. This is great family entertainment with rides for the kids, a variety of vendors and fireworks at night.

August: **Dutchess County Fair** (845-876-4001; dutchessfair.com), Dutchess County Fairgrounds, 6550 Spring Brook Avenue, Rhinebeck. Held toward the end of the month, Tuesday through Sunday 10am-midnight. Admission. For the largest and some say the best, county fair in the region, a stop at this event is in order. There are large display buildings, show arenas, a racetrack, food court vendors, rides, and more. Plenty of livestock is displayed, and name entertainment is offered in the evening. The colorful, noisy midway attracts all ages.

Livestock at the Dutchess County Fair: there are still dozens of small dairy farms in the county.

September: **Art Studio Views** (845-876-7578; artsnortherndutchess.org). Visit the private studios of over 25 Dutchess County artists; most are rarely open to the public. The studios are open on Saturday and Sunday of Labor Day weekend. The website lists hours and details.

Hudson River Valley Ramble (518-473-3835; hudsonvalleyramble.com). More than 100 guided walking, hiking, kayaking, biking, and equestrian events are held in 10 counties during the third weekend in September. There are several sites in Dutchess County included in the fun with planned activities. The website offers a schedule and locations.

Hudson Valley Wine & Food Festival (845-658-7181; hudsonvalleywinefest. com), Dutchess County Fairgrounds, 6550 Spring Brook Avenue. Rhinebeck. Open Saturday 11-6; Sunday 11-5. Admission. There are dozens of wine tastings, gourmet treats, farmers' markets, cooking demos, and live music at this annual celebration of Hudson Valley wines. Finger Lakes wineries are in attendance as well.

Hahn Farm Fall Festival (845-266-5042; Hahn farm.com), 1331 Netherwood Road, Salt Point, is held every weekend from mid-September through October, Saturday and Sunday 11-5. Children will enjoy the hayrides, corn maze, pony rides, and all kinds of family fun at this annual harvest celebration. Artisans demonstrate spinning, weaving and sheep shearing. Pumpkins are everywhere and they come in orange, white and warty varieties! The website has a schedule of events.

October: **Gathering of Old Cars** (845-889-8851), Staatsburgh State Historic Site, 75 Mills Mansion Road, Staatsburg. Open 11-4. Admission. This get-together for antique autos at Mills Mansion, is sponsored by the Red Hook Car Club. It's a wonderful way to visit the site and enjoy its grand location on the Hudson River.

NYS Sheep & Wool Festival (845-876-4001), Dutchess County Fairgrounds, 6550 Spring Brook Avenue, Rhinebeck. This is an amazing event with spinning, dyeing and weaving expos and livestock for sale. The weavers who attend have excellent products for sale and the festival is renowned throughout the Northeast and attracts an interesting dedicated clientele.

Pumpkin Festival (845-831-6962), Beacon Riverfront Park (adjacent to Metro North train station), 1 Ferry Plaza, Beacon. Free. Open noon-6. Enjoy music, environmental displays, food, and pumpkins at this riverfront festival. Those with children should not pass up this celebration.

November: **Holiday Crafts Fair** (845-431-8400), Dutchess Community College, 53 Pendell Road, Poughkeepsie. This is one of the county's largest Christmas fairs featuring craftspeople, food vendors and fun for the kids.

December: **Historic Hyde Park Christmas Celebration and Open House** (845-229-7770), Vanderbilt Mansion, 119 Vanderbilt Park Road (off Route 9), Hyde Park. This delightful annual event is usually held the first weekend in December. An array of activities, music, refreshments and beautiful holiday decorations delight visitors at the open house. The decorations continue throughout the month of December.

Sinterklaas in Rhinebeck (845-758-5519), an old Dutch tradition in the Hudson Valley, is an amazing festival held throughout the town on the first Saturday in December. Don't miss this celebration if you have young children. There are parades, performances of all kinds, open houses, a children's parade, art exhibits, Dutch treats, and, of course, Santa Claus. Dutchess County resident Jeanne Fleming has been coordinating this expanding event since the early 1980s.

A number of tree lightings, parades, and open houses take place at the various historic sites and great estates throughout the county during December. Check dutchesstourism. com for a complete list of these events if you visit the county during the holiday season.

Bard College is where many special events, lectures and concerts may be attended year-round.

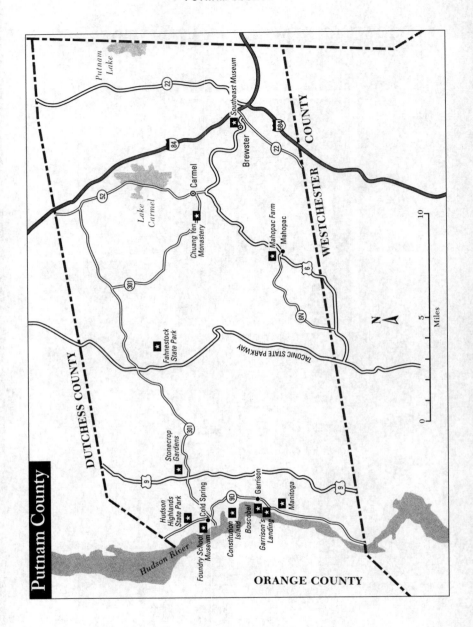

PUTNAM COUNTY

One of the gateways to the Hudson Highlands, Putnam County offers splendid river views, lots of outdoor entertainment, and a chance to see small-town America before it disappears completely.

In Cold Spring the tiny shops and riverside gazebo are charming reminders of a more leisurely past. The Federal mansion called Boscobel (which came within hours of being demolished) has been restored to its former elegance. A spring walk through the gardens there offers thousands of flowers in full color, blooming with scent. There are acres of wetlands, lakes, forests, and meadows in Putnam, beckoning the hiker, walker, and nature lover. A very different outdoor environment was created at Manitoga, where industrial designer Russel Wright constructed Dragon Rock, a unique home built into the wall of a quarry. In this county you can drive along rustic roads, smell apple blossoms, see houses that date from before the Revolution, stop at an art gallery, or just laze away an afternoon watching the Hudson River. Route 9D from the Bear Mountain Bridge goes past many historic areas. Route 9 is the old Albany Post Road and has been in constant use for more than two centuries. Just an hour from Manhattan, Putnam County can seem a century away, with a pace and a grace all its own.

VISITOR INFORMATION

Putnam County Visitors Bureau (845-808-1015), 40 Gleneida Avenue, Carmel 10512; tourputnam.org.

GETTING THERE

By car: Interstate 84, Route 684, the Taconic State Parkway, Routes 9 and 9D all go through the county.

By train: Metro North (Harlem and Hudson lines) stops in Brewster, Garrison and Cold Spring.

MEDICAL EMERGENCY

Putnam Hospital Center (845-279-5711); 670 Stoneleigh Avenue, Carmel.

VILLAGES

Cold Spring. This beautiful river town was founded in the 18th century and, according to legend, got its name from George Washington's comment on the temperature of the water in a local spring. The village received an economic boost in the 19th century when it became the site of one of the largest iron foundries in the country. West Point Foundry produced everything from weapons to some rather unusual furniture, and some pieces may be seen at the Tarrytown home of Washington Irving in Westchester County.

On Main Street you can visit several shops that specialize in everything from rare books and vintage clothing to knick knacks and brass beds. The best way to explore the village is to wander up and down Main Street. Make sure to continue down to the railroad tracks where you will find a plaque commemorating Washington's visit. The bandstand here was constructed for riverside concerts—now it provides a place to look across the Hudson to Storm King Mountain, which true to its name, is the center of many storms.

At the corner of Main and West streets, follow West Street south to Market to see the Chapel of Our Lady. This one-room Greek Revival chapel was built in 1834 for workers at the foundry; it's the oldest Roman Catholic church in the region and was one of the most popular subjects for painters of the Hudson River School. The chapel looks across the river, but you may have to wait to get in on weekends since it's a popular place for weddings.

Garrison. The Landing overlooks the Hudson River at the railroad station, and it's the town's hub. In 1969 the riverside gazebo was used as the set for filming the movie *Hello, Dolly!* Today the Landing is home to the **Garrison Art Center** (845-424-3960; garrisonartcenter.org), which has exhibits, workshops, and special events, including an art fair, throughout the year. The center is open Tuesday through Sunday 10-5.

HISTORIC SITES AND MUSEUMS

Boscobel (845-265-3638; Boscobel.org), 1601 Route 9D, Garrison-on-Hudson. Open April through December, Wednesday through Monday 9:30-5. Admission. If you only have time to visit one site in Putnam County, this is the one to see.

Standing on a bluff overlooking the Hudson River, the country mansion known as Boscobel looks as if it had spent all of its 200 years in peace and prosperity. But appearances can be deceiving. States Morris Dyckman, a Loyalist of Dutch ancestry, began building the mansion in 1805 for himself and his wife,

Elizabeth Corne Dyckman, and their family. But he died before it was completed. Designed in the Federal style, Boscobel was furnished with elegant carpets, fine porcelain, and furniture from the best workshops in New York. The house remained in the family until 1888; from then on it had various owners, including the federal government. In 1955, the government decided it no longer wanted Boscobel, and the house was sold for $35 to a contractor, who stripped it of many of its architectural details and sold them off. Local people were so incensed that they tracked down the sections that had been sold; they salvaged and restored the other parts of the

Boscobel, an estate overlooking the Hudson River, and moved to its present site in Garrison, was built in the 18th century by States Dyckman.

house, and, finally, purchased land on which to re-erect the building. Today visitors will see Boscobel as it was, complete with elegant staircase, fine decorative objects, and period furniture made by New York craftspeople. It is requested visitors wear broad heeled walking shoes to tour the home, as this helps preserve the floors and rugs. There is now an exhibition gallery featuring paintings by Hudson River School artists Frank Anderson, Samuel Colman, Jasper Cropsey, David Johnson, and John Ferguson Weir. Changing exhibits are shown throughout the season.

Boscobel's grounds are enchanting as well. At the Gate House you can see the home of a middle-class family of the era and explore the Orangerie, a 19th-century greenhouse. In spring and summer the gardens at Boscobel blaze with thousands of flowers, including tulips, daffodils, roses, pansies and wildflowers. Special events are held all season, including concerts, children's workshops, candlelight holiday tours and lectures. From mid-June through August, there is the annual **Hudson Valley Shakespeare Festival**, with several different plays performed outdoors on the grounds under a tent (845-265-9575; HVShakespeare.org). It's a wonderful way to see Shakespeare!

Chuang Yen Monastery (845-225-1819; baus.org), 2020 Route 301, Carmel. Open April through December, daily 9-5. Every Saturday at 1pm there is a public tour offered. The monastery houses the largest Buddhist statue in the Western Hemisphere, as well as many other unique shrines, statues, and pieces of art. The library has more than 70,000 volumes, the majority of them Buddhist texts. A morning meditation session and seminar is held every Sunday followed by a vegetarian lunch and visitors are welcome to participate.

Graymoor (845-424-3671; graymoor.org), 1350 Route 9, Garrison. Open year-round, daily 10-5. Free. Founded by the Episcopal Church in 1898, this historic site is home of the Franciscan Friars of the Atonement. Today the site is an ecumenical retreat center, with nature trails and access to the Appalachian Trail.

Putnam History Museum (845-265-4010; putnamhistorymuseum.org), 63 Chestnut Street, Cold Spring. Open March through December, Wednesday through Sunday 11-5. Admission. The original Foundry School served the children of Irish immigrants and apprentices who were employed at the West Point Foundry. Today the 1820 building is a small museum. Exhibits offer a look at local history, including Civil War artillery weapons (the Parrott gun was developed by a West Point officer) that were constructed here. There are small collections of paintings and furniture. There is a horse-drawn cutter once owned by Julia Butterfield, who is said to have received the sleigh from the tsarina of Russia.

The **West Point Foundry Preserve** is located past the museum, at the south end of Chestnut Street and Route 9D (80 Kemble Avenue, at bridge). This 93-acre landscape is on the National Register of Historic Places and is now owned by by Scenic Hudson, an organization that occasionally organizes tours of the area (845-473-4440; scenichudson.org). The ironworks that operated here from 1817 through 1911 were once the most important military supplier in the United States. The restored wetlands may be viewed from a short loop trail that follows Foundry Brook. An exciting future lies ahead for this public park since it has been selected to participate in a new federal program involving green landscape design, construction and management, the Sustainable Sites Initiative (SITES). The goal is to develop a world-class outdoor museum dedicated to the ironworks' role in America's emergence as an industrial superpower. Soon the park will be part of this national effort to create sustainable landscape and revolutionize the way public spaces are created. (It is unclear in the Trump Era if funding will continue for this project.)

Southeast Museum (845-279-7500; southeastmuseum.org) 67 Main Street, Brewster. Open April through December, Tuesday through Friday 9-3; Saturday 9-noon. Donation. This Victorian-style building houses a small museum with an eclectic local collection of items. There are permanent exhibits on the Borden Dairy Condensory (condensed milk was developed by a Putnam County resident), the construction of the Croton Water System (a project remarkable for engineering innovations), the American circus, Harlem Line Railroad, and a large collection of minerals from local mines. History of Putnam County is also a focus of this museum and there are special events throughout the year. For history buffs, **Old Southeast Church** (845-279-7429), 1664 Route 22, Brewster (Old Croton Turnpike), open June to Labor Day, Sunday 2-5, may be of interest. Free. Founded in 1735 by Elisha Kent, this is the church most tenant farmers of the area attended in the 18th century. The present structure was built in 1794 and guides in period dress take visitors through the church on summer Sunday afternoons.

Stonecrop Gardens (845-265-2000; stonecrop.org), 81 Stonecrop Lane, Cold Spring. Admission. Open April through October, Monday through Saturday 10-5; and on certain Sundays. This 63-acre tranquil refuge set above the village of Cold Spring and surrounded by the Hudson Highlands is the former home of Anne and Frank Cabot. There are 12 acres of magnificent gardens, including woodland, water, rock, and grass gardens. According to the British-born director, several student interns live and work at Stonecrop each year to learn gardening techniques. Summer is the time to see ferns as well as the wisteria pavilion, which overlooks the pond garden, and the enclosed flower garden is bursting with color during the warm-weather months. There are bamboo groves and foliage throughout the fall. Don't miss the horticultural rarities on display here, like the largest herbaceous plant in the world, native to Brazil. Every season has something beautiful to offer, so call in advance to see what's in bloom if you're a garden aficionado!

ACTIVITIES

Putnam is a small county but there are places to pick your own crops as well as weekly farmers markets where organic meats, fruits, vegetables, and breads are available. Travelers will find local honey, maple syrup and wine to take home, reminders of the bounty of the Hudson Valley.

FARMERS' MARKETS

Brewster (914-671-6262), 15 Mt. Ebo Road South (off Doansburg Road & Route 22), Brewster. Open mid-June through November, Sunday 10-2.

Cold Spring (845-265-3611), 1601 Route 9D, Boscobel, Garrison. Open May through October, Saturday 8:30-1:30.

Putnam Valley (845-528-0066), 729 Peekskill Hollow Road (Tompkins Corners Methodist Church), Putnam Valley. Open mid-June through September, Friday 3-7.

FARM MARKETS, PICK-YOUR-OWN FARMS

Green Chimneys Farm & Wildlife Center (845-279-2995), 400 Doansburg Road, Brewster, is open year-round, Saturday and Sunday 10-3, and offers organically grown vegetables raised by the students of the Green Chimneys School. Organized free tours of the farm and wildlife center are given on weekends.

Maple Lawn Farm Market (845-424-4093), 2461 Route 9, Garrison, is open daily March through December and stocks seasonal produce, baked goods, cider and Christmas trees.

Niese's Maple Farm (845-526-3748), 146 Wiccopee Road, Putnam Valley. Open Saturday and Sunday, 10-3. Since 1892, seven generations of the Niese family have been producing maple syrup and honey on this farm. During March through November there are pancake breakfasts on the weekends.

Ryder Farm (845-279-4161), 400 Starr Ridge Road, Brewster, has 125 acres of organically grown raspberries on its pick-your-own family farm, in operation for more than two centuries. Open May through November (call for hours since the season is weather dependent).

Salinger's Orchards (845-277-3521), 230 Guinea Road, Brewster, has a wide selection of local fruit and vegetables; a cider mill and bakery offer tempting treats to visitors. They produce over 3000 fruit pies each year baked in a glass enclosed kitchen at the market. Make sure to take one home! There are apple blueberry, strawberry, and peach. All are delicious and the price is reasonable. Open year-round, daily 9-5.

Saunders Farm (845-424-3150), 853 Old Albany Post Road, Garrison. Open year-round by appointment only. They specialize in certified Angus beef at this 140-acre cattle farm. Every year for a few weeks in October there is an outdoor sculpture exhibition on the farm with about 60 large works of art. Some hang from trees, others are scattered throughout the open fields. They are all for sale. This unusual outdoor museum may be temporary, but it's definitely worth a stop!

Tilly Foster Farm (845-228-4265), 100 Route 312, Brewster. Open year-round, daily 10-4. A picturesque 200-acre farm, this educational resource is open free to the public for picnics, hiking and fishing. There are tours of the farm one day each month, May through October. This is a great place to visit if you are traveling with children. There's a restaurant on the premises, *Tilly's Table*, with an enormous stone fireplace and two decks for alfresco dining. The menu features organically grown herbs and vegetables from the farm's gardens as well as locally sourced items.

Vera's Philipstown Farm Market (845-265-2151), 3091A Route 9, Cold Spring, offers fruit, vegetables, flowers, imported foods and is open March through December, daily 8:30-6; until 5 Sunday.

GOLF

The lush greens of Putnam County golf courses lure golfers of all abilities. Some of these courses are semi-private and might have special events or tournaments scheduled. All charge fees for use and cart rentals.

Centennial Golf Club (845-225-5700), 185 Simpson Road, Carmel. Open daily April through November. Enjoy a 27-hole, Larry Nelson-designed course; practice facilities, and world-class services.

Garrison Golf Club at the Garrison (845-424-3604), 955 Route 9D, Garrison, is open April through November, daily 7-7.

Highlands Country Club (845-424-3727), 955 Route 9D, Garrison, is open April through December, daily 7-6.

Putnam National Golf Club (845-628-4200), 187 Hill Street, Mahopac, has 18 holes and is 6750 yards in length. Open April through November, daily 7-6.

Vails Grove Golf Course (845-669-5721), 230 Peach Lake Road, Brewster, has nine holes. The course is open to the public April through November, weekdays 7:30-6, weekends after 12:30.

HIKING & OUTDOORS

Clarence Fahnestock Memorial State Park (845-225-7207), 1498 Route 301, east of the Taconic Parkway, Carmel. Open year-round. Free. This 14,000-acre park consists of swamp, lake, forest and meadow and was assembled through donations of land from private and state organizations. Several hiking trails, including part of the Appalachian Trail, wend in and out of the park; there are also fishing ponds, Canopus Beach, boat rentals, and ice-skating areas. The Fahnestock Winter Park section offers approximately ten miles of cross-country ski trails as well as a snowshoe area with marked trails. Visitors may rent both skis and snowshoes. Fees are charged for boats and for swimming, and you must bring your own equipment for fishing. The park also sponsors performing-arts programs and has provisions for camping, although you must call ahead to make reservations. The park's marked 1.5

mile Pelton Pond Nature Trail follows the perimeter of a pond formed when an old mine shaft was dammed. You can picnic in this area or watch the woods from a small pavilion. Hikers will want to look for the 8-mile stretch of Appalachian Trail that crosses the park, the Three Lakes Trail—with its varied wildflowers and views—and Catfish Loop Trail, which cuts through the abandoned settlement once known as Dennytown. Since many of these trails cross one another, you should look for signs and trail blazes along the main park roads, which include Route 301, Dennytown Road and Sunk Mine Road. If you plan to go fishing in the park, you will need a state license. Be sure to stop at park headquarters when you arrive. You can pick up a list of special events and free trail maps and fishing guides. Some facilities are accessible to the disabled.

Constitution Marsh Nature Preserve (845-265-2601); constitutionmarsh. org), Indian Brook Road, access off Route 9D, one-quarter mile south of Boscobel in Garrison. Trails are open daily, but visitors must make reservations if they want to take a tour. A National Audubon Society haven for nature lovers who enjoy birding along the river and spotting rare wildflowers in spring. There is a boardwalk to make viewing easier and a self-guided nature tour.

The renowned parrot gun, used during the Revolutionary War, was manufactured at the foundry in Cold Spring and this one remains in Riverfront Park in the village.

Hudson Highlands State Park (845-225-7207), Route 9D, Cold Spring. Open year-round, daily sunrise to sunset. There are about 6000 acres in this enormous park. A few particularly scenic hiking trails meander through the eastern portion of the Highlands, in Putnam County. The Breakneck Ridge Trail begins just north of the tunnel on Route 9D, two miles north of the village of Cold Spring. Look for the white blazes. The Washburn Trail begins on Route 9D, one mile north of Cold Spring, and passes an abandoned quarry, then rises steeply before reaching the summit. This trail ends at the beginning of the Notch Trail (blue blazes). The White Rock/Canada Hill Trail begins where the white-blazed part of the Appalachian Trail crosses Route 9 (at the junction with Route 403). Where the AT turns left to ascend the ridge, follow the yellow blazes, which end at the Osborn Loop (blue blazes). Continue to the junction with the Sugarloaf South Trail (red blazes). A side trip to the top of Sugarloaf South offers great views up the Hudson to West Point. The Osborn Loop turns south along the western flank of the mountain, then turns uphill to reach its southern terminus at the Appalachian Trail. Follow north along the ridge, and descend to the junction with the Carriage Connector. This loop is about 6.5 miles long. If you include the side trip up Sugarloaf South, add another mile. *NOTE: Sections are closed for repairs in 2018, so call before heading out.*

Lake Gleneida Walking Trail (845-808-1994). This 2.3 mile unpaved trail around Lake Gleneida begins at the intersection of Route 301 and Fowler Avenue in Carmel. There are trail markers, benches and several footbridges along the path. It's an easy walk and is recommended for families with young children.

Manitoga/Russel Wright Design Center (845-424-3812; russelwrightcenter. org), 584 Route 9D, Garrison. Open June through October for house and landscape tours. Reservations are required for tours, which are given, Saturday, Sunday and Monday at 11am and 1:30pm. Call ahead November through March as tours are by appointment only during those months. Admission. The name of this center is taken from the Algonquian word for "place of the spirit," and the philosophy of Manitoga lives up to its name. Here people and nature are meant to interact, and visitors are encouraged to experience the harmony of their environment. The center was designed by Russel Wright, who created a five-mile system of trails that focus on specific aspects of nature. The Morning Trail is especially beautiful early in the day, the Spring Trail introduces the hiker to wildflowers, and the Blue Trail wanders over a brook and through a dramatic evergreen forest (the trail system hooks up with the Appalachian Trail). You will find a full-size reproduction of a Native American wigwam constructed with traditional methods and tools. The site is used as an environmental learning center, and many special programs are offered. You can visit Dragon Rock, the grass-walled cliff house built by Wright. Manitoga is a place where human design and the natural world reflect and inspire each other.

Manitou Point Preserve (845-473-4440), 90 Mystery Point Road, Garrison. Take Route 9D north for two miles from Bear Mountain Bridge. Make a left on Mystery Point Road. Entrance is at the dead end. Open year-round dawn to dusk. This 136-acre retreat once belonged to the Livingston family. Enjoy four miles of lush trails that wind through Manitou Marsh, past woods and the Cooper Mine Brook ravine, along the banks of the Hudson River. You will pass the restored Livingston mansion, which is now the national headquarters for Outward Bound and not open to the public.

Taconic Outdoor Education Center (845-265-3773; nysparks.com), Clarence Fahnestock Memorial State Park, 75 Mountain Laurel Lane, Cold Spring. Free. This state-run center is situated on 300 acres and holds classes and workshops year-round for groups and organizations. There are four public program days annually. Call for dates. Boat, swim, fish, or stay overnight in one of the park's cabins and enjoy the experience at Highland Lodge (reservations for overnight camping required).

Other parks include **Pudding Street Multiple Use Area**, Pudding Street, Putnam Valley; **California Hill Multiple Use Area**, Gordon Road, Kent; **White Pond Multiple Use Area**, White Pond Road, Kent; **Big Buck Mountain Multiple Use Area**, Farmers Mills and Ressique Road, Kent; **Ninham Mountain Multiple Use Area**, Gypsy Trail and Mount Ninham Road, Kent; and **Cranberry Mountain Wildlife Management Area**, Stagecoach Road, Patterson. For more information on these areas, call 845-256-3000.

KAYAKING

Canopus Lake—This 105-acre lake, part of Fahnestock Memorial State Park, is accessible from a parking area on Route 301. You will need a NYS Taconic Region annual boat pass, which you can purchase at the park office. There are boat rentals here for use on the lake as well.

Constitution Marsh—Audubon New York has canoe and kayak tours of the marsh if you contact them directly for information.

East Branch of the Croton River—This river may be accessed from the Green Chimneys beach off Doansburg Road in Brewster only on evenings and weekends since it is used by the school during the week.

Stillwater Pond—This is a 55-acre pond that may be reached from the Taconic State Parkway (southbound, mile marker 29.6). If you use your own craft, you need a NYS Taconic Region annual boat pass. Stop at the park office to get a key (no charge). There is a road to the launch area by the parking lot.

Hudson River Expeditions (845-809-5936, hudsonriverexpeditions.com), 14 Market Street, Cold Spring. Open Memorial Day weekend through October, daily 9-6. If you want to take a kayak or canoe tour on the Hudson and would like the details organized for you, this is the place to contact. They offer options for all interests and abilities. The two offices: in Cornwall-on-Hudson in Orange County and in Cold Spring in Putnam County, aim to please!

WINTER SPORTS

ICE SKATING

Brewster Ice Arena (845-279-2229; brewstericearena.com), 63 Fields Lane, Brewster. Located near the intersection of I-84 and I-684, there are two Olympic-size indoor ice rinks here that offer public skating as well as hockey and figure-skating sessions. Lessons and rentals are available. The outdoor batting cages operate from April through October. A bar and restaurant are on the premises and the website lists latest schedule information.

SKIING

Thunder Ridge Ski Area (845-878-4100; thunderridgeski.com), 50 Thunder Ridge Road, Patterson. Open December through March, weather permitting, Monday through Friday 10-9; Saturday 9-9; Sunday 9-5. There are 30 trails and six lifts here (three chairs and three magic carpets) servicing several gentle slopes. This is an excellent place to introduce young children to the sports of skiing and snowboarding. There are some challenging advanced trails for experienced skiers as well as a terrain park for snowboarders. Night skiing is offered every day but Sunday. Temperatures here are more moderate than at other Catskill areas at higher elevations for those who don't "weather" extreme cold. Lessons are available at the ski school and there's a cafeteria and equipment rentals on the premises.

LODGING

The Garrison (845-424-3604), 2015 Route 9, Garrison 10524. ($$) This four-room inn is a truly special place in the Hudson Highlands with several historic stone structures on the property and magnificent views of the Hudson River at every turn. An ideal place for a romantic getaway, guests may enjoy a first-rate golf course, full-service spa, and fine dining on the premises. You will be transported back to another era, yet with all the modern amenities. Not recommended for children. Open year-round.

Heidi's Inn (845-279-8011), 1270 Route 22, Brewster 10509. ($)

This quiet, simple, comfortable inn has 40 rooms, all with private bath; 13 have a kitchenette. A continental breakfast is included with the reasonable room rates. Children are welcome. They are open year-round.

Hudson House Inn (845-265-9355), 2 Main Street, Cold Spring 10516. ($$) The second oldest continuously operating inn in New York State, Hudson House is completely restored and filled with antiques. In addition to quaint bedrooms, there's a cozy lounge, river views, and an exquisite garden during

most of the year. Thirteen rooms have private bath; two are suites. A full breakfast is served to guests. Children welcome. Open year-round.

Pig Hill Inn (845-265-9247), 73 Main Street, Cold Spring 10516. ($$) This Georgian brick town house is a most unusual place to stay. Each of the nine guest rooms is furnished in a different style, and most have a fireplace. And, if you fall in love with the rocking chair, or anything else in your room, you can purchase it. All rooms have private baths; two have Jacuzzi tubs. There's a gift shop on the first floor. Open year-round.

Pig Hill Inn on Main Street in Cold Spring.

WHERE TO EAT

DINING OUT

The Arch (845-279-5011), 1292 Route 22, Brewster. ($$$) Open Wednesday through Saturday 5-9; Sunday11:30-7:30. An elegant, intimate spot filled with antiques and separated into three small dining rooms with fireplaces and lots of windows. The chef specializes in Continental cuisine with a French touch. The menu changes seasonally; game is the specialty in fall. Reservations and jackets for men are required. Not recommended for children.

Clock Tower Grill (845-582-0574), 512 Clock Tower Drive, Brewster. ($$) Open Tuesday through Thursday noon-9; Friday noon-11; Saturday 5-11;

Sunday 3-9. Located in back of the Clock Tower Commons is a spacious restaurant where sliding barn doors separate the bar and dining room. Enjoy unpretentious farm-to-table entrees including shrimp and grits, cavatelli with sausage and kale, brandy-cured Long Island duck and bourbon-braised short ribs. Don't skip the mouth-watering desserts. Not recommended for children.

Cutillo's (845-225-8903), 1196 Farmers Mill Road, Carmel. ($$) Open Tuesday 5-10; Wednesday through Sunday noon-10. This family owned and operated restaurant serves classic Italian dishes—veal parmigiana, eggplant rollatini, manicotti—in a cozy informal atmosphere. I wish my hometown, Woodstock, had a restaurant like this one! Children are welcome.

The dining room at Hudson House, Cold Spring.

Hudson House (845-265-9355), 2 Main Street, Cold Spring. ($$) Open for lunch daily 11:30-3:30; dinner 5-9; Sunday brunch 11-3; dinner 3:30-8. Country touches fill this charming 1832 landmark building, and the dining rooms have Hudson River views. Specialties include steaks and cedar plank salmon. Desserts are superb and there is a children's menu.

Iron & Wine (845-878-6800), 3191 Route 22, Patterson. ($$) Open daily, except Tuesday, 11am-11pm. You will find tapas and small plates created with local ingredients. The flat breads, mussels, calamari, and accompanying cocktails are first-rate. They feature "Margarita Mondays" and occasionally paellas will be half price as well....definitely a bargain for the decent quality cuisine here. Not recommended for children.

Jaipore Royal Indian Cuisine (845-277-3549), 280 Route 22, Brewster. ($) Open daily for lunch noon-3; dinner 5-10. Enjoy a variety of Indian dishes (salads, breads, vegetables, soups, chicken, lamb and curries are just some of the choices) in a historic mansion that dates from 1856. Originally the home of a county judge, it became the residence of Mrs. Henry Ward Beecher in 1857. In the 1920s the building was a speakeasy and in the 1980s a topless bar. The buffet (always available at lunch) is a bargain and offers diners the opportunity to taste a little of everything. Children welcome.

Le Bouchon (845-265-7676), 76 Main Street, Cold Spring. ($$) Open daily noon-9; Friday and Saturday until 10. This brasserie/café is owned by a native of France's Alsace region. A couple of the tempting offerings include salmon strudel and escargot as well as three types of mussels and salad nicoise. Not recommended for children.

Luigi's Famiglia Cucina (845-225-4000), 62 Gleneida Avenue, Carmel. Open daily 11-10. ($$) Enjoy consistently well-prepared Italian fare: chicken marsala, steaks and seafood, everything is made to order. Portions are generous. Children welcome.

Ramiro's 954 (845-621-3333), 954 Route 6, Mahopac. ($$) Open Tuesday through Sunday 3:30-9. This delightful bistro with a full bar, fountain, and open kitchen serves first-rate Latin American cuisine. A spiral staircase leads upstairs to a more formal dining room along with an art gallery. Soups, corn cakes and empanadas are a few of the appetizers. Beef short ribs, fresh seafood, and enchiladas are offered as entrees. The restaurant opened in 2011 and has found a devoted clientele.

Rick's Seafood (845-621-2489), 545 Route 6, Mahopac. ($$) Open daily 9am-9pm. This comfortable restaurant with nautical décor is also a fish market. Enjoy coconut-crusted mahi-mahi, Chilean sea bass, and cod oreganato, to name a few of the popular creations here. Don't pass up the soups. The butternut squash lobster bisque and crab corn chowder are both excellent. Not recommended for children.

Riverview Restaurant (845-265-4778), 45 Fair Street, Cold Spring. ($$) Open Tuesday through Sunday for lunch noon-2:30; dinner 5-9. The contemporary American cuisine here is hearty, and the place is popular with locals. There's wood-fired brick-oven pizza, pasta, salads, steaks and seafood. Enjoy a river view while dining on the terrace, weather permitting. Don't forget to bring cash: NO credit cards are taken here! Children welcome.

Round Up Texas Smoked BBQ (845-809-5557), 2741 Route 9, Cold Spring. ($$) Open Tuesday through Sunday 11:30-8. Enjoy Texas-style dry-rubbed hickory-smoked brisket, sausage, ribs, chicken, and catfish, along with classic sides (cole slaw, creamed spinach, and more) in an informal atmosphere. Children welcome.

The terrace at Riverview Restaurant in Cold Spring.

Rraci's Ristorante Italiano (845-278-6695), 3670 Route 6, Brewster. ($$) Open for dinner Tuesday through Sunday 5-10. There are terrific salads and homemade pasta dishes, along with crab cakes, filet mignon and daily fish specials. The flagstone patio in the back offers a pleasant spot to dine with plants and green umbrellas at the tables, in the warm weather months. On the expensive side, as Italian restaurants go, but the food is usually excellent. Not recommended for children.

Thai Elephant 2 (845-319-6295), 2693 Route 22, Patterson. ($$) Open Tuesday through Thursday 11-10; Friday and Saturday until 11; Sunday 1-10. Housed in an old Colonial-style building with dark wood paneled walls and a fireplace, this Thai restaurant serves a variety of soups, curry dishes, and Pad Thai. There are several choices for vegetarians, including ginger tofu and eggplant basil tofu. Children welcome.

Valley at the Garrison (845-424-3604), 2015 Route 9, Garrison. ($$$) Open for dinner Thursday through Saturday 5:30-9; Sunday brunch 11-2:30. Contemporary American cuisine featuring the freshest seasonal ingredients from

Hudson Valley artisan farms is featured in this special spot. The dining room overlooks the Hudson River, and there are magnificent views of West Point and the surrounding mountains. There's outdoor dining in the warm weather months. Not recommended for children.

EATING OUT

Florrie Kaye's Tea Room (845-225-8327), 69 Gleneida Avenue, Carmel. ($) Open Tuesday through Sunday 11-5:30. This authentic British tearoom is a unique Hudson Valley attraction on the main street in Carmel. In addition to a wide variety of phenomenal teas, there's fair-trade coffee. Enjoy sandwiches, scones and wonderful petite cakes and cookies. Leave the kids home: this is a wonderful place for a women only lunch!

Florrie Kaye's Tea Room in Carmel is one of my favorite places to relax and enjoy lunch.

The Freight House Café (845-628-1872), 609 Route 6, Mahopac. ($) Open daily 8-3; Friday and Saturday 8-3 and 7-11. Located in a building constructed in 1872 as a railroad storage facility, this spacious, informal café is decorated with old prints, photos, antiques and books. It's a great spot to relax and enjoy hearty fare, including the all-day-long breakfast, a bowl of homemade soup or filet mignon steak sandwich. A family-run business with a friendly vibe, diners may watch their meals being prepared in the large open kitchen. Children welcome.

Gappy's (845-878-0800), 1323 Route 52, Carmel. ($) Open daily 11-10; Friday & Saturday until 2am; Sunday noon-9. Every town should have a restaurant like this one: inexpensive basic Italian fare made from scratch. Their lasagna is a specialty and their pizzas are great too. Eat in or take out and enjoy! Children welcome.

Gino's (845-628-1911) 597 Route 6, Mahopac. ($) Open Tuesday through Saturday11:30-9:30. This is the place to go for home-cooked Southern Italian specialties, from hearty portions of lasagna and manicotti to linguine with clam sauce and baked ziti. Their homemade whole-wheat pizza and pasta selections are excellent, and so are the focaccia sandwiches of grilled eggplant, chicken, or Portobello mushroom. There is a children's menu.

Greek Village (845-225-5882), 1856 Route 6, Carmel. ($) This informal luncheonette, located in a strip mall, has excellent lemon egg drop soup and gyros. If you are like me, and enjoy Greek cuisine, make sure to stop and enjoy an authentic dish or two when you're in the area. Children welcome.

Hudson Hil's (845-265-9471), 129-131 Main Street, Cold Spring ($) Open daily, except Tuesday, 8-4, for breakfast and lunch. They do serve dinner seasonally on Friday and Saturday nights. I loved the lunch I had at this eatery where they source fresh local ingredients for their soups, salads and sandwiches and have a great selection of home baked breads and desserts. I'm looking forward to going for breakfast when I'm in Cold Spring again early in the morning! Children welcome.

Red Rooster Drive-In (845-279-8046), 1566 Route 22, Brewster. ($) Open Sunday through Thursday 10-11; Friday and Saturday until 1am. An old-fashioned, immaculate drive-in with wonderful outdoor eating area is housed in an A-frame decorated with red-and-white stripes topped with a huge ice-cream cone. The kids will love the burgers, hot dogs, and fish and chips. For the more health- conscious, there's a charbroiled chicken breast sandwich on the menu. The milk shakes are one of the best items here, making this a great snack stop. The miniature golf course on the premises is owned and operated by the restaurant. Fast food with cachet! The kids will love it.

ENTERTAINMENT

Arts on the Lake (845-228-2685; artsonthelake.org), 640 Route 52, Carmel. Music, art exhibits, book signings, lectures; it's all here and there's something for every taste.

Brewster Theater Company (845-232-0739; brewstertheater.org), 26 Prospect Street, Brewster. This theater offers both drama and comedy year-round.

Garrison Art Center (845-424-3960;), 23 Garrison Landing, Garrison. Galleries, classes and programs for all ages.

Hudson Valley Shakespeare Festival (845-265-9575; hvshakespeare.org), Boscobel, 1601 Route 9D, Garrison.

Magazzino Italian Art (845-666-7202; magazzino.art), 2700 Route 9, Cold Spring. This new (2017) warehouse art space devoted to postwar and contemporary Italian art, may be visited year-around by appointment.

Philipstown Performing Arts (845-424-3900; philipstowndepot theatre. org), 10 Garrison Landing (at the train depot), Garrison. The performance schedule runs throughout most of the year and musicals, drama, comedy and children's theatre are produced here.

Putnam Arts Council (845-803-8622; putnamartscouncil.com), 521 Kennicut Hill Road, Mahopac. Art classes, exhibits, youth programs and more. The website has a full listing of events.

Southeast Cultural Arts Coalition (845-363-8330; culturalartsco.com), 67 Main Street, Brewster. This cultural center offers concerts, art exhibits and a variety of performances year-round.

SPECIAL EVENTS

January: **Winterfest** (845-265-3773), Taconic Outdoor Education Center, 75 Mountain Laurel Lane, Cold Spring. Free. Enjoy a pancake breakfast, nature walks, winter sports and more at this annual festival: it's wonderful to attend if you have young children.

March: **Sap to Syrup Maple Sunday** (845-265-3773), Taconic Outdoor Education Center, 75 Mountain Laurel Lane, Cold Spring. Free. Watch demonstrations of tapping trees and boiling and producing syrup. There is also a pancake breakfast!

June: **Snapping Turtle Walk** (845-265-3638), Boscobel, 1601 Route 9D, Garrison. In early June, female turtles crawl up the steep banks from their habitat in Constitution Marsh to lay their eggs. The program features live turtles from the marsh and a guided walk around the grounds to look for female turtles. The program begins promptly at 7:30am. **Hudson Valley Shakespeare Festival** (845-809-5750; 265-9575; hvshakespeare,org), Boscobel, 1601 Route 9D, Garrison. Reservations are required and the full schedule for the summer season is on the website.

July: **Fourth of July Celebration** at the bandstand at the end of Main Street includes fireworks after sunset, games and activities for the kids in the park, and usually a bike race. Free. **Summer Sunset Music Series**, at the bandstand on Main Street, Cold Spring. Free. Enjoy live music— jazz, folk, rock—usually on Sunday evenings. **Annual Putnam 4-H Fair** (845-278-6738). Veterans Memorial Park, 201 Gipsy Trail Road, Carmel. Friday through Sunday 10-7. Admission and parking fee. This is a true country fair, featuring animals, exhibits and live entertainment. There's a pig roast, pony rides, and fishing contest. The kids will love this event.

August: **Riverside Craft Fair** (845-424-3960), Garrison Landing, Garrison. Usually held on the third weekend in August, this craft fair features the work of about 70 artisans along the banks of the Hudson River. Open Saturday and Sunday 10-5; suggested donation $5 for adults. **Daniel Nimham Intertribal Pow Wow** (845-225-0381; 800-470-4584), Veterans Memorial Park, 201 Gipsy Trail Road, Carmel. Admission and parking fee. Enjoy Native American singers, dancers, crafters, and foods. A colorful festival that will be enjoyed by all ages.

September: **Big Band Evening and Sunset Picnic** (845-265-3638), Boscobel, 1601 Route 9D, Garrison. Admission. Bring a picnic supper and enjoy views of the Hudson River while dancing to the music of a 20-piece jazz orchestra, recreating the swinging sound of the big-band era. Reservations required. Annual Brewster **Founder's Day Street Fair** (845-279-2477), Main Street, Brewster. Free. Enjoy rides, live entertainment, vendors and fair food at this family-friendly event.

December: **Candlelight Tour of Boscobel** (845-265-3638), 1601 Route 9D, Garrison. Admission. Take a candlelight tour of Boscobel decorated for the holidays. Reservations required.

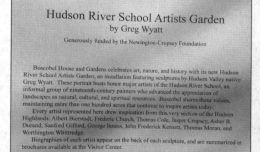

The Artists Garden at Boscobel in Garrison is a fascinating place to explore.

Croton Point Park in winter.

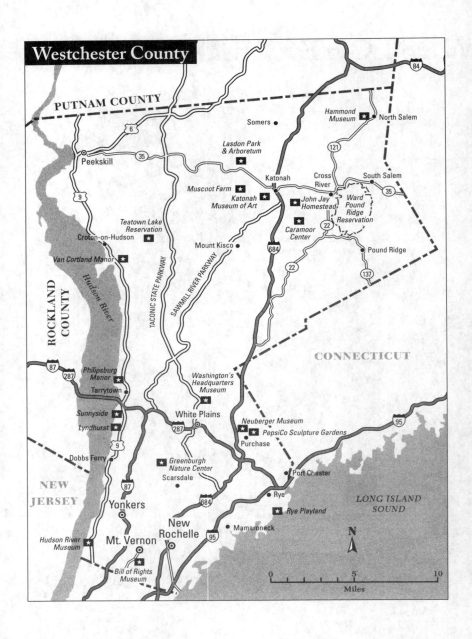

Westchester County

PUTNAM COUNTY

6

35

Peekskill

9

Somers ●

Lasdon Park & Arboretum ★

Hammond Museum ★   ● North Salem

121

Katonah

Cross River

South Salem

35

Muscoot Farm ★

Katonah Museum of Art ★

John Jay Homestead ★

Ward Pound Ridge Reservation

Teatown Lake Reservation

Croton-on-Hudson ★

Mount Kisco ●

684

Caramoor Center ★

22

● Pound Ridge

Van Cortland Manor ★

22

137

Hudson River

ROCKLAND COUNTY

TACONIC STATE PARKWAY

SAWMILL RIVER PARKWAY

CONNECTICUT

87
287

Philipsburg Manor ★

Tarrytown

Washington's Headquarters Museum ★

95

Sunnyside ★

Lyndhurst ★

White Plains

9

287

Neuberger Museum ★

★ PepsiCo Sculpture Gardens

Purchase

Dobbs Ferry ●

NEW JERSEY

87

Greenburgh ★ Nature Center

Scarsdale

684

Port Chester ●

Yonkers

● Rye

LONG ISLAND SOUND

Hudson River Museum ★

Mt. Vernon

New Rochelle

95

★ Rye Playland

● Mamaroneck

Bill of Rights Museum

N

0   5   10
Miles

WESTCHESTER COUNTY

H ome of the unexpected: Westchester—which calls itself the Golden Apple—can be a nature preserve, a riverfront mansion, a 17th-century Dutch house tucked just off the old Post Road, or a bustling shopping district. The county has made extraordinary attempts to preserve both its history and its natural environment. Although Westchester borders New York City, it's an area replete with parks that offer an enormous selection of children's activities and special events for visitors. Washington Irving described the enchantment of Westchester in his short stories, immortalizing Tarrytown and the Headless Horseman. On historic Route 9 the Gothic castle called Lyndhurst and its majestic grounds will awe visitors. From the Pinkster Festival in spring to December's candlelight tours of historic sites, the county is fun to explore year-round.

VISITOR INFORMATION

Westchester County Office of Tourism (914-995-8500; 800-833-WCVB), 148 Martine Avenue, White Plains 10601; tourismwestchestergov.com.

GETTING THERE

By car: Westchester is accessible from I-87, I-95, Route 684, and Route 9.

By bus: **Adirondack Trailways** (800-858-8555) offers service to various towns in Westchester from Port Authority in Manhattan. The Bee-Line System (914-813-7777) offers countywide bus service with more than 50 routes and express service to Manhattan.

By train: **Amtrak** (800-872-7245) provides service from New Rochelle to stations on the Boston-Washington Northeast corridor. There is service from Croton-Harmon and Yonkers to upstate New York, Montreal, Chicago, and points west. **Metro North** (800-METRO-INFO) operates commuter trains with 43 station stops in Westchester on three lines. There is daily service to Grand Center Station in Manhattan, as well as points north.

By air: **Westchester County Airport** (914-995-4860; westchestergov.com/airport), 240 Airport Road, White Plains, offers scheduled airline and charter services as well as corporate flights.

MEDICAL EMERGENCY

Hudson Valley Hospital Center (914-737-9000), 1980 Crompond Road, Cortlandt Manor.

White Plains Hospital (914-681-0600), 41 East Post Road, White Plains.

Northern Westchester Hospital Center (914-666-1254), 400 East Main Street, Mount Kisco.

Phelps Memorial Hospital Center (914-366-3590), 701 North Broadway, Sleepy Hollow.

HISTORIC HOMES

Caramoor Center for Music and the Arts (914-232-1252/5035; caramoor.com), 149 Girdle Ridge Road, Katonah. Open year-round for house tours by appointment. Admission. Built in the 1930s by lawyer and banker Walter Tower Rosen, this 117-acre estate was meant to be the setting for Rosen's magnificent collection of fine art from Europe and the Orient. The house was created in an interesting way: entire rooms (55 in all) from European villas were combined with an American "shell." The result is a unique, magical building that provides an architectural tour of the world in a few hours.

Lyndhurst, a Gothic Revival estate in Tarrytown, is operated by the National Trust for Historic Preservation.

Rosen's bedroom, for example, was taken from an Alpine cottage; in his wife's room is a headboard made for Pope Urban VIII; the music room is from a 16th-century Italian villa; portions of the outdoor theater are from the south of France. Throughout the house are thousands of breathtaking pieces of priceless needlework, tapestries, porcelain, furniture, and art, some of which date from the Middle Ages and China's golden age. Lectures are given by art historians who illustrate their talks with pieces from the collections.

Don't miss the exquisite gardens at Caramoor, where fine statuary is set among evergreens and flowers. This unusual home is also the site of a world-renowned summer music festival. The Venetian Theater is a showcase in itself and was built around 15th-century Venetian columns; operas and concerts take center stage on warm evenings, while chamber concerts are offered in the Spanish Courtyard. Concertgoers are allowed to picnic on the grounds before shows.

Kykuit (845-631-8200; hudsonvalley.org), 381 North Broadway, Sleepy Hollow. Tours begin from Philipsburg Manor. Open May through October, Thursday through Sunday, 10-5; month of October, daily except Tuesday, 10-5. Admission. Tours (there are five different options) are two hours in length and are not recommended for children under the age of 10. John D. Rockefeller, the founder of Standard Oil, delegated the task of building Kykuit, his home, to his son, John D. Rockefeller Jr. The neoclassical country house and its gardens were completed in 1913, and Kykuit remains one of the finest and best-preserved Beaux Arts homes in America. Make sure to see this home, even if your time in the county is limited. Governor Nelson Rockefeller lived here from 1960 to 1979. The gardens contain masterpieces by Henry Moore, Alexander Calder, and Louise Nevelson, and there are special tours that focus on the landscapes around the estate. The house is furnished with antiques, fine ceramics, and paintings; a coach barn contains vintage automobiles and carriages. paths among the dozens of different trees, ferns, and plantings.

Philipsburg Manor (914-366-6900; hudsonvalley.org), 381 North Broadway, Sleepy Hollow. Open April through mid-November, Wednesday through Sunday 10-4:30; November and December hours vary. Closed January through March. Admission. Once the center of a 17th-century estate of more than 50,000 acres, Philipsburg Manor was founded by Frederick Philipse, a Dutch immigrant. He arrived in America as a carpenter and built an empire of milling and trading businesses. For almost 100 years, the Philipse family was respected in the community. However, they fled to England as Loyalists during the Revolutionary War, and their lands were broken up.

Historic Van Cortlandt Manor (circa 1732), a stone and brick house overlooking the river in Croton-on-Hudson, now a National Historic Landmark, was originally an 86,000-acre tract granted to Stephanus Van Cortlandt as a patent by Royal Charter.

Tours of the manor begin in the basement, where the dairy and slave cooking quarters are located. The front hall contains documents like the 1750 house inventory—and advertisements for runaway slaves. The house was not the main residence of the family, so it was not furnished lavishly. The mill, still run by waterpower, continues to grind meal for the kitchen and turns out 500-1000 pounds of flour annually. The resident miller explains the intricacies of a millwright's job, how waterpower turns corn into flour.

Outside by the barn and outbuildings, costumed guides work the small farm and act out vignettes depicting life at the time. They show the North, too, depended on slavery for economic survival. This site has not shied away from the ugly, yet realistic aspects of early American culture; children will understand more about slavery by watching the dramatic enactments presented here. A clear sense of how America developed on the backs of different cultures is communicated here, a rarity anywhere. This progressive—and realistic—approach to colonial history is reason alone for families to visit this interesting site.

Van Cortlandt Manor (914-271-8981; hudsonvalley.org), 525 South Riverside Avenue, Croton-on-Hudson. Open late June through August, Friday through Sunday, by tour only at 10:30, 11:30, 12:30, 1:30 and 3. Admission. This manor originally consisted of 86,000 acres of land. The main floors of the present manor house were built in 1748; the house remained in the Van Cortlandt family until the middle of the 20th century. As supporters of the American Revolution, the Van Cortlandts were hosts to such luminaries as Washington, Franklin, and Lafayette. Inside the house there is a blend of styles and periods, reflecting the history of the family. One of the most impressive items is the fowling gun, a huge firearm that was fired into a flock of birds and reduced hunting time considerably. Outside, the gardens beckon flower lovers and the Long Walk—a brick path that leads to the **Ferry House,** a nearby inn and tavern—wanders by well-maintained flowerbeds and herb gardens. The Ferry House has been restored and furnished with Hudson Valley pieces and offers a rare look into the social life of the colonial period. Notice the familiar white-clay pipes—they were for rent, with the ends broken off for each new smoker.

Washington Irving's Sunnyside (914-591-8763; hudsonvalley.org), 3 West Sunnyside Lane (off Route 9), Irvington. Open May through mid-November, Wednesday through Sunday, 10-4. Admission. A grounds pass can be purchased at a reduced rate. The house is open by guided tour only; tours leave on the half hour. Washington Irving once referred to his home as being "as full of angles and corners as an old cocked hat," and the charming, wisteria-draped home of the author of *The Legend of Sleepy Hollow* and *Rip Van Winkle* is an original. Irving purchased the small estate in 1835 and soon began to remodel it, adding weathervanes, gables, and even an Oriental-style tower. There is much locally made furniture, and some furnishings from Irving's time. In fact, his desk and many of his books, remain. The kitchen was considered a modern wonder: A large hot-water heater was fed from the nearby pond by a gravity-run system. The grounds are carefully tended and overlook the Hudson River and the railroad tracks. Irving made a deal with the railroad, allowing it to pass through his land if trains would stop to pick him up for the trip to New York. You can stroll along the paths, picnic near the Little Mediterranean (a pond), watch the swans, see the icehouse and root cellar, and visit the "necessary."

SMALLER HISTORIC HOMES

Ever Rest, the Jasper Cropsey Homestead (914-478-1372; newingtoncropsey. com), 49 Washington Avenue, Hastings-on-Hudson. Open by appointment weekdays 10-1. Free. Cropsey was part of the Hudson River School of painters as well as an architect (he designed part of the New York City railroad system), and his Gothic home has about 100 of his works, including paintings and sketches. The artist's studio is part of the tour and there's a short video about Cropsey's life and times.

Horace Greeley House and New Castle Historical Society (914-238-4666; newcastlehistoricalsociety.org), 100 King Street, Chappaqua. Open Tuesday through Thursday and Saturday, 1-4; or by appointment. Free. A crusading editor of the New York Tribune, presidential candidate in 1872, foe of slavery, and a women's rights advocate, Greeley lived here during the summer months from 1864 to 1872. The furnished house is on the National Register of Historic Places and there's Greeley family furniture, papers, and books. The gardens include unusual species indigenous to the area and plants once used for medicinal purposes.

John Jay Homestead (914-232-5651; johnjayhomestead.org), 400 Jay Street, Katonah. Open May through mid-October, Wednesday through Sunday 10-4; late October through April, Thursday through Saturday, 1-4; Admission. This 18th-century farmhouse was home to five generations of Jays. As president of the Continental Congress and first chief justice of the Supreme Court, John Jay, the most famous family member, held some of the most influential appointments in government. He retired here in 1801. Family portraits grace the walls and the kitchen has an impressive beehive oven. The tour adds an interesting dimension to America's early years.

HISTORIC SITES

Lighthouse at Sleepy Hollow — the Tarrytown Lighthouse (914-366-5109), 299 Palmer Avenue, Sleepy Hollow. Tours are offered from mid-April through August, Sunday 1-3. The cast-iron tower dates back to 1883 and was operational until 1961, when navigational lights on the Tappan Zee Bridge made it obsolete. Twelve light keepers and their families resided in the five-story structure, and on the tour visitors will learn about their lives. There's plenty of parking in Kingsland Point Park, where the tours begin.

Old Dutch Church and Burying Grounds (914-631-4497/1123; olddutchburyingground.org), 42 North Broadway (Route 9), Tarrytown. There are cemetery tours Sundays at 2pm, Memorial Day weekend through October, for a fee. Visitors can take a self-guided tour for free. One of the oldest churches in New York State, this stout stone building was erected in 1685 and is still used for services. Surrounding the church is the fascinating Sleepy Hollow Cemetery, where visitors can read old Dutch and English tombstones. Washington Irving is buried here and the cemetery is reputed to be the spot where a headless Hessian ghost resided giving rise to The Legend of Sleepy Hollow. The gates are locked promptly at 4:30pm every day.

MUSEUMS

Hudson River Museum and Glenview Mansion (914-963-4550; hrm.org), 511 Warburton Avenue, Yonkers. Open year-round, Wednesday through

Sunday noon-5. July and August, Friday and Saturday until 8. Admission. Planetarium shows on Saturday and Sunday only at 12:30, 2 and 3:30. Admission. When financier John Bond Trevor built a 19th-century mansion called Glenview on a rise overlooking the Hudson River, he probably never envisioned it becoming a museum. But when the house was purchased by the city of Yonkers, that's what happened. Period artwork, clothing, furniture and decorative items are displayed throughout the mansion; the museum is located in a separate wing and contains science and art exhibit areas. Hudson Riverama includes permanent galleries with Hudson River-themed artwork. The Andrus Planetarium (the only public planetarium in the area and one of the few in the Northeast) can take you on a journey through the universe. The planetarium offers shows on weekends, and there are special events throughout the year, so it's best to check the website for a complete schedule.

Hudson Valley Center for Contemporary Art (914-788-7166; hvcca.org), 1701 Main Street, Peekskill. Open Friday 11-5, Saturday and Sunday noon-6. Tuesday through Thursday, by appointment only. Admission. This 12,000-square-foot museum contains changing exhibits and is a hub in Peekskill for the arts community. It's known as a venue for experimental art, and a visit will include a video presentation and sculpture exhibit. There are a variety of special programs offered year-round. After visiting the museum, stop at the Lincoln Depot (914-402-4318), 10 South Water Street, where a 3000-square-foot freight and passenger rail depot marks the spot where Abraham Lincoln stopped to greet New Yorkers on February 19, 1861 during his inaugural train journey to Washington D.C.

Katonah Museum of Art (914-232-9555; katonahmuseum.org), 134 Jay Street, Katonah. Admission. Open Tuesday through Saturday 10-5; Sunday noon-5. Admission. This lively teaching museum was founded in 1953 to display the best art of the past and present, and foster arts education. There are exhibits by museum members, an annual local studio tour, and changing displays, which may range from a look at the creations of fashion designers to Navajo rugs or modern art. Special events and shows are held year-round, and the museum is well worth a stop after walking around the charming village of Katonah.

Neuberger Museum of Art (914-251-6100; Neuberger.org), Purchase College Campus, 735 Anderson Hill Road, Purchase. Open Thursday through Sunday noon-5. Admission fee is waived the first Saturday of every month. Masterpieces of modern art by Avery, Hopper, O'Keeffe, Pollock, and others are displayed in several galleries at this extraordinary teaching museum. There is also an important collection of African art, and selections from Nelson's Rockefeller's collection of ancient art are exhibited. An outdoor sculpture area with works by Henry Moore, Andy Goldsworthy, and Alexander Liberman should not be overlooked. This is one of the county's finest cultural resources, with changing exhibitions. The museum offers workshops, panels, tours, performances, and concerts throughout the year. There's a gift shop and café on the premises.

Ossining Urban Cultural Park Museum (914-941-3189), 95 Broadway, Ossining. Open year-round Tuesday through Saturday 10-4. Ossining was once renowned as the home of Sing Sing prison, and this museum features replicas of prison cells as well as a model of the Old Croton Aqueduct and other exhibits about the town's history. Those interested in the prison will find this stop of interest.

SMALLER MUSEUMS

Peekskill History Museum (914-736-0473; peekskillmuseum.com), 124 Union Avenue, Peekskill. Open year-round, Saturday 1-4. Free. This local history museum, housed in the Herrick House, one of Peekskill's most famous Victorians, features exhibits relating to the city's history, including Revolutionary War cannons.

St. Paul's Church National Historic Site (914-667-4116; nps.gov/sapa), 897 South Columbus Avenue, Mount Vernon. Open year-round Monday through Friday 9-5; second Saturday of the month, noon-4. Free. Few people realize the 18th century libel trial of John Peter Zenger led directly to the establishment of the Bill of Rights in 1791. And all this took place in Mount Vernon. This site preserves the story and the tour begins at St. Paul's Church, founded in 1665 with one of the oldest working church organs in America. The Freedom Bell, sister of the Liberty Bell and cast at the same London Foundry, is located here. The church was used as a courthouse at one time and Aaron Burr presented cases here. There are both self-guided and guided tours available.

Somers Historical Society and Museum of the Early American Circus (914-277-4977; somersny.com), 335 Route 202, Somers. Open year-round, Thursday 2-4, or by appointment. An unusual museum in the historic Elephant Hotel, recalls the birth of the American circus in the 18th century. The hotel was built by showman, Hachaliah Bailey (a distant relation of the Bailey of Barnum & Bailey), and houses a museum full of circus memorabilia, posters, photos and exhibits of local history.

Square House Museum (914-967-7588; ryehistory.org), 1 Purchase Street, Rye. Open year-round, Tuesday through Friday, 9-4; Saturday 10-3. Admission. This 1760 Federal farmhouse and tavern once hosted George Washington; today the five restored rooms offer a look into 18th-century life. While here, I learned the term *bar and grill* derives from barkeepers having secured a wooden covering over the bar at night to avoid having liquor stolen.

Yorktown Museum (914-962-2970; yorktownmuseum.org), 1974 Commerce Street, Yorktown Heights. Open year-round, Tuesday and Thursday 11-4; Saturday 1-4, or by appointment. Free, but donations are welcome. A unique collection of dollhouses and miniature landscapes depicting Victorian homes, street scenes and stores is on display, are exhibits of Mohegan Indian life and local history.

GARDENS

Donald M. Kendall Sculpture Gardens at PepsiCo Headquarters (914-253-3150; pepsico.com), 700 Anderson Hill Road, Purchase. Open April through October, Saturday and Sunday 10-4. Free. Here, on 168 acres, visitors will see approximately 50 large sculptures by Rodin, Giacometti, Nevelson, Moore and Noguchi. Carefully landscaped with paths, reflecting pools, and fountains, the gardens (filled with trees, shrubs, and herbaceous plants) bloom from early spring until fall.

Hammond Museum and Japanese Stroll Garden (914-669-5033; hammondmuseum.org), 28 Deveau Road, North Salem. Open May through October, Wednesday through Saturday noon-4. Admission. This small Asian arts museum with a four-acre Japanese-inspired garden offers a chance to step back into the Edo period of Japanese history. Created by Natalie Hays Hammond in memory of her parents, these gardens actually are 13 small landscapes, including a Zen garden, as well as many species of trees and flowers (cherry, quince, azalea, iris, peony, among others). Each section is beautifully appointed and has a symbolic meaning. In the reflecting pool five water lilies represent humanity, justice, courtesy, wisdom, and fidelity. The museum displays a mix of art, antiques, and collectibles, but it is the gardens that must not be missed. A café on the grounds serves refreshments.

Lasdon Park and Arboretum (914-864-7268; lasdonpark.org) 2610 Route 35, Somers. Open year-round, daily 8-4. This lush 243-acre park has a 30-acre arboretum with a formal azalea garden, a magnolia and lilac collection, a rare native American-chestnut grove, and a dwarf conifer collection of pines, spruces, firs, and cypress. Another feature is the Chinese garden with plant species native to China, including cherry trees and butterfly bushes. There's a plant store on the premises.

Native Plant Center (914-606-7870; sunywcc.edu), Westchester Community College, 75 Grasslands Road, Valhalla. Open year-round daily dawn to dusk. This center informs visitors about the importance of low-maintenance native plants, which support birds, bees, and butterflies. The two-acre demonstration garden, named after Lady Bird Johnson, consists solely of plants and wildflowers indigenous to the northeastern United States. Designed for summer and fall color, no pesticides or fertilizers are used in the garden.

Pruyn Audubon Sanctuary (914-666-6503; sawmillriveraudubon.org), 275 Millwood Road (Route 133), Chappaqua. Open year-round, daily dawn to dusk. Free. Guided group tours are available by appointment. A 57-acre parcel of protected open space, this garden features more than 125 types of annual and perennial flowering plants selected to be food or nectar plants for butterflies and hummingbirds, including asters, irises, lavender lilies, and snapdragons. A drip pool attracts birds. More than 25 species of butterflies and moths and two dozen species of birds are drawn to the garden. Plants have identification labels.

September 11th Memorial Garden at Kensico Dam Plaza (914-328-1542; parks.westchester.gov), 1 Bronx River Parkway, Valhalla. Open year-round, daily 8-dusk. There is a garden of shrubs and perennials surrounding *The Rising*, a sculpture, Westchester County's memorial to those who lost their lives on September 11, 2001. The garden was designed with a wooded, natural appearance as a backdrop to the memorial. Both native and nonnative species were used in the garden. This moving tribute is worth a stop, if you are in the area.

ACTIVITIES

BICYCLING

Bicycle Sundays (914-231-4600; wpf.org). If biking is your passion, plan to take part in this Sunday event from May through September, except holiday weekends, from 10am-2pm. At that time, the Bronx River Parkway (16 miles of the highway) is closed to vehicular traffic. Call 914-864-PARK and request trail maps for the parkway, North County Trailway, South County Trailway, Briarcliff-Peekskill Trailway, and Old Croton Aqueduct State Historic Park, which all have free bike paths open year-round. In-line skating is also welcome in most of these areas. To obtain trail maps online, another website is westchestergov.com/parks.

Briarcliff-Peekskill Trail (914-864-PARK). This county-owned linear park runs 12 miles from Ossining to the Blue Mountain Reservation in Peekskill.

Bronx River Pathway (914- (914-864-PARK). This 807-acre park extends 13.2 miles in three distinct segments. It is excellent for road biking, hiking, and walking.

North County Trailway (914-864-PARK). There are 22 miles of county-owned trails, running from Mount Pleasant north to the Putnam County line in Yorktown Heights.

Old Croton Aqueduct State Historic Park (914-693-5259). This level, 26-mile trail from Croton Dam south to Van Cortlandt Park in the Bronx passes through 11 towns and offers striking panoramas of the Hudson River at several points. The trail follows the route of the aqueduct, which carried water to New York City from 1842 to 1955. Most of this structure lies beneath the trail and has been designated a National Historic Landmark.

South County Trailway (914-864-PARK). This 5.2 county-owned trail runs from Hastings to Elmsford..

Endless Trail Bikworx (914-674-8567), in Dobbs Ferry offers day-trip packages from Manhattan that include a round-trip train ticket to Dobbs Ferry as well as lunch at a restaurant stop.

Westchester Cycle Club (914-555-1212; westchestercycle club.org) organizes over 1000 bicycle rides for members throughout the county every year, on weekends as well as during the week. The membership dues are reasonable and entitle bike enthusiasts to access a library of 600 Westchester County bicycle routes to plan independent trips. Website has membership information.

BOAT CRUISES & ROWBOAT RENTALS

Croton Sailing School (800-859-7245; crotonsailing.com), 7 Elliott Avenue, Croton. Sailing lessons, charters and youth program are available seasonally. Check the website for details.

Franklin D. Roosevelt State Park (914-245-4434), 2957 Crompond Road, Yorktown Heights. Rowboat rentals on the lake and pond are available during the summer season.

Trinity Cruise Company (914-589-7773; trinitycruises.com), 12 Riverfront Green, Peekskill. Open mid-May through October, Wednesday through Sunday, for narrated sightseeing cruises and sunset cruises on the Hudson River. The *Evening Star* is a delightful cruise boat; website has a complete schedule of trips.

Wampus Pond (914-273-3230), 811 Route 128, Armonk. Rowboats available for rent from Memorial Day weekend through Labor Day weekends and holidays only.

BREWERIES & DISTILLERIES

Broken Bow (914-268-0900), 173 Marbledale Road, Tuckahoe.Open Thursday 5-8pm; Friday and Saturday 1-10; Sunday 1-5. This brewery is family owned and operated and they produce several beers which may be enjoyed in the beer garden on the premises.

Captain Lawrence Brewing Company (914-741-BEER), 444 Saw Mill River Road, Elmsford, is open Saturday and Sunday for tours. Call for hours: they vary with the season. This craft brewer produces several award-winning beers on the premises.

Peekskill Brewery (914-734-BEER), 47 South Water Street, Peekskill. Open daily noon to midnight. This is actually a taproom (on the first floor), pub (on the second floor) and restaurant (food available on both floors).

Located on South Water Street, across from the Peekskill train station, this converted bi-level industrial space houses a brewpub serving its own beers and a variety of comfort food.

There's live music on weekends and it's a fun place to stop for beer lovers!

StilltheOne Distillery (914-305-4437), 1 Martin Place, Port Chester. Tours are given by appointment only, Wednesday through Saturday. Made with pure honey, the Comb Vodka, Comb 9 Gin, and Comb Blossom Brandy produced at this distillery are all served at fine restaurants. It's an interesting operation, and the name refers to the lengthy marriage of the owners, Pelham Manor residents who opened the distillery in 2011.

Yonkers Brewing Company (914-226-8327), 92 Main Street, Yonkers. Open daily 11:30-10; Friday until 11pm; Saturday 10am-midnight; Sunday 1-10pm. There are several beers on tap here along with a full menu of bar food.

FAMILY FUN

The Cliffs (914-328-ROCK), 1 Commerce Street, Valhalla. Open year-round, Monday through Friday 10-10; Saturday 9-8; Sunday 9-6. Admission. This indoor rock climbing and fitness facility features over 13,000-square-feet of climbing suitable for all ages and abilities.

Funfuzion at New Roc City (914-637-7575; funfuziononline.com), 29 LeCount Place, New Rochelle. Open daily, including holidays, noon-midnight. Admission. This enormous indoor entertainment complex features six amusement venues. Kids can create their own fun experiences that incorporate video games, rides, glow in the dark bowling, miniature golf, pool, go-karts, and more.

iFLY (914-449-4359), 849 Ridge Hill Boulevard, Yonkers. Open Monday through Friday 11-9; Saturday and Sunday 9-9. Take flight at New York's only indoor skydiving facility. There is no parachute and no jumping, just a wall-to-wall cushion of air that gives you a realistic and safe free-fall experience.

LEGOLAND Discovery Center (866-243-0770), 39 Fitzgerald Street, Yonkers. Open Sunday through Thursday 10-7; Friday and Saturday 10-9. Kids will enjoy creating their own buildings and cars to survive the shaking "earthquake tables." There is also a soft-play area for young children, a 4-D film, and a video about how Legos are manufactured.

Muscoot Farm (914-864-7282; muscootfarm.org), 51 Route 100, Somers. Open year-round, daily 10-4. Free, but there are workshops here that do charge a fee. This showplace for farming techniques of the 19th century is a 777-acre interpretive farm offering a look at life in a bygone era. Built in 1865 by a pharmacist (muscoot means "something swampy" in a local Native American language), visitors can view a variety of farm animals and displays of vintage farm equipment, tour historic farm buildings, and enjoy hayrides on Sunday (May through October). Muscoot has a series of trails that wind through ferns and wildflowers, along which animals and birds make their homes. There are ponds, wetlands, and meadows to explore, as well.

Playland (914-813-7010; ryeplayland.org), 1 Playland Parkway (off I-95), Rye. Open daily, except Monday, June through Labor Day, 10-11pm; May & September weekends only. Admission. A true old-fashioned amusement park and National Historic Site, Rye's Playland is an architectural gem. Built in 1928, this was the first amusement park constructed according to a complete plan where recreational family fun was the focus. The family atmosphere and art deco style are still here to be enjoyed. Set on the beaches of Long Island Sound, Playland offers a 1200-foot boardwalk, swimming pool, gardens, saltwater boating pond, a beach, and of course, 50 rides and an amusement area. Seven original rides are still in use, including a carousel with a rare carousel organ and painted horses, the Dragon Coaster, a rare wooden roller coaster, and the Derby Racer (horses zip around a track). Fireworks and special entertainment, including free musical revues, go on all summer. In the winter there are three ice-skating rinks open to the public.

Wolf Conservation Center (914-763-2372; nywolf.org), 7 Buck Run, South Salem. Open Tuesday through Saturday 9-5; Sunday 9-3. There are live wolves in this private facility; the owners present a variety of programs for children and families throughout the year. Some are given in the evening, including the howling program! Check the website for current listings of events.

FARMERS' MARKETS AND FARMS

Even though Westchester is more developed than other Hudson River counties, farm stands provide fresh local produce during the summer and fall harvest seasons. Farmers' markets are held in many towns and they are a great way to sample the bounty of the county: these are a few of my favorites, but there are several others throughout Westchester.

Croton-on-Hudson Farmers' Market (914-923-4837). Municipal parking lot off Route 9. From early May through November, Sunday 9-2.

Larchmont Farmers' Market (914-923-4837), Metro-North Railroad parking lots off Chatsworth Avenue. Late April through mid-December, Saturday, 8:30-1.

Ossining Farmers' Market (914-923-4837), Corner of Main & Spring Streets. January through mid-May Saturday 9-1; late May through mid-December, 8:30-1.

Cabbage Hill Farm (914-241-2658), 115 Crow Hill Road, Mount Kisco, seeks to increase public awareness about sustainable agriculture through an educational working farm. They conserve rare and endangered breeds of animals here. On the first and third Sunday of every month, the 175-acre farm is open to the public by advance appointment. Make sure to see the greenhouses: one has an aquaponics operation where greens are grown year-round and are fed entirely from the fish tank water. The other greenhouse contains flowers and herbs, all organically grown. Crops are fertilized using compost made from the farm animals. A fascinating farm where a number of rare heritage breed animals may be seen. This is truly an unusual farm!

Harvest Moon Farm & Orchard (914-485-1210), 130 Hardscrabble Road, North Salem, offers tours. You can pick apples in the fall or shop at the stand year-round. They have fresh vegetables, jams and other local products. The store is open April through December, daily 9-6. And there is apple and pumpkin picking in season daily. The produce is first-rate and this is a popular place with local residents.

Hayfields (914-669-8275), 1 Bloomer Road, North Salem, is open Monday through Friday 7-7; Saturday and Sunday 8-6. This is one of my favorite farm markets in the county. In addition to local produce and flowers, they have terrific sandwiches, cookies and excellent coffee. So after shopping, I enjoy having a snack. This area of North Salem is quiet and pastoral, a perfect place to enjoy sitting at one of the picnic tables here with a sweet or savory snack and relaxing after shopping!

Hilltop Hanover Farm & Environmental Center (914-962-2368), 1271 Hanover Street, Yorktown Heights, consists of 187 acres with forest, pastureland, and buildings that date back to the 1600s, when the Underhill family owned the property. Children will enjoy the animals, and just about everyone will like the hiking trails here. They are open year-round Tuesday through Saturday 10-4; closed Sunday and Monday.

Rainbeau Ridge (914-234-2197), 49 David's Way, Bedford Hills. This working farm offers a variety of educational activities for children, including day camp in the summer months. There are cooking classes for adults. Open year-round; family owned and operated.

Stone Barns Center for Food & Agriculture (914-366-6200), 630 Bedford Road, Pocantico Hills, has a farm market and farm store open to the public year-round, Wednesday through Sunday 10-5. The center welcomes visitors to "unleash their inner farmer." The public is invited to participate in a farm-to-table program, enroll in an herbal infusions class, attend a farm-policy lecture, join a toddler in the little farmers program, or talk with the farmers. The public may tour the historical architecture at the center. Programs and activities change monthly with the weather and the seasons. There are programs to suit just about anyone's interest at this impressive venue.

Stone Barns Center for Agriculture in Tarrytown.

Stuart's Farm (914-245-2784), 62 Granite Springs Road, Granite Springs, is open April through October 9-6; November and December 9-5. They sell a large selection of fruits and vegetables in season and you can pick your own peaches, pears, apples, and pumpkins here.

Westchester Greenhouses (914-693-2935), 332 West Hartsdale Avenue, Hartsdale, is open from Easter to Christmas, 8:30-5:30. They offer annuals, perennials, cut flowers, fresh produce, jams honey and hayrides in October. You will find Christmas trees and wreaths after Thanksgiving.

Wilkens Fruit and Fir Farm (914-245-5111), 1335 White Hill Road, Yorktown. The bakery and market are open August through mid-December, daily 10-5. Pick your own apples and peaches in season. Choose and cut Christmas trees after Thanksgiving.

GOLF

Westchester is renowned for some prestigious professional golf tournaments hosted in the county. Five county-owned courses are open to the public.

Dunwoodie Golf Course (914-231-3490), 1 Grace Avenue, Yonkers. This is an 18-hole, par-70 course with a pro shop, driving range, snack bar, and restaurant.

Maple Moor Golf Course (914-995-9200), 1128 North Street, White Plains. This is an 18-hole, par-71 golf course with pro shop, snack bar, and restaurant.

Mohansic Golf Course (914-862-5283) 1500 Baldwin Road, Yorktown Heights. This is an 18-hole course, par-70 with pro shop, driving range, snack bar, and restaurant.

Saxon Woods (914-231-3461), 315 Mamaroneck Road, Scarsdale, is an 18-hole, par 71 course with pro shop, restaurant, and locker rooms.

Sprain Lake Golf Course (914-231-3481), 290 East Grassy Sprain Road, Yonkers, is an 18-hole, par-70, with pro shop, snack bar, and restaurant.

Semi-private golf courses include **Doral Golf Club** (914-939-5500), 975 Anderson Hill Road, Rye Brook (9 holes), and **Lake Isle Country Club** (914-961-3453), 660 White Plains Road, Eastchester (18 holes).

HIKING

There are over 40 county-owned parks in Westchester. These are some of my favorite places. For a more complete list, contact the **Department of Parks, Recreation and Conservation** (914-864-PARK; parks.westchestergov.com). Also go to **PARKS** section on page 478.

Franklin D. Roosevelt State Park (914-245-245-4434), 2957 Crompond Road, off the Taconic Parkway, Yorktown Heights, is open year-round, daily 8am-dusk and has hiking and cross-country ski trails, a huge outdoor pool (roughly an acre in size) that's accessible to the disabled, and boating on Mohansic Lake and Crom Pond.

Indian Brook Assemblage of The Nature Conservancy (914-244-3271), Mount Holly Road, Lewisboro, is really a 143-acre property that's a collection of three smaller parks and preserves maintained by The Nature Conservancy. Lakes, waterfalls, ponds, and trails make a perfect getaway for the outdoors lover, and the hiking here ranges from a leisurely walk to a challenging climb.

Marshlands Conservancy (914-835-4466), 220 Boston Post Road, Rye. Marked trails take hikers through fields and woods and along the seashore. This is a great spot for birders, and a small nature center offers exhibits on the natural history of Long Island Sound.

More hiking may be enjoyed at the **Mianus River Gorge** (914-234-3455), Mianus River Road, Bedford, and along the **Old Croton Aqueduct** (914-693-5259), Route 129, to the Croton Dam Plaza. The latter hike is 30 miles long, but hikers and cyclists can follow as much or as little of this trail as they desire. Note the plaza spillway which was considered an engineering marvel in its day. The **Westchester Wilderness Walk** (914-234-6992), Upper Shad Lane, Pound Ridge, is part of the Westchester Land Trust and includes 150 acres of woodlands, streams, and somewhat rugged terrain. There are four loops that meander through six miles of trails. The terrain is rather challenging on a couple of these trails.

SWIMMING

Those who want to go to a beach can enjoy the one at **Playland Park** (914-813-7010), 1 Playland Parkway, Rye. There are some other nice beaches as well:

Blue Mountain Reservation Beach (914-862-5275), 435 Welcher Avenue, Peekskill, has beaches, a pool, and extensive recreation areas.

Croton Point Park and Beach (914-862-5290), 1A Croton Point Avenue, Croton-on-Hudson, overlooks the Hudson River and has special events during the summer months. There's also a swimming pool, recreation hall, and playing fields.

Osceola Beach and Picnic Grounds (914-245-3246), 399 East Main Street, Jefferson Valley, is a good place to go with small children. There is a snack bar, picnic tables and an overall family atmosphere.

Spruce Lake at Mountain Lakes Park (914-669-5793), 201 Hawley Road, North Salem. This lake is open Saturday, Sunday and holidays only from

Memorial Day weekend through Labor Day. There's a sandy beach and picnic area making this a good place to go with young children. Rowboats and canoes are available to rent by advance reservation.

WINTER SPORTS

CROSS-COUNTRY SKIING

The following parks (914-864-PARK) have marked and groomed cross-country ski trails. Call before going to make sure there is skiing:

Blue Mountain Reservation, Cranberry Lake Preserve, Lenoir Preserve, Marshlands Conservancy, Mountain Lakes Park, Saxon Woods Park, Ward Pound Ridge Reservation

ICE SKATING

Since schedules vary from month to month, call the ice rinks for current skating sessions. Make sure to check specifically for figure skating, ice hockey, or freestyle time.

Ebersole Ice Rink (914-422-1390), 110 Lake Street, White Plains. There are public skating sessions daily for both ice hockey players and figure skaters.

Edward J. Murray Memorial Skating Center (914-377-6469), 348 Tuckahoe Road, Yonkers, is open daily for figure skating, speed skating, and ice hockey.

Hommocks Ice Rink (914-834-1069), 130 Hommocks Road, Larchmont, is open October through mid-June. Call for hours.

Ice Hutch (914-699-6787), 655 Garden Avenue. Mount Vernon. The indoor ice rink here opened in 1997 and offers public skating year-round as well as sessions for ice hockey and freestyle figure skating. There is a pro shop and concession on the premises.

Playland Ice Casino (914-481-5941), 1 Playland Parkway, Rye, is open from September through May. There are three indoor rinks offering freestyle, adult, and children's sessions.

Westchester Skating Academy (914-347-8232), 91 Fairview Park Drive, Elmsford, has two National Hockey League-size ice rinks with classes and rentals. Open year-round; call for hours.

PARKS

Westchester is filled with parks and nature preserves. Depending on where you will be visiting in the county, these are all excellent green spaces!

Blue Mountain Reservation (914-862-5275), 435 Welcher Avenue, Peekskill. Open year-round, daily, 24 hours. Situated in the northwestern part of the county, in addition to hiking, there's a large lake for swimming in this 1500-acre recreation area. Camping facilities are available in the Trail Lodge, which has a dining hall and large fireplace.

Colonial Greenway (914-864-PARK). This 15-mile unpaved trail goes through New Rochelle, Mamaroneck, Eastchester, and Scarsdale. No bikes are permitted and it is ideal for hiking or walking. Dogs are allowed if they are leashed. Areas encompassed by this greenway include Saxon Woods, the Hutchinson River Path, Twin Lakes County Park, Ward Acres, and the Leatherstocking Trail.

Cranberry Lake Preserve (914-428-1005), 1609 Old Orchard Street (off Route 22), North White Plains. Open Tuesday through Sunday 9-4. This preserve consists of 135 acres of unspoiled wetlands and hardwood forests. The park has a five-acre lake with trails and boardwalks, so visitors can observe life in an aquatic habitat. You'll also find cross-country ski trails and hiking. A small lodge offers occasional programs and there's a rock quarry here too.

Croton Point Park (914-862-5290), 1 Croton Point Avenue (off Route 9), Croton-on-Hudson. Open year-round, 8am-dusk. This 508-acre park, along the banks of the Hudson River, features a pool, canoe-launching area, recreation hall, and ball fields. The park is ideal for fishing, hiking and picnicking. Cabins, lean-tos, and facilities for tents and trailers are also available. This park is the largest peninsula on the Hudson River and the **Croton Point Nature Center** (914-862-5297) contains exhibits on local flora and fauna as well as local Native American history.

A winter view from Croton Point Park, a popular place for swimming, camping, and boating; this county park is where the Great Hudson River Revival festival is held annually in June.

Greenburgh Nature Center (914-723-3470), 99 Dromore Road, off Central Avenue, Scardsdale. Open year-round, daily 9:30-4:30. Situated on 32 acres, this innovative nature center offers visitors a chance to explore several environments, including woodlands, a vineyard, orchards, and cultivated gardens. Over 30 species of trees may be found in the preserve, along with wildflowers, ferns, and a number of songbirds. At the museum, see a Nunatak, an Inuit word meaning "hill of stone;" more than 100 animal exhibits; descriptive displays that explain the area's natural history; and a glass beehive. There are maps for a self-guided nature walk.

Marshlands Conservancy (914-835-4466), 220 Boston Post Road, Rye. Open year-round, daily dawn to dusk. There is an environmental education center here with changing exhibits and four saltwater aquaria at this 173-acre wildlife sanctuary. The unique character of the conservancy lies in the diversity of habitats preserved within it's boundaries, including woods, fields, ponds, and a salt marsh; paths throughout the property lead to these points of interest.

Rockefeller State Park Preserve (914-631-1470), 125 Route 117, Pleasantville. Open year-round, daily dawn to dusk. Find a variety of habitats here, including wetlands, woodlands, meadows, fields, and a lake. Miles of hiking trails, which during winter are cross-country ski trails, will delight outdoors lovers, and for horseback riders, there are bridle paths. The visitor center hosts exhibits of local and historical interest. This private land was opened to the public by the Rockefeller family.

Rye Nature Center (914-967-5150), 873 Boston Post Road, Rye. The grounds are open daily dawn to dusk; nature center open every day except Sunday, 10-4. This site is only 47 acres, but it's a good stop if you are traveling with children. The museum has exhibits of local plants and animals and there are some mini exhibits about nature. There is a 2.5-mile nature path that can be easily walked, even by the youngest and oldest travelers!

Scenic Hudson Park at Irvington (914-591-7736). From I-287, exit 9, take Route 9 south for 1.6 miles. At the light turn right onto Main Street and continue to the end. Make a right on North Astor Street, make a left on Bridge Street, cross the railroad tracks, and continue bearing to the left. The park is on the right. This 12-acre site, with views of the Manhattan skyline, the Palisades, and Tappan Zee Bridge, is continually being transformed into parkland. Scenic Hudson Land Trust saved the area from development. There is a promenade, boat launch, and ball fields.

Teatown Lake Reservation (914-762-2912, 1600 Spring Valley Road, Ossining. Take exit 134 off the Taconic Parkway, then follow Grant's Lane to Spring Valley Road. Open daily year-round from dawn to dusk; museum open Wednesday through Sunday 9-5. Free. This 1000-acre reservation has marked nature walks and 15 miles of hiking trails, a museum, and outdoor exhibits. Wildflowers are abundant here in the spring with more than 230 species native to the area on a two-acre island. Guided tours of the island are offered April through September. Visitors may enjoy watching waterfowl and other animals at a large lake; inside the museum are live exhibits of local animals and plants.

Ward Pound Ridge Reservation (914-864-7317), 6 Reservation Road, Pound Ridge. Open daily year-round, 8am-dusk. Parking fee. Ward Pound Ridge is the largest park in Westchester, covering over 4300 acres. There are 35 miles of trails for cross-country skiing, sledding, hiking, and horseback riding. There are also several places to go fishing and to picnic. You can easily spend a day here. Year-round, on Saturday, there are nature programs for children at the *Trailside Nature Museum* (open Tuesday through Saturday 9-4).

Weinberg Nature Center (914-722-1289), 455 Mamaroneck Road, Scarsdale. The nature trail here is open year-round, daily from dawn to dusk. The *Trailside Museum* is open Wednesday through Sunday 9-5; during the summer months, Monday through Friday, 9-5. This sanctuary is home to a range of birds and wildlife, with a meadow, orchard, butterfly and hummingbird garden, Japanese-style Zen meditation garden, and outdoor Native American village. There are exhibits and programs in the museum and this is a great place to take young children.

Westmoreland Sanctuary (914-666-8448), 260 Chestnut Ridge Road, Mount Kisco. Open year-round, dawn to dusk. Nature museum is open Monday through Saturday 9-5; Sunday 10:30-5. Free. (Fees are charged for some workshops and special events.) This 625-acre sanctuary offers 8 miles of walking and hiking trails, wildlife displays, and exhibits of local natural history. This is an excellent site for a family visit.

LODGING

BED & BREAKFASTS

Westchester County is home to many hotels offering visitors several amenities. I am sorry to report in recent years the quality of service has declined and several of the hotels are in need of updating. They are generally overpriced for what they provide. Visitors who prefer B&B establishments will have difficulty finding one. Due to restrictive zoning regulations in most communities in the county, such businesses are rare. There are a few I discovered in the county that have high standards. I welcome your feedback if you stay in any of them.

Alexander Hamilton House (914-271-6737), 49 Van Wyck Street, Croton-on-Hudson 10520. ($$)

Apple Motor Inn (914-693-2900), 775 Saw Mill River Road, Ardsley 10502. ($)

Bedford Post Inn (914-205-3773), 954 Old Post Road, Bedford 10506.

Crabtree's Kittle House (914-666-8044), 22 Kittle Road, Chappaqua 10514. ($$)

Westchester Marriott (914-631-2200), 670 White Plains Road, Tarrytown 10591. ($$$) This hotel has 444 guest rooms, a heated

The Alexander Hamilton House in Croton-on-Hudson is one of the few bed & breakfast establishments in Westchester County.

indoor pool, sauna, spa, and fitness center. There are fine amenities—flat-screen TV, plush bedding, and marble bathrooms. *Cooper's Mill*, a terrific farm-to-table restaurant, serves a buffet breakfast every morning and specializes in American cuisine and an array of cocktails at lunch and dinner; *Ruth's Chris Steakhouse* serves excellent porterhouse steaks in an elegant atmosphere every evening after 5pm. There is also a sports bar, the *Tavern*, on the premises.

The location of this hotel is excellent, close to several of the historic attractions in Tarrytown. Of all the major hotels in Westchester County, this is the only one I would recommend: the accommodations, service and amenities are consistently well above average.

WHERE TO EAT

Westchester County is fortunate to have hundreds of restaurants, in all price ranges and to please all tastes. I wish I had the time—and the money—to sample all of them.... and the necessary space here to write detailed descriptions about these establishments!

The following DINING OUT places (about 55 in total) were selected from my personal experience traveling throughout the county in recent years. They represent a relatively small select sampling of the fine neighborhood restaurants throughout Westchester. Entries are minimal since I wanted to include as many places as possible. Check websites or call for days/hours restaurants are open. The county is large, so those in the DINING OUT section are grouped by geographic area. When you visit the county, try the broad spectrum of eateries—from Indian and Italian to Asian and modern American — found in this restaurant-intensive region of the Hudson Valley!

DINING OUT

Northwestern Westchester
(Including Peekskill, Croton, Ossining, Briarcliff, Yonkers)

Churrasquiera Ribatejo (914-941-5928), 39 Spring Street, Ossining. ($) This family-run Portuguese diner is an informal eatery, where you can watch your food being prepared on an open grill.

Gleason's (914-402-1950), 911 South Street, Peekskill. ($) Hearty American favorites are served in this popular restaurant located in a historic building. It's named after Jackie Gleason, a resident of the city in the early 1960s.

Ocean House (914-271-0702), 49 North Riverside Avenue, Croton-on-Hudson. ($) Enjoy seafood and fresh fish of all kinds in this cozy spot. I love their fish stew and clam chowder!

Ramenesque (914-930-1788), 1008 Main Street, Peekskill. ($) This informal Japanese café specializes in ramen bowls and this is what I suggest you order. The cucumber and crabstick salad was tasty too, but bowls are the way to go! Children welcome.

Ravenna Osteria (914-732-0292), 1099 North Division Street, Peekskill. ($) Authentic Italian cuisine and pizza beautifully prepared. This is what a neighborhood Italian restaurant should be—consistently good and reasonably priced! Children welcome.

Squire's (914-762-3376), 94 North State Road, Briarcliff Manor. ($) This informal pub, located in a strip mall, has been in business for nearly 50 years. Their Kobe beef burgers are excellent as are the buffalo chipotle burgers: this unpretentious eatery is definitely worth a detour if you're a burger aficionado!

Table 9 (914-737-4959), 92 Roa Hook Road, Cortlandt Manor. ($$) Whether you prefer quinoa bowls and grilled fish or burgers and steaks, there's something on this creative menu to suit your taste. The cocktails are first-rate and the atmosphere is sophisticated yet cozy. If you dine early (3 -5:45pm), check out the amazing specials. Open every day for lunch and dinner.

Zeph's (914-736-2159), 638 Central Avenue, Peekskill. ($$) Set in a reclaimed factory building, they serve American cuisine with a fresh twist. Outdoor patio in summer months is delightful and the food is first-rate.

The entrance to Blue Hill at Stone Barns, a fine restaurant in Westchester County.

Southwestern Westchester

(Including river towns of Tarrytown, Irvington, Hastings, Dobbs Ferry, Yonkers)

Blue Hill at Stone Barns (914-366-9600), 630 Bedford Road, Pocantico Hills. ($$$) Located on an 80-acre working farm, once a Rockefeller property, this fine restaurant celebrates the produce of the Hudson Valley; much of what is served is raised organically on-site. The food and service are excellent and the ambience is perfect for any special occasion.

Bridge View Tavern & Beer Garden (914-332-0078), 226 Beekman Avenue, Sleepy Hollow. ($) Here you will find gourmet food served in a pub setting overlooking the Hudson River. There's an outdoor beer garden in the warm weather months where diners may enjoy burgers, wings, veggie chili, calamari and mussels along with dozens of beer selections. Delightful!

Harper's Bar & Restaurant (914-693-2306), 92 Main Street, Dobbs Ferry. ($$) Standard American favorites are made with locally sourced ingredients here. The chef worked at *La Panetiere* in Rye, so expect fine fare but in a casual atmosphere.

Horsefeathers (914-631-6606), 94 North Broadway, Tarrytown. ($$) One of the first "grazing" restaurants in the county, they continue to offer burgers, steaks and overstuffed sandwiches. Casual and comfortable.

Mima Wine Bar (914-591-1300), 63 Main Street, Irvington. ($$) Fine Italian home cooking is the mainstay at this popular restaurant with over 20 wines by the glass. Handmade pasta with shrimp and Hudson Valley trout stuffed with capers, onion and tomato, are only a couple of the tempting entrees here.

MP Taverna (914-231-7854), 1 Bridge Street, Irvington. ($) Housed in a former warehouse by the Hudson River, this wonderful brasserie opened in 2012. Upscale comfort food including grilled fish, chicken and lamb entrees is offered, all with a Mediterranean accent. My favorite dish is the Greek paella.

Red Hat on the River (914-591-5888), 1 Bridge Street, Irvington-on-Hudson. ($$) From the rooftop bar, see the Tappan Zee Bridge to the right and the Manhattan skyline to the left. The restaurant is only a few feet from the Hudson River when dining alfresco. I've enjoyed grilled salmon and burgers here...desserts are worth sampling as well.

Santorini Greek Restaurant (914-631-4300), 175 Valley Street, Sleepy Hollow. ($$) You will find delicious homemade Greek specialties at terrific prices here. My moussaka was done to perfection and so was the chicken souvlaki. Greek salad or soup is included with all entrees. Servings are generous. Don't pass up the baklava!

Sushi Mike's (914-591-0054), 146 Main Street, Dobbs Ferry. ($$) Sushi lovers take note: the Fantastic Roll here is just that: wrapped in white seaweed, filled with salmon, tuna, yellowtail, flying fish roe, avocado and vegetables. Don't pass up this one!

X20 Xavier's (914-965-1111), 71 Water Grant Street, Yonkers. ($$$) On the Hudson River waterfront, enjoy fantastic international fare in a magical ambience. Chef-owner Peter X. Kelly, who owns three Rockland County restaurants, has preserved a century-old crumbling pier to bring this fine dining option to the city of Yonkers.

Zuppa (914-376-6500), 59 Main Street, Yonkers. ($$) This spacious, comfortable restaurant and bar serves imaginative Italian dishes. The wine list is excellent and so are the desserts.

Central Westchester
(White Plains, Ardsley, Larchmont, Hartsdale, Scarsdale)

Anna Maria Italian Restaurant (914-833-0555), 18 Chatsworth Avenue, Larchmont. ($$$) This welcoming family restaurant specializes in Italian comfort food. Anna Maria, the owner, was born in Naples, Italy and is always at the restaurant, making sure patrons are well served.

808 Bistro (914-722-0808), 808 Scarsdale Avenue, Scarsdale. ($$) The international fare in this informal dining spot includes something for every taste. Most offerings are both healthful and tasty and the place is popular with local residents.

Lusardi's (914-834-5555), The Northern Italian cuisine has a Mediterranean accent: homemade pasta stuffed with spinach and porcini mushrooms is one of my favorite entrees.

Meritage (914-472-8484), 1505 Weaver Street, Scarsdale. ($$) The New American fare here is consistently good. Most ingredients are local and organic; pastas are made on the premises.

Mulino's (914-761-1818), 99 Court Street, White Plains. ($$) Northern Italian cuisine is served at tables looking out on a courtyard garden with waterfalls. This popular gathering place with Westchester politicians serves rack of lamb, veal chop, fresh fish, and several tempting desserts.

Pete's Saloon (914-592-9849), 8 West Main Street, Elmsford. ($$) This informal eatery has a busy bar and serves classic American favorites: burgers, steaks, sandwiches, and salads. There are several beers on tap and live entertainment a couple of nights each week.

Plate's (914-834-1244), 121 Myrtle Avenue, Larchmont. ($$) This charming contemporary American restaurant with Asian, French and Italian influences serves pulled pork, ribs and brisket from the restaurant's smoker on Sunday. On the menu every day is duck, scallops, burgers from grass-fed beef topped with raw milk cheddar cheese, to name a few of the offerings.

Ray's Café (914-833-2551), 1995 Palmer Avenue, Larchmont. ($$) This Chinese restaurant serves Shanghai-style cuisine. You can even order crispy or steamed whole fish, prepared to order the way you like it!

Sazan (914-674-6015), 729 Saw Mill River Road, Ardsley. ($$$) Since there are dozens of small plates and appetizers at this Japanese restaurant, ordering a variety of them is a good way to sample the offerings. Noodle dishes are hearty and there's a sushi bar that seats eight.

Northeastern Westchester
(Bedford, Chappaqua, Katonah, Mt. Kisco, Pound Ridge, North Salem)

Aesop's Fable (914-238-3858), 13 King Street, Chappaqua. ($$) Eclectic seasonal fare from local farms as well as vegetables and herbs from the backyard garden in season. Enjoy tapas-style dishes, wood-fired pizza, pasta, salmon, steaks and vegetarian creations at this delightful new eatery.

Bacio Trattoria (914-763-2233), 12 North Salem Road, Cross River. ($$) This intimate restaurant featuring Mediterranean cuisine has a large outdoor patio for alfresco dining in the summer. The grilled calamari is excellent.

Beehive (914-765-0688), 30 Old Route 22, Armonk. ($$) Enjoy Mediterranean favorites, salads, wraps, burgers and sandwiches with phenomenal creative twists on these usual offerings. There's a children's menu and they serve breakfast, lunch and dinner every day. I love this place and wish the Beehive would open in Woodstock where I live!

Blue Dolphin (914-232-4791), 175 Katonah Avenue, Katonah. ($) This family restaurant in a diner-like building is a mainstay in town featuring Italian specialties.

Farmer & The Fish (914-617-8380), 100 Titicus Road, North Salem. ($$) This renovated 18th-century homestead has beamed areas around a central stone chimney with five acres in back of the restaurant where all kinds of vegetables and herbs are grown in season. Fish is the specialty of the house, including a tiered seafood tower for two. There's a raw bar and if you are a lobster lover, this is the place to order it.

La Camelia (914-666-2466), 234 North Bedford Road, Mount Kisco. One of the best Spanish restaurants you will find anywhere in the region, it is located in a 150-year-old landmark building.

La Cremaillere (914-234-9647), 46 Bedford Road, Bedford. ($$$) This renowned classic French restaurant offers a beautiful country setting in which to enjoy chateaubriand, duck and rack of lamb. Reservations suggested. Leave the kids home!

Lalibela (914-864-1343), 37 South Moger Avenue, Mount Kisco. ($$) Ethiopian cuisine here is served on a large central tray lined with flatbread for scooping the food that is usually stewed. Knives and forks are available by request. There are several fresh salads, vegetable and lentil dishes.

Le Fontane (914-232-9619), 137 Route 100 (corner of Routes 100 & 139), Katonah. ($$) Traditional Southern Italian cuisine featured on seasonal menus with all the usual favorites. They have been around over 30 years and are a mainstay in town.

Moderne Barn (914-730-0001), 430 Bedford Road, Armonk. ($$) Excellent contemporary American cuisine with Mediterranean influences enhanced by locally sourced seasonal produce is served here. The dining space, a renovated furniture barn, features booths with long banquettes. Nice bar too.

Neo Bistro and Sushi Bar (914-244-9711), 69 South Moger Avenue, Mount Kisco. ($$) The combined flavors of the East and West meet here: like sushi tortilla filled with tuna, salmon, cilantro, and guacamole. I enjoyed the green tea crème brulee for dessert. Interesting tasty choices!

121 (914-669-0100), 2 Dingle Ridge Road, North Salem. ($$) This is a wonderful neighborhood restaurant serving dishes like creamy potato leek soup, crisp fried calamari, wood-fired oven pizzas, ribs, roasted chicken and sandwiches.

Pho Corner Bistro (914-242-1662), 740 North Bedford Road, Bedford Hills. ($$) Open Wednesday through Monday 11-9. Located on the corner of a strip mall, this is an extraordinary Vietnamese eatery. There are rice-paper rolls with shrimp, tasty banh mi sandwiches, and pho (rice-noodle soup). The variety of bowls should please every taste although the menu selections aren't vast. Don't miss the Vietnamese coffee after your meal! A rather small venue, I don't suggest Pho for families with children. It's a popular place for take-out with their local clientele.

Southeastern Westchester
(Mamaroneck, New Rochelle, Port Chester, Rye)

Agostino's (914-235-6019), 336 Pelham Road, New Rochelle. ($$) This family-owned and operated Italian restaurant offers house-made pastas, traditional entrees and an extensive wine list. Specialties of the Abruzzi region are featured and the service is excellent. Children welcome.

Alba's (914-937-2236), 400 North Main Street, Port Chester. ($$$) The large elegant dining room with Oriental-style rugs throughout serves fine traditional Northern Italian cuisine. Enjoy veal, chicken, seafood, steaks and pasta here. It can get noisy on busy weekend nights. Not recommended for children.

Coromandel Cuisine of India (914-235-8390), 30 Division Street, New Rochelle. Authentic Indian cuisine served in an atmosphere with Indian décor and music. Tandoori specialties and classical curries are the mainstays on the menu.

Da Giorgio (914-235-2727), 77 Quaker Ridge Road, New Rochelle. ($$) This cozy restaurant specializing in traditional Italian cuisine is located in a shopping center. There are more than a dozen pasta dishes to choose from, along with several veal and risotto selections.

Elia Taverna (914-663-4976), 502 New Rochelle Road, Bronxville. ($$) An inviting Greek restaurant serving first-rate salads, grilled lamb chops, spanakopita and chicken souvlaki. Enjoy fine Greek fare at affordable prices.

Emilio (914-835-3100), 1 Colonial Place, Harrison. ($$$) This Italian restaurant is housed in a colonial-style house. The spinach lasagna and wild-mushroom ravioli are my favorite dishes here. The menu changes seasonally; interesting game dishes are served in the winter.

Le Panetiere (914-967-8140), 530 Milton Road, Rye. ($$$) Housed in a building dating back to the early 19th century, with a Provencal interior featuring exposed beams and stucco walls, this is one of the finest French restaurants in the Hudson Valley. It's a great place to go to celebrate a special occasion. There is usually a prix-fixe menu available.

Le Provencal Bistro (914-777-2324), 436 Mamaroneck Avenue, Mamaroneck. ($$) Home-style French bistro with comfort foods like lamb sirloin and chicken with lentils and carrots. For dessert, there's chocolate mousse cake among the choices. Children welcome.

Piero's (914-353-2049), 123 Halstead Avenue, Harrison. ($$) Fine Italian cuisine is served for both lunch and dinner in elegant surroundings. Originally located in Port Chester for 20 years, they re-located to Harrison in 2015 and still have a dedicated following.

Q Authentic Barbecue Restaurant & Bar (914-933-7427), 112 North Main Street, Port Chester ($) Hearty Midwestern-style barbecue is served at long, crowded tables. There's a bustling atmosphere in this family restaurant where barbecued brisket, pork ribs, wings and sausage smoked on the premises, are the mainstays. And kids love to watch their meal being prepared in the glassed-in kitchen.

Rosa's La Scarlitto Restaurant (914-777-1667), 215 Halstead Avenue, Mamaroneck. ($$$) Chef Rosa Merenda and her husband, Angelo, usually greet patrons and recommend particular dishes. The cuisine is authentic Italian in the style of Bari. Homemade gnocchi is made with ricotta rather than potatoes, and melts in your mouth. Dining here is pricey; not recommended for children.

Rosemary & Vine (914-481-8660), 29 Purchase Street, Rye. ($$) Enjoy Mediterranean food daily, except Sunday, for breakfast lunch and dinner. There's live jazz Wednesday from 7-9pm. The organic offerings feature lots of choices for vegetarians. I love this place: the fare is healthful and well prepared.

Scalini Osteria (914-337-4935), 65 Pondfield Road, Bronxville. ($$) An intimate, romantic trattoria serving regional Italian specialties like clams and mussels fra diavolo, grilled calamari with chopped vegetables, and pasta with wild boar sausage. The menu changes seasonally and grilled fish entrees are always available. Dine alfresco on the courtyard patio in the summer.

Sonora (914-933-0200), 179 Rectory Street, Port Chester. ($$) Latin American regional cuisine is served here. Quesadillas filled with lobster and avocado drizzled with crème fraiche. Paella surrounded by a whole lobster filled with clams, mussels, sea scallops and shrimp. Go out of your way to dine here: it's definitely a treat!

Underhill's Crossing (914-337-1200), 74 ½ Pondfiled Road, Bronxville. ($$) The eclectic Asian-fusion cuisine ranges from pizza, sandwiches and burgers, to veal, lamb, and salmon entrees. All dishes are prepared to order. Open since 1994, this restaurant is popular with local residents.

EATING OUT

There are hundreds of terrific informal eateries dotting Westchester County. I've selected some of my favorites to feature here. As you travel the county you will discover a few to your liking; if so, do let me know!

Araras Coffee and More (914-831-5439), 406C Mamaroneck Avenue, White Plains. ($) Open daily, except Sunday, this is the place to go for superior coffee. The eatery is owned and operated by two Brazilian women who serve up the best coffee in the city!

The Blue Pig in Croton-on-Hudson is a fun place to relax and enjoy first-rate homemade ice cream.

Arthur Avenue Wood-Fired Pizza (914-747-2611), 59 Marble Avenue, Pleasantville. ($) This informal eatery serves up some of the best pizza you'll have anywhere. Arthur Avenue in the Bronx is renowned for its Italian specialties, including breads of all kinds and pizza and this is a taste of the Bronx in Westchester. Mangia!

Bean Runner Café (914-737-1701), 201 South Division Street, Peekskill. ($) This vibrant community hub combines a café, music, and an art gallery. Breakfast and lunch choices include omelets, paninis, wraps and salads. There's live music on weekends and a children's playroom on the premises.

Blue Pig (914-271-3850), 121 Maple Street, Croton-on-Hudson. ($) Homemade ice cream here, with flavors like cinnamon walnut and espresso Oreo, is made daily from scratch using local milk. No fillers or preservatives will be found in anything created here. The ice cream sandwiches made with chocolate chip cookies and brownies are memorable. There's a nice garden patio too!

Chappaqua Station (914-861-8001), 1 Station Plaza, Chappaqua. ($$) Enjoy breakfast, lunch or supper here. There are several home-baked items, cookies and desserts as well as great coffee drinks made to order. The atmosphere is informal and this is a delightful place to stop for a bite any time of day.

Growlers Beer Bistro (914-793-0608), 25 Main Street, Tuckahoe. ($) The craft beer list is huge, and the food includes items like gumbo, pulled pork sandwich, rosemary chicken burger, smoky baby back ribs, and Growler burgers, made with a mix of beef, pork, and veal. Fries are topped with bacon, parsley and Parmesan cheese. It can get quite noisy and crowded here on weekends, so be forewarned.

Kelly's Sea Level (914-967-0868), 413 Midland Avenue, Rye. ($) This local spot is open daily serving generous portions of all the American favorites, as well as shepherds pie and fish & chips, at amazingly reasonable prices. There are several beers on tap and the atmosphere is "homey," according to owner Jerry McGuire who lives next door.

Kurzhals Coffee (914-208-0158), 900 Main Street, Peekskill. ($) Open daily 6:30am-7pm; Friday and Saturday until 8pm. Sunday 7-7. Located in one of the oldest masonry buildings in the area, dating back to 1836, this was once a place to recruit Union soldiers during the Civil War. Later the Kurzhals Brothers operated a successful hardware store here. In the past two decades the store has been abandoned. Gabriel Arango now offers ethically sourced coffee, roasted in small batches from two local roasters. Milk and cream comes from Hudson Valley Fresh. This is a wonderful place to relax and enjoy coffee, iced or hot, any time of year!

La Tulipe Desserts (914-242-4555), 455 Lexington Avenue, Mount Kisco. This European-style patisserie has phenomenal marzipan, handmade truffles, lemon tartlets with meringue cones, and an array of tempting treats. The owner hails from Holland and went to culinary school in Paris. The finest ingredients are used in all the creations in this unassuming oasis of desserts.

Little Kabab Station (914-242-7000), 31 East Main Street, Mount Kisco. ($) This tiny eatery is designed for take-out, but the menu is surprisingly large. Everything is prepared to order with fresh ingredients: Tandoor roasted kebabs, curries, and biriyanis. The Indian rolls are great if you're in the mood for a quick snack.

Little Drunken Chef (914-242-8800), 36 East Main Street, Mount Kisco. ($) Joining several "Little" restaurants in town, this fun place opened in 2015 and

This casual restaurant serving wines by the glass on South Division Street in Peekskill features live music in the evenings.

features tapas and oysters. There's a sidewalk patio, full bar and D.J. cage for late night hours with music.

Modern Restaurant & Pizzeria (914-633-9479), 12 Russell Avenue, New Rochelle. ($) One of the oldest pizza parlors in the county, the original brick oven was built in the early 20th century and is still in use. An old-fashioned Italian family restaurant serving pasta, steaks and seafood but I recommend the pizza!

Pollo a la Brasa Misti (914-939-9437), 110 North Main Street, Port Chester. ($) Authentic Peruvian fare is served in this no-frills eatery with a largely immigrant clientele. The name of the place is also one of the popular entrees: chicken served with rice and salad, a mainstay in Peru. Desserts are homemade and delicious.

The Parlor (914-478-8200), 14 Cedar Street, Dobbs Ferry ($$) This terrific pizza parlor has an extensive menu with salads, pastas and other flavorful creative twists on basic fare. If you love pizza, do not miss this neighborhood eatery!

Twelve Grapes Music & Wine Bar (914-737-6624), 12 North Division Street, Peekskill. ($$) New American cuisine featuring light entrees, pizza and pasta dishes like mushroom ravioli. There's live music Thursday through Saturday and at Sunday brunch.

Walter's Hot Dogs (no phone here!), 937 Palmer Avenue, Mamaroneck. ($) They're open daily from noon to 6 for hot dogs that have received national attention. Walter Warrington, founder of this unusual eatery, keeps locals coming back for singles and doubles (two on one bun). A must-stop for aficionados of this American classic!

ENTERTAINMENT

Arts Westchester (914-428-4220; artswestchester.org), 31 Mamaroneck Avenue, White Plains. Free. There are changing art exhibits year-round featuring the work of local artists, live music and dance, in a historic building. The website lists cultural events throughout the county.

Bendheim Performing Arts Center (914-472-3300), jccmw.org), 999 Wilmot Road, Scarsdale. This theater, with more than 200 seats, offers musical and theatrical performances, comedy acts, lively lectures with leading intellectuals, and a variety of children's programs.

The Capitol Theatre (914-937-4126; capitoltheatre.com), 149 Westchester Avenue, Port Chester. A full schedule of rock groups throughout the year.

Caramoor Center for Music & the Arts (914-232-5035; caramoor.org), 149 Girdle Ridge Road, Katonah. This Katonah Landmark is home to the annual Caramoor International Music Festival, one of the top five outdoor festivals in the country for six weeks every summer. The two outdoor theaters are filled with the world's best classical, operatic and jazz artists.

Emelin Theatre (914-698-0098; emelin.org), 153 Library Lane, Mamaroneck. Founded in 1972, this theater offers exceptional entertainment including drama, family programs, classical music folk, jazz, bluegrass, films and lectures.

The historic Paramount Theater, a former film venue, now showcases a variety of entertainment in downtown Peekskill.

Hudson Stage Company (914-271-2811; hudsonstage.com), 19 Whippoorwill Road (North Castle Public Library), Armonk. This is the home of the county's Actors' Equity non-profit theatre, producing original plays and staged readings throughout the year.

Jacob Burns Film Center (914-747-5555; burnsfilmcenter.org), 364 Manville Road, Pleasantville. If you are in the area, check out this three-screen theater that features foreign, independent, documentary, and classic films. There are offerings year-round in this historic theater, which dates from 1925. In 1987 it closed its doors, but was able to re-open in 2001. There are thousands of memberships that were sold and this cinema has drawn moviegoers from all over the county. You don't have to be a member to attend a film!

Paramount Hudson Valley (914-739-2333; paramounthudsonvalley.com), 1008 Brown Street, Peekskill. This restored 1000-seat palace of the 1930s offers arts and entertainment from classical to pop. There are independent films and drama offered throughout the year. (This was where I went to see movies back in the 1950s and 1960s while growing up in nearby Shrub Oak. It was the only place within miles to see a film.)

Performing Arts Center (914-251-6200; artscenter.org), SUNY Purchase. There are several theaters here that offer dozens of events annually in dance, classical music, jazz, drama, and more.

Tarrytown Music Hall (914-631-3390; tarrytownmusichall.org), 13 Main Street, Tarrytown. This national landmark dates from 1885. The 840-seat theater has Queen Anne, Victorian, and art deco elements, and it is home to the Jazz Forum Arts Series, comedy, dance, children's theater, classical and folk music.

Westchester Broadway Theatre (914-592-2222; broadwaytheatre.com), One Broadway Plaza, Elmsford. Enjoy popular musical revivals in this dinner theater where all 450 seats have a great view of the stage. Before the show, there's a three-course meal served at your table. This is the longest-running year-round Equity theater in the state of New York!

Westchester Community College (914-606-6262; sunywcc.edu), 75 Grasslands Road, Valhalla. A mix of musical, dance and theatrical performances are offered here, as well as a film series.

SELECTIVE SHOPPING

Westchester County is often synonymous with shopping! The county has many charming downtown shopping districts in villages like Briarcliff Manor, Pleasantville, Chappaqua, Mount Kisco, Bedford, and Katonah. The best way to see the interesting boutiques, bookstores, and specialty shops is to wander through these towns at a leisurely pace. A few of examples of what you may find: **Yellow Monkey Antiques** (914-763-5848), 792 Route 35, Cross River, with 8000 square feet of elegant European country furniture, glassware, china and linens. Another of my favorite places in

The Coop, on South Division Street in Peekskill, is chock-full of interesting treasures.

the county is **Riverrun Rare Books** (914-478-1339), 12 Washington Avenue, in Hastings-on-Hudson (open daily 11-4), with more than 200,000 books in categories ranging from Shakespeare and James Joyce to history, travel, and art. There are over 10,000 American fiction titles alone. Used and rare book aficionados won't want to miss this gem!

Kelloggs & Lawrence (914-232-3351), 26 Parkway, Katonah is open daily 8-6; until 5 on weekends. Since 1887, this hardware store has sold a wonderful array of interesting gift items and clothing, in addition to hardware. A barrel filled with peanuts in their shells may be found at the front door!

SHOPPING CENTERS

Cross County Shopping Center (914-968-9570), 8000 Mall Walk, Yonkers. Open daily 10-9:30. This is the county's largest mall, with more than one million square feet of space across several buildings, joined by a promenade.

Galleria Mall at White Plains (914-682-0111), 100 Main Street, White Plains. This four-story mall has several levels of parking for over 125 stores as well as a large food court.

Vernon Hills Shopping Center (914-472-2000), 700 White Plains Road, Eastchester. There are several upscale stores here and hours vary with the establishment. It is not an enclosed mall, but an outdoor shopping center.... great for walking around on a beautiful day!

The Westchester (914-683-8600), 125 Westchester Avenue, White Plains. There are more than 100 fine stores in this 830,000-square-foot mall, featuring upscale amenities like valet parking, bronze sculptures and marble floors.

SPECIAL EVENTS

March: **Hudson Valley Restaurant Week** (914-232-6538; hudsonvalleyrestaurantweek.com). From Sunday through Friday, mid-month, *Also In November*, nearly 100 restaurants throughout the region participate offering a three-course lunch for $20.95 and a three-course dinner for $29.95.

April: **Sheep to Shawl** (914-631-8200), Philipsburg Manor, 381 North Broadway, Sleepy Hollow. Admission. Scottish border collies exhibit their sheepherding skill, plus you can enjoy shearing, wool dyeing, and cloth weaving demonstrations at this annual spring event.

May: **White Plains Cherry Blossom Festival** (914-422-1336), Ternure Park on Lake Street, White Plains. Free 11:30-5. You may enjoy Asian-influenced activities and entertainment amid the flowering cherry blossom trees; origami workshops, Taiko drummers, tea ceremonies, and karate exhibitions. **Blessing of the Animals** (914-669-5033; hammondmuseum. org), 28 Deveau Road, North Salem. Held on the first Sunday in May, rain or shine, this colorful tradition at the Hammond Museum begins with a bagpiper leading a procession into the garden for a blessing of the animals by a Native American leader, a rabbi, a Catholic priest, a Zen Buddhist priest, and an interfaith minister. Have your pet on a leash or in a crate. The festivities usually begin at 2pm, but check the website to be sure. **Crafts at Lyndhurst** (914-631-4481; artrider.com), 635 South Broadway (Route 9), Tarrytown, is held in *both May and September*. Admission. This spectacular crafts fair has become a Westchester tradition for over 30 years. Craftspeople attend from across the country, including potters, jewelers, fiber artists and glassmakers. There's a children's tent and food vendors offer an array of treats.

June: **Great Hudson River Revival** (800-67-SLOOP), Croton Point Park, 1A Croton Point Avenue, Croton-on-Hudson. Admission. This weekend long riverside festival of art, music and environmental activism is held to support the work of the historic sloop *Clearwater*. Musical performances by major talent may be enjoyed in this outdoor venue. And founder of the festival and folk legend, Pete Seeger, is watching over it all! **Juneteenth Parade** (914-737-3400) is held on a Saturday afternoon in mid-June in Peekskill. Admission. This is the oldest and longest-running African-American celebration in U.S. history marking the day when the nation's last slaves learned they were free. In addition to the parade that begins on Park Street at 2pm, there are gospel, rap and other performances, as well as lots of food vendors. It all takes place at Riverfront Park. **White Plains Outdoors Arts Festival** (914-422-1336), Tibbets Park, White Plains. Free. An outdoor showcase of the work of fine artists, craftspeople, and sculptors from the region. Performances, demonstrations, and a variety of food vendors. **Peekskill Artist District Open Studios** (914-734-1894), downtown Peekskill. Free. Visitors can meet more than 35 artists in their studios and see an array of artwork on the first Friday of the month until 9pm. Guided tours of galleries, art studios, and residential lofts in and around the growing downtown art district are available. *Mid-June through mid-August*: **Caramoor International Music Festival** (914-232-1252), 149 Girdle Ridge Road, Katonah. Admission. This internationally renowned outdoor music festival features chamber music, opera, jazz and pops. Picnicking is allowed on the magnificent grounds.

July: **Fourth of July Fireworks**: **Mamaroneck** (914-777-7784), Mamaroneck Harbor; **New Rochelle** (914-654-2086), Five Island Park; Playland (914-813-7000), **Rye**; **Yonkers** (914-377-6450), City Recreation Pier. **Independence Day Festivities** (914-591-8763), Sunnyside, **Tarrytown**. Admission. Celebrate July 4th in 19th-century style, with a pie-judging contest, town ball game, and juggling. Picnicking on the grounds is permitted.

September: **Church Tower Walk** (914-667-4116), St. Paul's Church National Historic Site, 897 South Columbus Avenue, Mount Vernon. Spring, summer, and fall, every other Friday afternoon at 3pm. Visitors may enjoy a guided tour up the wooden staircase in the 235-year old church tower, which leads to the historic 1758 Freedom Bell, cast in London at the same foundry that produced the Liberty Bell of Philadelphia. **Armonk Outdoors Art Show** (914-273-9706), North Castle Community Park, Armonk. Admission. This juried art show and sale of fine art includes works in oil, acrylic, and watercolor, as well as photography, sculpture and mixed media.

October: **Tarrytown Halloween Parade** (914-631-8389), Broadway to Patriot's Park. Free. People of all ages parade down Broadway in costume, and the array of floats will delight just about anyone. **Great Jack-O'Lantern Blaze** (914-631-8200), Van Cortlandt Manor, 525 South Riverside Avenue, Croton-on-Hudson. This amazing festival celebrating Halloween includes pumpkin carving and creating amazing lanterns for the holiday. Call for exact date.

November: **Chappaqua Antiques Show** (914-238-4666), West Orchard Elementary School, 25 Granite Road, Chappaqua. Held the first weekend in November, Saturday and Sunday 10-6, this show has become a tradition in town with dozens of vendors from around the Northeast.

December: **Frosty the Snowman Parade & Holiday Tree Lighting** (914-273-2420), Armonk. Free. Steve Nelson had the village of Armonk in mind when he composed his famous song and fairy tale about Frosty the Snowman in 1949. The event is held on the second Saturday afternoon in December with cars decorated in holiday lights and Santa ringing the siren from the fire department's oldest engine. There are rides for the kids and more at this colorful celebration. **Holiday Candlelight Evenings** (914-631-8200), Sunnyside, 3 West Sunnyside Lane, Irvington. Admission. Enjoy special holiday tours of the candlelit historic site on weekend evenings in December with caroling and hot cider around the bonfire. **A Very Dutch Holiday at Lyndhurst** (914-631-4481), 635 South Broadway (Route 9), Tarrytown. The elaborately decorated mansion is a sight to behold during weekend evenings in December. Enjoy live music and dessert treats in a festive atmosphere. Call for days and times.

NOTES